ROTISSERIE
LEAGUE
BASEBALL

2004 Edition

Contents

When Okrent published the rules in 1980 in the magazine *Inside Sports*, who could have known what it would lead to?

— Jay Lovinger

Bob Sklar laid the groundwork for the Rotisserie League years before, in Ann Arbor Michigan. Using "imaginary money," Sklar and a few sociologists and historians selected various major league players at the beginning of each season, and their performance — batting average and ERA — determined the winner, who got a blue ribbon, or something. Sklar had been a teacher of mine at the University of Michigan, my parents actually paying hard-earned tuition dollars so that I could receive Official Wisdom from some nut who picked players for a nonbetting contest. I had long sought to improve on the Assistant Professors League, or whatever it was called. In 1980 I found the answer. True, Sklar laid the seed, but his game was to the Rotisserie League as rounders is to the 1927 Yankees.

— Dan Okrent

OUR OWN 2004 ALL-STAR TEAM

James Benson
John Benson
Marc Bowman
Stacey Brandner
Lary Bump
Bill Gilbert
Bill Gray
Peter Graves
Chad Hodgdon
David Luciani
Stephen Lunsford
Jack Magruder
John Manuel
Fred Matos
LaVelle E. Neal III
Glen Waggoner
Kevin Wheeler
Doug White

THE SECRET TO WINNING

by

Glen Waggoner

Flash back to Spring Training, 2003. You're pouring over your stat sheets and your magazines and your brand-new copy of this book. You're checking in, every morning, on the Internet news links to newspapers in every major league city. You've done a Google search for every Web site with the words "Rotisserie" and "Fantasy", and you're a third of the way through the 2,983 or so hits. You've committed the last five issues of *Baseball America* to memory. You've run your Benson Draft Software 23 times with as many core scenarios. It's all coming together, and you're peaking at just the right time because ... *your Draft is tomorrow!*

But first, take this simple T/F quiz on What's to Come in 2003:

1. The defending champs, the halo-flying Anaheim Angels, will win fewer games than the low-budget Royals.

2. Bill Mueller lifetime (.286) will lead the AL in batting *and* drive in 85 runs (vs. lifetime best: 59).

3. Esteban Loaiza will win more games than Randy Johnson and Curt Schilling *combined*.

4. Each member of the Devil Rays' starting OF —Aubrey Huff, Rocco Baldelli and Carl Crawford—will get 175 hits, the only OF in baseball to do so.

5. The Giants will become the first World Series team to trade its ace (Russ Ortiz), lose a 100-RBI man (Jeff Kent) and a manager (Dusty Baker), get

zero pitches from its closer (Robb Nen)—and still win 100 games.

6. Virtually the same Braves lineup that barely outscored the D-Rays in 2002 will score more runs than any Braves team since 1897.

7. Jose Guillen, Vernon Wells, Preston Wilson, Javy Lopez and Mike Lowell will each hit 30 homers or more. Shawn Green, Pat Burrell, Mike Piazza, Troy Glaus, Ryan Klesko and Brian Giles will not.

8. Mark Loretta, Marcus Giles, Mark Grudzielanek, Scott Podsednik and Michael Young will each .300 or better. Larry Walker, Bernie Williams, John Olerud, Mike Piazza and Roberto Alomar will not.

9. Rod Beck, Joe Borowski, Tim Worrell, Lance Carter and Rocky Biddle will each get 20+ saves. Billy Koch, Robb Nen, Kazuhiro Sasaki, Kelvim Escobar and Antonio Alfonseca will not.

10. The Cubs and the Red Sox will both come within five outs of going to the World Series.

How'd you do?

Yeah, me too: 0 for 10.

Humbling, isn't it, trying to make sense out of this game. That's why we come back to it, season after season. That's why we throw out our old lists every fall, make new ones, and enter this spring's Draft confident that we're going to do better.

Then, once the season begins, and our boys stumble out of the box, and our ace closer goes down, and our high risk-high reward pick (a Rockies pitcher? a can't-miss rookie?) turns out all risk and no reward, we go to the trade market. Last summer, sitting in a strong third-place position, I made a deal that I was absolutely certain would push me forward, at least to second and maybe to the top: a big banger (Richie Sexson) who's an arguable keeper next year at $22 for three lesser regulars who, collectively, will make up Sexson's RBIs and HRs, plus a solid starter (Matt Clement). The result? The Goners sink to 6th.

The moral? The ball takes some really funny bounces, even—especially—in Rotisserie League Baseball.

This season, as always, you face a lot of tough questions: Is Barry Bonds (45, 90, .341 at age 40) *ever* going to slow down? Is Larry Walker 16, 79, .284 at age 37 on Opening Day) done—at least as a premium Rotisserie player? Is Jason Giambi (41, 107 but .250 and no good knees) worth big bucks? Mike Piazza? Alfonso Soriano? Jimmy Rollins?

Pitching's even tougher to call. Always has been, always will be. Which of these guys did you pick to finish in the top 10 in NL ERA last spring: Brandon Webb, Hideo Nomo or Luis Hernandez? (Thought so). If you guessed right (and put your money where your mouth was) on even one of those, you probably also figured that Ryan Franklin and Darrell May would have ERAs under 4.00 in the AL (the rough equivalent of 3.50 in the NL). Oh, and you obviously had Dontrelle Willis (14-6, 3.30, NL Rookie of the Year, savior of baseball in South Florida) in your Farm System, didn't you? *Didn't you?*

Once again, I'm guessing that most of us overlooked middle relievers. (I know I did.) In the NL, Joe Nathan, Luis Ayala and Oscar Villareal combined for more wins than Roy Oswalt, Kirk Rueter and Matt Morris had in more than twice as many IP. (And the first three cost, what, a twentieth of what the latter three fetched in your Draft?) In the AL, because starters in close games don't have to be pinch-hit for, there are fewer unsung middle innings heroes, but wouldn't you have preferred to have Bruce Kim and LaTroy Hawkins (for $2-3 combined) and their 17 wins instead Derek Lowe (for mid-double figures) and his 17 W's?

As always, though, making the right call on closers turned out to be the most confounding task. In the AL, only nine closers had 20 saves or more (actually, the dropoff was from 16 to 15). In the NL, 16 guys had 20 saves or more, but I'm not sure whether that's a blessing or a curse. And do you plunk down large dollars for a bona fide, guaranteed, take-it-to-the-bank ace (Mariano Rivera, John Smoltz)? Or do you spend a fraction of that on a bullpen by committee? Hey, it didn't work out so well for the Red Sox, but you'd have been hugging yourself all winter had you bought Rocky Biddle and Danny Kolb for 10 cents on the dollar for what somebody else paid for Billy Wagner.

So what does all this mean? Three things: it's that time of year again (Play Ball!); it ain't over 'til it's over; and you really need to read the rest of this book.

Oh, yeah—one more thing: the secret to winning. That's easy. Spend the first three months after the Super Bowl thinking about nothing, *nothing*, but your Rotisserie team. (But I don't need to tell you that, do I?) And be lucky.

Really lucky.

1

Ground Rules

OFFICIAL CONSTITUTION OF
ROTISSERIE LEAGUE BASEBALL

Preamble

We,

*the people of the Rotisserie League, in order
to spin a more perfect Game,
drive justice home,
kiss domestic Tranquility good-bye,
promote the general Welfare
in Tidewater—where it's been
tearing up the International League—and secure the
Blessings of Puberty to ourselves
and those we've left on Base,
do ordain and establish this
Constitution for Rotisserie League Baseball,
and also finish this run-on sentence.*

ARTICLE I. OBJECT

To assemble a lineup of 25 National League or 23 American League baseball players whose cumulative statistics during the regular season, compiled and measured by the methods described in these rules, exceed those of all other teams in the League.

ARTICLE II. TEAMS

There are 12 teams in a duly constituted Rotisserie League composed of either National League or American League players.

> **NOTE:** If you choose to play with fewer teams, be sure to make necessary adjustments so that you acquire approximately 80% of all available players at your auction draft. You could have a six-team league using American League players, for example, and draft only from among your seven favorite AL teams. Unless you reduce the available player pool proportionately to reflect a reduced number of teams, you'll never learn to appreciate the value of a good bench.

> **NOTE:** Do *not* mix the two leagues. It's unrealistic and silly, it's not the way the big leagues do it, it means you end up using only All-Stars and established regulars, and it's fattening. (On the other hand, if you *do* mix leagues, we're not going to call out the Rotisserie National Guard or anything.)

ARTICLE III. ROSTER

A team's active roster consists of the following players:

1. **NATIONAL LEAGUE PLAYERS**
   Five outfielders, two catchers, one second baseman, one shortstop, one middle infielder (either second baseman or shortstop), one first baseman, one third baseman, one corner man (either first baseman or third baseman), two utility players (who may play any non-pitching position), and ten pitchers.

2. **AMERICAN LEAGUE PLAYERS**
   The same, but only one utility player and nine pitchers. The utility player is called a designated hitter, consistent with the AL's insistence on perpetuating that perversion of the game.

ARTICLE IV. AUCTION DRAFT DAY

A **Major League Player Auction** is conducted on the first weekend after Opening Day of the baseball season. Each team must acquire 23 players at a total cost not to exceed $260 in the American League, or 25 players at a cost not to exceed $280 in the National League. A team need not spend the maximum. The League by general agreement determines the order in which teams may nominate players for acquisition. The team bidding first opens with a minimum salary bid of $1 for any eligible player, and the bidding proceeds around the room at minimum increments of $1 until only one bidder is left. That team acquires the player for that amount and announces the roster position the player will fill. The process is repeated, with successive team owners introducing players to be bid on, until every team has a squad of 23 players, by requisite position, for the American League, or 25 players for the National League.

- Don't get hung up on the bidding order; it's irrelevant. Do allow plenty of time; your first draft will take all day.
- Players eligible at more than one position may be shifted during the course of the draft.
- No team may make a bid for a player it cannot afford. For example, a team with $3 left and two openings on its roster is limited to a maximum bid of $2 for one player.
- No team may bid for a player who qualifies only at a position that the team has already filled. For example, an AL team that has acquired two catchers, and whose utility or DH slot is occupied, may not enter the bidding for any player who qualifies only at catcher.
- Players who commence the season on a major league team's disabled list are eligible to be drafted. If selected, they may be reserved and replaced upon completion of the auction draft. (See **Article XII**.)

NOTE: Final Opening Day rosters for all National League or American League teams will be needed on Auction Draft Day. Because some teams don't make their final roster moves until the last minute, even *USA Today's* rosters, published on Opening Day, have holes. The best way to get the most complete, updated rosters is with membership in the **Rotisserie League Baseball Association**. (See the Front Office chapter for information on how to join.)

A **Minor League Player Draft** is conducted immediately following the major league auction, in which each Rotisserie League team may acquire players (a) who are not on any National/American League team's active roster; and (b) who still have official rookie status, as defined by major league baseball.

NOTE: The major league rule reads: "A player shall be considered a rookie unless, during a previous season or seasons, he has (a) exceeded 130 at-bats or 50 innings pitched in the major leagues; or (b) accumulated more than 45 days on the active roster of a major league club or clubs during the period of a 25-player limit (excluding time in the military service)."

- Selection takes place in two rounds of a simple draft, not an auction.
- In the first season, the selection order shall be determined by drawing paired numbers from a hat (that is, positions 1 and 24, 2 and 23, and so on, in a 12-team league).
- In subsequent years, the selection order in each of the two rounds is determined by the order in which the teams finished in the previous season. In leagues with 12 teams, the 6th place team selects first, proceeding in descending order to the 12th place team, which is in turn followed by the 5th, 4th, 3rd, 2nd, and 1st place teams.
- The price and subsequent salary upon activation of each farm system player drafted is $10.
- See **Article XIII** for rules governing farm systems.

NOTE: The order of selection stated above represents a change from early years of Rotisserie baseball, when teams selected in reverse order of the final standings of the preceding season's pennant race. By awarding the first selection to the highest finisher among second-division teams instead of the last team, we seek to offer an incentive to teams to keep plugging and a disincentive to finish last (in the past, a last place finish would be "rewarded" with the first farm-draft pick).

ARTICLE V. POSITION ELIGIBILITY

A player may be assigned to any position at which he appeared in 20 or more games in the preceding season. If a player did not appear in 20 games at a single position, he may be drafted only at the position at which he appeared most frequently. The 20 games/most games measure is used only to determine the position(s) at which a player may be drafted. Once the season is under way (but after Auction Draft Day), a player becomes eligible for assignment to any position at which he has appeared at least once. In American League versions, players selected as DH's may qualify at any position (i.e., they need not have appeared in 20 games as DH the preceding season). In National League versions, players selected for the utility slot may qualify at any position.

Two of the official major league sources for determining player eligibility are the National League's *Green Book* and the American League's *Red Book*. Both list appearances by position under fielding averages. The *Red Book* lists all players who appeared as designated hitters the preceding season. Circulating an eligibility list by position before Auction Draft Day saves a lot of time. Prepare one yourself in March, when the *Green Book* and *Red Book* are published. Or obtain it with membership in the **Rotisserie League Baseball Association** - our list is available at least five months earlier, so you'll be able to spend the winter doing something worthwhile. Spend a few minutes before your auction to settle eligibility questions and assign eligibility to rookies. When in doubt, use common sense (instead of knives) to resolve disputes.

ARTICLE VI. FEES

The Rotisserie league has a schedule of fees covering all player personnel moves. No money passes directly from team to team. No bets are made on the outcome of any game. All fees are payable into the prize pool and are subsequently distributed to the top four teams in the final standings. (See **Articles VIII** and **IX**.)

1. **BASIC:** The cumulative total of salaries paid for acquisition of a 23 man roster on Auction Draft Day may not exceed $260 in the AL or $280 in the NL.

2. **TRANSACTIONS:** $10 per trade (no matter how many players are involved) or player activation (from reserve list or farm system). In a trade, the team that pays the fee is subject to negotiation.

3. **CALLUP FROM FREE AGENT POOL:** $25 for each player called up from the free agent pool.

4. **RESERVE:** $10 for each player placed on a team's reserve list (see **Article XII**).

5. **FARM SYSTEM:** $10 for each player in a team's farm system (see **Article XIII**).

6. **ACTIVATION:** $10 for each player activated from the reserve list or farm system.

7. **WAIVERS:** $10 for each player claimed on waivers (see **Article XV**).

8. **SEPTEMBER ROSTER EXPANSION:** $50 (see **Article XVI**).

ARTICLE VII. PLAYER SALARIES

The salary of a player is determined by the time and means of his acquisition and does not change unless the player becomes a free agent or is signed to a guaranteed long-term contract. (See **Article XVII.**)

- The salary of a player acquired in the major league draft is his auction price.
- The salary of a player called up from the free agent pool during the season is $10.
- The salary of a player activated from a team's farm system during the season is $10.
- The salary of a player claimed on waivers is $10.
- The salary of a player called up during September Roster Expansion to supplement the 23-man roster (AL) or 25-man roster (NL) is $25 if he is drawn from the free agent pool. (See **Article XVI.**)

NOTE: Because you can commit only $260 for salaries on Auction Draft Day ($280 for NL), and because you will keep some of your players from one season to the next, salaries are *extremely* important, particularly after the first season ends and winter trading begins. Would you trade Barry Bonds for Steve Finley? The Giants wouldn't. But a smart Rotisserie League owner just might make such a deal in the *offseason*, if Bonds' salary was $35 higher, because the difference between Bonds' and Finley's auction price is enough to buy a frontline starter and an everyday outfielder. Maintaining accurate, centralized player-personnel records of salary and contract status is the most important task of the League Secretary, who deserves hosannas from the other owners for all the work he does.

NOTE: The $260/$280 salary limit pertains to Auction Draft Day *only*. After Auction Draft Day, free agent signings and acquisition of high-priced players in trades may well drive up a team's payroll.

ARTICLE VIII. PRIZE MONEY

All fees shall be promptly collected by the League Treasurer, who is empowered to subject owners to public humiliation and assess fines as needed to ensure that payments are made to the league in a timely fashion. The interest income from this investment can be used to defray the cost of a gala postseason awards ceremony and banquet. The principal shall be divided among the first four teams in the final standings as follows:

- 1st place - 50%
- 2nd place - 20%
- 3rd place - 15%
- 4th place - 10%
- 5th place - 5%

ARTICLE IX. STANDINGS

The following criteria are used to determine team performance:

- Composite batting average (BA)
- Total runs scored (R)
- Total home runs (HR)
- Total runs batted in (RBI)
- Total stolen bases (SB)

- Composite earned run average (ERA)
- Total innings pitched (IP)
- Total wins (W)
- Total saves (SV)
- Composite ratio: walks (BB) + hits (H), divided by innings pitched (IP)

Teams are ranked from first to last in each of the eight categories and given points for each place. For example, in a 12-team league, the first-place team in a category receives 12 points, the second-place team 11, and so on down to 1 point for last place. The team with the most total points wins the pennant.

NEW CATEGORIES IN 2003 - Astutue readers will notice that runs scored and innings pitched are new categories beginning in 2003, thus making a total of ten categories. Taditionalists dedicated to the "standard eight" categories are free, of course, to continue in their set ways. The addition of runs and innings will render unnecessary the following rules, which have been the source of much argument, although again traditionalists may keep them:

THE FENOKEE IP REQUIREMENT - A team must pitch a total of 900 innings to receive points in ERA and ratio. A team that does not pitch 900 innings maintains its place in ERA and ratio ranking but receives zero points in both of these categories. (Thus, a team that finished third in ERA but did not have 900 IP would receive no points in that category. The fourth-place team in ERA would still receive 9 points.) This rule was passed in 1988 in response to an "all-relief" strategy attempted by the Okrent Fenokees in the 1987 season. The strategy was not successful because Swampmaster Dan Okrent abandoned it after six weeks or so. But it might have worked, in more disciplined hands. Hence the rule.

THE FENOKEE AB REQUIREMENT - A team must have 4250 at-bats in the season. A team that does not have 4250 at-bats maintains its place in the batting average ranking but receives zero points in that category. This rule was passed in 1991 in response to an "all-pitching" strategy attempted by the Okrent Fenokees in 1990. This time, the Beloved Founder and Former Commissioner-for-Life assembled an All-Star pitching staff, Tony Gwynn, and 13 Ken Oberkfells (the 1990 equivalent of a Greg Colbrunn type of player, i.e., guys who didn't play enough to bring down Gwynn's "team" BA). The BFFCL hoped to amass pitching points, by spending excessively on top pitchers and dominating all pitching categories, while scoring at the top of the BA category and scoring one point each in the other offensive categories to squeeze into the first division. The strategy was not successful because the Swampmaster abandoned it after six weeks or so. But it might have worked, in more disciplined hands.

The addition of new cumulative statistics, one each in hitting and pitching, combined with the elimination of the Fenokee rules, will create an open invitation for any disciplined owner now to attempt the Fenokee methods.

- Pitchers' offensive stats are *not* counted, mainly because they don't appear weekly in *USA Today*. Nor are the pitching stats of the occasional position player called in to pitch when the score is 16-1 after five innings and the relief corps is hiding under the stands.
- In cases of ties in an individual category, the tied teams are assigned points by totaling points for the rankings at issue and dividing the total by the number of

teams tied.

- In cases of ties in total points, final places in the standings are determined by comparing placement of teams in individual categories. Respective performances are calculated and a point given to each team for bettering the other. Should one team total more points than the other, that team is declared the winner.
- Should the point totals still be equal, the tie is broken by adding each team's *total runs scored* at season's end (the object of the game on the field being to score more runs than the opposition). This new tie-break method thus leave *the number of innings pitched* as a separate and final tie-breaker.

ARTICLE X. STATS

The weekly player-performance summaries published in *USA Today* beginning in April constitute the official data base for the computation of standings in Rotisserie League Baseball.

> **NOTE:** When we first started out, we used *The Sporting News*. Not for nothing was the Holy Bible known to baseball people as *The Sporting News* of religion. But that was then, and this is now. When *USA Today* began to appear daily everywhere, American culture changed. Whether the newspaper was sitting outside a hotel room door, or in one of those vending boxes that takes two quarters (and which might be a reason to walk a mile during the heat of a July pennant race) Rotisserians changed their ways of thinking about the world. With the advent of the internet, *The Sporting News* has once again become a viable daily source. So has STATS Inc. Just the same, it is fitting and proper for everyone in every league to have the same final source authority as the last word, considering that these various sources don't always agree the day after the season ends.

- The effective date of any transaction for purposes of statistical calculation is the Monday (AL) or Tuesday (NL) *before* the commencement of play on those days. This is because weekly stats have traditionally appeared in *USA Today* on Tuesday for AL games through the preceding Sunday and on Wednesday for NL games through the preceding Monday.
- Reporting deadlines should be established as close to these breaks as possible but not later than the start of any game at the beginning of a new reporting period. Noon on Monday (AL) or Tuesday (NL) makes sense.
- Transactions recorded on Auction Draft Day, including trades and callups to replace disabled players, are effective retroactive to Opening Day. Transactions occurring after Auction Draft Day but before the closing date of the first cumulative summaries to appear in *USA Today* in April are effective the Monday (AL) or Tuesday (NL) immediately after the first closing date.
- Performance stats of a player shall be assigned to a Rotisserie League team only when he is on the active 23-man or 25-man roster of that team. It is common for a player to appear on the roster of more than one Rotisserie League team during the season because of trades and waiver-list moves. Even a player who is not traded may spend time on a team's reserve list, during which period any numbers compiled for his major league team do not count for his Rotisserie League team.
- Standings shall be tabulated and issued in a regular and timely fashion, as determined by the league owners.

> **NOTE:** Keeping score is the only part of Rotisserie League Baseball that isn't any fun. Unless you're computerized, it's tedious and time-consuming. And even if your league does have a computer wonk on board, it still means he or she can't

take a vacation between Opening Day and early October. (God forbid your league should go a week without standings!) The best solution: Let the official stat service authorized by the Founding Fathers do all the heavy lifting for you (see Front Office chapter).

A season is a season, as reported in *USA Today*. Sometimes a team may play a 163rd game as a one-game "playoff." Live with it, and enjoy the extra excitement. Or tell your stat service (now, not in October) that you want to end the season after 162 games, no matter what, and offer to pay extra for a special cutoff.

ARTICLE XI. TRADES

From the completion of the auction draft until August 31, Rotisserie League teams are free to make trades of any kind without limit, except as stipulated below, *so long as the active rosters of both teams involved in a trade reflect the required position distribution upon completion of the transaction.* No trades are permitted from September 1 through the end of the season, or between frozen roster submission and Auction Draft Day. Trades made from the day after the season ends until rosters are frozen on April 1 prior to Auction Draft Day are not bound by the position distribution requirement.

> **NOTE:** This means that if Team A wants to swap Vladimir Guerrero to Team B for Curt Schilling any time between Auction Draft Day and the trade deadline, Team A will have to throw in a bum pitcher and Team B a duff outfielder to make the deal. During the off-season, the two could be dealt even-up.

- Trades do not affect the salaries or contract status of players.
- Each trade is subject to the $10 transaction fee. The fee is not affected by the number of players involved in the trade.
- Unless you want knife fights to break out among owners, prohibit all trades involving cash, players to be named later, or "future considerations." Trust us.

> **NOTE ON DUMPING:** "Dumping" is the inelegant but scientifically precise term used to describe what happens when a team out of contention gives up on the season and trades to a contending team its most expensive talent and its players who will be lost to free agency at the end of the year, typically for inexpensive players who can be kept the following season. A "dumping" trade is always unbalanced, sometimes egregiously so, with the contending team giving up far less than it gets, and the noncontending team giving up much more in order to acquire a nucleus for the following season. While this strategy makes sense for both clubs, extreme cases can potentially undermine the results of the auction draft, which should always be the primary indicator of an owner's ability to put together a successful team. To guard against this, we have in the past employed rigid and restrictive Anti-Dumping measures to control trades between contenders and noncontenders. But in light of major shifts in international politics and economics in recent years, we decided in 1993 that these restrictive measures tended to inhibit rather than enhance the playing of the game. Accordingly, we swept away all Anti-Dumping legislation in 1993. We did so with some trepidation, but we felt the benefits of a free market would outweigh the potential for abuses. We were right. Let freedom ring.

If your league still wants Anti-Dumping legislation, see **Article XXI.**

ARTICLE XII. THE RESERVE LIST

A team may replace any player on its 23-man (or 25-man) roster who is:

- placed on the **disabled list**
- **released**
- **traded** to the other league
- **sent down** to the minors by his major league team

To replace such a player, a Rotisserie League team must first release him outright or place him on its reserve list. A team reserves a player by notifying the League Secretary and paying the $10 transaction fee. A reserved player is removed from a team's active roster at the end of the stat week (on Monday or Tuesday) - when formal notification is given - and placed on the team's reserve list. There is no limit to the number of players a team may have on its reserve list. Reserving a player protects a team's rights to that player.

A team has two weeks to take action once a player is placed on the disabled list, released, traded to the other league, or sent to the minors by his major league team. If no action is taken, the position is frozen open until the original player's return, and no replacement may be made, except as provided under **Article XIV** after the All-Star game.

- *A suspended player may not be reserved, released, or replaced.*

NOTE: When we first wrote that, we were thinking about the old-fashioned things players might do to get themselves suspended - Bill Madlock hitting an umpire (1980), say, or Gaylord Perry throwing spitter (1962 to 1983), although he was suspended for doing it only once (1982). Then came the drug suspensions of 1984 and afterward. We have decided to consider players suspended for substance abuse as if they were on the disabled list, and allow teams to replace them.

- Once a specific action has been taken to remove a player from its 23 or 25-man roster (via release or placing him on the reserve list), a team is then free to select any eligible player from the free agent pool of players not already owned by another Rotisserie League team. The salary assigned to a player selected from the free agent pool is $10; the callup fee is $25 (see **Article VI**).
- If the same player is claimed by more than one team in a given week, he goes to the team ranking lowest in the most recent standings.
- Every reserve move must be accompanied by a concomitant replacement move (i.e., a team may not reserve a player without replacing him).
- Placing a player *on* the reserve list and activating a player *from* the reserve list are *each* subject to a $10 transaction fee.
- The callup takes effect as soon as it is recorded by the League Secretary, although the player's stats do not begin to accrue to his new team until Monday (AL) or Tuesday (NL) of the week the League Secretary records the callup.
- Player moves are to be made in accordance with the player's status as of the transaction reporting deadline. For instance, if a player is active on his major league roster on the transaction reporting deadline, he cannot be reserved, even though he was on the DL earlier in the reporting period.
- A player on a Rotisserie League reserve list may not be traded *unless* the replacement player linked to him is also traded.
- A replacement player may be traded or otherwise replaced (e.g., in case of injury, he could be reserved and a free agent called up to fill his slot). In such a case, the newly acquired player becomes linked to the original reserved player. To avoid

even the appearance of collusion, a replacement player traded from one team to another may not be traded back to his original team for three reporting periods.

- When a player on a reserve list returns to active major league duty, he must be **reinstated** to the active 23 or 25-man roster of his Rotisserie League team *two weeks* after his activation or be **waived**. Failure to notify the League Secretary shall be considered a waiver of the player on the reserve list. A player may not be **reinstated** or **waived** until he has been activated by his major league team.

NOTE: Intended to prevent stockpiling of players, this rule is tricky to monitor. Daily newspaper transaction columns and telephone sports information lines don't always catch every single major league roster move. The clock starts ticking when the League Secretary *is made aware of* a player being reactivated. By the way, "two weeks" means two full reporting periods and may actually be as long as two weeks plus six days (as in the case of a player being reactivated the day after a reporting deadline). In fairness, and because this game is not full-contact karate but a game played among friends, an owner should be given warning by the League Secretary that time is up and he will lose a player if he doesn't make a move. Especially if there are extenuating circumstances (i.e., anything from retracing Livingston's steps in Africa to just plain laziness).

NOTE: The League Secretary being "made aware" requires some objective evidence so that Secretaries cannot be subjected to phone calls with some content such as, "You have been made aware, because I just made you aware." Be cautious about media "announcements." It is not unusual for a major league team's media director (or the field manager, or some other official) to announce in a post-game interview that the team has decided to call up one player and send down another player. or to put one on the DL while activating another. Such communications often occur the night before the transaction is actually communicated to the league office. And if you think Rotisserie League Secretaries can be fussy, they are easy, compared to the MLB bureaucracy. Awareness of player moves should thus be linked to some agreed-upon source of actual transactions, so that league Secretaries never have to rely on what somebody heard on the radio or saw on television.

- When a player is reinstated to the active 23 or 25-man Rotisserie League roster from a team's reserve list, the player originally called up to replace him must be waived, unless the replacement player or the original player can be shifted to another natural opening on the roster for which he qualifies.
- If the replacement player is replaced (e.g., he is injured, put on reserve, and a free agent is called up), then *his* replacement becomes linked to the original player on the reserve list.
- A player reinstated from the reserve list may not displace any active player on the Rotisserie League team's 23-man roster *other than* his original replacement (or his successor).

NOTE: The intent of all this is to minimize the benefit a team might derive from an injury. Say Jeff Bagwell breaks his wrist (nah, could never happen again) and you call up the inevitable Greg Colbrunn to replace him. Bagwell comes back. What you'd like to do is activate Bagwell, keep Colbrunn and waive your other corner man, who hasn't had more than five at-bats any week since the season began. Our rules say you can't, on the premise that *a team is not ordinarily helped by an injury to a key player.* We know the big leagues don't handle it this way, but art doesn't always imitate life. No owner should be let off the hook freely after drafting a player who rarely plays.

ARTICLE XIII. FARM SYSTEM

If a farm system player is promoted to the active roster of a major league team at any time during the regular season *prior* to September 1 (when major league rosters may expand to 40), his Rotisserie League team has *two weeks* after his promotion to **activate** him (at any position for which he qualifies) or **waive** him.

- The fee for activating a player from a team's farm system is $10.
- If a farm system player is activated, the player displaced from the 23-man or 25-man roster to make room for him must be placed on waivers, *unless* the farm system player can be activated into a natural opening, in which case no waiver is required. **Example:** One of your pitchers is placed on a major league disabled list; you reserve him and activate a pitcher from your farm system who has been called up by his major league team.
- Once brought up from its farm system by a Rotisserie League team, a player may not be returned to it, although he may be placed on a team's reserve list in the event he is returned to the minor leagues by his major league club.
- A farm system player not brought up to a team's 23-man or 25-man roster during the season of his initial selection may be kept within the farm system in subsequent seasons upon payment of an additional $10 per year, so long as he retains official rookie status and the League Secretary is duly notified on April 1 each year, when rosters are frozen. (See also **Article XVIII.**) If the player makes the majors on Opening Day, the owner must choose to freeze him ($10) or release him.
- A team may have no more than three players in its farm system.
- A farm system player may be traded during authorized trading periods, subject to prevailing rules governing transactions, as may a team's selection rights in the minor league draft.

NOTE: This means that a team could acquire and exercise as many as three farm system draft picks, providing that it does not exceed the maximum of three players in its farm system at a given time.

ARTICLE XIV. SIGNING FREE AGENTS

Active major league players not on any Rotisserie League team's roster at the conclusion of the auction draft become free agents. During the course of the season the pool of free agents may also include minor league players not in any Rotisserie League farm system (see **Article XIII**) who are promoted to an active major league roster; waived players who are not claimed; and players traded from the "other" major league. Such players may be signed in the following manner.

From Opening Day Until the All-Star Game. Free agents may be called up to replace players placed on a Rotisserie League team's reserve list as outlined in **Article XII**. The only exception to **Article XII's** provisions for signing free agents during this period is that a player traded into the league from the "other" major league or signed by a team within the league as a free agent may be signed by a Rotisserie League team with its **Free Agent Acquisition Budget (FAAB)**, as described below.

After the All-Star Game. From the All-Star Game until the last weekly transaction deadline before September 1, free agents may be signed, without limit in number, but within the limitations of a Rotisserie League team's **Free Agent Acquisition Budget:**

- Each team shall have, for the purpose of acquiring free agents during the course of the season, a supplementary budget of $100.
- At the deadline established by each league for recording weekly transactions, a team may submit a sealed bid for one or more free agents.
- The minimum bid shall be $5; the maximum shall be the amount remaining in a team's **FAAB**.
- A free agent so selected goes to the highest bidder. If more than one team bids the same amount on a player, and if that amount is the highest bid, the player goes to the team that is lowest in the most recently issued standings.
- The salary of a free agent signed in this manner is his acquisition price. His contract status is that of a first-year player.
- In addition to the player's acquisition price, a team signing a free agent must pay the $25 transaction fee for calling up free agents as set forth in **Article VI**.
- For each free agent that it signs, a team *must* at the same time waive or release a player at the same position from its *active* roster. If on a major league team's *active* roster, such a player is *waived*. If he has been placed on a major league team's disabled list, *released*, traded to the "other" league, or demoted to the minors, such a player is released and may not be acquired by a Rotisserie League team until he is once again on a major league roster.
- A free agent signed for a salary in excess of $10 (i.e., more than the customary call-up fee for replacement players) is deemed to have a guaranteed two-year contract. If such a player is not protected the following season (i.e., if he is released into the free agent pool at the time rosters are frozen on April 1), then a contract buyout fee in the amount of twice his salary or $100, whichever is greater, shall be paid by the team owning his contract at the time.
- If a Rotisserie League team loses a player to the "other" league in an interleague trade, then the team's available **FAAB** dollars are increased by an amount equal to the lost player's salary.

NOTE: If a team wishes to replace an injured player and reserve him, it must use the mechanism described in **Article XII**; it may not use the FAAB process without releasing the player. The highest FAAB bid gets the free agent regardless of DL (and here is the only possible relief to replace a frozen roster slot as defined in **Article XII**; justice derives from the price paid to fix the problem).

NOTE: The provision regarding players acquired for a sum in excess of the customary $10 callup fee is intended to discourage frivolous bidding for free agents. It is also intended to make teams who are most likely to benefit from signing costly free agents — that is, teams still in the race for the first division — pay for it dearly, by making such players expensive to dump the following spring.

NOTE: Set up a simple, common-sense mechanism for handling the "sealed bid" part of the **FAAB** process. Nothing elaborate is needed. Price Waterhouse need not be called in. Don't permit bidders to make contingency bids (e.g., "If I don't get Ruth at $29, then I'll bid $25 for Gehrig, and if I don't get Gehrig ... ") unless your League Secretary doesn't have a day job.

ARTICLE XV. WAIVERS

Under certain conditions, a Rotisserie League player may be waived.

- When a player on a Rotisserie League team's reserve list is activated by his major league team, either he or the player called up earlier to replace him *must* be placed on waivers (see **Article XII**).
- When a team activates a player from its farm system, except into a natural opening (see **Article XIII**), the player dropped from the 23-man or 25-man roster to make room for him *must* be placed on waivers.
- A player no longer on the active roster of his major league team and whose Rotisserie League position is taken by a player activated from the reserve list or farm system may not be placed on waivers but *must* be released outright.
- A player placed on waivers is no longer eligible to be claimed if he is sent down to the minors, traded to the other league, or is placed on the DL by his major league team.

NOTE: This is to prevent a team from picking up a disabled list player on waivers merely for the purpose of releasing him and replacing him with a player of higher quality from the free agent pool.

- The waiver period begins at noon on the Monday (AL) or Tuesday (NL) after the League Secretary has been notified that a player has been waived and lasts one week, at the end of which time the player shall become the property of the lowest-ranked team to have claimed him. To make room on its roster, the team acquiring a player on waivers must assign the player to a natural opening or waive a player at the same position played by the newly acquired player.
- Waiver claims take precedence over the replacement of an injured, released, or demoted player who has been put on reserve. That is, a player on waivers may be signed by a team with a roster opening at his position only if no other team lower in the standings claims the player on waivers.
- A team may acquire on waivers *no more* than one player in a given week, but there is no limit to the number of players a team may acquire on waivers during the season.
- A player who clears waivers — that is, is not claimed by any team — returns to the free agent pool.
- The fee for acquiring a player on waivers is $10. The salary of a player acquired on waivers shall be $10 or his current salary, whichever is greater. His contract status shall remain the same.
- A player with a guaranteed long-term contract may *not* be waived during the season. He may, however, be released and replaced if he is traded to the "other" league.
- A player may be given his outright release *only* if he is
        (a) unconditionally released,
        (b) placed on the "designated for assignment" list,
        (c) sent to the minors,
        (d) placed on the "disqualified" list,
        (e) traded to the "other" major league, or
        (f) placed on the disabled list.

ARTICLE XVI. SEPTEMBER ROSTER EXPANSION

If it chooses, a team may expand its roster for the pennant drive by calling up additional players after September 1 from the free agent pool, its own reserve list, or its own farm system. A team may call up as many players as it wishes, subject to payment of appropriate fees as outlined below, except that at no time may the number of active players on its roster exceed 40.

- The order of selection for September Roster Expansion is determined by the most recent standings, with the last-place team having first selection, and so on. During this 24-hour period, September Roster Expansion claims take precedence over waiver claims and routine callups to replace players who are disabled, released, or traded to the other league by their major league teams. This selection order pertains until midnight, September 2, *only,* after which time a team forfeits its order in the selection process, though *not* its right to make a selection. Selection after midnight, September 2, is on a first-come, first-served basis. Also, after midnight, September 2, waiver claims and routine callups to fill natural openings take precedence over September Roster Expansion claims.
- Players are selected in a round by round draft format. If, after a selection, no other team wishes to claim a player, a team may then claim as many players consecutively as it wishes up to the 40-man roster limit.
- The performance stats of players called up during September Roster Expansion start to accrue on the Monday (AL) or Tuesday (NL) after the League Secretary has been notified of the player's selection.
- The fee for expanding the roster in September is $50 per player.
- The salary assigned to a September callup from the free agent pool is $25. The salary of a September callup from a team's reserve list or farm system is the salary established at the time he was previously acquired (on Auction Draft Day, or subsequently from the free agent pool, or via waivers).

NOTE: A device for heightening the excitement for contending teams and for sweetening the kitty at their expense, September Roster expansion will generally not appeal to second-division clubs (who should, however, continue to watch the waiver wire in the hope of acquiring" keepers" for next season at a $10 salary).

ARTICLE XVII. THE OPTION YEAR AND GUARANTEED LONG-TERM CONTRACTS

A player who has been under contract at the same salary during two consecutive seasons and whose service has been uninterrupted (that is, he has not been waived or released, although he may have been traded) must, prior to the freezing of rosters in his third season, be released; signed at the same salary for his option year; or signed to a guaranteed long-term contract. If **released**, the player returns to the free agent pool and becomes available to the highest bidder at the next auction draft. If signed at the same salary for an **option year**, the player must be released back into the free agent pool at the end of that season. If signed to a **guaranteed long-term contract,** the player's salary in each year covered by the new contract (which commences with the option year) shall be the sum of his current salary plus $5 for each additional year beyond the option year. In addition, a signing bonus, equal to one half the total value of the long-term contract but not less than $5, shall also be paid.

NOTE: This rule is intended to prevent blue-chippers, low-priced rookies who blossom into superstars, and undervalued players from being tied up for the duration of their careers by the teams who originally drafted them. It guarantees periodic transfusions of top-flight talent for Auction Draft Day and provides rebuilding teams something to rebuild with. And it makes for some interesting decisions at roster-freeze time two years down the pike.

- In determining a player's status, "season" is understood to be a full season or any fraction thereof. Thus, a player called up from the free agent pool in the middle of the 1998 season and subsequently retained at the same salary without being released in 1999 (even though he may have been traded) enters his option year in 2000 and must be released, signed at the same salary for an option year, or signed to a long-term contract.

- A team may sign a player to only one long-term contract, at the end of which he becomes a free agent.
- Option-year and long-term contracts are entirely transferable, both in rights and obligations; the trade of a player in no way affects his contract status.
- If, during the course of a long-term contract, a player is traded from the National League to the American League (or vice versa), the contract is rendered null and void. The team that loses the player's services shall be under no further financial obligations.
- In all other cases-specifically *including* sudden loss of effectiveness — a team must honor the terms of a long-term contract, as follows: A player with such a contract *may* be released back into the free agent pool (that is, not protected on a team's roster prior to Auction Draft Day), but a team that chooses to do so must pay into the prize pool, above the $260 or $280 Auction Draft Day limit, a sum equal to *twice* the remaining value of the player's contract or $100, whichever is greater.

ARTICLE XVIII. ROSTER PROTECTION

For the first three seasons of the League's existence, each team must retain, from one season to the next, *no fewer than* 7 but *no more than* 15 of the players on its 23-man or 25-man roster. After three seasons, this minimum requirement is eliminated, the maximum retained. The minimum is removed because, after three seasons, a team might find it impossible to retain a specific minimum because too many players have played out their option.

- The names of players being retained must be recorded with the League Secretary by midnight, April 1. Specific notice must also be made at that time of any guaranteed long-term contract signings and farm system renewals of players still in the minors (farm system players who make Opening Day rosters must be frozen at $10 or released).
- The cumulative salaries of players protected prior to Auction Draft Day are deducted from a team's $260 or $280 expenditure limit, and the balance is available for acquisition of the remaining players needed to complete the team's 23-man or 25-man roster.
- The League Secretary should promptly notify all teams in the League of each team's protected roster, including player salaries, contract status, and amount available to spend on Auction Draft Day.
- Failure to give notice of a guaranteed long-term contract for a player in his option year will result in his being continued for one season at his prior year's salary and then released into the free agent pool. Failure to renew a farm system player's minor league contract will result in his becoming available to all other teams in the subsequent minor league draft.
- A farm system player whose minor league contract is renewed on April 1 and who subsequently makes his major league team's active roster may at his Rotisserie League owner's option, be added to the protected list of players on Auction Draft Day (and another player dropped, if necessary, to meet the 15-player limit), or he may be dropped and made available in the auction draft. He may not be retained in his Rotisserie League team's farm system.

NOTE: The April 1 roster-protection deadline was originally set to correspond with the end of the major leagues' spring interleague trading period, a defunct rite of spring that still gives us a week or so to strategize. Until you know who the other teams are going to keep, you won't know for sure who's going to be available. And until you know how much they will have to spend on Auction Draft Day, you won't be able to complete your own predraft budget. So April 1 it is; don't fool with it.

ARTICLE XIX. GOVERNANCE

The Rotisserie League is governed by a Committee of the Whole consisting of all team owners. The Committee of the Whole may designate as many League officials as from time to time it deems appropriate, although only two - the League Secretary and the League Treasurer - ever do any work. The Committee of the Whole also designates annually an Executive Committee composed of three team owners in good standing. The Executive Committee has the authority to interpret playing rules and to handle all necessary and routine League business. All decisions, rulings, and interpretations by the Executive Committee are subject to veto by the Committee of the Whole. Rule changes, pronouncements, and acts of whimsy are determined by majority vote of the Committee of the Whole. Member leagues of the **Rotisserie League Baseball Association** may appeal to the RLBA for adjudication of disputes and interpretation of rules. The Rotisserie League has three official meetings each year: Auction Draft Day (the first weekend after Opening Day), the Midsummer Trade Meeting (at the All-Star break), and the Gala Postseason Banquet and Awards Ceremony. Failure to attend at least two official meetings is punishable by trade to the Minnesota Twins.

ARTICLE XX. YOO-HOO

To consecrate the bond of friendship that unites all Rotisserie League owners in their pursuit of the pennant, to symbolize the eternal verities and values of the Greatest Game for Baseball Fans Since Baseball, and to soak the head of the League champion with a sticky brown substance before colleagues and friends duly assembled, the **Yoo-Hoo Ceremony** is hereby ordained as the culminating event of the baseball season. Each year, at the awards ceremony and banquet, the owner of the championship team shall have a bottle of Yoo-Hoo poured over his or her head by the preceding year's pennant winner. The Yoo-Hoo Ceremony shall be performed with the dignity and solemnity appropriate to the occasion.

> **NOTE**: If Yoo-Hoo, the chocolate-flavored beverage once endorsed by soft-drink connoisseur Yogi Berra, is not available in your part of the country, you have two options: (a) send up an alternative beverage, one chosen in the Yoo-Hoo spirit, as a pinch-hitter, or (b) move.

ARTICLE XXI. THE IN-SEASON SALARY CAP

Having written a Constitution which at first excluded any anti-dumping provisions, then included the most elegant and finely-detailed anti-dumping rules existing anywhere on the planet thus ensuring domestic tranquility, and then repealed these anti-dumping provisions thus securing the blessings of liberty for all posterity, we decided to place the 1998 version of anti-dumping provisions in this carefully-chosen location, after the Yoo Hoo Article of the Constitution, where it can later be removed, re-added, or refined as we see fit, without affecting our Article numbering system any further, and we did all this without losing our ability to construct a run-on sentence.

There is more at issue here than player-dumping. The broader theme might be described as "roster excesses." Dumping can create rosters with team salaries in excess of $400. Throw in some FAAB spending such as would have transpired if the Kenny Lofton trade of 1997 had occurred just a few days later, think $99, and it becomes easy to envision a team salary over $500.

Experience has taught us that big roster excesses, if left unchecked, are not in the best interests of Rotisserie League Baseball. In 1997 we tested an idea called the in-season salary cap. We liked it. We always knew that a salary cap on Auction Draft Day is essential; now we know that a salary cap during the season can also be helpful. Here it is:

In a duly-constitiuted Rotisserie League, from Auction Draft Day until the end of the major league season, no team's salary may exceed the Auction Draft Day salary limit by more than $40. Specifically, in the American League with an Auction Draft Day salary limit of $260, the in-season limit is $300. In the National League with an Auction Draft Day Salary limit of $280, the in-season limit is $320.

ROTISSERIE ULTRA
The Rules of Play

Turn Up the Volume

Rotisserie Ultra requires more scouting, more planning, more wheeling, and more dealing. You move players off and onto your active roster as often as you want to. You ride guys on hot streaks, then ditch them when they go cold. You buy free agents. You bring along youngsters all the way from the low minors. You swing complicated, multiplier deals. You build a strong bench with waiver moves to carry you through injuries and slumps.

Does playing Rotisserie Ultra mean giving up all pretense of having a normal life? No, you should keep up that pretense as long as you can. It does mean that you're not going to have a lot of time for scuba diving the Great Barrier Reef, reading Joyce, learning to play the saxophone, paneling the rec room, or having a catch with your kid this summer. You're going to be busy, Bucky - or you're going to be in the second division.

Remember that the Sturgeon General himself — Peter Gethers, owner of Peter's Famous Smoked Fish - has warned that playing Rotisserie Ultra *before you're ready* can lead to "sensory overload, stress-related insomnia, pattern baldness, hot flashes, and premature ejaculation."

We recommend that fledgling leagues play the regular version of the game, become acclimated to its demands and pressures, and shake out owners who can't stand the heat of a pennant race before moving on to Ultra. Stay within yourselves, walk before you run, take it one game at a time, and floss regularly. Only then should you consider Ultra. After all, we can't have everybody in America having too much fun all at once.

Editor's Note: *Many of the rules in the Official Constitution of Rotisserie League Baseball also apply to Rotisserie Ultra, so we decided not to repeat every line of fine print that applies to both, except as needed for clarity. That means that the "Rules of Play" that follow for Rotisserie Ultra should be read together with the original Constitution. If you can't handle that assignment, you're going to have real trouble with Rotisserie Ultra.*

ULTRA I. THE ROTATION DRAFT

After the conclusion of the auction draft, in which teams acquire their 23-man or 25-man active rosters for a sum not to exceed $260 or $280, owners successively draft up to 17 additional players in 17 separate rounds of selection (15 in the NL). Initially, players acquired in this fashion comprise a team's reserve roster.

- Any baseball player is eligible for this draft. Exception: in National League versions, no player on the roster or in the minor league organization of an American League team may be selected; and, in American League versions, the opposite is true. Eligible players include (in the NL version, by way of example) previously undrafted NL players, NL owned minor leaguers, unsigned players, Japanese players, high school or college players, and the kid down the block with the great arm.
- In the rotation draft, owners are not required to select players by position. They may select all pitchers, all position players, or a mix.
- The order of selection for each of the 17 rounds is determined by the order of finish in the previous season. In leagues with 12 teams, the 6th place team selects first, proceeding in descending order to the 12th place team, followed by the 5th, 4th, 3rd, 2nd, and 1st place teams.

NOTE: For leagues switching over from Rotisserie League rules to Rotisserie League Ultra rules, the first two rounds of the rotation draft follow the order of the former farm system draft. Only players who have rookie status and are not on a major league 25-man roster or disabled list may be selected in these two rounds. This protects the property rights of teams that may have acquired additional farm system draft picks or improved their draft position via trades prior to the shift to Rotisserie League Ultra.

ULTRA II. THE RESERVE ROSTER

A team's reserve roster consists of those players acquired through the rotation draft, through trades, through demotions from the active roster, or through waiver claims. Any transaction (e.g., trade, demotion, waiver claim) that increases the size of the reserve roster beyond 17 players must be accompanied by a concomitant transaction (e.g., trade, promotion, waiver) that simultaneously returns the reserve roster to its maximum 17 (15 in the NL).

ULTRA III. FEES

1. **Basic:** The cumulative total of salaries paid for acquisition of a 23-man or 25-man active roster on Auction Draft Day may not exceed $260 (or $280 for NL).

2. **Reserve Roster:** There are no fees payable for the acquisition of players for the 17-man reserve roster.

3. **Transactions:** $10 per trade (no matter how many players are involved).

4. **Waivers:** $10 for each player claimed on waivers.

5. **September Roster Expansion:** $50 for each player added to a team's active roster in September.

ULTRA IV. PLAYER SALARIES

The salary of a player is determined by the time and means of his acquisition and does not change unless the player becomes a free agent by means of release or is signed to a guaranteed long-term contract.

THE EXTRA PITCHER OPTION

The Extra Pitcher Option allows a GM to realize the full potential of Ultra. Let's say you have the usual 9 pitchers and 14 position players (or 10 and 15) on your active roster, and your team starts slipping in wins. Presto! You send down the outfielder hitting .227 in your utility slot and promote a good middle innings guy from your reserve roster. In AL leagues, you must still have a DH, two catchers, and three middle infielders, so the 10th pitcher must come at the expense of a corner or an outfielder.

The Extra Pitcher Option provides more action, sweetens the pot through additional transaction fees, and is simple to administer and monitor. You can change the mix back and forth as frequently as you wish, provided only that the total number of active players does not exceed 23 for the AL and 25 for the NL, and that at no time do you have more than 14 active position players (15 for NL) or more than 10 active pitchers (11 for NL).

After hearing from leagues around the country regarding their experience with the Tenth Pitcher Option, we decided to leave it as just that — an option. Some leagues, particularly those using AL players, found it awkward to implement because of the DH. Others thought it was okay for Ultra but not regular Rotisserie. Still others simply didn't like it. Many made the transition smoothly.

Hey, that's why we call it an Option.

- The salary of a player acquired in the auction draft is his auction price.
- The salary of a player acquired in the rotation draft is determined as follows: If the player was selected in the first round, $15; rounds 2-6, $10; rounds 7-12, $5; rounds 13-17, $2.
- The salary of a player claimed on waivers is $10 or his previous salary, whichever, is greater. His contract status remains the same.

ULTRA V. TRADES

From the completion of the rotation draft until noon on the Monday ((AL) or Tuesday (NL) on or following August 31, teams are free to make trades of any kind without limit (except as indicated in **Ultra VI**, below). However, at no time can any team have on its active roster more players at a particular position than allowed under the rules of the auction draft (see **Article III** of the Official Constitution of Rotisserie League Baseball). A team may, however, be under-represented at a position. So long as these strictures are adhered to in the immediate wake of a trade, teams may trade any number of players, at any position, irrespective of the number or position of players being received in such trade (except, again, as indicated below in **Ultra VI**).

- At no point may a team have more than 17 players on its reserve roster (15 players in the NL) or more than 40 players on its active and reserve rosters combined.
- At no point may a team have more than 23 players on its active roster (25 for NL), except during the September Roster Expansion period (see **Ultra X**).
- No trades of any kind may be made between September 1 and October 15, nor between April 2 (Roster Freeze Day) and the conclusion of the rotation draft on Auction Draft Day.

ULTRA VI. ANTI-DUMPING

Players in the last year of a guaranteed contract or playing out their option year and players with a salary of $25 or more are considered "asterisk" players. Such players may be traded only under the following conditions:

- One team may trade asterisk players to another team provided that for each asterisk player traded, one is received in the same deal.
- The above notwithstanding, a team may trade one asterisk player to another team without an asterisk player coming in return or receive one asterisk player without giving one up, but may make only one such unbalanced trade in the course of the season.
- Between October 15 and Roster Freeze Day, asterisk players on winter rosters may be traded without restrictions whatsoever.

ULTRA VI-A. ANTI-DUMPING REPEALED

Effective Opening Day, 1993, Article **Ultra VI** (above) was repealed. The text of **Ultra VI** is left in place so that newcomers to **Ultra** will know just what is being done away with.

ULTRA VII. MOVEMENT BETWEEN ACTIVE ROSTER AND RESERVE ROSTER

An owner may demote a player from the active roster to the reserve roster, or promote a player in the reverse direction, at any time and for any reason, such promotions to take effect with the subsequent stat deadline (Monday noon for AL leagues, Tuesday noon for NL leagues). However, no player may be demoted without being replaced on the active roster by an eligible player — that is, a player who fulfills position eligibility requirements (which may include shifting another active player into the demoted player's position and the promoted player into the shifted player's position) and who is currently on a major league roster and not on a major league disabled list.

- **Exception:** If the acquisition of an active player in a trade places the acquiring team's active roster above the positional limit (e.g., more than two catchers), a player at that position may be sent down without the need for the recall of another player.
- A player acquired by trade from another team's active roster is considered active with the acquiring team on the effective date of the trade, unless the acquiring team chooses (or is compelled by roster restrictions) to demote him. Similarly, a player acquired in a trade from another team's reserve roster is considered to be reserved with the acquiring team, unless the acquiring team promotes him.

ULTRA VIII. SIGNING FREE AGENTS

Active major league players not on any Rotisserie League team's active roster or reserve roster at the conclusion of the auction draft become free agents. During the course of the season the pool of free agents may also include minor league players not on any Rotisserie League team's reserve roster who are promoted to an active major league roster; players traded from the "other" major league; and waived players who are not claimed. Beginning one week after the first standings report, and continuing through the season until the last weekly transaction deadline before September 1, such free agents may be signed, without limit, in the following manner:

- Each team shall have, for the purpose of acquiring free agents during the course of the season, a supplementary budget of $100, known as its **Free Agent Acquisition Budget (FAAB)**.

- At the deadline established by each Rotisserie League for recording weekly transactions, a Rotisserie League team may submit a *sealed* bid for one or more free agents.
- The minimum bid shall be $5; the maximum shall be the amount remaining in a team's **FAAB**.
- A free agent so selected goes to the highest bidder. If more than one team bids the same amount on a player, and if that amount is the highest bid, the player goes to the team that is lowest in the most recently compiled standings.
- The salary of a free agent signed in this manner is his acquisition price. His contract status is that of a first-year player.
- For each free agent that it signs, a team *must* at the same time waive or release a player from its *active* roster.
- If a free agent signed for a salary of $25 or more is not protected on the subsequent April 1 Roster Freeze, then the owner of his contract at the time must pay into the prize pool a buyout fee of twice his salary or $100, whichever is greater.

NOTE: The reason for the pre-September 1 deadline is to prevent Rotisserie League teams from completely restocking with $5 players when the major leagues expand their rosters to 40 in September.

NOTE: The mechanics of the "sealed bid" process will vary from league to league. Where practicable, as in leagues that have weekly meetings, the sealed bid should be just that — a bid sealed in an envelope that is opened at the meeting. In other cases, it may be more efficient to recruit a disinterested party to record all bids and report them to the League Secretary for action. Whatever mechanism you devise, keep matters in perspective. These aren't the secrets to nuclear fusion, for Einstein's sake! So try to balance the gee of security with the haw of mutual trust.

ULTRA IX. WAIVERS

Players are placed on waivers (a) when they cannot be accommodated on a team's active or reserve roster, because of space and/or positional limitations; and (b) under the rules governing the winter roster (see **Ultra XI**).

- The waiver period commences at noon on the Monday (AL) or Tuesday (NL) immediately following the team's notification of waiver to the League Secretary and extends for one full reporting period (i.e., one week). At the conclusion of that week, if the player is unclaimed, he goes into the free agent pool, and may be acquired by a team only as outlined in **Ultra VIII**, above.
- Waiver claims are honored according to the inverse order of the standings effective the week before the close of the waiver period.
- A team may reclaim a player it has waived only if all other teams in the league decline to claim him.
- The fee for acquiring a player on waivers is $10. The salary of a player acquired on waivers shall be $10 or his current salary, whichever is greater; and his contract status shall remain the same.
- Only a player currently on a 25-man major league roster (i.e., not on a disabled list) may be claimed on waivers.
- A player traded to the "other" league may not be placed on waivers.
- A player on a guaranteed long-term contract may not be placed on waivers, even in the final year of his contract.

ULTRA X. SEPTEMBER ROSTER EXPANSION

If it chooses, a team may expand its roster for the pennant drive by promoting from its reserve roster an *unlimited* number of players, as the post September 1 active-roster size expands to a maximum of 40 players. Such players may play any position.

> • September expansions can be effective no earlier than noon on the Monday (AL) or Tuesday (NL) immediately following August 31. Expansions made later in September become effective the subsequent Monday or Tuesday at noon.
> • A fee of $50 must be paid for every promotion that increases the active-roster size beyond 23 (or 25 for NL). Player salaries are not affected by such promotions.

ULTRA XI. WINTER ROSTER

Effective October 15, each owner is required to submit to the League Secretary a list of 23 players (25 for NL), irrespective of position, taken from its combined active and reserve rosters, but one not including any players who have concluded their option year or the last year of a guaranteed long-term contract. This group of players becomes the winter roster.

> • Immediately after the submission of winter rosters, a waiver period concluding at noon, November 1, begins. By inverse order of the final standings in the season just ended, teams may select no more than one player from that group of players not protected on a winter roster, again with the exception of players who have concluded their option year or the final year of a guaranteed long-term contract. On claiming such a player, the claiming team must, in turn, waive a player from its own winter roster. Players thus waived become eligible for a second round of waiver claims, for a period of one week, that are conducted the same fashion. Unclaimed players from the first waiver period are no longer eligible.) The process continues until there is a week in which no one is claimed.
> • All winter-waiver claims cost the claiming team $10, to be paid into the league treasury for the coming season.
> • The salary of a player claimed on winter waivers is $10 (or his current salary, whichever is greater), and he shall be deemed to be commencing the first year of a new contract with the coming season.
> • After October 23, winter rosters may exceed or fall below 23 (or 25) players through trading action. Whatever size the roster, however, any successful claim of a player on waivers must be accompanied by the placing of another player from the claiming team on waivers.

ULTRA XII. ROSTER PROTECTION

Roster protection in Rotisserie League and Rotisserie League Ultra is identical (see **Article XVIII**), except as follows:

> • The cumulative salaries of frozen players are deducted from a team's $260 or $280 expenditure limit in the auction draft, and the balance is available for the acquisition of the remainder of a team's active roster. However, salaries of players frozen on April 1 who are not on 25 man major league rosters on Auction Draft Day do not count against the $260 or $280 limit.
> • Frozen players not on 25-man major league rosters count against the limit of 17 players on Draft Day reserve rosters, and the salaries they carry must be paid into

the league treasury on Draft Day. In addition to the 15 players that a team may protect from its winter roster of active and reserve roster players, a team may also protect an additional 3 players on its reserve roster, provided that such players have rookie status and have never been active on a Rotisserie League team.

• Players frozen may include players who have spent the entire previous season on a reserve roster — typically because they played only in the minor leagues. Even so, such players who are subsequently frozen are deemed to be in the second year of their contract with their Rotisserie League Ultra team.

• Assignment of frozen players to a reserve roster position is at the owner's discretion. That is, an owner with a $10 minor leaguer carried over from the pre ceding year might, for strategic reasons, assign that player to the 17th position in the rotation draft, thus forgoing a $2 pick. Or the owner might assign the player to the first round and forgo a $15 pick. The assignment of frozen players by all teams will be made before the rotation draft commences.

NOTE: Some Ultra Leagues believe that the clock on minor leaguers should not start ticking until they are promoted to the majors, as in Rotisserie Regular. We feel this would tie up too many players and eventually undermine the auction draft. Effective in 1991, we increased the number of $2 and $5 players in the rotation draft (see **Ultra IV**). That should facilitate building a farm system and encourage protection of key players without providing the blanket protection of freezing the clock. This is called a compromise.

Let There Be Lite !

Great ideas often have implausibly pedestrian beginnings.

Isaac Newton was sitting under an apple tree, thinking he would like something sweet but tart and loaded with vitamin A, when the principle of gravity fell into his lap. A man who loved martinis a bit too much, Eli Whitney got his big inspiration when his wife yelled from the kitchen, "Keep your cotton picking hands off that gin!" And because somebody else was picking up the tab, Daniel Okrent, down from his rustic estate in western Massachusetts to join Manhattan friends for lunch, found himself eating snails and making history over a decade ago in the then-fashionable East Side bistro La Rotisserie Francaise, instead of wolfing down a grease-on-white-with-mayo at his favorite New York restaurant; and thus the world was deprived of Blimpie League Baseball.

Maybe there's something in the water up there in the Berkshire Mountains, or maybe there's just nothing else to do, but a few years back yet another bucolic Edison stumbled out of the backwoods with a new widget. Fortunately, BFFCL Okrent recognized his nearby neighbor's creation as an inspired variation on a great theme, an ingenious mechanism for filling an important sociocultural need, a cleverly constructed design with possible commercial potential.

So we stole it.

That's how we are able to bring you the newest version of The Greatest Game for Baseball Fans Since you - know - what, Rotisserie Lite! But before we do, common courtesy requires us to say a few words about the country bumpk ... ah, *squire* whom we city-slickered into giving away his invention for a handful of T-shirts and the promise to spell his name right.

Tony Lake (that's L-A-K-E) is a man for all seasons, though he definitely prefers summer. A hardscrabble farmer then biding his time between crops as a circuit-riding professor of international politics at several pricey New England colleges, Farmer-Professor Lake has been President Clinton's National Security Adviser and the highest-ranking Rotisserian in the world. He is a terminal Boston Red Sox fan who started playing Rotisserie League Baseball almost a decade ago, when BFFCL Okrent sold him a copy of the rules for 40 acres and a mule. Farmer-Professor Lake says the idea for Rotisserie Lite came to him one day near the end of the 1989 season when he was sitting on his tractor thinking about the Middle East situation.

"Late that season I suddenly found myself going sane," the tiller-scholar recalls. "I caught myself reading boxscores to find out who won, not just to see how my players had done. Some days I even read the front page first. Clearly, I was in trouble."

The academic-agrarian attacked the problem by identifying what he liked best and least about Rotisserie Ultra play in the League of Nations where his team — the Smuts Peddlers — had always been a strong contender. I like boxscores, and I like listening to games on the radio," he says. "I don't like the lure of trading, because it appeals to extreme type-A personalities like Okrent. I was spending too much time thinking about trades instead of about foreign policy or that funny sound my tractor was making."

While unwilling to go cold turkey (he still plays in the League of Nations), Farmer-Professor Lake did go looking for a halfway house. He found it when he founded the Washington Slo-Pitch League, a six-team outfit whose owners hail mostly from the nation's capital. (The mayor of the founder's hometown was awarded a one-third ownership in a franchise as a hedge against local tax increases. So far it's worked.)

"I see the game we play in Slo-Pitch as a halfway house in either direction," Farmer-Professor Lake says. "If you've never played Rotisserie before, it's a great way to learn what it's all about. And if you've been playing it too hard or too long, it helps you recapture the whimsy, and whimsy is the whole point of Rotisserie in the first place."

Thanks, Tony. We needed that.

ROTISSERIE LITE
The Rules of Play

Same Auction Draft!   **No Farm System!**
Same Stat Categories!   **No Reserve List!**
Same Yoo-Hoo!   **No Money!**

Editor's Note: The following rules were lifted from the unwritten constitution of the Washington Slo-Pitch League, with several embellishments and alterations of our own to give them a bogus air of originality. Please note that we were too lazy to repeat all the pertinent rules of Rotisserie Regular that also apply in Rotisserie Lite. That means you'll have to go back and read the **Official Constitution of Rotisserie League Baseball** *to figure out what we're talking about.*

LITE I. FEWER TEAMS

A Rotisserie Lite League using National League or American League players is composed of six teams.

> • With only six teams, Rotisserie Lite Leagues have shorter (and probably more orderly) auction drafts, fewer friendships to wreck, and less trouble squeezing into a telephone booth.

LITE II. ONLY SEVEN MAJOR LEAGUE TEAMS

A Rotisserie Lite League uses players from only seven major league teams.

> • Resist the temptation to draw players from an entire league or — worse still — to mix the two leagues. "Lite" doesn't mean "soft." By restricting the talent pool, Lite owners will need to scout as diligently as do Rotisserie Regular and Rotisserie Ultra owners. You'll have to learn which middle innings relievers can be counted on for the greatest number of quality innings, which non-regular corner men will get the most at-bats; and which fourth outfielders will deliver 40 or more RBI. In other words, you'll have to become a better, more knowledgeable fan. And isn't that the Rotisserie Way?
> • Using players from only seven major league teams helps an owner new to the world of Rotisserie to draw on his or her strength. After all, we all start out as fans of a particular team, which means that we enter the Rotisserie world knowing and liking one team better than others. What better place to start?

LITE III. NO MONEY

Each team has 23 Lite Dollars (L$) to spend at the auction draft to acquire a full roster of 23 active major league players, with a minimum salary and minimum bidding increments of 10 cents. But real money is not used.

> • "The intensity of feeling in Rotisserie is unrelated to money anyhow," says Farmer-Professor Lake. "If you play for traditional Rotissestakes - 260 real dollars for 23 real players — it's enough to be irritating if you lose, but not enough to buy a new car if you win. So what's the point?"
> • Using L$ still requires an owner to manage the team budget and cope with the exigencies of free market competition for the services of Matt Williams, Mo Vaughn, and other superstars at the auction draft. Farmer-Professor Lake promises that your throat goes dry and your heart palpitates when the bidding hits L$2.70 for Greg Maddux, the same as when it crosses $30 for baseball's best pitcher in regular Rotisserie. This means that a kid owner can have just as much Rotissefun as a parent owner without having to beg for an advance against the next six months of allowances.
> • Playing for L$ also makes a team owner feel a little less hysterical when the *Baseball America* and *Baseball Weekly* subs come due.

LITE IV. MONTHLY TRANSACTIONS

Transaction Day occurs once a month, on the Monday (AL) or Tuesday (NL) before stats appear in *USA Today.* The first Transaction Day falls on the first Monday or Tuesday in May. Except for the All-Star Break Trading Period described below, all Rotisserie Lite roster moves are restricted to Transaction Day.

> • On Transaction Day, a Rotisserie Lite team may release players (a) placed on a major league disabled list; (b) demoted to the minor leagues; (c) traded to the other division or to the other major league; or (d) released by their major league team, *without limit* from its current roster and replace them with players from the free agent pool who qualify at the same position. Players may not be reserved. Even players on major league disabled lists must be released if their Rotisserie Lite owner chooses to replace them. Released players go into the free agent pool and maybe claimed on the *next* Transaction Day.
> • Player moves on Transaction Day shall take place in reverse order of the most recent standings, with the lowest team in the standings having the right of first claim on a player from the free agent pool. While there is no limit on the number of players a team may release and replace, a team may make only one transaction at a time. That is, the last-place team in a six-team league may not make a second transaction until all other teams in the league have had an opportunity to make a transaction.
> • As there is no reserve list in Rotisserie Lite, an owner whose star player is on his major league team's disabled list and isn't scheduled to come off for another two weeks will have to make a strategic call: Ride out the injury and retain the player under contract; or release him into the free agent pool and call up a replacement immediately.
> • The salary of a player claimed from the free agent pool on Transaction Day is L$1.

LITE V. TRADE RESTRICTIONS

Except for a two-week trading period ending with the last out of the All-Star Game, no trades are permitted in Rotisserie Lite.

> • All trades during the trading period take effect on the first pitch of the first regular season game after the All-Star Game.
> • A Rotisserie Lite team may trade only one player with a salary of L$2 or more to any one team.

LITE VI. SAME SCORING CATEGORIES

Standings shall be determined on the same basis as in Rotisserie Regular and Rotisserie Ultra - that is, according to each team's cumulative performance over the course of a full season in eight statistical categories: home runs, RBI, stolen bases, and batting average for batters; wins, saves, ERA, and ratio (hits plus walks divided by innings pitched) for pitchers.

> • A team receives points in each category according to its relative position. In a six-team league, the leader in home runs would receive six points, the second-place team five points, and so on. The team with the highest point total wins the Rotisserie Lite pennant.
> • Standings should be compiled and distributed weekly.

LITE VII. LONG-TERM CONTRACTS

The same rules governing the option year and long-term contracts that complicate an owner's life in Rotisserie Regular and Rotisserie Ultra shall also pertain in Rotisserie Lite. (See **Article XVII** of the Official Constitution.)

> • **Exception:** A player under a long-term contract in Rotisserie Lite may be released and replaced at any time without penalty, subject only to the restrictions regarding player transactions.

LITE VIII. ROSTER PROTECTION

On April 1, each team may protect a certain number of players according to the following schedule: The team that finished first the preceding year may protect a maximum of 7 players; all other teams, a maximum of 10 players. There is no minimum requirement.

Editor's Postscript: As you play Rotisserie Lite, let us know what you think. It takes a long time to turn a piece of coal into a diamond. We particularly want to hear from you about new wrinkles, adaptations, and changes that we might scarf up for the next year's book.

> • Yes, this makes it a lot harder to build a dynasty. But trust us: One Harry Stein loose on the land is more than enough.
> • Trading is not permitted over the winter on the grounds that Rotisserie Lite owners have better things to do with their time. Particularly those who also play Rotisserie Regular or Rotisserie Ultra.

LITE IX. YOO-HOO

As there is no prize pool to divvy up in Rotisserie Lite, the Yoo-Hoo running down a Rotisserie Lite pennant winner's face and trickling into the corners of his or her mouth will taste all the sweeter, if you can imagine such a thing.

NEW RULES FOR THE NEW MILLENNIUM!

New Millennium Rotisserie? Yes! A new millennium doesn't come along every day, you know. Thus the 21st annual proceedings of the Rotisserie League Baseball Association brought us into the 21st century by including a Constitutional Convention for the first time since 1979. The one and only official rule-making body in the Free World has spoken.

Don't be jumping to the conclusion that the Founding Fathers like change just for the sake of change, however. Although the RLBA's leadership includes a wide variety of political philosophies, there is a universal appreciation for tradition. Don't forget: the "B" stands for baseball. If anything, the new rules embody the New Conservatism.

People say: you can't turn back the clock. But those who make the rules know that any clock can indeed be turned back. If the clock is off, turning it back may be exactly the right thing to do. Progress means getting closer to where you want to be, and sometimes progress means turning back.

The movement for new rules arose from a recognition that a draft day bargain isn't what it used to be. True sleepers have become too rare. Too many people have too much of the same information, which is all too easily available. The thrill of knowing about a good player, when no one else in your league knows about that player, is a key element of fun which has been diminished in the Rotisserie world as we enter the new millennium.

Another key element of fun that could use some beefing up is the possibility of a spectacular error by a fellow owner. There hasn't been a good laugh on Auction Draft Day, since Valerie was unaware that Bob Horner had gone to Japan. There are just too many good lists available too easily. Benson's forecasts have been almost as good as Zoltan's. And now Baseball Weekly has that auction, with everyone and their uncle analyzing it to death for two weeks before the real Auction Draft Day. And so on.

The revival of traditional Rotisserie's thrill of victory, and agony of defeat, is obtainable from one simple adjustment: insert one year of time lapse in between Draft Day and the beginning of the Rotisserie season. That's right ... on Draft Day 2004, you draft your team for the 2005 season. We started in 2001. What better time to make this adjustment, than at the dawning of the new millennium?

Editor's Note : *Many of the rules in the **Official Constitution of Rotisserie League Baseball** also apply to New Millenium Rotisserie, so we decided not to repeat every line of fine print that applies to both, except as needed for clarity. That means that the "Rules for Play" that follow for New Millenium Rotisserie should be read together with the original Constitution. If you can't handle that assignment, you're going to have real trouble with New Millenium Rotisserie.*

ARTICLE I. OBJECT
Change the words "regular season" to "the next year's regular season."

ARTICLE II. TEAMS

No changes.

ARTICLE III. ROSTER

No changes.

ARTICLE IV. AUCTION DRAFT DAY

Change the words "the baseball season" to "the baseball season preceding the year of Rotisserie scoring."

> **NOTE:** Playing by the new rules of the new millennium, owners may wish to draft players who have gone to Japan or achieved some other post-rookie sta tus while remaining attractive for the future. Finding the next Cecil Fielder might be fun, but opening the doors to Japan could also open the doors to drafting players from "the other league," if the rookie status rule didn't apply. For a full open-door policy, simply adopt the rules of Double Ultra as pre sented after this new constitution.

> **STRATEGY TIP:** During the Minor League Player Draft, don't forget to fo cus on the top prospects of big-market clubs from "the other league."

ARTICLE V. POSITION ELIGIBILITY

Change "Once the season is under way (but after Auction Draft Day)" to "After Auction Draft Day."

ARTICLE VI. FEES

No changes.

ARTICLE VII. PLAYER SALARIES

No changes.

ARTICLE VIII. PRIZE MONEY

No changes.

ARTICLE IX. STANDINGS

No changes.

> **NOTE:** The year preceding the official year of Rotisserie scoring (e.g. the year 2004, if you are drafting players in April 2004 for scoring during the 2005 season) may be scored as an unofficial exhibition season. Just be careful to avoid the temptation to take it seriously.

ARTICLE X. STATS

No changes.

ARTICLE XI. TRADES

Change "August 31" to "August 31 of the Rotisserie scoring year." Change "end of the season" to "end of the Rotisserie scoring season." Remove the sentence which begins, "Trades made from the day after the season ends ..."

ARTICLE XII. RESERVE LIST

Reserve List provisions take effect only during the official Rotisserie scoring season (e.g. 2005 for teams drafted in April 2004).

ARTICLE XIII. FARM SYSTEM

Change the words "during the regular season" to "during the regular season of the year of Rotisserie scoring."

All farm system activation requirements are postponed until Opening Day of the official Rotisserie scoring season. Neither the 25-man major league rosters during the year preceding Rotisserie scoring, nor the 40-man major league rosters during the winter preceding Rotisserie scoring, have any effect on farm activation requirements.

ARTICLE XIV. SIGNING FREE AGENTS

Change "From Opening Day" to "From Opening Day of the Rotisserie scoring season." Change "during the course of the season" to "during the course of the Rotisserie scoring season."

THE OPENING DAY FAAB OPTION: Facing the reality that **FAAB** bids will be numerous and highly important as soon an Opening Day finally rolls around for the official Rotisserie scoring season (e.g. Opening Day 2005 for teams drafted in April 2004) leagues may choose to have an Opening Day **FAAB** auction, live and in-person, on or around the first Saturday after Opening Day of the scoring season. Given what's at stake when the first **FAAB** bids take effect, it would be wise to have the whole league present, anyway, when the sealed envelopes are opened; having a real live **FAAB** auction could be faster, easier and more fun.

FAAB INCREASE OPTION: Given what's at stake in the first **FAAB** Auction, whether it is by sealed bids or live and in-person, leagues may choose to add $100 to each team's **FAAB** allocation, making a supplementary budget of $200 total.

ARTICLE XV. WAIVERS

No changes.

NOTE: Waivers occur only during the year of Rotisserie scoring.

ARTICLE XVI. SEPTEMBER ROSTER EXPANSION

Change "September 1" to "September 1 of the Rotisserie scoring season."

ARTICLE XVII. THE OPTION YEAR AND GUARANTEED LONG-TERM CONTRACTS

All provisions are subject to re-adoption of Article XVIII.

ARTICLE XVIII. ROSTER PROTECTION

Roster protection provisions become optional. A league may choose to move back into conventional "this year" Rotisserie, by going through the normal roster protection cycle after the end of the first year of Rotisserie scoring. Another option is to release all players and start fresh every year (if the release-all-players option is followed, don't forget to draft teams for the 2005 season, in April of 2004, so that you don't arrive in April 2005 with nobody to root for).

ARTICLE XIX. GOVERNANCE

No changes.

ARTICLE XX. YOO-HOO

No changes.

ARTICLE XXI. THE IN-SEASON SALARY CAP

No changes.

> **NOTE:** If the **FAAB** Increase Option is adopted, increase the in-season salary cap by $20.

ARTICLE XXII. WHAT TO DO FOR THE YEAR 2004

Skip a year of competition? Never! Draft a team for 2004 right now.

DOUBLE ULTRA

Rotisserie Leagues for Real Men

Double Ultra is for fans and competitors who are already playing in two or more leagues (one AL and one NL) or those who haven't tried two leagues yet but nonetheless guess they can handle the job of following a thousand players every year. The concept is simple: you own an Ultra franchise which consists of a 40-man American League roster and a 40-man National League roster. What makes it one franchise and one league is combined scoring. There are 20 stat categories: AL batting average, NL batting average, AL home runs, NL home runs, etc.

One of the many good aspects of Double Ultra is that it eliminates, or at least mitigates, the effect of a star play being traded to "the other league." When there is an interleague trade in Double Ultra, the franchise that owned the player in the old league, now owns the same player in the new league. The ownership transfer occurs by adding the traded player to the Ultra list in the new league, and waiving any player from the Ultra list to make room for the new arrival. This transaction has no effect on any other transactions or fees. The claiming team simply pays a one-time waiver fee. The salary and contract status of the traded player remain what they were in the former league.

> **NOTE:** Because a team's fortunes can change suddenly due to interleague trades, Double Ultra encourages everyone to pay attention all year, or at least until the August 31 major league trading deadline, no matter how bad their team may seem in the early going.

2

The Inner Game

GENESIS

It was in the 1970's when we got together with Bob Sklar, who was a professor at the University of Michigan. Sklar had played a primitive game like Rotisserie. And then it was in the winter of 1979-1980. In January we had lunch at La Rotisserie Francaise, to get organized. We didn't know Glen Waggoner then. He was a dean at Columbia. Peter Gethers brought in Glen. Rob Fleder was from Esquire, Bruce McCall from the New Yorker at the time. Bruce did the team logos. His team was The McCall Collects, and he really got us into doing team newsletters. He did the official crest. He was very active in the team names, the ballparks, all of that. Also there was Valerie Salembier. Dan knew her. She was in advertising sales. Dan Okrent, Steve Wulf, Michael Pollet, Cork Smith. Six of us gathered that day in January; later there would be eleven.

- Lee Eisenberg

INTRODUCTION TO THE INNER GAME

America's Greatest Game

"Next to religion, baseball has furnished a greater impact on American life than any other institution." — President Herbert Hoover

If baseball is the national pastime, Rotisserie baseball is the new national passion. Simply stated, Rotisserie is a contest to see who can pick the best players. The elegant parts include how you pick the players, and what happens after you pick them.

There is something uniquely American about assembling a baseball team. A hundred years ago, anyone with enough time and money could field a world class team and watch them play. Soon, however, professional leagues and contracts locked up all the best players. Today, you need to be named Rupert Murdock with 475 million dollars burning a hole in your pocket, or spend 20 years building a close friendship with a Chairman and CEO of a $6 billion entertainment conglomerate, just to think about owning and operating a major league baseball team. Fortunately, there are some less expensive and faster ways to test your player-selection skills. Youngsters can assemble fantastic teams using baseball cards as markers: Todd Helton at first base, Alfonso Soriano at second, and so forth. (If the card enthusiasts are serious, they can look at the stats on their cards, and total up the numbers of their imaginary rosters for comparison.) Various tabletop and computer games, such as Diamond Mind and APBA leagues, can begin with a pre-season draft. All kinds of office pools and homemade contests revolve around questions like which hitter will slug the most home runs, and which pitcher will win the most games each year, suggesting various possibilities for roster-based competition.

When a writer tries to tell people about Rotisserie leagues, the usual problem is getting bogged down in details. The game has many dimensions and can become complex quickly. Focusing on any one aspect too early will obscure the big picture. The game is built around a full baseball season, so it takes about seven months to play. There are a thousand professional players who might be a factor in the big leagues in any one year, so there is a long list of possible roster candidates. These big dimensions are one of the qualities that makes the game so much fun for such a long time.

If you like simple games, stay with tic-tac-toe or connect-the-dots. There are some simplified variations of Rotisserie baseball, but all of them are multifaceted. To get an idea of what we're dealing with, consider this following metaphor: Its like poker with fifteen players at the table, and twenty packs of cards in use. If you find this image stimulating rather than repulsive, you have the potential to be a great Rotisserian.

Rotisserie League Baseball leads a phenomenal surge in the popularity of games that create imaginary baseball teams on paper. The participants become "owners," and each group of rival roster-builders is called a league. They meet in late March or early April to select their players for the coming year. The winner is decided by totaling the actual player performances in October, and seeing whose players did the best in certain predetermined statistical categories.

There is widespread use of the term "fantasy league" to describe Rotisserie and other contests that put real players and real statistics onto rosters that exist only for the people who create them. While it may be a fantasy to visualize a double play going from Alex Rodriguez to Alfonso Soriano to Todd Helton there is nothing unreal about the competitions that assemble and manage these rosters. If Rotisserie is "fantasy baseball," then chess is "fantasy warfare," and the American Equestrian Team is "fantasy cavalry." The people who enter into these contests are not pretending anything; they are simply doing their best to win an elegant and time-honored competition.

Rotisserie League Baseball (a federally registered trademark of the RLBA, Inc.) is named for a New York restaurant, La Rotisserie Francaise, where the game's founding fathers launched their original competition in 1980. The restaurant is long gone, so don't expect a cabbie to take you there during your next visit to the Big Apple; you would have a better chance of finding Ebbets Field.

Several years ago John Benson teamed with Randy Baron to publish a two volume set of Rotisserie Baseball wisdom. John is in his third decade as the leading authority on Rotisserie Baseball. John and Randy were instrumental in the early development of Rotisserie strategy. John's "think tank" would have never been built if he and Randy hadn't joined forces in the late 1980's. Randy is more than an extremely knowledgeable, tough Rotisserie competitor; among other things, he's one of the finest Duplicate Bridge players in the world; and he is a true gentleman who has our thanks for agreeing to help us with this work.

The following essay is the finest work we've ever encountered on the subject of winning Rotisserie baseball. It is a must read. While it may look like a daunting task, don't bypass this section for the player profiles yet. We'll get to that in short order. Our mission this year is to give you the best information on player outlook and statistics ever. We'll tell you how the players are going to do, and give you all the numbers that matter, but by reading this section first, you will look at the game in a different way, and you will become a better competitor.

Having an idea of how players will do is important, but knowing what you're doing with the players before you draft them is the most critical aspect of Rotisserie success. Baseball players don't always do as we expect. Such uncertainty adds vitality to the game, but the Essentials of Winning Rotisserie Baseball will add clarity and provide a means to navigate through the turbulent 2004 season. A strong draft is a must. It's nearly impossible to win if you don't draft well and John's essay will show you how to identify opportunities, forecast player values, bid correctly, deal with changes, and stay on track to win your league.

FREE SPRING UPDATE

Get ready for Draft Day by visiting-- **www.johnbenson.com**

and clicking on "Free Spring Update."

New 2004 forecast dollar values for all players will be available in mid March

THE FOUR ESSENTIALS OF WINNING
ROTISSERIE BASEBALL

Winning Rotisserie baseball is a lot like winning the Ryder Cup in golf, just more complex. There are a thousand golfers on the course, grouped into teams of 25 by interested observers. It takes over six months to play a round, and many golfers enter or leave the field while the game is in progress. You root for 23 to 40 golfers, not just one, and you must choose them based on certain specified classifications and criteria. If one of your chosen golfers breaks a leg, you can pick another golfer. And one more minor detail: your golfers are competing in four different tournaments, simultaneously, all on the same course.

These little complexities make it difficult for many people to see the big picture. Most writers and analysts have adopted a worm's eye view, not a bird's eye view. They choose one of two methods to avoid any comprehensive attempt at dealing with the whole game:

(1) Some see the complexity, and turn away from it entirely. They choose to write about the fun of the game, how to get started, the fascinating twists and turns, and the joy of winning. If they give advice, it is anecdotal, always entertaining, and seldom rigorous. These subjects have their place in Rotisserie literature; indeed I have just trudged through them myself. It isn't easy to write about the rules and technical aspects of Rotisserie baseball and its offshoots, without being anecdotal and humorous. I have respect for the people who tackle these subjects. But winning is another question, and some writers never get to it.

(2) Some authors seize on one small aspect of the game. Like the blind men touching parts of an elephant in the poem by John Godfrey Saxe, they make valid observations but fail to see the whole beast. Therefore they draw false conclusions. Feeling a leg, they say the elephant is like a tree. Touching his trunk, they think they have found a type of snake. Then one grabs the tusk, and says the elephant is a sort of spear. They are all right, and all wrong.

The favorite elephant-part for Rotisserie analysts is the question of player valuation: given a set of player stats, what is the dollar value that should be assigned to them? This is an important question that must be addressed somewhere in the subject of winning Rotisserie baseball, but it is hardly the beginning or the end, or even a big part of the middle.

People get hung up on valuation just because it is the one aspect of Rotisserie that separates it from other contests to see who can pick the best players. People play in leagues using APBA or Diamond Mind Baseball, and they pick their players at the start of the season, but they don't have an auction. People play simple contests like "let's see who can pick a lineup that hits the most homers this year," and they don't worry about dollar values, either.

At the core, Rotisserie is just a game to pick the best players at the start of the season. The way the game works, someone with superior auction skills will have a definite edge over someone who lacks such skills, but the key is knowing the players, not knowing arithmetic.

For the coming baseball season, which would you rather know ...

(a) Which rookie pitcher is going to win 18 games with a 2.98 ERA? Or:

(b) What will be the relative scarcity and precise value of a home run, versus a stolen base, in the American League this year?

I hope you said (a). If I had told you, in April 2002, that Alfonso Soriano was going to become a 40/40 player, you would have had a big advantage over the people who didn't have a clue that such a performance was coming, even if those people knew all about the value of a home run and a stolen base, and you didn't.

You would have done just fine in the auction, with little knowledge of player valuation. If you look at Rotisserie baseball as a year-long game of skill, there are four essentials to winning, and you have to be good at all of them (or very lucky) if you want to win your league:

1. Forecasting player performance.
2. Assigning value and rankings based on forecasted statistics.
3. Conducting the draft or auction.
4. Managing your roster after the draft.

It is intuitively obvious that number 1 (forecasting) is the most important; if you can see the future better than others, you should win. And yet number 2 (valuation) receives more attention than forecasting in an awful lot of books and essays about this game.

If you mess up number 3 (conducting the draft), your work on (1) and (2) can be undone. You need skills to assemble a good roster during the course of an auction; and you must not make any blunders on money management. Three bad minutes in a draft or auction can undo three months of preparation. The main issue is simply taking care, however. If you write the wrong address on a letter when you mail it, the work that went into your letter-writing might be wasted. But when you read a book about how to compose a letter, you don't want half of it devoted to address accuracy.

Player valuation simply isn't a complex issue, and precision in valuation simply isn't relevant. You can argue for months about the question of whether a player's value is going to be $27 or $29, given a certain performance level, but you're wasting too much valuable time with such nitpicky questions.

Before the auction, you should be thinking about the underlying performance level: how much is this player going to play during the season, where will he appear in the batting order, who is batting in front of him and behind him, what ballpark he's playing in this year, and how healthy and consistent he has been. And if you know all these things (or at least know as much as you can find out without becoming obsessive in your research), and if you know that his value is likely to be around $28 (plus or minus a buck or two), well then you should stop thinking about that player and start thinking about some other player. Certainly you should be thinking about player performance before the draft, not thinking about whether he will be a little over $28 or a little under $28 this year.

During the auction, you should be watching the other owners, and keeping track of the money, rosters, and available players. If you sit there agonizing about whether you should bid $27 of $29 for the star first baseman Joe Bimbleman, then the whole game is going to pass you by. Try playing poker with a calculator as your main focus, and you will see what I mean.

There are some sophisticated quantitative techniques that can be used to your advantage during an auction, but the complex parts involve questions about your probability of getting a certain player at a certain price at a certain moment, not the question of valuation arithmetic.

In the following chapters, we will review each of the four essentials. They will be given attention appropriate to their relative importance, which is (roughly):

Forecasting player performance - 40%
Valuation based on expected stats - 20%
Conducting the draft or auction - 20%
Managing the roster (trades, injuries, etc.) - 20%

You may quibble with my percentages, but you cannot deny the necessity for competence in all four areas.

Without good forecasts, your valuations will be useless. People who came to their 2002 auctions with a precise "knowledge" of what Alfonso Soriano had been worth during 2001 didn't find this "information" very useful; what they needed to know was that Soriano was improving and developing rapidly.

Without a rational valuation method, your forecasts will not always lead to wise draft decisions. For example, if you use some half-baked formula that home runs are worth 25 cents apiece, and stolen bases are worth 20 cents apiece, etc., and you value all players accordingly, and you end up with $4000 of calculated value in a ten-team league that has only $260 per team ($2600 total), then your values based on $4000 will have you overbidding for every name that comes up. (At least you will fill out your roster quickly and can go home early.)

You have to conduct your draft or auction rationally. You can't win your league if your plan is "pay any price necessary to get Barry Bonds." Likewise, you can't use your first round pick to draft Randall Simon (or bidding $30 for him) just because he was a friend of yours in high school. And there is more to the auction/draft than just being scientific. If you go to an auction and bid up to full, calculated value, without recognizing the independent dynamics of competitive bidding, you will never finish higher than third even if your forecasts and valuations are perfect. In an auction with ten owners, there will be ten different opinions of what each player is worth. From your point of view, every time someone buys a player for a price higher than you had expected, that owner will be wasting some money. Over the course of an auction, a great deal of money gets wasted, meaning that prices must drop (from your point of view) later in the auction, when there is relatively more talent available and less money available than there was at the beginning of the auction. Understanding this concept and being patient will work wonders.

Finally, if you traded your two top outfield stars for a couple of flashy rookie pitchers on April 30, you have probably wasted your scouting, your valuation, and your successful draft.

SCOUTING AND FORECASTING

LAST YEAR'S NUMBERS

Some time before Draft Day, possibly as early as October if you follow this game year round like I do, you are going to find yourself staring at last year's numbers and studying them intently. Everybody does it. In fact, that's the problem with last year's numbers. Everybody gets them in *USA TODAY* right after the season ends, and everybody looks at them all winter. Some people study last year's numbers excessively. When you get to the point where you find yourself remembering the numbers without having to look them up, I would say you have studied them more than enough.

My advice is to spend less time looking at last year's numbers. True, you have to start somewhere, and last year's numbers are a convenient starting point. I will even tell you why they are convenient:

- The calendar year is the official "accounting period" for major league baseball records and championships, etc.
- Last year covers the same length of time that you are now trying to forecast, i.e. one season.
- Existing data are usually sorted and analyzed by year: last year, the year before, two years ago, etc.
- Almost all publications, stats on disk, web sites, etc. are focused on last year.
- Your league standings from the previous year are based on the one-year period.

The main problem with last year's numbers is that there is TOO MUCH material focused on last year. It is too easy to get your hands on last year's stats, all exquisitely computerized and scrutinized and summarized, that there is an overwhelming temptation to stop after you have seen enough of last year's numbers, because you are fed up with them. After spending 600 hours during the winter, reviewing stats to the point of having them almost memorized, you feel justified in calling it quits. You know that you have studied just as hard as anyone else in your league. Isn't that enough?

The problem is not that you must study MORE, but that you must study DIFFERENT. I am advising you to spend LESS time studying last year's numbers. They make you blind, after a while.

Part of the problem is that everyone else in your league will also know last year's numbers, backwards and forwards, because they have been deluged with the same "information" that you have. To win a Rotisserie baseball league, you must have new ideas, some insight, some different way of looking at the past. When everybody uses the same information exclusively, the game becomes a contest to see who can perform the most rigorous manipulations of last year's numbers. That is not much fun, and (even worse) it will make your performance mediocre.

My advice is to put last year's numbers into a new context, as fast as possible after you receive them. Keep a historical file on a computer, if you can. Dump the most recent year's numbers in, as soon as you get them, and produce a new "model" of long term performance. A quick and dirty method to put career stats into context, is to weight them, say 50%, 33%, and 17% for the past three years, and create a "weighted average" annual performance.

Another important step you can take is to break down last year's numbers into first half and second half. We'll discus the subject of second half numbers shortly. Other publications that aim to educate you about this game are just beginning to see the importance of analyzing second half numbers.

You don't have to wait for my annual books to start analyzing second half numbers. Save a file of stats at the All-Star break, and when you get the full year numbers, just subtract the first half to get the second half. You can begin scrutinizing the second half before the LCS is finished, and it will do you more good than scrutinizing those full year numbers that have always caught your attention in October.

Need more ideas? Robert O. Wood invented the method of splitting a veteran player's career into ten equal parts, so that every player has a "first decile" equal in significance to every other player's first decile, based on plate appearances rather than days on a roster. You can do the same thing yourself, and look at the "last decile" instead of last year.

If any new activity can simply get your attention away from last year numbers, it is a worthwhile activity. You can transform last year numbers into per-at-bat statistics and then make comparisons. You can match last year against two years ago, and do a "fluctuation analysis" to see who is most improved and who is fading fastest. You can combine the two methods and compare per-at-bat numbers for current year versus per-at-bat for the previous year.

Anything you can do to move your attention away from last years numbers will offer you a competitive advantage. You will be inundated with last year's numbers anyway, from everywhere you look, everything you read, everyone you listen to. Don't waste your time looking for last year's numbers. They will find you. I guarantee it.

Finally, my Forecast Draft Software will do most of the above for you, and more, even with graphs, saving dozens or hundreds of hours for creative thinking instead of arithmetic.

INTRODUCTION TO FORECASTING:
THINK "CONTEXT!"

If you get one lesson from this essay, let it be this: put all numbers and ideas into context, and you will play this game better.

The watchword in winning Rotisserie baseball is "context." If you see some fact or number that catches your eye — take a superstar performance in winter ball for example — put that piece of information into context. Is the player on a major league roster? Has he ever before done anything similar in baseball? Does he have a good chance to play, or is he waiting in line behind Alfonso Soriano or Jeff Bagwell, with no chance of being traded? If he does get to play, will he bat leadoff or cleanup like he did in Puerto Rico this winter, or will he bat ninth and be used only against occasional lefty pitchers? If he collected a pile of saves in winter ball, does he have a realistic chance to be his team's closer this year, or is there a high-paid healthy veteran ahead of him in the bullpen hierarchy?

There are four types of people who play Rotisserie baseball: (1) those who are good and know it, (2) those who are good but underrate their own abilities, (3) those who are novices and know it, and (4) the most dangerous group to deal with — those who think they know what they are doing, when they don't.

Some readers who fall into this fourth category will have problems as a result of reading this essay, because they will take things out of context. They will reveal their narrow-minded approach by drawing false inferences based on over-generalization. For example, they will say, "Benson uses second half stats to forecast performance for the coming year. Bimbleman had a good second half, so Benson must like him." Or: "Benson uses a player's age to forecast improvement. Bimbleman is age 26 this year, so Benson must like him." You get the idea. If you hear anybody making general statements that indicate a lack of perspective and a tendency to seize on one idea taken out of context, get them into your league, because they make excellent, cash-paying fish.

The single most important context is one that you must describe for yourself: the strength of your own Rotisserie league and your competitive situation within that league. One of the most popular pre-draft questions from people who call me for advice is: "Who's a good sleeper?" That's an impossible question to answer for someone who is not familiar with what your competitors know and what they don't know. Tell me everything everybody in your league knows, and then I can tell you what they don't know.

Here is an example of context. Back in March 1997, I often recommended Tony Womack as a "sleeper." At that time, he only had two major league steals, but he'd stolen 37 bases for the

Bucs minor league affiliate, Calgary, and he'd been caught only 12 times; a 76% success rate. I'd been watching him for several years in the Pirates organization and could see that he had great speed and the attitude a manager loves. Tony was willing to play any position. He just wanted a chance and when the Pirates financial woes forced them to trade away Carlos Garica, Jay Bell, Orlando Merced and Denny Neagle, it became clear they had to look to their top minor leaguers to fill several positions created by the fire sale trades. The prospects Pittsburgh acquired were not going to be ready in most cases, and the only place the Pirates could turn was to their high minors and players like Tony Womack. Womack, with experience as an infielder and an outfielder would make an excellent sleeper, and his speed could be valuable even if he were used in a utility role. I thought he could steal at least 20 bases. He stole 60.

It was amusing to note the variety of reactions when I gave Womack's name as a sleeper. Some said, "Oh, everybody knows about Womack; he's obvious; I need someone obscure." Other people said: "Tony who? What team is he on?" This diversity was further evidenced in actual Rotisserie auctions in April 1997. Womack sold for under $6 in a third of all auctions; and yet he sold for prices of $14 or higher in almost a third of all auctions, as well. It was obvious what happened: In many leagues, two or more people saw Womack as a source of 20-plus steals and the price soared. In numerous other leagues, only one bidder (or nobody) attached much value to Womack, and his price stayed very low.

So the context of your league could make a player worth $2 or $20 on any given Draft Day, depending on what people know (or what they think they know). To do well in your league, you really have to assess the competitive situation accurately. From reading this essay, you cannot possibly find out what your competitors know, or don't know. You must do that competitive intelligence work on your own. So study your competition, and think "context."

MARCH MADNESS

So you have a joined a Rotisserie league, and you want to prepare for Draft Day. Where do you start? Hopefully, you have enough time to do some meaningful homework. If you just got into this Rotisserie league on Thursday, and your draft is tomorrow, you have a problem. The best you can do is grab some of the spring training annuals at your newsstand, and find a book with some projected dollar values for the coming year.

The fastest cram course — and lots of people have been using this last-minute method for several years — is to get this year's *Benson Baseball Annual, Benson Draft Software* and *johnbenson.com Private Pages* direct from the publisher at 800-707-9090 (203-834-1231 from Canada), and look at the forecast stats and $ values for the coming year. It's amazing how many people call a few days before their draft. Having the book and software helps you during the draft, but studying them for a couple of weeks or longer is a much better idea. They are written later than this book and reflects more recent news.

People who follow baseball during the winter — or at least start watching during spring training — do much better than people who wait until the last minute to start preparing for their draft. There is a natural flow to the distillation of talent, starting during September of the previous season, when rosters expand, and moving through the instructional leagues, winter ball, and up to the last few days of spring training. It is much easier to understand the significance of daily events if you have been following this whole process and have a sense of perspective and direction that each team is taking.

We have to enter this cycle at some point, to begin explaining how you will answer the questions: who is going to play, and how well are they going to do? To provide a starting point, we will assume that you are joining a league about two weeks before opening day, say near the end of spring training. From that point, you will have time to review a variety of information before Draft Day. If you started before March 20, so much the better.

SPRING TRAINING: WHO'S PLAYING?

The first thing you want to do in March is to look at spring training box scores, and see who's playing. Using this method, you would have found Cecil Fielder in 1990, even though he wasn't included in any of the so-called spring training annuals. Fielder, who went on to hit 50-plus home runs when such an achievement happened only once every 15 years, will remain in these pages for many years as the best example of a player known to those who follow spring training and unknown to those who don't. Fielder had been in Japan, and so he wasn't in anyone's "last year stats" analysis. If you watched spring training, however, you would have noticed that Cecil had been hitting home runs — three in one game.

Usually I don't give a lot of weight to spring training performance statistics, except to the extent that they influence management's decision about who makes the team and who doesn't. What I do watch closely is the presence or absence of competition for each position on the field.

Back in spring training 1990, you would have noticed that Cecil Fielder didn't have a lot of competition for the Tigers first base job (the elderly Dave Bergman, maybe?) and that the Tigers didn't have a regular DH, either. That information would have told you that Cecil was likely to play. Looking into his major league track record before he went to Japan in 1989, you would have found that Cecil had 31 home runs in 506 career at-bats for Toronto, and that he was just a kid when he produced those numbers. I am getting ahead of myself, however. The point is that you should look at who's playing during spring training, as a starting point for each season.

There are a few cautions to exercise while you are staring at spring training box scores. We have already mentioned that the statistics themselves don't mean much. The only important statistic is playing time. For several years, I kept track of spring training stats and compared them to actual performance during the official season that follows. What I found was:

1. Good hitters with an established major league track record will usually do well during the official season, regardless what they do during spring training. A poor spring training is not a tipoff that a veteran has faded. If you find a serious injury, that's significant, but a .150 batting average doesn't mean anything. Veterans who have already earned their roles may be experimenting with new batting stances or new methods of guess-hitting during spring training; also they may be simply enjoying the sun. Seriously, most of the veterans are merely trying to get their timing down, and hit some balls up the middle.

2. Bad hitters, with years of major league experience proving they are bad hitters, are likely to continue their weak hitting during the regular season, even if they hit .400 during spring training.

3. Hitters with no major league track record (i.e. the rookies) might be able to win a spot on their team's Opening Day roster with a hot spring training performance, but their stats during the actual season will be consistent with their minor league track record regardless what happened during spring training. Again, the spring training stats really don't mean anything. It amazes me how some major league teams can make significant roster decisions on the basis of performance during spring training. For those with a long memory, think of Scott Pose or Jim Lindeman, and you get the idea. The games are noncompetitive, and the statistical sample is so small as to be near meaningless. Anyone can hit .400 for a month, especially when the pitchers are not seriously trying to get the batters out. All organizations have years of accumulated stats and scouting reports, etc. It makes no sense to think that three hot weeks in a spring training camp are

enough to displace years of evidence. Anyway, you don't have to make the same mistake. Ignore the stats and just look at playing time.

Another caution when dealing with spring training box scores is to watch out for trial periods, especially during the early weeks. Most teams will eventually put their "real" Opening Day lineup on the field, day after day, to tune up for the regular season. During the first three weeks of March, however, you will often see a backup candidate playing the same position every day, while the veteran (who is already assured that he has the starting job) will sit on the bench, pinch-hit, or occasionally appear out of position. There is no fixed date when these experiments must come to an end; I think you can usually see the real lineup of every team by March 25 each year, but you should get some outside confirmation before concluding that a regular player has been displaced, even if it's two days before Opening Day and the veteran still hasn't appeared much.

Another caution: try to ignore "split squad" box scores. Split squad games (usually marked "SS" in the newspaper) occur when a team plays two games on the same day. For example, the Yankees may play one game at home against the White Sox at Tampa, and another game versus the Blue Jays in Dunedin at the same time; obviously they must field two teams. Long ago, management might have split the team into an A squad and a B squad, but in recent years it has been common practice to put at least two star players in each lineup when a team must split. (Is it possible that somebody actually considers the box office aspect of spring training games?) There are some subtle methods to elicit real information from split squad box scores, such as trying to identify the token stars on an otherwise second-rate squad, or looking for efforts to pair up certain shortstops and second basemen, etc., but it is better to forget the split squad box scores completely unless you are extremely familiar with a team's roster.

For those who go to spring training, do not be impressed by one-game performances. Every player in a major league camp is good enough to go 5 for 5, or to pitch six perfect innings, on any given day. If you see them that day, you will be tempted to think that you have inside information. You don't. You simply saw one professional athlete performing at his peak on one given day. Even week-long performances can be visually deceptive as to a player's speed and power.

Sometimes, whole major league organizations become deluded about a particular player during spring training. When I was in St. Petersburg during the last week of March in 1987, the aforementioned Jim Lindeman was playing every day for the Cardinals, smashing torrid line drives every time he swung the bat. And he sparkled in the field, flying through the air for incredible catches and cutting down runners with superhuman throws. The Cardinals saw the same things I saw, and concluded that a .251 batting average at Louisville in 1986 was a good enough springboard to the majors, given this terrific month of March. So the Cards traded away Andy Van Slyke and installed Lindeman in right field. He hit .208 and returned to Louisville before the year was over. Van Slyke made the Pirates into a contending team, immediately.

Watching spring training can be a full-time job. I know, because I do it. You get up in the morning, have coffee with other writers and scouts, scan the internet, and then catch one game in the afternoon and one in the evening. If your vacation plans don't allow room for all this activity, you can always subscribe to Benson's Private Pages on the internet (800-707-9090) or call me during spring training or any time at (203-834-1231) to make an appointment.

SECOND-HALF STATS

Baseball information comes in annual doses, and then gets filed away under annual classifications. We can say simply the "1969 Mets" or "1988 Dodgers" or "2002 Angels" or "1986 World Series" and people immediately visualize specific players and accomplishments. Everything significant in baseball gets a year attached to it, and almost every year has its signature personalities. Try free association, either way: 1951? Bobby Thompson. Roger Maris? 1961.

Statistics, in particular, are stated in terms of per-year totals and averages. If you say, "Joe Bimbleman once hit 25 homers" that means 25 in one year. If you say, "he has 25 homers" that means this year. Almost all of the big questions in baseball are questions about one year: Does the team have a 20-game winner? Is this guy a "40/40" player? You don't have to say "per year," because everyone knows that's what you mean: one year.

During any given season, there is a natural tendency for observers to focus on whatever evidence has become available so far "this year" and to attach undue significance to these partial results, as if they were just as important as any previous annual results. When Scott Erickson was leading the league with a 1.83 ERA half way through 1991, he got just as much attention and respect at that point as he would have earned by posting a 1.83 ERA for a full year. This one brilliant half-season had an effect on popular thinking for the next ten years, that Erickson was really capable of pitching at this level, if he could just be healthy and get a few breaks. There was no other evidence available to contradict or modify the stated results up to that point in time. Indeed, in mid 1991 many people were looking back at Erickson's 1990 performance and noting the 1.35 ERA during September as confirmation that the new superman was for real. Nobody was saying, "Hey, it's only half a year of great performance ... he will probably have an ERA over 4.00 in the second half, and finish the season with an ERA around 3.00." Everyone was inclined to believe that "so far this year" was synonymous with "this year in total."

Early results always stick in our memory. Take April for example: I still remember that Graig Nettles once hit nine home runs in April. Ron Cey got eleven homers in April one year. It was big news at the time. In both cases, the players suddenly became normal again, and finished their seasons with not-so-memorable totals of 20-something homers. Still, those memories of April surges linger. Did you ever hear excited conversation about somebody hitting nine or eleven homers during July? Nobody gets national attention for hitting nine homers during July. By midseason, you would need a dozen homers in a month to get anyone to lift an eyebrow. If you hit a dozen homers in April, people talk about the Hall of Fame.

We get a steady flow of numbers during the season. On April 30 we look at April stats and think about them. On May 31 we look at April-May stats and reflect further. On June 30 we look at April-May-June numbers, and on July 31 we look at April-May-June-July. The cumulative effect of all this looking at numbers is that April gets over-emphasized in our thinking. So does May. And June.

When do we stop and look at every player's isolated July-August performance? Or August-September? The later months just don't ever get the whole national population of fans looking at their results, but April-May results get that kind of scrutiny in print and broadcast media, because on May 31 all the stats they have to talk about are April-May stats.

In the late 1980's, I took a liking to second-half numbers. To some extent I liked them because they were the "underdogs" of the statistical world. They were ignored, overlooked, and under-appreciated. Another reason why I liked second-half stats was that they gave me an advantage over the people who didn't know about them. Although they are underappreciated, second-half stats are potentially more important than first-half stats, because they are more recent history, more indicative than those first-half numbers which stick in memory.

I didn't invent the idea of looking at second-half numbers, of course. It is an old baseball axiom that a rookie's true value is measured in his second tour around the league, after pitchers have had time to study him, i.e. during the second half of his rookie season. Matt Nokes hit .289 as a rookie, but his performance changed during the season; he hit way over .300 in the first half, and .251 in the second half. He remained a .251 hitter for most of his career.

If you want to win Rotisserie baseball, you better get used to the idea of studying second half numbers. Many magazines and annuals have started focusing on second half numbers, just as I predicted they would when I started including them in my first annual book in January 1989. Last year's second-half numbers are, after all, more recent evidence than the first-half numbers that get so much attention. The second half of the preceding year is chronologically close to the period that we are trying to predict. Events that occurred early in the preceding year are less relevant than events that occurred late in the preceding year because the older events are chronologically more remote.

In a baseball forecast context, events that happened ten years ago are meaningless. A two-year-old event is possibly meaningful, but is still suspect because of its age. Events just one year old are more relevant than two-year-old events, and things that happened late last year are usually more meaningful than those that happened early last year. Second-half stats give us a picture, a valuable little snapshot, in which the more remote events of the previous year (i.e. April, May and June) have been eliminated.

If *something happened* during the preceding year that changed a player's abilities and output, that "something" will be more heavily reflected in the second-half numbers than in the full year numbers. If whatever it was that happened, such as change in role or a physical improvement or deterioration, happened on July 4th, that event will be fully reflected in second-half statistics, 50% reflected in full year statistics, and not-at-all reflected in first-half statistics of the prior year.

As we all know, many things can happen during the long baseball season. A hitter may be moved in the batting order. The players batting in front of him or behind him in the batting order may change, or be changed. The player's whole team may be changed. Opposing defense may be relocated to a hitter's disadvantage, or his own fielding position may be shifted and have an adverse, or favorable, effect on his hitting. All these factors affect statistics even when a player's innate skills, attitude, concentration, and total playing time remain exactly the same.

Skills can change, too. A young hitter may learn (finally!) to lay off the high fastball, or to go the other way with an outside pitch. He may learn such things gradually over the course of several years, he may learn them during one season, or he may learn them suddenly on July 4th. An older hitter may lose some speed and get to first base on time less often, or he may lose his ability to get around on a fastball. Or pitchers may simply learn that the old man can no longer jerk their fastball into the seats. Word spreads fast among pitchers around a league.

Rookies, not veterans, are most susceptible to opposing pitchers and managers learning something that is going to impair their hitting performance. As noted above, the cornerstone of the "second-half theory" is the old baseball axiom that a rookie's true ability can be seen in his second tour around the league, i.e. in the second half of the season.

In January 1989 I began publishing details of second-half numbers, including dollar values based on second-half performance, and the response was overwhelming. Even though I didn't invent second-half analysis (that baseball axiom about rookies is at least ninety years old) I am proud to be the first person who pursued this idea extensively, in print, for Rotisserie and forecasting purposes.

My enthusiasm for second-half numbers has been such that people (who should know better) have at times suggested that second-half stats are the sole basis for my forecasts and predictions. It is flattering to have people think of "Benson's idea" whenever they hear about second-half scrutiny, but it is obviously silly to turn that association around backwards, and say "second-half stats method" whenever they hear someone say "Benson forecast."

Quoting from the first ten editions of the *Rotisserie Baseball Annual*: "Second-half annualization is definitely useful, but it is just one tool available. When you finally make a determination and put your money where your mouth is, you should have considered numerous factors and various points of view, not just second-half performance."

Forecasting is not a mathematical exercise. There is no such thing as a "mechanical forecast" except in the world of people who don't know what they are doing. You may start a forecast process with a mechanical projection, but that is the beginning of the forecast, not the end. My method is to make an individual scrutiny of every single player, including original information directly from players, coaches and managers. Within the part that is purely analytical, second-half stats are just one more place where people should look for clues. I stress the importance of looking, because so many people don't look, and they don't see.

Drafting players for Rotisserie purposes is a lot like hiring people for professional positions. In hiring, there are several steps that should be followed. You should look at credentials. You should interview. You should check references. You should give a pre-employment physical exam. But when somebody says, "That manager hires his people on the basis of physical exams," they are showing their ignorance of the total process.

So keep things in perspective, and you will find all kinds of nuggets that give you an edge in Rotisserie competition. When you like players for numerous reasons (the right age, the right ballpark, the right situation on the right team, and a good second half in the previous season) then you are on the right track. For our most recent this-year forecasts, get *Benson's Private Pages* and/or *Forecast Draft Software* (800-707-9090 or 203-834-1231).

THE PROBLEM WITH STARTING PITCHERS

One of the most complex problems faced by Rotisserians and major league executives alike, is the scouting of talent for starting pitcher roles. Although the problem is complex, I don't recommend that you spend a great deal of time on it. During the winter and spring training, your time would be better spent on other questions.

The best approach to starting pitchers is simple: Just make a list of "OK" candidates, go to the draft or auction looking for bargains, and hope for good luck during the season. You can reach the point of diminishing returns very quickly when you scrutinize starting pitchers. Consider the "Cy Young curse" as a starting point: the very best starting pitcher from the previous season is often not a good selection in the next season.

Starting pitchers are the most unreliable, unpredictable, unpleasant group of people in the world, statistically speaking that is. Even within a major league team, they are a sub-group unto themselves. They have their own habits and unique superstitions. Starting pitchers generally don't like to talk with media people on the day they are scheduled to pitch; some of them won't even talk to their own teammates, for fear of damaging their concentration. How many hitters are so careful about preparing for a game?

Pitchers are not crazy to put so much emphasis on concentration. There is something about the art of pitching that causes a tiny shift in performance to produce a tremendous difference in measured results. The same pitcher might win 18 games one year and just 8 the next. A pitcher with an "established" career ERA of 3.50 is always capable of producing an ERA as low as 2.50 or as high as 4.50 in any given season. It happens all the time. These big changes in stats can occur with no observable change in physical abilities. When a pitcher actually experiences a change, such as learning a new pitch, or losing some velocity due to injury, you can see him soar to stardom or disappear from the major leagues completely in a very short time.

Hitters are much more predictable. Statistically, they usually perform within a predictable range. Variations of more than 10% or 15%, compared to historic averages, are uncommon in most of the stat categories. A career .250 hitter might hit .225 or .275, but not likely outside that range. Someone who has produced an average of 75 RBI per year might rise or fall by 15 RBI, but he will usually hit in the range of 60 to 90, by just staying healthy and active.

Think about the difference between a good hitter and a bad hitter. A good hitter hits around .300 or better (or say .290 if it makes you happier — the lower the number, the stronger the conclusion that we are building, but it really makes no difference). A bad hitter hits .215 (the actual Mendoza Line — you could look it up). Would you say then, that a "bad" hitter is 215/300 or 72% as good as a "good" hitter. If you think .285 is a good average, then Mario Mendoza is more than 72% as good as a good hitter.

The bad hitter (.215 average) makes an out 78.5 % of the time. A good hitter (.300 average) makes an out 70.0 % of the time. Only 8.5% of the time does a good hitter get a hit when a bad hitter would make an out. The .215 hitter and the .300 hitter do the "same thing" statistically (either both make an out or both get a hit) 91.5 % of the time. You could argue that a bad hitter, based on batting average, is 91% as good as a good hitter; while a bad pitcher is only half as good as a bad pitcher, based on earned run average.

You may quibble with the percentages and stat categories. The above numbers are not intended to be rigorous mathematics. They are intended only to make the point: there is a big, big difference in stats between the best and worst pitchers in baseball, much more variation than you find among hitters. And that variation will continue to grow. And the same pitcher can produce big variations from year to year. That point is a cornerstone of common sense when you play Rotisserie. Pitcher performance just isn't consistently predictable within a useful, reliable range.

Does a pitcher's actual performance — the way he throws the ball, and in what sequence or situation — change that much from year to year? I don't believe it can, because active major league pitchers are all at the highest level in a large pyramid of talent. If there are about 400 pitchers (the rosters plus the DL.) in major league ball at any given moment, that is 400 people out of about 100 million males between the ages of 18 and 40 in the U.S., Canada, and the Central American / Caribbean area. How good are those 400? All of them are absolutely excellent! How big is the real skill difference between the best and the worst among those 400? Pretty darn small.

Conclusion? The stats we use to measure pitchers, especially ERA and wins, tend to magnify and exaggerate the real differences in quality of performance. On any given day, a tiny factor like a skinned knuckle, a hangnail, a sore toe, or a mental problem like bank account or spouse worries — or a pesky reporter who asked an irritating question — can have a surprising impact on a pitcher's observable performance, while the same factors in a hitter's life could be completely invisible for a week or longer. Did the pitcher really throw much different when he had a bad day? Not likely. If his motion or pitch selection really looked that bad, the pitching coach and manager would notice right away, and make a change. Very seldom can the best observers in the universe detect anything visible, until it is too late, and by then the stats are cast.

What do you do about it? When you do your scouting and forecasting, spend less time and effort on starting pitchers. Follow a few simple rules. Look for tall, healthy, hard-throwing lefties who pitch for winning teams in huge ballparks. You can't have all these criteria every time you choose a pitcher, but you can try to get as many as possible crammed into each selection. We have more advice about starting pitchers in the chapters covering Draft Day and roster management, but you start on the right path by allocating your scouting and forecasting time wisely. Struggling to identify the fifth starter on each team is NOT a worthwhile use of time. The person you end up identifying is probably going to have negative value anyway. He will likely be near the bottom of those 400 pitchers in the big leagues. Spend your precious time thinking about the fourth and fifth outfielders and identifying the likely DH against righty pitching on every team. These hitters are roster assets; they won't hurt you, and they will often rise in value (predictably) during the season.

SCOUTING FOR SAVES

While you should save time by not scouting the starting pitchers too extensively, you must put some solid effort into your examination of bullpens. Saves are a critical category in every Rotisserie league. For a good bullpen, you need to know all the proven ace relievers whose teams will not change their stopper role. After the established closers and co-closers, look for hard-throwers who have setup and support roles, especially on teams with unsettled bullpen situations. Veterans with a track record of success in a setup role will usually be favored over talented newcomers, and ex-closers (like Rod Beck) have a way of finding some save situations, although you should make an effort to know every pitcher who will be competing for those precious saves.

The game's top analysts have repeatedly proven that successful performance in the saves category correlates highly with victory in Rotisserie baseball. Mike Dalecki, for example, has made annual examinations of a large population of leagues, using regression analysis and correlation coefficients to check which categories are the key to victory.

All of the above advice applies to your search for saves: look at long-term track records, last year and second-half stats, and September box scores. During the winter, look for overlaps and vacancies. Roster analysis is especially important when you are looking for saves. An average major league team will win 81 games, and about half of those victories will produce a save. So there are only about 40 saves to go around on each pitching roster. That number won't change much because of the talent in the bullpen.

A major league team can increase its home-run output by filling the lineup with sluggers. But talent won't have a huge impact on the total number of saves. (Note that a bad closer gets a save in about 75% of his save situations; a good closer gets about 85%, not much difference.) In 2002, you could have put John Smoltz, Billy Koch and Troy Percival all on the same major league roster, and you still couldn't get more than about 55 saves in total; it just isn't mathematically possible. You have to look at the competition within each roster, not just the track records of the candidates to get saves.

The numbers game can work to your advantage, too. Even the worst major league team wins about 60 games every year, meaning that 30 or more saves will be recorded by the bullpen on that team. Finding the best reliever on a bad staff can easily add 20 saves to your team stats. Sometimes the ace relievers on weak teams get even more saves than the ace relievers on good teams, because (as Bill James showed) when a weak team wins a game, it is more likely that the score will be close. When a strong team wins a game, it is more likely to be a 12-5 affair with no save for anyone. So picking the ace relievers from the winningest teams will not be a sure way to get the ace relievers with the most saves. Look at Mike Williams in 2002. Bullpens always produce value, even on teams that don't have more than one starter worth considering.

Searching for saves is complicated by the fact that one of your most important tools — examination of spring training box scores — is not very useful. How can you find saves during spring training? Saves are very scarce to begin with. If a pitcher gets one save a week, that's 26 over the course of a season, so one save per week is a very high output. During spring training, the true ace reliever might get only one or two saves, while a marginal reliever might get lucky and record three or four saves. You can't define roles by looking at the save statistic.

One spring training stat that I like to scrutinize is Games Finished (GF). Looking at a box score and seeing an established ace reliever working the ninth inning (and only the ninth inning) gives you a definite indication that the team views him as a closer, no matter what the score was in that game. The manager made a decision to use him in the final inning of that spring game, regardless what the score may have been. It was just a workout. The team is treating him like an ace reliever, meaning that management discretion is working in his favor. The GF column tells us a great deal about what the manager and the front office are thinking.

Aside from the GF stats, you can look for any pitcher being used for exactly one inning per outing during spring training. Starting pitchers can be spotted, because they work three innings, then four, five, or six. The candidates to get saves will almost always be used one inning at a time, or maybe two at the most.

The "who's going to play" part of the question is worth considering carefully while you are looking for save artists during the preseason, despite all these difficulties. In late March, most teams are fielding the same lineups that they plan to use during the regular season. Even when a manager parades out a hoard of pitchers, his starter is usually a "real" starter, and his closer is usually someone who will be given the ball to finish games in July and August.

STAYING IN SHAPE DURING THE WINTER

For year-round baseball fans and analytical types, the offseason presents a marvelous opportunity. The numbers finally stop changing long enough to allow some in-depth analysis beyond anything that would be practical during the summer when new numbers keep spewing out every day. Here are some ideas to get a head start on "next year" any time after last year ends. Remember, as we keep saying, your ultimate goal is to come up with a forecast for the coming season: who is going to play, and how well are they going to do?

The broadcast media generally turn their attention away from baseball during the winter, but the specialized print media and their websites follow baseball year round. *USA TODAY* has joined the reliable veteran, *The Sporting News*, in providing in-depth coverage during the offseason. And *Baseball America* is especially strong on coverage of minor leaguers and rookies. I recommend getting all three by subscription, including their web content. You can find them at any good newsstand, but having a complete library will pay off at times. My web content, *Benson's Private Pages*, formerly called *Benson's Baseball Monthly*, now updated continuously year round, is promoted extensively in this book, because it helps you.

If you suffer baseball withdrawal during the winter, and find that printed matter and web content just isn't enough to get you through until spring training, you can always look for winter baseball on the Spanish-language cable TV stations. The winter ball playoffs usually get onto one of the cable sports stations. As a last resort, you can always pull out a videotape of a game from the previous season. For scouting purposes, I like to tape at least one game of every team playing against a righty starter and a lefty starter, every year. For fun, you can tape a game without watching it, and pull it out on a cold winter evening for some out-of-season viewing.

PAYING ATTENTION TO WINTER LEAGUES

Like any short record of baseball statistics, 170 at-bats in winter ball can be misleading. Winter ball stats, assuming that a player has been a regular throughout the winter season, are no more significant than the major league stats that you see around May 20 each year. Some of the high-flyers will fall back to earth, and some of the slow-starters will come on strong. Combine the statistical insignificance with the fact that winter ball games are not the most serious competition in the world, or the highest level of play, and you could make a strong argument that the numbers aren't worth any more than a passing glance.

But if you think again about the major league stats and standings that you see in mid May, you realize that there are some valuable clues about who is doing better or worse than they did the year before. After 170 at-bats, you can often see who is going to be successful among the rookie crop, which veterans are in danger of losing their jobs, and which pitchers are getting powerful results from those new pitches they have been developing.

Winter ball stats give similar clues. You get indications, and hints which, in combination with other information that you have accumulated, may lead you to make some accurate assessments and come up with some valuable insights. To give you a feeling for the kind of insights that you can get from winter ball numbers, here are some of the classic cases in Rotissehistory.

Greg Maddux went to Venezuela and produced a 7-4 record for last place Zulia, with an ERA of 1.49 and a ratio of 1.07 in 96 innings. Maddux had struggled through a 6-14 season with a 5.61 ERA for the Cubs the year before. Do you think he was a good starter for a price of $1 or $2 that April? Maddux, of course, went 18-8 with a 3.18 ERA for the Cubbies after that winter performance.

Doug Jones reached age 30 with only nine major league saves in ten years as a pro. Then one winter, the soft-throwing Jones led the Puerto Rican League in ERA with 0.51 and a ratio under 0.91, with a strikeout/walk ratio of better than 3:1. All Jones did was get 37 saves for Cleveland during the regular season, and then 32 the next year, and 43 the year after that, with ERA's of 2.27, 2.34, and 2.56.

When Roberto Alomar was a 19-year-old middle infield prospect who had never appeared in the major leagues, he hit .302 with 31 runs scored in 199 at-bats. He went on to have a very successful rookie season.

Jose Rijo once had a reputation as a wild man (meaning poor control of the strike zone) until he produced an ERA of 1.81 and a ratio of 0.88 in the Dominican league, while walking only 11 in 55 innings. The year before, he had been demoted to the minor leagues after walking 100 batters for the Oakland A's. After that winter performance, Rijo not only returned to the major leagues; he also produced a 13-8 record with a 2.39 ERA and a 1.12 ratio. The walks were never again much of a problem.

The anecdotal evidence goes on and on. Among the stars who put up huge numbers in winter before going on to good rookie seasons have been Carlos Baerga, Edgar Martinez, Ramon Martinez, Greg Vaughn, and many others. There are two cautions, however.

(1) Winter ball performances are just one indicator. There has to be a job opening on the major league roster, before any player can accomplish anything. You can use winter ball stats to confirm what you already believe, but you aren't likely to get any wholly new ideas by following the winter leagues. I liked Edgar Martinez, Roberto Alomar and many others as major league prospects, long before they had their good winter numbers. The outstanding performances just enhanced my interest. As we keep telling you, think context, before reaching any conclusions.

(2) Pitchers who work hard in winter ball have a strong tendency to weaken in August of the following season. They simply get tired. If you end up with a successful acquisition based on winter league performance, consider trading them in late July.

SEEING THE FUTURE

During the winter, you can do a great deal of spade-work for next year by keeping track of changes. Winter meetings usually produce a flurry of activity every year, with trades and free agent signings (and some talented free agents going unsigned or leaving for Japan, or returning from Japan). In October, if you have time to start that early, write down a list of who was playing each position on every team at the end of the previous season, and keep this list up-to-date as players come and go during the winter. You may, of course, rely on other people to do this for you (or buy my Forecast Draft Software which includes winter depth charts), but you will never marshal any marvelous insights while reading published winter analyses. Things change right up until the end of spring training. Starting with a full set of raw data lets you develop your own unique perspective while keeping every player in perspective.

You can put your lists on a computer, or just scribble them on a piece of paper. For a few years beginning in the late 1980's I used to move magnetic name-tags on a visual board, to make sure no player got lost in the shuffle. My Forecast Draft Software ended that low-tech era while adding a huge arsenal of functionality. Whatever method you use, you will be amazed to see the gaping holes and excess/overlaps that occur during the winter. You can be sure that major league GM's are looking at the same information, and you can often foresee their roster moves long before anything gets into the news.

One of the biggest problems with scouting and forecasting is that the people who make roster decisions in major league baseball often change their minds, or don't have a clear vision of the future in the first place.

Given the numerous variables and uncertainties, no one expects you to assemble a Rotisserie team full of players who will all hold their value or get better. On a 23-man roster you are going to have a couple of disappointments; it's part of the game. Your job in managing a Rotisserie team is simply to do the best you can. For dealing with the question, "Who's going to play?" your best tactic is just to do your homework.

Even beginners should prepare for Draft Day by writing down their expectations about who has the starting job on each team at each position. (At this point you find one more reason to pick either the AL or NL, not both: you can cut in half the number of players and positions that need watching.) It's OK to start with one of the spring training preview magazines or (better yet) a publication like *USA TODAY* or *The Sporting News* that attempts to project starters for you. Don't stop with a published list, however. Do some kind of research on your own, such as checking box scores to verify what you have read. And stay current on trades and injuries. By writing your own list instead of using someone else's, you at least accept responsibility for the thought process, and you might very well come up with a good idea or two just by going through the motions of thinking. You need something somewhere that isn't held in common by everyone in your league.

To compete in any serious league, you will want to make depth charts, not just lists of starting lineups. The more thoroughly you answer the question "what if ... ?" the better you will do in any league. Usually it's not too hard to see who plays a backup role at each position. From last year's records, you can see who got the call when the regular was hurt or resting. From spring training box scores, you can see who else is being considered and tested by management. Minor leaguers often enter into the picture. Managers often help you out by telling, during spring training, who is the starter and who is next in line at each position. It pays to do your homework.

As you get near Draft Day, your primary objective is to identify the players who have starting jobs on Opening Day. If your Draft Day is the first weekend after the major league season starts, you will only have to look at few box scores to see who is playing. The harder part, and the key to victory over the course of a long season, is to find some of the lesser role players who have good chances to emerge with increased playing time during the season. The $1 players and the last-round picks who end up having decent seasons are the main difference that separates winners and losers.

The factors to watch are players' ages, abilities, track records facing righthanded and lefthanded pitching, durability/injury history, and personal preferences of the manager and general manager who control the team. During your search and review of starting players, you will find some starters who aren't quite as secure as their peers on other teams. Older players, those who are injury-prone, those who have been platooned in the recent past, and players who have found their way into the manager's doghouse are all logical candidates to give up some of their playing time during the year ahead.

When you look at the backup players during your "what if" reviews, you will find the same names filling the contingency slot at multiple positions. For example, a young good-hitting utility infielder has at least four clear chances to win a big increase in playing time. The second baseman, third baseman, or shortstop could get hurt or traded. Any of them might slump badly. And the utilityman might hit .330 as an occasional substitute, attracting more attention and winning greater consideration as a regular.

When you start doing your homework, you will find numerous study aides. One of your first problems will be separating the wheat from the chaff among all the materials that purportedly are there to help you. There is a great deal of chaff out there, and there always will be. We have already recommended several reliable publications.

We have made some general suggestions on how to spend your time during the winter. If you have a draft in two weeks, not all of these are going to be applicable this year. But if you are getting started in, say, January or February, most of them will apply, and all will be useful sometime during the next year.

There is no such thing as too much preparation for your draft. There are some unproductive ways to spend your time, however, such as over-scrutinizing starting pitchers as we have mentioned. We will leave the subject of scouting and forecasting with one further caution:

DON'T BET THE RANCH ON ROOKIES

Unless you have a two-year plan to become gradually competitive with a weak, new franchise in an ongoing league, you don't want a roster full of rookies. The hype is overwhelming and drives up perceived values beyond anything reasonable. Baseball card dealers, major league scouts, fans returning from spring training, team media offices, and everybody you can think of, keep introducing "the next Ted Williams" and "the next Tom Seaver" every year as an annual ritual. Don't listen to them.

Rookies are like lottery tickets. If you get one and win it's great. But you should approach them as entertainment, not investments. Another parallel with lotteries: people who get lucky will go around telling everyone they know, incessantly; the people who waste their money time after time just don't talk about it. The vast majority of rookies do not live up to expectations. Consider the much-touted Hank Blalock and Sean Burroughs in 2002, and you will see what I mean.

Even if you know for a fact that a rookie has the potential to hit .300 with 20 homers, you can't win if you go out and pay the going rate for a .300, 20-homer hitter. The best you can do is get what you pay for, and break even. That's not how to win a Rotisserie league. You need to buy players for less than they're worth. And if you ever pay up to full value, you want a proven veteran, not an untested kid. Everyone talks about rookies in terms of potential. Even when the prognosticators are right about the talent, it may take two or three years for a talented youngster to reach his potential.

In the draft/auction chapter, we have some suggestions on how you can benefit from rookie hype. The basic idea is to get the other guys all excited about rookies, and let them suffer with them. Everybody wants Jose Cruz or Juan Gonzalez, and everybody ends up with Jose Gonzalez. This is one bandwagon you don't want to ride on.

VALUATION

So you have a list of players. And you have answered the questions (as best you can): who is going to play, and how well are they going to do? You have written down, or obtained, a list of expected stats for every player available in your draft. Now you are ready to assign rankings and dollar values. Even if you have a simple draft, I recommend that you use dollar values to do your rankings at each position, because you will get a list that says not only who's better, but how much better they are than the next player on your list; this information will be valuable at times during the draft.

If you want to see actual formulas and calculation examples, get *Rotisserie Baseball - Playing for Blood* from Diamond Library (800-707-9090 or 203-834-1231). There isn't any higher mathematics involved here; it's all addition, subtraction, multiplication, and division. Anyone is capable of following the arithmetic, or doing it themselves. But we believe that beginner/intermediate players are not likely to be do-it-yourself valuation enthusiasts. And there are numerous printed sources of valuation lists for every player, including the forecasts that appear every year in *The Rotisserie Baseball Annual*, and the updates that appear right up until Draft Day in *Benson's Private Pages* and Forecast Draft Software. If you are not going to do your own value calculations, put some thought into choosing a good source when you obtain them. The values in this book are good, but they are before spring training.

There is no "right" valuation method. You just need a rational method that works in your league, and to know your league better than anyone else does. One of the first tipoffs to people who don't know what they're talking about is the claim, "My method is right!" Our recommendation is that you put some energy into choosing a source of dollar values. We hope you will choose the "Benson" sources and buy our annual books, web content, and Forecast Draft Software, but the main point is to use any source or method that makes you feel comfortable going into your draft or auction. The advice in this chapter will help you see who knows what they're doing, and who doesn't, when it comes to valuation methods.

The valuation problem isn't really very complicated, although people have written whole books about it. You have $260 per team. In the old ten-team National League, that's $2600 total.

We will use the ten-team league as an example throughout this chapter, because it makes much of the arithmetic easier. If you are valuing players in a twelve-team league, you will have $3120 to account for ($260 x 12).

Whatever method you use, there are certain checks and balances that must be included. We are giving you a fairly complete list of these tests for reasonableness, to help you evaluate the valuation methods. Any method that passes all of these tests will yield essentially the same answers; the only significant differences in values will result from differences in the stats that are forecast for each player.

Before giving you our general guidelines for rational valuation, I have some broad comments about the valuation process itself. One of the biggest problems that you will encounter when you deal with valuation, whether you simply pick up a printed list, follow someone else's recipe, use my Forecast Draft Software, or do everything yourself, is that too many people jump into the valuation arithmetic without stopping to think about what they are doing, and why. The danger in going straight to the arithmetic is that you create an illusion that your results are "answers" and that you have considered everything that needs to be considered.

The exercise is to take the $2600 in your league, and assign it to 230 players who will be taken during your auction. I will give two analogies to illustrate the process of player valuation: business valuation and the "game of chance" valuation.

Business valuation is the closest parallel to player valuation. A player is a package of value, involving future events that are unknown (but can be reasonably estimated) at the time you do your valuation. When you value a company or a property, you go through various steps. One of the most obvious steps is to look at recent sales of similar assets. I use actual average prices paid in last year's auctions, nationwide, for every player, based on a sample of about two hundred leagues. It's no more complicated than looking up a stock price in the newspaper, to see the actual price as of yesterday's close. Also, if you want, you can go through actual calculations to see what a player "earned" in the previous season, or half-season, or previous two years on average, or any time period, following the same methods as if you were a doing a valuation for the coming season.

The more important question when you buy a business, or a ballplayer, is what's going to happen in the future. That's why you need a specific statement of what you expect for stats in the coming season. Back in April 2002, it didn't do you a whole lot of good to know what Vernon Wells "earned" in 2001. Nor would it have been the most useful piece of information to know what Edgar Martinez earned in 2001, when you went into your 2002 draft. In the first case, you had a young and improving player who had not enjoyed a full season in the majors, and in the latter case, you had an old and fading player with a history of being easily injured. And age is not the only criterion that would favor looking forward rather than looking backward.

Continuing the business valuation scenario, you do various calculations after you have formed your vision of the future. A business generates cash flows, and has a residual or liquidation value as well. So you calculate the present discounted value of future cash flows, and the current value of proceeds from contemplated sell-off of assets after you buy the business, and you end up with a precise calculation of value, to the penny if you want it.

You also find that business valuation people know how to deal with uncertainty. When a company is at risk because of increased competition, a shrinking total market for their products or services, unstable management, or any other factor, the business valuation process takes these factors into consideration. The net value reflects various adjustment for contingencies, all based on the judgment of the evaluator. If you looked behind the net dollar value, you would find a "base case" value and also a specific amount deducted to account for risk. There might be an upward, add-on value, if the risk is near zero, and the company has obvious upside potential.

In Rotisserie player valuation, the best way to handle risk is to deal with it during the auction. Your "base case" is your calculated value, which is almost always different from what you want to bid in an auction, anyway. The next chapter explains how to adjust your bids to reflect risk and other factors.

The business valuation method illustrates two problems that arise whenever you do Rotisserie player valuations:

(1) Your calculated value may be way off, compared to the actual market value of the asset in question. One of the main reasons why there were so many corporate takeovers during the 1980's was that people doing these calculations on businesses would keep coming up with calculated "answers", showing that many companies were worth much more than the selling price of their stock. So people with money would simply buy the stock, and own the company, at a price far below the calculated value. In one notable case, the mining company AMAX published its own valuation calculations in a full page ad in the *Wall Street Journal*, to assure stockholders that their stock was worth much more than the current selling price; this action helped to prevent a takeover. The point is: you can calculate all you want, but when it's time to buy, calculated value may be far different from the price that buyers are paying right now in the real world.

(2) Even if calculations could somehow reflect market conditions and get at true values, no two people are ever going to come up with exactly the same calculated answer, except by coincidence. There are too many variables involved, and too many choices and assumptions required to reach an answer. Whenever I see calculated values showing "accuracy" to the penny, I become suspicious of the source. Players are never worth $8.72 or $20.39, because you can't bid $8.72 or $20.39. The rules say you have to bid $8 or $9, or choose between $20 and $21. Precision and accuracy are not the same thing. A pitcher who throws ten consecutive pitches exactly belt high, and exactly nine inches outside, has excellent precision, but his accuracy isn't very good.

The other analogy that I want to apply to player valuation, the "game of chance" parallel, emphasizes the importance of context. You may ask the question, "How much is a player worth if he hits .308 with 11 homers, 55 RBI, and 11 stolen bases?" The mechanical, formula-oriented people who "calculate" player values will jump to give you an answer, but they can answer only for the average roster in the average league. It's sort of like answering the question: "How much are three kings worth, in a game of stud poker?" You may calculate that, in an average game, three kings will win 85% of the time, and the average pot is $50, so three aces must be worth $50 X .85, or $37.50. All very simple, except that when you play stud poker and see three aces showing in another hand, you can take your calculated value and put it ... well, you know.

Player valuations, boiled down to simple answers expressed in one number, can be misunderstood and misused. The more you say, "This is the correct value," the more danger there is of misuse. No player has any value, except in the context of an auction with real bidders and real money (or just real "points") being bid. You simply cannot take a player out of context and assign a value to him, although people keep trying to do that, all the time.

VALUATION GUIDELINES

1. You must account for all of the money in the auction. If you have ten teams with $260 each, your total values (excluding any negative players) must add up to $2600. If you end up with $2580 or $2640, don't worry about it; you are within 1% or 2%, which is close enough for bidding purposes. When you get that close, you should stop calculating and start spending time on other questions, like following the news to see which player situations have changed since you started doing your valuation. If your total values add up to $3300 or $1900 when you wanted to account for $2600, then you need to go back and re-think your methods.

2. You must have the correct number of pitchers and hitters with positive value. If your league has ten teams with 14 hitters and 9 pitchers on each team, you want a valuation list that gives you positive value for 140 hitters and 90 pitchers. If you run a little bit over, say 145 hitters or 93 pitchers, don't be too concerned. If your 140th hitter is worth $1, it is very likely that your 141st hitter will also be worth $1, and so will the 142nd. Likewise, the 90th pitcher, the 91st, and the 92nd are all likely to have a $1 value.

3. The last (140th) hitter and the last (90th) pitcher must have a $1 value. No one is going to pay $2 when there is no one bidding against them. And bids of $0 or negative amounts are not allowed. After nine teams have filled out their pitcher slots, the last team can buy any pitcher for $1. The last pitcher always sells for $1 in every real auction, unless the bidder has lost track of what's happening, or is a fool. You want your player valuations to reflect these realities.

4. The last player in each position "pool" must be worth $1. A lot of people miss this point, because hitters are somewhat fungible, but it's the same principle as the hitter/pitcher separation. The key point is that there is more than one auction going on. Once you get all your pitchers, you are GONE from the auction for pitchers. The same thing is true of catchers and other positions. There is a bit of overlap, but basically we have a separate auction for catchers, and separate auctions for corner men (1B/3B), middle infielders (2B/SS) and outfielders. In every auction, you reach a point where there is only one owner who has a slot open in each player position pool. That owner is not going to pay $2 or $5 when there is no one bidding against him.

It amazes me that some people can't see how the roster rules affect player values. If you believe that all hitters are interchangeable, then it shouldn't make any difference if the rules require five outfielders, or four, or six. And some people actually make this statement. Now try to picture a league that requires only one outfielder per team. With ten teams in the league, the top ten outfielders will all be sought-after. And then the DH/utility slots are all likely to be filled with outfielders, because you will have some star players who didn't make the top ten list for outfielders. Then what? Well, you can look for some outfielders who qualify at other positions, but you are still going to end up facing the fact that vast majority of outfielders simply don't fit onto anybody's roster. If you have a list of 55 outfielders worth $1 or more, you can take the bottom half of that list and throw it away. Also: how much will a superstar outfielder be worth in the one-outfielder league? There won't be that much difference between the best outfielder and the worst outfielder after the rosters are filled ... so you will find that Vladimir Guerrero isn't worth $40; he is worth perhaps $15, because he is $15 more valuable than the "last" outfielder.

Official Rotisserie rules are designed to create balance from one position to another. This careful design gives an illusion that position rules don't matter when you assign player values. The fact is that the major league talent pool changes from year to year. You may have lots good-hitting middle infielders one year, and very few the next. If you ignore these differences, in the long run you are going to waste valuable information, and lose.

5. You must allocate separate budgets for hitters and pitchers. They do not compete in the same stat categories, so you have to make a policy decision, how much of the total $2600 should you spend pursuing the four hitting categories, and how much should you spend on the pitching categories.

We say "policy decision," not "calculation," because no one has yet calculated the theoretically correct answer to the question, how the money should be allocated to hitting and pitching. One writer may say it's simple: half of all points are awarded for pitching, and half are awarded for hitting, so you should allocate half of the money to each group. Thus, you assign $1300 to pitching and $1300 to hitting, and for nine pitchers you end up with an average $14 value and an average value of $9 for hitters.

This 50/50 approach is appealing in its simplicity, but it ignores the fact that pitcher performances are highly unpredictable. When you build a Rotisserie roster, or assemble an investment portfolio, or run a business, you don't want risk. People pay to avoid risk. You buy insurance, for example. Predictability, on the other hand, has value. "Blue chip" stocks often sell for more than the calculated value of the underlying assets and cash flows, because the companies are stable. People are willing to pay extra for stability. In Rotisserie, they are willing to pay extra for hitters, and they pay less for pitchers. Someday someone (probably an insurance underwriter by profession) will give us the correct calculations to discount pitcher values and enhance hitter values, but no one has done it yet.

Another writer may say that 70/30 is the correct hitting/pitching allocation, because three of the eight categories (batting average, ERA, and BPI ratio) should be assigned zero value, while the other five categories deserve all the attention when you allocate money. Thus hitters end up with three "meaningful" categories, while pitchers have only two, and the arithmetic works through to 70/30.

The error of this theory is the assumption that the "middle of the pack" hitter has a zero value in the batting average category, because those in the top half have positive value, and those in the bottom half have negative value, and the category as a whole is worth zero. But I say the average hitter is not a zero value in batting average. If the league total batting average is .265 for the whole league, and you have a whole team of .265 hitters, you don't get a zero in batting average. You get five or six points. With an average BA, you are in the middle of the pack, not at the bottom. The 70/30 theory cannot explain where those five or six points come from, or the five or six points each for the team with the average ERA and the average pitcher's baserunner per inning ratio. (Credit Mike Dalecki with first elucidating this fallacy in the 70/30 theory.)

Personally, I don't spend a great deal of time trying to calculate the pitcher/hitter allocation. I let the market speak for itself, just as I look in the paper or check a financial website to see the current prices on stocks and commodities. I am more interested in knowing what happens in real, live auctions. The results are astoundingly consistent. Every year, nationwide, people spend 65% of the total auction money on hitting and 35% on pitching. There isn't much variation. Old leagues, new leagues, AL, NL, whatever: fully 95% of all leagues fall within a narrow range of 63% to 67% on hitting, so there's your answer. In a real auction, 65% of the money is going to be spent on hitting.

Just two more points on 65/35 answer:

(a) We are talking about league totals, not spending within your unique roster. There is nothing wrong with spending 50% of *your* money on pitching, or 80% of your money on hitting. Indeed, you should always be ready to grab any players at bargain prices, whether they are hitters or pitchers. You can always trade one for the other. The point is simply that you should allocate your TOTAL league $2600 (or $3120) using the 65/35 breakdown to get player values. Once you have your valuation lists, you can buy any players you want.

(b) The risk factor for pitchers is reduced considerably if you have the freedom to activate, demote or waive any pitcher at any time. Bad pitcher stats are most painful when you simply can't do anything to get the bad pitcher off your roster. When you buy a "good" pitcher, part of the price includes risk avoidance: a lifetime 3.00 ERA may not guarantee a great season, but it gives assurance that a horrible season is less likely than would be the case if the pitcher had a 4.50 lifetime ERA.

If you play by the rules of Rotisserie Ultra, or have other rules that allow easy removal of bad pitchers, you can allocate less money to pitching. In an Ultra auction, you can allocate 70% or even 75% to hitters, and then wait to see which pitchers emerge to have good seasons, and which ones collapse, and change your selections as the season unfolds.

THE VALUATION "RECIPE"

The following process is illustrated with actual examples (again, 800-707-9090 or 203-834-1231) in *Rotisserie Baseball - Playing for Blood*. The general flow, without the numbers, is:

1. Separate your pitching/hitting money, as described above.

2. Sort all players by position. If you have your player names and forecast stats on a computer disk, put one assigned position (first baseman, second baseman etc.) next to each player's name.

Whether you are scratching notes on paper or using a computer, you need to know who qualifies at what position, before you can start drafting or bidding. Many players qualify at multiple positions. The standard rule is that, if a player played 20 or more games at that position last year, or if he played that position more than any other, or if he has already played that position this year before Draft Day, then he qualifies. For reasons explained below, you should initially assign positions according to the probable scarcity of talent at each position. Every player qualified at multiple position should be clearly indicated as such, because you might need that information during the draft.

Until you get into your draft or auction, you can't tell exactly which positions are going to be toughest to fill. Odd evnts can happen, such as bidders using their DH or utility slots to take players qualified at second base or shortstop. Back in 1991, I actually saw a league come within one player of running out of qualified shortstops, because several people chose a shortstop for their middle infield (either second base or shortstop) position, and some put shortstops at their "DH or any/utility" position. We actually came within one name of running out of qualified shortstops; Dave Anderson, not memorable for any other reason in baseball history, was the last one left. After him, I don't know what we would have done. Anyway, the point is to know multiple eligibilities, because you might need them.

The probable scarcity, and the order in which you should assign position eligibilities, is as follows. First, classify every player who qualifies at catcher. Second, identify everyone who qualifies at a middle infield position; it doesn't make a whole lot of difference, because they are somewhat interchangeable, but I mark shortstops first, and then second basemen. Third, you identify corner infielders (I mark the third basemen, then the first basemen). Finally come the outfielders who don't qualify at any other position.

3. Total the number of "units" in each stat category. If you are valuing 2003 forecast stats, add up the total number of home runs, RBI, etc. in your forecast stats for 2003 for all players. For batting average, the unit is a base hit that elevates you in the standings. If the worst team batting average in your league is .250, then every hit by which a player exceeds .250 will be one unit. In the pitching categories, the units for ERA and BPI ratio are innings, to the extent that IP exceed the average number of innings that would go with average earned runs and baserunners that would be given up by the average pitcher on the last place team in your league. Some players will have negative value in batting average, ERA, and BPI ratio. A few players will have a negative value even after you add in the value of other categories, if they have a very bad BA, ERA, or ratio.

4. Spread the allocated money for pitchers and hitters among the available stat units. Then add up a value for each player.

5. Make adjustments to account for the number of players required at each position. My method begins with an arbitrary total of much more than $2600 or $3120, so that every player's value is initially inflated. You can then remove value from all players, a little more or less depending on their positions, until you get down to the correct total of $2600 (ten teams) or $3120 (twelve teams). Again, the details are explained in *Rotisserie Baseball - Playing for Blood.*

6. Make a few final "sanity" checks. Go back to the four points under "Valuation Guidelines" above.

Aside from these basics, your main effort is to know your own personal league economics. Every league is different. If you have two owners both convinced that Choo Choo Coleman is worth $30, and both of these owners have $30 to spend when Choo Choo's name comes up, he is going to sell for $30. And if NOBODY believed that Choo Choo was worth more than $1, nobody is going to bid $2 or $3 when his name comes up.

We will refer to value calculations repeatedly when you get into the subject of draft tactics and strategies in the next chapter.

DRAFT DAY

Some people never want to stop preparing. I know one guy who takes a transistor radio into the draft room, just to make sure he doesn't miss any late-breaking news. There is surely some value in knowing if a star player breaks his leg during your draft, but the chance of that happening is fairly remote. On balance, the distraction of ongoing news is probably not a good idea. My friend with the radio has never drafted a seriously-injured player in six years, but he hasn't won his league in six years, either. My advice is to find a colleague who will follow the news for you and provide any necessary updates, while you concentrate on building a roster.

At some point, you must shift your attention away from preparation and start saying which players you want, and how much you want them. It is vital to get your mind focused entirely on the player selection process. Preparation is necessary to success in a draft, but once you get to the first name in the first round, you are engaged in an all-absorbing struggle where the key factors are concentration, memory, personal organization, quick-thinking, perception, ability to see every decision from your opponents' point of view, and (last but not least) stamina.

If you haven't been in a draft before, you are in for a real treat. Every draft has its own life. There will be twists and turns and surprises every minute. Your draft will develop its own sense of humor and its own competitive sub-plots, as people seize on themes and enhance them hour after hour. From an amusement point of view, there is nothing quite like a Rotisserie draft or auction. If you let your imagination conjure up an image of the most fun you have ever had playing any sport or game, combined with an exciting social occasion, you will begin to get a feeling for what is involved in a Rotisserie draft.

As an intellectual competition, there are numerous parallels that come close to describing what's involved in a draft. The concentration level is right up there with tournament chess and bridge. The competitive excitement is similar to high stakes poker. The intellectual strain is comparable to a tough, six-hour final exam, something like taking the college entrance exams or the law boards. From my own experience, I can tell you: it is easier to manage your way through the CPA exam than to maintain your focus through a Rotisserie draft (and the CPA exam is designed to hit you with all kinds of new and different questions, just to see if you can keep your head while not being dogmatic). The single phrase that seems to carry over from the academic world and apply to Rotisserie draft performance is "exam generalship."

There is no scoreboard during a draft (unless you have my Draft Software with projected standings at all times during the draft), so the participants can only guess how well they are doing at any point in time. At the end of the draft, most people have a distorted view of how well they did. There is a phenomenon that I call the "inverse ignorance ratio" in self assessment. Smarter owners generally focus on all their missed opportunities and mistakes, and they see the good moves made by others; people with good rosters usually feel bad at the end of their draft. The less astute owners are more likely to be pleased with their rosters; they got the one or two players who were at the top their "want list" (no matter what the price) and won't see the error of their ways until the season is half finished.

So, when the time comes, you must get absorbed in the draft. Still, there are some final items of preparation that must be completed, after you finish your scouting and forecasting and valuation, but before you start putting names on your roster. You can help yourself by taking some last steps to get ready for the draft itself:

PLAN YOUR DECISION-MAKING PROCESS

"Process?" you may ask. "What process?" If you simply take a list of players and values to your auction, and keep bidding until your roster is full, that doesn't take a whole lot of planning, does it? No, but you are not going to win that way, either. Winning takes a little planning.

First consider whether you can bring a friend or partner to the draft with you. Some leagues don't allow partners to help during a draft, but most of them tolerate or even encourage the presence of colleagues and assistants. If you can bring along another person or two, that could be a big advantage. The best-functioning team I ever saw had three people doing separate jobs. One of them kept track of which players were taken and which were available. Another kept track of how much money each team had spent, and what positions remained vacant at each point. The third person sat at the draft table and actually did the bidding for players; he was especially responsible for studying the faces of the other owners and looking for bluffs, anxiety, and opportunities. My draft software does all these things, except watch the faces of other owners and make the bids.

Three participants per team could put 36 people in a draft room, and I admit that sounds a little excessive. But you shouldn't overlook the fact that an ally or two can help. And if you bring someone with you, it is vital to have a clear division of labor, and to work out your roles before going to the draft. In case you are thinking of it, don't try changing roles in the middle of a draft, even if you are 50/50 partners. You will both lose your train of thought and end up doing worse.

After partnership, another big question is whether your league allows computers in the draft room. Many leagues prohibit computers. Most of those prohibitions sprung up in the mid 1980's when a good laptop PC cost about $6000. Since more people now have portable computers, most leagues tolerate them. The key point is that you should know what your league allows, make your preparation match the league's general practice, and try to influence the rule yourself if you have a preference.

GET YOUR TOOLS READY

The following information is essential preparation:

(a) You need one master list of players available, on which you will indicate or cross off players as they are taken. This list should indicate position eligibility and your dollar values if you are having an auction. The main point is that you must be able to see instantly who is available, and this list must be flawless throughout the auction. If you don't list every available player before you start, you are just wasting information that is available with little or no cost or effort.

Another key point is that you should have one primary list showing players taken. If you have various lists, sorted by position, sorted in alphabetical order, etc., and try to cross off players taken on all these lists, you will waste valuable effort and take attention away from the draft by trying to keep multiple lists current.

(b) You need a list of players sorted by eligible position. The master list mentioned above could be sorted by position, or you could have subsidiary lists. Within each position listing, you should rank the players from top to bottom, and show the dollar value for each name.

(Assign dollar values even if you are not following the auction format; you will see why, shortly.)

(c) You need a roster worksheet for each of your opponents, on which you can enter the players taken and see at a glance which positions are filled and which are vacant. One bid sheet with a column for each roster will do the job nicely. You can quickly glance down a roster and see which positions are vacant, and you can quickly look across each position row and see which teams have vacancies.

(d) You need a worksheet showing money spent and money remaining for each team, if you use an auction. The "money" sheet can be the same as the roster list described in (c) above. Obviously, you need a sharp pencil or a fine point pen, because you will have to write small.

(e) In addition to these "must" lists, you will probably want various other lists that might be useful in certain situations during the draft. Some of these will be obvious when you read our advice on draft tactics. Some of the popular lists are:

- "Likely Overbid" players, e.g. last year's World Series heroes, last year's top starting pitchers, highly publicized rookies, all rookie pitchers who are supposed to be good, and older players who were top stars five years ago.

- "Safe Pitchers" (low value, low risk, basically a bunch of low-ERA middle relievers).

- Injured players (any list from a newspaper or injury update service will do), so you can see at a glance, who has what wrong with them.

- Fake lists: with all these lists floating around, somebody is going to look over your shoulder some time during the auction; it happens in every league, unavoidably. Make a list that includes a mixture of players you like and players you don't like; put circles and arrows around a couple that you don't like.

If your draft is in a relatively small, crowded room, arrange your lists to reflect that fact. Recognize that you can't spread out too much. Get a clipboard so you won't be dropping your lists or getting them mixed up. Put your fake list on top. Practice flipping through your lists before the draft starts, so you won't have to go through a learning curve after the draft starts. If your draft is run by phone or online through a computer modem, and you have complete privacy, take advantage of that fact. Cover your walls like a "war room" full of useful information.

The image of all these lists and things to keep track of during the draft might make your head spin, especially if you haven't done it before. To be sure, it is possible to overdo your list making, and end up with a lot of paper that isn't useful. Here are a few ideas to keep things under control:

For your first draft or auction, use just one master list, sorted by position and by value within position. In future years, you can add other lists after you have perceived a need for them.

If something has to give during the auction, let it be keeping track of other people's money. You will give up a small competitive edge by not knowing every owner's financial condition at every moment, but it's better to give up a little edge than to become totally confused. Any time during the auction when you find yourself losing track of who's been taken, you are trying to do too much. Concerning money, beginners should lobby to have their league's auctioneer keep a running tab and review it frequently during the auction.

Use combinations and overlays to consolidate your lists. Color highlight pens are extremely useful. Using just the one master list, for example, you could highlight players you want to bring up for bid early in orange, highlight pitchers who are OK but not great with yellow, highlight sleepers with blue, etc.

Take a break and clear your head some time before the draft. Get a good night's sleep. One of the world's greatest Rotisserians, John Tippler, will never win his league, because he doesn't follow this advice. John's fellow owners know that he likes to party. So, for the past eight years, they have always found a way to see that he is suitably amused the night before Draft Day. Poor John goes to spring training, studies intensely, prepares copious lists loaded with insight, and always finishes fourth or fifth because of a bad draft.

Some people need to put away their player lists and rankings for a full day or two. The more homework you have done, the longer you need to relax and get your mind clear. Even those people who have just pulled together a few notes on the morning before their draft, are well advised to take a half hour respite before their draft actually starts. If you see someone poring over their lists as they walk into the draft room, you are looking at a loser.

We don't advocate taking a vacation to the extent that you might miss some vital news, but you could consider taking your spouse out for dinner on the night before Draft Day (they won't see you again for six months, you know); just get back in time to catch the baseball news on TV. On Draft Day, you can benefit from taking a ten minute walk and breathing some fresh air before getting started. The point is: don't be talking to yourself or re-ranking players when you sit down to start drafting. Be ready and be sharp.

CONDUCT OF THE DRAFT

One of main benefits of good preparation is that it makes you relaxed and confident. If you haven't been to a draft before, you should get one point perfectly clear: EVERYBODY in the draft is going to make mistakes. Good preparation will help you minimize your mistakes; you can never eliminate them entirely. During the draft, it is critical to put mistakes behind you, moment by moment, and focus on the next problem. Never let yourself waste even one second brooding during the draft. You have the whole summer to feel sorry for yourself; use your draft time for drafting players thoughtfully.

Before we go any farther, memorize this principle: do NOT go to an auction believing that you must get any particular player. It is OK to have a list of, say, five or ten power hitters of which you "must" get at least one, and five or ten ace relievers from which you plan to get one, etc. But it is not OK to go to your auction thinking, "I must get Mark McGwire." You can do that if you want, of course, but you will be playing for the fun of owning Mark McGwire, not for the fun of winning your league. Take your pick.

While you are trying to keep your own mistakes to a minimum, you can do all kinds of things to help your opponents make large and frequent errors. It takes a little experience to learn which people are most susceptible to which kinds of errors, but there are some general themes that always work on somebody.

Sit back during the early stages.

One of the great truisms of Rotisserie auctions is that prices are higher in the beginning of the auction, when everyone has lots of money to spend, and everyone has a vacancy at every position — so everyone can bid on every player. During the early stages of the auction, you don't want to buy players. You hope that the players you want will not come up early; you hope they will come up later in the auction.

When it's your turn to nominate a player early in the auction, bring up someone likely to be in demand, generating bids in excess of value. You want to focus on players who are most difficult to value, e.g. rookies, starting pitchers in general, players who have just had surprising seasons (either good or bad), players who have changed teams (or better yet, changed leagues), and anyone who is doing anything new or different such as playing a new position or playing for a new manager.

Some types of players are almost always overvalued. Here are some ideas to help you stimulate excessive bids by your opponents.
- Last year's World Series heroes are always popular; everybody loves a winner. The more publicity they got, the more overbidding their names will generate.
- Home town favorites are sure bets to attract high bids. Focus especially on the most promising youngsters and the starting pitchers on your home town team.
- Bring up your opponents' favorite players, regardless of team. The single most important competitive intelligence that you can collect before your draft is: who are the favorite players of each of the other owners?
- Think of rookies who have received the most publicity. Visualize magazine covers, Rookie All-

Star Teams in the major newspapers, the most recent Minor League Player of the Year, hot baseball cards, etc.

- Nominate pitchers who were top starters (especially Cy Young winners) about three or four years ago. You want famous names.

The ploy of bringing up names you don't want will usually work consistently through the first third of an auction (say about eight rounds), sometimes longer. Even as a beginner, you will get a feel for that point, when you see two or three consecutive players sell for a "fair" price, or go as bargains.

There is one important caution to keep in mind when bringing up players you don't want: never bid $1 on anyone unless you are willing to take them for $1. There is no assurance that someone is going to take you off the hook. You might think that someone should always be willing to pay $2 for the pitcher who won the Cy Young award four years ago, but if he had ERA's over six in both of the past two seasons, you might be the only person bidding.

Look for bargains.

The players likely to sell for less than they are worth are the opposites of those types listed above. What's the opposite of a home town favorite? A hated rival, of course. If you live in Boston, Yankees will be cheap. If you live in San Francisco, the bargains will be Dodgers, and in LA the Giants will be underappreciated.

What's the opposite of famous? The tiny media markets are great places to look for Draft Day bargains. Players from San Diego, Seattle, Milwaukee, Houston, and the other smaller cities will be the best bargains.

What's the opposite of a rookie pitcher? A veteran hitter, of course. Some of the best bargains are those unexciting, never All-Star, regular players who just keep getting 500 at-bats, year after year. You don't want a fancy-fielding shortstop with a .220 lifetime batting average, but a second baseman who consistently hits .275 with 8 homers, 40 RBI, and 11 SB will usually be underappreciated, unless he has done something to attract attention.

What's the opposite of a World Series hero? A nobody on a losing team fits the bill pretty well. You want the opposite of fame. To find these players, look for at-bat totals that surprise you on the high side. When you find yourself thinking, "What? He got 480 at-bats last year and the year before? I thought he was a bench jockey," then you have found yourself a candidate for a bargain.

WAIT FOR THE "END GAME"

Just as players sell for too much during the early rounds, they sell for too little near the end. This whole phenomenon exists in all leagues, but is very much at work in leagues with several beginners doing the bidding. I can remember one auction back in 1988, when the astute Brian Spectacle kept very careful track of money and rosters, and said, "Vince Coleman, $2," in the twentieth round. All the people who had enough money to bid $3 didn't have any outfield or utility slots open, and everyone who had a vacant slot couldn't bid $3. There were about 30 seconds of strained silence while everyone looked at each other; it seemed like about an hour, and it never happened again.

Remember these points: Try to save some money for the end, so that you don't finish up taking bums for $1 apiece when you could be buying genuine stars for $3 or $4. You don't want to be left with lots of money and no talent to spend it on, but you don't want to miss the bargains at the end, either. If you do a good job of not spending too much early, and a decent job of keeping track, you should be in good shape at the end of the auction.

Knock out other teams' toppers.

If your league has topper rights, you don't want those toppers (except your own of course) coming into play near the end of the auction when prices are low. You want people to pay the highest possible prices if and when they exercise their topper rights. Obviously, you want to bring up other people's best topper players as early as possible, when prices will be high. In the Compuserve Palmer league of 1991, I went into the auction with a large collection of topper rights that I had carefully assembled through winter trading. Much to my dismay, I found that all my toppers were blown off within the first few rounds. I felt like the Iraqi air defense system during the first few minutes of Desert Storm: boom, boom, gone.

OPTIMAL BIDDING

Another axiom of auction economics is that people are going to have different opinions of what each player is worth. Some 15 years ago, I published a study of actual prices paid in a hundred auctions nationwide, and highlighted the case of Alvin Davis for example. Davis, at the time, was a model of consistent performance. He was worth exactly $20 according to every method of calculating value, and, sure enough, $20 was always the *average* price paid for Alvin Davis. But if you looked at all these auctions, you could see that Alvin cost as much as $37 in one auction, and sold for $25 to $30 in many. On the low end, he was available for $16 or less in about one fifth of all auctions, and he sold for $10 or less, in about one tenth of all auctions.

Whenever a player sells for more than you think he's worth, that's good news for you. In a new league with twelve teams and $260 per team, you start the auction with a rational list that shows 276 players worth $1 or more, and $3120 total value for all these players. When a $10 player (on your list) sells for $20 (which may have been the value on someone else's list), you now see $3100 of money remaining, and players worth $3110. Then if a $5 player sells for $10, your list shows talent worth $3105 still remaining, but only $3090 left to spend.

Simply stated, prices are bound to fall; there is less money chasing more talent, every time someone overpays. Near the end of the auction, you may find $200 worth of talent remaining, and only $15 of cash still in circulation; the bargains are imminent.

This phenomenon works, from your point of view, even if everyone else is rational. Other people assign value to players who you think are worthless. After the auction ends, some of the players that you thought were worth $1 or $2 or even $5 will remain untaken, because people came to the auction with different ideas of who was valuable and who wasn't. And among the players where everyone agreed that the player was worth something, there were differing opinions about how much each was worth.

From your point of view, lots of money gets wasted in every auction. Just by glancing at any record of actual prices paid in last year's auctions, you will find numerous prices that approach absurdity. The reason is that you have not only differences of opinion about value, but you also have people bidding irrationally, e.g. "I don't care if I win, I just want to own Jason Giambi."

On average, the median price paid in a large number of auctions is exactly equal to true value. But that means: half the time people are paying too much, and half the time they are paying too little. The quantity of money that gets wasted is very large, and can be measured accurately.

Easier than counting "wasted" dollars and re-calculating values, you can tell the probability (using nationwide averages) that you will succeed buying a player at 90% of value, 80% of value, 50% of value, etc. For example, a star hitter can be bought for under 80% of value, about one fifth of the time. That may not sound like much frequency, but it means (roughly) that if you bid 75% of value on five star hitters, you will get one of them. It happens, and history proves it happens.

The main issue is patience. Four times out of five, the optimal bid (say, 80% of the calculated value of a star hitter) won't work. You have to be patient to get that one time in five, and you can't be picky about getting your favorite players. Patience and flexibility will yield profits.

You know your "profit" when you buy a player. If you get a $20 (calculated) value for $14, that's a $6 profit. Optimal bids can be calculated by simply taking each incremental price ($1, $2, $3, etc.) and for each price, list the possible profit ($), and the probability of getting that player at that price. I can tell you the probability, based on hundreds of auctions nationwide. A $6 profit, with 20% probability of successful bid, means that you have an Expected Value of $1.20: (0.20 probability X $6.00 potential profit). Every time you bid $14 on a $20 star hitter, you have an average profit of $1.20. Four times out of five, you get nothing, but one time out of five, you get a $6 profit.

If you bid higher, you increase the probability of buying a player, but you decrease the profit. If you bid lower, you decrease the probability but increase the possible profit. The optimal bid is simply the point at which your multiplication (probability times profit) yields the highest answer.

The conclusion of optimal bidding studies is that you should try very, very hard to bid no more than 85% of a player's calculated value. Unless the player is a star hitter or an established ace reliever, you shouldn't be bidding more than 70% of calculated value. By refusing to bid higher, you will accumulate money for the end of the auction, when prices drop. I get dozens of letters from people every summer, telling me the same story: "After many years of finishing near the bottom, I finally tried optimal bidding. I sat through the auction and didn't buy ANY players until the eighth round. It was painful. People kept looking at me and teasing me. All my favorite players were already sold by the time I started bidding. I got a bunch of no-names. I am in first place by a wide margin. Now everybody thinks I'm a genius. Thank you."

If the mathematics of optimal bidding didn't become completely clear by now, don't worry about it. *Rotisserie Baseball - Playing for Blood* has a more complete presentation of this subject, with the original raw data, graphs, tables, etc. Just remember these points: (1) bid low, and (2) be patient.

BUDGETING

Optimal bidding is the most useful tool that you can bring to an auction, but you need more. If your league is well-established with a high level of competition, the bids are going to be in a narrower range than what you find in the "average" league. It is conceivable that you could get to the end of your auction, and find that all the remaining excess value is in low-value players. In other words, you might be able to get several players worth $5 or more for $1 apiece at the end of the auction, but you might be unable to spend all your money because there aren't enough high value players left to bid on.

The last thing you want to do is finish the auction with unspent money. You want to pack as much value as possible onto your roster. To do that, you might have to pay up to full, calculated value for certain players in certain situations. These situations are most likely to arise in ongoing leagues where most of the good players have been retained and won't be available in the auction. To prevent this problem, you need roster budgeting: allocating certain dollar amounts to certain positions.

For a beginner, or for a new league, you are not likely to need much work on budgeting, but we are covering the subject, so you can start thinking about it. The basic idea is that you need certain components somewhere on your roster in order to win. For a new league starting from scratch, you should look at all the available players, and count how many are worth $20 or more. If you see 36 defined "stars" in your twelve-team league, your fair share would be three of the star players.

For simplicity, assume we are talking about players worth $20 to $40 apiece, $30 on average, in the star category. (You can find the actual numbers by looking at your own value lists for your own league.) In this example, if you have $260 to spend on your whole team, then these three players might cost you an average of $30 apiece, or $90 in total.

At the start of your auction, you need to allocate $90 for these three star players. That doesn't mean you intend to pay $90 for them; you hope to get $90 worth of talent in these three players, while paying under $75. But you recognize, at the outset, that you MIGHT need $90.

Obviously, you need a list of players who meet the "star" criteria. You may have a definition other than "worth $20 or more." In fact, you can make this as complicated as you want, and have separate budgets for "superstar hitters," and "high value outfielders," and any categories that you choose to define, and your budgets and categories can overlap.

In this simple example, just picture a budget of up to $90 for three "high value" players. Remember, you cannot set your sights on any particular player, so you make a list of, say, fifteen players who qualify for this category. The longer your list of acceptable candidates, the better you are going to do. And you have to be flexible. Your top candidate might have a calculated value of $40. With a long list, you might go all the way down to $19 or $18 value.

You have to use judgment and keep track of who's available. Until you get down to the end of your list, you just wait and wait. But when you see that you are down to the last few players from your pre-defined star list, you start bidding aggressively, up to 100% of calculated value. When you are down to the last player on your list, if you don't have three of them already, bid aggressively again (up to 100% of calculated value).

If you miss all of the "good" players in the star category, you must make two changes: (1) you start bidding aggressively on players who come close to meeting the standards you have set for each category, and (2) you shift some of your $90 "star" budget to the remaining players. For example, if you were pressed into spending $30 each for two stars, and don't have any other players worth over $20, you can allocate the unspent $30 to get two $15 players, where you had planned to get one $29 player and one $1 player.

While making these changes in tactics, you still don't bid over full, calculated value for any player. You don't need three $30 players to win your league. If you end up with a bunch of $18 players that you got for prices like $8 or $9, you can easily trade your bargain-priced regular players for high-price superstars, later in the year.

The main point of roster budgeting is that you want to start the season with some kind of foundation in high-value talent. Note that I say "want to" and not "have to." During the auction, you need to recognize situations where it is appropriate to bid up to full value. Budgeting is the easiest method to help you recognize those situations when they arise.

DRAFT INFLATION

All of the above discussion of "value" is based on a new league with all teams having empty rosters. An ongoing league with retained players will usually have some form of "draft inflation."

Simply stated, draft inflation occurs when the value of players retained exceeds the salaries at which these players are retained. Everyone keeps their best bargain-price players, so they will have more money in their auction. If you retain a player worth $20, for a salary of $10, you are removing more talent than money. It's exactly the opposite of what happens early in an auction when people are over-paying for players. By retaining players at favorable salaries, everyone is, in effect, starting the auction with a number of bargain purchases. When the Draft Day auction starts, there is less talent and more money at the beginning of actual bidding, so prices must be adjusted upward.

Draft inflation is fully explained in *Rotisserie Baseball - Playing for Blood*. If you are joining a new league, or any league with no retentions, you don't have to account for draft inflation. But if you are playing in an ongoing league with retained players, especially when owners keep players at low salaries, you need to adjust all of your calculated values to reflect the actual money and the actual value of players that will be available in your auction. Like everything else covered here, my draft software keeps track of inflation for you, and adjusts values continuously during the auction.

THE SIMPLE DRAFT-PICK METHOD

If your league selects players with a simple rotating draft, your Draft Day is going to be much simpler. You can live without optimal bids, or roster budgeting, and you don't have to keep track of your money or anyone else's. You just have to name players, and they are yours. The "simple" draft has its own complexities and unique twists and turns, however.

The simple draft usually does a better job of separating and rewarding those who are well-prepared. So the first item to check is that you have thorough lists and rankings at each position. In an auction format you can bring up any old name with a price of $1, and hope that somebody will take you off the hook if the player is a bum. At least it's possible that you can be saved. In a draft, once you name a player, he's on your roster.

Your mission during a draft isn't very complicated. You just have to identify the best player available each time it's your turn. The only reason you have to watch your opponents is because their actions might affect your definition of "best" at any point.

FOCUS ON POSITION SCARCITY

The key issue in a draft format is to make sure that you don't get shut out and miss all the good players at any position. For this reason, the "skill positions" of catcher, shortstop, and (to a lesser extent in most years) third base and second base, all get special attention. The scarcest player type is the ace reliever; they often disappear within the first few rounds.

When making a selection, the question that you want to ask yourself is: "If I don't get this particular player now, who is going to be available next time its my turn. This is the point where dollar values can help you, even though you aren't having an auction. Each player's dollar value also answers the question: "What happens if I don't get any of the 'good' players and end up with the last guy at this position?" A $25 player, by definition, is worth $24 more than the last guy at that position.

Suppose you look at your list of outfielders, and see the next eight available players are worth $25, $25, $24, $24, $23, $22, $21, and $21, respectively. You don't feel any sense of urgency about grabbing the top outfielder. Now suppose you look at shortstops, and your available list shows the top shortstop is worth $19, the second best is $11, and the rest are worth $9 or less. In this situation, you would probably choose the $19 shortstop, not the $25 outfielder. In the shortstop pool, you see a drop of $8 or more following the next shortstop selection. In the outfield pool, you are not likely to drop more than $4 in value by waiting until the next round.

Keeping track of other teams' rosters is especially critical in a draft. In the above example, you might want to look deeper than eight players on your outfielders available list. If there will be twenty picks before you get to choose again, and most of the other teams have three or four vacancies for outfielders, while their shortstop positions are almost all filled, the $25 outfielder might be the better selection. You need some judgment and some good luck, but the point to keep in mind is simple: try to foresee what will happen if you don't take the highest-value player on your list. Very often, taking a player with a lower "raw" value is a better idea.

Knowing that a team has filled up a particular position can give you a big advantage. Suppose, for example, that you are trying to choose between two players in the fifteenth round. Both have a value of $9 according to your list. One is a shortstop, and one is a third baseman. Say you are picking in the ninth position in a twelve-team draft. The tenth, eleventh and twelfth teams will pick after you. Then the order reverses, and the twelfth, eleventh and tenth teams will choose again, and then its back to your turn. If you look at the rosters, and see that these other three teams are all filled at shortstop, middle infield, and utility, your answer is simple: you take the third baseman, knowing that the shortstop must come around to you again.

Even more important than shortstops and catchers, make sure you draft an ace reliever or two. In an auction you can react to the ace reliever situation as it unfolds, and bid aggressively if and when it becomes necessary. But in a draft, you can find yourself cut off from the saves category and helpless to do anything about it. Every draft has a life of its own, and you have to watch what other people are doing, but as a general rule, you should aim to get one ace reliever among your first three picks, and try for another soon. If you have both AL and NL teams to choose from, you can wait longer before you get shut out, but you also need twice as many ace relievers to get your fair share. Just figure there is less than one ace reliever per major league team, and count how many will be in your draft.

Put the squeeze on other teams.

While you are trying to bob and weave to get the most out of your own draft picks, look for opportunities to diminish the value of other teams' draft picks. Focus especially on teams that you perceive as rivals, if you think you are a contender.

One general tactic is that you want to be a leader, not a follower, when choosing which position to fill. When there have just been several picks of starting pitchers, don't take a starting pitcher. You will just be conceding a deficit compared to the other teams, when you take the next-best starting pitcher. After several people take pitchers, go for the best available hitter. After a run on outfielders, take the best infielder or the best relief pitcher. Throughout the draft, keep asking yourself: "Which position hasn't been mentioned for a long time?" And check your list for that position before making your selection. You will find some pleasant surprises.

If you don't let other teams put the squeeze on you, that means you are successfully putting the squeeze on the other guys. You can be aggressive and pro-active along these lines. If you see that seven teams haven't yet taken a shortstop, and the best available shortstops are worth $7, $6, $4, $3, $1 and $1 respectively, you could start a run on shortstops by taking the one worth $7. If the other teams are paying attention, the next three picks might be those three shortstops worth $6, $4, and $3. You will have locked in a profit relative to those who picked after you, and you will have condemned some teams to living with the worst $1 shortstops.

Don't jump at starting pitchers early.

If you get one ace starter within your first six picks, that's enough. There are many more starting pitchers than any other types of player, so you won't see big drops in value when you ask that question: "What happens if I don't take the best available starting pitcher now?" In a roundabout way, waiting for starting pitchers in a draft is like allocating your money in favor of hitters in an auction format.

At the end of the draft, don't grab a bunch of bad starters, even if you have a strict innings pitched requirement. It is safer to get some harmless middle relievers, and then trade for starting pitchers after you see which ones are likely to have good seasons. If you don't invest heavily in starting pitchers, you will be strong in hitting and relief pitching, and people will be coming to you with trade proposals.

In summary, whether you use a draft or an auction, the main idea is to pack as much value as possible onto your roster. You don't need "balance," although it's nice. The end of the draft means you are beginning a six-month journey on roster management, and you just want to be well supplied before you start.

ROSTER MANAGEMENT

Draft Day is the most important date on the Rotisserie calendar, but the baseball season lasts a full six months. Anything can happen. One or two mistakes can undo your Rotisserie roster after the season starts. Conversely, with good management and a few career years, just about any team can take first place in any given season.

Trading activity varies considerably from one league to another. In some leagues, people can get carried away with the fun of pushing famous names around like pawns. In leagues that churn players continuously, the sharpest trader is often the best bet to become champion. If the draft is just a prelude to six months of trading frenzy, your beginning roster may not even matter all that much, except that it must include some good bargaining chips for all the activity that begins when the trading bell rings.

Most leagues adopt the philosophy that trading is an adjunct to the basic contest, and that the winner should be decided primarily by his ability to build a winning roster before the season starts, and then manage it through a long summer of contingencies. Even if your league frowns on free-wheeling Finleyism, however, you want to be on the active end of the spectrum within your league.

Trading allows you to balance your statistics and move value into the categories where you get the most benefit. You can't get this "liquidity" if you don't trade, and you won't stumble across any marvelous opportunities if you aren't in the trade market.

Most leagues take steps to stop trades that look like collusion. There are all kinds of rules against lopsided trades, ranging from simple "not allowed" statements, to elegant formulas that define exactly what's allowed and what isn't. The problem is: while you can legislate against collusion, you cannot legislate against stupidity — and some owners are prone to make serious blunders in the trade market.

We are about to give you numerous tips on "beating" your trade partners. While playing to win, try to fit these tactics into the unique culture of your league. Winning is less fun when it leaves eleven people angry at you. One suggestion: if you have that "uh oh" feeling about a trade being too lopsided, you are probably going to wish you hadn't done it. So don't.

DON'T TRY TO LOOK TOO SMART

A modest trader is a happy trader. Nobody wants to trade with a know-it-all. Everyone is wary when dealing with a known shark. Even worse than the shark is the person who thinks he's a shark. After every trade, he tells everyone who will listen, how and why he took the other guy to the cleaners ... and then he wonders why no one else wants to trade with him.

There are several simple tactics to keep a low profile. Try these methods:

1. Don't overwhelm people with information. It is fine to describe the good features of your own players and the weaknesses of your opponent's. But if you overdo it, you will merely annoy people.

2. Early in the year, make a bad trade. We are not suggesting that you should give up a star for garbage; just make an impression. You can capture attention without giving up much. For example, trade a player of small (but obvious) value, for someone who is overwhelmingly worthless, knowing that you can dispose of the worthless player. People will always chuckle when they remember what you did right after the draft. This method is similar to the old poker maxim: make sure you get caught bluffing (once) early in the game.

3. Remind people of your worst trades. When you trade a lot, you are bound to have bad luck occasionally. Use that bad luck to your advantage, by reminding people what you did. We know one clever owner who kept his trade machinery running smoothly for a decade, by always reminding people that he had traded Eric Davis for Mitch Webster in May 1986.

STUDY BEFORE YOU TALK

There are two sure ways to lose credibility as a trader: (1) offer a player the other guy doesn't need, or (2) ask for a player the other guy can't afford to give up. The converse of this statement is that you can gain credibility by doing your homework. Study the other guy's roster from his point of view, and you will make a good impression when you start talking.

BE PATIENT

Don't ask immediately for the player you really want. Talk in general terms initially, such as, "You need starting pitchers, and I need home runs." If your objective is to get Jason Giambi, there is one sure way to drive the price sky-high: call up and say, "I want Jason Giambi." If you talk generally about trading a star pitcher for a power hitter, you might get a pleasant surprise. It's always better when you don't have to bring up the name you want. Another pleasant surprise might be that you don't have to give up as much as you thought.

Talk about the other team's needs, not your own. Nobody wants to hear about what you need, and if you keep saying things like, "nine home runs would raise me five points in the standings," those home runs are going to become extremely expensive. If the other guy needs stolen bases, that should be your main topic of conversation.

When you get a good offer, ask for a little more. It rarely hurts to ask. Try for something small, like "Would you throw in Jones?" And if the other guy says no, or he wants to think about it, you can immediately accept his original offer: "Oh, nevermind, we can just do what you want."

ALWAYS TRY TO HELP BOTH TEAMS

The best way to bargain, especially after you get to know the other owner, is to say: "Look, let's examine our rosters together and see where we shift values around so that we both come out better." Follow classic negotiating tactics. Keep talking about the good features of the players you are offering to trade away, and keep talking about your opponent's needs.

APRIL-MAY TRADES

One of the standard sucker moves in every league is taking new owners to the cleaners in April and May. After joining a competition based on statistics, beginners are overwhelmingly prone to attach too much significance to their first few weeks of stats and standings reports. Everyone wants feedback. They are dying for an answer to the question: "How well did I do on

Draft Day?" The "inverse ignorance ratio" tells us that wise owners always think they had a bad draft; less-astute owners always think they did well; and newcomers always have vague anxiety.

The first half of the season is also the time when most teams are active in the trade market, for several reasons. Trade opportunities are most plentiful when everyone is still in the hunt. And most leagues have a deadline, after which you cannot make trades. So if you're not in the trade market during the first half of the season, you could miss it completely.

During the early part of each season, you will see many extremes of player performance, some good and some bad. April statistics are the most dangerous numbers in baseball. When a hitter goes 1 for 17 in July, his batting average drops from .250 to .240, and nobody even notices. When a hitter goes 1 for 17 in April, his batting average is posted as .058, and everyone thinks he should be sent back to the minors (if he's young) or released (if he's old).

Some of the better baseball commentators won't even mention batting average during April. They will say "three for ten" or "nine for thirty" or whatever the real stats are. When you say a three-for-ten hitter is "hitting .300" you are stretching the truth a bit.

If you want proof of silliness in April numbers, pick up any newspaper from the last week of April, a year ago. If you have a good player performing poorly, don't panic. I will always remember that Tony Gwynn was hitting .237 in June 1988. Would you have unloaded him, or waited for the second half when he hit .400 and went on to win the NL batting crown?

MAKING SENSE OUT OF YOUR STANDINGS

During April, May, and even June, you will find that your league standings are highly volatile from week to week. In many leagues, the standings remain volatile right up to the end of the season.

The commonest mistake concerning standings is to overreact during the first few weeks. Many people call me in April-May in a state of panic; they're in tenth place, 20 points out of first. I ask them, "But how does your roster FEEL?" Is it a tenth place roster? Or do you just have some underperformers?" On May 15 you can tell a lot more about the future outlook for your team by looking at your players' established performance, than you can by looking at their performance in the current season.

MIDSEASON ANALYSIS

By late June or early July, your standings begin to become meaningful. The following advice on "manipulating" the standings is intended to be used during the second half of the season. It would be silly to try these ideas during April or May. You must be open-minded about the fact that you can win (or lose) any category by changing your roster during the first half of the year.

Like the game of baseball itself, Rotisserie offers myriad possibilities and surprise endings. Standings can tell you the probabilities of winning, if you know how to read the numbers, but Rotisserie standings can also be very misleading. A "safe" fifteen point lead can evaporate in a week.

One reason Rotisserie standings can change faster than "real" baseball standings, is that there is more at risk every day. When the Mets and Dodgers take the field, there is only one game at stake, even if the score becomes 27-0. But whenever a pitcher takes the mound, his Rotisserie owner is at risk for unlimited damage. Ask anybody who owned Jim Clancy and Bob Forsch (two good pitchers who gave up a combined 17 earned runs in one game) in August 1989.

Another reason why a big lead in a Rotisserie league might evaporate quickly, is that standings points are not all equal. Some points are very fragile, or "unsettled" as I like to call them. If you are one home run ahead of the next closest competitor in the home-run category, that's worth one point, but you can lose that point with one swing of the bat. If you are 24 homers ahead of the next guy, that's also worth one point; but a point based on 24 home runs isn't going to evaporate in one day.

The key to managing your roster, especially later in the season, is to find the true meaning of your league standings. Think about the standings in terms of player performance in the real world. You can see that 24 home runs represent a great half season from a great home-run hitter. If it's July 1, and you are looking at a 24 home-run lead or deficit, think of that as "about two thirds of a season from a 36-homer guy," and you will keep your perspective.

The standings are not some external force that determines whether your team is good or bad; the standings are a passive set of numbers that can be manipulated. Some standings can be downright misleading.

TRADE AWAY "WASTED VALUE"

With a 31 home-run lead over your closest opponent, you could lose 30 homers without losing a point in the standings. One month from one very hot slugger would be 10 home runs (that's a pace of 60 per year). So you could trade away one slugger, or even two, without risking much in the HR category.

Almost every team has wasted value somewhere. If you cannot find any category where you lead your closest opponent by a wide margin, you have done a fine job of midseason roster management AND you have been lucky.

USE TRADES TO IMPACT CRITICAL CATEGORIES

The same way you look at unsettled points to plan your own strategy, you can look for teams that have unsettled points in the categories where you can afford to help. You should give special consideration to teams that can take points away from your arch rivals.

Your main purpose in trading is to improve in the categories that you need most. Sometimes, however, you cannot find anyone who is willing and able to give you what you need. What do you do then?

As the trading deadline approaches, you have to be increasingly open-minded. If you tried and failed to swap for the players you need, consider just "giving" a player to a team that can take points away from your closest rival.

Finally, some people just won't trade, even when you're willing to give more than you get. In such cases, you can still give free advice and insight, telling them how to manage their roster in a way that will help them while taking points away from your arch rival.

KNOW WHEN IT'S OVER

The commonest mistake in long-term strategy is the dogged pursuit of fifth place. Long after a money-winning finish is impossible, many owners keep fighting to get the best possible standing. While this activity is helpful for league interest and can also produce small benefits like getting a high minor league draft pick the next spring, it is generally better to get focused on "next year" sooner rather than later, and begin managing your roster accordingly. You simply do better when you concentrate on one year or the other.

The ideal time to shift your attention, from this year to next year, may vary according to factors other than standings. You need to look at the quality of opportunity available in pursuing each alternative. If you want to play for this year, but no one will trade you the established players you need to be competitive, it may be time to shift your strategy toward the youngsters.

If you think you want to build for next year, but find that all the low-salary, emerging stars are being pursued by every team in the league, you might seize an opportunity by trading away all your low-priced talent for high-salaried stars who can help you this year. Bad rosters can be miraculously transformed in rare cases when the league attitude is too lopsided toward next year.

DO YOUR PLAYER-DUMPING BEFORE IT'S TOO LATE

Don't wait until the night before your trading deadline to begin moving your high-salary players. The top teams in your league may all look lucky, but there is a good chance that their owners simply know more about this game than you do, or at least they knew more on Draft Day and/or managed their draft better than you did.

Talk to other owners all summer, and LISTEN extensively. When you start hearing, "You can't keep that guy at $40, and you're out of the money this year anyway," you have waited too long. So listen carefully for subtler suggestions along those lines, and start making your moves before your personal trade market deteriorates.

Knowing your main goal is critical all year, every year, whether you're playing for this year or next. The worst thing you can do is to have NO strategy and make no adjustments. So, formulate a vision of the future. Define where you want to be when the season ends. Make a list of the steps necessary to get there. And execute!

DEALING WITH INJURIES

What two letters spell "agony" for major league managers and Rotisserie owners alike? "DL" is the ominous notation meaning that the forces of nature have removed your player from active service, often for unknown duration. At any point in time, you might find 10% of the player population on the Disabled List. To each Rotisserie owner, that means about two and half players. The DL is very much a part of this game.

When a player gets hurt, his owner always has two questions: (1) How long will this injured player be out? And (2) When they come back, will their performance return to normal? Usually, these questions don't have clear-cut answers. So what do you do?

1. Build a roster that can absorb injuries. Obviously, this process starts on Draft Day, but players change roles and teams during the season, and you often have to pursue the players you want through trades after the season starts. No amount of planning is going to make you totally safe, but some simple tactics can cushion the impact of injuries. For example, get a setup reliever from the same major league team as your ace closer.

Fourth outfielders and top utility men from the same major league teams as your Rotisserie stars make good insurance. When the star player gets hurt, you get the benefit of increased playing time from the backup player. Often these reserves are available in trade for minimal prices after the draft ends. Trading one part-time player for another is a good way to break the ice in the trade market, and you can help another owner by giving him a backup for his star player.

2. Be realistic about "medical information." Like "military intelligence" and "a quick wait," medical information has an elusive quality. The questions are always objective; the answers are always unclear. I don't have to wish I had a nickel for every time someone has asked me, "When is Joe Bimbleman going to play again?" I collect at least two dollars for every such question, and the answer always begins with the statement of fact: I can tell you a definite time frame when he is NOT going to play, because that kind of fact can often be found within the realm of "information."

If you talk to the players themselves, you soon discover the vast uncertainty that surrounds every injury. Healing is a complex, invisible, and frequently mysterious process, far removed from the precise world of clocks and calendars. The manager doesn't know; the doctor doesn't know. Heck, the player himself doesn't know.

Here are two general tips to make an educated guess: (1) look at other players who have previously had a similar injury can be enlightening, and (2) professional athletes usually heal faster than us mortal humans. When the team doctor says four to six weeks, I tend to guess closer to four, initially, and when six weeks go by with no sign of imminent return, I tend to become extremely pessimistic, because the injury was probably worse — sometimes much worse — than originally estimated.

Notwithstanding the superior healing ability of the average pro athlete, the best policy from the outset is to be pessimistic for roster management purposes. If you act on the belief that healing will be slow, then you might get a pleasant surprise. If you guess wrong on the optimistic end of the spectrum, you can lose on two counts.

Sometimes injuries can create opportunities. One obvious benefit is that you get access to the free agent pool. The Yankees got a net benefit when Wally Pipp felt too ill to play, and Lou Gehrig stepped in. It is a good idea to be familiar with your league available list all the time, but you should really take a long, hard look when you have a disability. You might get a pleasant surprise.

COMPETITIVE INTELLIGENCE

Every large corporation has someone in charge of competitive intelligence. If you don't know what the competition is up to, you will have trouble beating them. In Rotisserie leagues, the key point is that you must study other people's rosters and moves, not just your own. It is amazing how many smart owners plod through their Rotisserie seasons with only brief looks at the opposition. You can create amazing benefits by knowing your opponent's point of view.

In addition to finding underperformers on your opponents' rosters, there are two other benefits to be obtained through "competitive intelligence".
(1) You can find the needs and weaknesses (and/or surplus numbers) in the other rosters, and
(2) You can find prejudices in your opponents' player selections, and take advantage of them.

Competitive intelligence doesn't always produce immediate benefits. Usually, it takes patience to accumulate information and bring it into play at just the right moment. Over the course of a long season you can accumulate a great deal of information just by communicating with your fellow owners. Some leagues don't have too much communication, but if you play in a "quiet" league, that just creates more relative value for whatever information you can get.

Don't limit your league friendships to just two or three owners. Ignoring two thirds of your league is not going to help you be informed. Make an effort to know everybody. Ask about where your opponents went to school. If you didn't know before Draft Day, spend the summer finding out who their favorite players are.

Some owners are going to approach you with outrageous trades and silly requests. Don't turn them off too abruptly. Any time you get a trade offer, no matter how ridiculous, stay calm. If someone offers you Randy Velarde for Derek Jeter, just ask him to explain how he views this trade as helping both teams (a perfectly reasonable request, and much more productive than slamming down the telephone).

Whenever someone is trying to rob you, they should be willing to talk extensively. Talking to an astute owner, you might be able to pick his brain and get some insight into league standings or other owners' mentalities. And if the guy with the outrageous trade offer is just a dope, you might find out how to take advantage of him. If he thinks Velarde is so great because of his experience and ability to play multiple positions, maybe you can steer the conversation toward trading him another, similar player from your roster, for someone better.

ANTICIPATE MOVES BY THE OPPOSITION

Good chess players try to look several moves ahead. The competitor who is never surprised is never beaten. In Rotisserie, it pays to look around at everyone else's roster, and try to anticipate their next moves, whenever you have a choice to make yourself.

You can also gauge the future availability of free agents by looking at all players in the current pool. If your league has three or four decent catchers lying around untaken, there is usually no reason to hurry when grabbing any one of them. Looking at every team's roster, to see who needs a catcher, you can tell even more about the chances that one of them might be taken soon.

When you see a horde of pitchers ready to come off the DL, you can expect a richer supply of talent to be available soon. If you have a replacement to make, it's often worth waiting a week, especially when pitching is involved.

There is a lot more to roster management than just these few tips. We could write a whole book about it. In fact, we have written almost a whole book about it: *Rotisserie Baseball - Playing for Blood*.

TOOLS OF THE TRADE

The world was different in 1988. We had no *Baseball Weekly*, no *ESPN.com*, no Baseball Tonight, no *STATS.com*, no Baseball America *Prospect Handbook*, no cornucopia of websites spewing daily information and insight. *The National* had not yet appeared and then disappeared. Box scores contained only the scantiest information. Spring training was still full of camps where fans could walk onto the practice fields and sit on a bench with the players. The world has certainly changed. Some of the changes are good, while some of the new sources of "information" might better be described as distractions.

Time management has become the biggest issue. Just a decade ago, the problem was that we had the time, but we didn't have enough information. Sure, we were frenzied in our pursuit of information, and it often seemed like we were short of time, but remember how many nights we stayed up — even those of us with "instant" online access to the news wires — waiting for the West Coast box scores. That's right: waiting. And at other times, we bought morning newspapers only to find that they were missing half the previous night's games. Once again, we had to wait another day for Tuesday's "late night box scores" to appear in Thursday's papers.

Today, staying informed is easy, raising two implications: (1) staying informed isn't exactly a competitive advantage, because everyone is doing it; and (2) there is a new challenge to use information wisely, displacing the old challenge to find the information in the first place.

This essay was originally intended to launch immediately into a series of tips about where to find the best information, but as soon as I sat down and started thinking about the purpose of all this information, I decided to take a step back and say a few words about questions like context and thinking about the big picture. I do that a lot. Don't worry. I will get to the details, and there will be plenty of them.

If you want to visualize a goal for your information-gathering activities, this is it: maintain a critical mass of knowledge, so that whenever news breaks, you can take advantage immediately, without doing too much research. That means knowing every major league team's depth charts, the top setup men, who were the last players cut in spring training and how they are doing in the minors, which utility infielders will be converted into full-time substitutes after someone else gets injured, and which utility guys stay on the bench because the manager loves their flexible package of pinch-hitting, pinch-running, and late-inning double-switch replacement at any of four positions. Without this context, your instant access to information won't be worth as much as it could be.

It is extremely useful to learn to think like major league managers and GM's do. Get to know them. Never miss a mid-winter interview of a GM. Always get the managers' postgame quotes — and commit them to memory — when they explain why they made the moves they did. Hal McRae actually had an answer to that question which set him off in Kansas City a few years ago, if you followed the conversation that led up to that little motivational tempest.

Study history. Superficially, it may seem like a waste of time to read books that were written during the 1980's, but the old Bill James Abstracts are loaded with critical thinking and clear explanations which can help you today. Most of those managers — and some of the players — are still around. And the new people moving into top jobs in baseball today were all around during the 1980's (even Randy Smith, who benefited from sharing work experiences with his father, Tal Smith). The questions, decisions and philosophies are all the same as they were 15 years ago.

The impact of James' thinking on the usefulness of today's instant information cannot be overstated. It was James who designed the network of pitch-by-pitch game scorers who now make STATS On Line in-progress box scores possible. Long ago, he foresaw the need for access to details — not because he is so fascinated with minutiae, but because he can see the big picture.

If you are reading this advice a week before Draft Day, don't drop your *Baseball Weekly* and rush to the library to read George Will's book, *Men At Work*; but do plan to do some summer reading along those lines (Will has another book coming), and do a lot more reading next winter. On this foundation you can build your context, that critical mass of knowledge which makes information useful.

Now for your daily homework. Read all box scores and game stories; there are only 15 per day. Rather than focusing on who had a big game and who didn't, focus on what changed, maybe even before the game started: who's in and out of the lineup, who's up or down in the batting order, which obscure reliever pitched the eighth inning to protect a one-run lead, and which relievers got mop-up duty. There is no source that can rival *USA Today* in print. In the on-line world, the undisputed champ is STATS, Inc. I will give you four examples of what STATS On Line can do for you. I could give a hundred. To see what's available in 2004, go to www.stats.com or call them at 1-800-63-STATS.

In-progress Box Scores:

Why wait for the conventional news services to file their results after the game is over? Often I need to make a pitcher decision, and I can't wait for the Seattle game to finish. So I log onto STATS and check to see how a certain pitcher is doing. If he's got a two-hit shutout going in the seventh inning, I feel good about him. If he left with one out in the fifth inning and six runs in, that tells me something important, too.

Merely seeing the starting lineups can be useful. Remember what I just said about things changing before a game even starts. And seeing that a player has already stolen a base in the second inning can tell you plenty about how his hamstring is feeling — hours before your competition has the same information.

Statistical Profiles:

If you have seen the STATS player profiles, with stat splits, home/road, grass/turf, day/night etc., you have only seen the tip of the iceberg, and you are looking at last year's numbers. How would you like to know how a given pitcher is doing against every team in the league, in

June or July this year? It's there, in STATS Fantasy Advantage, updated continuously as the season unfolds.

Game Logs:

Imagine going through every newspaper from April to August, to find out how and when a player's performance has changed. What is a player's batting average, since he came off the DL three weeks ago? When is the last time he stole a base? Is he striking out more than usual? Has he been drawing enough walks to downplay a low batting average? It's all there. You can scan the whole season, even a whole career, day by day, or you can name the date and see everything that has happened since then.

Whenever I need to choose a pitcher, I look at his last three or four starts, and focus on strikeout/walk ratio. Give me five pitchers to choose from, and I can instantly tell you which one is on top of his game right now.

Player Portfolio:

This one is my favorite, because I play in so many leagues that it can be difficult to remember who's on what roster. I type my teams into STATS On Line (they save all the info for me) and then I can check each day's results, last week, two weeks, or even look at the upcoming schedule and see instantly who's going to Colorado.

The Player Portfolio saves me literally dozens of hours every month, hundreds of hours every season. And here is a tip on how to get even more benefit than tracking your own players: put in each league's available list, and see instant comparisons when you need to choose a substitute. Sometimes I even put in an arch rival's roster, especially when he's got pitchers headed for Colorado.

With STATS On Line, I find that the mountain of newspapers which used to blockade my office has gradually disappeared. When I do buy a paper, I can recycle it immediately, knowing that the same info can be found any time I need it, as fast as my modem can tap in.

And then there is my own *Benson Baseball Annual*, a book that I view as a sort of Rotisserians' Baseball Abstract, spiced up with the best insights from a year of interviewing players, managers, coaches and GM's. The writing goes team by team, position by position, telling who's going to play, who's in reserve, and why ... all the way down to the minors. The 2003 edition is going to be astoundingly current. *The Annual* also delivers the best and latest thinking in Rotisserie arts and sciences.

Diamond Library publishes other books, including this one you're reading, and *Future Stars*, which is represented with meaty excerpts here in the official Rotisserie Farm Report.

The *Benson Private Pages* deliver a year-round update of *The Benson Baseball Annual*. Glen Waggoner once said here in these pages that Benson's Updates are worth six points in the standings, so I guess the only question is whether you care about six points. *Benson's Private Pages* exceed 500 pages per year.

For STATS products and services, call 800-63-STATS.

For Diamond Library, call 800-707-9090 or 203-834-1231 or visit johnbenson.com on the web for a closer look.

The Rules, Simplified

1. Rotisserie League teams are made up of real, live major league baseball players, selected at an auction draft that takes place at the beginning of the season (typically on the first weekend following Opening Day).

2. Each team in a Rotisserie League is composed of 25 players taken from the active rosters of the National League or 23 players from American League teams. A Rotisserie League drawn from National League or American League players should have 12 teams. You can, however, have fewer teams.

3. A team consists of five outfielders, two catchers, one second baseman, one shortstop, one middle infielder (either 2B or SS), one first baseman, one third baseman, one corner man (1B or 3B), one utilityman (NL) or designated hitter (AL), and nine pitchers. National League rosters have two utilitymen and ten pitchers since 1998.

4. Players are purchased at an open auction. Spending is limited to $260 per team for the American League, or $280 per team for the National League. (If you don't want to use money, call them units or pocorobas or whatever. The point is resource allocation.) Teams may spend less. The first bidder opens the auction with a minimum bid of $1 for any player. The bidding then proceeds around the room (at minimum increments of $1) until only one bidder is left. The process is repeated, with successive owners introducing players to be bid on, until every team has a complement of 23 players from the American League or 25 players from the National League.

5. A player is eligible to be drafted for any position at which he appeared in 20 or more games the preceding year. If he did not appear in 20 games at any one position, he is eligible for the position at which he appeared the most times. Once the season starts, a player qualifies for a position by playing it once. Multiple eligibility is okay.

6. Trading is permissible from Auction Draft Day until midnight August 31. After every trade, both teams must be whole — that is, they must have the same number of active players at each position that they had before the trade.

7. If a major league player is put on the disabled list, sent to the minors, traded to the other league, or released, he may be replaced by a player from the free agent pool of unowned talent. Replacement must be made by position. The original player may either be released or placed on his Rotisserie team's reserve list. A team may not release, reserve, or waive a player without replacing him with another active player.

8. Cumulative team performance is tabulated in five offensive and five pitching categories:
- Composite batting average (BA)
- Total home runs (HR)
- Total runs scored (R)

- Total runs batted in (RBI)
- Total stolen bases (SB)
- Composite earned run average (ERA)
- Total wins (W)
- Total linnings pitched (IP)
- Total saves (SV)
- Composite ratio: walks (BB) + hits (H), divided by innings pitched (IP), also known as baserunners per inning, (BPI or B/I), or walks and hits per inning pitched (WHIP).

9. Teams are ranked from first to last in each of the eight categories. For example, in a twelve-team league, the first-place team receives 12 points, the second-place team 11 points, on down to one point for last place. The team with the most points wins the pennant.

10. Prize money is distributed as follows: 50% for first place, 20% for second, 15% for third, 10% for fourth, and 5% for fifth. Even more important, the owner of the winning team receives a bottle of Yoo-Hoo — poured over his/her head.

"Do I have to play for money?" No! People who can't play golf unless they have some money attached to the outcome are the same people who will want to invest $260 (or $26 or $2.60) in their Rotisserie team. Unlike the big league version, Rotisserie League Baseball can be played for very little money, or none at all. You can play for pennies, Cracker Jack prizes, or nothing at all and still have fun. Just be sure to keep the ratio of "acquisition units" to players at 260/23 (or 280/25 — it's about 11.25 per player either way) for each team on Auction Draft Day.

"What do I do if it's May 15 and I've just gotten around to reading this book? Wait till next year?" Absolutely not! That's second-division thinking! You can start anytime! Put your league together, hold your auction draft, and deduct all stats that accrue prior to that glorious day. Or enjoy the certainty of getting six weeks worth of stats with every player acquired. Next year, start from scratch.

USA Stats
THE BEST STAT SERVICE IN THE GAME

3

Scouting Report

ABREU, BOBBY - OF - BL - b: 3/11/74 $32

Abreu is a forecaster's dream. He's reliable and will play at least 150 games and he consistently hits .300, belts 20 homers, steals 20 bases and rings up 90 RBI. In right field, his play is above average. No flaws, no biases in performance. Abreu is a player.

	AB	R	HR	RBI	SB	BA
2001 Philadelphia	588	118	31	110	36	.289
2002 Philadelphia	572	102	20	85	31	.308
2003 Philadelphia	577	99	20	101	22	.300

ALFONZO, EDGARDO - 3B - BR - b: 11/8/73 $13

Alfonzo struggled mightily in the first half of 2003, but was able to come back and put up solid numbers in the second half, when he hit close to .300 with improved power numbers. He is capable of playing second and third well, though he much prefers being on the left side of the infield. Alfonzo always has been a selective hitter and sometimes that works to his disadvantage, as pitchers will take advantage of his patience to frequently get ahead in the count. Still, the hitters with good knowledge of the strike zone are the ones who are most likely to bounce back after a disappointing season. He is going to be a dependable hitter for several more years, even if he never becomes the superstar many thought he would be earlier in his career. He should hit about .280 with 20 to 25 homers this year.

	AB	R	HR	RBI	SB	BA
2001 New York - NL	457	64	17	49	5	.243
2002 New York - NL	490	78	16	56	6	.308
2003 San Francisco	514	56	13	81	5	.259

ALMONTE, ERICK - SS - BR - b: 2/1/78 $0

After Derek Jeter went on the disabled list on opening night, the Yankees brought up Almonte for his first extended major league playing time. He received attention by batting .300 or better for his first eight games, but quickly dipped down into a range more in line with his professional career norm. The 6'2", 200-pound Almonte doesn't look fluid in the field; he committed 12 errors in 31 games. After going back to Triple-A Columbus, he went on the disabled list because of a strained ligament in his left knee. Almonte seems destined to become no more than a utility infielder.

	AB	R	HR	RBI	SB	BA
2003 New York - AL	100	17	1	11	1	.260

ALOMAR, ROBERTO - 2B - BB - b: 2/5/68 $13

There are some who thought that Alomar struggled after he left Cleveland because he couldn't handle playing in New York. There is no evidence of that, however, since he spent half of 2003 with the White Sox and put up nearly identical numbers to the year and a half he was with the Mets. Alomar's best days are obviously behind him. His bat is slow, meaning he can't hit for average or power. Most of his speed is gone as well, leaving him a shadow of his former self in the field and on the basepaths. While he isn't going to put up fantastic numbers again, he could be a regular for another year or two, because he is experienced enough to not embarrass himself. Somebody will take a chance on him this year and give him a starting spot.

	AB	R	HR	RBI	SB	BA
2001 Cleveland	575	113	20	100	30	.336
2002 New York - NL	590	73	11	53	16	.266
2003 NY - NL/CHI - AL	516	76	5	39	12	.258

ALOMAR, SANDY - C - BR - b: 6/18/66 $2

If Alomar were any other player he would long have been sent into retirement. However, what he now lacks in hitting ability, he makes up for in other areas. He has virtually no power anymore and draws few walks, in part because pitchers simply aren't afraid to throw him strikes. He has slipped some defensively as well, though he doesn't embarrass himself behind the dish and still calls a good game. Alomar is so well respected by nearly everybody in the game that he will have no trouble finding a place to play if he wishes to continue his career. He is no longer capable of playing every day, though many clubs would view him as a valuable addition as a backup and mentor to both the starting catcher and pitchers.

	AB	R	HR	RBI	SB	BA
2001 Chicago - AL	220	17	4	21	1	.245
2002 New York - NL	283	29	7	37	0	.279
2003 Chicago - AL	194	22	5	26	0	.268

ALOU, MOISES - OF - BR - b: 7/3/66 $17

Alou has really shown his age over the past two seasons. His bat has significantly slowed, meaning he isn't able to pull pitches with authority like he was only a few years ago. He has enough experience to still post a reasonable batting average, and he will still take a walk, even if he is no longer an above average hitter. A subpar defender, Alou has little range, is not able to cover much ground in the outfield and makes many bad decisions in the field. Alou can be a contributor for a few more seasons, although it's likely his days of being an All-Star are long gone. Don't expect him to make a dramatic improvement.

	AB	R	HR	RBI	SB	BA
2001 Houston	513	79	27	108	5	.331
2002 Chicago - NL	484	50	15	61	8	.275
2003 Chicago - AL	565	83	22	91	3	.280

AMEZAGA, ALFREDO - SS - BB - b: 1/16/78 $1

A diminutive utility infielder, Amezaga got his first extended trial in the majors late last season. After hitting .347-3-45 at Triple-A with 14 steals in 22 tries, Amezaga struggled at the plate in the big leagues. With additional experience, he should be able to hit for an acceptable average with minimal power. Defensively, Amezaga is fine at second base or shortstop, but doesn't quite have the arm strength teams like to see at third base. While Amezaga has excellent speed, his minor league steal success rate indicates that he may have difficulty posting big stolen base numbers in the majors. He was expected to serve as a backup infielder at the major league level this season.

	AB	R	HR	RBI	SB	BA
2002 Anaheim	13	3	0	2	1	.538
2003 Anaheim	105	15	2	7	2	.210

ANDERSON, GARRET - OF - BL - b: 6/30/72 $26

Anderson has been the picture of consistency over his nine full major league seasons. A dependable high-average hitter, he is also a good bet to hit 30 home runs and drive in 100 runs in any given year. He doesn't like to take many walks, but manages to put the ball in play most of the time. While he is not a big base stealing threat, Anderson will pick up several steals a season and runs the bases well. He has above-average range in left field. Anderson has been one of the most durable players in the game, rarely missing more than a handful of games in a season. He is in his prime and should remain a premier everyday player.

	AB	R	HR	RBI	SB	BA
2001 Anaheim	672	83	28	123	13	.289
2002 Anaheim	638	93	29	123	6	.306
2003 Anaheim	638	80	29	116	6	.315

ANDERSON, MARLON - 2B - BL - b: 1/6/74 $13

Anderson has been a maddeningly inconsistent player who hasn't made much of some obvious physical skills. He had a promising callup in 1998, but had to go back to the minors after a disappointing rookie year. He's a fast runner who doesn't steal bases even on the rare occasions when he does reach base. He doesn't belong at the top of the order, but he doesn't hit well with runners on base, limiting his effectiveness lower in the lineup. His biggest improvement in 2003 was his ability to hit lefty pitchers, actually hitting for higher average against them. He continued to have trouble turning double plays. Offensively, he's mediocre at best, even for a second baseman, and his position as a starting second baseman could be in jeopardy.

	AB	R	HR	RBI	SB	BA
2001 Philadelphia	522	69	11	61	8	.293
2002 Philadelphia	539	64	8	48	5	.258
2003 Tampa Bay	482	59	6	67	19	.270

ATKINS, GARRET - 3B - BR - b: 12/12/79 $4
Atkins, the first three-time All-American in UCLA history, had his best minor league season as he reached the final rung of the system ladder in his first year at Triple-A Colorado Springs in 2003 and was a September callup by the parent Rockies. Get used to him. Atkins has the look of a hitter - he has good plate discipline and can drive the ball the opposite way. Atkins has only played third base for two seasons after beginning his pro career at first base, and he is still learning the subtleties of the position. Nevertheless, Atkins was expected to open spring training as the top candidate for the starting third base position, which Colorado has had trouble filling since Vinny Castilla went away in 2000.

	AB	R	HR	RBI	SB	BA
2003 Colorado	69	6	0	4	0	.159

AURILIA, RICH - SS - BR - b: 9/2/71 $13
After having one monster season followed by one poor campaign, Aurilia settled in and had the kind of year one would expect out of a guy with his ability. Aurilia has line drive power, so certainly his 27 homer season of 2001 was an aberration. He lacks the patience at the plate required to be a big-time slugger. While he is quick enough to play shortstop reasonably well, he is no basestealing threat. Aurilia has been consistent and dependable throughout most of his career, so expect at least a couple more seasons in line with what he did in 2003.

	AB	R	HR	RBI	SB	BA
2001 San Francisco	636	114	37	97	1	.324
2002 San Francisco	538	76	15	61	1	.257
2003 San Francisco	505	65	13	58	2	.277

AUSMUS, BRAD - C - BR - b: 4/14/69 $4
Ausmus gets a lot of playing time because he is one of the top defensive catchers in the game. He can stop a running game and he is excellent at inspiring confidence in a pitching staff. He has been especially effective in working with Houston's young, inexperienced pitchers. He is very durable, catching over 100 games for 10 straight years. Ausmus was a consistent .260 hitter with limited power for most of his career. However, he has been considerably below that level in two of the last three years. He will remain a regular catcher as long as he maintains his defensive capabilities but he will not be an asset to a Rotisserie team in any category.

	AB	R	HR	RBI	SB	BA
2001 Houston	422	45	5	34	4	.232
2002 Houston	447	57	6	50	2	.257
2003 Houston	450	43	4	47	5	.229

BAERGA, CARLOS - 1B - BB - b: 11/4/68 $1
Baerga suffered a finger injury in spring training when his hand was caught in a car door during a freak windstorm in Tucson, but by then Baerga already had made such a strong impression that he was a gimme to make the club after signing a minor league contract with Arizona before the 2003 season. A switch-hitter, Baerga has a quick, short batting stroke that enables him to

handle just about everything a pitcher can throw up there. He is line drive hitter who uses the whole field and can still drive the ball out of the park, but 20-homer seasons of his youth are gone forever, in part because he is no longer a regular. He is a bubbly personality and a pleasure in the clubhouse, another reason he fits well as a veteran. He can play every infield position but shortstop and thrives as a pinch-hitter. Back in shape after getting sloppy a few years ago, his ability to swing the bat gives him a leg up in a battle for a bench position.

	AB	R	HR	RBI	SB	BA
2002 Boston	182	17	2	19	6	.286
2003 Arizona	207	31	4	39	1	.343

BAGWELL, JEFF - 1B - BR - b: 5/27/68　　　　　　　　$25

Bagwell has been one of the top players in the game for his entire 13-year career. He has hit over 30 home runs in each of the last 8 seasons and has averaged over 115 runs batted in over this period. He is also an excellent defensive player and has outstanding baseball instincts. He had shoulder surgery following the 2001 season and has been noticeably hampered in his throwing in the last two years. A consistent .300 hitter for most of his career, he has failed to reach that level in each of the last three years. He is experiencing a slow decline in production but should continue at close to an All-Star level for two or three more years if his shoulder holds up.

	AB	R	HR	RBI	SB	BA
2001 Houston	600	126	39	130	11	.288
2002 Houston	571	94	31	98	7	.291
2003 Houston	605	109	39	100	11	.278

BAKO, PAUL - C - BL - b: 6/20/72　　　　　　　　$0

A notoriously weak hitter, Bako stays around because he is a lefthanded swinger with a good knowledge of the strike zone, plays good defense, and doesn't complain about being a reserve. Bako, who only once has received more than 234 at-bats in a single season, has next to no power and struggles to keep his batting average above water, meaning not even a decent amount of walks can help his cause much. While he is a solid backstop, adept at blocking balls in the dirt, he is destined to finish out his career playing once a week at best.

	AB	R	HR	RBI	SB	BA
2001 Atlanta	137	19	2	15	1	.212
2002 Milwaukee	234	24	4	20	0	.235
2003 Chicago - NL	188	19	0	17	0	.229

BALDELLI, ROCCO - OF - BR - b: 4/1/81　　　　　　　　$27

In 2002, Baldelli advanced three levels in the Tampa Bay system, from Single-A to Triple-A, posting strong all-around numbers at each stop. In his first season in the majors last year, he didn't dissapoint. Baldelli is an awesome athlete, possessing excellent speed, a strong arm and is developing his power. He doesn't draw many walks and strikes out quite a bit, but that's not uncommon for a hitter his age. He has the ability to play all three outfield positions and could develop into a legitimate number three hitter in the future.

	AB	R	HR	RBI	SB	BA
2003 Tampa Bay	637	89	11	78	27	.289

BANKS, BRIAN - OF - BB - b: 9/28/70　　　　　　　　$0

Banks first reached the majors with the Brewers in 1996 but he's always been a reserve player. He's only had one season with more than 200 at-bats but he's a useful pinch hitter and an inexpensive backup in the outfield and first base. He can also catch.

	AB	R	HR	RBI	SB	BA
2002 Florida	28	3	1	4	0	.321
2003 Florida	149	14	4	23	2	.235

BARAJAS, ROD - C - BR - b: 9/5/75 $0

Barajas is a solid catch-and-throw guy, the kind of guy who has enough marketable defensive skills to make himself useful to a team that does not need a lot of offense from its second catcher. He handled Curt Schilling and Miguel Batista for the better part of two years with the Diamondbacks. Barajas made an offensive adjustment in the second half of the 2002 season that resulted in an ability to drive the ball to his pull field, left, but pitchers caught up to him again in 2003 and he struggled near the Mendoza line. Unless his offense improves, he is a career backup at best.

	AB	R	HR	RBI	SB	BA
2002 Arizona	154	12	3	23	1	.234
2003 Arizona	220	19	3	28	0	.218

BARD, JOSH - C - BB - b: 3/30/78 $0

Bard should be a number one catcher somewhere but highly touted Victor Martinez is in his way in Cleveland and Bard's immediate future is dependent on how quickly Martinez develops. On his own merit, Bard is a good defensive catcher with a fairly live bat but he will lose the starting battle to Martinez at some point and that will relegate Bard to an occasional start. Given the chance, Bard is too good and too young to settle in as a backup catcher.

	AB	R	HR	RBI	SB	BA
2002 Cleveland	90	9	3	12	0	.222
2003 Cleveland	303	25	8	36	0	.214

BARRETT, MICHAEL - C - BR - b: 10/22/76 $3

Barrett was beset by hip and hand injuries and he missed a significant portion of the season and he was not reactivated until mid September. Usually when a young player is slowed by an injury, the discussion is about a wasted season and what-ifs are kicked around but for Barrett, last year's injuries, while painful, might buy him more time to prove that he can hit and should be a starting catcher. He went into the 2003 season as the number one catcher but he ended up playing and catching less than Brian Schneider, who was listed as Barrett's backup but who now appears to be a better catcher than Barrett. Barrett will get a chance to re-establish himself but it won't be a slam dunk.

	AB	R	HR	RBI	SB	BA
2001 Montreal	472	42	6	38	2	.250
2002 Montreal	376	41	12	49	6	.263
2003 Montreal	226	33	10	30	0	.208

BATISTA, TONY - 3B - BR - b: 12/9/73 $11

Batista's exaggerated open stance makes him one of the majors' most recognizable players at the plate. He's not likely ever to hit for a high average, because his stance and movement put major holes in his swing on both the inside and outside corners. But if a pitcher makes a mistake against him, watch out! Batista is a major power threat and run producer, especially for a player who so infrequently hits safely. His offensive performance has declined during the second half of each of the last four seasons; last year he was a Mendoza Line hitter against lefthanders. Batista is not a good defensive player. He already has moved from shortstop, and his range at third base has come under fire.

	AB	R	HR	RBI	SB	BA
2001 TOR/BAL	579	70	25	87	5	.238
2002 Baltimore	615	90	31	87	5	.244
2003 Baltimore	631	76	26	99	4	.235

BAUTISTA, DANNY - OF - BR - b: 5/24/72 $5

Bautista had a very disappointing 2003 season, which had the promise of being his best. Bautista

---

came into spring training as an everyday player for the first time in his 10-year major league career, although he did not hit well enough to hold the job and eventually lost it when Arizona acquired Raul Mondesi at the trading deadline. Bautista created high hopes - and a job for himself - when he hit .325 with six homers before suffering a season-ending shoulder dislocation in May, 2002. Healthy again from surgery, he was not the same player in 2003. Bautista is blessed with athletic gifts. He is a powerful man who can drive the ball to both alleys, although his power seemed to vanish a year ago. He is more of a natural athlete than a natural outfielder; he has a strong arm, although he occasionally misses the cutoff man. He appears to be back as an outfield reserve and steady bench player, probably his best role, anyway.

	AB	R	HR	RBI	SB	BA
2001 Arizona	222	26	5	26	3	.302
2002 Arizona	154	22	6	23	4	.325
2003 Arizona	284	29	4	36	3	.275

BAY, JASON - OF - BR - b: 12/8/73 $16

After failing to emulate other small market teams that grew by dealing veterans for young talent, the Pirates finally got one right when they sent Brian Giles to the Padres for Bay and Oliver Perez. Had Bay not broken his wrist in May, the Padres might have been reluctant to trade him. He's hit for power and average in the minors and he can steal bases. It's hard to conceive of Bay not making it fairly big.

	AB	R	HR	RBI	SB	BA
2003 SD/PIT	87	15	4	14	3	.287

BELL, DAVID - 3B - BR - b: 9/14/72 $0

Of immediate concern is Bell's bad back that forced him to miss a third of the season. He tried to come back the final week to help the Phillies in their last ditch drive for a wild card berth but he was out of action after just two games. It was a gutsy try but again, the concern is how his back will behave in 2004. If he's healthy and can play every day, note that Bell has played and hit well when he's part of a strong team.

	AB	R	HR	RBI	SB	BA
2001 Seattle	470	62	15	64	2	.260
2002 San Francisco	552	82	20	73	1	.261
2003 Philadelphia	297	32	4	37	0	.195

BELL, JAY - 2B/3B - BR - b: 12/11/65 $0

Bell's 2003 season could only be described as playing out the string. A first-round draft pick of the Twins in 1984, he transformed himself during his career from a sacrifice-bunting shortstop to a power-hitting (in 1999, at least) second baseman. He was neither of those last year, when he was used most often as a pinch-hitter even though he batted just .139 against lefthanders and had one extra base hit all season. Bell has batted lower than .200 in each of the last two years, and seemed likely to retire.

	AB	R	HR	RBI	SB	BA
2001 Arizona	428	59	13	46	0	.248
2002 Arizona	49	3	2	11	0	.163
2003 New York - NL	116	11	0	3	0	.181

BELLHORN, MARK - 2B/3B - BB - b: 8/23/74 $3

If Bellhorn were Norman Greenbaum, the 2002 season was his "Spirit in the Sky." Heretofore journeyman Bellhorn slugged a career-high 27 home runs with the Cubs in 2002 but crashed back down to earth in 2003 while playing for the Cubs and Rockies, whom he joined after being traded for Jose Hernandez in late June. A switch-hitter, Bellhorn is patient at the plate and not afraid to get into deep counts while waiting for a pitch he can drive. He has good power from both sides of the plate and is a dead pull hitter from the right side. Although Bellhorn is big for an

---

infielder at 6'1", 205, he has adequate range and hands at both second base and third base, probably his best position. He is not a base-stealing threat but will get a couple a year. Bellhorn was expected to be a candidate for a reserve infield position, although he could horn his way into a more regular if he returns to his 2002 form.

	AB	R	HR	RBI	SB	BA
2001 Oakland	74	11	1	4	0	.135
2002 Chicago - NL	445	86	27	56	7	.258
2003 CHI - NL/COL	249	27	2	26	5	.221

BELLIARD, RONNIE - 2B/3B - BR - b: 4/7/75 $8

A new lease on life worked wonders for Belliard, who after virtually fading into oblivion in Milwaukee was a big hit in Colorado in 2003. Although Belliard came into spring training after suffering a broken thumb in winter ball, a continuation of the injury bugaboo that slowed him with the Brewers, he quickly asserted himself and won the starting second base position as a non-roster invitee. After losing his second base job, his power and his confidence after Milwaukee signed Eric Young in 2002, Belliard returned to his previous form as a steady top-of-the-order hitter, although he tailed off in the second half. He uses the whole field and can drive the ball into the gaps, although he is a 10-homer man at most. Because of his willingness to work counts, Belliard draws more than his share of walks. Belliard has above average speed and stole 33 bases in his final full minor league season, although he has not refined his skills in the majors and has never even hit double figures. His speed helps him at second base, his best position, and was expected to be the regular second baseman entering spring training.

	AB	R	HR	RBI	SB	BA
2001 Milwaukee	364	69	11	36	5	.264
2002 Milwaukee	289	30	3	26	2	.211
2003 Colorado	447	73	8	50	7	.277

BELTRAN, CARLOS - OF - BB - b: 4/24/77 $36

With the Royals unexpectedly in the playoff hunt late into the 2003 season, it was hard to believe they were considering trading their best player; such are the mysteries of small-market baseball. Because Beltran was arbitration eligible after 2003 and expected to become a free agent after 2004, the Royals wanted to see what they could get for him before it became difficult to trade him. Ultimately, they kept him in Kansas City to assist with their pennant drive. Despite missing half of April with a strained oblique muscle, Beltran was clearly the most productive Royals hitter, leading the team in most hitting categories and placing among league leaders in steals, triples and batting average. Beltran became just the sixth player of the modern era to reach 100 RBI, 100 runs scored and 30 steals in a season for the third time. He has worked to become more patient at the plate and is learning to make the most of chances to drive the ball for extra bases. Beltran runs very well, gliding over large tracts of outfield to run down many a fly ball; he makes the occasional spectacular play, including home run robbery, and throws fairly well although a hyperextended right elbow suffered in August limited his throwing the rest of the year. Beltran seems to be able to steal bases at will; he has been caught just 12 times in 132 tries over the last four seasons. After receiving a large sum for one final year in Kansas City, Beltran is expected to become a free agent; the Royals will likely trade him if they are unable to sign him, as seems likely.

	AB	R	HR	RBI	SB	BA
2001 Kansas City	617	106	24	101	31	.306
2002 Kansas City	637	114	29	105	35	.273
2003 Kansas City	521	102	26	100	41	.307

BELTRE, ADRIAN - 3B - BR - b: 4/7/78 $12

Beltre possesses enormous physical gifts, although they have not translated into the All Star-caliber player Los Angeles hoped for. Beltre has good power and is strong enough to take the ball out of the park in both gaps. He is a free swinger that gets himself into trouble when he tries

---

to do too much, however, chasing high fastballs or breaking pitches on the outside. He has above average speed, although he has not learned to translate that into the stolen base. He has a rocket for an arm, one of the two or three best infield arms in the major leagues, although he compromises that gift with so-so range and is prone to an occasional lapse in concentration. Beltre, only 25, was expected to be the starting third baseman.

	AB	R	HR	RBI	SB	BA
2001 Los Angeles	475	59	13	60	13	.265
2002 Los Angeles	587	70	21	75	7	.257
2003 Los Angeles	559	50	23	80	2	.240

BENARD, MARVIN - OF - BL - b: 1/20/70 $0

Benard, normally a dependable and reliable backup outfielder, missed most of last season with recurring knee problems. When he's healthy, he has line drive power and a decent eye at the plate. Before he hurt his knee, he was a speedy player capable of stealing more than 20 bases a year, and a quality defensive outfielder. Benard, whose knee bothered him nearly all of the season, had yet another knee operation three days after the end of the regular season. He is going to have to go to spring training and prove himself healthy before he gets another shot in the big leagues.

	AB	R	HR	RBI	SB	BA
2001 San Francisco	392	70	15	44	10	.265
2002 San Francisco	123	16	1	13	5	.276
2003 San Francisco	71	5	0	4	1	.197

BENNETT, GARY - C - BR - b: 4/17/72 $1

Bennett missed a month because of a sprained medial collateral ligament in his right knee following a collision at home plate in April, although he returned to become a semi-regular in San Diego's continuing merry-go-round behind the plate. Bennett does not have much power, and he finally adjusted his stance while with Colorado in 2002, spreading his feet and trying to hit the ball back up the middle. He is more a defensive than offensive catcher, and his quick hands and feet enabled him to frame balls well and keep everything in front of him. He handles a staff well, and his arm is a little better than average. Bennett finished strong, driving in 10 runs in August, his major league high in a month, and was expected to maintain his job as a platooner.

	AB	R	HR	RBI	SB	BA
2001 COL/NY - NL/PHI	131	28	3	15	0	.244
2002 Colorado	291	26	4	26	1	.265
2003 San Diego	307	26	2	42	3	.238

BERG, DAVE - 2B - BR - b: 9/3/70 $0

A utility player who is comfortable playing at any position other than catcher, Berg isn't a big bat nor is his glove outstanding enough to earn him a spot in the lineup. Suffering through unexplained fatigue for much of last season, he spent more time on the shelf than usual. Not blessed with either power or speed, Berg doesn't walk enough to be of much use as a pinch-hitter and so his role is limited to being an emergency replacement type. Clearly good enough to play in the big leagues, he will be fight to win a spot in his customary utility role but he is little threat to crack a regular lineup over the long run.

	AB	R	HR	RBI	SB	BA
2001 Florida	215	26	4	16	0	.242
2002 Toronto	374	42	4	39	0	.270
2003 Toronto	161	26	4	18	0	.255
2002 Montreal	123	24	0	7	10	.187

BERKMAN, LANCE - OF - BB - b: 2/10/76 $25

A Number 1 draft choice by the Astros in 1997 after an outstanding college career at Rice,

Berkman emerged as one of the top hitters in the game in 2001 and 2002. However, his production declined somewhat in 2003 as his numbers were down in every category. He plays hard, runs well and has a strong work ethic. He has become an excellent left fielder and his only significant weakness is that he doesn't hit as well righthanded as he does lefthanded. Berkman can be expected to rebound from his sub-par 2003 season and play at an All-Star level as he enters the prime years of his career.

	AB	R	HR	RBI	SB	BA
2001 Houston	577	110	34	126	7	.331
2002 Houston	578	106	42	128	8	.292
2003 Houston	538	110	25	93	5	.288

BERROA, ANGEL - SS - BR - b: 1/27/80 $23

Much-heralded phenom Angel Berroa lived up to his billing as he put together a season full of defensive highlights and potent hitting and was the 2003 AL Rookie of the Year. Berroa struggled early with the glove, usually making his errors on routine plays, but then settled into a groove and was one of the better fielding shortstops in the game for most of the summer. He has good range and a strong arm, and has quickly learned the nuances required to succeed at the major league level. Meanwhile, at the plate, Berroa was near the top of a talented rookie class, hitting for power and average as well or better than most. Berroa is a free-swinger who will get caught up in the moment by trying too hard to jack a ball out of the park. He does better when he stays back and relies on his quick bat to generate line drives and his superior upper-body strength to lift the ball over the wall occasionally. Berroa runs well enough to steal 30 bases and he has already learned enough to be an above-average baserunner. He was used in several different spots in the Royals batting order in 2003, including a trial as a leadoff hitter in September; his combination of power and speed can let Berroa succeed almost anywhere in the order. In 2004, avoiding the sophomore jinx will be Berroa's challenge. He'll need to improve his patience at the plate, and try not to hit everything out of the park.

	AB	R	HR	RBI	SB	BA
2001 Kansas City	53	8	0	4	2	.302
2002 Kansas City	75	8	0	5	3	.227
2003 Kansas City	567	92	17	73	21	.287

BETEMIT, WILSON - 3B/SS - BB - b: 11/2/81 $0

Wilson Betemit has often appeared on lists of top minor league prospects because he has all the tools any scout could love; he's been compared physically to Alfonso Soriano, which is not as wild an exaggeration as that might sound. Betemit has a strong arm and good range, although he has been prone to spells of overplaying balls into unnecessary errors; Betemit shifted primarily to third base in 2003. He has above-average speed and decent pop in his bat from both sides of the plate. Still, Betemit lacks necessary plate discipline; he fanned an alarming 115 times in 478 at-bats during a mildly disappointing season at Triple-A Richmond in 2003. It was yet another setback for Betemit, who missed a large part of 2001 with ankle and back injuries that also caused him to start 2002 in a serious funk. Betemit remains a top prospect, but the Braves have to be wondering if his talents will ever be given full reign.

BIGBIE, LARRY - OF - BL - b: 11/4/77 $0

When the Orioles brought Bigbie back up in late July, he was batting .350 at Triple-A Ottawa. Installed as the regular left fielder, he gradually improved his major league average, crossing the .300 line in early September with a 3-for-5 day against the Red Sox and didn't fall below that mark again. He has had similar gradual improvement in his five pro seasons. The next step, the one that could take him above average major league status, would be to develop more power. Last year's total of 12 homers in the minors and majors was his career best. Bigbie is an excellent defensive outfielder who has made just one error in parts of three major league seasons. He has a good enough arm to throw out runners who try to test him.

	AB	R	HR	RBI	SB	BA
2001 Baltimore	131	15	2	11	4	.229
2002 Baltimore	34	1	0	3	1	.176
2003 Baltimore	287	43	9	31	7	.303

BIGGIO, CRAIG - 2B - BR - b: 12/14/65 $16

Biggio was one of the top second basemen in baseball for over a decade. He made a successful switch to center field in 2003 and will play there again in 2004. He continues to bat at the top of the order as he has throughout his career and a recent study ranked him fourth among the all-time best leadoff hitters. Once a league leader in stolen bases, Biggio has lost a couple of steps and no longer is a serious base stealing threat. Biggio's career peaked in 1997-1998 with two outstanding seasons. He has experienced a steady decline in production since then as would be expected for a player in his late thirties. This will continue in 2004 as he is now no better than an average player.

	AB	R	HR	RBI	SB	BA
2001 Houston	617	118	20	70	7	.292
2002 Houston	577	96	15	58	16	.253
2003 Houston	628	102	15	62	8	.264

BLAKE, CASEY - 1B/3B - BR - b: 8/23/73 $11

The problem that Blake faces is that he's just getting started in the majors and he'll be 30 years old before the season ends. Blake played well enough to earn the starting nod at third for 2004, but he's not a long term solution. He showed good power but he has a rather slow bat and he fanned over one hundred times last year. It would be no surprise to see Blake quickly fall into a platoon role. He'll be hard pressed to duplicate his 2003 performance.

	AB	R	HR	RBI	SB	BA
2001 MIN/BAL	37	3	1	4	3	.243
2002 Minnesota	20	2	0	1	0	.200
2003 Cleveland	557	80	17	67	7	.257

BLALOCK, HANK - 3B - BL - b: 11/21/80 $18

One of the best young hitters in baseball, Blalock arrived in a big way in 2003. Hitting for power and average, Blalock staked his claim for a starting third base spot and should be there for years to come. He has a sweet lefty swing that can generate power to the gaps, particularly against right-handed pitching. Blalock did not hit well against lefties last season and was platooned, but will likely see more time against them this season, which could depress his batting average slightly. There is no longer any consideration of moving him to another position.

	AB	R	HR	RBI	SB	BA
2002 Texas	147	16	3	17	0	.211
2003 Texas	567	89	29	90	2	.300

BLANCO, HENRY - C - BR - b: 8/29/71 $1

With Javy Lopez hitting everything out of the yard in Atlanta, Henry Blanco's reserve catcher role shrunk even more than usual. He remained Greg Maddux's personal catcher, but even that job was dissolved in September by Lopez's powerful bat as the Braves decided they needed the extra power from Lopez in the post-season — even during Maddux's starts. Blanco is an especially weak-hitting backup catcher; he has just occasional power and has struggled to stay above .200 in his two seasons with the Braves. Blanco makes poor contact at the plate and is a below-average baserunner. Fortunately, he does excel as a backstop; he handles pitchers well, does a fine job of blocking pitches in the dirt, and is adept at throwing out potential basestealers, which makes him all the more valuable as Maddux's catcher since Maddux does a poor job of holding baserunners. Blanco's future will be similar to his recent past, as a deep reserve catcher prized mostly for his defensive ability.

	AB	R	HR	RBI	SB	BA
2001 Milwaukee	314	33	6	31	3	.210
2002 Atlanta	221	17	6	22	0	.294
2003 Atlanta	151	11	1	13	0	.199

BLOOMQUIST, WILLIE - 3B - BR - b: 11/27/77 $3

Super-sub Bloomquist earned his keep by playing six different positions — all four infield spots and both corner outfield posts — in 2003, sticking all year after a strong showing in the September, 2002, stretch drive. Bloomquist, the Pacific-10 Conference player of the year at Arizona State in 1999, drives the ball to the gaps and has better than average speed, averaging 25 stolen bases a year in four minor league seasons. He was a shortstop in college and has the range and arm to play that position, although he is athletic enough to adapt. He was expected to cement his spot as a backup player this season.

	AB	R	HR	RBI	SB	BA
2002 Seattle	33	11	0	7	3	.455
2003 Seattle	196	30	1	14	4	.250

BLUM, GEOFF - 2B/3B - BB - b: 4/26/73 $7

Blum has established himself as a valuable utility player who can play in both the infield and outfield. His best position is third base but he doesn't hit well enough to be a full time regular at the position. He played very well at second base when Jeff Kent was injured last year reinforcing that his greatest value is as a versatile switch-hitting utility player. He hits much better from the left side where he is a dead pull hitter. Blum is expected to again fill a utility role in 2004 and should produce at a similar level as in 2003.

	AB	R	HR	RBI	SB	BA
2001 Montreal	453	57	9	50	9	.236
2002 Houston	368	45	10	52	2	.283
2003 Houston	420	51	10	52	0	.262

BONDS, BARRY - OF - BL - b: 7/24/64 $32

By now it should be apparent to everyone that Bonds is the best baseball player on the planet, and one of the best who ever lived. He was, by all objective accounts, the top player in the game for the third straight season in 2003, despite suffering through a summer in which his father was dying of cancer. In all reality, there isn't a player out there who is all that close to Bonds. Albert Pujols, for all the (deserved) attention he got for his fine 2003 campaign, still had a slugging percentage that was about 60 points less than Bonds, and an on-base percentage that was about 90 points less. Despite his age, Bonds has shown absolutely no signs of slowing down in recent years. Even if he takes a couple of steps back, he will still be even with Pujols and the other top sluggers in the game.

	AB	R	HR	RBI	SB	BA
2001 San Francisco	476	129	73	137	13	.328
2002 San Francisco	403	117	46	110	9	.370
2003 San Francisco	390	111	45	90	7	.341

BOONE, AARON - 3B - BR - b: 3/9/73 $23

Boone began the year moving to second base for the Reds, but soon was back at third base with the Yankees. He also went from a run-producing spot in Cincinnati's lineup to the lower third of New York's order. Most of his batting ratios and his stolen base percentage overall were up from what was a breakthrough power year in 2002 — and he reached a career high in RBI. He was errorless in his 19 games at second base and at third was more error-prone, but with greater range than before. Boone hits righthanders better than he does lefties. He adjusted well after a slow start in the AL, and should have more good years ahead of him.

	AB	R	HR	RBI	SB	BA
2001 Cincinnati	381	54	14	62	6	.294
2002 Cincinnati	606	83	26	87	32	.241
2003 CIN/NY - AL	592	92	24	96	23	.267

BOONE, BRET - 2B - BR - b: 4/6/69 $27

The underpublicized Boone became the only third second baseman in the 20th century to record three consecutive 100-RBI seasons when he once again broke triple-digits in his third season in Seattle. (Hall of Famer Charlie Gehringer and Bobby Doerr are the others.) Boone has terrific plate coverage and can drive the outside pitch over the fence in right. A third generation major leaguer, he also pulls his hands in well to handle the inside pitch. Boone is at the elite level as a defender, an athletic glove man who has smooth hands and a quick turn on the doubleplay. Boone took his game up another notch when he set a career stolen base record in 2003. He ranks among the consummate second basemen in the game and was expected to provide middle-of-the-order production again this season.

	AB	R	HR	RBI	SB	BA
2001 Seattle	623	118	37	141	5	.331
2002 Seattle	608	88	24	107	12	.278
2003 Seattle	622	111	35	117	16	.294

BORCHARD, JOE - OF - BB - b: 11/25/78 $0

Borchard, who was a star in both baseball and football at Stanford, is one of the best athletes around. There is little that he can't do on the baseball diamond as he can hit for average and power. He also has a fantastic arm and is an outstanding defensive outfielder. He isn't slow, though he doesn't show any willingness to steal bases. Borchard belongs in the big leagues and will hit if he ever gets a chance to play regularly. The White Sox never gave him a chance last year, dumping him after only a handful of starts. He could get another shot there, though he likely would be better off starting off fresh with another organization.

BORDERS, PAT - C - BR - b: 8/29/71 $0

Borders grew to know northern I-5 well in 2003, making four trips from Triple-A Tacoma to Seattle as the third catcher. Borders did not play much, but was just happy to be there, having turned 40 in May and having just 44 major league at-bats since 1998. Borders is no longer the player he was when he won the World Series MVP in 1992, although he can still swing the bat. He has lost most of the little speed he had. He was expected to open the season in Triple-A, as he has the last five years, and hope for an opening.

BORDICK, MIKE - 3B/SS - BR - b: 7/21/65 $6

One of the better defensive shortstops around and a classy guy, Bordick has underrated power and a decent batting eye. He won the starting shortstop job from Chris Woodward for much of last season and while he was playing regularly there even late in the year, he was mulling retirement at season's end. If he were to return this season for another go-around, he would face a similar situation as he did last spring, where he went into the season as a backup infielder who stood a chance to gain a starting spot in the case of injury or ineffectiveness of the incumbent.

	AB	R	HR	RBI	SB	BA
2001 Baltimore	229	32	7	30	9	.249
2002 Baltimore	367	37	8	36	7	.232
2003 Toronto	343	39	5	54	3	.274

BOWEN, ROB - C - BB - b: 2/24/81 $0

Bowen is on the verge of a major league career just because he can catch and throw. He provides a good target for pitchers and has a cannon for an arm. Offense? That remains to be seen. Bowen had severe contact problems in the minors until 2003. How severe? Teammates gave him the game ball the day he went over .200. Bowen, to his credit, didn't stop there and his bat earned him a promotion to Triple-A, and eventually to the majors as an emergency catcher. He's a switch hitter with some strength, so the potential is there. But he's not to the point where he can land on a major league roster, yet.

BRADLEY, MILTON - OF - BB - b: 4/15/78 $8

Bradley, a high potential but slow to develop player, showed marked improvement late in 2002 and last year he met expectations and made everyone happy. Bradley's attitude problems may not be completely resolved and it's unwise to predict an improvement in temperament for a volatile man but, if he keeps his nose clean, he still has a significant upside and this year or next, Bradley will be a 30-homer, 30-steal player.

	AB	R	HR	RBI	SB	BA
2001 MON/CLE	238	22	1	19	8	.223
2002 Cleveland	325	48	9	38	6	.249
2003 Cleveland	377	61	10	56	17	.321

BRAGG, DARREN - OF - BL - b: 9/7/69 $0

At this point in his career Bragg is just bench strength. He can play every outfield position and still has a little basestealing speed. His chances to play are limited to infrequent starts coupled with pinch-hitting and late inning defensive work.

	AB	R	HR	RBI	SB	BA
2002 Atlanta	212	34	3	15	5	.269
2003 Atlanta	162	21	0	9	2	.241

BRANYAN, RUSSELL - 3B - BL - b: 12/19/75 $3

Branyan has tape measure power but his all-or-nothing swing usually ends up in his return to the dugout and putting his bat away in the rack. Although he's no Brooks Robinson, Branyan plays well enough at third base and he's adequate in left field and at first base. His history of long slumps at the plate has kept him from being a starter.

	AB	R	HR	RBI	SB	BA
2001 Cleveland	315	48	20	54	1	.232
2002 Cincinnati	378	50	24	56	4	.228
2003 Cincinnati	176	22	9	26	0	.216

BROUSSARD, BEN - OF - BL - b: 9/24/76 $8

In spring training Broussard was chosen to start over Travis Hafner but he was injured and unable to play until mid-May. Hafner capitalized on the opportunity and even when Broussard played when Hafner was injured, Hafner reclaimed the job outplaying Broussard. Hafner is also a year younger than Broussard, although at age 28, Broussard's future is still bright, but he must improve. 2003 was clearly an audition for both Hafner and Broussard and no team needs to carry two lefthanded batting first basemen.

	AB	R	HR	RBI	SB	BA
2002 Cleveland	112	10	4	9	0	.241
2003 Cleveland	386	53	16	55	5	.249

BROWN, ADRIAN - OF - BB - b: 2/7/74 $2

Brown's game is built almost entirely on speed. In 12 pro seasons, he hasn't hit more than seven home runs. After his average dropped nearly 100 points in two years with the Pirates, both they and the Devil Rays let him go. The Red Sox signed him, but even in an all-star season at Triple-A Pawtucket, he had just five homers and 32 RBI — but with 34 stolen bases. That speed and good defense in center field landed him on Boston's postseason roster. At this stage of his career, Brown makes a good Triple-A insurance policy as an extra outfielder.

	AB	R	HR	RBI	SB	BA
2001 Pittsburgh	31	3	1	2	2	.194
2002 Pittsburgh	208	20	1	21	10	.216

BROWN, DEE - OF - BL - b: 3/27/78 $0

There's no question that Dee Brown is a superior athlete. Unfortunately, he has been unable to convert his raw athleticism to baseball talent. Brown platooned in left and rightfield the first two months, and hit an important homer during the Royals season-opening winning streak; that was the season highlight for Brown as he quickly lost playing time to lesser-known players. A sprained wrist in May put him on the shelf until July. By the time he returned in July, Brown was barely an afterthought for the Royals; he played sparingly and managed just eight hits the last seven weeks of the season. Brown has a powerful swing, although he has an extremely poor batting eye, often swinging at bad pitches and letting good ones go for called strikes. Brown runs very well, although he has not always made good use of his speed in the outfield or on the bases. He is confined to a corner outfield role and his arm is merely average, limiting his utility in rightfield. Brown remains a raw talent who is looking more and more like a failed prospect. In 2004, Brown has an uphill battle to gain even a deep bench role in the majors.

	AB	R	HR	RBI	SB	BA
2001 Kansas City	380	39	7	40	5	.245
2002 Kansas City	51	5	1	7	0	.235
2003 Kansas City	132	16	2	14	1	.227

BRUNTLETT, ERIC - SS - BR - b: 3/29/78 $0

Bruntlett, a shortstop, was a ninth-round draft choice out of Stanford by the Astros in 2000. Despite moving up to the Double-A level in only his second season, he has not been considered a top prospect. He played most of the 2003 season at Triple-A New Orleans, batting .259 with 2 home runs, 27 runs batted in and 9 stolen bases in 84 games. He was called up to Houston when Jeff Kent was hurt and played well enough to compete for a utility role at the major league level in 2004. He is not likely to hit well enough to be a major league regular.

	AB	R	HR	RBI	SB	BA
2003 Houston	54	3	1	4	0	.259

BUCHANAN, BRIAN - 1B/OF - BR - b: 7/21/73 $5

A big athlete, Buchanan has shown signs of being able to be a big-time power hitter, averaging a home run every 20 at-bats in spot duty with Minnesota and San Diego the last three seasons. Predominately a pull hitter, Buchanan can use both gaps. He has surprising speed and will steal a base if not tended. The trouble is finding a place for him to play. Buchanan has played first base and both corner outfield positions with the Padres, and while he tries he is not particularly graceful defender. A hard worker, Buchanan was expected to open the season as a multi-position reserve and pinch-hitter.

	AB	R	HR	RBI	SB	BA
2001 Minnesota	197	28	10	32	1	.274
2002 San Diego	227	31	11	28	2	.269
2003 San Diego	198	29	8	29	6	.263

BUCK, JOHN - C - BR - b: 4/1/80 $1

Buck has been Houston's top catching prospect and was on track to reach the major leagues in 2004. However, he missed a good part of the 2003 season playing at Triple-A New Orleans when he broke his wrist in a collision at first base. He batted .255 with 2 home runs and 39 runs batted in while playing in only 78 games. Buck was voted the best defensive catcher in the Pacific Coast League in the Baseball America poll. He is slated to play at the major league level in 2004 but he may not be ready. He can be expected to struggle offensively until he gets established.

BURKE, CHRIS - 2B/SS - BR - b: 3/11/80 $0

Burke was a first round draft choice by the Astros out of the University of Tennessee in 2001. After a disappointing season when he was rushed to the Double-A level in 2002, he did much better when he repeated that level in 2003. He had a .301-3-41-34 season and had as many walks (57) as strikeouts. He was named to the Texas League All Star team as a utility player and was named the best defensive second baseman in the Texas League by Baseball America. Burke has divided his time between shortstop and second base and it is not yet clear where he will play in the future. He needs a year at Triple-A but he is on track for a major league career.

BURKE, JAMIE - C - BR - b: 9/24/71 $0

Burke is a light hitter who would have been in another profession many years ago were he not a catcher. He has little power (his minor league career best is eight home runs), though he can hit for average. He also is capable of playing first, third and a little in left field. Burke had a fine season in Triple-A last year, hitting .322, but then again, 32 year old players with as much experience as he should be able to succeed in the minor leagues. He saw brief action with the White Sox late in the season. Given the lack of quality catchers, it's likely Burke will resurface again this year. He is not going to be trusted with regular duty, however, and he'll likely spend considerable time in the minor leagues once again.

BURKS, ELLIS - OF - BR - b: 9/11/64 $0

Burks will be 40 in September and given his age and tattered knees, he will earn his keep as a DH. He can still play left field if needed, but playing defense aggravates his knees. Just let him sit and hit because he can still pound the ball, because he's much, much healthier and stronger when protected from the rigors of daily outfield play. His bat is still quick with a lot of power, but knee problems have taken their toll on his speed, and is no longer the basestealer he was eralier in his career.

	AB	R	HR	RBI	SB	BA
2001 Cleveland	439	83	28	74	5	.280
2002 Cleveland	518	92	32	91	2	.301
2003 Cleveland	198	27	6	28	1	.263

BURNITZ, JEROMY - OF - BL - b: 4/15/69 $12

Burnitz returned to form somewhat with both the Mets and Los Angeles in 2003, although it now appears that he will be more of a .230 hitter the rest of his life rather than the .270 hitter he was in his earlier days. He is a little too eager at the plate, almost jumping at pitches. While that works when he sees fastballs, pitchers have learned to feed him slow offerings and let him a) pull them foul or b) turn them into harmless outs. Burnitz does have big-time power and will still drive a mistake out of the park. He adjusted and handled lefties a little better in 2003, but they still give him trouble. Burnitz is a quality right fielder, with a strong and accurate arm and decent range. A 20-20 guy in his rookie year, Burnitz like a lot of power hitters now eschews the running game, although he is more than capable of stealing 10-15 bases a year. He is a good baserunner. He was expected to be the starter in right field, although his low average and frequent strikeouts compromise his chance to be a middle-of-the-order hitter for a contender.

	AB	R	HR	RBI	SB	BA
2001 Milwaukee	562	104	34	100	0	.251
2002 New York - NL	479	65	19	54	10	.215
2003 NY - NL /LA	464	63	31	77	5	.239

BURRELL, PAT - OF - BR - b: 10/10/76 $10

Hmm?? How often has this happened? Burrell entered 2003 already established as a young stud — no, make that a bona fide star. He's hit beautifully from age 24 on and then at 27, when he's most likely to step on the gas, he falls of a cliff. Why? Did his eyesight go bad? Was it Bowa? Was it a personal problem? Was it laziness created by having the security of a new, six-year, fifty million dollar contract? Was it having to make his personal deposit in a specimen cup? He has to turn it around. Has to. Another year like 2003 and talk may turn from "another Mike Schmidt"

---

to "another Joe Charboneau."

		AB	R	HR	RBI	SB	BA
2001	Philadelphia	539	70	27	89	2	.258
2002	Philadelphia	586	96	37	116	1	.282
2003	Philadelphia	522	57	21	64	0	.209

BURROUGHS, SEAN - 3B - BL - b: 9/12/80 $13

Power papa Jeff Burroughs led off only when the batter before him made the final out of an inning, but son Sean was a hit in that role the final five weeks of the season and appears to be a candidate to remain there in 2003. Burroughs is a line drive hitter who uses the whole field and can drive the ball into the gaps. He has good strike zone discipline and does not swing at bad balls. While he makes good contact, he has not learned to identify the pitches he can turn into home runs. That may come with age. He is a natural ballplayer; he has average speed but makes good decisions on the bases and will take the extra base. After experimenting at second base in 2002, Burroughs played strictly third in 2003 and made strides. He has an above-average arm. Burroughs, only 23, will be a fixture of third base for years to come.

		AB	R	HR	RBI	SB	BA
2002	San Diego	192	18	1	11	2	.271
2003	San Diego	517	62	7	58	7	.286

BYRD, MARLON - OF - BR - b: 8/30/77 $26

Byrd began the season under pressure and given such high expectations, you have to like the fact that a rookie hit over .300 in the heat of a pennant race and he stayed hot when Bowa had him bat leadoff after he'd been hitting eighth for the first half of the season. Byrd passed all tests. He might struggle as pitchers adjust to him but he's a solid hitter with a fine eye and strike zone judgment and after the pitchers work him over little, he'll still find a way and keep his average in the .300 range.

		AB	R	HR	RBI	SB	BA
2002	Philadelphia	35	2	1	1	0	.229
2003	Philadelphia	495	86	7	45	11	.303

BYRNES, ERIC - OF - BR - b: 2/16/76 $8

Byrnes began the 2003 campaign as Oakland's leadoff hitter, and was doing a pretty good job at the plate. He lost his starting spot, however, with a truly dreadful second half of the season that saw him hit only .171 with only 11 extra base hits. Byrnes has a decent eye at the plate, though he sometimes gets into trouble by trying to do too much. While the Athletics kept trying to get him to be more selective at the plate, he clearly pressed too much after the All-Star break. Byrnes has some speed, which allows him to play center reasonably well. Like most Oakland players, he was not allowed to attempt many stolen bases. Byrnes is not a young player, so it doesn't appear that he has much of a future. He could be a regular for another couple of seasons, though he could just as easily settle into a reserve role.

		AB	R	HR	RBI	SB	BA
2001	Oakland	38	9	3	5	1	.237
2002	Oakland	94	24	3	11	3	.245
2003	Oakland	414	64	12	51	10	.263

CABRERA, JOLBERT - 2B/OF - BR - b: 12/8/72 $6

Shot in the buttocks during an attempted car-jacking in his native Colombia before the 2002 season, Cabrera gave Los Angeles a kick of his own in 2003, when he had his best major league season while serving primarily as a platoon second baseman. Cabrera, a hacker, can drive the ball into the gaps - he averaged a double every 11 at-bats last season. He does not look to walk; at the same time he usually puts the ball in play. He has good speed and with regular work could steal 10-15 bases a year. Cabrera is a strong defender almost anywhere on the field. With good

---

athleticism and range and a strong arm, he is an above-average defender anywhere on the field. Cabrera was expected to be a valuable platoon player/situational sub.

	AB	R	HR	RBI	SB	BA
2002 CLE/LA	84	8	0	8	1	.143
2003 Los Angeles	347	43	6	37	6	.282

CABRERA, MIGUEL - 3B/OF - BB - b: 4/18/83 $18

Cabrera is a most impressive young player and he will quickly become a star. He is discriminating at the plate and while some righthanders can give him trouble, he murders lefties and he will improve against right handed pitchers in shot order. He is not especially light on his feet but he is adequate at third base and he filled in well during Mike Lowell's absence but he played more in left field when Lowell was able to go, so left field may be his permanent home.

	AB	R	HR	RBI	SB	BA
2003 Florida	314	39	12	62	0	.268

CABRERA, ORLANDO - SS - BR - b: 3/2/74 $25

Cabrera rebounded from back trouble which led to a down year in 2002. His range improved as did his hitting and he had the best year of his career. Cabrera batted over 600 times in 2003 and showed power, speed and a renewed ability to hit for average. Cabrera signed a one year contract with the Expos for the 2003 season and his improved performance last year made him one of the hottest commodities for 2004. He is still in the prime of his career.

	AB	R	HR	RBI	SB	BA
2001 Montreal	626	64	14	96	19	.276
2002 Montreal	563	64	7	56	25	.263
2003 Montreal	626	95	17	80	24	.297

CAIRO, MIGUEL - 2B/OF - BR - b: 5/4/74 $3

The only time when Cairo has been a starter was when he was with the expansion Devil Rays, and even then it was only out of necessity. Cairo is a dreadful hitter who has absolutely no power. He has a decent eye at the plate, though he doesn't draw many walks because pitchers know he is a relatively easy out. The only way he has lasted as long as he has is because he can play three infield positions as well as the two corner outfield spots. Cairo's only real value is his versatility, so there is a decent chance he will have to start the season in Triple-A and wait for an injury to get him back to the big leagues.

	AB	R	HR	RBI	SB	BA
2002 St. Louis	184	28	2	23	1	.250
2003 St. Louis	261	41	5	32	4	.245

CALLOWAY, RON - OF - BL - b: 9/4/76 $7

Calloway got his shot when Vladimir Guerrero was injured and now, with Guerrero moving on, Calloway will have another chance to win a job in right or left field. While he has a reputation as a power and speed guy, he showed little of either last year and he didn't play well enough last year to position himself in spring training as the man to beat.

	AB	R	HR	RBI	SB	BA
2003 Montreal	340	36	9	52	9	.238

CAMERON, MIKE - OF - BR - b: 1/8/73 $19

Junior Who? Cameron has had better numbers than the super star he replaced, Ken Griffey, since joining Seattle in 2000 after Griffey forced a trade with Cincinnati. Cameron has big-time power to both alleys - he had a four-homer game in 2002 - and has a decent eye, drawing his share of walks. The downside? He swings through way too many pitches and his strikeout totals are always among the highest in baseball. With his speed, the more he puts the ball in play, the better. He was a 25-30 guy in both 2001 and 2002, although his numbers fell off a year ago. He has great range in center field, a big asset in big Safeco Field, and a strong arm, although he is prone to the careless miscue. He was expected to be the regular in center field, although the ball is in his court as far as making the plate adjustments necessary to move up from the No. 6 spot in the order.

	AB	R	HR	RBI	SB	BA
2001 Seattle	540	99	25	110	34	.267
2002 Seattle	545	84	25	80	31	.239
2003 Seattle	534	74	18	76	17	.253

CASEY, SEAN - 1B - BL - b: 7/2/74 $13

Casey is a big man and he looks like a power hitter but he is the polar opposite of Russ Branyan in that he just tries to meet the ball, and he has been a starter for years. Casey usually hits singles but not enough to contend for a batting title. Casey pops only about six extra base hits a month and most are doubles, not homers. Among all first baseman, Casey was near the top in games played and at-bats but his offense was barely good enough to place him in the top twenty among major league first baseman, and his production on a per at-bat ratio, is worse. Casey is slow afoot and while he was not counted on for a home run explosion it is fair to ask why Casey did not hit for more power after it became clear that Cincinnati's new park clearly favored hitters. Nothing happened and it's hard to fathom why a major league club, day after day, is content to trot out a first baseman that hits a home run about once every 45 at-bats in this live ball, small park era. Casey's contract is for the kind of money that the Reds were eager to shed during their great purge of 2003, yet no pennant contender expressed interest in Casey and that says it all.

	AB	R	HR	RBI	SB	BA
2001 Cincinnati	533	69	13	89	3	.310
2002 Cincinnati	425	56	6	42	2	.261
2003 Cincinnati	573	71	14	80	4	.291

CASH, KEVIN - C - BR - b: 12/6/77 $0

Blessed with a good throwing arm, Cash has decent and developing power and incredible confidence receiving tough pitches. He struggled terribly after being recalled by Toronto in early August and while he is expected to gain more power, he has never been one to take walks nor hit for average in the minor leagues and his over-eagerness at the plate has been exemplified by his limited ability to take walks at Triple-A Syracuse last year. Apparently not yet ready for prime time, Cash will be competing for a big league starting job but is more likely headed back for full time duty in the minors rather than a backup catching role in the majors. We will see him again by September and he stood an outside shot to win the regular catching spot in the majors with an outstanding spring.

	AB	R	HR	RBI	SB	BA
2002 Toronto	14	1	0	0	0	.143
2003 Toronto	106	10	1	8	0	.142

CASTILLA, VINNY - 3B - BR - b: 7/4/67 $11

Vinny Castilla enjoyed a mild Renaissance in 2003. While he didn't deliver the outstanding power from his seven seasons in Colorado, he hit for power and average better than he'd done since leaving the Rockies. Castilla is a fastball hitter who will attack the first hittable pitch, looking to drive it out of the ballpark. Although he will hit a mistake pitch a long way, Castilla fares poorly against pitchers with fine control. His penchant for swinging at high fastballs means pitchers can climb the ladder with him, or work pitches away from him until they are unreachable. At the hot corner Castilla displays good range and a strong arm. He has lost a step, but makes up for it with superior positioning. He runs the bases like the 36-year-old slugger he is, although he avoids foolish baserunning mistakes by staying within his limits.

	AB	R	HR	RBI	SB	BA
2001 TB/HOU	538	69	25	91	1	.260
2002 Atlanta	543	56	12	61	4	.232
2003 Atlanta	542	65	22	76	1	.277

CASTILLO, LUIS - 2B - BB - b: 9/12/75 $26

Castillo was hobbled with leg and ankle problems for some of the 2003 season, which explains his career low 21 steals and career high 19 unsuccessful attempts to steal (since becoming a regular player in 1999). He's a more mature major leaguer now and he evolved by playing high stakes, pennant race baseball where it is imperative to think of the needs of the team rather than personal stats. With healthy wheels Castillo will hit .310 and steal 40 bases in 2004.

	AB	R	HR	RBI	SB	BA
2001 Florida	537	76	2	45	33	.263
2002 Florida	606	86	2	39	48	.305
2003 Florida	595	99	6	39	21	.314

CASTRO, JUAN - 2B/3B/SS - BR - b: 6/20/72 $1

Castro is a fine defensive performer and would make a quality backup infielder. Shortstop is his best position, but he can also fill in quite well at both second and third base. His offensive shortcomings are obvious. He has slight power and struggles to keep his batting average at respectable levels. However, his attitude is superior and he never complains about not being an everyday player.

	AB	R	HR	RBI	SB	BA
2001 Cincinnati	242	27	3	13	0	.223
2002 Cincinnati	82	5	2	11	0	.220
2003 Cincinnati	320	28	9	33	2	.253

CASTRO, RAMON - C - BR - b: 3/1/76 $0

Castro has been the Marlins backup catcher for his entire five year major league career. He's talented but hasn't had an opportunity to prove himself as a big leaguer. His defensive skills are solid and given a chance to start, Castro has the ability to hit 15 to 20 homers. He is a bit of a wild swinger and he probably won't hit much for an average, but on the right team, he could be put to use.

	AB	R	HR	RBI	SB	BA
2002 Florida	101	11	6	18	0	.238
2003 Florida	53	6	5	8	9	.283

CATALANOTTO, FRANK - OF/DH - BL - b: 4/27/74 $12

Officially converted from a second baseman to an outfielder, Catalanotto started well but slumped for much of the second half. An aggressive line drive hitter, he is good at getting on base even though he prefers not to take walks. His defense is adequate and last year, he showed he is fully recovered from an injury-plagued 2002 season. Though he hits plenty of doubles, he doesn't have much power. He projects as the bigger half of a platoon, probably as a right fielder. A team that needed a regular second baseman could still move him back to that position but either way, he's destined to spend much time on the bench against lefties.

	AB	R	HR	RBI	SB	BA
2001 Texas	463	77	11	54	15	.330
2002 Texas	212	42	3	23	9	.269
2003 Toronto	489	83	13	59	2	.299

CEDENO, ROGER - OF - BB - b: 8/16/74 $16

The last two years, Cedeno has hardly looked like the player who set a Mets record with 66 stolen bases and batted .313 in 1999. He put on weight, which has slowed him down on the bases and at bat without adding appreciable power. Thus, that reduction in speed has taken away most of his game. He seems to think of himself as a power hitter, and he has so little patience at the plate that he no longer is a good leadoff hitter. Cedeno's defense continued to be poor, but the Mets had to use him in right or center field.

	AB	R	HR	RBI	SB	BA
2001 Detroit	523	79	6	48	55	.293
2002 New York - NL	511	65	7	41	25	.260
2003 New York - NL	484	70	7	37	14	.267

CHAPMAN, TRAVIS - 3B - BR - b: 6/5/78 $0

Using an unconventional batting stance, Chapman has hit fairly well in the minors but you have to wonder if he can maintain his equilibrium in the majors. He's shown a little power in minors and he should be able to hit about .260 with ten homers if he plays a full year in the majors.

CHAVEZ, ENDY - OF - BL - b: 2/7/78 $10

Chavez had the look of a sleeper last year and all signs were positive for him. A sleeper needs a chance to play and Chavez did, playing far more than ever but his only offensive tool is speed enough to steal 30 to 40 bases. His relatively puny stolen base total in 2003 was disappointing. He's still young and if he improves against righthanded pitching, we might still see him swipe 30 to 40 bags.

	AB	R	HR	RBI	SB	BA
2001 Montreal	77	4	0	5	0	.208
2002 Montreal	125	20	1	9	3	.296
2003 Montreal	483	66	5	47	18	.251

CHAVEZ, ERIC - 3B - BL - b: 12/7/77 $0

The one big thing keeping Chavez from being a true superstar is his inability to hit lefthanded pitching. Overall, his numbers look quite good, especially considering he has played in one of the worst parks for hitters in the big leagues throughout his career. However, a closer look shows that he has never been able to hit southpaws, and even more troubling, he has given no indications that he is learning. In 2003, his batting average against lefties was barely above .200 and his slugging percentage was well below .400. His defense, now much improved, and his competitive spirit has kept him in the lineup every day so far. However, that isn't going to last much longer. Being a lefthanded hitter will ensure he opens this season as a starter, though no team is likely to keep putting what amounts to an automatic out in the lineup if it can be avoided.

	AB	R	HR	RBI	SB	BA
2001 Oakland	552	91	32	114	8	.288
2002 Oakland	585	87	34	109	8	.275
2003 Oakland	588	94	29	101	8	.282

CHAVEZ, RAUL - C - BR - b: 3/18/73 $17

Chavez is a catcher who was originally signed by Houston in Venezuela in 1990. He played briefly for Montreal and Seattle in the late 1990s before returning to the Houston organization where he is held in high regard because of his makeup. He has appeared in the major leagues in 6 seasons but has only about 100 at-bats. Chavez is solid defensively which may provide an opportunity for more major league playing time. He had a .273-6-47 season at Triple-A New Orleans in 2003, splitting time between catcher and third base. Chavez is an adequate backup major league backup catcher but would not provide much offense.

	AB	R	HR	RBI	SB	BA
2003 Houston	37	5	1	4	0	.270

CHEN, CHIN-FENG - OF - BR - b: 10/28/77 $0

Power is his forte, but Chen needs to make more consistent contact if he's going to hit for an acceptable average against major league pitching. His numbers with the Dodgers' Triple-A team last year were solid, but there is room for improvement. He could challenge for a major league job in spring training, but will probably need a little more seasoning.

CHOI, HEE SEOP - 1B - BL - b: 4/1/78 $1

Choi is a big, strong kid who can really hit, although his 2003 campaign never got off the ground. Originally slated to be the starting first baseman, those plans were changed when the Cubs acquired Eric Karros. Then he suffered a serious head injury chasing a popup during an interleague game against the Yankees. Choi has the ability to hit lefthanders well, and is starting to develop into more of a power hitter. It should be evident that Choi, who was banished to Triple-A in August, is not going to get any kind of real shot with the Cubs. With any other organization he still would be considered a top prospect, and he still likely will have a productive big league career. Only that isn't likely to happen with the Cubs.

	AB	R	HR	RBI	SB	BA
2002 Chicago - NL	50	6	2	4	0	.180
2003 Chicago - NL	202	31	8	28	1	.218

CHRISTENSON, RYAN - OF - BR - b: 3/28/74 $0

Christenson's stock fell after Oakland let him go in 2000. He's now bouncing around the minors and fills in for a while on a weak major league team like the Brewers and Rangers. He is not a good hitter, but he has some speed and is a reliable utility outfielder.

	AB	R	HR	RBI	SB	BA
2002 Milwaukee	58	5	1	3	0	.155
2003 Texas	165	22	2	16	2	.176

CINTRON, ALEX - SS - BB - b: 12/17/78 $16

Cintron was recalled from Triple-A Tucson when injuries plagued the Arizona infield early in 2002, and he was so impressive that the Diamondbacks traded Tony Womack in the second half (they would have let him leave via free agency in the offseason regardless) to allow Cintron to become the regular shortstop. Cintron's thickish, heavy-legged body has drawn comparisons to that of Alex Rodriguez, and Cintron flashed some unexpected power when given the opportunity to play regularly. A switch-hitter, Cintron can drive the ball from both sides of the plate and has a good eye. He is not afraid to take a walk and seldom strikes out. He is not a stolen base threat. He is a solid fielder at three infield positions, and he has enough range and enough arm to play shortstop at the major league level. He appears to be the top candidate for the starting shortstop position in a competitive Arizona infield.

	AB	R	HR	RBI	SB	BA
2002 Arizona	75	11	0	4	0	.213
2003 Arizona	448	70	13	51	2	.317

CIRILLO, JEFF - 3B - BR - b: 9/23/69 $0

Cirillo butted heads with former Seattle skipper Lou Piniella, and many believed a managerial change to the more mellow Bob Melvin would enable Cirillo to return to his form as a two-time All Star. It didn't work. Cirillo, who had 53 doubles and 115 RBIs for Colorado in 2000, has topped those numbers in his two seasons combined with the Mariners. A line-drive hitter, he seems to have lost his aggressiveness at the plate, becoming defensive without the ability to drive the ball. He is a good defender and has a strong arm, good hands and decent range. He has better than average speed but he virtually stopped trying to steal a base last year, perhaps because he was hardly ever on base. Nothing was guaranteed in spring training after losing his job at third to Carlos Guillen down the stretch last year.

	AB	R	HR	RBI	SB	BA
2001 Colorado	528	72	17	83	12	.312
2002 Seattle	485	51	6	54	8	.249
2003 Seattle	258	24	2	23	1	.205

CLARK, BRADY - OF - BR - b: 4/18/73 $10

A nondrafted free agent who signed in 1996, Clark's perseverance paid off as he spent 2003 in the major leagues as the fourth outfielder in Milwaukee. Like many Brewers in that look-see season, Clark set numerous career bests in his first extended look. Clark has good pop to the gaps and understands the strike zone, not afraid to work deep into counts to wait for his pitch. He had two 25-steal seasons in the low minors, although he has curtailed his running in short stints in the majors. He has the speed to run once he gets comfortable. He has only average range and arm strength. He was expected to compete for a reserve outfield role.

	AB	R	HR	RBI	SB	BA
2001 Cincinnati	129	22	6	18	4	.264
2002 CIN/NY - NL	78	9	0	10	1	.192
2003 Milwaukee	315	33	6	40	13	.273

CLARK, HOWIE - 3B - BL - b: 2/13/74 $0

Confident at just about any position except behind the plate, Clark showed absolute confidence as a hitter in his brief trials with Toronto last season. While no one should expect him to top .300 in the long run, he is a bit overaggressive at the plate and has little power. He has no trouble putting the ball in play but he doesn't project to maintain a high average and never has been a home run hitter. Clark will be trying to win a spot on the bench as a utility player. As recently as a year ago, there had been a remote chance he would win a job as a second baseman but now, he's the type of player who stands a good chance to get a couple of hundred at-bats with limited production.

	AB	R	HR	RBI	SB	BA
2002 Baltimore	53	3	0	4	0	.302
2003 Toronto	70	9	0	7	0	.357

CLARK, TONY - 1B - BB - b: 6/15/72 $2

Clark's status as a team leader has taken a dive after two bad years with two different teams. His power returned somewhat last season, when he was the Mets' home run leader after they traded Jeromy Burnitz. The 6'7" switch hitter had so much trouble with righthanded pitchers that the Mets sometimes used righthanded-hitting Jason Phillips against them. Clark hits a high percentage of balls in the air, which has combined with his decreased power to create more outs during his at-bats. He is a sure-handed fielder. For the third consecutive winter, Clark was a free agent.

	AB	R	HR	RBI	SB	BA
2001 Detroit	428	67	16	75	0	.287
2002 Boston	275	25	3	29	0	.207
2003 New York - NL	254	29	16	43	0	.232

CLAYTON, ROYCE - SS - BR - b: 1/2/70 $6

Clayton, playing with his third team in four seasons, struggled in his return to the NL with Milwaukee, compiling his worst batting average in his 11 seasons as a major league regular. He strikes out way too much for a player who must use his speed. He had trouble catching up with a major league fastball and is susceptible to the outside breaking ball, often getting himself out by swinging at questionable pitches. While his offense is plummeting, Clayton's glove work remains solid. His range, once outstanding, remains above average, although his arm strength is only OK. He turns the doubleplay well. Once a threat to steal 20-30 bases a year, Clayton has given up on the running game and had a career low in 2003. He is nearing the end of the line. His best chance to start was if Milwaukee picked up his option as insurance for rookie Rickie

Weeks.

	AB	R	HR	RBI	SB	BA
2001 Chicago - AL	433	62	9	60	10	.263
2002 Chicago - AL	342	51	7	35	5	.251
2003 Milwaukee	483	49	11	39	5	.228

COLBRUNN, GREG - 1B - BR - b: 7/26/69 $0

Colbrunn is one of the best pinch-hitters in the game, although it was difficult to tell last year because he missed so much time because of injuries. He underwent surgery to repair torn cartilage in his right wrist on July 15 and missed the rest of the year. Colbrunn is a line drive hitter who does not get cheated at the plate, smoking the ball even on his outs. He can turn around any fastball and tears up lefthanders. He has home run power. He is a solid clubhouse presence and a true gamer. Colbrunn's defense is average at best, and while he played some third base at Arizona in 2002 is probably only a first baseman/DH at this stage of his career. He was expected to fill the role health robbed him of in 2003, as a pinch-hitter and situational substitute.

	AB	R	HR	RBI	SB	BA
2001 Arizona	97	12	4	18	0	.289
2002 Arizona	171	30	10	27	0	.333
2003 Seattle	58	7	3	7	0	.276

CONINE, JEFF - 1B/OF - BR - b: 6/27/66 $14

Conine began last season as the Orioles' star. He finished it back in Florida, where he was an original Marlin, leading that team back into the postseason for the first time since he left after the '97 season. After a slow start, he helped his new/old team with three homers in his last five regular-season games, and with some uncharacteristically good defense in left field. Conine totaled more homers than in any year since 1996, so he still has something left in his tank. He hits righthanded or lefthanded pitching, so he can remain an everyday player until his decline inevitably begins.

	AB	R	HR	RBI	SB	BA
2001 Baltimore	524	75	14	97	12	.311
2002 Baltimore	451	44	15	63	8	.273
2003 BAL/FLA	577	88	20	95	5	.282

CONTI, JASON - OF - BL - b: 1/27/75 $0

Conti got a late look with Milwaukee last season after previously putting in major league time with Arizona and Tampa Bay. Conti has a short, compact swing and can put the ball in play, although he struck out excessively in a short time with the Brewers. He has good speed and could steal 10-15 bases a season if he played regularly, which is problematic because of his struggles at the plate . He has a center fielder's range and a right fielder's arm. He was expected to have a chance at a major league roster if he adjusted his hitting approach, because the other skills are there.

	AB	R	HR	RBI	SB	BA
2002 Tampa Bay	222	26	3	21	4	.257
2003 Milwaukee	48	3	2	7	0	.229

COOMER, RON - 1B - BR - b: 11/18/66 $0

Have bat, will travel. Coomer is a veteran journeyman who has good power and can drive the ball into both gaps. He handles the fastball well and has a good approach at the plate, not afraid to wade deep into a count and take a walk if he doesn't get his pitch. He hammers lefthanders and is a 15-homer, 75-RBI type in a regular role, although those days seem behind him. Coomer came up as a third baseman, although his only viable position these days is first base. He has not attempted a stolen base in three years and is a station-to-station base runner. Because of his hitting acumen, he was expected to find a role as a righthanded bat off the bench this season.

	AB	R	HR	RBI	SB	BA
2001 Chicago - NL	349	25	8	53	0	.261
2002 New York - AL	148	14	3	17	0	.264
2003 Los Angeles	125	11	4	15	0	.240

CORA, ALEX - 2B - BL - b: 10/18/75 $6

Look up "little ball" in the dictionary ... Cora, brother of long-time major league middle infielder Jose Cora, brings the same m.o. to the park — slap the ball into a hole and make plays in the field. Once in a blue moon, Cora will drive an inside pitch over the fence in right. What he mainly does is hit the ball where it is pitched while defending the plate, neither walking nor striking out abundantly. He recognizes breaking balls well. He does not have much better than average speed and never has stolen more than seven bases in a season. He came up as a shortstop and has the superior range and arm to play that position, so the move to second base the last two seasons has been a piece of cake. He has wonderful hands and turns the double play well. He was expected to be no worse than a platoon second baseman this season, and could return to regular status with a little more offensive firepower.

	AB	R	HR	RBI	SB	BA
2001 Los Angeles	405	38	4	29	0	.217
2002 Los Angeles	258	37	5	28	7	.291
2003 Los Angeles	477	39	4	34	4	.249

CORDERO, WIL - 1B - BR - b: 10/3/71 $10

Cordero had his best season in a while in 2003. The former shortstop is now affixed to first base and he can easily field this position. His power is respectable but mild when compared to the power hitting first baseman in the major leagues. He's effective against lefthanded pitchers, hitting over .320 against them last year, which suggests that he should be platooned but he can still hold his own against right handed pitching and he's cheap.

	AB	R	HR	RBI	SB	BA
2001 Cleveland	268	30	4	21	0	.250
2002 Montreal	161	22	6	30	2	.267
2003 Montreal	436	57	16	71	1	.278

CORDOVA, MARTY -/DH - BR - b: 7/10/69 $0

Cordova, the American League Rookie of the Year in 1995, batted in 111 runs for the Twins the next year. Since then, we have seen just bits and pieces of that promise — a few home runs here, a stolen base there, an outfield assist somewhere else. Last April, he played four games in the outfield and threw out two runners. Then he missed the remainder of the season after undergoing Tommy John surgery. Cordova's skills have clearly eroded, he hasn't acquired good strike-zone judgment as he has matured and he's likely to begin this season back on the disabled list.

	AB	R	HR	RBI	SB	BA
2001 Cleveland	409	61	20	69	0	.301
2002 Baltimore	458	55	18	64	1	.253
2003 Baltimore	30	5	1	4	1	.233

COUNSELL, CRAIG - 3B/SS - BL - b: 8/21/70 $7

Counsell missed two months in 2002 simply by being Counsell - he slid hard into second base in a vain attempt to break up a double play (when is the last time Barry, Sammy or Manny even pretended to hit the dirt in that situation) and suffered a broken finger. When Counsell returned, he could not knock the rust off his game and suffered through his worst season in his four with Arizona. A gritty player who recites the fundamentals each night before he goes to bed, Counsell is one of the best hit-and-run batters in the National League and will steal a base despite not having stolen-base speed. He can handle the glove at three infield positions. While his range and bat are best suited to second base, he played more games at third base than any other Arizona player following Matt Williams' release two months into 2003. Despite a subpar season Counsell is in no danger of losing his roster spot, although his position is undetermined. His best chance to start will be at shortstop, although a super-sub role as a "regular irregular" seems more likely.

	AB	R	HR	RBI	SB	BA
2001 Arizona	458	76	4	38	6	.275
2002 Arizona	436	63	2	51	7	.282
2003 Arizona	303	40	3	21	11	.234

CRAWFORD, CARL - OF - BL - b: 10/14/77 $30

Crawford, just 22, is an incredible talent. He gave up a football scholarship to Nebraska to sign with the Devil Rays and made it to the majors by the time he was 20. Crawford emerged as a premier stolen base threat in 2003, and demonstrated that he's learning how to deal with major league pitching faster than they are learning how to deal with him. His power is still developing as he learns how to drive the ball, and he had a very strong second half last season, indicating that he's unlikely to have a sophomore slump.

	AB	R	HR	RBI	SB	BA
2002 Tampa Bay	259	23	2	30	9	.259
2003 Tampa Bay	630	80	5	54	55	.281

CREDE, JOE - 3B - BR - b: 4/26/78 $11

Like many of the White Sox sluggers, Crede was so unbelievably bad in the first half of the season that not even a strong second half could make his overall numbers look good. Crede hit only .225 with virtually no power before the All-Star break, though he rebounded to have a fine second half. Crede struggled early because he was too aggressive at the plate. Because he swung at so many pitches early in the count, opposing hurlers realized they didn't have to do much to get him out. He was much more patient in the second half of 2003, and that should bode well for this year. He put up consistent numbers in the minors and there is no reason to think that he won't be a productive big league hitter. He should hit about .280 and approach 25 home runs this season.

	AB	R	HR	RBI	SB	BA
2001 Chicago - AL	50	1	0	7	1	.220
2002 Chicago - AL	200	28	12	35	0	.285
2003 Chicago - AL	536	68	19	75	1	.261

CRISP, COCO - OF - BB - b: 11/01/79 $13

A young, improving player, Crisp was called up to fill holes in the Cleveland outfield in June and he demonstrated speed on the base paths but no sign of being a great base stealer. He's a slap hitting switch-hitter but he strikes out too much. He is not a long ball threat and he has a weak throwing arm. Crisp has the speed to cover the territory in center or right, but his arm is strictly left field. Left field is usually where they play a slow guy with a big bat. The once power-laden Indians need a few bombers in the lineup and Crisp's best chance to become a regular is as a table setter. Right now, he gets caught much too often attempting to steal. If he becomes a standout 40-50 bags a year guy, he's got a career in front of him but, as it stands now, players like Crisp are a dime a dozen.

	AB	R	HR	RBI	SB	BA
2002 Cleveland	127	16	1	9	4	.260
2003 Cleveland	414	55	3	27	15	.266

CROSBY, BOBBY - SS - BR - b: 1/12/80 $5

The rising star of Oakland's farm system the past couple of years, Crosby finally made it to the big leagues during the last month of 2003. He was used very sparingly by the Athletics, however, who were in a fierce battle with Seattle for the AL West title. Crosby was dynamite for Sacramento last season, hitting above .300 while getting on base nearly 40 percent of the time and clubbing 62 extra base hits (including 22 home runs). Certainly he can't be expected to put up those numbers in his first full season in the big leagues. However, given his age, there is no reason to think that he won't contend for the rookie of the year award this season, and be one of the best shortstops in the game a few more years down the road.

	AB	R	HR	RBI	SB	BA
2003 Oakland	12	1	0	0	0	.000

CRUZ, DEIVI - SS - BR - b: 11/6/72 $7

The Orioles didn't re-sign Mike Bordick before last season, so they signed Cruz instead. He looked like an up-and-coming shortstop when he batted .302-10-82 for the 2000 Tigers at age 24. However, that was two years before more strenuous visa screening revealed that he was three years older than he admitted being. So he joined the legion of foreign players who were older than the Orioles realized. At bat, Cruz acts as if he knows his time is limited, rarely wasting an opportunity to swing at a pitch — any pitch. Still, Cruz is a better-than-average run producer for a shortstop, even batting in the .250-.260 range. He's also a reliable fielder. Not a championship-caliber player, but good enough to start for also-ran teams.

	AB	R	HR	RBI	SB	BA
2001 Detroit	414	39	7	52	4	.256
2002 San Diego	514	49	7	47	2	.263
2003 Baltimore	548	61	14	65	1	.250

CRUZ, ENRIQUE - SS - BR - b: 11/21/81 $0

Cruz made the jump from Single-A in 2002 to the major leagues in 2003 after being a Rule 5 draftee from the New York Yankees, although his numbers in very limited playing time made it apparent that the 21-year old was not ready. A lean and lanky hitter, Cruz has the raw tools to make it. He hits the ball where it is pitched, although his plate discipline was exposed by veteran major league hurlers. Cruz stole 33 bases twice in the Yankees' system and runs well. Primarily a third baseman in the minors, he played all three infield positions last season, when he was a victim of being rushed. He was expected to return to the minor leagues for a full season of reps in 2003.

	AB	R	HR	RBI	SB	BA
2003 Milwaukee	71	6	0	2	0	.085

CRUZ, JOSE - OF - BB - b: 4/19/74 $14

While Cruz pounded southpaw hurlers last season, the switch-hitting right fielder struggled nearly all of the year against righthanded pitching. He never was able to feel comfortable hitting from the left side of the plate, and hit for virtually no power there. The good news is that Cruz showed remarkable discipline, drawing 102 walks, which was 31 more than his previous best. Righthanded pitchers continually throw him high and inside fastballs, and Cruz simply cannot handle those pitches well. While it's obvious that Cruz is never going be a superstar, he still is a decent everyday player. He will have to hit better lefthanded, however, if he wants to keep playing every day.

	AB	R	HR	RBI	SB	BA
2001 Toronto	577	92	34	88	32	.274
2002 Toronto	466	64	18	70	7	.245
2003 San Francisco	539	90	20	68	5	.250

CUDDYER, MICHAEL - OF - BR - b: 3/27/79 $0

Cuddyer opened 2003 in the majors but was sent to the minors after struggling at the plate and losing his starting spot. In addition to outfield work, Cuddyer also played third base and debuted at second base while in the minors, which is a good way to increase his value. A former first-round draft pick, Cuddyer has great power potential and has hit well in clutch situations in the minors.

He's just about ready for major league duty and probably would be playing everyday if he came up with a team that had openings in the outfield.

	AB	R	HR	RBI	SB	BA
2001 Minnesota	18	1	0	1	1	.222
2002 Minnesota	112	12	4	13	2	.259
2003 Minnesota	102	14	4	8	1	.245

CUST, JACK - DH - BL - b: 1/16/79 $0

We've heard a lot about Cust as a power-hitting prospect since he hit 32 homers in the Single-A California League in 1999. What we haven't heard is that he's a man without a defensive position, a cavalier baserunner giving away outs and a hitter who takes too many strikes and falls behind in the count. Perhaps that's why the Orioles were the third organization in three years for the former Diamondbacks first-round draft pick. Given more playing time last year than in his two earlier major league trials, Cust produced more than he had. A good finish showed promise for a more successful 2004 season as a DH.

	AB	R	HR	RBI	SB	BA
2002 Colorado	65	8	1	8	0	.169
2003 Baltimore	73	7	4	11	0	.260

DAMON, JOHNNY - OF - BL - b: 11/5/73 $24

Damon has tantalized his three teams with the talent that allowed him to bat .327 with 16 homers, 88 RBI and a league-leading 46 stolen bases in 2000. He has batted better than .300 in only one other major league season, and the only time he exceeded any of the other figures was when he hit 18 homers for the Royals as a 24-year-old in '98. He was able to run with usually station-to-station Boston well enough to become the first Red Sox player with consecutive seasons of 30 steals since Tris Speaker — in 1912, Fenway Park's first season. Damon is a good but not excellent leadoff batter. He has scored more than 100 runs in each of the last six seasons, but doesn't reach base more than about 35 per cent of the time because he neither walks nor strikes out often. He has good range but a limited arm in center field.

	AB	R	HR	RBI	SB	BA
2001 Oakland	644	108	9	49	27	.256
2002 Boston	623	118	14	63	31	.286
2003 Boston	608	103	12	67	30	.273

DAUBACH, BRIAN - 1B - BL - b: 2/11/72 $2

Daubach has become the quintessential lefthanded bat off the bench. Although he's always had a little bit of power, he cannot hit lefthanded pitching and as a result has not been able to keep a starting spot. In 2003 he came to the plate only 16 times all season with a southpaw on the mound. That, combined with the fact that he realistically can play only first base, makes him less valuable. He's not a strong defender, either, as he lacks the quick reflexes that most outstanding fielding first sackers possess. Daubach will be back this year, though he won't play any significant role.

	AB	R	HR	RBI	SB	BA
2001 Boston	407	54	22	71	1	.263
2002 Boston	444	62	20	78	2	.266
2003 Chicago - AL	183	26	6	21	1	.230

DaVANON, JEFF - OF - BB - b: 12/8/73 $13

DaVanon finally got an opportunity to play semi-regularly in the majors last year and didn't waste it. DaVanon has decent power and is a disciplined hitter. On the bases, DaVanon has good speed and is capable of double-digit steals. Defensively, he can play all three outfield positions, but is better at the corners than in center. His age works against him becoming an established starter, but DaVanon has proved that he can be a valuable fourth outfielder on a major league team.

	AB	R	HR	RBI	SB	BA
2001 Anaheim	88	7	5	9	1	.193
2002 Anaheim	30	3	1	4	1	.167
2003 Anaheim	330	56	12	43	17	.282

DAVIS, BEN - C - BB - b: 3/10/77 $2

Davis is a big, good-looking athlete whose numbers have not caught up with his body. He has tried to be more aggressive since coming to Seattle in 2002 and had strong numbers for a platoon player last year. A switch-hitter, Davis has the skills to be a regular, but he still needs to develop a better concept of the strike zone. He is a free swinger, and pitchers know it. Davis has a big-time arm, and after improving his footwork was one of the toughest catchers to steal against in the AL. He is an average runner, although he will finesse a stolen base or two a year. He was expected to make a run at the fulltime starting job this season.

	AB	R	HR	RBI	SB	BA
2001 San Diego	448	56	11	57	4	.239
2002 Seattle	228	24	7	43	1	.259
2003 Seattle	246	25	6	42	0	.236

DAVIS, J.J. - OF - BR - b: 10/25/78 $0

A player can only be considered a prospect for so long. He was the Pirates number one pick in 1997 but he has been developing slowly. Davis just hasn't cut it and now a new and younger crop of prospects are coming on board and Davis is probably out of the Pirates plans.

	AB	R	HR	RBI	SB	BA
2003 Pittsburgh	35	1	1	4	0	.200

DeJESUS , DAVID - OF - BL - b: 12/20/79 $0

With just two pro seasons under his belt, David DeJesus jumped from Double-A to the majors for a cup of coffee in September, 2003. DeJesus is an excellent contact hitter who has an outstanding batting eye. While striking out less than he has walked, DeJesus has consistently posted an on-base average near .400 as he has climbed quickly through the Royals farm system. DeJesus has only gap power and although he has decent speed it isn't enough for him to be a top of the order, slash-and-run kind of hitter. He's limited to a corner outfield spot in regular use and his arm is average for right field. DeJesus' long-term future depends a lot upon how much power he's able to develop as he fills out his lanky six-foot frame; for now he has the look of a fourth outfielder.

DELGADO, CARLOS - 1B - BL - b: 6/25/72 $24

One of the most powerful and patient hitters in the majors, Delgado has become a perennial Triple Crown threat, especially as he rebounded in 2003 to more typical performance after a subpar year by his own high standards in 2002. Always willing to go the opposite way to settle for a base hit, Delgado suffered through minor knee problems in mid-summer last year that limited him to DH action but the problem never interfered with his performance and he continued to perform throughout the season. Obviously, he's the starting first baseman and a number three of four hitter who will continue to be a recurring MVP candidate.

	AB	R	HR	RBI	SB	BA
2001 Toronto	574	102	39	102	3	.279
2002 Toronto	505	103	33	108	1	.277
2003 Toronto	570	117	42	145	0	.302

DELLUCCI, DAVID - OF - BL - b: 10/31/71 $3

Few major leaguers hustle as aggressively and intelligently as Dellucci, both in the field and on the bases. Last season he was batting at about his career norm, in the .260s before slumping during a July when he didn't drive in a run. The Yankees liked what they'd seen of him in the 2001 World Series, and acquired Dellucci in the Raul Mondesi trade to play right field and add a lefthanded bat. He didn't hit for New York, and in late August went on the disabled list because of a sprained ankle. Dellucci returned for the postseason. His difficulty hitting lefthanders limits him to a platoon role.

	AB	R	HR	RBI	SB	BA
2001 Arizona	217	28	10	40	2	.276
2002 Arizona	229	34	7	29	2	.245
2003 AZ/ NY - AL	216	26	3	23	12	.227

DeROSA, MARK - 2B/3B/SS - BR - b: 2/26/75 $4

Despite being edged out of his semi-regular second base job by Marcus Giles, DeRosa found his way into the Braves lineup more often in 2003 than in 2002. His ability to play third base and shortstop gave manager Bobby Cox more options in how to use DeRosa. He's an above-average fielder at second and third base and an adequate fill-in at shortstop; DeRosa can also be used at the corner outfield positions in a pinch. At the plate, DeRosa has gap power but struggled to make consistent contact last year, fanning in almost twenty percent of his at-bats. DeRosa is not an especially speedy baserunner. Even if Giles had not emerged as a solid regular in 2003, it is unlikely DeRosa would have won the full-time job at second base. He's a utility man whose best role is off the bench or making spot starts to spell regulars, and even that role will be severely challenged should he remain with the Braves in the near term.

	AB	R	HR	RBI	SB	BA
2001 Atlanta	164	27	3	20	2	.287
2002 Atlanta	212	24	5	23	2	.297
2003 Atlanta	266	40	6	22	1	.263

DIAZ, EINAR - C - BR - b: 12/28/72 $0

Diaz is a solid, if unspectacular, catcher, capable of starting for a major league team. He has little power or speed, and should be expected to hit in the mid-.200s. A free swinger, Diaz draws very few walks and generally posts a very low on-base average. Diaz is, however, a good contact hitter, and usually puts the ball in play. His overall skills are good enough to enable him to play regularly in the big leagues, hitting at the bottom of the batting order.

	AB	R	HR	RBI	SB	BA
2001 Cleveland	437	54	4	56	1	.277
2002 Cleveland	320	34	2	16	0	.206
2003 Texas	334	30	4	35	3	.257

DiFELICE, MIKE - C - BR - b: 5/28/69 $0

Since becoming the Devil Rays regular catcher in their inaugural season, Mike DiFelice has gradually reverted to a reserve role. In 2003, he earned a job out of spring training as a non-roster invitee, and eventually spelled Brent Mayne for the Royals as the backup backstop. DiFelice displayed unusual power in 2003, and earned more playing time than a nominal backup; he also was an unusually good hitter against lefty pitchers in 2003, making him an especially good complement to lefthanded hitting Mayne. DiFelice showed a fiery disposition and earned brief notoriety for an on-field explosion against the Twins in which he was quickly ejected, then littered the field with debris from the dugout. DiFelice is merely average behind the plate; he has been able to control opposing baserunners well enough, but pitchers have a greater tendency to give up runs in bunches when DiFelice is handling them. Despite a career-best season with the bat, DiFelice remains a replacement-level backup catcher who is unlikely to start more than a third of his team's games.

	AB	R	HR	RBI	SB	BA
2001 TB/AZ	170	14	2	10	1	.188
2002 St. Louis	174	17	4	19	0	.230
2003 Kansas City	189	29	3	25	1	.254

DREW, J. D. - OF - BL - b: 11/20/75 $15

A fearsome hitter when healthy, Drew has suffered through numerous ailments in recent years that have cut down on his ability to drive the ball. He played hurt all of 2003, first fighting through knee problems leftover from offseason surgery, and then from a pulled muscle in his stomach, and both injuries prevented him from being much of a threat at the plate. Drew has never played in more than 135 games in any one season because of injuries, therefore he should be expected to spend at least a couple of weeks on the disabled list again this year. However, if he should remain healthy for a whole season, he would put up big-time power numbers while hitting at or slightly above .300.

	AB	R	HR	RBI	SB	BA
2001 St. Louis	375	80	27	73	13	.323
2002 St. Louis	424	61	18	56	8	.252
2003 St. Louis	287	60	15	42	2	.289

DUNCAN, JEFF - OF - BL - b: 12/9/78 $0

Hurting for outfield help, New York brought Duncan up from Double-A Binghamton and liked what they saw as he played more games in center field than any other Met. Though he hit well in the lower minors and last year batted .288 with 24 steals in the Eastern League, Duncan was overmatched by major league pitching — especially lefthanders, against whom he went 1-for-15. He's barely a year removed from Single-A ball, so it's likely he would start the 2004 season in Triple-A and be called up to the majors if he hits well.

	AB	R	HR	RBI	SB	BA
2003 New York - NL	139	13	1	10	4	.194

DUNN, ADAM - OF - BL - b: 11/9/79 $13

Once a can't miss superstar, Dunn has missed too often to warrant continued accolades. Dunn came into the league in 2001 with a reputation as a power hitter and while his power is real, his reputation caused pitchers to work him too carefully, as evidenced by Dunn's 128 walks in 2002. However, his 128 walks were offset by 170 strikeouts and the book on Dunn changed in 2003 from, "Work the corners and don't give him anything to drive," to "Challenge him with breaking stuff and make him swing the bat." A player that fans 170 times and bats .249 as he did in 2002, should be challenged, and either he'll step up and raise his average 40 points, cut his whiffs and belt 40 homers or he'll struggle, which lanky Texan Dunn did in 2003. He was hard pressed to keep his average above the .200 mark all year but he managed to hit enough hanging curves out of the park to keep some believing that he is still a budding superstar. He was bothered by a sore thumb and he played infrequently as the season wore down. Dunn is only age 24 so he has time to develop but he needs a lot of work. Dunn plays adequately in left field, a bit less so in right and he also filled in at first base when Sean Casey needed a break. Eventually, first base will be Dunn's main position. Dunn is even tempered and a hard worker, which has drawn praise, but there are others who wish Dunn would go a little nuts after one of his 14 for 100 slumps, just to show a sense of urgency.

	AB	R	HR	RBI	SB	BA
2001 Cincinnati	244	54	19	43	4	.262
2002 Cincinnati	535	84	26	71	19	.249
2003 Cincinnati	381	70	27	57	8	.215

DURAZO, RUBE - 1B/DH - BL - b: 1/23/74 $13

It seemed only natural that Durazo wound up with Oakland in 2003. With his smooth swing and exceptional knowledge of the strike zone, Durazo is exactly the kind of player that Athletics' general manager Billy Beane covets. Durazo, once thought to be a liability against lefthanded throwers, acquitted himself in 2003. He got well over 500 at-bats last season, which meant he played nearly every day, and actually hit better against the southpaws, with a batting average about 30 points higher and a slugging percentage about 40 points greater. He has little speed, not that it mattered much to Oakland, who attempt fewer steals than almost any other team in baseball. While Durazo isn't going to be a superstar, he should be expected to perform much as he did last year.

	AB	R	HR	RBI	SB	BA
2001 Arizona	175	34	12	38	0	.269
2002 Arizona	222	46	16	48	0	.261
2003 Oakland	537	92	21	77	1	.259

DURHAM, RAY - 2B/ - BB - b: 11/30/71 $13

Durham is a disciplined, professional hitter who knows how to make the most out of hitting in the leadoff slot. He consistently hits between .280 and .295 and is more than willing to take a walk to set things up for the power hitters in the lineup. Durham is solid defensively, too. He doesn't have the greatest range or strongest arm, though he makes up for that by knowing how to play hitters. Hitting ahead of Barry Bonds in San Francisco's lineup last year meant he attempted by far the fewest stolen bases of his career. However, given the right situation he still is capable of pilfering more than 20. Durham has at least a few more productive seasons left. Expect him to be one of the better hitting second basemen in the game again this year.

	AB	R	HR	RBI	SB	BA
2001 Chicago - AL	611	104	20	65	23	.267
2002 Chicago - AL	564	114	15	70	26	.289
2003 San Francisco	410	61	8	33	7	.285

DYE, JERMAINE - OF - BR - b: 1/28/74 $1

Dye's offense clearly suffered the last two seasons, and missed two months in 2003 after separating his right shoulder, and upon returning in September, still struggled at the plate, hitting under .200. Dye is a superb defensive player and can use his speed to track down balls many players couldn't catch. He should bounce back this year and have a better season, especially if he winds up playing his home games in a much more forgiving ballpark.

	AB	R	HR	RBI	SB	BA
2001 KC/OAK	599	91	26	106	9	.282
2002 Oakland	488	74	24	86	2	.252
2003 Oakland	221	28	4	20	1	.172

ECKSTEIN, DAVID - SS - BR - b: 1/20/75 $14

A prototype leadoff hitter, Eckstein is a five-foot-eight package of hustle and energy. He has great strike zone judgment, excellent speed and makes good contact. Capable of playing either of the middle infield positions, Eckstein is a steady fielder. Last season, Eckstein had more than his share of nagging injuries, including arm, shoulder, hand and hamstring problems. He also suffered through an extended slump in early 2003 for the first time in his career. With his speed and ability to get on base, however, Eckstein should continue to be at the top of the lineup on an everyday basis in 2004.

	AB	R	HR	RBI	SB	BA
2001 Anaheim	582	82	4	41	29	.285
2002 Anaheim	608	107	8	63	21	.293
2003 Anaheim	452	59	3	31	16	.252

EDMONDS, JIM - OF - BL - b: 6/27/70 $18

Edmonds was having a typical season in 2003 during the first half, when he was arguably one of the top players in the National League. Unfortunately, a series of injuries dogged him the rest of the way and put a damper on what might have been a fantastic year. It just proves that when he's healthy, Edmonds is one of the top hitters around. He has a great knowledge of the strike zone, meaning he can pick his pitches to hit. He will hit for power and average and play Gold Glove level defense in the outfield. About the only thing he does not do well is run, primarily because he is trying to protect his body by not taking any unnecessary chances. If healthy, Edmonds will hit .300 with over 40 homer runs; if not, he can play through pain and still produce better than most.

	AB	R	HR	RBI	SB	BA
2001 St. Louis	500	95	30	110	5	.304
2002 St. Louis	476	96	28	83	4	.311
2003 St. Louis	447	89	39	89	1	.275

ELLIS, MARK - 2B - BR - b: 6/6/77 $9

Ellis is a steady type of player, one who doesn't have enough offense to stand out in a crowd, yet one who is good enough to keep from embarrassing himself. He has a decent eye at the plate, combined with line drive power. He also has enough speed to hit near the top of the lineup, even on a team that doesn't like to steal many bases. A decent, if unspectacular, defensive second baseman, he also has the ability to fill in at short and third if needed. Ellis can be an adequate second baseman for a club who doesn't have any other options. However, he will get pushed out of the way the minute a more accomplished hitter comes along.

	AB	R	HR	RBI	SB	BA
2002 Oakland	345	58	6	35	4	.272
2003 Oakland	553	78	9	52	6	.248

ENCARNACION, JUAN - OF - BR - b: 3/8/76 $22

Encarnacion has stabilized as a hitter and he should continue to hit .275 with 20 to 25 homers and 20 stolen bases. Defensively, he will play an adequate right field as long as he is protected by a Roadrunner in centerfield.

	AB	R	HR	RBI	SB	BA
2001 Detroit	417	52	12	52	9	.242
2002 CIN/FLA	584	77	24	85	21	.271
2003 Florida	601	80	19	94	19	.270

ENSBERG, MORGAN - 3B - BR - b: 8/26/75 $16

Ensberg had a productive college career at USC where he ranked third on the school's career home run list behind Mark McGwire and Geoff Jenkins. He moved steadily through the Astro organization and opened the 2002 season as the starting third baseman. He didn't hit enough to keep the job but he was ready when he received another opportunity and had a productive season. He provides the power and solid defense required of a third baseman. He is moving into the prime years of his career and should contribute at an above-average level for a starting third baseman. As a major league regular, he should be capable of consistent production at the .280-25-85 level.

	AB	R	HR	RBI	SB	BA
2002 Houston	132	14	3	19	2	.242
2003 Houston	385	69	25	60	7	.291

ERSTAD, DARIN - OF - BL - b: 6/4/74 $11

Erstad's speed and athleticism have been his primary strengths over his major league career. When healthy, he has the speed and technique to be among the league leaders in stolen bases while providing strong defense in center field. His hitting has been up and down during his career, with alternating good and bad years. While he is not a power hitter, he can occasionally help his team with the long ball. Last year, Erstad was limited by a tendon problem in his right hamstring that effectively wrecked his season. There is a possibility that Erstad could be moved to a corner outfield spot or first base to help keep him healthy, although Erstad would be among the less productive offensive players at such positions.

	AB	R	HR	RBI	SB	BA
2001 Anaheim	631	89	9	63	24	.258
2002 Anaheim	625	99	10	73	23	.283
2003 Anaheim	258	35	4	17	9	.252

ESCOBAR, ALEX - OF - BR - b: 9/6/78   **$3**

After tearing his ACL in a 2002 spring training game, Escobar spent the rest of the 2002 rehabbing, not playing. In 2003, he was with Triple-A Buffalo where he led the entire Indians organization with 24 home runs. Called up to Cleveland, Escobar played well and he continued to hit with authority. Escobar is better off playing every day for the Indians than toiling again in the minors. The one time five tool prospect still seems to have all his tools. He is a first rate right fielder with a strong and an increasingly accurate arm. If he plays right field all year, he will be among the major league leaders in outfield assists.

	AB	R	HR	RBI	SB	BA
2001 New York - NL	50	3	3	8	1	.200
2003 Cleveland	99	16	5	14	1	.273

ESTALLELA, BOBBY - C - BR - b: 8/23/74   **$0**

Estellela has Popeye arms below Olive Oyl shoulders, and shoulder problems have forced him onto the disabled list for the second half of both 2002 and 2003. Estellela has big-time power and can drive a fastball out of any park, not just his latest home in Coors Field. Yet he has a longish swing and has yet to master pitch recognition and strike zone discipline. He is a free swinger and can be fooled on breaking pitches, often getting himself out. Estellela strikes out once every 3.5 at-bats, an awful ratio for such limited rewards. He does not have a strong arm and can be run against. Estellela would be great as a contestant Home Run Derby; as a major league player, he is a fringe reserve at best.

	AB	R	HR	RBI	SB	BA
2002 Colorado	112	17	8	25	0	.205
2003 Colorado	140	17	7	21	2	.200

ESTRADA, JOHNNY - C - BB - b: 6/27/76   **$0**

No matter how well Johnny Estrada plays he'll forever be hung with the tag of having been traded for Kevin Millwood; it's fortunate for Estrada that he is actually a skilled catcher in his own right. He has a fine arm and the Braves compare him defensively to Eddie Perez. A switch-hitter with fairly good power, Estrada has shown fine on-base skills in the high minors. He tends to be an aggressive hitter, although he makes consistent contact and avoid strikeouts. Estrada led Triple-A Richmond with a .328 batting average and 66 RBI, and his .393 on-base percentage was also tops on the club. The solid season at Richmond included MVP honors in the Triple-A All-Star game and earned Estrada another trip to the bigs as he got an occasional start after his September callup. Estrada is poised to become a big-league regular; he has nothing left to prove in the minors.

	AB	R	HR	RBI	SB	BA
2001 Philadelphia	298	26	8	37	0	.228
2003 Atlanta	36	2	0	2	0	.306

EVERETT, ADAM - SS - BR - b: 2/2/77   **$8**

Everett is a shortstop with outstanding defensive skills. Originally signed by Boston, he was traded to the Astros for Carl Everett after the 1999 season and has been regarded as the team's shortstop of the future. After beginning his fourth year at Triple-A, he became the starting shortstop for Houston in May 2003, replacing Julio Lugo. He took advantage of the opportunity and solidified the defense while hitting better than expected. Everett can be overpowered by good pitching and will not hit for power or average. However, his defense and speed should keep him in the lineup as a bottom-of-the-lineup regular.

	AB	R	HR	RBI	SB	BA
2001 Houston	3	1	0	0	1	.000
2002 Houston	88	11	0	4	3	.193
2003 Houston	387	51	8	51	8	.256

EVERETT, CARL - OF - BB - b: 6/3/71 $18

Everett was a better player last season, due mostly to his surgically repaired knee being fully healthy for the first time in a couple of seasons. He is a strong player who can hit the ball a long way. His biggest drawback is his lack of discipline at the plate. He is a very impatient hitter, one who swings at far too many balls down and out of the strike zone. His knee problems also have made him a subpar outfielder and it's likely that he will be close to a full-time designated hitter for the rest of his career. Everett, who has several much-publicized incidents in Boston, has been calm and collected for most of the past two seasons. Assuming he stays healthy, and that his temper doesn't get the best of him, he can hit 25 to 30 homers and drive in about 100 this season. He likely won't put up All-Star caliber numbers, though he should be a reasonably productive player for another two or three seasons.

	AB	R	HR	RBI	SB	BA
2001 Boston	409	61	14	58	9	.257
2002 Texas	374	47	16	62	2	.267
2003 TEX/CHI - AL	526	93	28	92	8	.287

FEBLES, CARLOS - 2B - BR - b: 5/24/76 $4

All signs pointed to 2003 being a pivotal year in Carlos Febles' career. Unfortunately for Febles, he continued to regress and when the club ran out of options, he was released. Febles missed three weeks after injuring his ring finger trying to bunt and when he returned, Desi Relaford had become the starting second baseman. Febles was considered to be a very good team player whose skills never reached their expected talent level. Royals GM Allard Baird was demonstrably upset about having to cut Febles and was quick to re-sign him to a minor-league deal once he cleared waivers. At his best, Febles is a solid defensive second baseman who has above-average speed and occasional power. Too often, however, he has had difficulty making contact at the plate, making him a liability despite his good defense. Febles is still young enough and has enough inherent talent that he can rebuild his career, although at this point he has an uphill battle.

	AB	R	HR	RBI	SB	BA
2001 Kansas City	292	45	8	25	5	.236
2002 Kansas City	351	44	4	26	16	.245
2003 Kansas City	196	31	0	11	8	.235

FELIZ, PEDRO - 3B - BR - b: 3/27/75 $4

Feliz isn't nearly the prospect he was once considered now that he has been found to be two years older than previously reported (he was born in the spring of 1975 instead of 1977). That said, he isn't a bad hitter. He has plenty of power in his bat, though he doesn't walk nearly enough and doesn't have a lot of speed or basestealing ability. He is a dependable third baseman who possesses good quickness and an accurate throwing arm. Given the fact that he will turn 29 in April, it isn't likely that Feliz is suddenly going to walk even 50 times a season. While he will provide good power off the bench, he isn't disciplined enough to keep a starting spot.

	AB	R	HR	RBI	SB	BA
2001 San Francisco	220	23	7	22	2	.227
2002 San Francisco	146	14	2	13	0	.253
2003 San Francisco	235	31	16	48	2	.247

FICK, ROBERT - 1B - BL - b: 3/15/74 $9

The Braves signed Robert Fick during the off-season hoping to add a potent lefty bat to their increasingly menacing lineup. Fick was expected to play first base regularly, but instead lost time in April to a right shoulder strain. His power fell off and he went into a serious second-half slide to end up sharing the firstbase job with Julio Franco and Matt Franco down the stretch. Fick has a good batting eye, as might be expected of a player who began his career as a catcher, but he gets into long stretches where he tries to pull the ball too much. Pitchers have learned to keep the ball away from Fick, getting him to ground out when he tries to pull the outside pitch. Fick is an average first baseman who can also play right field, a position he learned in his last year in Detroit. As a catcher, his arm is strong but erratic; his throwing from first base and right field has been more accurate. Fick's attitude has been questioned in the past although that didn't seem to be a problem in 2003. Instead, Fick was confronted with a substantial second-half slump which resulted in a down year. If he can show more consistency over the course of the season, Fick can regain a full-time job at first base.

	AB	R	HR	RBI	SB	BA
2001 Detroit	401	62	19	61	0	.272
2002 Detroit	556	66	17	63	0	.270
2003 Atlanta	409	52	11	80	1	.269

FIGGINS, CHONE - OF - BB - b: 1/22/78 $11

A middle infielder by trade, Figgins was pressed into center field duty last season and acquitted himself well enough to be considered a viable utility player. Figgins is a short, speedy type who, lacking any power, tries to slap the ball to all fields. If he can hit in the high .200s, Figgins can help a big league team. Last season, Figgins went .312-4-30 in 68 Triple-A games before making the jump to the majors. His most likely major league role for this year is as a Tony Phillips-type utility player, subbing for injured regulars and serving as a pinch-runner.

	AB	R	HR	RBI	SB	BA
2003 Anaheim	240	34	0	27	13	.296

FINLEY, STEVE - OF - BL - b: 3/12/65 $21

Finley is a supremely conditioned athlete who shows no signs of slowing down despite the fact that he will turn 39 in spring training. The active career leader with more than 100 triples, Finley still has the speed to turn gappers into three-base hits and track down balls in both gaps from his spot in center field. A physiology major in college, Finley understands his body and tends to it well. His conditioning program is rigorous; his pregame meal is a tin of tuna. He remains a dead pull hitter, although he has learned to take the outside pitch to left-center a little more as a concession to pitching patterns. Not only is he one of the fastest players in the league, he is perhaps the best base runner. He consistently reads the ball off the bat accurately and cuts the bases expertly, maintaining a first-to-home speed that is among the best in the game. He even was used in the leadoff spot in 2003 as his team searched for a good combination. He will be the starting center fielder in the final year of a two-year deal done before last year.

	AB	R	HR	RBI	SB	BA
2001 Arizona	495	66	14	73	11	.275
2002 Arizona	505	82	25	89	16	.287
2003 Arizona	516	82	22	70	15	.287

FLAHERTY, JOHN - C - BR - b: 10/21/67 $0

Flaherty played an important role by giving the Yankees a viable catching alternative who would allow them to rest Jorge Posada and not leave a cipher in their offensive lineup. A former starting catcher with the Tigers, Padres and Devil Rays, Flaherty reached double figures in home runs. Flaherty also had a higher success rate than the Yankees' starter in throwing out base stealers. The native New Yorker might have played even more in 2003 if Posada wasn't also better at hitting against lefthanders. But at least Flaherty had a chance to catch for a playoff team for the first time since 1996.

	AB	R	HR	RBI	SB	BA
2001 Tampa Bay	248	20	4	29	1	.238
2002 Tampa Bay	281	27	4	33	2	.260
2003 New York - AL	105	16	4	14	0	.267

FLOYD, CLIFF - OF - BL - b: 12/5/72 $18

Before last season, Floyd signed with the Mets, his fourth team in two years. He wanted to make an impression on his newest new team and shed his label of being injury-prone. Despite a sore right heel, he tried to play hurt. Finally, in August, the combination of pain and the Mets' hopelessness was great enough to cause him to undergo Achilles surgery. The only apparent effect on his play was that he couldn't run well. For the sixth consecutive season, he batted .288 or better. Because he was one of New York's few power sources, pitchers worked around him so he had a career best walk/strikeout ratio. When he's ready to play this season, he should hit well.

	AB	R	HR	RBI	SB	BA
2001 Florida	555	123	31	103	18	.317
2002 FLA/MON/BOS	520	86	28	79	15	.288
2003 New York - NL	365	57	18	68	3	.290

FORD, LEW - OF - BR - b: 5/4/68 $3

Lew Ford has lined himself up to grab a 2004 spot on a major league roster. Ford has good speed and a solid arm. He can play all three outfield spots, but is most comfortable in left. He has a short, quick swing that has impressed scouts. He doesn't get jammed much and can come off the bench and get a hit. The only drawback is that he's pretty much a pull hitter. But his speed, arm and stroke makes him a perfect backup outfielder. With some experience, he could develop into an everyday player.

FORDYCE, BROOK - C - BR - b: 5/7/70 $2

Fordyce made the most of the greatest amount of playing time in his nine major league seasons. He hit about .300 after the All-Star break, after Geronimo Gil's anemic bat took him out of the lineup. Fordyce is an aggressive, if impatient, hitter. He won't wait out pitchers, but he makes good contact. He showed better power before coming over from the White Sox in 2001. Fordyce is below average at throwing out base stealers, but is considered a positive influence on his teammates. He also endeared himself to management by participating in a blood bank, one of owner Peter Angelos' favorite charitable endeavors.

	AB	R	HR	RBI	SB	BA
2001 Baltimore	292	30	5	19	1	.209
2002 Baltimore	130	7	1	8	1	.231
2003 Baltimore	348	28	6	31	2	.273

FOX, ANDY - 2B - BL - b: 1/12/71 $0

Fox has a job because he plays every infield position, except for catcher. Fox can also play the outfield. He has little power or speed, but he is still able to hit around .250 hitter so don't go by his .194 bating average last year. He will almost certainly return to a reserve role this season, but he has shown that he can fill-in capably when needed.

	AB	R	HR	RBI	SB	BA
2001 Florida	81	8	3	7	1	.185
2002 Florida	435	55	4	41	31	.251
2003 Florida	108	12	0	8	1	.194

FRANCO, JULIO - 1B - BR - b: 8/23/61 $3

Despite celebrating his 42nd birthday in August, Julio Franco remained a viable hitter for the Braves in 2003, delivering a good batting average and occasional power while sharing a first base job with Robert Fick and Matt Franco. He still has surprising agility around the first base bag, and decent speed on the basepaths. A patient hitter, Franco displays a batting stance that has prompted many a broadcaster to advise, "kids, don't try this at home" as he stands knock-kneed with the bat wrapped around his head, pointed at the pitcher. He unravels from this stance while swinging, so pitchers who can ruin his timing will have success against Franco. Because of his advanced age, it is hard to believe Franco will continue to have a significant future as a ballplayer, but as long as he can produce like he has the last few years, he'll continue to get a chance.

	AB	R	HR	RBI	SB	BA
2001 Atlanta	90	13	3	11	0	.300
2002 Atlanta	338	51	6	30	5	.284
2003 Atlanta	197	28	5	31	0	.294

FRANCO, MATT - 1B - BL - b: 8/19/69 $0

The Braves see Matt Franco as a good clutch hitter and they use him most often as their primary lefty bat off the bench. Yet, Franco has struggled as a pinch-hitter, batting below .200 in more than a hundred appearances in that role the last three years. A more successful role for Franco has been to platoon at first base, where he wields an above-average glove; he can also play either corner outfield position in an extreme emergency. Franco has just average speed, but he will try for an extra base when the opportunity presents itself. He's a hard-nosed player who provides intangibles such as being a clubhouse leader and the Braves seemed to be enamored of him. But if Franco cannot hit better in a pinch-hitting role, it is hard to see how he can contribute enough to the team to warrant a big-league roster spot in 2004.

	AB	R	HR	RBI	SB	BA
2002 Atlanta	205	25	6	30	1	.317
2003 Atlanta	134	11	3	15	0	.246

FREEL, RYAN - OF - BR - b: 3/8/76 $7

At age 28, Freel has neither the ability nor the time to develop into a regular. He is utility player whose best position is second base but he can play third, left and center fairly well. He was in the majors last year because the Reds were stuck with Wily Mo Pena and they needed a guy who could fill in, in the outfield and infield so they could overcome the roster drag of keeping Pena in the majors. Freel will probably see more time in the minors this year than he did in 2003.

	AB	R	HR	RBI	SB	BA
2001 Toronto	22	1	0	3	2	.273
2003 Cincinnati	137	23	4	12	9	.285

FULLMER, BRAD - DH - BL - b: 1/17/75 $9

Fullmer missed over half of last season with a ruptured right patella tendon, but was expected to be ready for spring training. A muscular hitter with good power to right and center field, Fullmer generally puts the ball in play. He has decent speed for a first baseman/DH and will generally steal few bases each year. Lefties with good breaking stuff have given him trouble, so Fullmer has generally been platooned. Since he is below average defensively, Fullmer's best niche is as a designated hitter. If healthy, Fullmer can be expected to get at least 400 at-bats in a full season.

	AB	R	HR	RBI	SB	BA
2001 Toronto	522	71	18	83	5	.274
2002 Anaheim	429	75	19	59	10	.289
2003 Anaheim	206	32	9	35	5	.306

FURCAL, RAFAEL - SS - BR - b: 8/24/80 $27

Entering the 2003 season at the age of 25, Rafael Furcal made expected progress as a hitter, increasing his power output while reducing his strikeout rate. Furcal swung at fewer bad pitches as he hit leadoff for the Braves, one of the most potent offensive clubs in recent memory, so it should be no surprise that he placed among league leaders in runs scored; he also was among leaders in hits, triples, steals and was the league's most difficult batter to double up. Furcal combines his moderate power with outstanding speed; he led the Braves in steals and was caught just twice all year. Furcal seemed to be able to steal at will, but was held back because the club used more of a power-hitting approach than one-run strategies like stolen bases; if pressed into making more attempts, Furcal could steal 50 bases in a season. Although he made history by turning just the 12th unassisted triple play in major league history, it was a disappointing season for Furcal on defense. He made far too many careless errors at shortstop and often got into a mechanical funk which caused his throws to sail. With Wilson Betemit and others progressing in the Braves farm system, Furcal will need to improve his defense at shortstop or move to third base. Either way, he'll remain one of the game's better young hitters in 2004.

	AB	R	HR	RBI	SB	BA
2001 Atlanta	324	39	4	30	22	.275
2002 Atlanta	636	95	8	47	27	.275
2003 Atlanta	664	130	15	61	25	.292

GALARRAGA, ANDRES - 1B - BR - b: 6/18/61 $7

Although Galarraga is long past his prime and is not longer young enough to withstand the rigors of everyday duty, he still has some punch left in his arms. The gray-haired slugger started a little more than half the time for the Giants last year and thrived in that part-time role. While Galarraga talked about retiring late in 2003, he was expected to play at least one more season. He is only two home runs away from 400 in his career, and that is a mark that Galarraga wants to achieve. He still has the ability to hit lefthanded pitchers with authority, so bringing him back for another year would not be the worst thing for a club to do.

	AB	R	HR	RBI	SB	BA
2001 TEX/SF	399	50	17	69	1	..256
2002 Montreal	292	30	9	40	2	.260
2003 San Francisco	272	36	12	42	1	.301

GARCIA, JESSE - 2B - BR - b: 9/24/73 $0

For the last three years, Jesse Garcia has been like the 26th man on the Braves' 25-man roster. Whenever they need to fill an opening for an infielder, Garcia gets the call. Mostly, though, he bides his time at Triple-A Richmond. In 2003, Garcia again hit over .300, but again did not translate that hitting into major league success. He's an aggressive, slap hitter who rarely walks and doesn't strike out much, either. Garcia has good wheels; he was second with 29 steals for Richmond and was often used as a pinch-runner in his big-league stints. Garcia handles middle infield duty well enough, but his disappointing on-base ability - despite his good batting average - will limit his overall usefulness.

	AB	R	HR	RBI	SB	BA
2001 Atlanta	5	3	0	0	6	.200
2002 Atlanta	61	6	0	5	0	.197
2003 Atlanta	10	6	0	2	0	.400

GARCIA, KARIM - OF - BL - b: 10/29/75 $7

For the second consecutive year, the Yankees acquired Garcia in midseason. This time he stuck, and batted .305 over the season's final 52 games. Garcia is one of the majors' most extreme streak hitters. When he's on, he's an extremely dangerous power hitter. But just as quickly as he gets into a hot streak, his batting can fall into a deep depression. For example, after returning to the Indians in 2002, he hit 16 homers and drove in 52 runs in 51 games. Last season, he was batting just .194 in 24 games for the Tribe. In a platoon role, mostly in right field, for New York, he battered righthanders at a .321 rate. Garcia hasn't stolen a base in the majors since 1999.

	AB	R	HR	RBI	SB	BA
2001 Cleveland	45	8	5	9	0	.311
2002 NY - AL/CLE	202	30	16	52	0	.297
2003 CLE/ NY - AL	244	25	11	35	0	.262

GARCIAPARRA, NOMAR - SS - BR - b: 7/23/73 $29

No player in Boston is more popular than Garciaparra. Last season wasn't his best, but it was one when he avoided most of the nagging injuries that have kept him out in the past. Garciaparra showed better speed in 2003, as evidenced by his increased numbers of stolen bases and triples. He is an extremely aggressive hitter; pitchers sometimes can get ahead of him by making him chase pitches off the plate. Garciaparra neither walks nor strikes out often, and is extremely dangerous against lefthanders. In the field, he earned another shot at remaining a shortstop by cutting down his errors. However, his range also decreased. He may be playing third base not too far into the future.

	AB	R	HR	RBI	SB	BA
2001 Boston	83	13	4	8	0	.289
2002 Boston	635	101	24	120	5	.310
2003 Boston	658	120	28	105	19	.301

GERMAN, ESTEBAN - 2B - BR - b: 12/26/78 $0

German was perhaps the fastest player in Oakland's minor league system last year, and his 32 stolen bases for Triple-A Sacramento is an indication that the Athletics believed that he could be a real force on the basepaths. German doesn't have a lot of power, and it's unlikely that he would hit even 10 homers in the big leagues. He did improve his swing last season and began to hit many more doubles. His speed also makes him a gifted fielder who has great range at second base. If he can earn a starting spot this spring, German could end up challenging for a stolen base title. He is incredibly fast, will hit around .300 and loves to take a walk. He would make an excellent leadoff hitter.

GERUT, JODY - OF - BL - b: 9/18/77 $16

Gerut had a brilliant year for someone who had never played an inning of major league baseball. He took over as the regular outfielder for Cleveland in the wake of the disabilities of Matt Lawton, Milton Bradley and Ellis Burks. A sophomore slump is a possibility for Gerut, for no better a reason than he is a sophomore. Expect a bit of a fall off.

	AB	R	HR	RBI	SB	BA
2003 Cleveland	480	66	22	75	4	.279

GETTIS, BYRON - OF - BR - b: 3/13/80 $0

Byron Gettis is a bundle of athletic talent who developed slowly until 2003 when he burst upon the Double-A Texas League by challenging for the league batting and RBI titles. An undrafted free agent who eschewed an opportunity to play college football in 2000, Gettis is an excellent defensive outfielder who uses his above-average speed well and has a strong throwing arm. He had made gradual progress through two seasons in Single-A ball, hitting for a bit of power and getting on base at a decent rate. In 2003 he added a lot of power while improving his on-base rate to lead Wichita in nearly every offensive category. With Alexis Gomez's disappointing season, Gettis has moved into a position to challenge for the everyday centerfield job should Carlos Beltran leave Kansas City. A repeat of his 2003 success in 2004 would make Gettis a front-runner for regular major league duty by 2005.

GIAMBI, JASON - 1B/DH - BL - b: 1/8/71 $21

Did Giambi begin to grow old in 2003? Did his eyes bother him? Or was it just a bad year with a season-long slump? He had the lowest average of his nine-year career, with a 64-point drop from the year before and a 92-point decline since 2001. Lefthanders absolutely ate Giambi up, holding him to a .192 average, but he batted just .267 against righties. He struck out a career-high 140 times but refuting the eye-problem theory, he hit better at night than during the day. Giambi appeared to be out of his slump when he batted .373 during June, but he was just a .226 batter after the All-Star game.

	AB	R	HR	RBI	SB	BA
2001 Oakland	520	109	38	120	2	.342
2002 New York - AL	560	120	41	122	2	.314
2003 New York - AL	535	97	41	107	2	.250

GIAMBI, JEREMY - DH - BL - b: 9/30/74 $7

Jason Giambi's little brother has shown only flashes of the same ability. And if you thought Jason had a bad 2003 season, it was a picnic compared to Jeremy's. After showing power and on-base ability in Oakland and Philadelphia, he signed with the Red Sox before last season. The year ended Aug. 1 for him because of shoulder surgery, which was one reason why he contributed little to the Sox at the plate. David Ortiz took the role anticipated for Giambi, and ran with it. Still, Giambi walked about once every six plate appearances and stole his first base in the majors.

	AB	R	HR	RBI	SB	BA
2001 Oakland	371	64	12	57	0	.283
2002 Philadelphia	313	58	20	45	0	.259
2003 Boston	127	15	5	15	1	.197

GIBBONS, JAY- OF - BL - b: 3/2/77 $15

Gibbons had a breakthrough year in 2003, the kind of year the Orioles envisioned when they made him a Rule 5 draft pick in 2000. He drove in 100 runs for the first time, and had a career-best .277 average. That was largely because, for the first time in the majors, he hit for almost the same average against lefthanded pitchers that he did against righties. Though he's not considered to have a good arm, he has been able to throw out overly aggressive baserunners. Gibbons slumped late in the season. However, especially if he gets some help in the lineup, he should become a dangerous run producer.

	AB	R	HR	RBI	SB	BA
2001 Baltimore	225	27	15	36	0	.236
2002 Baltimore	490	71	28	69	1	.247
2003 Baltimore	625	80	23	100	0	.277

GIL, BENJI - 2B/SS - BR - b: 10/6/72 $0

In parts of eight major league seasons, Gil has had two solid years at the plate - 2001 and 2002. His performance last season was more typical of his early career. At best, Gil is a decent backup, capable of playing all four infield positions. He does not hit well enough to play regularly, although he has a little speed and can hit an occasional home run. Gil strikes out a lot and is one of the toughest hitters in the major leagues to walk. He was expected to compete for a backup infield job this spring.

	AB	R	HR	RBI	SB	BA
2001 Anaheim	260	33	8	39	3	.296
2002 Anaheim	130	11	3	20	2	.285
2003 Anaheim	125	12	1	9	5	.192

GILES, BRIAN - OF - BL - b: 1/20/71 $23

Giles is one of the most underrated good players in the major leagues. Wanting to add some clout for their first season at Petco Park in 2004, the Padres obtained him for prospects Jason Bay and Eric Cyr last August. Giles brings the complete package to the plate. He has hit 35 or more homers four times in the last five seasons with a short powerful swing that makes him hard to fool. He turns well on inside pitches and can drive the outside pitch to the opposite gap. He has good strike zone knowledge and does not chase bad pitches as pitchers often try to work around him. Giles is not a pretty runner, although he is faster than he looks. He is aggressive and looks to steal a base. He can play all three outfield positions, although his range and arm are best-suited for left. In left, he is a premier player. Giles was expected to open the season as a corner outfielder, and should return to 35-110 form.

	AB	R	HR	RBI	SB	BA
2001 Pittsburgh	576	116	37	95	13	.309
2002 Pittsburgh	497	95	38	103	15	.298
2003 PIT/SD	492	93	20	88	4	.299

GILES, MARCUS - 2B - BR - b: 5/18/78 $23

Perhaps the most unlikely member of the Bombardier Braves, Giles had a breakout year in 2003, hitting for a high average and above-average power while holding down a spot near the top of the batting order; it was an outstanding season for Giles after splitting most of the previous two years with Mark DeRosa. Giles rebounded nicely from a concussion suffered in a collision with Mark Prior; it cost him an appearance in the All-Star game, but two weeks later Giles recorded hits in nine straight at-bats, one shy of the National League record. Giles is an aggressive hitter who takes advantage of pitchers who don't want to give him a free pass in front of the meat of the Braves batting order. Finesse pitchers who can hit spots will give Giles the most trouble, although he will punish mistakes. Giles maintains his aggressiveness in the rest of his game, too. His fielding errors usually come as a result of trying to make an impossible fielding play, and he has run into some outs on the bases. Giles teams with Rafael Furcal to give the Braves one of the best keystone tandems in baseball.

	AB	R	HR	RBI	SB	BA
2001 Atlanta	244	36	9	31	2	.262
2002 Atlanta	213	27	8	23	1	.230
2003 Atlanta	551	101	21	69	14	.316

GINTER, KEITH - 2B/3B - BR - b: 5/5/76 $7

Ginter, one of the victims of a bizarre hotel robbery and assault while with Houston several spring trainings ago, made a statement in his first season of full-time major league duty in Milwaukee. Ginter set career highs in all categories when finally getting a chance to start both at second base and third. He has a short, quick stroke with which he generates surprising power for a man his size. He knows the strike zone and will take a walk, although his aggressive approach also leads to strikeouts. His speed is slightly above average, although he is not fast enough to be a stolen base threat. A second baseman in the minors, Ginter was more scrappy than fluid at either second or third in 2003, although his fielding percentage at third was good. He was expected to compete for a starting job at second base, his best position.

	AB	R	HR	RBI	SB	BA
2001 Houston	1	0	0	0	0	.000
2002 Milwaukee	81	7	1	8	0	.235
2003 Milwaukee	358	51	14	44	1	.257

GIRARDI, JOE - C - BR - b: 10/14/64 $0

Back problems dogged Girardi from spring training on, and limited the veteran backstop to a career low number of games played. He had been living on inflated offensive numbers from a three-year stint in Colorado, and the respect he got from New Yorkers from his time with the Yankees. He has had virtually nothing to offer the previous couple of seasons, and it wasn't a surprise that age and injuries finally caught up with him in 2003. Girardi is about done as a big league player. He might be able to squeeze another year out of his body, though it is more likely that he won't be able to convince a team to take a chance on him.

	AB	R	HR	RBI	SB	BA
2001 Chicago - NL	229	22	3	25	0	.253
2002 Chicago - NL	234	19	1	13	1	.226
2003 St. Louis	23	1	0	1	0	.130

GLANVILLE, DOUG - OF - BR - b: 8/25/70 $4

While Glanville offers next to nothing at the plate at this point in his career, he is not the worst ballplayer around. He is a dependable outfielder and he has some speed, which gives him some value as a late-inning replacement, either in the field or on the basepaths. Earlier in his career he was good for 25-30 steals a year, though his current inability to get on base consistently means he is no longer a significant threat to run. It should be obvious, given that his slugging percentage is less than .350 combined over the last two seasons, that Glanville is not going to be an everyday player. However, he should be able to latch on with a club who is looking for a veteran who won't

---

grumble about playing time.

	AB	R	HR	RBI	SB	BA
2001 Philadelphia	634	74	14	55	28	.262
2002 Philadelphia	422	49	6	29	19	.249
2003 TEX/ CHI - NL	246	24	5	16	4	.264

GLAUS, TROY - 3B - BR - b: 4/1/77 $13

A dead-fastball hitter, Glaus has a classic righthanded power swing, pulling the ball to left and left-center field. Glaus sees a lot of pitches; he strikes out a lot and draws his share of walks as well. Although he has hit better than .250 only once in his major league career, Glaus is a solid run producer. He has surprisingly good speed and good base running technique. Glaus is a good fielder at third base. Last season, he missed most of the last half with a torn right rotator cuff that he was planning to rehabilitate without surgery. The Angels were hopeful that Glaus would be healthy by the start of spring training.

	AB	R	HR	RBI	SB	BA
2001 Anaheim	588	100	41	108	10	.250
2002 Anaheim	569	99	30	111	10	.250
2003 Anaheim	319	53	16	50	7	.248

GOMEZ, CHRIS - 2B - BR - b: 6/16/71 $1

A former starting shortstop, Chris Gomez has embraced the utility role. He's learned to play second and third base, making him the perfect late inning defensive replacement. There's still some pop in his bat, but has not been much of a pinch-hitter. The major drawback is his knees. The wear and tear and surgeries on them have taken their toll, but Gomez doesn't use it as an excuse. He shakes off bad games or slumps well and blends in well with clubhouse chemistry. He's just not an every day player at this stage of his career.

	AB	R	HR	RBI	SB	BA
2001 SD/TB	301	37	8	43	4	.259
2002 Tampa Bay	461	51	10	46	1	.265
2003 Minnesota	175	14	1	15	2	.251

GONZALEZ, ADRIAN - 1B - BL - b: 5/8/82 $1

Gonzalez was a 2000 first-round pick of the Marlins out of high school. He has progressed slowly but steadily through the minors and should challenge for a roster spot sometime in 2004. He projects as a high-average hitter with good power, but it may be a couple of years before his power kicks in. Gonzalez fields well enough to play first base in the majors.

GONZALEZ, ALEX - SS - BR - b: 2/15/77 $8

His .256 batting average and 18 home runs were career bests for Gonzalez. Given his age Gonzalez should be able to maintain his power and bring his average up 10 or 15 points but that represents the limit of his offensive output: 20 home runs and a .270 average with little speed. Gonzalez is only a bit above average in the field.

	AB	R	HR	RBI	SB	BA
2001 Florida	515	57	9	48	2	.250
2002 Florida	151	15	2	18	3	.225
2003 Florida	528	52	18	77	0	.256

GONZALEZ, ALEX S. - SS - BR - b: 4/8/73 $9

Cubs skipper Dusty Baker soured on Gonzalez in the second half of last season, and with good reason. Gonzalez, while equaling his career best home run mark with several weeks still remaining in the year, did nothing else at the plate. Opposing pitchers were able to exploit his tendency to swing at pitches far outside the strike zone, and when he became shaky in the field he quickly fell out of favor with Baker. Gonzalez isn't quite as bad as his 2003 numbers. Given

---

a starting spot, he would perform about as he did from 2000-02, where he hit about .250 with 15-18 homers. However, his performance last season means he will have to earn an everyday position in spring training, and he doesn't have the kind of ability to stand out in a crowd. It's likely that he will spend this season in a reserve role.

	AB	R	HR	RBI	SB	BA
2001 Toronto	636	79	17	76	18	.253
2002 Chicago - NL	513	58	18	61	5	.248
2003 Chicago - NL	536	71	20	59	3	.228

GONZALEZ, JUAN - OF/DH - BR - b: 10/16/69 $10

When he is healthy, Gonzalez is a big-time power threat, especially against lefty pitching. Over the last few years, health has been a major issue for Gonzalez, and last year he was sidelined for an extended period with a strained calf muscle. Not the type to play through an injury, Gonzalez is unusually susceptible to missing playing time in any given season. His talent is undeniable, and the two-time MVP still has the ability to put together a big year if everything goes well. When Gonzalez gets on a hot streak, he can carry a team for weeks at a time.

	AB	R	HR	RBI	SB	BA
2001 Cleveland	532	97	35	140	1	.325
2002 Texas	277	38	8	35	2	.282
2003 Texas	327	49	24	70	1	.294

GONZALEZ, LUIS - OF - BL - b: 9/3/67 $24

Having found an oasis in the desert since arriving in 1999, Gonzalez led Arizona in virtually every run production category again in 2003. His unorthodox, wide-open stance works for him, and that is all that matters. He sets up a la Brian Downing, although in the opposite batters box, with his front foot exaggerated toward the line and his back foot on the chalk. As a result, he seldom gets jammed, as was once his problem, and instead can drive the inside pitch to right and right-center. Opponents started pounding him outside, but he has been able to get the fat part of the bat on those pitches, also. He is smart and aggressive enough to steal a base or two, but half a dozen is his limit. He plays a deep left field to keep the ball in front of him and has a limited arm because of shoulder surgery years ago while in the Houston organization, although he is acrobatic enough to steal home runs by scaling the 8-foot fence at Bank One Ballpark. He signed a three-year, $30 million contract extension that will keep him the starting left fielder through 2006. He has 30-homer, 110-RBI pop.

	AB	R	HR	RBI	SB	BA
2001 Arizona	609	128	57	142	1	.325
2002 Arizona	524	90	28	103	9	.288
2003 Arizona	579	92	26	104	5	.304

GONZALEZ, RAUL - OF - BR - b: 12/27/73 $0

It took Gonzalez nine years to get to play above Double-A. Now it seems as if it will take nine more to get him out of the Mets outfield, even though he contributes almost nothing to their offense. Last season, when he played in 107 games, he did show some of the plate discipline that he developed during those years in the minors. He slumped badly after the All-Star break, batting .202 with no homers. The roly-poly Gonzalez, listed at 5'9" and 190 pounds, hustles and runs faster than he would appear able. Think of him as Benny Agbayani without the power.

	AB	R	HR	RBI	SB	BA
2002 CIN/NY - NL	104	13	3	12	4	.260
2003 New York - NL	217	28	2	21	3	.230

GOODWIN, TOM - OF - BL - b: 7/27/68 $8

Goodwin is able to stick around despite having limited ability because he knows his role and doesn't complain about not being in the starting lineup. He never had any power in his bat, and now struggles at times just to get on base regularly. Goodwin had some leg problems in 2003, an indication that he is losing much of his speed. He can provide help to a club looking for a late-inning defensive replacement or a bat off the bench. However, asking him to do anything more is asking for a whole lot of trouble. Don't be surprised if he has to go to Triple-A and spend time there before getting playing time in the majors this year.

	AB	R	HR	RBI	SB	BA
2001 Los Angeles	286	51	4	22	22	.231
2002 San Francisco	154	23	1	17	16	.260
2003 Chicago - NL	171	26	1	12	19	.287

GRACE, MARK - 1B - BL - b: 6/28/64 $0

Grace opted to give it one more shot in 2003, signing a one-year contract with an option worth $1.75 million in guaranteed salary. It was hard to blame him for taking the money rather than moving into the broadcast booth, but Grace's skills were eroded to the point that he could not get into the lineup despite the fact that Arizona's offense was puny all year. Grace's bat slowed to the point that he had difficulty pulling the ball, and he could barely put into play balls that he routinely turned into gap doubles earlier in his 15-year career. Grace remained a solid defender and motivating clubhouse presence, but it was clear that he was at the end of the line. Grace talked in the spring about staying in the game as a coach or manager when his playing days were over, and he would be a viable candidate for any major league coaching vacancy.

	AB	R	HR	RBI	SB	BA
2001 Arizona	476	66	15	78	1	.298
2002 Arizona	298	43	7	48	2	.252
2003 Arizona	135	13	3	16	0	.200

GRAFFANINO, TONY - 2B/3B/SS - BR - b: 6/6/72 $5

Graffanino is a nice guy to have around. He can play all four infield positions relatively well, and while his offense isn't good enough to make him a starter, he won't embarrass anybody if he needs to fill in for a few days because of an injury. He has a good knowledge of the strike zone, and a little bit of pop in his bat, which makes for a good guy to have coming off the bench to hit in the late innings. Graffanino has never been a full-time player since making his big league debut in 1996, and he won't become one this season. Expect him to keep his current role, which could include a start or two a week against lefthanded pitching.

	AB	R	HR	RBI	SB	BA
2001 Florida	145	23	2	15	4	.303
2002 Chicago - NL	229	35	6	31	2	.262
2003 Chicago - NL	250	51	7	23	8	.260

GREEN, SHAWN - OF - BL - b: 11/10/72 $23

Green finally told reporters what insiders suspected for most of 2003, that his numbers were down because he was trying to play through an injury. Green underwent shoulder surgery after the 2003 season, the least productive of his last half-dozen as a full-fledged regular. Green has a quick and ferocious bat, and he is able to attack and drive anything on the inner half. (He is one of the few lefthanded hitters who starts against Randy Johnson, and he holds his own.) While the shoulder injury deprived him of home run power, Green still maintained his ability to drive the ball into both gaps. He is a selective hitter and works deep into counts waiting for his pitch. Green has very good speed and is an intelligent baserunner. A 30-30 man in 1998, Green does not run as much as he once did but still is very capable of stealing 10-15 bases should he choose. He covers a lot of ground, charges the ball well, and has an above-average if not cannonesque arm. Green was expected to be the No. 3 or 4 hitter and everyday player, although there was talk he might be moved to first base.

	AB	R	HR	RBI	SB	BA
2001 Los Angeles	619	121	49	125	20	.297
2002 Los Angeles	582	110	42	114	8	.285
2003 Los Angeles	611	84	19	85	6	.280

GREENE, TODD - C - BR - b: 5/8/71 $0

Greene has resurrected his career as a backup catcher in the big leagues. He is only adequate behind the plate, but hits for much more power than the average catcher and can serve as a platoon DH or backup first baseman as well. Greene is a low-average hitter and its almost impossible for him to take a walk, attributes that will keep him from playing regularly in the future.

	AB	R	HR	RBI	SB	BA
2001 New York - AL	96	9	1	11	0	.208
2002 Texas	112	15	10	19	0	.268
2003 Texas	205	25	10	20	0	.229

GREER, RUSTY - DH - BL - b: 1/21/69 $0

Greer has become the poster child for orthopedic surgeons everywhere. Since he last played in 2002, he has undergone shoulder surgery and has had a ligament transplant in his left elbow. Knee and hip surgeries were also on the horizon for Greer, but he had some thought of delaying those in an attempt to play toward the end of the coming season. If Greer succeeds in playing at all in 2004, it will likely be just a few games toward the very end of the season.

	AB	R	HR	RBI	SB	BA
2001 Texas	245	38	7	29	1	.273
2002 Texas	199	24	1	17	1	.296
2003 Texas	199	24	1	17	1	.296

GRIEVE, BEN - DH - BL - b: 5/4/76 $4

Grieve has regressed since 2001. His power numbers have fallen off, his batting average has dropped and strikeout rate has stayed high. He needs to improve his mental approach to the game. He missed most of 2003 to injuries including an infected thumb, a blood clot, and rib removal surgery. Even with a full recovery to his health, Grieve will have to start producing again if he doesn't want to wind up spending even more time on the bench.

	AB	R	HR	RBI	SB	BA
2001 Tampa Bay	542	72	11	72	7	.264
2002 Tampa Bay	482	62	19	64	8	.251
2003 Tampa Bay	165	28	4	17	0	.230

GRIFFEY, KEN JR. - OF - BL - b: 11/21/69 $4

My Kingdom for a Hearse! Being in shape or out of shape doesn't seem to matter, does it? Griffey actually worked out and got into shape in the winter and he lasted exactly five games before he dislocated his shoulder diving for a ball. It's almost unnerving to watch Griffey on the field because he still looks and sometimes plays as we remember him in his prime. Griffey is still a very good center fielder and he still effortlessly whips his hands through the hitting zone and balls well struck rocket off his bat and go far into the night. His physical deterioration is surreal; a man's body worn fragile from the stresses of housing the most superhuman, natural abilityever seen in the game.

	AB	R	HR	RBI	SB	BA
2001 Cincinnati	364	57	22	65	2	.286
2002 Cincinnati	197	17	8	23	1	.264
2003 Cincinnati	166	34	13	26	1	.247

GRISSOM, MARQUIS - OF - BR - b: 4/17/67 $18

Grissom surprised nearly everyone in 2003, putting together a solid season as a starter, perhaps his best since 1996. He fit perfectly in the Giants batting order, and took advantage of hitting ahead of Barry Bonds. He got plenty of pitches to hit and he took advantage of that opportunity to post the second highest batting average of his career. He has lost much of his speed and is no longer a consistent threat on the basepaths. He has enough experience, however, to steal the occasional base. Expect Grissom to return at least a little closer to reality this year. He lacks the patience at the plate to be a consistent leadoff hitter, meaning he is much more likely to hit around .250 than he is to hit .300 again.

	AB	R	HR	RBI	SB	BA
2001 Los Angeles	448	56	21	60	7	.221
2002 Cincinnati	343	57	17	60	5	.277
2003 San Francisco	587	82	20	79	11	.300

GROSS, GABE - OF - BL - b: 10/21/79 $3

A top athlete who was the starting quarterback for Auburn as a freshman, Gross had already exceeded expectations in 2003 by graduating from Double-A and holding a batting average around .290 with power for much of the time in Triple-A. In 2002 he had his share of problems, mostly during the first half of the season. His batting average was .238 that year. The main issue was quickness with his hands, and Gross has answered the skeptics this year. His arm is good enough for right field in the majors.

GRUDZIELANEK, MARK - 2B - BR - b: 6/30/70 $13

The Cubs fell in love with Grudzielanek from day one last year. He was a consistent, though unspectacular, hitter all season and provided the organization with the type of veteran player that it loves to have in the lineup. Still, it's hard to see why he was so popular with fans and management. He has next to no power – not even the short power alleys in Wrigley Field could help him there – and has no speed or basestealing ability. He is relatively solid with the glove, though his range is limited and he rarely comes up with a play worthy of the highlight reel. While Grudzielanek will be a starter again this season, he will hold onto that job only until someone better comes along.

	AB	R	HR	RBI	SB	BA
2001 Los Angeles	539	83	13	55	4	.271
2002 Los Angeles	536	56	9	50	4	.271
2003 Chicago - NL	481	73	3	38	6	.314

GUERRERO, VLADIMIR - OF - BR - b: 2/9/76 $35

Back trouble shelved him for seven weeks in early June. When he returned, he hit the way he always does, which is better than just about any player in the game. Frank Robinson pulled him off the field in the Expos last home game so that the fans could give the free agent the kind of cheer that the best player in Expos history should receive, so they booed him. They should have turned off the lights then and there and sent everyone home and the team to Portland.

	AB	R	HR	RBI	SB	BA
2001 Montreal	599	107	34	108	16	.307
2002 Montreal	614	106	39	111	40	.336
2003 Montreal	394	71	25	79	9	.330

GUIEL, AARON - OF - BL - b: 10/5/72 $13

The second most powerful bat in the Royals lineup, behind Carlos Beltran did not belong to Mike Sweeney; Aaron Guiel hit as many homers as Sweeney, and was the only Royals player besides Beltran to slug over .500. Despite not being recalled to the majors until the end of May, Guiel worked his way from the bench to a starting role. Once given the leadoff job, Guiel showed outstanding on-base ability as well as unexpected power. He'll work the count as a leadoff hitter but will pull the ball for extra bases when hitting in an RBI spot. Although he's not the smoothest of outfielders - nor the fastest - Guiel gets the job done with good reads and a fearlessness both in the outfield and on the bases; his arm is adequate for rightfield. Guiel was very close to quitting baseball altogether not long ago. Now, after nearly a decade and a thousand at-bats in the minors, he's earned at least a big-league platoon role.

	AB	R	HR	RBI	SB	BA
2002 Kansas City	240	30	4	38	1	.233
2003 Kansas City	354	63	15	52	3	.277

GUILLEN, CARLOS - 3B/SS - BB - b: 9/3/75 $8

Guillen, a shortstop since being acquired from Houston in the Randy Johnson trading deadline deal in 1998, became the regular third baseman down the stretch in 2003 and had two five-RBI games at that position. He struggled with pelvis and groin injuries but otherwise was the same guy, a slasher who puts the ball in play from both sides of the plate. He does not have the kind of power managers look for on the corner infield, however. Guillen has good plate discipline and gets more than his share of walks for a "little ball" guy, although his speed which is only average and inability to steal a basis doom him to a lower spot in the order. He is a solid defender with major league-caliber range and arm at shortstop. He was expected to play an integral role in the infield, whether at shortstop or third base.

	AB	R	HR	RBI	SB	BA
2001 Seattle	456	72	5	53	4	.259
2002 Seattle	475	73	9	56	4	.261
2003 Seattle	388	63	7	52	4	.276

GUILLEN, JOSE - OF - BR - b: 5/17/76 $19

Overall, Guillen had a fantastic 2003 season, especially since he began the season in the minor leagues. Given a chance in Cincinnati when Ken Griffey Jr. went on the DL in the first week of the campaign, Guillen responded by consistently hitting the ball before he was traded to the Athletics. In the American League, Guillen's weaknesses were exploited regularly and he struggled more often. He has a poor knowledge of the strike zone and consistently chases balls well off the plate. Guillen has some speed, though his over-aggressiveness costs him on the basepaths. He has one of the best outfield arms in all of baseball and saves plenty of runs with his throwing ability. It's certainly possible that Guillen has figured things out and will be a productive player this season. However, it's much more plausible that Guillen will drop back to his career levels. He just has too many holes in his swing to be a legitimate and consistent offensive threat.

	AB	R	HR	RBI	SB	BA
2001 Tampa Bay	135	14	3	11	2	.274
2002 Cincinnati	240	25	8	31	4	.238
2003 CIN/OAK	485	77	31	86	1	.311

GUTIERREZ, RICKY - SS - BR - b: 5/23/70 $0

Cleveland signed the former Cubs shortstop and moved him to second base to replace Roberto Alomar in 2002. In 2003, he worked hard and tried to come back from spinal fusion surgery but, he was not ready and had to shut it down for the year after playing only fifteen games. Even at age 34, Gutierrez will be on a major league roster if he's healthy, because he has good plate discipline with a good batting eye. He doesn't have much power or basestealing speed.

	AB	R	HR	RBI	SB	BA
2001 Chicago - NL	528	76	10	66	4	.290
2002 Cleveland	353	38	4	38	0	.275
2003 Cleveland	50	2	0	3	0	.260

GUZMAN, CRISTIAN - SS - BB - b: 3/21/78 $15

Guzman is entering an crucial period in his career. He's in the final year of his multi-year contract and really hasn't put up the numbers worthy of such a deal. He strikes out too much for someone who doesn't have a lot of power. Then again, he doesn't hit the ball over the fence much for someone with decent strength. He can run, but doesn't steal many bases. He doesn't walk or consistently bunt well. He's adequate in the field. Guzman is an enigma because the physical

---

tools are there. He hasn't put them together since being an All-Star in 2001.

		AB	R	HR	RBI	SB	BA
2001	Minnesota	493	80	10	51	25	.302
2002	Minnesota	623	80	9	59	12	.273
2003	Minnesota	534	78	3	53	18	.268

GUZMAN, EDWARDS - 3B - BL - b: 9/11/76 $0

Guzman was the other player that the Expos got along with Livan Hernandez when they sent Jim Brower to the Giants in 2002. In addition to filling in at both corner infield spots, Guzman also filled in a few times as a catcher, which does nothing but help his chance to stay in the majors. Guzman suffers from the same problem that plagues all of Expos utility men. He can't hit.

		AB	R	HR	RBI	SB	BA
2001	San Francisco	115	8	3	7	0	.243
2003	Montreal	146	15	1	14	0	.240

HAFNER, TRAVIS - 1B/DH - BL - b: 6/3/77 $7

Hafner and Ben Broussard split duty at first base for the Indians in 2003, but Broussard played more. The Indians favor Broussard and had Broussard not been injured early in the year, Hafner could well have spent most, if not all of the 2003 season in the minors. To his credit, Hafner took advantage of Broussard's injury and, he hit well enough to make the Indians notice, if not quite rethink their first base plans for 2004. At this point, Hafner must be considered a minor asset for a cost-conscious, rebuilding team. He is a decent first baseman and he has moderate power but, he because he lacks game experience or eye-popping potential, he's on the bubble.

	AB	R	HR	RBI	SB	BA
2003 Cleveland	291	35	14	40	2	.254

HAIRSTON, JERRY - 2B - BR - b: 5/29/76 $6

Hairston was off to the best start of his career — stealing bases, turning double plays and walking more than he struck out, like the leadoff batter the Orioles envisioned. Then a broken right foot sidelined him in May. By the time he returned in September, Brian Roberts had established himself as a major league second baseman. Hairston's foot still wasn't right; he didn't even attempt a stolen base after his return. If Hairston can move well enough to show better-than-average range in the field and steal bases, his career path could remain upward. However, a move to shortstop or to another team seemed in order for him.

		AB	R	HR	RBI	SB	BA
2001	Baltimore	532	63	8	47	29	.233
2002	Baltimore	426	55	5	32	21	.268
2003	Baltimore	218	25	2	21	14	.271

HALL, BILL - 2B/SS - BR - b: 12/28/79 $2

Hall, Milwaukee's minor league player of the year in 2001, got his first extended major league time in 2003 and showed possibilities. Hall had 18 homers in 2001 and showed similar pop with the Brewers. A free-swinger, Hall has the ability to drive the ball into the gaps for extra bases and with his speed can take the extra base. He needs to work on reading moves but has the ability to steal 10-15 bases a year. Hall has a good arm and showed superior range while playing more than a dozen games at both second base and shortstop late in 2003. Hall was expected to contend for a starting middle infield spot, likely shortstop, as the Brewers go to a youth movement.

	AB	R	HR	RBI	SB	BA
2003 Milwaukee	142	23	5	20	1	.261

HALL, TOBY - C - BR - b: 10/21/75 $5

Hall struggled at the plate in 2003 but proved he's capable of producing double-digit home runs in the course of a season. He's a good-looking hitter for a catcher and if he learns to take more pitches, he should start producing decent numbers.

	AB	R	HR	RBI	SB	BA
2001 Tampa Bay	188	28	4	30	2	.298
2002 Tampa Bay	330	37	6	42	0	.258
2003 Tampa Bay	463	50	12	47	0	.253

HALTER, SHANE - 2B/3B/SS - BR - b: 11/8/69 $2

Halter is a Jack-of-many-but-not-all-trades. He played most often at third base but he spent some time at every infield position except catcher. As soon as someone appears that can play every infield position — including catcher — and maybe hit above .225, the 35-year-old Halter will be given a gold watch, the thanks of a grateful nation and bus fare to Toledo.

	AB	R	HR	RBI	SB	BA
2001 Detroit	450	53	12	65	3	.277
2002 Detroit	410	46	10	39	0	.239
2003 Detroit	360	33	12	30	2	.217

HAMMOCK, ROBBY - C - BR - b: 5/13/77 $6

An example of perseverance, Hammock spent five years in the minor leagues following his college career at the University of Georgia before a final polishing in the Arizona Fall League in 2002 proved his readiness for the majors. Hammock, drafted as a catcher out college, has developed into an Eli Marrero jack-of-most-trades, a player with enough agility and athletic ability to play both corner infield spots and both corner outfield spots along with his natural position. Hammock is a line-drive hitter with good power, averaging a home run about every 20 at-bats in his rookie season in 2003. He has decent range in the field and can handle pitchers. His versatility makes him an asset, and his strong rookie season suggests he could challenge for the starting catching position on a team that needs all the offense it can get.

	AB	R	HR	RBI	SB	BA
2003 Arizona	195	30	8	28	3	.282

HAMMONDS, JEFFREY - OF - BR - b: 3/5/71 $0

It's not Hammonds' fault that he got to spend a year playing for the Rockies and hitting in Coors Field. He certainly is not the first below average hitter to put up what appear to be good numbers hitting in the rarified air in Denver (see Charlie Hayes and Dante Bichette). However, the fact that he was released by the lowly Brewers last year, who said they'd rather play John Vander Wal and Brady Clark instead of Hammonds, should explain everything. Hammonds has never been a consistent hitter because he will swing at almost anything. He also is a poor fielder. He doesn't possess good instincts in the field, nor does he have enough speed to make up for his inadequacies. He also has a weak arm. There are enough teams that need help in the outfield for Hammonds to stick around for another year or two. Don't expect him to make much of a contribution, however.

	AB	R	HR	RBI	SB	BA
2001 Milwaukee	174	20	6	21	5	.247
2002 Milwaukee	448	47	9	41	4	.257
2003 MIL/SF	132	22	4	13	1	.242

HANSEN, DAVE - 1B - BL - b: 11/24/68 $0

Hansen has 15 career pinch-hit home runs and over 100 pinch-hits, stats that elegantly sum up his major league career. Hansen has batted more than 150 times in a season only once since 1993, and that was for the Hanshin Tigers in Japan in 1998. Hansen is a good pinch-hitter because he has a solid approach at the plate - he knows the strike zone, lays off marginal strikes and puts the ball in play. He can play both corner infield positions, although he is only an average fielder and is out there only to give a regular a rest. He will not run, which is a good thing he has been successful on only 4 of his 11 major league stolen base attempts. He was expected to assume his customary role as a pinch-hit specialist this season.

	AB	R	HR	RBI	SB	BA
2003 San Diego	135	13	2	15	1	.244

HARRIS, LENNY - 3B - BL - b: 10/28/64 $0

The all time major league leader in pinch hits is age 39. He fills in occasionally at third and in the outfield and he can catch what he can reach but he can't cover much ground now.

	AB	R	HR	RBI	SB	BA
2001 NY - NL	135	12	0	9	3	.222
2002 Milwaukee	197	23	3	17	4	.305
2003 CHI - NL/ FLA	145	14	1	8	1	.193

HARRIS, WILLIE - OF - BL - b: 6/22/78 $1

A true speedster, Harris could be an offensive force at the top of the lineup if he could ever find a way to get on base consistently. While he has blazing speed, he is often overmatched at the plate. He has real trouble getting around on better than average fastballs, and he has yet to learn how to read breaking pitches. He is gifted defensively, and there is a chance that he could earn a spot as a platoon player, either at second or in center fielder, because of that. However, he had only two hits in 19 at-bats in 2003 against lefthanded pitching, meaning that there is little hope of him being a regular at this point in his career.

	AB	R	HR	RBI	SB	BA
2001 New York - NL	135	12	0	9	3	.222
2002 Chicago - AL	163	14	2	12	8	.233
2003 CHI - AL/FLA	137	19	0	5	12	.204

HART, BO - 2B - BR - b: 9/27/76 $10

A hot start when he was first called up from Triple-A inflated Hart's value and worth both with the Cardinals' brass and the fans in St. Louis. He hit .460 in his first 50 at-bats with the Cardinals, though his numbers went down steadily after that, and by the end of the season, after the return of Fernando Vina, he was starting only a couple of days a week. He has no power at all, can't hit for a high average, and is only a marginal defender. Hart can stick around if he is willing to go back and forth between Triple-A and the majors a few times a season and be the last guy on the roster. Asking him to even play two or three times a week, is asking for trouble.

	AB	R	HR	RBI	SB	BA
2003 St. Louis	296	46	4	28	3	.277

HARVEY, KEN - 1B/DH - BR - b: 3/1/78 $9

One of several Royals rookies who played significant roles in 2003, Ken Harvey had a rollercoaster year. Following a record-setting MVP season in the 2002 Arizona Fall League, Harvey attained instant cult-hero status during the Royals fast start with several clutch hits and a game-winning homer. He fell into disuse as interleague play began then was suddenly thrust into a full-time job when Mike Sweeney was lost to a back injury. Harvey wilted under the workload of everyday play and also had trouble staying healthy himself; he suffered a shoulder injury in a first base collision with J.D. Drew, then reinjured himself swinging the bat a short while later. Harvey's power fairly disappeared in the second half and he was reduced to a platoon role as the pennant race wound down. Harvey's inexperience showed in the field as he was often out of position on balls hit to the right side of the infield. He runs the bases slowly; his below-average footspeed was long ago further diminished by multiple foot injuries. Hardly the most graceful athlete on the field, Harvey has an aggressive approach at the plate and displays a severe uppercut swing which helps generate power, but makes him vulnerable to pitchers who do more than just throw fastballs down the middle. Harvey is a likeable young player with a lot of talent, but also a lot of holes in his game. He has a long way to go to become a star, and he can start by reducing his strikeouts and learning to hit the breaking ball in 2004.

	AB	R	HR	RBI	SB	BA
2003 Kansas City	485	50	13	64	2	.266

HATTEBERG, SCOTT - 1B - BL - b: 12/14/69 $7

One of the stars of last year's somewhat controversial book, Moneyball, Hatteberg failed to live up to all the hype during the 2003 season. Overall, Hatteberg's numbers look much better when compared against catchers (he started out as a backstop with the Red Sox in the mid 1990s). As a first baseman, however, his offense leaves much to be desired. While he is exceedingly patient at the plate, he has limited power. And while it's true that the ballpark in Oakland helps the pitchers, his numbers away from home weren't significantly better. Hatteberg also has no speed and often stumbles around in the field, though he is better than when he initially started playing first base. For most teams, he would be a part-time player.

	AB	R	HR	RBI	SB	BA
2001 Boston	278	50	3	25	1	.245
2002 Oakland	492	58	15	61	0	.280
2003 Oakland	541	63	12	61	0	.253

HELMS, WES - 3B - BR - b: 5/12/76 $8

Helms became the second third baseman in Brewers franchise history to hit at least 20 home runs. The first? Tommy Harper, with 31 in 1970, back when Bud Selig was just a car dealer who bought the team and moved it from Seattle in 1969. (Eddie Mathews doesn't count; all his homers were with the Braves.) Helms, free of the chains of the Atlanta system, flourished as a regular in his first season as a starter. He has big power to left field, although like many power hitters he can have trouble with outside breaking pitches and overswings, causing strikeouts. He does not run well and is smart enough to know it, playing it station-to-station. He is not a great fielder, and Atlanta tried him at first base and the outfield at times in their system. He was expected to be the regular third baseman again this year.

	AB	R	HR	RBI	SB	BA
2001 Atlanta	216	28	10	36	1	.222
2002 Atlanta	210	20	6	22	1	.243
2003 Milwaukee	476	56	23	67	0	.261

HELTON, TODD - 1B - BL - b: 8/20/73 $33

Helton continues to keep company with the best who have ever played. Helton and Joe DiMaggio are the only two players in baseball history to have at least 25 homers and 95 RBIs in their first six seasons, and Helton became the only player in history to have three seasons with at least 50 doubles, 30 homers and 100RBIs when he got his 50th double of the 2003 season in September. Helton has it all. He has a patient approach at the plate and is not afraid to lay off a pitch just out of the zone in order to pounce on one that is. He has quick, powerful stroke and can put the ball in play from foul line to foul line, although as he has more experience he has learned to drive the ball to right field more often. He is the only active major league with a slugging percentage over .600. Helton does not have great speed, although he usually is good for a few stolen bases a year when he catches the defense napping (he was an option quarterback at Tennessee, remember, before becoming the eighth player taken in the 1995 draft). He worked hard on his defense, to the point he is a two-time Gold Glove winner. He is a potential .350-42-145 first baseman every year in the near future, and will again occupy the No. 3 spot.

	AB	R	HR	RBI	SB	BA
2001 Colorado	587	132	49	146	7	.341
2002 Colorado	553	107	30	109	5	.329
2003 Colorado	583	135	33	117	0	.358

HENDERSON, RICKEY - OF - BR - b: 12/25/58 $2

Remember this. No matter how long Henderson hangs on, no matter how many weak grounders he hits in his final days, Henderson will always be the best leadoff hitter in the history of baseball. So do not judge him now. A first ballot Hall of Famer (the numbers say he should be the first unanimous selection), Henderson played in an independent league until catching on with the Dodgers when injuries struck late last summer. He no longer explodes on high fastballs and drives them out of the park. Nor does he coax many walks or steal many bases. Still, Henderson does have better-than-average speed and a want-to that will not quit. He was expected to keep trying, although a roster spot is a long-shot.

	AB	R	HR	RBI	SB	BA
2001 San Diego	379	70	8	42	25	.227
2002 Boston	179	40	5	16	8	.223
2003 Los Angeles	72	7	2	5	3	.208

HERMANSEN, CHAD - OF - BR - b: 9/10/77 $0

Hermansen had 80 home runs in the Pittsburgh farm system from 1997-99 but has never been able to sustain that offense in his many chances in the majors. Hermansen has a big swing and is a misser — even when he finds a fastball he likes, he often cannot catch up to it. When he puts the ball in play, he can drive it to the gaps and beyond. He has been tried in the middle infield and center field, and is athletic enough to play those spots adequately. He has 10 to 15 stolen base potential, although that requires a regular role, something he has not earned. He was expected to enter spring training fighting for a backup job.

	AB	R	HR	RBI	SB	BA
2001 Pittsburgh	55	5	2	5	0	.164
2002 PIT/CHI - NL	43	3	1	3	7	.209
2003 Los Angeles	25	2	0	2	0	.160

HERNANDEZ, JOSE - 3B/SS - BR - b: 7/14/69 $9

Jose Hernandez is a player that has been neither star, nor failure, nor trouble maker, but he evokes inordinately strong negative reactions from many people. Hernandez has gas in his tank but he will forever be branded by being pulled from the lineup of the lowly Brewers before 2002 ended because he was about to set a record for striking out. So? He hit 49 homers for those Brewers in two years but they wanted Royce Clayton and Wes Helms. Clayton can't hit a lick and he can't pick it any better than Hernandez and Helms still is not as good as Hernandez, but Hernandez moves on to a suddenly powerless Colorado team and then to Chicago and he finally ends up buried in the rubble of Pittsburgh. Three moves in a season are very tough and all things considered, he had a fairly good year. What do people want from him? Would they leave Hernandez alone if he was just a glove man who hit .218 with one homer but only struck out only 50 times a year? Is Hernandez skewered because he strikes out a lot for a shortstop? He'll whiff, sure, but he can still go deep twenty times a year and he has a good glove. Deal with it.

	AB	R	HR	RBI	SB	BA
2001 Milwaukee	542	67	25	78	5	.249
2002 Milwaukee	525	72	24	73	3	.288
2003 COL/CHI-NL/PIT	519	58	13	57	2	.225

HERNANDEZ, RAMON - C - BR - b: 5/20/76 $8

Hernandez had by far his best season as a hitter in the big leagues in 2003. He batted more than 20 points above his career average and displayed a little more power. He doesn't walk much, especially for a guy who had spent his entire career with the Athletics. Hernandez is regarded as one of the better signal callers in baseball. He has good quickness behind the plate, which helps him save many more balls in the dirt, and he will consistently throw out nearly 40 percent of runners trying to steal. Since last season was his first above average year, it is unlikely that he is going to take another giant step forward. Expect him to hit about .260 with 15 to18 homers.

	AB	R	HR	RBI	SB	BA
2001 Oakland	453	55	15	60	1	.254
2002 Oakland	403	51	7	42	0	.233
2003 Oakland	483	70	21	78	0	.273

HESSMAN, MIKE - OF - BR - b: 3/5/78 $0

Despite leading the Richmond Braves in homers the last two seasons and earning International League honors, Mike Hessman is not considered an especially good prospect. Hessman has the stereotypical power-hitting approach, often overswinging and chasing unhittable pitches, but generating good power when he does make contact. His brief big-league debut in 2003 was a microcosm of his minor league career, full of whiffs and power hitting. Hessman looks very much like the classic Triple-A power hitter who can not make the transition to the bigs. But, if he can cut his strikeout rate from one in four - as it was for Richmond in 2003 - Hessman has a chance to stick with a big-league club as an extra bat off the bench, especially considering that he is equally adept at playing either corner infield or outfield spot.

	AB	R	HR	RBI	SB	BA
2003 Atlanta	21	2	2	3	0	.286

HIDALGO, RICHARD - OF - BR - b: 7/2/75 $22

Hidalgo had a breakout season in 2000, hitting for both average and power. After his production declined in 2001 and slipped even further in 2002, he rebounded in 2003 with an excellent year. He has played all three outfield positions but is strongest in right field with his rifle arm which led the National League in outfield assists in 2003. Hidalgo has a strong work ethic and has made some necessary adjustments to use the whole field. He has excellent power and should be capable of more seasons similar to 2003 but not up to his career year in 2000 (.314-44-122-13).

	AB	R	HR	RBI	SB	BA
2001 Houston	512	70	19	80	3	.275
2002 Houston	388	54	15	48	6	.235
2003 Houston	514	91	28	88	9	.309

HIGGINSON, BOB - OF - BL - b: 8/18/70 $9

He's given an ultimatum to Detroit to trade him but due to his high salary and fading skill, there are no takers and the Tigers won't swallow enough of his contract to make something happen. His poor performance has caused any interest in him to fade and it appears that Higginson's flame has gone out and he is merely content to collect one of the more indefensible salaries in the major leagues. Even at his best Higginson wasn't worth what the Tigers paid him in 2003 — $11,500,000 — which is slightly higher than Gary Sheffield's salary.

	AB	R	HR	RBI	SB	BA
2001 Detroit	541	84	17	71	20	.277
2002 Detroit	444	50	10	63	12	.282
2003 Detroit	469	61	14	52	8	.235

HILL, BOBBY - 2B - BB - b: 4/3/78 $0

If Hill is not at second base on opening day for the Pirates, there is no justice. Pokey Reese is a better fielder but Hill is no slouch and he could have started for the Pirates two years ago but he had to wait out Don Baylor and then Dusty Baker in Chicago and they tend to play guys with a long past, rather than a long future. Figure Hill to cover a .265 average with 25 steals and eight home runs.

	AB	R	HR	RBI	SB	BA
2002 Chicago - NL	190	26	4	20	6	.253
2003 CHI - NL/PIT	7	1	0	0	0	.286

HILLENBRAND, SHEA - 1B/3B - BR - b: 7/27/75   **$16**

Hillenbrand is a first class hitter. He drives the ball to left field with the best of them, and he is a better fit at Bank One Ballpark in Arizona rather than Fenway Park because his line drives get over the fence for homers instead of ricocheting off the Green Monster for doubles. A streaky hitter, he can carry a team when he is hot. At the same time, once you have seen Hillenbrand hit, you have just about seen it all. He is such a free-swinger than he almost never walks, which is hard to imagine since pitchers do fear him. Hillenbrand is a liability at third base; his range is suspect and his arm is erratic. He played more first base than third for Arizona after being acquired for Byung-Hyun Kim after the D'backs gave up on Matt Williams two months into 2003, although that position also was an adventure. He has no speed and is not a threat to take the extra base. He was expected to be the starting third baseman, but first base was always an option considering Arizona's glut of infielders.

	AB	R	HR	RBI	SB	BA
2001 Boston	468	52	12	49	3	.263
2002 Boston	634	94	18	83	4	.293
2003 BOS/AZ	515	60	20	97	1	.280

HINCH, A.J. - C - BR - b: 5/15/74   **$0**

Hinch bounced to Detroit from Cleveland by way of Kansas City. It is hoped that the Tigers have come to the conclusion that Brandon Inge has had ample opportunity to fail and he's not the catcher that they thought he was. Hinch has never had a good opportunity but he is a much better catcher than Inge and at 30 he may be ready to contribute some offense.

	AB	R	HR	RBI	SB	BA
2001 Kansas City	121	10	6	15	1	.157
2002 Kansas City	197	25	7	27	3	.249
2003 Detroit	74	7	3	11	0	.203

HINSKE, ERIC - 3B - BL - b: 8/5/77   **$15**

After an American League Rookie of the Year Award in 2002, Hinske struggled for the first couple of months last year only to discover that he had been playing with a broken hamate bone for the first part of the year. After spending about a month on the disabled list, Hinske came back and looked much more confident offensively than he had in the first part of season. An extra-base machine who can take walks, Hinske's fielding woes of the first part of 2002 resurfaced last year and he will have to become more confident with the glove if he's to remain a third baseman for the long term. Even with his problems with the glove, he's the starting third baseman for now.

	AB	R	HR	RBI	SB	BA
2002 Toronto	566	99	24	84	13	.279
2003 Toronto	449	74	12	63	12	.243

HOCKING, DENNY - 2B/3B - BB - b: 4/2/70   **$0**

Denny Hocking is a great athlete who can play almost any position on the field. Even as he gets older, his arm remains one of the best around. Since he's played every position except catcher, he has a vast knowledge of the game and uses it to his advantage. His offense has been in decline in recent years, and he doesn't hit nearly as well righthanded as he does lefthanded. Hocking remains one of the best utility players in the game, which works in his favor as he was expected to enter free agency after the 2003 season.

	AB	R	HR	RBI	SB	BA
2001 Minnesota	327	34	3	25	6	.251
2002 Minnesota	260	28	2	25	0	.250
2003 Minnesota	188	22	3	22	0	.239

HOLLANDSWORTH, TODD - OF - BL -b: 4/20/73   **$0**

The oft-injured Hollandsworth has been in the majors for nine years and he's played more than

100 games only three times. Hollandsworth has a fairly live bat and should he remain healthy and play a full season, he'd hit 15-18 homers.

	AB	R	HR	RBI	SB	BA
2001 Colorado	117	21	6	19	5	.368
2002 COL/TEX	430	55	16	67	8	.284
2003 Florida	228	32	3	20	2	.254

HUDSON, ORLANDO - 2B - BB - b: 12/12/77 $8

Hudson plays hard and has developed into an above-average fielding second baseman with good instincts. Even though he was brought up through an organization that emphasizes on-base percentage, Hudson has not developed the needed ability to take walks and it limits his offensive potential, especially considering he has only minor power and speed. Beyond that, he has real trouble against lefties and some have argued that he would be better served to give up switch-hitting altogether if he is to keep a full-time job. He's a starting second baseman but if his struggles against lefties continue early into this season, his everyday status is not assured.

	AB	R	HR	RBI	SB	BA
2002 Toronto	192	20	4	23	0	.276
2003 Toronto	474	54	9	57	5	.268

HUFF, AUBREY - 1B/OF/DH - BL - b: 12/20/76 $24

Huff is a patient hitter with 30-plus home run power and demonstrated in 2003 that he has the ability to hit .300 or better. Huff's defense is less than spectacular, but his bat will keep him in the lineup, even if it has to be as the designated hitter. He was the best offensive player for the Devil Rays in 2003, finishing strong and raising hopes for an even better season in 2004.

	AB	R	HR	RBI	SB	BA
2001 Tampa Bay	411	42	8	45	1	.248
2002 Tampa Bay	454	67	23	59	4	.313
2003 Tampa Bay	636	91	34	107	2	.311

HUMMEL, TIM - 3B - BR - b: 11/18/78 $1

The Reds ended the 2003 season with the need to replace Aaron Boone at third base and Hummel may have been the answer — and a sleeper. He was buried in the White Sox organization before the Reds took him as the PTBNL in the deal that sent reliever Scott Sullivan to the Sox. Hummel had a strong high school and college career and he was ranked 43rd among Baseball America's Top 100 prospects. Hummel can play second base and shortstop but he played most frequently at third base for the White Sox Triple-A Charlotte club. Hummel hit .284 with 15 home runs for Charlotte and he is solid on defense at all three infield positions.

	AB	R	HR	RBI	SB	BA
2003 Cincinnati	84	9	2	10	0	.226

HUNDLEY, TODD - C - BB - b: 5/27/69 $3

Hundley returned to Los Angeles in 2003 but missed the middle four months of the season after undergoing surgery to alleviate a nerve problem in his lower back. A former 41-homer All-Star in 1996, Hundley has been reduced to a platoon player (at best) who can do one thing — hit an occasional homer against a righthanded pitcher. Hundley tries to pull everything and can drive a mistake, but that's about it. A nominal switch-hitter, Hundley is so weak from the right side that he seldom sees time against lefties. Arm surgery robbed him of any semblance of a throwing arm, and opponents can run at will when he starts. He does not move well behind the plate and is absolutely no threat on the bases. His skills have eroded to the point that he is, at best, a situational lefthanded hitter.

	AB	R	HR	RBI	SB	BA
2001 Chicago - NL	246	23	12	31	0	.187
2002 Chicago - NL	266	32	16	35	0	.211
2003 Los Angeles	33	2	2	11	0	.182

HUNTER, TORII - OF - BR - b: 7/18/75　　　　　　$19

One of the game's most likable players, Hunter is one of a few center fielders who plays excellent defense and can drive in runs. The two-time Gold Glove winner sacrifices his body to take hits away from the opposition and can throw runners out. Offensively, his swing is a little long; he chases pitches out of the strike zone and he strands too many runners in scoring position. But hits the ball to all fields and through work with hitting coach Scott Ullger, really wears out curve balls. He's hitting his prime and could have a big offensive year.

	AB	R	HR	RBI	SB	BA
2001 Minnesota	564	82	27	92	9	.261
2002 Minnesota	561	89	29	94	23	.289
2003 Minnesota	581	83	26	102	6	.250

IBANEZ, RAUL - 1B/OF - BL - b: 6/2/72　　　　　　$19

Largely ignored by mainstream media, Raul Ibanez is, nevertheless, a dangerous lefty hitter. In 2003, Ibanez again hit for a fine average and supplied a strong RBI bat in the middle of the Royals lineup to finish the season with one of the top batting averages in the league against righthanded pitching. Ibanez is fairly aggressive at the plate; he primarily looks for a fastball which he'll try to drive for extra bases. He is constantly tinkering with his stance and his swing, it helps even out his production during the season and eliminate any long hitless stretches. Despite a slight power drop-off in 2003, Ibanez was one of the Royals most productive hitters. He has worked hard to make himself a passable outfielder although he still mis-reads some fly balls and his sub-par arm is exposed in rightfield; Ibanez also handled occasional first base duties well enough, too. He won't steal a lot of bases, but Ibanez has enough speed to take the extra base when necessary. Likeable and intelligent, Ibanez has had to work hard for everything he has gotten in the majors and that experience has helped make him a strong clubhouse presence; several young Royals hitters praised Ibanez's positive influence during the club's breakout season. A big payday was anticipated for the new free agent after the 2003 season as the Royals made it an off-season priority to bring back their productive lefty bat.

	AB	R	HR	RBI	SB	BA
2001 Kansas City	279	44	13	54	0	.280
2002 Kansas City	497	70	24	103	5	.294
2003 Kansas City	608	95	18	90	8	.294

INFANTE, OMAR - SS - BR - b: 12/26/81　　　　　　$0

Infante was the Tigers opening day shortstop but he was error prone and he didn't hit and the Tigers sent him to Toledo in June and he continued to hit poorly. Infante was not recalled until the last week of the season. Although he will become a more reliable fielder, he has never shown any offensive ability and he must improve at the plate if he is going to be a starter.

	AB	R	HR	RBI	SB	BA
2002 Detroit	72	4	1	6	0	.333
2003 Detroit	221	24	0	8	6	.222

INGE, BRANDON - C - BB - b: 5/19/77　　　　　　$0

If Inge has a major league future it will be as a backup catcher on a team that has a number one catcher who can hit right handed pitching, which Inge clearly cannot do. Last year Inge was backed up by Matt Walbeck and A.J. Hinch. Only the Tigers seem blind to fact that Inge should back up Walbeck, Hinch or, anybody else.

	AB	R	HR	RBI	SB	BA
2001 Detroit	189	13	0	15	1	.180
2002 Detroit	321	27	7	24	1	.202
2003 Detroit	330	32	8	30	4	.203

IZTURIS, CESAR - SS - BB - b: 2/10/80 $7

Izturis is another who excels at the small man's game. A few years into switch-hitting, Izturis still looks more comfortable from his natural right side, from which he can drive the ball into the gaps. He is still learning his swing from the left side, where he can be overmatched but is making strides. He smartly concentrates on putting the ball in play and using his excellent speed. Izturis is still learning to read pitchers' moves, although he has the ability to steal 20 bases. He had four 20-stolen base seasons in the Toronto minor league organization. He is a fine glove man, with great range, a strong arm and supple hands. He makes most plays look easy. He was expected to be the starting shortstop for seasons to come after continuing to improve offensively.

	AB	R	HR	RBI	SB	BA
2001 Toronto	134	19	2	9	8	.269
2002 Los Angeles	439	43	1	31	7	.232
2003 Los Angeles	558	47	1	40	10	.251

JACKSON, DAMIAN - 2B/OF - BR - b: 8/16/73 $5

Jackson's major league career hasn't reached the potential he showed in the minors, but he has become a viable utility player. His speed makes him an effective base stealer and pinch runner. For Boston in 2003, Jackson played every position but catcher and pitcher. His fielding history has been one of good range, but frequent errors. Jackson has been with five major league teams; it's highly likely he could play for more clubs before his career is over.

	AB	R	HR	RBI	SB	BA
2000 San Diego	470	68	6	37	28	.255
2001 San Diego	440	67	4	38	23	.241
2002 Detroit	245	31	1	25	12	.257
2003 Boston	161	34	1	13	16	.261

JENKINS, GEOFF - OF - BL - b: 7/21/74 $13

Jenkins is a premier power hitter that only injuries can stop. He put up quality numbers despite missing the final five weeks of the season with a fractured thumb, that after a dislocated ankle cost him 3 1-2 months in 2002 and shoulder and thumb injuries cost him two months in 2001. Jenkins has a quick, whipping stroke and can drive the ball to all fields, foul line to foul line. He is a big swinger who is not afraid to strike out, and he can have trouble with breaking balls. He has above-average speed and stole 11 bases in his last full season, although he has abandoned the running game as his injuries have mounted. He gets to a lot of balls in left field and has the arm for the position. The left field starter and middle of the order hitter, Jenkins could hit 35 homers and drive in 110 runs if he can play a full season.

	AB	R	HR	RBI	SB	BA
2001 Milwaukee	397	60	20	63	4	.264
2002 Milwaukee	243	35	10	29	1	.243
2003 Milwaukee	487	81	28	95	0	.296

JETER, DEREK - SS - BR - b: 6/26/74 $25

Jeter suffered a separated left shoulder while sliding on opening night, and even into October anytime anything went wrong at bat or in the field, commentators blamed that on his shoulder. Missing more than a month reduced all of his counting stats to full-season career lows. After his average dipped below .300 in 2002 for the first time in five years, he was in contention for the batting title until the final day last season. He and Alfonso Soriano are so proficient against lefthanders (.370 average for Jeter in '03) that they helped reduce the Yankees' traditional trouble with southpaws. After nine seasons in the majors, his basestealing and defensive skills are down somewhat. Regardless, he should remain a top-of-the-order offensive force.

	AB	R	HR	RBI	SB	BA
2001 New York - AL	614	110	21	74	27	.311
2002 New York - AL	644	124	18	75	32	.297
2003 New York - AL	482	87	10	52	11	.324

JIMENEZ, D'ANGELO - 2B - BB - b: 12/21/77 $12

Entering his prime years at age 26 and with three big league seasons under his belt, Jimenez' defense is still better than his offense. He has begun to mature into a reliable hitter although his power and ability to steal bases are rated fair and poor respectively. It's unlikely that Jimenez will develop significantly in the power category and while he has good speed he has yet to develop base stealing skills and he tends to kill rallies. Management has him on a short leash but if Jimenez is to be a sleeper in the near future, it will be as a base stealer.

	AB	R	HR	RBI	SB	BA
2001 San Diego	308	45	3	33	2	.276
2002 SD/Chicago - AL	429	61	4	44	6	.252
2003 CHI-AL/CIN	561	69	14	57	11	.273

JOHNSON, CHARLES - C - BR - b: 7/20/71 $5

Johnson regained his power in his first season in Coors Field in 2003, but the rest of his game appears to have leveled off at a place far below his previous four-Gold Glove standard. Johnson, who likes the ball low and outside where he can extend his arms, has struggled to get his average above .250 and continues to have trouble with breaking pitches and fastballs up in the zone. Never fast, he has become one of the slowest runners in the game, station-to-station only. He has a strong arm - he tied the Colorado franchise record by catching three potential base-stealers in one game May 17 - but reaches for too many balls rather than square up in a good blocking position. He was expected to open the regular season as the starter, but he's old for a catcher.

	AB	R	HR	RBI	SB	BA
2001 Florida	451	51	18	75	0	.259
2002 Florida	244	18	6	36	0	.217
2003 Colorado	356	49	20	61	1	.230

JOHNSON, KELLY - SS - BL - b: 2/22/82 $0

Once considered among the best Braves prospects (Baseball America listed him third in 2001), Kelly Johnson has lost some of the star stature he earned as a supplemental first-round draft pick in 2000. He moved up a level in 2003, but without standout results, hitting .275 with six homers and 45 RBI for Double-A Greenville, including losing a month of the season to elbow tendinitis. Johnson had shown very good power at lower levels while displaying above-average strikezone judgment; both skills were rarely in evidence at Greenville. Meanwhile, his defensive work remained spotty and will eventually force him to move to the outfield or third base; he has been passed on the Braves' depth charts by several other infield prospects. Johnson runs well, which would help in a shift to the outfield, but he'll have to hit for more power and regain his batting eye before he can again be labeled a top prospect.

JOHNSON, MARK - C - BL - b: 9/12/75 $0

Johnson's best asset is that he is a lefthanded hitting catcher. He is a dependable receiver, though he has been a notoriously weak hitter in his six seasons in the big leagues. He has a good knowledge of the strike zone and is more than willing to take a walk. While he also has a little bit of pop in his bat, he has never hit above .250 in any season. Johnson is going to have to go back to the minors and earn another trip to the big leagues. Even if he is productive in Triple-A, he is not going to be trusted to play anything more than a reserve role.

	AB	R	HR	RBI	SB	BA
2001 Chicago - AL	173	21	5	18	2	.249
2002 Chicago - AL	263	31	4	18	0	.209
2003 Oakland	27	3	0	3	0	.111

JOHNSON, NICK - 1B/DH - BL - b: 9/19/78 $11

Johnson broke through last season with his highest batting average since 1999, when he was in Double-A. He was batting .300 until finishing the season in an 0-for-17 slump. Other than that, he was very consistent, hitting for nearly the same average against lefthanders as against righties, but with less power. As in the minors, Johnson walked more often than he struck out and showed an aptitude for being hit by pitches. After missing more than two months because of a stress fracture in his right hand, he became the Yankees' regular first baseman. Johnson is above average defensively.

	AB	R	HR	RBI	SB	BA
2001 New York - AL	67	6	2	8	0	.194
2002 New York - AL	378	56	15	58	1	.243
2003 New York - AL	324	60	14	47	5	.284

JOHNSON, REED - OF - BR - b: 12/8/76 $13

Johnson came from nowhere last year to secure a spot as a regular outfielder and while he showed typical rookie inconsistency, he also demonstrated a strong stroke and a surprisingly good ability to put the ball in play. He has decent but unexciting power and though he was above .300 for much of the season, shouldn't be expected to hit anywhere close to that in the long run. Not patient enough to be the leadoff hitter, which is where he was often tried last year, Johnson stands an excellent chance to be a fourth outfielder type who gets plenty of playing time. With the exception of his batting average, his 2003 season gives a good indication of what should be expected for a repeat performance this year.

	AB	R	HR	RBI	SB	BA
2003 Toronto	412	79	10	52	5	.294

JONES, ANDRUW - OF - BR - b: 4/23/77 $22

Many people had Andruw Jones pegged to suddenly improve his game to another level in 2003 as he reached the magical age of 26 in April. It didn't happen. Instead, Jones continued to be one of the most consistent power threats in the majors — he has averaged 35 homers and 105 RBI over the last four years — while still playing centerfield as though it were his destiny. Jones runs fluidly all over the outfield; his great range and above-average arm have helped him win many well-deserved Gold Gloves. He makes hard plays look easy and tests TBS camera crews as he comes out of nowhere to make impossible catches. Jones has stopped trying to steal bases much anymore which is probably for the best because he has never used his speed well on the basepaths. At the plate, Jones has a powerful swing which has increasingly become less level as Jones tries to hit home runs. He succeeded often enough in 2003 to be among league leaders in homers and RBI, but his uppercut swing and pull mentality also caused him to lead the Braves in strikeouts. As Jones suffered through an awful August slump that dropped his batting average more than 20 points, his free-swinging approach came under unusual scrutiny. He's still one of the best young players in the game and is entering the prime of his career, but for Jones to reach that next level he'll need to learn a bit more patience at the plate and stop trying to pull everything.

	AB	R	HR	RBI	SB	BA
2001 Atlanta	625	104	34	104	11	.251
2002 Atlanta	560	91	35	94	8	.264
2003 Atlanta	595	101	36	116	4	.277

JONES, CHIPPER - OF - BB - b: 4/24/72 $26

Braves fans have come to expect success from their team. For the last decade, they have Larry Wayne "Chipper" Jones to thank for a lot of that success. Because he has been so consistent, Jones tends to escape attention lavished on some of the game's best players, but he is one of the best switch-hitters in baseball and always an offensive threat. Jones has an outstanding batting eye; he has walked more often than striking out for six years in a row and has posted an on-base percentage over .400 each of those seasons. Although he is no longer a home run crown candidate, Jones continues to drive in runs because he makes sure he gets a good pitch to hit. In 2003, Jones tied the National League record with his eighth straight 100-RBI season and finished among league leaders in RBI, walks, and OBP. The weakest of the three Braves outfielders, Jones is barely average in leftfield and has an infielders arm, one reason that many people expect he'll eventually move to first base. Jones has just average speed and has ceased trying to steal bases. Because he has such good strikezone judgment and is able to consistently hit for power and average from both sides of the plate, Jones will remain one of the better hitters in baseball, whether he plays left field or moves back to the infield.

	AB	R	HR	RBI	SB	BA
2001 Atlanta	572	113	38	102	9	.330
2002 Atlanta	560	90	26	100	8	.327
2003 Atlanta	555	103	27	106	2	.305

JONES, JACQUE - OF/DH - BL - b: 4/25/75 $20

Jones is a good, but streaky, hitter. He has the gift of being able to hit the ball out to both left and right field. He can run, although he doesn't steal bases. And he's learning to hit better against lefthanded pitchers. He chases pitches (especially the high ones) and doesn't walk much at this stage of his career. But he's getting a little more selective every year. Since this is the last year of his contract, he could go on a salary drive and put up big numbers. He covers as much ground as anyone in left field. His only drawback is his tendency to either loft or ground his throws from the outfield.

	AB	R	HR	RBI	SB	BA
2001 Minnesota	475	57	14	49	12	.276
2002 Minnesota	577	96	27	85	6	.300
2003 Minnesota	517	76	16	69	13	.304

JONES, JASON - OF - BB - b: 10/17/76 $0

In a little more than three months at Triple-A last season, Jones hit .288-9-55 before getting his first major league callup. He's a bit old to be considered a prospect, but he could see some action as an injury replacement or backup at the big league level. Jones is a first baseman by trade who was shifted to the outfield corners last season. He has occasional power and can hit for a respectable average with a good eye at the plate.

	AB	R	HR	RBI	SB	BA
2003 Texas	107	11	3	11	0	.215

JORDAN, BRIAN - OF - BR - b: 3/29/67 $4

Jordan missed the final three months of 2003 with a strained left patella tendon, although he is expected to be ready for 2004. He is an aggressive, attacking player — what would you expect out of a former NFL defensive back? His hitting approach is to identify fastballs and drive them to left and left-center. Because of that pitchers try to work him with breaking balls. When he is in a zone, he takes those pitches to right and is a very tough out. Jordan hammers lefthanders and is at his best in the clutch, as he proved down the stretch in 2002. A knee injury two years ago robbed him of his stolen base speed, although he remains a threat to take the extra base or to take out a middle infielder while breaking up a double play. Jordan has good range and charges balls well, and his arm is well above average as a left fielder. Jordan was expected to return to play as a regular left fielder and middle of the order hitter.

	AB	R	HR	RBI	SB	BA
2001 Atlanta	560	82	25	97	3	.295
2002 Los Angeles	471	65	18	80	2	.285
2003 Los Angeles	224	28	6	28	1	.299

KAPLER, GABE - OF - BR - b: 8/31/75 $7

In 1998, Kapler was a minor league player of the year, with 28 homers and 146 RBI in 139 Double-

A games. He hasn't come close to that level since; 18 homers, 72 RBI and a surprising 23 stolen bases are his major league high-water marks. Thus, the Tigers, Rangers and Rockies passed him along, and he ended up as a platoon outfielder against lefthanders for Boston last season. Most fans first came to know Kapler as a well muscled player in TV ads. Therein, his critics say, lies his problem. Kapler has bulked up to the point that making quick movements, such as throwing or swinging a bat, becomes difficult.

	AB	R	HR	RBI	SB	BA
2001 Texas	483	77	17	72	23	.267
2002 Colorado	315	37	2	34	11	.279
2003 COL/BOS	225	39	4	27	6	.271

KARROS, ERIC - 1B - BR - b: 11/4/67 $7

Karros rebounded after two straight dreadful seasons with a decent year with the Cubs. That was due mostly to the fact that Dusty Baker used him in a platoon with Hee Sop Choi and Randall Simon most of the 2003. He still has many holes in his swing, which are exposed more often against the hard throwers in the league. He never was a fast player, and age has robbed him of any speed. His reflexes also have slowed, making him only an average defender. Used judiciously Karros can repeat his 2003 numbers. However, if he should become an everday player once again, expect disastrous results.

	AB	R	HR	RBI	SB	BA
2001 Los Angeles	438	42	15	63	3	.235
2002 Los Angeles	524	52	13	73	4	.271
2003 Chicago - NL	336	37	12	40	1	.286

KATA, MATT - 2B/3B - BB - b: 3/14/78 $6

Kata first made a name for himself as a "Killer B," one of the Arizona minor leaguers who managed to make things happen when summoned to replace the regulars during major league spring training games in 2002. He has since become a "Baby 'Back," one of the young farm system products around whom the Diamondbacks plans to build their team - and their marketing strategy - from now on. Kata is a scrappy switch-hitter who can play three infield positions. He has exceptional range at second base, and 2003 teammate Mark Grace compared him to former Cub Gold Glover Ryan Sandberg at that position. Kata has gap power from both sides of the plate and has above average speed, although that has yet to translate into stolen bases at the major league level. He knows how to play the game and was expected to have the inside track at a reserve infield spot at the major league level.

	AB	R	HR	RBI	SB	BA
2003 Arizona	288	42	7	29	3	.257

KEARNS, AUSTIN - OF - BR - b: 5/20/80 $10

Kearns was healthy for about six weeks of the 2003 season. He hurt his right shoulder in a home plate collision on May 21 and he was in pain from that point until he was finally put of the DL on July 8. Kearns planned to return in August but the pain persisted and he had surgery to repair the labrum, rotator cuff and AC joint in his right shoulder. Despite the injury Kearns was playing well and showing the kind of improvement expected of a budding young star. He's good to go for spring training so just add 30 points to his batting average and double everything else from 2003 and that's where he will be this year.

	AB	R	HR	RBI	SB	BA
2002 Cincinnati	372	66	13	56	6	.315
2003 Cincinnati	292	39	15	58	5	.264

KELTON, DAVID - OF - BR - b: 12/17/79 $0

The Cubs had been touting David Kelton as a future superstar for a couple of years, though it is hard to see why. He hasn't hit consistently in the high minors and he does not have enough power to be a corner infielder or corner outfielder. All in all, Kelton would be a mediocre everyday player in the big leagues. He won't be able to take anybody's starting spot away, either at third or in the outfield, and he doesn't have enough speed or the ability to get on-base enough to make him useful at the top of the lineup. He has all the markings of the classic Triple-A player. Although he is good enough to hit those pitchers, he is not good enough to stick around for long stretches of time in the big leagues.

KENDALL, JASON - C - BR - b: 6/26/74 $18

Pittsburgh used to have a slogan that said, "We're playing Hard Ball." Now, all the cash-strapped Pirates play is Horror-Ball and the main attraction of Pittsburgh's freak show is Kendall, who has hit over .300 for five of his eight major league seasons and his .325 average last year brought his career batting average to .304, but how bad is it when your catcher stars in the local production of "The Rickey Henderson Story?" How many catchers have ever been used as a table setter let alone used in such a way for their entire career? Kendall used to steal bases but my goodness, the man just caught 145 games and he's 30 years old! Last year he was caught seven times in fifteen attempts and over the last four years he's been gunned down forty one times! There are many reasons why this team is in the tank but none more revealing than feeling the need to green light a 30- year-old catcher who has been caught stealing forty one times in four years. Mark Cuban, won't you please come home?

	AB	R	HR	RBI	SB	BA
2001 Pittsburgh	606	84	10	53	13	.266
2002 Pittsburgh	545	59	3	44	15	.283
2003 Pittsburgh	587	84	6	58	8	.325

KENNEDY, ADAM - 2B - BL - b: 1/10/76 $17

Speed is the most consistent part of Kennedy's game, and he can be counted on to steal somewhere around 20 bases in a full season. As he has matured, Kennedy has developed occasional power at the plate as well. Early in his career, Kennedy drew very few walks, but he is becoming a more patient hitter as he matures. He is a much weaker hitter against lefthanded pitching, a fact that leaves him somewhat vulnerable to being platooned.

	AB	R	HR	RBI	SB	BA
2001 Anaheim	478	48	6	40	12	.270
2002 Anaheim	474	65	7	52	17	.312
2003 Anaheim	449	71	13	49	22	.269

KENT, JEFF - 2B - BR - b: 3/7/68 $22

Despite a somewhat undeserved reputation as a poor defensive player, his offense is strong enough to rank him as one of the top second basemen in the major leagues for the last seven years. He has consistently hit for both power and average. His production in 2003 was a little below his usual standard largely due to a wrist injury that sidelined him for almost a month and affected his swing for a longer period of time. He should be able to continue to produce at close to this level for a couple more years as he enters the decline phase of his career.

	AB	R	HR	RBI	SB	BA
2001 San Francisco	607	84	22	106	7	.298
2002 San Francisco	623	102	37	108	5	.313
2003 Houston	505	77	22	93	6	.297

KIELTY, BOBBY - OF/DH - BR - b: 8/5/76 $11

Traded by Minnesota in the Shannon Stewart trade, Kielty is a player with good power, an excellent batting eye, an above-average throwing arm and confidence enough to play any outfield position. He's not a super producer relative to most major league left fielders and he suffered through an assortment of irritating but minor injuries in the middle of last season. He's good enough to stick around for a while and his speed is underrated and certainly not reflected in his stolen base totals. He's going to be battling to be the everyday left fielder this season.

	AB	R	HR	RBI	SB	BA
2001 Minnesota	104	8	2	14	3	.250
2002 Minnesota	289	49	12	46	4	.291
2003 MIN/TOR	427	71	13	57	8	.244

KINGSALE, EUGENE - OF - BB - b: 8/20/76 $0

A native of Aruba who never quite blossomed in the Baltimore chain before being claimed off waivers by Seattle in 2001, Kingsale made strides in the second half of 2002 when given regular playing time in San Diego, but struggled in 2003 with the Tigers. He went on the DL in June, then was sent to the minors. A switch-hitter with a lanky frame, Kingsale developed into more than just a slap-hitter with wheels as he got more work. He is still overpowered at the plate, but has showed an ability to put the ball in the gaps. He has the speed to track down balls in the gaps, but Kingsale is not a true center fielder; he is better suited for left. He finished last season as a free-agent.

	AB	R	HR	RBI	SB	BA
2002 SEA/SD	219	27	2	28	9	.283
2003 Detroit	120	11	1	8	1	.208

KINKADE, MIKE - OF - BR - b: 5/6/73 $0

Kinkade has proven he can hit Triple-A pitching, although he has not translated that into big league success. He has good power and can drive fastballs to his pull field, which is left. He has a good eye and will take a walk, although his big swing results in a lot of strikeouts. He came up as a third baseman in the Milwaukee chain although he has played mostly outfield and first base in recent seasons. He is only a fair fielder; he plays because of his offensive potential. He batted .370 against lefties last season and was expected to compete for a bat-off-the-bench role.

	AB	R	HR	RBI	SB	BA
2001 Baltimore	160	19	4	16	2	.275
2002 Los Angeles	50	7	2	11	1	.380
2003 Los Angeles	162	25	5	14	1	.216

KLASSEN, DANNY - 3B - BR - b: 9/22/75 $0

Klassen began his career as a shortstop but he's played all around the infield. He remains a talented athlete and he's not an automatic out, with good pop for a middle infielder and soft hands. Given a legitimate chance, the 29-year-old Klassen can be a useful utility infielder.

	AB	R	HR	RBI	SB	BA
2003 Detroit	73	9	1	7	0	.247

KLESKO, RYAN - 1B - BL - b: 6/12/71 $14

Klesko's 2003 season ended on Labor Day, when he underwent surgery to repair a damaged AC joint in his right shoulder. Early reports indicate the surgery was successful, and Klesko was expected to be fine this season. Klesko is a power hitter with speed, and it is virtually impossible to get a fastball by him on the inner half of the plate. He drives that pitch into the gap or over the fence. His plate coverage on the outer half has gotten better, limiting pitchers' options. Once a darkhorse candidate to become the first 30-30 man in San Diego franchise history, Klesko no longer is a threat to steal because of balky knees. He remains a better-than-average runner, however, and is OK at first base, his best position. The days of playing him in the outfield appear over, although San Diego does have a plethora of corner players. Klesko should be primed for another 25-100 season this year.

	AB	R	HR	RBI	SB	BA
2001 San Diego	538	105	30	113	23	.286
2002 San Diego	540	90	29	95	6	.300
2003 San Diego	397	47	21	67	2	.252

KONERKO, PAUL - 1B - BR - b: 3/5/76 $11

Konerko had one of the weirdest seasons in recent memory last year, failing miserably nearly every night before the All-Star break, then turning it around and beating up on AL pitching seemingly on a nightly basis. Konerko is a polished, experienced hitter with a good eye at the plate and it is surprising that he struggled for as long as he did. He has good power, though he seems content at times to settle for singles and doubles instead of waiting for a mistake to hit over the fence. He was a DH more in 2003 than in previous seasons, mostly because of his offensive struggles, and should still be considered a solid defensive first baseman. While Konerko is not consistent enough to be the masher that he was the second half of last season, he is nowhere near as bad as he was in the first three months of the season. Expect him to level off and perform as he did in 2001-02, where he hit a little less than .300 with close to 30 home runs.

	AB	R	HR	RBI	SB	BA
2001 Chicago - AL	582	92	32	99	1	.282
2002 Chicago - AL	570	81	27	104	0	.304
2003 Chicago-AL	444	49	18	65	0	.234

KOONCE, GRAHAM - 1B - BL - b: 5/15/75 $0

Much was made of the season Koonce had in Triple-A a year ago, when he beat up unmercifully on minor league pitching (34 home runs and 115 RBIs). However, Koonce should have been expected to put up big numbers considering he was in his 10th season of professional ball. He has always been a disciplined hitter who has gotten on base regularly, and if given a chance, Koonce could likely perform better than a lot of weak hitting first baseman around (like Sean Casey, Randall Simon, Ben Broussard or even … Scott Hatteberg). However, given his age and lack of big league experience, it's much more probably that he will be a backup in the field and a lefthanded bat off the bench.

KOSKIE, COREY - 3B - BL - b: 6/28/73 $17

Koskie is one of the few third baseman in the game who can hit and field well. He studies pitchers well and works hard to maintain his swing. Sometimes he gets too picky at the plate and takes more strikes than he should. But he can drive the ball to the opposite field and runs well enough to steal a few bases. A former hockey goalie, Koskie has good reflexes at third base and has improved his throwing substantially through work with the coaching staff. Koskie's 2004 option needed to be picked up.

	AB	R	HR	RBI	SB	BA
2001 Minnesota	562	100	26	103	27	.276
2002 Minnesota	490	71	15	69	10	.267
2003 Minnesota	469	76	14	69	11	.292

KOTSAY, MARK - OF - BR - b: 12/2/75 $13

Kotsay is a try-hard guy who gets the most out of his tools, which are above average to begin with. He struggled to maintain his form in 2003, however, after suffering a sprained lower back in May and missing more than two weeks. Some thought he attempted to come back too soon, before his body was ready, and his numbers seemed to agree. Kotsay is a line drive hitter who has learned to aggressively turn on an inside pitch and drive it out of the park, although he is more likely to sting the ball into the gaps. He is an extra-base threat because of his speed, which is above average. He has a top-of-the-order batting eye and is not afraid to get deep into counts. He is a fearless defender, patrolling the alleys with abandon. He has great instincts both in the field and on the bases and is a 12-15 stolen base guy. He has a strong and accurate arm. Kotsay was expected to be a fixture in center field for years to come.

	AB	R	HR	RBI	SB	BA
2001 San Diego	406	67	10	58	13	.291
2002 San Diego	578	82	17	61	11	.292
2003 San Diego	482	64	7	38	6	.266

LAMB, MIKE - DH - BL - b: 8/9/75 $0

Lamb is a Quadruple-A type player capable of hitting for average at the major league level but little else. He lacks speed and power, and although he is versatile enough to play the corner infield and outfield positions, he is below average defensively across the board. Lamb would be a useful reserve on a deep team, serving as a lefty bat off the bench, but is unlikely to see significant playing time in the big leagues anytime soon.

	AB	R	HR	RBI	SB	BA
2001 Texas	284	42	4	35	2	.306
2002 Texas	314	54	9	33	0	.283
2003 Texas	38	3	0	2	1	.132

LANE, JASON - OF - BR - b: 12/22/76 $0

Lane batted .517 with 4 home runs in the 1998 College World Series as a junior in leading USC to the Championship. However, he did not get drafted until the Astros selected him in the sixth round after his senior year. Moving up a level each year, Lane had a breakout MVP season in 2001 at Double-A (.316-38-124-14). He has spent most the past two seasons with Triple-A New Orleans but has impressed in brief trials with Houston both years. His progress was stalled in 2003 when he missed several weeks with an abdominal injury. Lane can handle all three outfield positions and he runs well and plays hard. He should be in the major leagues to stay in 2004, probably as a fourth outfielder.

LANGERHANS, RYAN - OF - BL - b: 2/20/80 $0

A minor prospect of raw talents, Ryan Langerhans reached the majors briefly with Atlanta for the second straight year. Langerhans began the season at Double-A Greenville where he'd finished 2002 as the club's Player of the Year. He again displayed decent power and speed there, although he occasionally had trouble making consistent contact, striking out once every four at-bats. After making the Southern League All-Star team, Langerhans had a mid-season callup to Triple-A Richmond where he continued to show some power, although his whiff rate didn't improve. In the field Langerhans is limited to a corner outfield spot where his good speed can help him outrun his mistakes. Langerhans is a superior athlete who is still learning to put his talent to use on a baseball field; he needs a couple of full high-minors seasons to further refine his talent, and projects as a fourth or fifth outfielder and a good lefty bat off the bench once he reaches the majors for good.

LARKIN, BARRY - SS - BR - b: 4/28/64 $3

Last year Larkin said that 2003 could be his last year as a regular and he was closer to the truth than he wanted to be. Clearly, Larkin wanted to keep playing baseball but after a nasty contract negotiation with Reds CEO John Allen, Larkin stormed off saying that he was finished playing for Cincinnati because he'd been insulted by the Reds take it, or leave it offer, of $500,000 plus incentives, for one more year. Larkin was preparing to cold call other teams for a job when Expos manager Frank Robinson brokered a deal by telling Larkin that he needed to wear a Reds uniform and not that of another team, when his career ended. On the last day of the season, Larkin and Allen sat down and shook hands on a deal very similar to the one that Larkin had rejected. It called for more up front salary plus incentives, for one more year with the Reds, after which Larkin will be traded to the Reds front office in a posiiton to be named later.

	AB	R	HR	RBI	SB	BA
2001 Cincinnati	156	29	2	17	3	.256
2002 Cincinnati	507	72	7	47	13	.245
2003 Cincinnati	241	39	2	18	2	.282

LARSON, BRANDON - 3B - BR - b: 5/24/76 $0

Larson had the starting third baseman's job handed to him in spring training and the potential to poke 30 homers in the Reds cozy new ball park but he opened in Cincinnati by going 4 for 48 and he was demoted to Triple-A Louisville in mid April. He was recalled in July and had another clear shot to start at third when the Reds traded Aaron Boone but by then Larson was banged up and he finally shut it down in August and had arthroscopic surgery to repair damage to his labrum, rotator cuff and biceps tendon in his left arm. After his recall from Louisville, Larson was just 5 for 41. In addition to the procedure on his left arm, he's had laser eye surgery to sharpen his vision but there is no operation that will permit him to hit breaking stuff. He was one of the Reds young prospects last year but after the Reds salary purge, Larson, at age 28 is now one of their older players and one who's done nothing to establish himself as a major league player.

LaRUE, JASON - C - BR - b: 3/19/74 $5

As a catcher, LaRue improved last year. At the plate it was a mix of good and bad. After being charged with 20 passed balls in 2002, LaRue cut way down in that category last year. Of course, it's hard to give up passed balls when hitters dig in and tee off on the cookies tossed by most of the Reds staff in 2003, but in general, LaRue was solid. He found the power hitting environment of the Great American Ballpark to be to his liking and while his average fell, his power rose. LaRue should have his best year at the plate in 2004.

		AB	R	HR	RBI	SB	BA
2001	Cincinnati	364	39	12	43	3	.236
2002	Cincinnati	353	42	12	52	1	.249
2003	Cincinnati	379	52	16	50	3	.230

LAWTON, MATT - OF/DH - BL - b: 11/3/71 $10

Lawton has never been a true power hitter but he belted fifteen home runs in a 353 at-bats last year which, on a per at-bat basis, is his career best but it leads to a problem. Injuries limited Lawton to less than 400 at-bats and Lawton is one of the highest paid players on the restructuring Indians roster. Making nearly seven million a year, Lawton has to play every day; which leads to another problem and while Lawton is not as fragile as, say, Jeffrey Hammonds, he's gone the distance (over 500 at-bats) only twice in his nine year career. His surgically repaired right shoulder bothered him last year and it affected his throwing. If his throwing arm doesn't come around, he could become an expensive platooner.

		AB	R	HR	RBI	SB	BA
2001	MIN/NY - NL	559	95	13	64	29	.277
2002	Cleveland	416	71	15	57	8	.236
2003	Cleveland	374	57	15	53	10	.249

LECROY, MATTHEW - C/DH - BR - b: 12/13/75 $10

A booming bat has landed Matthew LeCroy in the middle of a major league batting order. LeCroy is barely adequate as a catcher (his throwing holds him back) and is still learning first base (although he's made good progress). He's a designated hitter with the ability to carry teams when hot. In fact, he passed the career 600 at-bat mark in 2003 with nearly 30 homers and over 100 RBI. Twins officials believe that LeCroy also has, "plus-makeup," that helps him in pressure situations. He hasn't reached the arbitration stage yet, so there's good bang for the buck.

		AB	R	HR	RBI	SB	BA
2002	Minnesota	181	19	7	27	0	.260
2003	Minnesota	345	39	17	64	0	.287

LEDEE, RICKY - OF - BL - b: 11/22/73 $2

Ledee was around in case Marlon Byrd was not up to the task which Byrd was, but Ledee was a key lefthanded hitter against righthanded pitching, against whom he hit all of his thirteen homers in only 247 at-bats.

		AB	R	HR	RBI	SB	BA
2001	Texas	242	33	2	36	3	.231
2002	Philadelphia	203	33	8	23	1	.227
2003	Philadelphia	255	37	13	46	0	.247

LEE, CARLOS - OF - BR - b: 6/20/76 $26

Lee was one of the few White Sox hitters who was productive in the first half of the 2003 season. Overall, Lee has been somewhat slow to develop. He became a full-time player when he was only 22 years old, and many expected him to quickly become an All-Star. While he wasn't bad, he never came close to being a dependable hitter until last season. Lee has a lot of power, although he said last year that he would rather hit more singles and doubles than try and hit 40 or more homers. His biggest drawback is his lack of patience at the plate. He will swing at the first halfway decent pitch he sees, rather than trying to work deep into the count and find a better one. He has decent speed, and his ability to read a pitcher's pickoff throw, makes him a fine basestealer. Though not a superstar, Lee is a fine player and he can be expected to produce much as he has the past couple of seasons.

	AB	R	HR	RBI	SB	BA
2001 Chicago - AL	558	75	24	84	17	.269
2002 Chicago - AL	492	82	26	80	1	.264
2003 Chicago - AL	623	100	31	113	18	.291

LEE, DERREK - 1B - BR - b: 9/6/75 $24

Good timing. Lee signed a one year contract with Marlins in 2003 and then he went out and had a career year. He hasn't peaked yet. Within the next two years, he will hit more than 40 home runs.

	AB	R	HR	RBI	SB	BA
2001 Florida	561	83	21	75	4	.282
2002 Florida	581	95	27	86	19	.270
2003 Florida	539	91	31	92	21	.271

LEE, TRAVIS - 1B - BL - b: 5/26/75 $13

After his 2001 season, Lee was expected to progress his offense, but took a step backward in 2002. In 2003, he missed most of April to a strained oblique muscle and struggled in May and June, but a strong July contributed to Tampa Bay re-signing him for 2004, where he was expected to be their first baseman. Lee follows in the tradition of Rico Brogna, as a slick-fielding first baseman who lacks power at the plate. He has developed into a good hitter against lefty pitching, and if he can remain injury-free this year, he may have his career year.

	AB	R	HR	RBI	SB	BA
2001 Philadelphia	555	75	20	90	3	.258
2002 Philadelphia	536	55	13	70	5	.265
2003 Tampa Bay	542	75	19	70	6	.275

LIEBERTHAL, MIKE - C - BR - b: 1/18/72 $14

Lieberthal has been written off for the past four years, primarily because he's a catcher and he's had some serious injuries and after what he did last year, they'll call it a last gasp and write him off again. Look, he had a very good year in every aspect. He hit a career high .313, he hit over .300 against left and righthanded pitchers and he hit in the clutch. Plus he caught 131 games. Go ahead, write him off.

	AB	R	HR	RBI	SB	BA
2001 Philadelphia	121	21	2	11	0	.231
2002 Philadelphia	476	46	15	52	0	.279
2003 Philadelphia	508	68	13	81	0	.313

LOCKHART, KEITH - 2B - BL - b: 11/10/64 $0

Lockhart's career appeared to be nearing an end in San Diego last season, when he had his fewest at-bats of any major league season since 1994 after missing almost two months with a strained lower back. He still has very occasional power, although his bat speed has deteriorated. A serviceable second baseman, Lockhart had limited opportunity there last season. It is really the only spot on the field he can play. He has only one stolen base in the last three years. After making San Diego's roster as a spring training invitee on a minor league contract, Lockhart was expected to be on the outside looking in when reserve infield positions were allotted this spring.

	AB	R	HR	RBI	SB	BA
2001 Atlanta	178	17	3	12	1	.219
2002 Atlanta	296	34	5	32	0	.216
2003 San Diego	95	18	3	8	0	.242

LoDUCA, PAUL - C/1B - BR - b: 4/12/72 $11

Lo Duca continues to be a top quality major leaguer, although his production has dropped slightly in each of his last two seasons after becoming a regular in 2001. Not a big man, Lo Duca seems to wear down with all those innings behind the plate. He can drive high fastballs out of the park — ask Randy Johnson — and has a good knowledge of the strike zone. Lo Duca is aggressive yet seldom swings at a bad ball, and identifies breaking pitches right away. Like hitters of yore, he shortens up with two strikes and tries to find a hole. He is an above average runner, although the time behind the plate has taken some of his speed away and he no longer looks to steal. He is smart on the bases. Lo Duca handles pitchers well and has a good throwing arm, although his accuracy is suspect. He was expected to be the regular catcher and hit high in the order, although he can take a turn at first.

	AB	R	HR	RBI	SB	BA
2001 Los Angeles	460	71	25	90	2	.320
2002 Los Angeles	580	74	10	64	3	.281
2003 Los Angeles	568	64	7	52	0	.273

LOFTON, KENNY - OF - BL - b: 5/31/67 $24

After struggling just to find a place to play before the 2003 season, Lofton proved he can still play. He provided the Cubs the spark they were looking for when he replaced the injured Corey Patterson in center field. He immediately became the leadoff man the club had been seeking for several seasons, and provided tremendous veteran leadership in the clubhouse. While he has slowed somewhat and is no longer a threat to steal 50 bases a year, he will still use his accumulated basestealing knowledge to be among the league leaders. Lofton is past his days as an All-Star, though he has enough left to be among the best leadoff hitters around. For this season, expect him to perform as he did in 2003.

	AB	R	HR	RBI	SB	BA
2001 Cleveland	517	91	14	66	16	.261
2002 CHI - AL/SF	532	98	11	51	29	.261
2003 PIT/CHI - NL	547	97	12	46	30	.296

LONG, TERRENCE - OF - BR - b: 2/29/76 $8

Long was a dreadful hitter most of the 2003 season, but still kept his starting job because the Athletics had a couple other starters who were even worse. Long has little power and chases too many bad pitches to be effective hitting near the top of the order. He also has little patience at the plate, especially for a guy who spent the last four full seasons in Oakland. Long is not a good defensive outfielder. He has been moved around all three positions in recent years as the A's desperately tried to find a place to hide him in the outfield. He wound up splitting time equally in 2003 between left and right. Long will be a starter this season only if there is not a better alternative. It won't be long before his bat pushes him into a reserve role.

	AB	R	HR	RBI	SB	BA
2001 Oakland	629	90	12	85	9	.283
2002 Oakland	587	71	16	67	3	.240
2003 Oakland	486	64	14	61	4	.245

LOPEZ, FELIPE - DH - BB - b: 5/12/80 $0

Lopez arrogantly frittered away a starting job in Toronto and then he blew another in Cincinnati. Why? Lopez' problem is that he acts as if he is a better player than he is. Well, he's right. He is better than he looks and he can play shortstop spectacularly well. At times he makes bonehead plays and then he acts as if it's someone else's fault. His hitting is spotty and he'll never hit like Nomar or A-Rod but he will smooth out and mature. All he needs to do is comport himself like a professional ballplayer and he will have a starting job handed to him.

	AB	R	HR	RBI	SB	BA
2001 Toronto	177	21	5	23	4	.260
2002 Toronto	282	35	8	34	5	.227
2003 Cincinnati	197	28	2	13	8	.213

LOPEZ, JAVY - C - BR - b: 1/5/70 $18

Not many players have a breakout season in their tenth full big-league season, but Javy Lopez enjoyed an entirely unexpected offensive explosion in 2003. After totalling just 28 homers the past two seasons, Lopez hammered 43 in 2004, nearly as many homers as he had RBI in the entire previous season. Lopez attributed much of his recent success to being totally healthy, and having a renewed focus. He makes no excuses about swinging for the fences; batting near the bottom of the RBI portion of the Braves lineup afforded him the opportunity to "go for it," and National League pitchers suffered as a result. Despite missing a few games here and there with a variety of nicks and bruises, Lopez was among league leaders in homers and total bases, and set a new major league record for homers by a catcher; only Barry Bonds had a better homer-to-at-bat ratio than Lopez. His offensive output was so extreme that near season's end he was given catching duty even for Greg Maddux, his first time catching Maddux in five years. Lopez is a below-average defensive catcher who has little mobility and a relatively weak arm; he runs the bases slowly and poorly. The timing of Lopez's breakout season was fortuitous; he became a free agent at the end of the season.

	AB	R	HR	RBI	SB	BA
2001 Atlanta	438	45	17	66	1	.267
2002 Atlanta	347	31	11	52	0	.233
2003 Atlanta	457	89	43	109	0	.328

LOPEZ, MENDY - 1B - BR - b: 10/15/74 $0

After spending the better part of eight seasons in the Royals farm system, Mendy Lopez shuttled between three other teams from 2000 to 2002, then returned to the Royals as a spring training non-roster invitee. He made the club for Opening Day and enjoyed his strongest season to date, and first spent entirely on a major league roster. Lopez lost two months to an injured right calf muscle, then became an important reserve over the final two months of the season. He made at least one appearance at every defensive spot on the field except catcher and centerfield, helping to rest the club's regulars. Normally a weak-hitting glove man, Lopez showed a bit more pop with the bat in 2003. However, Lopez is best used in a reserve role. He's a good baserunner who can play many different positions; he knows his role and is comfortable coming off the bench.

	AB	R	HR	RBI	SB	BA
2001 HOU/PIT	58	8	1	7	0	.241
2003 Kansas City	94	13	3	11	2	.277

LORETTA, MARK - 2B - BR - b: 8/14/71 $15

San Diego did not get into the pennant race or the headlines last season, which kept Loretta one of the best-kept secrets of 2003. Signed as a free agent in December, Loretta was among the NL leaders in hits and batting average most of the year, returning to the form he showed in the late 1990s with Milwaukee before nagging injuries slowed him. Loretta is a line drive hitter who can drive the ball in the gaps. He uses the entire field and set a career high in homers in 2003 while also having four hitting streaks of at least 10 games. He has good discipline at the plate and puts the ball in play, a top hit-and-run man and bunter. He has great hands and a good arm, and is capable of playing all four infield positions, although shortstop is a bit of a reach. His best position is second base, and he will open the season as the regular there after signing a two-year contract extension late last year.

	AB	R	HR	RBI	SB	BA
2001 Milwaukee	384	40	2	29	1	.289
2002 MIL/HOU	283	33	4	27	1	.304
2003 San Diego	589	74	13	72	5	.314

LOWELL, MIKE - 3B - BR - b: 2/24/74 $18

In spite of many teams being interested in Lowell and the mid season arrival of Miguel Cabrera, Lowell remained with the Marlins all year because they got hot and were in playoff race. Lowell again battled injuries but he was one of baseballs home run leaders in the first half then, his power vanished in the second half — before he broke his hand in late August. Lowell should keep his power in the mid to high twenties but at his age and with his injury history, it's likely that his 32 home runs in 2003 will be his career peak.

	AB	R	HR	RBI	SB	BA
2001 Florida	551	65	18	100	1	.283
2002 Florida	597	88	24	92	4	.276
2003 Florida	492	76	32	105	3	.276

LUDWICK, RYAN - OF - BR - b: 7/13/78 $5

Ludwick is only a fair outfielder but his bat may be strong enough to earn him the Indians fourth outfielder job. If Gerut, Crisp or Escobar flounder, Ludwick will get a long look and he has the kind of power that the Tribe badly needs.

	AB	R	HR	RBI	SB	BA
2002 Texas	81	10	1	9	2	.235
2003 TEX/CLE	162	17	7	26	2	.247

LUGO, JULIO - SS - BR - b: 11/16/75 $14

Lugo was waived by the Astros last May in connection with charges of assault of which he was later acquitted. He was picked up by the Devil Rays as their regular shortstop to replace the injured Ordonez. Lugo is a versatile player; ideally suited to be a utility man having played both second base and shortstop and outfield, but has proved himself capable of handling an everyday job. He runs well and has occasional power. Based on his 2003 performance, he could be a regular again this year, and is capable of a .280-15-60-15 season.

	AB	R	HR	RBI	SB	BA
2001 Houston	513	93	10	37	12	.263
2002 Houston	322	45	8	35	9	.261
2003 HOU/TB	498	64	15	55	12	.271

MABRY, JOHN - OF - BL - b: 10/17/70 $0

Mabry, expected to be a major contributor as a pinch-hitter and situational substitute, was hampered by a shoulder injury and did not play much in 2003. Mabry has great power against righties and is a good situational hitter. He has a great eye and works counts to his advantage. Mabry can play all four corners, although he is best suited to the infield, and is a conscientious guy who understands his role. He has limited speed but is a savvy baserunner. Mabry was secure in his role as a valuable reserve with a quality bat.

	AB	R	HR	RBI	SB	BA
2001 STL/FLA	154	14	6	20	1	.213
2002 Oakland	214	28	11	43	1	.276
2003 Seattle	104	12	3	16	0	.212

MACHADO, ROBERT - C - BR - b: 6/3/73 $0

Machado became the Orioles' "defensive" catcher when they called him up from Triple-A Ottawa to replace Geronimo Gil. Machado's only salable skills are his ability to throw out base stealers and his hitting success against lefthanded pitchers. Those have enabled him to earn jobs briefly with six different major league teams. Unfortunately for Machado, Baltimore starting catcher Brook Fordyce also hit lefties exceptionally well. There should be another job for Machado as a once-a-week catcher and defensive replacement.

	AB	R	HR	RBI	SB	BA
2001 Chicago - NL	135	13	2	13	0	.222
2002 Milwaukee	211	19	3	22	0	.261
2003 Baltimore	49	8	1	3	0	.265

MACIAS, JOSE - 3B/OF - BB - b: 1/25/74 $3

Macias is valuable as a utility capable of playing any infield or outfield position and is the most versatile defensive player the Expos had last year. Macias filled in everywhere but catcher, shortstop and first base. Although Macias is a switch-hitter, he doesn't hit for average or power from either side and he's no threat to steal bases. It should be noted that he hit only .180 on the road last year.

	AB	R	HR	RBI	SB	BA
2001 Detroit	488	62	8	51	21	.268
2002 Montreal	338	43	7	39	8	.249
2003 Montreal	272	31	4	22	4	.239

MACKOWIAK, ROB - OF - BL - b: 6/20/76 $6

It's nice when a player like Mackowiak makes it. He's far from being a tools guy, but he busts his tail and earns his paycheck when he has the chance. The Pirates are a mess but Mackowiak played less in 2003 than in 2002 and regardless of whether that's a sign of chaos or order, it's a bad sign for Mackowiak. Plus they have to evaluate a lot of new faces hauled in during their fire sale of Lofton and Giles, which is more bad news for Mackowiak.

	AB	R	HR	RBI	SB	BA
2001 Pittsburgh	214	30	4	21	4	.266
2002 Pittsburgh	385	57	16	48	9	.244
2003 Pittsburgh	174	20	6	19	6	.270

MAGRUDER, CHRIS - OF - BB - b: 4/26/77 $0

Magruder has limited ability and at age 27, the profile of a career minor leaguer. He's a short, chunky guy who has been with three organizations. He has shown occasional power, but is mostly a gap hitter, and he can swipe a few bases with his good speed. He has a good glove and can play all three outfield positions but the best possible role he could have in the majors is that of a reserve outfielder, pinch-hitter, and pinch-runner.

	AB	R	HR	RBI	SB	BA
2002 Cleveland	258	34	6	29	2	.217
2003 Cleveland	26	3	1	3	0	.346

MARRERO, ELI - OF - BR - b: 11/17/73 $4

Marrero's best asset is his versatility. He can play all over the field, including behind the plate, first, third and the corner outfield positions. He quickly became a favorite of manager Tony La Russa, who has done everything he can over the past few years to get Marrero in as many games as possible. A former catcher, Marrero has a little power, is deceptively quick and will steal more bases than most former backstops will. Although he is not particularly gifted defensively, he won't hurt his team anywhere he plays. He is not good enough to play every day, though he can perform reasonably well in a limited role.

	AB	R	HR	RBI	SB	BA
2002 St. Louis	397	63	18	66	14	.262
2003 St. Louis	107	10	2	20	0	.224

MARTIN, AL - DH - BL - b: 11/24/67 $0

Martin is a veteran outfielder whose star has been diminishing since 1999, missing all of 2002 with an elbow injury. He began the 2003 season on the Devil Rays with the expectation that he would be the everyday DH, starting opening day at that position but by the middle of June, it was apparent that he wasn't able to hold on to that job. He plays almost exclusively against righthanded pitching, and at this stage of his career, he is no longer guaranteed a platoon role, and will have to compete for a backup outfield spot.

	AB	R	HR	RBI	SB	BA
2001 Seattle	283	41	7	42	9	.240
2003 Tampa Bay	238	19	3	26	2	.252

MARTINEZ, EDGAR - DH - BR - b: 1/2/63 $15

Martinez, thriving at 40, continued to make a run at all the DH records. He still has the best career average among DHs and is No. 2 in home runs and RBIs behind Harold Baines. With a strong April, he will pass Baines in those categories this year. Martinez is a perfect hitter - patient enough to wait for his pitch, aggressive enough to drive it into the gaps or over the fence. Martinez is not afraid to work deep in the count waiting for his pitch. He uses the entire field, and while he strikes out now and again still never seems to get fooled. After being bothered by leg problems the previous two years, Martinez stayed injury-free in 2003. He is defensively in the one-year-at-a-time stage, although after breaking Ken Griffey Jr.'s franchise record for total bases last April seemed to have enough in the tank for another year at DH.

	AB	R	HR	RBI	SB	BA
2001 Seattle	470	80	23	116	4	.306
2002 Seattle	328	42	15	59	1	.277
2003 Seattle	497	72	24	98	0	.294

MARTINEZ, RAMON - 2B/3B/SS - BR - b: 10/10/72 $3

Martinez isn't terribly gifted, though he has a knack for making the most of his opportunities. He did enough for the Cubs late last season to take the starting shortstop spot from Alex Gonzalez and quickly became a fan favorite in Chicago for his hustle in the field. Although he has a little bit of power at the plate, he is often overmatched when facing the better pitchers in the league. He is dependable enough to stick around for a few more years as a reserve, though he isn't quite good enough to make anybody believe he can play every day.

	AB	R	HR	RBI	SB	BA
2001 San Francisco	391	48	5	37	1	.253
2002 San Francisco	181	26	4	25	2	.271
2003 Chicago - NL	293	30	3	34	0	.283

MARTINEZ, TINO - 1B - BL - b: 12/7/67 $13

Martinez has been a steady performer for more than a decade, though he has declined noticeably in the last two seasons. Most of the reason is because Martinez has had real difficulty hitting lefthanded pitching. It got so bad late last season, when he barely hit .210 against southpaws, that he was used basically in a platoon over the last half of the season with Eduardo Perez playing against the lefties. At this point in his career, he doesn't have nearly enough power to justify playing a corner infield position, even as a platoon player, and his defense, while adequate, isn't enough by itself to keep him in the lineup. Martinez might be able to squeeze another decent year or two out of his body, though it won't be long before he gets pushed out of the way by a younger, more prolific hitter.

	AB	R	HR	RBI	SB	BA
2001 New York - AL	589	89	34	113	1	.280
2002 St. Louis	511	63	21	75	3	.262
2003 St. Louis	476	66	15	69	1	.273

MARTINEZ, VICTOR - C - BB - b: 12/23/78 $5

Right now, Martinez is a good hitter and better at the plate than behind it. His throwing arm is suspect and as the Cleveland pitching staff tends to allow a lot of base runners, it seems that a good throwing catcher is a must have. How important is it that Martinez start at catcher? Well, he can hit; he's hit well everywhere. Last year in Triple-A Buffalo, Martinez batted .328 although he hit only seven homers. The Indians are not far into a rebuilding mode so Martinez might as well get his feet wet and work on his defensive shortcomings but, it would be a shame if his hitting is compromised by the grind of becoming a catcher. He's good no doubt, but we're not talking Johnny Bench here.

	AB	R	HR	RBI	SB	BA
2002 Cleveland	32	2	1	5	0	.281
2003 Cleveland	159	15	1	16	1	.289

MATEO, HENRY - 2B - BB - b: 10/14/76 $1

Mateo's major offensive asset is speed. Mateo is very quick and he knows how to steal. He could lead many teams in steals but he'd have to play a lot and that's not likely to happen as he's not particularly adept on defense and he's far from being a tough out.

	AB	R	HR	RBI	SB	BA
2002 Montreal	23	1	0	0	2	.174
2003 Montreal	154	29	0	7	11	.240

MATEO, RUBEN - OF - BR - b: 2/10/78 $0

Mateo was a major beneficiary of regular playing time after the injuries and salary purge the Reds experienced in 2003. Mateo may be getting his game together and the regular work certainly helped. He's still young at age 26 and whatever he is going to be for the rest of his baseball career, he will become this year. A slow start could end any thoughts of Mateo ever starting again but if he gets out of the blocks well, and he can, a once promising career will be back on track.

	AB	R	HR	RBI	SB	BA
2001 Texas	129	18	1	13	1	.248
2002 Cincinnati	86	11	2	7	0	.256
2003 Cincinnati	207	16	3	18	0	.242

MATHENY, MIKE - C - BR - b: 9/22/70 $3

An awful hitter, Matheny has stayed in the everyday lineup the last four seasons because St. Louis skipper Tony La Russa loves his defense and pitch-calling ability. He has hit above .250 only once in his career and doesn't even hit many doubles, much less a lot of home runs. He gets by because of the way La Russa believes he is able to handle a pitching staff. Matheny will always have trouble hitting his weight, but he'll have a job for as long as he and La Russa remain in St. Louis. If either one leaves, however, it will be difficult for Matheny to keep his job, as not many other skippers will be willing to live with his weak offense.

	AB	R	HR	RBI	SB	BA
2001 St. Louis	381	40	7	42	0	.218
2002 St. Louis	315	31	3	35	1	.244
2003 St. Louis	441	43	8	47	1	.252

MATOS, JULIUS - 3B - BR - b: 12/12/74 $0

A journeyman middle infielder with almost a decade of minor-league experience under his belt,

Matos came to the Royals as a non-roster invitee to spring training camp, then spent most of the summer at Triple-A Omaha where he had one of his best seasons at the plate. Matos was recalled shortly before the All-Star break for a brief major league look, then recalled again for good early in August, taking over the club's reserve infield role after Desi Relaford became the regular second baseman. He earned some regular play himself as the Royals rested some of their dinged-up starters and he filled the holes rather well. Matos has primarily been a shortstop in the minors; he has good range and quick hands, so he's capable of handling spot duty anywhere on the infield. Despite his decent season with the bat, Matos is not expected to hit much in the bigs. He runs well and is capable of making an occasional start on the infield to give a regular a day off. In 2004, Matos can be a useful spare part on a major league team, or he'll bide his time at Triple-A waiting for an opportunity.

	AB	R	HR	RBI	SB	BA
2002 San Diego	185	19	2	19	1	.238
2003 Kansas City	57	7	2	7	1	.263

MATOS, LUIS - OF - BR - b: 10/30/78 $22

Matos was one of the majors' biggest surprises in 2003. He had a .212 major league average over parts of three seasons when Baltimore brought him up from Triple-A Ottawa last May. By June, he batted .500 for his first nine games with the Orioles, and though he predictably tailed off, his average didn't go below .300. He hadn't batted that high before last season and he had reached double figures in homers in the minors only in 1999. Matos has enough speed to be among a major league's top 10 base stealers. He's a good center fielder, but not as good as his speed, arm and reputation indicate.

	AB	R	HR	RBI	SB	BA
2001 Baltimore	98	16	4	12	7	.214
2002 Baltimore	31	0	0	1	1	.129
2003 Baltimore	439	70	13	45	15	.303

MATSUI, HIDEKI - OF - BL - b: 6/12/74 $17

"Godzilla" arrived in New York touted as a power hitter after slamming 50 home runs in Japan in 2002. In the U.S., he turned out to be a line-drive hitter with gap power, a patient hitter and a fundamentally sound left fielder and baserunner who played every game. Despite his limited power, Matsui was one of the Yankees' leading run producers, nearly matching his 107 RBI from the year before. He hit lefthanders and righthanders for the same average. Matsui had 13 outfield assists. If not quite the slugger's deal, he justified the contract the Yankees gave him.

	AB	R	HR	RBI	SB	BA
2003 New York - AL	623	82	16	106	2	.287

MATTHEWS, GARY - OF - BB - b: 8/25/74 $10

After a 2002 season in which he looked to be Baltimore's center fielder of the future, Matthews was waived by the Orioles in late May, 2003, and claimed by San Diego, which had injury problems in the outfield and was in desperate need of a warm body. Matthews appears to have the skills to follow in his father's footsteps as a long-time major leaguer. He has good speed and has some pop, although he is not a home run hitter. He has good range and an average arm. Something keeps him from holding a permanent job, however, and he was expected to enter spring training as a reserve outfielder with potential.

	AB	R	HR	RBI	SB	BA
2001 PIT/CHI - NL	405	63	14	44	8	.227
2002 NYM/BAL	345	54	7	38	15	.275
2003 BAL/SD	468	71	6	42	12	.248

MAYNE, BRENT - C - BL - b: 4/19/68 $5

The Royals hot start in April included power from an unexpected source: Brent Mayne. After connecting for just six homers over the previous three seasons, Mayne bashed four in his first 14 games as he hit over .300 in the first month. However, Mayne's bat cooled over the remainder of the season as he managed just 15 RBI the next four months, leaving Royals fans struggling to remember the Mayne, or at least the last time he contributed with the bat. At his best, Mayne can be a patient hitter who will work the count, make contact and draw walks, and he'll add some extra-base hits along the way. His bat has slowed quite a bit in recent years and he's easily overmatched by hard-throwers. The Royals don't really expect much from Mayne at the plate anyway; they prize his defensive ability and how he handles their young pitchers. He blocks pitches well and is above-average at gunning down would-be base thieves despite a barely adequate arm. Mayne runs well enough for a 35-year-old catcher; he doesn't take unnecessary chances on the basepaths. Advancing age and dwindling offensive abilities signal a fast-approaching end for Mayne. Still, he should be able to hang around as a backup backstop for a couple more years before hanging up the spikes.

	AB	R	HR	RBI	SB	BA
2001 COL/KC	326	28	2	40	1	.285
2002 Kansas City	326	35	4	30	4	.236
2003 Kansas City	372	39	6	36	0	.245

McCARTY, DAVE - 1B - BR - b: 11/23/69 $0

The last thing the Red Sox seemed to need was another first baseman/outfielder, yet they claimed McCarty on waivers from Oakland in August. The Athletics had brought him up in July after he'd shown good power at Triple-A Sacramento. With the Sox, he played sporadically and hit well enough that they used him as a pinch hitter. Boston, his ninth organization and seventh major league team, also had him work out as a pitcher. He showed a fastball at up to 90 mph, and entered spring-training with a chance to tryout on the mound.

	AB	R	HR	RBI	SB	BA
2001 Kansas City	200	26	7	26	0	.250
2002 KC/TB	66	5	2	4	0	.136
2003 OAK/BOS	53	6	1	8	0	.340

McCRACKEN, QUINTON - OF - BB - b: 3/16/70 $2

A former defensive back for Steve Spurrier at Duke, McCracken struggled as a backup right fielder and bench player in 2003. McCracken suffered a career-threatening torn anterior cruciate ligament in his right knee in 1999 and after years of rehab appeared to back on his game in 2002, hitting .309 and working his way into the starting lineup late that August. He was unable to duplicate those numbers in 2003, when he struggled to put the ball in play. Although he has never had much sock, McCracken had trouble driving the ball into the gaps. He lost most of his speed after his knee surgery and relies on being fundamentally sound. He covers a lot of ground in the outfield, although his arm is only average. In the final year of a two-year contract, McCracken was expected to open the season as an outfield reserve.

	AB	R	HR	RBI	SB	BA
2001 Minnesota	64	7	0	3	0	.219
2002 Arizona	349	60	3	40	5	.309
2003 Arizona	203	17	0	18	5	.227

McDONALD, JOHN - 2B/3B/SS - BR - b: 9/24/74 $0

McDonald gets a little major league playing time every year. While he is a reliable fielder, he's never hit well enough to make a serious run at a full time major league job. McDonald first saw extensive playing time with the Indians in 2002 as an injury replacement. Normally a shortstop, he did a good job filling in at second base. McDonald has a good-field, no-hit reputation, and his best role may be as a reserve infielder, late inning defensive replacement or pinch-runner.

	AB	R	HR	RBI	SB	BA
2002 Cleveland	264	35	1	12	3	.250
2003 Cleveland	214	21	1	14	3	.215

McEWING, JOE - 2B/SS - BR - b: 10/19/72 $1

The crowd-pleasing McEwing hustled at every one of the seven positions he played in 2003, but when the dust cleared he hadn't really done much to help himself, his team or any remaining Rotisserie owners. He neither hits for power nor works counts to get on base often. Once McEwing does reach base, he is a smart, selective base stealer. Defensively, he's strongest at second base, where he played more often after the Mets traded Roberto Alomar. In September, McEwing batted 55 times with no RBI and no extra-base hits. He was a free agent after the season.

	AB	R	HR	RBI	SB	BA
2001 New York - NL	283	41	8	30	8	.283
2002 New York - NL	196	22	3	26	4	.199
2003 New York - NL	278	31	1	16	3	.241

McGRIFF, FRED - 1B - BL - b: 10/31/63 $1

McGriff passed Joe DiMaggio and Wille Stargell to reach 34th place on the major league career RBI list last season, although that might have been his last hurrah. McGriff missed about two months with groin and adductor muscle injuries and had the worst statistical season in his long, productive major league career. He no longer drives the ball the way he once did, although he still has good power when he gets his arms extended. McGriff's speed has abandoned him, and he is now a below average runner no longer capable of even the surprise stolen base. His range has become limited at first, although he still has a nice touch around the bag. McGriff struggled against lefties, finishing under the Mendoza Line, and ended the 2003 season as a platoon player. At 41, that may be his best usage this season.

	AB	R	HR	RBI	SB	BA
2001 TB/CHI - NL	513	67	31	102	1	.306
2002 Chicago - NL	523	67	30	103	1	.273
2003 Los Angeles	297	32	13	40	0	.249

McLEMORE, MARK - 3B/SS - BB - b: 10/4/64 $7

McLemore has developed into a "regular irregular," an accomplished veteran who is comfortable at three infield positions and in left field while bringing speed and a line drive bat to the lineup. A switch-hitter, McLemore concentrates on putting the ball in to utilize his speed, which remains a factor even as he nears 40. His good eye makes him a good fit at the top of the order, although his average hurts. He has good range at second base and not as much at shortstop, although he is adequate there. He gets to a lot of balls in the outfield. He can still steal and base and is good at taking the extra base. He was expected to play a similar role this season.

	AB	R	HR	RBI	SB	BA
2001 Seattle	409	78	5	57	39	.286
2002 Seattle	337	54	7	41	18	.270
2003 Seattle	309	34	2	37	5	.233

McMILLON, BILLY - OF - BR - b: 11/17/71 $2

McMillon is one of those guys that seemingly just slipped through the cracks somewhere along the way. He did everything he could in the minor leagues to show that he belonged in the bigs, yet he was never given the opportunity to play every day. He shows flashes of brilliance occasionally, mostly because he has good discipline at the plate. He has a little bit of pop in his bat, though he has lost much of his speed over the past few years. McMillon is clearly better than a lot of fourth and fifth outfielders, though he will have a hard time making the Opening Day roster this season because of his age and relative lack of experience. Still, he should resurface once again by mid-season and provide a little spark off the bench.

	AB	R	HR	RBI	SB	BA
2001 DET/OAK	92	7	1	14	1	.217
2003 Oakland	153	15	6	26	0	.268

MELHUSE, ADAM - C - BB - b: 3/27/72 $1

Melhuse has been in professional baseball for 11 seasons, yet he has less than 200 at-bats in the major leagues. His skills behind the plate aren't enough to keep him in the bigs full time, nor is he a good enough hitter to keep him out of the minors. He hit well enough in very limited action for Oakland last season, though he strikes out far too much to be a consistent batter. There is a good chance Melhuse's career is over. Even if he signs another contract, and plays well enough in the minor leagues to earn a promotion, he will be one of the last guys off the bench. He just doesn't have enough experience in the major leagues to be trusted in a more demanding role.

	AB	R	HR	RBI	SB	BA
2001 Colorado	71	5	1	8	1	.183
2003 Oakland	77	13	5	14	0	.299

MENCH, KEVIN - OF - BR - b: 1/7/78 $3

Mench followed a fine rookie season in 2002 with an injury-marred campaign last year. After missing over a month with a strained oblique muscle, Mench was optioned to Triple-A for a month. Then, a month after his return, he suffered a broken wrist when he was hit by a pitch. Despite the setbacks, Mench is a strong candidate to be an everyday player in 2004. He has good power potential and is an aggressive hitter who crowds the plate. Defensively, he is adequate in left or right field, but it is his bat that will keep him in a major league lineup.

	AB	R	HR	RBI	SB	BA
2002 Texas	366	52	15	60	1	.260
2003 Texas	125	15	2	11	1	.320

MENECHINO, FRANK - 2B - BR - b: 1/7/71 $0

It's really hard to believe that Menechino spent the entire season in Oakland. Knowing his limitations, the Athletics used him sparingly, as he started only 24 games the entire season. He was more selective at the plate last season, though it wasn't enough to make up for his other weaknesses. He has no speed and does not have a strong arm, which means second base is his only real position. Menechino will have to have an outstanding spring in order to make the Opening Day roster. Most likely, he will start the season in the minor leagues and hope to earn a promotion in midseason.

	AB	R	HR	RBI	SB	BA
2001 Oakland	471	82	12	60	2	.242
2002 Oakland	132	22	3	15	0	.205
2003 Oakland	83	10	2	9	0	.193

MERCED, ORLANDO - OF - BL - b: 11/2/66 $1

Merced was the runner-up to Jeff Bagwell for Rookie of the Year in 1991 and enjoyed a nine-year career before he was unable to land a major league job in 2000. After a brief stint in Japan, he finished the 2000 season in the Astros minor league system. He returned to the major leagues in 2001 and enjoyed two productive seasons as a part-time player, but last year his production fell, and had difficulty getting on base, posting an on-base percentage less than .300. He can play both the outfield and infield corner positions. He has been a capable pinch-hitter and performed well in a platoon role in the past, but can't be expected to win more than a backup outfielder role for this season.

	AB	R	HR	RBI	SB	BA
2001 Houston	137	19	6	29	5	.263
2002 Houston	251	35	6	30	4	.287
2003 Houston	212	20	3	26	3	.231

MERLONI, LOU - 3B/SS - BR - b: 4/6/71 $1

Merloni is a decent utility player who has some offensive ability, but he doesn't seem destined for full-time major league duty. He's been shuttled back and forth between the majors and minors by the Red Sox and Padres over the past several seasons, but many feel he was better than some of the players they stuck with. He's also got a great attitude and he works hard, both important qualities in a reserve.

	AB	R	HR	RBI	SB	BA
2001 Boston	146	21	3	13	2	.267
2002 Boston	194	28	4	18	1	.247
2003 SD/BOS	181	24	1	18	2	.265

MICHAELS, JASON - OF - BR - b: 5/4/76 $1

Pat Burrell's teammate at the University of Miami and with the Phillies, Michaels is a better outfielder with a stronger throwing arm. Michaels saw a little action when Marlon Byrd was injured but he's 28 and he's only had brief activity in the majors. He's not a good hitter but he can fill in adequately in the outfield. He did blast lefthanded pitchers with a .382 batting average.

	AB	R	HR	RBI	SB	BA.
2002 Philadelphia	105	16	2	11	1	.267
2003 Philadelphia	109	20	5	17	0	.330

MIENTKIEWICZ, DOUG - 1B - BL - b: 6/19/74 $12

Former Twins manager Tom Kelly used the word, "moxie," to describe how Doug Mientkiewicz plays first base. He covers plenty of ground and has outstanding reflexes to dig errant throws out of the dirt. He leads the team in ice packs, as he accumulates plenty of bruises and teammates rally around him because of his determination. He's no Jim Thome at the plate, but takes good at-bats and sprays the ball around the field. Statistics show that Mientkiewicz is one of the best clutch hitters in the league.

	AB	R	HR	RBI	SB	BA
2001 Minnesota	543	77	15	74	2	.306
2002 Minnesota	467	60	10	64	1	.261
2003 Minnesota	487	67	11	65	4	.300

MILES, AARON - 2B - BB - b: 12/15/76 $0

Miles has some power, though he likely will not hit a ton of homers in the big leagues. He has the ability to hit mistakes hard and line them into the outfield gaps for doubles. While he has decent speed, his poor judgment on the basepaths keeps him from being a basestealing threat. Because Miles doesn't hit a lot of homers or steal a lot of bases, he is going to have a hard time winning a starting spot in spring training. He likely will begin the season in the minor leagues again. He will be one of the first in line if an injury occurs, however.

MILLAR, KEVIN - 1B/OF - BR - b: 9/24/71 $16

Millar had an eventful winter before the 2003 season. First, he signed a contract with a Japanese team. After having misgivings because of strained international relations, and possibly because the Red Sox had claimed him on waivers from Florida, a deal among the three teams freed him to play for Boston. Though his batting average suffered last season, he had career highs in homers and RBI (and in stolen bases) as some of his doubles turned into homers. Because he hits the ball to all fields, more of his line drives can make it over the fence on the road than over the Green Monster at Fenway. Millar slumped badly after the All-Star break, but remained a crowd favorite because he plays so hard.

	AB	R	HR	RBI	SB	BA
2001 Florida	449	62	20	85	0	.314
2002 Florida	438	58	16	57	0	.306
2003 Boston	544	83	25	96	3	.276

MILLER, CORKY - C - BR - b: 3/18/76 $1

Miller handles himself well behind the plate and that will buy him some playing time in the majors. He just doesn't have the talent or durability to be a first string major league catcher.

	AB	R	HR	RBI	SB	BA
2001 Cincinnati	49	5	3	7	1	.184
2002 Cincinnati	114	9	3	15	0	.254
2003 Cincinnati	30	4	0	1	0	.267

MILLER, DAMIAN - C - BR - b: 10/13/69 $3

It's hard to believe that Miller was an All-Star only two seasons ago. Though he was never a top-notch offensive threat, he fell on hard times in the last couple of seasons as he reached the age where most catchers start experiencing a decline in their abilities. He especially struggled, as many catchers often do, late in 2003, ostensibly worn down by the rigors of catching most days. Although he never has been much of a hitter for average or power, Miller is more than willing to take a walk. Regarded as a fine defensive backstop, he will be able to keep his starting job for another year or two.

	AB	R	HR	RBI	SB	BA
2001 Arizona	380	45	13	47	0	.271
2002 Arizona	297	40	11	42	0	.249
2003 Chicago - NL	352	34	9	36	1	.233

MIRABELLI, DOUG - C - BR - b: 10/18/70 $1

Mirabelli has built an eight-year major league career as a backup catcher, with more job security in 21st-century baseball than any position other than lefthanded reliever. Mirabelli's game has been well suited to Fenway Park, though he didn't hit lefthanders as well last year as in the past. He did make strides toward losing his gig last season — when his power, on-base ability and throwing all took steps backward even though he had slightly more playing time. There will be a backup job for him somewhere in 2004, even if he has to go back to the minors for a while.

	AB	R	HR	RBI	SB	BA
2001 TEX/BOS	190	20	11	29	0	.226
2002 Boston	151	17	7	25	0	.225
2003 Boston	163	23	6	18	0	.258

MOELLER, CHAD - C - BR - b: 2/18/75 $2

Moeller was handed the Diamondbacks' starting catching position after veteran Damian Miller was traded to the Chicago Cubs at the 2002 winter meetings, and Moeller opened the 2003 season as if he would keep the job all year. He was hitting over .300 at the All-Star break before tailing off. He has good pop to both alleys, although he is such a free-swinger that he occasionally gets himself out swinging at pitchers' pitches. While Moeller worked well at times with fellow former Southern California product Randy Johnson, some Arizona pitchers preferred another battery mate in 2003 for defensive reasons. Moeller has an erratic arm and threw out only one in four potential base-stealers. Moeller again will be among the candidates for the starting catching position, although the likelihood of catcher-by-committee again appears great.

	AB	R	HR	RBI	SB	BA
2001 Arizona	56	8	1	2	0	.232
2002 Arizona	105	10	2	16	0	.286
2003 Arizona	239	29	7	29	1	.268

MOHR, DUSTAN - OF - BR - b: 6/19/76 $6

Mohr can hit a little bit and play solid defense. But he's still looking for everyday duty. What holds him back is his high strikeout rate for a part-time player, as well as occasional lapses in the field and on the basepaths. Mohr deserves credit for remaining confident and coming up with occasional big plays to keep the coaching staff mindful of his talents. A very muscular player, Mohr can knock the ball out of the park but needs to focus on making solid contact and staying away from the strikeout.

	AB	R	HR	RBI	SB	BA
2001 Minnesota	51	6	0	4	1	.235
2002 Minnesota	383	55	12	45	6	.269
2003 Minnesota	348	50	10	36	5	.250

MOLINA, BENGIE - C - BR - b: 7/20/74 $7

A good defensive catcher with a little pop in his bat, Molina is an everyday player when healthy. Last season, a broken wrist caused Molina to miss most of September, but overall it was still Molina's best season since 2000. Although a free swinger, he makes good contact at the plate and uses the whole field. One of the slowest runners in the league, Molina hits into a lot of double plays and has stolen only one base in his big league career. Molina's defensive abilities will continue to assure him of a starting role. He provides better-than-average offense for a catcher.

	AB	R	HR	RBI	SB	BA
2001 Anaheim	325	31	6	40	0	.262
2002 Anaheim	428	344	5	47	0	.245
2003 Anaheim	409	37	14	71	1	.281

MONDESI, RAUL - OF - BR - b: 3/12/71 $20

Acquired by Arizona at the 2003 trading deadline to supply much needed pop, Mondesi delivered during his short time. He has great physical gifts but was available after wearing out his welcome with another club, this time the Yankees. Mondesi has 30-30 - heck, 40-40 - tools but never seems to apply himself enough to get there. He has a terrific arm and with a head transplant would make a perennial All-Star caliber right fielder. He was expected to be the starting right fielder, because it is hard to give up on that raw ability.

	AB	R	HR	RBI	SB	BA
2001 Toronto	572	88	27	84	30	.252
2002 TOR/NY - AL	569	90	26	88	15	.232
2003 NY - AL/AZ	523	83	24	71	22	.272

MONROE, CRAIG - OF - BR - b: 2/27/77 $8

Monroe's career took an interesting upturn in 2003. He was given an opportunity to play on a fairly regular basis for the Tigers and he hit the long ball for a team that is dreadfully short of power. Monroe's performance should earn him a shot to start or at least serve as a fourth outfielder.

	AB	R	HR	RBI	SB	BA
2001 Texas	52	8	2	5	2	.212
2002 Detroit	25	3	1	1	0	.120
2003 Detroit	425	51	23	70	4	.240

MORA, MELVIN - OF - BR - b: 2/2/72 $7

The early part of Mora's 2003 season was like Tom Cruise's character in "Risky Business": "Time a' your life, eh, kid?" The second half was an entirely different story. Mora, always a good line drive hitter, has developed discipline at the plate that helped him break out of the gate with a .349 average at last year's All-Star break. But after the break, he started swinging for the fences more, struck out twice as often as he walked and for the second consecutive year was a sub-.200 hitter. The only reason Mora's final season stats stayed impressive was that he batted just 69 times because of a sprained left knee. Mora has played extensively in the infield, but is best suited as an outfielder.

	AB	R	HR	RBI	SB	BA
2001 Baltimore	436	49	7	48	11	.250
2002 Baltimore	557	86	19	64	16	.233
2003 Baltimore	344	68	15	48	6	.317

MORBAN, JOSE - SS/DH - BB - b: 12/2/79 $0

Morban had played three seasons, never above low Single-A, when the Orioles selected him in the 2002 Rule 5 draft from the Rangers organization. With an already thin roster and little realistic chance in the pennant race, Baltimore chose to keep him on its active roster. His game is speed (100 steals in the minors) and defense. He showed some power (eight homers in both 2001 and '02), but batted no higher than .260 during those years. Those also were the skills he showed in his limited major league exposure last season. He's likely to be a starting shortstop in Double-A or Triple-A ball after a season of winter ball in the Dominican Republic.

	AB	R	HR	RBI	SB	BA
2003 Baltimore	71	14	2	5	8	.141

MORDECAI, MIKE - SS - BR - b: 12/13/67 $0

A 35 year-old career utility player who somehow seems to always play for a pennant contender. Of course, he comes cheap but, a Rabbit's foot is cheaper. Last season he played every infield position except catcher.

	AB	R	HR	RBI	SB	BA
2001 Montreal	254	28	3	32	2	.280
2002 MON/FLA	151	19	0	11	2	.203
2003 Florida	89	11	2	8	3	.213

MORNEAU, JUSTIN - DH - BL - b: 5/15/81 $4

Morneau has the potential to be a hitting machine but needs to make adjustments after making his major league debut in 2003. Morneau has great hand-eye coordination and great power. He can hit any fastball, but struggled when he began to chase breaking balls and changeups. That was chalked up to inexperience, because he does have a good batting eye and is expected to lay off those pitches. His defense? A work in progress. He'll see more big league time in 2004 but probably won't threaten to become a regular until 2005.

	AB	R	HR	RBI	SB	BA
2003 Minnesota	106	14	4	16	0	.226

MORRIS, WARREN - 2B - BL - b: 1/11/74 $6

Morris was called up from the minors and he played every day in Detroit and enhanced his chances of staying in the majors for a while as a utility infielder. Morris is not a long term solution. Detroit is simply waiting for Santiago and Infante to mature into the SS / 2B combo they hope to be. Morris played as well as he could so, more power to him but at his age, 2003 could be his career year and should easily be his peak, as far as playing time is concerned.

	AB	R	HR	RBI	SB	BA
2001 Pittsburgh	103	6	2	11	2	.204
2003 Detroit	346	37	6	37	4	.272

MUELLER, BILL - 3B - BB - b: 3/17/71 $17

Before 2003, Mueller was known as a scrappy third baseman with a knack for getting on base. He came out of the season as one of the American League's leading hitters and a major force behind Boston's postseason push. After signing with the Red Sox as a free agent, he started and finished strong, bouncing back from a June downturn. Mueller's new home park helped him even more than Wrigley Field had when he was with the Cubs, leading the AL in batting average.

Has he reached a new talent level, or is he merely coming off a career year? Most players in their 30s don't sustain a sudden jump in performance.

	AB	R	HR	RBI	SB	BA
2001 Chicago - NL	210	38	6	23	1	.295
2002 CHI - NL/SF	366	51	7	38	0	.262
2003 Boston	524	85	19	85	1	.326

MUNSON, ERIC - 3B - BL - b: 10/3/77 $2

Former catching prospect Eric Munson was the third sacker for the Tigers until he was sidelined in August for fracturing his thumb, and missed the rest of the season. He is a line drive power hitter with a live bat who has potentional to be a big time run producer. Even though he's got decent power, he hasn't hit well enough to ensure himself a starting role.

	AB	R	HR	RBI	SB	BA
2001 Detroit	66	4	1	6	0	.152
2002 Detroit	59	3	2	5	0	.186
2003 Detroit	313	28	18	50	3	.240

MYERS, GREG - C/DH - BL - b: 4/14/66 $8

Myers had a career least year and for someone in his late thirties, he has great power and a much more confident hitting approach than he had for most of his career, especially in his exceptional newfound ability to turn on inside pitches. No longer blessed with even an average throwing arm, Myers' days behind the plate are certainly numbered and while he can still contribute offensively, he is poised to return to being a useful bench player who doesn't play often. He's good enough to be a backup catcher for most teams but he won't play as much as he did last year.

	AB	R	HR	RBI	SB	BA
2001 BAL/OAK	161	24	11	31	0	.224
2002 Oakland	144	15	6	21	0	.222
2003 Toronto	329	51	15	52	0	.307

NADY, XAVIER - OF - BR - b: 11/14/78 $7

Nady, one of the best prospects in the San Diego chain after being a No. 2 draftee in 2000, was rushed to the big leagues when injuries struck the parent Padres in 2003. He has good power, although his plate coverage and pitch recognition are typical of young long-ball hitters. He underwent Tommy John surgery on his right elbow after the 2001 season, and his outfield arm is only average. Nady is not particularly fast but will surprise with a stolen base. He was expected to open the season at Triple-A, entering spring training.

	AB	R	HR	RBI	SB	BA
2003 San Diego	371	50	9	39	6	.267

NEVIN, PHIL - 1B/OF - BR - b: 1/19/71 $16

The "Phil Nevin - left field" experiment went bust early in spring training, when Nevin suffered a dislocated left shoulder March 7 while trying to make a diving catch in his new position. He missed 102 games because of the injury, taking with him the greater part of the San Diego offense. A former No. 1 overall pick in the draft, Nevin has prodigious power and can turn around anyone's fastball, Randy Johnson's included. Nevin also has learned to protect the outer half of the plate, thereby cutting down on his strikeouts. While he does not have great speed, he is aggressive and daring on the bases and is gung-ho about breaking up a double play. Although he has a strong arm, he is not a good defender because of his slow feet and limited range. He was moved to the outfield because he had so much trouble at third base. Nevin was expected to open the season as an everyday starter and cleanup hitter, although offseason movement around him was to determine his position.

	AB	R	HR	RBI	SB	BA
2001 San Diego	546	97	41	126	4	.306
2002 San Diego	407	53	12	57	4	.285
2003 San Diego	226	30	13	46	2	.279

NIEKRO, LANCE - 1B - BR - b: 1/29/79 $0

Blessed with a big league surname, Niekro is trying to make his mark at the plate, unlike his famous father and uncle. He has the ability to hit the ball to all fields and has demonstrated in the past that he can hit for a little power. He needs to improve his eye at the plate after walking only 41 times in four minor league seasons. Niekro started out at third base, but was moved to first after suffering a shoulder injury in 2001 which required surgery. He is going to have trouble hitting for enough power to justify playing a corner infield position, though he could wind up being a decent righthanded hitting part of a platoon at first.

NIVAR, RAMON - OF - BR - b: 2/22/80 $0

Speed and defense are Nivar's calling cards at this point in his career. Nivar, formerly known as Ramon Martinez, came up through the minors as a middle infielder, but his immediate future is as a center fielder, where he has Gary Pettis-type range. At Double-A and Triple-A last season, Nivar hit a combined .345 with six homers, 49 RBI and 15 steals. At the major league level, however, the offensive part of Nivar's game has not yet arrived, and it may take another year or so before he is a contributor at the plate in the big leagues. Because of his defensive skills, he should play frequently even if he doesn't hit well.

	AB	R	HR	RBI	SB	BA
2003 Texas	90	9	0	7	4	.211

NIX, LAYNCE - OF - BL - b: 10/30/80 $7

Nix got a taste of the majors over the last half of 2003, and did not disappoint. He is ultimately expected to hit for average and power, but is still developing as a hitter. Like many young hitters, he lacks patience and needs better strike zone judgment. In a half-season at Double-A last year, Nix hit .284-15-63 with nine steals. A brief tutorial in Triple-A might benefit Nix, but he has a good chance of opening 2004 as a platoon outfielder, starting against righthanded pitching.

	AB	R	HR	RBI	SB	BA
2003 Texas	184	25	8	30	3	.255

NIXON, TROT - OF - BL - b: 4/11/74 $16

Nixon had the best year of his career in 2003, even though he missed most of September because of a calf injury. As he has matured, predictably he has added weight and power. Last year, he had career highs in batting average, home runs and on-base and slugging percentages. Over the past three seasons, Nixon has averaged about 90 RBI. He's very dangerous against righthanded pitching; if he could hit lefthanders better, Nixon would be considered a star. He's not fast, but has a good arm and covers ground well enough to be considered one of the majors' best right fielders.

	AB	R	HR	RBI	SB	BA
2001 Boston	535	100	27	88	7	.280
2002 Boston	535	81	24	94	4	.256
2003 Boston	441	81	28	87	4	.306

NORTON, GREG - 3B - BB - b: 7/6/72 $0

Norton, a journeyman through his six-year major league career, found a niche as a pinch-hitter in his third season in Colorado in 2003. Norton, a switch-hitter, threatened John Vander Wal's franchise record of 28 pinch hits but still finished with the most in the majors. Norton has been much more effective as a lefthander hitter in his career, where he has shown good power and the ability to drive the ball to all fields. All but four of his career homers have come as a lefty. He has decent plate discipline and is not afraid to take a walk, although he still can be overmatched

---

on occasion. He is not a good fielder, the main reason he never could stake claim to a third base position that has been open to all comers this millennium in Denver. He can take a turn at first if pressed. Norton was expected to open the season comfortably ensconced on the bench as a pinch-hitter/platoon infielder this season.

	AB	R	HR	RBI	SB	BA
2001 Colorado	225	30	13	40	1	.267
2002 Colorado	168	19	7	37	2	.220
2003 Colorado	179	19	6	31	2	.263

NUNEZ, ABRAHAM O. - 2B/SS - BB - b: 3/16/76 $4

Nunez has been around a while and he should not be confused with the Abraham Nunez that plays for the Marlins but we get them mixed up all the time so how can we warn you not to? Confuse away because neither of them are very good ball players right now, although the Marlins version will have a better career than this fellow who is best described as a second string utility player. He got to play when Pokey Reese was lost for the season in 2003 but if the Pirates keep 40 year old Jeff Reboulet for another year, Nunez would have to see the writing on the wall.

	AB	R	HR	RBI	SB	BA
2001 Pittsburgh	301	30	1	21	8	.262
2002 Pittsburgh	253	28	2	15	3	.233
2003 Pittsburgh	311	37	4	35	9	.248

OJEDA, AUGIE - SS - BB - b: 12/20/74 $0

It remains one of the biggest mysteries in baseball, but Ojeda was one of the most popular players the Cubs had the past couple of seasons. He offers nothing as a ballplayer, not speed, power, the ability to hit for average or draw walks, nor defense. Yet he kept getting chances with the Cubs for four straight seasons. There is virtually no chance that any other organization would give him a shot, so expect his career to mercifully come to an end the moment the Cubs finally give up on him.

	AB	R	HR	RBI	SB	BA
2001 Chicago - NL	144	16	1	12	1	.201
2002 Chicago - NL	70	4	0	4	1	.186
2003 Chicago - NL	25	2	0	0	0	.120

OJEDA, MIGUEL - C - BR - b: 1/29/75 $0

Ojeda, a fixture behind the plate for the Mexico City Red Devils since 1995 after spending parts of two seasons in the Pittsburgh organization, made his first appearance in the major leagues when San Diego purchased his contract in May after having grown weary of one-time regular Wiki Gonzalez. Ojeda, a native of the northern Mexico state of Sonora, has good power and can drive the ball in the alleys. He developed into a hitting machine south of the border — 14 homers, 41 RBI, in 42 games with the Red Devils before joining the Padres last season, 19 homers and 80 RBI, with a .352 average in 2002. Ojeda is a good athlete and has good speed for a catcher, with the ability to steal a half-dozen bases. His catching skills are adequate. Ojeda was expected to be in mix for a reserve catching spot.

	AB	R	HR	RBI	SB	BA
2003 San Diego	141	13	4	22	1	.234

O'LEARY, TROY - OF - BL - b: 8/4/69 $0

O'Leary is one of those players who winds up playing for teams who think they can contend because of name recognition alone. He is a weak hitter with no power, defensive or basestealing ability, yet he continues to be on somebody's major league roster. O'Leary has been dreadful at the plate for four straight seasons, and one of these days all 30 big league clubs are going to wise up and send him not-so-gracefully into retirement. Even if that doesn't happen this year, he will not be anything approximating a decent hitter. At this point in his career, it will be a challenge for him to offer anything noteworthy.

	AB	R	HR	RBI	SB	BA
2001 Boston	341	50	13	50	1	.240
2002 Montreal	273	27	3	37	1	.286
2003 Chicago - NL	174	18	5	28	3	.218

OLERUD, JOHN - 1B - BL - b: 8/5/68 $13

Look up underrated in the dictionary ... Olerud is a valuable commodity and one of the best two-way first basemen in the game. He is so smooth, his playing style appears almost effortless at the plate and in the field, and his quiet nature belies his controlled aggressiveness. Olerud has great plate coverage and uses the whole field, lining doubles down both lines. He is a patient hitter who is not afraid to go deep in a count to get the pitch he wants, and he will take a walk if he does not get it. Olerud is a solid gloveman, a perennial Gold Glove candidate who not only has great range but also has perfected the one-hop scoop. He is not fast but makes smart decisions on the bases. He was expected to again be a mainstay at first base and in an RBI spot in the order.

	AB	R	HR	RBI	SB	BA
2001 Seattle	572	91	21	95	3	.302
2002 Seattle	553	85	22	102	0	.300
2003 Seattle	539	64	10	83	0	.269

OLIVO, MIGUEL - C - BR - b: 7/15/78 $4

It only took a few weeks for Olivo to take the starting job away from Sandy Alomar, Jr. last season. While he didn't have a great year, he was solid enough defensively to allow the White Sox to stick with him. Olivo has a chance to wind up being a solid hitter. He is plenty strong and it's likely he will develop more power in another year or so. While he also is quite fast for a backstop – he stole 29 bases in Double-A in 2002 – it isn't likely he will many opportunities to run in the big leagues. Olivo is no better or worse than many starting catchers in the big leagues. As a result, it is unlikely that he will be able to keep his starting spot for extended periods of time.

	AB	R	HR	RBI	SB	BA
2003 Chicago - AL	317	37	6	27	6	.237

OLMEDO, RAY - SS - BB - b: 5/31/81 $0

At age 23, Olmedo's hitting is not a match for his defense, which is very good at second base. Olmedo will never be a great hitter but he battles and he's a tough out. He still must learn to be more patient with pitchers who nibble.

	AB	R	HR	RBI	SB	BA
2003 Cincinnati	230	24	0	17	1	.239

ORDONEZ, MAGGLIO - OF - BR - b: 1/28/74 $30

Consistently one of the most underrated players in the game, Ordonez puts up great numbers year after year, yet is rarely mentioned as one of the better hitters in the game. Ordonez has superb plate discipline, good power and will both score and drive in plenty of runs. He is also a good defender, with a strong arm, who does a lot in the field to help his ballclub. Ordonez ran much more earlier in his career, and while he has retained much of the speed he had, playing with improved and more experienced hitters has meant a decline in his stolen base attempts. Overall, expect Ordonez to perform exactly as he has the past 4-5 years.

	AB	R	HR	RBI	SB	BA
2001 Chicago - AL	593	97	31	113	25	.305
2002 Chicago - AL	590	116	38	135	7	.320
2003 Chicago - AL	606	95	29	99	9	.317

ORDONEZ, REY - SS - BB - b: 11/11/72 $2

Ordonez possesses a great glove but has struggled with the bat. After the 2002 season, where he hit for low average and no power and also committed 19 errors, the Mets traded him to Tampa Bay. In early May last season he sprained his left knee, later revealed as a torn ligament. He underwent surgery in late June and was expected to be out for 9 months. He was having a career-year offensively, hitting .328, and also homering 3 times, tying his season record. Ordonez was not expected to return to the Devil Rays in 2004.

	AB	R	HR	RBI	SB	BA
2001 New York - NL	461	31	3	44	3	.247
2002 New York - NL	460	53	1	42	2	.254
2003 Tampa Bay	117	14	3	22	0	.316

ORTIZ, DAVID - 1B/DH - BL - b: 11/18/75 $15

The Twins didn't have room on their roster or in their budget for Ortiz, and he attracted surprisingly little interest in free agency before last season. He was the center of attention down the stretch in 2003, with dramatic hit after dramatic hit to lead the Red Sox into the playoffs. Overcoming the injuries that held him back in his first six major league seasons, Ortiz had a career year. He can hit the ball with power to all fields, so he was well suited to playing home games at Fenway Park. Lefthanders continued to give him trouble. Despite his size and the fact that he's typecast as a designated hitter, Ortiz is quick enough to play first base more than adequately.

	AB	R	HR	RBI	SB	BA
2001 Minnesota	303	46	18	48	1	.234
2002 Minnesota	412	52	20	75	1	.272
2003 Boston	448	79	31	101	0	.288

OSIK, KEITH - C - BR - b: 10/22/68 $0

Osik, a long-time journeyman in the Pittsburgh chain, made the Milwaukee squad as a non-roster invitee in spring training and made the most of it as a platoon catcher, albeit in an unusual platoon. A righthanded hitter, Osik did most of his work against righthanded pitchers but still set career highs in games, at-bats and doubles while adding a career-high 10-game hitting streak. He has very little power although he can take the ball where it is pitched. He has a better-than-average arm. He was expected to fight for a backup catching position again this season.

	AB	R	HR	RBI	SB	BA
2001 Pittsburgh	120	9	2	13	1	.208
2002 Pittsburgh	100	6	2	11	0	.160
2003 Milwaukee	241	22	2	21	0	.249

OVERBAY, LYLE - 1B - BL - b: 1/28/77 $0

After a record-setting blitz through the Arizona minor league system, Overbay came back down to earth in his first season in the major leagues in 2003. He was given the starting first base job when Erubiel Durazo was traded to Oakland at the winter meetings but failed to hold onto it, eventually being returned to Triple-A Tucson in the late summer for more seasoning. Overbay is not a great athlete but has made himself into a gifted hitter through constant repetition with his sweet swing. He can direct the ball from foul line to foul line, preferring to hit it where it is pitched. He can drive the ball to both gaps or dead center. Although he does not have great power, a Mark Grace-like 15-20 home runs a season does not seem beyond his capabilities. Overbay's range at first base is adequate, although he will never be another Grace, who served as a his mentor/ tutor in 2003. Overbay is in the lineup for his bat; if that does not come around, watch out. He was expected to open spring training as the everyday first baseman, but with Shea Hillenbrand on the roster could have competition for the job.

	AB	R	HR	RBI	SB	BA
2003 Arizona	254	23	4	28	1	.276

OWENS, ERIC - OF - BR - b: 2/3/71 $6

Speed is the key component of Owens' game. He's at his best when hitting the ball on the ground to take advantage of his quickness to first base. Owens is capable of hitting for average with minimal power. With sufficient playing time, Owens can be among the league leaders in steals in any given season; however, at this point in his career, he is no more than a fourth outfielder, and playing time is not a given. Owens can play any of the three outfield positions adequately.

	AB	R	HR	RBI	SB	BA
2001 Florida	400	51	5	28	8	.252
2002 Florida	385	44	4	37	26	.270
2003 Anaheim	241	29	1	20	11	.270

PALMEIRO, ORLANDO - OF - BL - b: 1/19/69 $5

A fourth outfielder if there ever was one, Palmeiro does a decent job with what skills he has. He is limited offensively by his total lack of power (three total home runs in his first 1,500 big league at-bats). Also, Palmeiro simply cannot hit lefthanded pitching, thereby guaranteeing that he will never be an everyday player. And while he can hit for a decent average, he really does not have enough power to justify taking up a starting spot in the outfield. His defense is adequate, as he can go get the ball even if his arm is somewhat weak. Still, after winning the World Series with the Angels in 2002, he now has a name people recognize, and that will be enough to land him a reserve role for the next couple of years.

	AB	R	HR	RBI	SB	BA
2001 Anaheim	230	29	2	23	6	.243
2002 Anaheim	263	35	0	31	7	.300
2003 St. Louis	317	37	3	33	3	.271

PALMEIRO, RAFAEL - 1B/DH - BL - b: 9/24/64 $19

Now more a DH than an everyday first baseman, Palmeiro can still swing the bat with authority. He is no longer much of a threat to hit .300, but 30 homers and 100 RBI in a full season is a conservative figure for Palmeiro. The question is whether he will get a full season's worth of at-bats in 2004, the answer to which largely depends on where he signs. Although he has missed very few games over the past eight seasons, at this stage of his career Palmeiro could find himself being rested more frequently. After a lengthy slump early last summer, Palmeiro recovered to post a strong performance in August.

	AB	R	HR	RBI	SB	BA
2001 Texas	600	98	47	123	1	.273
2002 Texas	546	99	43	105	2	.273
2003 Texas	561	92	38	112	2	.260

PATTERSON, COREY - OF - BL - b: 8/13/79 $14

By all accounts, Patterson had a breakthrough season in 2003, one that ended prematurely because of a torn ACL in his left knee. He hit consistently for the first time in the big leagues and provided much more power than he had before. While he still didn't draw hardly any walks, he showed improved patience at the plate and he swung at far fewer balls out of the strike zone. Patterson's performance last season guaranteed him a starting spot this year, and there is no reason to think he'll suffer a complete relapse at the plate. Do look for him to cut way back on his running game to prevent his knee from further injury. He was expected to be ready for the start of the season, though it wouldn't be a big surprise at all if he has to miss a few weeks to make sure his knee is fully healed.

	AB	R	HR	RBI	SB	BA
2001 Chicago - NL	131	26	4	14	4	.221
2002 Chicago - NL	592	71	14	54	18	.253
2003 Chicago - NL	329	49	13	55	16	.298

PAUL, JOSH - C - BR - b: 5/19/75 $0

While Paul once was thought to have the potential to be an everyday catcher in the major leagues, he has not been able to put up anything close to reasonable numbers at the more advanced levels. Paul has never hit for power and his lack of plate discipline made him far too easy of an out for the more experienced pitchers. Paul is about out of chances. He'll catch on with somebody's Triple-A team, however there is little chance that he will hit enough to make anybody think about having him even as a reserve in the big leagues.

	AB	R	HR	RBI	SB	BA
2001 Chicago - AL	139	20	3	18	6	.266
2002 Chicago - AL	104	11	0	11	2	.240

PAYTON, JAY - OF - BR - b: 11/22/72 $20

Payton is the best hitting left fielder in Colorado since Dante Bichette (a moment of silence for one of the greatest marketing t-shirts ever, "Bichette Happens") and the best fielder at that position in franchise history since being obtained from the New York Mets at the 2002 trading deadline. Payton is a perfect fit at Coors Field, a natural line-drive hitter in a park where line drives can carry over the fence. He drives the ball well to both gaps with a short, powerful swing, and set career highs in virtually every offensive caterogy in 2003. Pitchers once could get him out with sliders, although that is no longer the case. Payton has a better than average arm and has the range to play center field if needed. He has above-average speed in the field and on the bases, although he has not been able to translate that into stolen bases and steals far fewer - four, five bags a year - than he could. Payton was expected to open the season as the starting left fielder and a run producer in either the No. 2 or No. 6 spot in the order.

	AB	R	HR	RBI	SB	BA
2001 New York - NL	361	44	8	34	4	.255
2002 Colorado	445	69	16	59	7	.303
2003 Colorado	600	93	28	89	6	.302

PENA, CARLOS - 1B - BL - b: 5/17/78 $12

Pena was expected to have a big year but he didn't quite have one and he may never have a huge Carlos Delgado-type power year in Detroit's large park. Pena needs more seasoning but he will improve this year and he'll make a run at thirty homers and flash gold glove ability at first base. Pena will also hit for average and knock runs in by the bundle as soon as the Tigers find some talent with which to surround him. He is going to be their go-to guy for years.

	AB	R	HR	RBI	SB	BA
2001 Texas	62	6	3	12	0	.258
2002 Detroit	397	43	19	52	2	.242
2003 Detroit	452	51	18	50	4	.248

PENA, WILY MO - OF - BR - b: 1/23/82 $2

For the second year in a row Pena's contract means that he must be on the major league roster or the team will risk losing him. At this point it's clear that Pena has raw ability but his lack of minor league seasoning will make his move to productivity a longer, slower process. When he played, he only proved that he should be playing no higher than at Double-A level and not in the major leagues. In his last full season in the minors in 2002, Pena hit only .255 and then he was glued to the pine in Cincinnati to rot away with only 40 at-bats over the first four months of 2003 before the Reds threw in the towel and traded, sold or fired everyone in the Queen City and let Pena play a little. What's the over and under on the number of "injury rehab" trips to Louisville that the Reds will be able to pull off with Pena in 2004?

	AB	R	HR	RBI	SB	BA
2002 Cincinnati	18	1	1	1	0	.222
2003 Cincinnati	165	20	5	16	3	.218

PERALTA, JHONNY - SS - BR - b: 5/28/82 $0

Peralta has a very good glove at third and short but at age 21 on opening day, Peralta will spend more time in the minors. He can't hit yet but his defense is major league. If his bat comes around a bit, he can be a regular at short. In 2003, he was called up from Triple-A Buffalo to replace an injured Omar Vizquel, but was sent back down the same month to make room for Rickey Gutierrez. John McDonald then got injured, and Peralta was called up again in July, as a backup for the middle infield and third base.

	AB	R	HR	RBI	SB	BA
2003 Cleveland	242	24	4	21	1	.227

PEREZ, ANTONIO - 2B - BR - b: 1/26/80 $3

With Ordonez out for the year, Perez saw playing time as a backup to the middle infield and got some starts at second base. Perez is an above-average fielder with good range and can steal some bases but if he's going to be more than a backup infielder, he'll need to improve with the bat. He does make consistent contact, and might be able to hit for average and power if he develops. On teams thin in the middle infield, such as the Devil Rays, Perez could get the opportunity to prove himself in a greater role.

	AB	R	HR	RBI	SB	BA
2003 Tampa Bay	125	19	2	12	4	.248

PEREZ, EDDIE - C - BR - b: 5/4/68 $3

After a wasted 2002 season in the American League, Perez returned to the NL and set career-highs in virtually every offensive category as part of a catching platoon in Milwaukee. Perez hammered lefties, hitting over .330 against them, while establishing personal bests in homers, RBI, doubles and at-bats. He has good power to the alleys. He is a very slow runner who is not a threat take the extra base or steal a base. His defensive tools still need work, and he does not slow down an opponents' running game much despite an OK arm. He was expected to be at least a platoon starter this season.

	AB	R	HR	RBI	SB	BA
2001 Atlanta	10	0	0	0	0	.300
2002 Cleveland	117	6	0	4	0	.214
2003 Milwaukee	350	26	11	45	0	.271

PEREZ, EDUARDO - OF - BR - b: 9/11/69 $5

Perez might finally have found his role in the big leagues after nearly 11 years of trying. He pounded southpaws last season and earned himself regular duty for the first time since 1997. He was used primarily against lefthanders, though he likely would have had his career best at-bat totals had he not missed a few weeks late in the season after having an emergency appendectomy. While he has no speed at this point in his career, he is smart enough to be able to play multiple positions adequately. Perez can handle lefties more than well enough to succeed in a platoon role. However, he is not adept enough at hitting righthanded hurlers to play every day.

	AB	R	HR	RBI	SB	BA
2002 St. Louis	154	22	10	26	0	.201
2003 St. Louis	253	47	11	41	5	.285

PEREZ, NEIFI - 2B/SS - BB - b: 2/2/75 $4

Perez is simply a dreadful hitter who doesn't do much of anything right at the plate. He swings at everything, basically refusing to take a walk. He also can't hit for average or any power, as his

---

career .384 slugging percentage would indicate. Despite having good speed, he does not steal bases successfully, having been caught nearly half the time he has attempted to run in his career. Perez is a good defensive player, meaning he will have the opportunity to play another year or two as a backup and a late-inning replacement. He absolutely cannot be expected to hold down a spot in the everyday lineup.

	AB	R	HR	RBI	SB	BA
2001 COL/KC	581	83	8	59	9	.279
2002 Kansas City	554	65	3	37	8	.236
2003 San Francisco	328	27	1	31	3	.256

PEREZ, TIMONIEL - OF - BL - b: 4/8/75 $8

Things looked so promising for Perez and the Mets just four years ago, when he came up late in the season and sparked them in the playoffs. After a poor 2001 season, he bounced back to bat .295 the next year before falling off again last season. Perez's biggest problem is that he can't hit lefthanders, so he's likely to remain a platoon player. He almost always puts the ball in play, but doesn't hit it very hard. Though Perez is quick enough and a good enough outfielder to play in center, his arm could limit him to left field.

	AB	R	HR	RBI	SB	BA
2001 New York - NL	239	26	5	22	1	.247
2002 New York - NL	444	52	8	47	10	.295
2003 New York - NL	346	32	4	42	5	.269

PEREZ, TOMAS - 2B/3B - BB - b: 12/29/73 $3

Returning to switch-hitting in 2002, Perez posted career highs in homers and RBI, then in 2003, increased his RBI output. He started games at every infield position except catcher last year, and has learned how to hit against righthanded pitchers. Every team needs a capable utility infielder and the Phillies are happy to have Perez.

	AB	R	HR	RBI	SB	BA
2001 Philadelphia	135	11	3	19	0	.304
2002 Philadelphia	212	22	5	20	1	.250
2003 Philadelphia	298	39	5	33	0	.265

PERRY, HERBERT - 1B - BR - b: 9/15/69 $0

After a career year in 2002, Perry once again succumbed to the injury bug that has plagued him throughout his big league career. Season-ending shoulder surgery in June was followed by arthroscopic surgery on both knees. He was expected to be ready for spring training. When healthy, Perry is capable of hitting for average with decent power. At this stage in his career, coming off major surgeries, a backup spot is more likely than a starting role.

	AB	R	HR	RBI	SB	BA
2001 Chicago - AL	285	38	7	32	2	.256
2002 Texas	450	64	22	77	4	.276
2003 Texas	24	1	0	2	0	.167

PETRICK, BEN - OF - BR - b: 4/7/77 $0

Petrick was once the catcher of the future for the Rockies, but since 2001, he has shown that catcher is not his optimal position. He was a three-sport high school star who is very athletic, runs well, and could steal 15 bases if given enough playing time. Petrick can play the outfield, first base or catch and that serves him well as long as he's playing for a weak team that fills the roster with cheap players who play multiple positions. He is also hampered by a weak bat which is typical of utility players and weak teams. He was expected to to challenge for a bench position, most likely in the outfield.

	AB	R	HR	RBI	SB	BA
2001 Colorado	244	41	11	39	3	.238
2002 Colorado	95	10	5	11	0	.211
2003 COL/DET	122	18	4	12	0	.221

PHELPS, JOSH - DH - BR - b: 5/12/78 $9

Phelps has an explosive bat with great power and an improving batting eye. He struggled for much of the first half of last season but rebounded in the second half, even given limited playing opportunities. Once thought to be a future catcher, Phelps is a below average defensive player and so that opens up first base as the only defensive position he can play, which so far has limited his introduction to the majors as a DH. He's going to be battling for an everyday spot in the middle of the lineup and if he were to start this season in the American League, he would be again limited to either DH or first base. He's likely to see continued improvement and big power numbers should be expected if he gets plenty of playing time.

	AB	R	HR	RBI	SB	BA
2002 Toronto	265	41	15	58	0	.309
2003 Toronto	396	57	20	66	1	.268

PHILLIPS, BRANDON - 2B - BR - b: 6/28/81 $2

Phillips was an excellent shortstop before the Indians converted him to second base. While he didn't hit and he ran his mouth a little too much, Phillips handled the move to second base well enough to make the Indians front office smile. Phillips was the asking price for Bartolo Colon when Colon was traded to the Expos in 2002. Omar Vizquel still has a year remaining on his contract and when he's done, Phillips might return to short. Phillips will improve markedly as a hitter and he will be more diplomatic as he matures. He has a very bright future.

	AB	R	HR	RBI	SB	BA
2002 Cleveland	31	5	0	4	0	.258
2003 Cleveland	370	36	6	33	4	.208

PHILLIPS, JASON - C/1B - BR - b: 9/27/76 $12

Injuries to Mike Piazza and Mo Vaughn last year gave Phillips his first big chance in the big leagues, and he made the most of it. A catcher in the minors, he beat out Tony Clark for playing time at first and compiled the highest batting average of any Met. Phillips, recognizable by the goggles he wears on the field, moved up after a .346 start in 22 games at Triple-A Norfolk. He was batting .300 for the Mets until the season's final three games. He has good strike zone judgment and doubles power, and is considered a good defensive catcher.

	AB	R	HR	RBI	SB	BA
2003 New York - NL	403	45	11	58	0	.298

PIAZZA, MIKE - C - BR - b: 9/4/68 $7

Piazza had the least productive season since he began playing regularly in 1993. The major reason was a strained right groin muscle that limited him to 68 games. But that wasn't all. Piazza's batting average and home run rate went down for the third consecutive season. He could be the slowest player in baseball; he hasn't stolen a base since 2000. Piazza's defense behind the plate is so bad that as soon as he hits the handful of homers he needs to set the major league catcher career record for homers, he seems certain to move to first base. He looked shaky in his one game at that position last season.

	AB	R	HR	RBI	SB	BA
2001 New York - NL	503	81	36	94	0	.300
2002 New York - NL	478	69	33	98	0	.280
2003 New York - NL	234	37	11	34	0	.286

PIERRE, JUAN - OF - BL - b: 8/14/77 $39

The Kenny Lofton of the 21st century. There's nothing like a grinding pennant race to bring out the very best in a player and last year's race did just that for Pierre. Without the uplifting effects of a pennant race this year, a letdown could cost Pierre 20 steals and 20 points from his batting average.He hits well against both lefties and righties, and succeeded in walking more than striking out.

	AB	R	HR	RBI	SB	BA
2001 Colorado	617	108	2	55	46	.327
2002 Colorado	592	90	1	35	47	.287
2003 Florida	668	100	1	41	65	.305

PIERZYNSKI, A.J. - C - BL - b: 12/30/76 $14

Pierzynski has been accused of playing with too much of an edge, but it's that edge that's made him one of the best catchers in the game. Pierzynski has very good size and strength and is expected to hit with more power as he gains experience. His hand-eye coordination is excellent, as he can foul off pitches and wear down pitchers. Poor strike zone judgment keeps him from being a big run producer, but he's still a .300 hitter. Pierzynski calls a very good game and can control the running game. Look for his production to increase as he matures.

	AB	R	HR	RBI	SB	BA
2001 Minnesota	381	51	7	55	1	.289
2002 Minnesota	440	54	6	49	1	.300
2003 Minnesota	487	63	11	74	3	.312

PODSEDNIK, SCOTT - OF - BL - b: 3/18/76 $38

Podsednik — the first "d'" is silent — made a not-so-quiet run at the NL Rookie of the Year award in his first season as a starter in Milwaukee, which made the waiver claim of the season by signing him in October, 2002. Podsednik, a second-round draftee of Texas in 1994, had nine minor league seasons under his belt before getting his break. Podsednik is the classic "little ball" type with a touch of pop. He can drive the ball to his pull field, although he is quite satisfied to put the ball in play and use his frontline speed to make things happen. Podsednik was 2 runs short of becoming the fourth rookie in major league history to hit .300 with 40 stolen bases and 100 runs. Ichiro Suzuki (2001), Shoeless Joe Jackson (1911) and Tommy Barrett (1900) did it. Podsednik has the speed and know-how to stay in the 40 stolen base range. He has good range and an average arm. He was expected to be the starting center fielder and leadoff hitter after his spectacular coming out party.

	AB	R	HR	RBI	SB	BA
2002 Seattle	20	2	1	5	0	.200
2003 Milwaukee	558	100	9	58	43	.314

POLANCO, PLACIDO - 2B/3B - BR - b: 10/10/75 $17

A few years ago, Polanco was known for his glove, but last year he developed some power, which he should maintain but not improve upon. His main task is to learn to play several infield positions well. His hitting is a little icing on the cake. The free-swinging Polanco makes good contact, rarely walks or strikes out, and hits pretty well against lefthanded pitching.

	AB	R	HR	RBI	SB	BA
2001 St. Louis	564	87	3	38	12	.307
2002 Philadelphia	548	75	9	49	5	.288
2003 Philadelphia	492	87	14	63	14	.289

POSADA, JORGE - C - BB - b: 8/17/71 $16

Unlike Javy Lopez bouncing back with a monster year, Posada has made steady progress since he has played in the majors. That meant that in 2003 he reached career highs in home runs and RBI, a batting average above his career norm and his best walk/strikeout ratio since 1997. He answered critics who said he tends to tire late in the season by batting .320 after the All-Star break. Throughout his career, he has hit lefthanders better than righties. Posada is an underrated defensive catcher who can throw out basestealers in key situations, as he did during the postseason.

	AB	R	HR	RBI	SB	BA
2001 New York - AL	484	59	22	95	2	.277
2002 New York - AL	511	79	20	99	1	.268
2003 New York - AL	481	83	30	101	2	.281

PRATT, TODD - C - BR - b: 2/9/67 $1
Pratt has been in and out of the majors for 12 years as one of the better backup catchers in baseball. He knows what he's doing behind the plate and he still has a little juice in his bat. He's been known to devour lefthanded pitching but last year he actually did better against righthanded pitchers.

	AB	R	HR	RBI	SB	BA
2001 PHI/NY - NL	173	18	4	11	1	.185
2002 Philadelphia	106	14	3	16	2	.311
2003 Philadelphia	125	16	4	20	0	.272

PUJOLS, ALBERT - 1B/OF - BR - b: 1/16/80 $36
Pujols doesn't walk nearly as much as the other top power hitters in baseball, though nobody can argue with the results. He is still a patient hitter, however, and won't go chasing after balls in the dirt or ones that are a foot outside. He has outstanding athletic ability, as evidenced that he is able to play third, left and at first base without hurting the team defensively. He also has some speed, though he does not attempt to steal many bases. Ultimately he will end up playing first base, though he will still spend considerable time in the outfield for another year or two. Outside of Barry Bonds and Alex Rodriguez, there really aren't any other players in the game with his kind of talent. Even if he is, as rumored, a few years older than his listed age, he still will have many more MVP-type seasons left in his career.

	AB	R	HR	RBI	SB	BA
2001 St. Louis	590	112	37	130	1	.329
2002 St. Louis	590	118	34	127	2	.314
2003 St. Louis	591	137	43	124	5	.359

PUNTO, NICK - 2B - BR - b: 11/8/77 $0
Punto was the International League's All-Star shortstop in 2002, and is a prototypical leadoff hitter, with good on-base and steal ability. The 5'9", 170 pound, Punto will improve his hitting but he'll never hit for power. It is unlikely that he'll ever be a regular at any time in his career but as a utility player, Punto gives his team a reliable glove at second, short and third base.

	AB	R	HR	RBI	SB	BA
2003 Philadelphia	92	14	1	4	2	.217

QUINLAN, ROBB - 1B - BR - b: 3/17/77 $1
Quinlan has a track record of hitting for high averages in the minor leagues. He got his first cup of coffee in the big leagues last season, and the results were the same. Quinlan lacks the kind of power teams need in a first baseman, which may limit his opportunities in the majors, but he can hit. He also has good speed for a first sacker and can steal the occasional base. In more than half a season at Triple-A last year, Quinlan hit .310 with nine homers and ten stolen bases. Quinlan was expected to split time between Triple-A and the majors this season.

	AB	R	HR	RBI	SB	BA
2003 Anaheim	94	13	0	4	1	.287

RAINES JR., TIM - OF - BB - b: 8/31/79   <u>$0</u>

Cal Ripken Jr. was an infinitely better player than his father. In the Raines family, the generational talent levels are reversed. Tim Jr. did get at least some of his dad's speed gene, and is a good defensive player. But offensively, he's so lost he should take a compass up to the batter's box. You might think Junior is young enough to grow into a major league role, but consider that Rock Raines was a month younger than his son's 2003 age when he batted .298 with 90 stolen bases in 1983. The younger Raines' best shot is as a defensive replacement and pinch runner.

	AB	R	HR	RBI	SB	BA
2003 Baltimore	43	4	0	2	0	.140

RAMIREZ, ARAMIS - 3B - BR - b: 6/25/78   <u>$16</u>

When the Cubs acquired Ramirez from Pittsburgh in late July they put a convenient spin on the deal. The Cubs said that Ramirez was a young player with tremendous potential and they envisioned him being a fixture for them at third base for many years to come. While it's true that all of that could wind up happening, the facts are that Ramirez has done little in the past couple of seasons to make any objective person think that. Ramirez still swings at anything and everything that's close to the plate, doesn't run the bases well at all, and he's accused of being unalert on the field . Given his age, it's reasonable to expect some improvement in the next year, although it is unlikely that he will ever become a perennial All-Star.

	AB	R	HR	RBI	SB	BA
2001 Pittsburgh	603	83	34	112	5	.300
2002 Pittsburgh	522	51	18	71	2	.234
2003 PIT/CHI - NL	607	75	27	106	2	.272

RAMIREZ, MANNY - OF/DH - BR - b: 5/30/72   <u>$28</u>

Ramirez has been one of the major league's most dangerous hitters for nearly a decade. There's probably not a better hitter alive against lefthanded pitchers. The problem is that he isn't dangerous when he isn't playing. Last season's 154 games marked a career high, but he took a lot of heat for missing a key series against the Yankees because he said he was ill. Ramirez has become a less aggressive hitter; in 2003 for the first time he walked more often (a career-high 97 times) than he struck out. The downside was that his 104 RBI were his fewest since 1997. The left fielder has a better arm than most people realize; last year he reached double figures in assists for the fourth time in his career.

	AB	R	HR	RBI	SB	BA
2001 Boston	529	93	41	125	0	.306
2002 Boston	436	84	33	107	0	.349
2003 Boston	569	117	37	104	3	.325

RANDA, JOE - 3B - BR - b: 12/18/69   <u>$13</u>

Often overlooked because he doesn't hit a ton of homers, Joe Randa has been a steadying influence for the Royals, and a solid contributor with the bat and glove. In 2003, Randa had his best all-around season, hitting for a useful average and producing a fair number of runs while playing an outstanding third base. The Royals managed to stay in the pennant race down to the last week of the season at least partly because of Randa's red-hot bat; after missing two weeks in July due to a strained oblique, he batted .345 with 38 RBI over the last nine weeks of the season. Even when plagued by an inconsistent batting stroke early in the season, Randa was productive; he was among league leaders in sacrifice bunts for the season. Randa is one of those rare players who can produce in several different roles. Moved to an RBI spot in the order years ago, Randa became a more aggressive hitter. Returned to the number two spot in 2003, he again became more patient. Randa has quick reflexes around the bag at third, and an accurate arm. He has been prone to occasional streaks of errors, but avoided that in 2003, committing just seven errors all year. Randa hasn't been a speedy baserunner for several years, but still runs the bases intelligently. Although Randa, a free agent after the season, wants to return to Kansas City, the club wasn't interested in the long-term deal Randa was expected to seek. Still, the Royals prize Randa for his glove, productive bat and leadership so they intended to pursue him aggressively.

	AB	R	HR	RBI	SB	BA
2001 Kansas City	581	59	13	83	3	.253
2002 Kansas City	549	63	11	80	2	.282
2003 Kansas City	502	80	16	72	1	.291

RANSOM, CODY - SS - BR - b: 2/17/76 $0

Ransom is a gifted defensive player who simply hasn't been able to hit more advanced pitching. While he has been capable of playing shortstop in the big leagues for several years now, he struggles badly at the plate. He has yet to display any willingness to take pitches. Instead, he goes after anything close and frequently gets himself out. Because of his weakness at the plate, it is going to be tough for Ransom to stick in the big leagues for more than a few weeks at a time.

	AB	R	HR	RBI	SB	BA
2003 San Francisco	27	7	1	1	0	.222

REBOULET, JEFF - 2B - BR - b: 4/30/64 $0

Reboulet usually begins his season in the minors and then he waits for the phone to ring. Reboulet should be playing beer league softball by now but he's a smart veteran and the smartest thing the elderly Reboulet did was to sign with the Pirates organization and wait for an opportunity when something hits the fan in Pittsburgh. His value comes from his glove, not his bat.

	AB	R	HR	RBI	SB	BA
2003 Pittsburgh	261	37	3	25	2	.241

REDMAN, TIKE - OF - BL - b: 3/10/77 $13

Redman has real speed and he just may have figured out how to steal bases. In the minors last year, Redman grabbed 42 bags before the Pirates recalled him in early August and he added seven more for Pittsburgh. Redman has a quick stroke but little power and homers will be rare for him. What he can do is run and he should use his speed and slap the ball around and if he can bring his newly acquired base stealing ability to Pittsburgh, they should have plenty of work for him. He had excellent late season stats, batting .330 with 3 homers and 7 steals but he won't post a batting average nearly that high if he sticks for a full season.

	AB	R	HR	RBI	SB	BA
2003 Pittsburgh	230	36	3	19	7	.330

REDMOND, MIKE - C - BR - b: 5/5/71 $0

Redman is good enough behind the plate to be a starter but he can't hit which is not a major concern for most major league teams but it is, nevertheless, worth mentioning. Over the past three years, he's hit over .300 against lefthanded pitchers, so he may find himself as a temporary platooner at best.

	AB	R	HR	RBI	SB	BA
2001 Florida	141	19	4	14	0	.312
2002 Florida	256	19	2	28	0	.305
2003 Florida	125	12	0	11	0	.240

REESE, POKEY - 2B - BR - b: 6/10/73 $2

The Pirates are on a youth movement and Reese is 30 years old while Bobby Hill is 26 and overall a far better player than Reese. In 1999, Reese has a career year at the plate but that has since proved to be a fluke and won't happen again as Pokey cannot hit and while he can pick it, he's just too fragile to play every day. What else can he do other than to serve as a late inning defensive replacement and start a game a week?

		AB	R	HR	RBI	SB	BA
2001	Cincinnati	428	50	9	40	13	.224
2002	Pittsburgh	421	46	4	50	12	.264
2003	Pittsburgh	107	9	1	12	6	.215

RELAFORD, DESI - 2B/3B/OF - BB - b: 9/16/73 $12

Super-sub Desi Relaford did absolutely everything the Royals needed as a substitute starter and as a bench player. He made starts at five different positions around the infield and outfield, with only a little loss to the team's overall defense, and he eventually won the regular second base job. Relaford added an offensive spark when he was in the lineup, and also contributed a number of big hits off the bench; he played a large role in the club's outstanding start. Relaford was dinged up over the course of the season, but played through the various injuries; his most significant problem was a hand injury which forced him to bat exclusively from the left side, with noticeably diminished success against lefthanded pitchers thereafter. He runs well and shows a veteran's poise on the bases. As the Royals' primary off-season acquisition, Relaford was a revelation. It remains to be seen if Relaford can handle everyday duty at one position; he may again thrive better in a return to a well-used bench role.

		AB	R	HR	RBI	SB	BA
2001	New York - NL	301	43	8	36	13	.302
2002	Seattle	329	55	6	43	10	.267
2003	Kansas City	500	70	8	59	20	.254

RENTERIA, EDGAR - SS - BR - b: 8/7/75 $32

Renteria was expected to be a superstar when he first came up as a youngster with the Marlins in 1996. While that hasn't happened, he has made himself into one of the better shortstops around. A skilled glove man with an extremely strong arm, Renteria now is able to hit for average and provide a little bit of pop in his bat. While he won't challenge guys like Alex Rodriguez or Nomar Garciaparra, he is a steady and reliable bat, one that can be used in the middle of the lineup. Renteria has a ton of experience now, and there is no reason to think that he will suddenly stop hitting. Expect at least a couple more years of a .300 average, with 15-18 homers.

		AB	R	HR	RBI	SB	BA
2001	St. Louis	493	54	10	57	17	.260
2002	St. Louis	544	77	11	83	22	.305
2003	St. Louis	587	96	13	100	34	.330

REYES, JOSE - SS - BB - b: 6/11/83 $29

The brightest spot in a dsmal 2003 season for the Mets was Reyes' arrival. They resisted the temptation to bring him up from the minors until June. He struggled for the first month, batting .205. Reyes went 2-for-5 on July 1, and was en fuego the remainder of the season. He batted .335 and stole 11 bases in six weeks after the All-Star break before joining many of his teammates on the disabled list because of a sprained left ankle. Reyes' future is every bit as bright as painted by his selection as USA Today's Minor League Player of the Year for 2002.

		AB	R	HR	RBI	SB	BA
2003	New York - NL	274	47	5	32	13	.307

REYES, RENE - OF - BB - b: 2/21/78 $1

A former catcher until a right knee injury forced him into the outfield, Reyes may have the highest ceiling of any young position player in the Colorado organization. Reyes, a switch-hitter, has a short yet powerful batting stroke and can drive the ball into the gaps and beyond, a stroke that enabled him to win two minor league batting titles in his five years while working his way up the organizational ladder. A tremendously gifted athlete, Reyes was the 2001 Sally League MVP while stealing 53 bases with a .322 batting average at Asheville ... and that was the season after he underwent surgery to remove torn cartilage from his knee. He can play first base, although he is fast enough to be in the outfield. Reyes had a couple of cups of coffee with the parent Rockies in 2003 and was expected to enter spring training as a candidate for a backup role this year.

	AB	R	HR	RBI	SB	BA
2003 Colorado	116	13	2	7	2	.259

RIOS, ARMANDO - OF - BL - b: 9/13/71 $1

Rios is a good glove man who hangs around as the 24th or 25th man on the roster because he doesn't complain about not being a starter. Rios is limited offensively. He doesn't have a lot of power, and he isn't patient enough at the plate to get on base regularly. Being lefthanded helps his cause, as it lets him see action late in games as part of a double switch, or as a defensive replacement. Rios can stick around another year or two, though it is likely that he will have to spend at least part of the season in Triple-A. He is not going to be a regular, even if his club is crippled by injuries.

	AB	R	HR	RBI	SB	BA
2001 SF/PIT	321	38	14	50	3	.260
2002 Pittsburgh	208	20	1	24	1	.264
2003 Chicago - AL	104	4	2	11	0	.212

RIVAS, LUIS - 2B - BR - b: 8/30/79 $14

Rivas has been in the majors three years and is starting to baffle the coaching staff. He's good enough to be a Gold Glove fielder. He's good enough to provide some offense. But he hasn't taken the next step. He had a two-month stretch in 2003 where he was functional at the plate, thanks to games of pepper with coaches that helped him stay on the ball. Rivas chases bad pitches and sometimes has mental lapses when it is time to move runners over. He's a good basestealer, but doesn't reach base enough to flaunt it. He'll continue to start, but the wait is on for him to realize his potential.

	AB	R	HR	RBI	SB	BA
2001 Minnesota	563	70	7	47	31	.266
2002 Minnesota	316	46	4	35	9	.256
2003 Minnesota	475	69	8	43	17	.259

RIVERA, CARLOS - 1B - BL - b: 6/10/78 $0

Rivera has had some decent numbers in the minors and he likes to hack but he needs to get the bat on the ball occasionally. He shouldn't, but say he plays first base for the Pirates every day in 2004, Rivera would hit .215, fan 180 times and hit 15 homers.

	AB	R	HR	RBI	SB	BA
2003 Pittsburgh	95	12	3	10	0	.221

RIVERA, JUAN - OF - BR - b: 7/3/78 $0

Few outfielders have arms as strong and accurate as Rivera's. Last year, after batting .325 in 79 games at Triple-A Columbus, he became a platoon right fielder for the Yankees. Though Rivera didn't hit for as high an average in the majors, he was equally proficient as a run producer because he pounded lefthanders for a .340 average. Rivera finished the season on a high note, with five homers and 10 RBI in his last nine games, and a .375 average in September. The question is whether that finish was a legitimate indication that he can retain at least a platoon position in 2004.

	AB	R	HR	RBI	SB	BA
2001 New York - AL	4	0	0	0	0	.000
2002 New York - AL	83	9	1	6	1	.265
2003 New York - AL	173	22	7	26	0	.266

ROBERTS, BRIAN - 2B - BB - b: 10/9/77 $17

Jerry Hairston's broken foot gave Roberts his best chance for playing time in the majors, and he literally ran with it. Within eight days of his recall from Triple-A Ottawa, Roberts had hit two grand slams against the defending world champions. After that, he made contact, reached base at an acceptable leadoff level and continued to steal bases at a high success rate. Roberts and Hairston have battled for playing time the last three years. The Orioles tried Roberts at shortstop, but his arm isn't strong enough for that position. He was much more proficient in 2003 as a second baseman. For the son of a college coach, Roberts doesn't seem to be an instinctive player, but his physical skills should keep him in a lineup as a second baseman or DH.

	AB	R	HR	RBI	SB	BA
2001 Baltimore	273	42	2	17	12	.253
2002 Baltimore	128	18	1	11	9	.227
2003 Baltimore	460	65	5	41	23	.270

ROBERTS, DAVE - OF - BL - b: 5/31/72 $19

Roberts became only the third Dodger with back-to-back 40 stolen base seasons in 25 years when he reached that plateau late in a 2003 season that was shortened by a hamstring injury that caused him to miss 37 mid-year games. Roberts, who did not become a major league regular until he was 30, knows his role - he slaps at the ball and tries to use his speed to advance. He has virtually no power, not even into the gaps, and has only 37 extra-base hits in 810 at-bats in his two seasons in Los Angeles. He can be overpowered at the plate, although he is a skilled bunter who pushes it past the pitcher with the best of them. He combines raw speed with an extensive knowledge of pitchers and their moves, and could steal 55 to 60 bases as an everyday player. He gets a good jump on balls, compensating for an arm that is below average. Roberts was expected to be the regular center fielder and leadoff hitter, although his offense is only fair.

	AB	R	HR	RBI	SB	BA
2002 Los Angeles	422	63	3	34	45	.277
2003 Los Angeles	388	56	2	16	40	.250

ROBINSON, KERRY - OF - BL - b: 10/3/73 $3

Robinson has only one ability that is above average, and that is his speed on the basepaths. A notoriously weak hitter, he has poor strike zone judgment, no power and struggles to keep his batting average near acceptable levels. But because of his speed, which helps him in the field as well, clubs can justify keeping him around as the 24th or 25th guy on the roster. Robinson isn't going to be any more of a player than he was the past two or three season. He would be a disaster as a regular, and there is a good chance that he will have to spend at least some time this season in the minor leagues.

	AB	R	HR	RBI	SB	BA
2001 St. Louis	186	34	1	15	11	.285
2002 St. Louis	181	27	1	15	7	.260
2003 St. Louis	208	19	1	16	6	.250

RODRIGUEZ, ALEX - SS - BR - b: 7/27/75 $35

Arguably the most valuable position player in the game, Rodriguez is a Hall of Fame-caliber player at the peak of his skills. He is a Triple Crown threat and MVP candidate in any given season. Defensively, he is one of the best shortstops in baseball, and he is also capable of stealing 20 bases in a season with a high success rate. Despite having to play on substandard teams the last few years, A-Rod has been the consummate professional on and off the field.

	AB	R	HR	RBI	SB	BA
2001 Texas	632	133	52	135	18	.318
2002 Texas	624	125	57	142	9	.300
2003 Texas	607	124	47	118	17	.298

RODRIGUEZ, IVAN - C - BR - b: 11/30/71 $20

There is a tendency to write off catchers once they pass age 30, but Rodriguez has lost nothing and last year he was able to display leadership and squire his team through a grueling pennant race, which they would not have won, or, even been in, if he were not on the team.

	AB	R	HR	RBI	SB	BA
2001 Texas	442	70	25	65	10	.308
2002 Texas	408	67	19	60	5	.314
2003 Florida	511	90	16	85	10	.297

ROLEN, SCOTT - 3B - BR - b: 4/4/75 $24

Rolen is gifted both with the bat and the glove. While not a superstar like Albert Pujols or Barry Bonds, he is an exceptional hitter. He has improved his knowledge of the strike zone over the past few seasons, meaning his strikeout total has dropped almost 50 percent from his first couple of years with the Phillies. He has power, though he will not hit as many homers as the league leaders, partly because of his willingness to simply put the ball in play to drive in a needed run. Rolen has had no major injury concerns the last three seasons, as he appeared in more than 150 games each year. He had some back problems while in Philadelphia, though those seem to have subsided now that he gets to play the vast majority of games on a grass infield. He has been remarkably consistent throughout his career, so expect more of the same this year.

	AB	R	HR	RBI	SB	BA
2001 Philadelphia	554	96	25	107	16	.289
2002 St. Louis	580	89	31	110	8	.266
2003 St. Louis	559	98	28	104	13	.286

ROLLINS, JIMMY - SS - BB - b: 11/27/78 $19

Has Rollins settled in as a .260-.275 hitter with a little speed? It looks that way. He's fanned over one hundred times for three straight years which is the primary reason that he struggles to get on base. Marlon Byrd took over from Rollins as the Phillies leadoff hitter and Rollins hit everywhere in the lineup but third or fourth. Rollins got most of his at-bats batting second and if he stays at the top end of the lineup and hits with Byrd on base and the big boys batting behind him, well let's just say that if Rollins can't hit better in the number two spot, .260-.275 is as good as he'll get and he'll slide down to the bottom of the order.

	AB	R	HR	RBI	SB	BA
2001 Philadelphia	656	97	14	54	46	.274
2002 Philadelphia	637	82	11	60	31	.245
2003 Philadelphia	628	85	8	62	20	.263

ROLLS, DAMIAN - 3B/OF - BR - b: 9/15/77 $13

Rolls missed much of the first-half of last season with a broken thumb. He has a power-hitters' build, yet is nimble enough to play infield position adeptly, seeing playing time at both third base and outfield. He plays hard, always looking to take an extra base or getting dirty while keeping the opposition from doing so. He isn't going to be a star, but can be effective as a platooner and can win a starting job with the right team.

	AB	R	HR	RBI	SB	BA
2001 Tampa Bay	237	33	2	12	12	.262
2002 Tampa Bay	89	15	0	6	2	.292
2003 Tampa Bay	373	43	7	46	11	.255

ROMANO, JASON - OF - BR - b: 6/24/79 $0

Romano is a handy guy who can play six positions, although he has yet to show he can hit at the major league level despite good minor league numbers. He hit .306 with 10 stolen bases in 216 at-bats at Triple-A last season and had several stints with parent Los Angeles. He can drive a fastball into the gaps and has triples speed, although he had trouble identifying a major league breaking ball last year. He has good speed and a strong arm, which makes him a better-than-average second baseman and a candidate to play every oufield spot. He had 100 stolen bases in a three-season stretch in the low minors. He was expected to compete for a reserve infield/outfield spot, and would be a solid contributor with a more consistent offense.

	AB	R	HR	RBI	SB	BA
2002 TEX/COL	91	17	0	5	6	.253
2003 Los Angeles	36	3	0	0	2	.083

ROSS, CODY - OF - BR - b: 12/23/80 $0

Ross is the kind of player the Tigers need to clone. He's not a big, slow banger, nor is he a banjo-hitting speed merchant. Cody Ross can play baseball. He has good power, good speed and he plays good outfield defense. He won't be a superstar but his minor league performance (.287 -20 homers - 15 steals for Triple-A Toledo) is within his grasp in the next year or two in Detroit.

ROSS, DAVE - C - BR - b: 3/19/77 $2

Ross' first major league home run came against Mark Grace in 2002, although Ross showed in 2003 that he can go deep on anyone, hitting double-digit dingers in part-time duty for a team that needed all the offense it could muster. Ross had two double-digit homer seasons in the minors and can drive the ball to his pull field, left. He has no speed and is an adequate defender, although he must polish his mechanics behind the plate. He was solidly entrenched as the backup catcher this season.

	AB	R	HR	RBI	SB	BA
2003 Los Angeles	124	19	10	18	0	.258

ROWAND, AARON - OF - BR - b: 8/29/77 $3

Rowand began last season as the starting centerfielder for the White Sox, though his offensive limitations meant the club finally had to find other options. Rowand's downfall is his lack of plate discipline. He draws next to no walks, a trait he has shown throughout his professional career. Even when he was putting up big numbers in the minor leagues he never took more than 38 walks in a single season. He is a decent outfielder, though he likely would be better suited playing one of the corner outfield positions rather than in center. It doesn't appear that Rowand is going to be an everyday player. He will have to show more patience at the plate to do that, and his career numbers indicate that just isn't going to happen.

	AB	R	HR	RBI	SB	BA
2001 Chicago - AL	123	21	4	20	5	.293
2002 Chicago - AL	302	41	7	29	0	.258
2003 Chicago - AL	157	22	6	24	0	.287

SADLER, DONNIE - 3B/OF - BR - b: 6/17/75 $0

Sadler's versatility sometimes lands him on a major league roster for extended periods, but he does not possess any significant offensive skills and thus is suited only for occasional backup work. Capable of playing any defensive position except catcher, Sadler is nevertheless adequate at best in the field. His most likely role for the upcoming season is as an all-purpose backup.

	AB	R	HR	RBI	SB	BA
2001 CIN/KC	185	28	1	5	7	.162
2002 Texas	98	16	0	7	5	.163
2003 Texas	131	27	1	5	4	.198

SALMON, TIM - OF/DH - BR - b: 8/24/68 $15

As he enters the latter stages of his career, Salmon remains a potent offensive force when healthy. He has a compact, powerful swing and good strike zone judgment. He can even steal a base or two when needed. Although his range in right field is nothing special, Salmon compensates with a strong and accurate arm. In 2003, Salmon served as the designated hitter when Brad Fullmer went down, but he was expected to return to the outfield on a regular basis this year. Salmon has been vulnerable to injuries over the years, and last season saw him miss time with back stiffness. Although he is a good bet to miss playing time at some point in the season due to minor injuries, Salmon can still be a productive player when in the lineup.

		AB	R	HR	RBI	SB	BA
2001	Anaheim	475	63	17	59	9	.227
2002	Anaheim	483	84	22	88	6	.286
2003	Anaheim	528	78	19	72	3	.275

SANCHEZ, ALEX - OF - BL - b: 8/26/76 $21

Sanchez is the same erratic performer that he was with the Brewers and he's largely unchanged from the player that he was as a minor leaguer in the Devil Rays system. At that point in his career, Sanchez attracted attention for his ability to steal 60 bases and bat over .300. The majors being tougher, Sanchez has still been able to steal a lot of bases and keep his batting average high, which is something that similar players have been unable to do in their trip from the minors to the majors. Sanchez came back from a broken leg but the injury did not hamper him on the base paths and he was among the league leaders in steals and he was the only Tigers outfielder to hit above .250. What does hamper Sanchez on the bases is that he gets thrown out a lot and he takes foolish chances; the worst of which was a comical attempt to steal home late in the year as the pitcher stood with the ball in his hand. Sanchez suddenly decided to break for home but the catcher was waiting for him before Sanchez got within ten feet of home plate. Sanchez was so out that he didn't even slide and then he walked back to the dugout, seemingly happy with himself for being aggressive. He walked toward manager Alan Trammell, who had endured a season of record setting futility. Trammell wearily rubbed his eyes and then he stared straight past his boneheaded center fielder, as if he were searching for Ty Cobb in the late summer shadows.

		AB	R	HR	RBI	SB	BA
2001	Milwaukee	68	7	0	4	6	.206
2002	Milwaukee	394	55	1	33	37	.289
2003	MIL/DET	557	58	1	32	52	.287

SANCHEZ, FREDDY - 3B - BR - b: 12/21/77 $3

Being a shortstop in the Red Sox farm system wasn't the easiest way to get to the majors, not with Nomar Garciaparra in the way. Sanchez was being groomed for the second base job until Todd Walker arrived. Now Sanchez is with Pittsburgh, and more doors are open for him here. Although Sanchez is already mature enough to be in the majors; he was Pawtucket's Player of the Year in 2002, he was overmatched at the plate in two brief trials, a september callup in 2002 and a brief midsummer stint in 2003. Given regular playing time, he projects to be a .290 hitter with some pop and a little speed.

		AB	R	HR	RBI	SB	BA
2002	Boston	16	3	0	2	0	.188
2003	Boston	34	6	0	2	0	.235

SANCHEZ, REY - SS - BR - b: 10/5/67 $3

Since 2001, Sanchez has played for five franchises - Kansas City, Atlanta, Boston, the Mets and Seattle - twice brought in at the trading deadline to shore up a weakness at shortstop. Sanchez is what he is - a solid contact hitter who is not going to break down any fences, averaging a home run every 100 games in his long major league career. He has better than average speed although that does not translate into stolen bases. His primary asset is in the field. He is a top quality defender at both second and short, with supple hands, great range and a strong arm. He will always find work in the middle infield, although his "small ball" game is best suited for a pitching-first contender.

	AB	R	HR	RBI	SB	BA
2001 KC/ATL	544	56	3	37	11	.281
2002 Boston	357	46	1	38	2	.286
2003 NY - NL/ SEA	344	33	0	23	2	.250

SANDBERG, JARED - 3B - BR - b: 3/2/78 $1

The Rays had slated Sandberg to begin 2003 as the starting third baseman, but instead began at Triple-A Durham, getting called up to the majors in May. He was the everyday starter for a month, but coudln't keep the job, being sent to the minors again and replaced by Damian Rolls. He got another call up from the minors at the end of July, but still failed to demonstrate any improvement in his offense. Sandberg showed pretty good power in his first extended stint in 2002 with 18 homers but he struck out almost every other at-bat and his average was less than stellar. Unfortunately, in 2003, Sandberg did not noticeably improve his strikeout rate, nor his batting average. If he wants to play everyday in the future, he will need to improve his ability to make more consistent contact and draw more walks. If he can improve in those areas, he has a chance to being similar to Aaron Boone.

	AB	R	HR	RBI	SB	BA
2001 Tampa Bay	136	13	1	15	1	.206
2002 Tampa Bay	358	55	18	54	3	.229
2003 Tampa Bay	136	15	6	23	0	.213

SANDERS, REGGIE - OF - BR - b: 12/1/67 $22

Two questions: First, who would be fool enough to sign Sanders to a multi-year contract? Secondly, how good could this guy have been had he really had the discipline, desire and commitment to bust his tail every year when he was in his prime? For the past three years, Sanders has been on single-year deals with the Diamondbacks, then with the Giants and last year with the Pirates. Having to justify his existence on a one year deal has had a strange motivational effect on Sanders and he has never hit as well as he has over these past three years. From age 33 to 35, Sanders has hit 87 homers. Let's hope this sinks in with every general manager in the game so that the players who put up some big numbers and then sit back and take a year or two off will understand the simple beauty of a one year, incentive-laden, carrot on a stick contract. Here it is, now go out and get it.

	AB	R	HR	RBI	SB	BA
2001 Arizona	441	84	33	90	14	.263
2002 San Francisco	505	75	23	85	18	.250
2003 Pittsburgh	453	74	31	87	15	.285

SANTIAGO, BENITO - C - BR - b: 3/9/65 $6

Santiago keeps plugging along, providing his teams with reasonably consistent offense, above average defense and veteran leadership. Other than 1996, when he clubbed 30 homers for the Phillies, his home run total has been in the low to mid teens almost every season. He had a lot of speed for a catcher early in his career, and while he is not a consistent threat, he will manage a few steals a year. Santiago has been remarkably consistent each of the last three seasons. Given that he is one of the fittest players in the game, he is likely to make it four straight good years in a row this season. Expect another season where he hits about .275 with 12-15 homers.

	AB	R	HR	RBI	SB	BA
2001 San Francisco	477	39	6	45	5	.262
2002 San Francisco	478	56	16	74	4	.278
2003 San Francisco	401	53	11	56	0	.279

SANTIAGO, RAMON - 2B/SS - BB - b: 8/31/81 $4

Santiago is still a weak hitter and the hope that he would mature physically and improve at the plate evaporated when his true age was found to be a couple of years beyond that stated on his birth certificate. His supposed youth and smooth fielding interested scouts at first but, no player that has misrepresented his age has reached stardom.

	AB	R	HR	RBI	SB	BA
2002 Detroit	222	33	4	20	8	.243
2003 Detroit	444	41	2	29	10	.225

SANTOS, ANGEL - 2B - BB - b: 8/14/79 $0

Santos is very young but to date he's just a typical "good field, no hit" middle infielder. He'll be working in the minors most of, if not all this year. In 2003, he was acquired by the Indians from the Red Sox and after 13 games with Triple-A Buffalo, where he was hitting .239 with 2 homers and eight RBI, was called up to the majors to replace an injured Rickey Gutierrez.

	AB	R	HR	RBI	SB	BA
2003 Cleveland	76	9	3	6	1	.224

SCHNEIDER, BRIAN - C - BL - b: 11/26/76 $3

When Michael Barrett was injured, Schneider proved that he can start and play every bit as well as Barrett does. Schneider is not a great hitter; few catchers are. He's competent behind the plate, and his throwing arm is a little better than Barrett's. He has decent speed and is a good baserunner and he will knock a dozen balls into the seats in 2004.

	AB	R	HR	RBI	SB	BA
2002 Montreal	207	21	5	29	1	.275
2003 Montreal	335	34	9	46	0	.230

SCUTARO, MARCO - 2B - BR - b: 10/30/75 $0

Scutaro went from the Mets to the Athletics on an October 2003 waiver claim. Between his seven years in Triple-A and his time in the majors, he also went from Marcos Skoo-TAHR-oh to Marco SCOOTER-oh. Whatever he's called, he has some power, some speed, some defensive skill and some on-base ability. Once or twice a week, he might display one of those talents, but not often enough to show he's anything more than a Quadruple-A player. Lefthanded pitchers gave Scutaro a lot of trouble last season, so even a platoon role in the majors doesn't seem likely for him.

	AB	R	HR	RBI	SB	BA
2002 New York - NL	36	2	1	6	0	.222
2003 New York - NL	75	10	2	6	2	.213

SEGUI, DAVID - DH - BB - b: 7/19/66 $2

Segui is at a stage in his career when he's an injury waiting to happen. Though he was a consistent .300 hitter between 1997 and 2001, during the past three seasons he has been on the disabled list five times, missing nearly 300 games. Injuries to his left wrist ended each of his last two years, and he underwent surgery during last season. Once a fancy-fielding first baseman, he now is more a platoon DH, for he doesn't hit lefthanders well, possibly because of the wrist injury. Segui had a year remaining on his contract, but his diminishing skills and risk of injury made his return for 2004 look shaky.

	AB	R	HR	RBI	SB	BA
2001 Baltimore	292	48	10	46	1	.301
2002 Baltimore	95	10	2	16	0	.263
2003 Baltimore	224	26	5	25	1	.263

SELBY, BILL - 3B - BL - b: 6/11/70 $0

Bill Selby had his career highlight in 2002 when he hit a walk-off grand slam homer off Mariano Rivera. At age 34, Selby has bounced around the minors for years with brief appearances in the majors. He once tried learning to catch to enhance his chance to stay in the majors. Now, he dabbles in the infield or left and can fill in at first, second and third. He had his fifth cup of coffee in 2003 and that should help the 33-year-old Selby's pension plan.

	AB	R	HR	RBI	SB	BA
2002 Cleveland	159	15	6	21	0	.214
2003 Cleveland	39	3	0	5	0	.103

SEXSON, RICHIE - 1B - BR - b: 12/29/74 $22

Sexson played every inning of every game at first base for Milwaukee, when he returned to 40-home run form for the second time in three years. He is the first player in franchise history to have two 40-homer seasons. Sexson has prodigious power to all fields, and once took Randy Johnson deep twice in a spring training game. A free-swinger, Sexson has great arm extension as has no trouble taking an outside pitch over the fence in center or right-center. He has set career highs in walks in each of his three seasons in Milwaukee, although that is more a function of opponents refusing to pitch to him than his selectivity. Sexson is reasonably athletic for his size and will surprise with a stolen base here or there. He plays above-average defense. He was expected to be a regular at first at Milwaukee, although there was a remote chance the Brewers will try to get something for him since he is in the final year of a contract worth $8 million in 2004.

	AB	R	HR	RBI	SB	BA
2001 Milwaukee	598	94	45	125	2	.271
2002 Milwaukee	570	86	29	102	0	.279
2003 Milwaukee	606	97	45	124	2	.272

SHEFFIELD, GARY - OF - BR - b: 11/18/68 $34

In 2003, Gary Sheffield showed why he is considered one of the most dangerous hitters in the game. He challenged for the National League lead in many hitting categories as he anchored one of Atlanta's best offensive teams ever. Few hitters can match his bat speed; he can catch up to any fastball and his well-refined batting eye lets him avoid swinging at bad pitches. Yet Sheffield will expand the strikezone, successfully, to drive in runs. Pitchers who change speeds and stay away from his power zones will have the most success. The current thinking about pitching to Sheffield is to feed him off-speed stuff to the outside edge of the strikezone, only pitching up or in with unhittable deliveries. Anyone foolish enough to try overpowering Sheffield with heat will pay the heaviest penalties and he will mash a mistake pitch that catches too much of the plate. Seeing Sheffield pinwheel his bat while impatiently waiting for the next offering can give even the hardiest pitcher pause. Sheffield showed an unusual dominance over lefty pitchers in 2003, but also hit righthanders very well indeed. Although he has lost a step on the bases and in the outfield, Sheffield is still a good baserunner who can steal a base when needed, and he still throws well enough for rightfield duty.

	AB	R	HR	RBI	SB	BA
2001 Los Angeles	515	98	36	100	10	.311
2002 Atlanta	492	82	25	84	12	.307
2003 Atlanta	576	126	39	132	18	.330

SHUMPERT, TERRY - DH - BR - b: 8/16/66 $0

A late bloomer, Shumpert has been in the majors more than 10 years and continues to make room for himself as a jack-of-all trades bench player because of his versatility. In 2003, he platooned at second base with Marlon Anderson for a while in April, but struggled with the bat, and later in the season missed more than a month with a strained right hamstring. Upon returning in September, Shumpert saw limited playing time, as an off-the-bench reserve, playing at second base, third base and the outfield last year. His defensive skills in the infield are adequate, but although he tries in the outfield, he is overmatched there. Shumpert is a line drive hitter with occasional power to left field, and has enough speed to turn long singles into doubles, and doubles into triples. He is 37, and can be expected to remain a bench player but may be challenged by youth for playing time.

	AB	R	HR	RBI	SB	BA
2001 Colorado	242	37	4	24	14	.289
2002 Colorado	234	30	6	21	4	.235
2003 Tampa Bay	84	14	2	7	1	.190

SIERRA, RUBEN - OF/DH - BB - b: 10/6/65 $5

After being rescued from Texas and receiving his second extra baseball life with the Yankees under Joe Torre, Sierra joined the gaggle of right fielders playing in the Bronx. His role more often was as a designated hitter or pinch-hitter. Sierra's speed and defensive ability is mostly gone. Sierra is better hitting lefthanded, so he plays much more often against righthanders. He is the active leader among switch-hitters in career home runs, which means he's near the end of the road. He has seemed to be there before, but resurrected his career after time in Mexican and the independent Atlantic League.

	AB	R	HR	RBI	SB	BA
2001 Texas	344	55	23	67	2	.291
2002 Seattle	419	47	13	60	4	.270
2003 TEX/NY - AL	307	33	9	43	2	.270

SIMON, RANDALL - 1B - BL - b: 5/26/75 $10

Simon can and will hit the ball a long way, though that will only happen when bat happens to meet ball. He has no ability to adjust to a pitch once he commits to swinging, giving the advantage to the pitcher in almost every situation. He's big and strong and literally swings as hard as he can every time he takes a hack at a pitch. He's also overweight, making him a liability on the basepaths and a substandard first baseman. Simon isn't a horrible player; just not a very good one. He will go through some stretches where he will hit the ball consistently, and with power, though he'll go through many more rough times where he won't be able to buy a hit. Although he won't be able to keep a starting spot, he might land a platoon role playing against righthanded pitchers, as he did with the Cubs in the last few weeks of the 2003 campaign.

	AB	R	HR	RBI	SB	BA
2001 Detroit	256	28	6	37	0	.305
2002 Detroit	482	51	19	82	0	.301
2003 PIT/CHI - NL	410	47	16	72	0	.276

SIZEMORE, GRADY - OF - BL - b: 8/2/82 $3

Sizemore's first three seasons as a pro yielded home run totals of 1,2 and 3, respectively. The jump to a dozen in 2003, as scouts have been predicting, indicates the extent to which Sizemore is now doing more than use all fields and put the ball in play sharply. He is a naturally gifted hitter and multi-sport star athlete. His mentality is also outstanding. Sizemore is a natural leader on and off the field. He ended last season realizing that his performance in the Arizona Fall League and in spring training would decide to a large extent what would happen to him in 2004.

SINGLETON, CHRIS - OF - BL - b: 8/15/72 $6

Singleton was given the chance of a lifetime in 2003 when he was made a starter for one of the most successful franchises in recent years. However, his woeful production at the plate left the Athletics, an organization who should have known better, scrambling for a replacement to put in the outfield. Singleton has next to no power, and though he is fast, he has no basestealing skills and winds up being caught stealing nearly as many times as he is successful. Singleton's dreadful defensive play means he will have a hard time finding a place to play this season. He could land somewhere as a lefthanded bat off the bench, though his days as a starter are most likely over.

	AB	R	HR	RBI	SB	BA
2001 Chicago - AL	392	57	7	45	12	.298
2002 Baltimore	466	67	9	50	20	.262
2003 Oakland	306	38	1	36	7	.245

SMITHERMAN, STEPHEN - OF - BR - b: 9/1/78 $0

He showed four category tools in Double A Chattanooga (.310-19-95-11), but Smitherman is another in the oversupply of young outfield prospects for the Reds. He was not expected to be on the opening day roster.

	AB	R	HR	RBI	SB	BA
2003 Cincinnati	44	3	1	6	1	.15

SNOW, J.T. - 1B - BL - b: 2/26/68 $4

Finally the Giants realized that J.T. Snow just isn't good enough to play every day. Snow platooned at first last year, getting nearly all of his starts when righthanded pitchers were on the mound. A former switch-hitter who gave up hitting righthanded several years ago, Snow is limited in what he can do at the plate. While he has always been willing to take a walk, he doesn't hit for a high average and he doesn't hit for the kind of power that most clubs want out of their first baseman. He is regarded as one of the top defensive first sackers in the game, however. Used judiciously, Snow can still play a little bit, though he would be a liability as an everyday player.

	AB	R	HR	RBI	SB	BA
2001 San Francisco	285	43	8	34	0	.246
2002 San Francisco	422	47	6	53	0	.246
2003 San Francisco	330	48	8	51	1	.273

SOJO, LUIS - 1B/2B/DH - BR - b: 1/3/66 $0

When the Yankees needed an experienced emergency replacement because so many of their infielders were injured, they looked to coach Luis Sojo. He was more a symbol of past success as a good team player and veteran role model rather than a major contributor. He did bat .400 (6-for-15) in four World Series. Sojo last had played in the 2001 Series, when he went 1-for-2 after batting just 79 times during that regular season. Last year was his 15th in the majors, during which he never batted as many as 400 times or drove in more than 43 runs. He's almost certain to return to an instructional position in 2004.

	AB	R	HR	RBI	SB	BA
2001 New York - AL	79	5	0	9	1	.165
2003 New York - AL	4	0	0	0	0	.000

SORENSEN, ZACH - 2B - BB - b: 1/3/77 $0

Think of Sorensen as a younger version of Bill Selby- a player who may be valuable to a Rotisserie team for at most a few weeks at a time. He was drafted by the Indians in 1998 in the 2nd round of the June draft, and got his first taste of the majors last year, getting called up from Triple-A Buffalo at the end of May to replace Bill Selby, who was struggling. Sorensen was sent back to the minors in August, but was a September callup.

	AB	R	HR	RBI	SB	BA
2003 Cleveland	37	2	1	2	0	.135

SORIANO, ALFONSO - 2B - BR - b: 1/7/78 $37

Soriano had a sandwich season, batting .371 in April and .348 in September, but no better than .275 in any month in between. Though all of his Rotisserie stats declined from the year before, his secondary averages improved, pointing toward improvement in years to come. Soriano remained an atypical leadoff batter, but his 38/130 walk/strikeout ratio and .338 on-base percentage were career highs. Leading off games, he averaged a home run every 10 at-bats and homered more often than he walked. He was a more selective basestealer, and had the highest success rate of his career. At second base, both his range and fielding percentage were career bests, so he might not have to move to the outfield.

	AB	R	HR	RBI	SB	BA
2001 New York - AL	574	77	18	73	43	.268
2002 New York - AL	696	128	39	102	41	.300
2003 New York - AL	682	114	38	91	35	.290

SOSA, SAMMY - OF - BR - b: 11/12/68 $25

The 2003 season was a tribute to Sosa's ability to stay focused on the diamond and ignore some pretty big distractions. He was able to survive the now infamous corked bat incident, which would have ruined the seasons of less resilient players. Honest mistake or not, Sosa was still able to put that behind him, as well as an early-season beaning that led some detractors to say he was afraid of the ball. While it's true his home run totals have declined somewhat in recent years, he is still a top flight power hitter. And Sosa has taken care of his body well enough over the years that he should have a few more All-Star seasons left before he heads to Cooperstown.

	AB	R	HR	RBI	SB	BA
2001 Chicago - NL	577	146	64	160	0	.328
2002 Chicago - NL	556	122	49	108	2	.288
2003 Chicago - NL	517	99	40	103	0	.279

SPENCER, SHANE - OF - BR - b: 2/20/72 $4

Spencer's best role is as the righthanded half of a platoon in left or right field. He has moderate power against lefty pitching, but tends to struggle against righthanders. Spencer has reached the point where he may change teams more frequently, as many teams might prefer a younger prospect to him. Wherever he plays, Spencer should be good for 300 at bats this season.

	AB	R	HR	RBI	SB	BA
2001 New York - AL	283	40	10	46	4	.258
2002 New York - AL	288	32	6	34	0	.247
2003 CLE/TEX	395	39	12	49	2	.251

SPIEZIO, SCOTT - 1B/3B - BB - b: 9/21/72 $13

As a versatile, switch-hitting utility player, Spiezio can almost always count on getting 400 or more at-bats, either filling in for injured players or getting spot starts at first, third or in the outfield, especially against righthanded pitching. Spiezio doesn't hit for a high average and has only modest power and barely average speed. His best asset as a hitter is a good eye at the plate, and he is a patient hitter who generally makes contact. Defensively, he is fine at first base and below average at his other positions. Due to his offensive and defensive limitations, Spiezio is an unlikely candidate to be handed a regular job on Opening Day, but by the end of the season he will have found his way into the lineup more often than not.

	AB	R	HR	RBI	SB	BA
2001 Anaheim	457	57	13	54	5	.271
2002 Anaheim	491	80	12	82	6	.285
2003 Anaheim	521	69	16	83	6	.265

SPIVEY, JUNIOR - 2B - BR - b: 1/28/75 $9

After signing a big contract extension in 2003 spring training, Spivey suffered through a disjointed year because of more hamstring problems, a bugaboo that has cost him time off and on from 2000. Spivey is a great physical specimen who has come of age as a second baseman. He has very good power for a middle infielder and can turn around anyone's fastball, having hit several of the longest home runs in Bank One Ballpark history in his short time there. After struggling with breaking pitches in his rookie season, Spivey made great strides with pitch recognition and plate coverage. While he is a free-swinger who still strikes out often, he no longer is fooled much. Spivey has vast range at second base and can cover ground from behind first base into short center field. He is adept at turning the double play; few are quicker to the bag to take the throw, which enables him to stay out of harm's way while making the relay. Spivey has the speed to be a 15-18 stolen-base guy in the future, although his injury kept him from running much in 2003.

He will be the everyday second baseman, and has the power to hit 20-25 home runs.

	AB	R	HR	RBI	SB	BA
2001 Arizona	163	33	5	21	3	.258
2002 Arizona	538	103	16	78	11	.301
2003 Arizona	365	52	13	50	4	.255

STAIRS, MATT - 1B/OF - BL - b: 2/27/68 $9

Stairs' lack of range hinders him in the outfield and his lack of ability to hit lefthanded pitching holds him back even more. What he does is to murder righthanded pitching for a high average and with power. He's 34 and he will become more of a liability in the field so his future in the NL is rather limited. In the AL, as a lefthanded DH, Stairs could probably get close to 400 at-bats and pop 30 homers.

	AB	R	HR	RBI	SB	BA
2001 Chicago - NL	340	48	17	61	2	.250
2002 Milwaukee	270	41	16	41	2	.244
2003 Pittsburgh	305	49	20	57	0	.292

STANLEY, HENRI - OF - BL - b: 12/15/77 $0

An undrafted free agent out of Clemson, Stanley has steadily moved up through the Astros organization and should move up another level to the major leagues in 2004. In 2003, he had a .292-11-48-15 season at Triple-A New Orleans. He does not have outstanding tools but has good strike zone judgment and has averaged 20 stolen bases and 10 triples in his three full minor league seasons. His on-base average in his minor league career is .388. Stanley's arm is not considered strong enough to play center field and he is likely to be a fourth or fifth outfielder in the majors.

STEWART, SHANNON - OF- BR - b: 2/25/74 $21

Stewart was traded to the Twins during the 2003 season and quickly raised his status as one of the best hitters in the game. Blessed with good hand-eye coordination, Stewart will foul off several pitches in an at-bat before either getting a hit or drawing a walk. He drives the ball to all fields and can knock a few pitches out of the park. His basestealing adds yet another dimension. He's a solid outfielder, but an old football injury has led to one of the weakest arms in the game. He's the leadoff hitter almost every team needs.

	AB	R	HR	RBI	SB	BA
2001 Toronto	640	103	12	60	27	.316
2002 Toronto	577	103	10	45	14	.303
2003 TOR/MIN	573	90	13	73	4	.307

STINNETT, KELLY - C - BR - b: 2/4/70 $0

A well travelled backup catcher, Stinnet can hit, but not well enough to start. When he finds work as a backup catcher, he'll get 150 at-bats.

	AB	R	HR	RBI	SB	BA
2001 Cincinnati	187	27	9	25	2	.257
2002 Cincinnati	93	10	3	13	2	.226
2003 CIN/PHI	186	14	3	19	0	.237

STYNES, CHRIS - 3B - BR - b: 1/19/73 $7

The perennially underrated Stynes found a home at third base in Colorado last season, setting career highs for games played and games started while playing his typical take-no-prisoners game. Stynes is a natural line drive hitter who uses the whole field and is more than capable of yanking a fastball into the seats. He is an aggressive baserunner, although with only average speed he is not a stolen base threat. He was considered more of a second baseman entering

2003, although he showed he had the arm and the glove to play third last year. He can take a turn in the outfield, too, and is not afraid to get himself dirty, diving for balls in the holes and in the gaps. Even after career highs in doubles and RBIs, however, Stynes will enter spring training with few assurances. He will battle for a regular position, although it is more likely he will return to his role as a supersub.

	AB	R	HR	RBI	SB	BA
2001 Boston	361	52	8	33	4	.280
2002 Chicago - NL	195	25	5	26	1	.241
2003 Colorado	443	71	11	73	3	.255

SURHOFF, B.J. - 1B/OF/DH - BL - b: 8/4/64 $6

The Orioles brought back Surhoff, who had some of his best years with Baltimore playoff teams during the late '90s. Injuries to a knee and quadriceps have limited him during the past two seasons, but he has batted better than .290 each year. At this stage of his career, with diminished speed, he's probably limited to playing first base or DH. Surhoff is a pro's pro whose leadership qualities make him far more valuable than his play on the field. On a limited basis — mostly because of his increasing injury history — he can also help a team win on the field.

	AB	R	HR	RBI	SB	BA
2001 Atlanta	484	68	10	58	9	.271
2002 Atlanta	75	5	0	9	1	.293
2003 Baltimore	319	32	5	41	2	.295

SUZUKI, ICHIRO - OF - BL - b: 10/22/73 $35

Suzuki joined Lloyd "Little Poison" Waner and Johnny Pesky as the other players to have 200 hits in each of their first three seasons when he reached that plateau again in 2003. Waner and Suzuki are the only ones to have done it in consecutive seasons, as Pesky missed time during World War II. Suzuki simply tries to make contact and let his speed do the work. He has great bat control and seems to get a running start from the plate with his shifty footwork. He also has learned to drive the ball in situations, reaching his major league best in homers. He is a terrific baserunner and base stealer, taking little time to read the moves of major league pitchers since his arrival in 2001. He is a 30-stolen base guy in a bad year. As a defender, he is a natural center fielder with a great break on the ball. Not only can he track down almost anything, he also has an arm so strong that he is seldom challenged. He was expected to be a fixture in the leadoff spot and in right field, an All-Star candidate again.

	AB	R	HR	RBI	SB	BA
2001 Seattle	692	127	8	69	56	.350
2002 Seattle	647	111	8	51	31	.321
2003 Seattle	679	111	13	62	34	.312

SWEENEY, MARK - OF - BL - b: 10/26/69 $0

Sweeney has played with five organizations in a nine-year career that lately has been spent just one step ahead of another trip to Triple-A. Sweeney has spent as much time in the minors as in the majors since 1999; he has played in the majors and at Triple-A every year since. For a big guy he does not have much power, although he can make contact and uses the entire field. He has limited speed and is not a threat to steal. His best position is first base, although he can take a turn at the corner outfield spots and has been used as a very occasion DH. Always on the fringes, Sweeney was expected to open spring training trying to play himself onto a roster as a pinch-hitter.

	AB	R	HR	RBI	SB	BA
2001 Colorado	89	9	3	11	2	.258
2002 San Diego	65	3	1	4	0	.169
2003 Colorado	97	13	2	14	0	.258

SWEENEY, MIKE - 1B/DH - BR - b: 7/22/73 $19

If you'd known before the season that Mike Sweeney would lose forty games to injury you might expect the Royals to again have one of the worst records in baseball. Yet, despite upper back stiffness that put Sweeney on the shelf for a quarter of the season — and severely limited his hitting for weeks after he was activated — the Royals offense actually improved in 2003. Still, the Royals did miss Sweeney and his RBI bat; he was at his best in RBI situations, placing among league leaders in hitting with runners on base and in hitting with runners in scoring position. Sweeney was among league leaders in several offensive categories when he went to the DL in June. After he returned in August it was strictly as a DH, which hurt the Royals because it limited their options with regard to the rest of their lineup. Sweeney's strong line drive stroke was hampered by the back injury too, and he suffered a significant drop-off in power hitting for the season. Also, although Sweeney is merely an average first baseman, he is better than those who replaced him in the field the rest of the way. Sweeney began to swing the bat as expected in September, hitting for power and average to all fields with his powerful line-drive stroke. He is expected to be healthy again in 2004 and once again contend for a batting title while hitting for above-average power. An unusual addendum to Sweeney's recently-signed contract affords the Royals with an option on his contract if they manage to finish above .500, so their surprising 2003 season was a big benefit in that respect, too.

	AB	R	HR	RBI	SB	BA
2001 Kansas City	559	97	29	99	10	.304
2002 Kansas City	471	81	24	86	9	.340
2003 Kansas City	392	62	16	83	3	.293

TAGUCHI, SO - OF - BR - b: 7/2/69 $0

A veteran of the Japanese professional leagues, Taguchi came to the States a couple of years ago only to spend most of his time in the minor leagues. A strong defender in the outfield, Taguchi has suffered in America because of his inability to hit more advanced pitching. He struggled mightily even in Triple-A, putting up next to nothing offensively, especially in the power department (10 extra base hits in 250 at-bats). Taguchi is going be hard pressed to stick around another year. If he doesn't land with the right organization, one that is desperate for outfielders, then he likely will have to look for work abroad.

	AB	R	HR	RBI	SB	BA
2002 St. Louis	15	4	0	2	1	.400
2003 St. Louis	54	9	3	13	0	.259

TATIS, FERNANDO - 3B - BR - b: 1/1/75 $0

By now, even Tatis must know that he can't play baseball very well. Injured again, he was done for the year in June. An old adage says that if a player has one good year a team will wait up four or five more to see if he can do it again. Last year marked five years since Tatis hit 34 homers in 1999 but since 1999 Tatis has hit a total of 37 homers and he's missed 294 games.

	AB	R	HR	RBI	SB	BA
2001 Montreal	145	20	2	11	0	.255
2002 Montreal	381	43	15	55	2	.228
2003 Montreal	175	15	2	15	2	.194

TAYLOR, REGGIE - OF - BL - b: 1/12/77 $3

Taylor is a backup outfielder but he stumbled last year after a surprisingly productive 2002 season. As bench strength, Taylor will hit erratically for the rest of his career. He is good in center and left and he can run and steal bases but his major flaw, and the reason he will never be a regular is that he cannot adjust to pitchers who adjust to him. He's a player for whom management must find at-bats by matching him up against pitchers that he can handle and that's a chore.

	AB	R	HR	RBI	SB	BA
2002 Cincinnati	287	41	9	38	11	.254
2003 Cincinnati	180	17	5	19	7	.217

TEIXEIRA, MARK - 1B/3B/OF - BB - b: 4/11/80 $18

Teixeira staked a claim to a roster spot in spring training last season and didn't waste it, finishing the season as the everyday first baseman for the Rangers. He also showed that he could play at the corner outfield positions, and that may be the most likely destination for Teixeira this year. Toward the end of the summer, Teixeira endured an extended slump, but that did not mar a fine rookie season in which Teixeira showed the power and athleticism that has led scouts to consider him a future star. He was expected to build on his rookie season as an everyday player in 2004.

	AB	R	HR	RBI	SB	BA
2003 Texas	529	66	26	84	1	

TEJADA, MIGUEL - SS - BR - b: 5/25/76 $24

Much was made of Tejada's extremely slow start in 2003, though when it was all said and done he had a pretty good season. Take away April, when he had only 18 hits in 112 at-bats, and Tejada's numbers resembled his stellar 2002 campaign, which culminated with an AL MVP award. Although Tejada isn't nearly as willing to take a walk as many players, that doesn't make him undisciplined. He simply tries to find a good pitch to hit and then takes a hack at it. He is also regarded as a superb defender and a true leader in the clubhouse. Tejada is one of the best shortstops in the game. If he were to ever play in a true hitter's park he would put up spectacular offensive numbers.

	AB	R	HR	RBI	SB	BA
2001 Oakland	622	107	31	113	11	.267
2002 Oakland	662	108	34	131	7	.308
2003 Oakland	636	98	27	106	10	.278

THAMES, MARCUS - OF - BR - b: 3/6/77 $0

Thames has moderate power and decent speed. He plays the field well enough to serve as a backup corner outfielder in the big leagues, but is more likely to shuttle to and from the majors depending on injuries at the major league level.

	AB	R	HR	RBI	SB	BA
2003 Texas	73	12	1	4	0	.205

THOMAS, FRANK - 1B/DH - BR - b: 5/27/68 $11

The Big Hurt was back in a big way last season. Finally completely healthy, Thomas easily was the most consistent hitter the White Sox had all year, and was one of the best in the entire American League. Thomas was back to his old self, hitting 40 home runs for the fourth time in his career, drawing a lot of walks and driving in a bunch of runs. (He would have had a lot more runs batted in had he not been the only guy on the team hitting his weight in the first half of the season). Possibly the main reason for his turnaround was his ability to hit the high and inside pitch. A slight change in his stance allowed him to pull that ball into left field and turned what had been a big weakness into a strength. As a result, there is no reason to think that Thomas won't be a productive hitter again this season.

	AB	R	HR	RBI	SB	BA
2001 Chicago - AL	68	8	4	10	0	.221
2002 Chicago - AL	523	77	28	92	3	.252
2003 Chicago - AL	546	87	42	105	0	.267

THOME, JIM - 1B - BL - b: 8/27/70 $25

Thome is, of course, one of the premier sluggers of the last decade. His power stats are consistent and hugely impressive. The only flukiness in his career chart is that in 2002, he fanned only 139 times, the year that he was baseball's premier free agent-to-be and, the player that would undoubtedly sign the heftiest free agent contract of the year, which the MLBPA dearly hoped would raise the bar for other "lesser" free agents. So, in 2002 Thome hits a career high fifty two homers in a low 480 at-bats and his strikeouts, which had been in the 180 range for three straight years, suddenly, at age 32, fall way down to 139. On his own in the NL in 2003, Thome still pounded the ball out 47 times but it required an additional 98 at-bats to do it and he hit five fewer homers and he fanned 42 more times than he did in his walk away year. What's up with that?

	AB	R	HR	RBI	SB	BA
2001 Cleveland	526	101	49	124	0	.291
2002 Cleveland	480	101	52	118	1	.304
2003 Philadelphia	578	111	47	131	0	.266

TORREALBA, YORVIT - C - BR - b: 6/19/78 $3

Torrealba basically spent the past two seasons being an intern to Benito Santiago. He never was a highly regarded prospect coming up through San Francisco's farm system, though he made steady progress after being signed when he was only 16 years old. Even if he lacks enough power to make a strong impression at the plate, he is more than capable defensively. He always has had a strong throwing arm and he learned a lot the past two years from Santiago about how to handle a pitching staff. This could be the year that Torrealba winds up being the everyday catcher. He won't make anybody forget about Mike Piazza, though he has enough defensive ability to hold onto the starting spot.

	AB	R	HR	RBI	SB	BA
2001 SF/ATL	6	0	0	2	0	.500
2002 San Francisco	136	17	2	14	0	.279
2003 San Francisco	200	22	4	29	1	.260

TORRES, ANDRES - OF - BB - b: 1/26/78 $0

Torres got a chance to play for the Tigers and he showed a good glove and instincts in the outfield. Torres' defense is ahead of his offense and while he's not a good hitter, he has speed. His 27 stolen bases at Triple-A Toledo last year were down from 42 the year before.

	AB	R	HR	RBI	SB	BA
2002 Detroit	70	7	0	3	2	.220
2003 Detroit	168	23	1	9	5	.220

TUCKER, MICHAEL - OF/DH - BL - b: 6/25/71 $12

Michael Tucker was on his way to new career highs in several hitting categories when he fouled a pitch off his right leg in early August. The broken leg wasn't detected right away, but eventually forced him to the disabled list. Although he was expected to miss the rest of the season, Tucker worked hard to rehab and was available in the final week of the season. Tucker is a free-swinging, first-pitch, fastball hitter who has power to the opposite field, but he'll get into a funk after hitting a homer by becoming too power conscious. He is at his best when he keeps a short, level stroke and tries to hit liners to the opposite field. A streaky hitter, Tucker won't hit for a high average and his strikeout rate is too high for a batter with only moderate power. Miscast as a leadoff hitter, Tucker was maligned for his poor on-base ability; this became less of a factor once he moved to an RBI spot in the order later in the season. Tucker has decent speed and is a better basestealer than his 2003 results would indicate. He uses his speed well in the outfield; his arm is barely adequate for rightfield. Even though he tends to be inconsistent during the course of the season, Tucker's overall production for the year makes him one of the steadiest players in the game. Although he's not a good pinch-hitter, Tucker is a good fit in a platoon role as lefty pitchers give him a hard time.

	AB	R	HR	RBI	SB	BA
2001 CIN/CHI - NL	436	62	12	61	16	.252
2002 Kansas City	475	65	12	56	23	.248
2003 Kanses City	389	61	13	55	8	.262

TYNER, JASON - OF - BL - b: 4/23/77 $1

Tyner is a good contact hitter although he hasn't learned how to take a pitch. He's a good bunter with virtually no power although he is good in the clutch. He can often outrun his mistakes; he has sufficient range in left or center field although his arm is too weak for right field. In 2003, he served as a backup outfielder for the Devil Rays. His success in the future will depend largely on how much he learns to work the count in his favor.

	AB	R	HR	RBI	SB	BA
2001 Tampa Bay	396	51	0	21	31	.280
2002 Tampa Bay	168	17	0	9	7	.214
2003 Tampa Bay	90	12	0	6	2	.278

UGUETO, LUIS - 2B - BB - b: 4/1/78 $0

Ugueto is a prime example of the down side of the Rule 5 draft. He was forced to remain on Seattle's major league roster after they selected him in 2002, and his limited playing time — 23 at-bats — hindered his development. He has above-average speed and has good range n the middle infield. Ugueto has been used primarily as a pinch-runner in his brief time in the majors, and was expected to begin the season in the minors to get some reps.

URIBE, JUAN - SS - BR - b: 7/22/80 $7

Uribe made a remarkable comeback from a broken bone in his foot suffered in spring training and spent the second half of the season as the starting shortstop in Colorado after the Rockies dumped Jose Hernandez in a cost-saving move. Uribe, who made his major league debut in 2001 at the age of 21, appears to be making strides at the plate and regained some of the pop in his bat upon his return. He has a jerky batting style, a stop-and-start approach that requires high maintenance. He is a fluid defender with a cannon for an arm. Not only can he go in the hole and keep a ball in the infield, he can throw out even the fleetest runners from there. His errors usually come as a result of concentration lapses, since he has great physical tools. He has better than average speed, although he has not learned the art of stealing bases. He was expected to open the season as the starting shortstop.

	AB	R	HR	RBI	SB	BA
2001 Colorado	273	32	8	53	3	.300
2002 Colorado	566	69	6	49	9	.240
2003 Colorado	316	45	10	33	7	.253

UTLEY, CHASE - 2B - BL - b: 12/17/78 $6

Utley's first major league hit was a grand slam so, he'll always have vivid memories of his rookie year, but looking down the road, his future doesn't seem to be that bright. Utley shuttled between Philadelphia and Triple-A Scranton and filled a void created by an injury to Placido Polanco. Utley is not a defensive wizard but, he has a live bat and somebody likes him in Philadelphia. Even so, his playing time will be minimal this year.

	AB	R	HR	RBI	SB	BA
2002 Detroit	70	7	0	3	2	.200
2003 Philadelphia	134	13	2	21	2	.239

VALENT, ERIC - OF - BL - b: 4/4/77 $0

At UCLA, Valent was in the spotlight when he became one of three players in PAC 10 history to hit 30 home runs in a season. The other two are Mark McGwire and Troy Glaus. Unlike McGwire and Glaus, Valent has not made much of a splash in the majors, where he's had two cups of coffee; with the Phillies in 2001-02, and last year with the Reds. Valent can play all three outfield position but he has spent most of his time in right. He has a strong, accurate arm and he is now learning to play first base. His career was slowed with Philadelphia because of their bias toward veterans but he is still highly regarded and he's been a productive hitter in the minors.

	AB	R	HR	RBI	SB	BA
2001 Philadelphia	41	3	0	1	0	.098
2003 Cincinnati	42	3	0	1	0	.214

VALENTIN, JAVIER - C - BB - b: 9/19/75 $0
Valentin was once on the fast track to becoming the Twins starting catcher. He spent 2000,2001, and 2002 at Triple-A Edmonton. During spring training of the 2003 season, he was acquired by the Brewers then traded to the Devil Rays to be a backup catcher for Toby Hall. Valentin does possess good catcher tools; he can throw very well and pitchers have credited him for having a nice tight strike zone. He now finds himself on the outisde looking in to a possible role as a backup catcher.

	AB	R	HR	RBI	SB	BA
2003 Tampa Bay	135	13	3	15	0	.222

VALENTIN, JOSE - SS - BB - b: 10/12/69 $12
Valentin has been remarkably consistent in his first four seasons with the White Sox. Although his batting average declined all four years, he hit between 25 and 28 homers and averaged more than 70 RBIs each year. That's not A-Rod territory, though it isn't certainly isn't half bad for a shortstop. While Valentin has said he prefers to play shortstop, he is a below average fielder there. He also would become a more productive player if he saw some time at third or in the outfield as he did in 2001-2002. If he winds up moving around the diamond more, expect his offense, particularly his batting average, to increase. If not, he'll do as well as in the past.

	AB	R	HR	RBI	SB	BA
2001 Chicago - AL	438	74	28	68	9	.258
2002 Chicago - AL	474	70	25	75	3	.249
2003 Chicago - AL	503	79	28	74	8	.237

VANDER WAL, JOHN - OF - BL - b: 4/29/66 $5
Vander Wal, one of the best pinch-hitters in the game, started in a platoon in right field for Milwaukee in 2003, and his numbers extended accordingly. A 13-year major leaguer, Vander Wal is a solid line drive hitter who can take the ball out of the park to his pull field. He is a good low-ball hitter and has a good eye, although he strikes out a lot because of his aggressive approach. Vander Wal set a major league record with 28 pinch hits in strike-shortened 1995, and he is probably best-suited as a pinch-hitter on a contender. But everyone wants to play, and who can blame him for taking a shot? He is an average corner outfielder with an OK arm. He was expected to be a solid reserve, and perhaps even a prime-time player, this season.

	AB	R	HR	RBI	SB	BA
2001 PIT/SF	462	58	14	70	8	.268
2002 New York - AL	219	30	6	20	1	.260
2003 Milwaukee	327	50	14	45	1	.257

VARITEK, JASON - C - BB - b: 4/11/72 $11
Varitek was the least heralded of the Red Sox having a career year in 2003. However, his season was top-heavy. At the All-Star break, he had about equaled his production from his previous two full seasons — with a .306 average, 16 homers and 56 RBI. He hit lefthanders for a higher average, and righthanders for better power. Varitek slumped miserably down the stretch. Varitek fit in well with a team stressing offense and neglecting defense. He again had one of the lowest caught-stealing percentages among American League catchers.

	AB	R	HR	RBI	SB	BA
2001 Boston	174	19	7	25	0	.293
2002 Boston	467	58	10	61	4	.266
2003 Boston	451	63	25	85	3	.273

VAUGHN, MO - 1B - BL - b: 12/15/67 $0

Vaughn has been a big disappointment for the Mets in more ways than one. He is listed at 6'1" and 275, but probably weighed more. That size affected his mobility and his ability to get around on pitches. Thus, his performance was far less than New York expected when it traded Kevin Appier for Vaughn after the 2001 season. The Mets expected something more like the slugger who had more than 30 homers in six consecutive seasons. Instead, he has played just 166 games in his two years with the Mets because of an arthritic left knee. The extra weight he carries makes that ailment even more serious, and it could end his career.

	AB	R	HR	RBI	SB	BA
2002 New York - NL	487	67	26	72	0	.259
2003 New York - NL	79	10	3	15	0	.190

VAZQUEZ, RAMON - SS - BL - b: 8/21/76 $8

Vazquez missed 33 games with a strained abdominal muscle in the middle of the season and when he returned moved out of the leadoff spot in favor of Sean Burroughs. Vazquez has a quick and selective bat and can find the gaps, although he does not have home run power by any means. Returned to his natural shortstop position last season after playing second base in 2002 and showed good instincts, sure hands and a strong arm. He turns the doubleplay well, although his range is only major league average at best. He has good speed and is learning how to steal bases, putting up a career high last year. Vazquez was expected to be in a fight with former No. 1 draftee Khalil Greene for the starting shortstop position this spring, although a roster spot as at least a backup middle infielder seemed secure.

	AB	R	HR	RBI	SB	BA
2001 Seattle	35	5	0	4	0	.229
2002 San Diego	423	50	2	32	7	.274
2003 San Diego	422	56	3	30	10	.261

VELANDIA, JORGE - SS - BR - b: 1/12/75 $0

Velandia has spent parts of six seasons in the majors, almost entirely as a defensive replacement. He has batted just 179 times in 150 games. Last year, he was one of the home run leaders of a punchless team at Triple-A Norfolk with 11, but batted just .235 there. When he replaced the injured Jose Reyes with the Mets during September, Velandia had the most at-bats of his career. He didn't hit for average, but was able to get on base and hit with runners in scoring position. This season, he'll likely remain a Triple-A insurance policy.

	AB	R	HR	RBI	SB	BA
2003 New York - NL	58	6	0	8	0	.190

VENTURA, ROBIN - 1B/3B - BL - b: 7/14/67 $8

Ventura, acquired by Los Angeles from the Yankees at the 2003 trading deadline, played out the season as a platoon first baseman. Ventura still has that sweet stroke that enables him to use the whole field and drive the ball to right. He hangs in well against lefties although he seldom plays against them any longer. A career-full of injuries has taken its toll, limiting his range considerably at third base. Once a Gold Glover, Ventura can still charge slow rollers and make the barehand pickup and throw with the best of them, however. Never fast, Ventura is perhaps the slowest non-catcher in the game, although he recognizes that and takes no chances. Because of eroding defensive skills, Ventura was expected to compete for a platoon role this season.

	AB	R	HR	RBI	SB	BA
2001 New York - NL	456	70	21	61	2	.237
2002 New York - AL	465	68	27	93	3	.247
2003 NY - AL/LA	392	42	14	55	0	.242

VIDRO, JOSE - 2B - BB - b: 8/27/74 $19

On both ides of the ball, Vidro is among baseball's finest second basemen. He played on a bad right knee for much of the second half of 2003 but his average and power held up and he hit over .300 every month until September. His knee condition is not chronic and he's expected to have a strong year in 2004.

	AB	R	HR	RBI	SB	BA
2001 Montreal	486	82	15	59	4	.319
2002 Montreal	604	103	19	96	2	.315
2003 Montreal	509	77	15	65	3	.310

VINA, FERNANDO - 2B - BL - b: 4/16/69 $7

Vina never was an above average hitter, though he managed to be a steady contributor by playing exceptional defense and doing some of the little things to help teams win ballgames. He wasn't blessed with a lot of speed or power, though at his best he managed to hit a lot of doubles and steal more bases than expected. Vina missed a whole chunk of the season last year with a badly torn hamstring. While he returned to action late in the campaign, that is the kind of injury that can hinder a player over and over again, especially at Vina's age. While his days as a starter are likely over, he certainly will be able to find a job as a backup on a team looking for veteran leadership.

	AB	R	HR	RBI	SB	BA
2001 St. Louis	631	95	9	56	17	.303
2002 St. Louis	622	75	1	54	17	.270
2003 St.Louis	259	35	4	23	4	.251

VITIELLO, JOE - OF - BR - b: 4/11/70 $2

He's 34 and he's got bad wheels but Vitiello can still sting the ball. Had he not played on banged up legs for the majority of his career, Vitiello's name would be far better known than it is today. He devours lefthanded pitchers. Why he is not a fixture as an AL designated hitter is a mystery but credit Expos GM Oscar Minaya, who knows the 'Vitiellos' of the world better than anyone else.

	AB	R	HR	RBI	SB	BA
2003 Montreal	76	12	3	13	0	.342

VIZCAINO, JOSE - 2B/SS - BB - b: 3/26/68 $0

Vizcaino is a versatile switch-hitting utility infielder who has played for seven different major league teams since breaking in with the Dodgers in 1990. The highlight of his career was a game-winning hit for the Yankees in the 2000 World Series. He surprised with a career year in 2002 but failed to repeat in 2003 after a slow start and a broken bone in his wrist that sidelined him for 2 months. A shortstop through most of his career, he is steady defensively and is equally at home at second base and third base. He is one of the best utility infielders in the game and could continue in that role for another year or two.

	AB	R	HR	RBI	SB	BA
2001 Houston	256	38	1	14	3	.277
2002 Houston	406	53	5	37	3	.303
2003 Houston	189	14	3	26	0	.249

VIZQUEL, OMAR - SS - BB - b: 4/24/67 $9

In 2002, Vizquel set personal career highs in homers, RBI and slugging percentage. He's a switch-hitter, and in past years he had some trouble hitting lefties. Last season, he injured his right knee and underwent surgery in June and later in September. He was expected to be ready for spring training.

	AB	R	HR	RBI	SB	BA
2001 Cleveland	611	84	2	50	13	.255
2002 Cleveland	582	85	14	72	18	.275
2003 Cleveland	250	43	2	19	8	.244

WALBECK, MATT - C - BB - b: 10/2/69 $0

Walbeck was signed by Detroit to back up Brandon Inge. If he appears on a major league roster, it's in response to a sudden emergency. Since 1993, Walbeck has been a solid back up catcher in the majors, who has an accurate arm and can call a good game. However, he has never hit well.

	AB	R	HR	RBI	SB	BA
2002 Detroit	85	4	0	3	0	.235
2003 Detroit	138	11	1	6	0	.174

WALKER, LARRY - OF - BL - b: 12/1/66 $19

Walker is one of most gifted athletes to play this game, although that was not as evident in 2003 as it has been in seasons past. A fixture in right field in Colorado since 1995, Walker had career lows for a healthy season in virtually every offensive category since his rookie year in Montreal in 1990, and some wondered if age (37) and his injury history were finally catching up to him. Walker and manager Clint Hurdle verbally sparred near the end of 2003, an exchange some saw as an attempt to motivate Walker for this season. Walker vetoed a proposed trade to Arizona before 2003, and the idea the Rockies considered him expendable seemed to grate. For whatever reason, Walker did not drive the ball as he had in past seasons, when 30 homers and a .300 average were a given. He remains one of the best baserunners in the game, although he longer is a base-stealing threat. Walker still has a better-than-average arm, although right shoulder surgery years ago has reduced it from cannon status. He was expected to be the starting right fielder and hit in the heart of the order again. Critics, take heed. The last time Walker had such a poor offensive season (an injury-shortened 2000), he rebounded to hit .350 with 38 homers.

	AB	R	HR	RBI	SB	BA
2001 Colorado	497	107	38	123	14	.350
2002 Colorado	477	95	26	104	6	.338
2003 Colorado	454	86	16	79	7	.284

WALKER, TODD - 2B - BL - b: 5/25/73 $15

Of all the off-season offensive acquisitions for Boston, Walker was the least effective. He hit better than .300 in his new home park, but lefthanders tied him in knots to the extent that he was platooned on occasion with Damian Jackson or Lou Merloni. Walker is a good contact hitter with enough power to drive the ball into the gaps. He has been a consistent .290-type hitter with double-digit home runs, and he reached a career high in RBI in 2003. The Sox treat defense as a less-than-necessary evil, so they could live with Walker's limited range and hands.

	AB	R	HR	RBI	SB	BA
2001 COL/CIN	551	93	17	75	1	.296
2002 Cincinnati	612	79	11	64	8	.299
2003 Boston	587	92	13	85	1	.283

WARD, DARYLE - 1B - BR - b: 6/27/75 $0

Ward suffered though a lost season in 2003 with Los Angeles, when a wrist injury sidelined him early and he spent most of the final two months at Triple-A. Ward, always a big-time prospect, appeared to have turned the corner in 2002 with Houston. He is a strong man with natural power to all fields, and he uses that approach to takes pitches where they are pitched. He is a student of the game and is rarely caught off guard, which makes his 2003 season all the more out of character. While Ward has grown up with the game and has good instincts, he can get too heavy to be a good baserunner or defender. His best position is first base, although he has been forced into left field most of his career. He was expected to bounce back and become a valuable reserve and situational starter this season.

	AB	R	HR	RBI	SB	BA
2001 Houston	213	21	9	39	0	.263
2002 Houston	453	41	12	72	1	.276
2003 Los Angeles	109	6	0	9	0	.183

WELLS, VERNON - OF - BR - b: 12/8/78 $27

Considered one of the top prospects in baseball just a few years ago, Wells finally responded to the hype; he posted his best campaign yet in his first full season with a guaranteed spot in the lineup. Wells' power continues to improve as he develops his upper body strength and his seasonal totals didn't do justice to the actual improvement he displayed. Hitting .230 in April with just three home runs brought down, what was in fact, a breakthrough season for Wells in which he looked like a completely different hitter by the middle of May, being much more confident and selective. Even with the improvement he is a bit too aggressive and could take more walks. He starts 2003 as the everyday center fielder and should put up even better power numbers and drive in more runs.

	AB	R	HR	RBI	SB	BA
2001 Toronto	96	14	1	6	5	.312
2002 Toronto	608	87	23	100	9	.275
2003 Toronto	678	118	33	117	4	.317

WERTH, JAYSON - OF - BR - b: 5/20/79 $0

A former first round pick of the Baltimore Orioles, the plan had been for Werth to become an everyday outfielder last season but an injury to his wrist in spring training held him back and he never did get on track, ultimately ending up spending most of his season with the Blue Jays' Triple-A Syracuse team, where he struggled miserably. Werth has above-average power but showed a surprising newfound impatience at the plate last year and he will have to regain his strike zone judgement if he's to crack a big league lineup. He goes into this season battling for a job as a reserve outfielder and is more likely headed back to the minors to start this season.

	AB	R	HR	RBI	SB	BA
2002 Toronto	46	4	0	6	1	.261
2003 Toronto	48	7	2	10	1	.208

WHITE, RONDELL - OF - BR - b: 2/23/72 $12

As the Royals most important offensive addition to their pennant drive, Rondell White was expected to immediately be a run producer and he delivered. Although the usual assortment of nagging injuries kept White out of the lineup for ten games after his deadline trade from San Diego to Kansas City, White hit for a good average and displayed a powerful bat. White has an aggressive power stroke; he's a first-pitch hitter who is prone to chasing unhittable fastballs out of the strikezone and can be tied up by sharp breaking stuff. He strikes out a bit too much for a moderate power threat, but makes up for it by hitting for a good batting average. Despite repeated knee injuries, White runs well enough to cover a lot of ground in the outfield, but isn't an especially good baserunner. A weak arm has relegated White exclusively to leftfield duty. Once again a free agent, White was expected to move to yet another team, following a trend that has seen him play for five different organizations in the last four years. If White can manage to stay healthy for a full season he could again have the kind of season his early years in Montreal promised.

	AB	R	HR	RBI	SB	BA
2001 Chicago - NL	323	43	17	50	0	.307
2002 New York - AL	455	59	14	62	1	.240
2003 SD/KC	488	62	22	87	1	.289

WHITEMAN, TOMMY - SS/3B - BR - b: 7/14/79 $0

Whiteman was drafted by Houston in the sixth round in 2000 from the University of Oklahoma. He is a shortstop and a Native American from the Crow Nation. After batting over .300 at the low-A level in both 2001 and 2002, he had a .261-13-70-3 season at Double-A Round Rock in 2003, tailing off at the end of the year. He is somewhat erratic defensively, particularly on throws, committing 36 errors in 2003. He may move to third base as he advances. He has potential but must improve his plate discipline as well as his defense to challenge for a major league job, possibly in 2005.

WIDGER, CHRIS - C - BR - b: 5/21/71 $0

A reasonably dependable defensive backstop, Widger has little to offer at the plate, which is the main reason he has played for four different clubs in the last three seasons. He slaps at the ball, often trying just to make contact, and as a result he has little or no power. He is also impatient and draws few walks. Widger spent some time at first and in the outfield while on an injury rehab assignment for a back injury, and that extra versatility will make him a little more valuable. Although he likely will latch on with somebody this season, he won't be asked to play a lot, and won't produce when he does.

	AB	R	HR	RBI	SB	BA
2002 New York - AL	64	4	0	5	0	.297
2003 St. Louis	102	9	0	14	0	.235

WIGGINTON, TY - 3B - BR - b: 10/11/77 $13

Wigginton batted .302 in 111 at-bats for the 2002 Mets, yet few believed he could be their everyday third baseman going into last season. He ended up playing virtually every day and leading the team in most offensive categories. He might have played too much, in fact, for he tailed off to a .236 batting average after the All-Star break. Wigginton isn't fast, but picked his spots well enough that he was thrown out just twice trying to steal. He played passable defense. Wigginton twice hit 20 or more homers in the minors, and is likely to show more power than in his rookie year.

	AB	R	HR	RBI	SB	BA
2002 New York - NL	116	18	6	18	2	.302
2003 New York - NL	573	73	11	71	12	.255

WILKERSON, BRAD - 1B/OF - BL - b: 4/1/76 $17

Wilkerson didn't move permanently to first base but he played there enough to qualify in 2004 as a first baseman and as an outfielder. He's got fine plate judgment and he should hit at least .285 this year. While he won't suddenly have a huge power explosion, his home run output will rise yearly and level off in the low 30s over the next four years. He'll hit at least 23 homers this year.

	AB	R	HR	RBI	SB	BA
2001 Montreal	117	11	1	5	2	.205
2002 Montreal	507	92	20	59	7	.266
2003 Montreal	504	78	19	77	13	.268

WILLIAMS, BERNIE - OF - BB - b: 9/13/68 $18

Williams missed 44 games in 2003, the first year since 1994 that he didn't bat at least .305. He also had his lowest power totals since that season. Williams clearly had lost at least half a step in the field and on the bases even before undergoing knee surgery during last season. Shoulder injuries have reduced the strength in his throwing arm. He remained an intelligent baserunner

---

who wasn't caught stealing all year and a selective hitter who walked more often than he struck out. Williams hits lefthanders somewhat better than he hits against righties. It's possible that he could be moved from center to left field this year.

	AB	R	HR	RBI	SB	BA
2001 New York - AL	540	102	26	94	11	.307
2002 New York - AL	612	102	19	102	8	.333
2003 New York - AL	445	77	15	64	5	.263

WILLIAMS, GERALD - OF - BR - b: 8/10/66 $0

After eleven straight years of major league action, utility outfielder Williams barely made it twelve in 2003 when he was called up from the minors in September. He's age 38 and he should consider retirement rather than endure another long season of minor league bus rides and the faint hope of being called up to the majors.

	AB	R	HR	RBI	SB	BA
2001 TB/NY - AL	279	42	4	19	13	.201
2002 New York - AL	17	6	0	0	2	.000
2003 Florida	31	5	0	3	3	.129

WILSON, CRAIG - C/1B/OF - BR - b: 11/30/76 $10

Signing Reggie Sanders was a blow to Wilson's development and an unnecessary move by the Pirates who thought fans would become interested if some of their players used to be famous. The Pirates really wanted to trade Sanders for prospects late in the year but they couldn't and that kept Wilson on the bench. Near seasons end, Wilson began to play more and his bat came alive and he hit a dozen homers in the final two months of the year. With no specific position available, it appears that the Pirates have the King Kong of utility players as Wilson's bat needs to be in their lineup and he can play right and left field, first base and catcher.

	AB	R	HR	RBI	SB	BA
2001 Pittsburgh	158	27	13	32	3	.310
2002 Pittsburgh	368	48	16	57	2	.264
2003 Pittsburgh	309	49	18	48	3	.262

WILSON, DAN - C - BR - b: 3/25/69 $4

Wilson remains one of the better defensive catchers in the game, and pitchers love throwing to him. He blocks balls well and has a strong and accurate arm, helping to dissuade an opponent's running game. He has become a situational hitter, featuring a short swing and looking to put the ball in play rather than drive it out of the park. His 10-homer seasons are a thing of the past. He does not walk as much as he should. He was expected to compete for the starting job, and while his best offensive days are behind he will always have a job because of his defensive skills.

	AB	R	HR	RBI	SB	BA
2001 Seattle	377	44	10	42	3	.265
2002 Seattle	359	35	6	44	1	.295
2003 Seattle	316	32	4	43	0	.241

WILSON, ENRIQUE - SS - BB - b: 7/27/73 $0

Wilson gained some notoriety during the 2003 season because of his success in hitting Pedro Martinez. Other than that, Wilson would fill in when an infielder had a slight injury or was being rested. Because he had great difficulty hitting lefthanders, Wilson yielded playing time to Erick Almonte while Derek Jeter was sidelined during the season's opening weeks. Once a highly regarded shortstop prospect who stole 23 bases in Double-A and batted .306 in Triple-A, Wilson put on weight without adding strength or power. He also turned out to be two years older than he had claimed. A utility player is the most he can be.

	AB	R	HR	RBI	SB	BA
2001 PIT/NY - AL	228	17	2	20	0	.211
2002 New York - AL	105	17	2	11	1	.181
2003 New York - AL	135	18	3	15	3	.230

WILSON, JACK - SS - BR - b: 12/29/77 $8

Two years ago, Wilson was a "good field - no hit" shortstop. Now he's beginning to hit. Despite the hype, there still aren't many shortstops that hit very well and while Wilson is clearly nowhere near the caliber of A- Rod, Nomar or Jeter, he's improving and he has become useful. Expect him to show improvement on offensive again this year.

	AB	R	HR	RBI	SB	BA
2001 Pittsburgh	390	44	3	25	1	.223
2002 Pittsburgh	527	77	4	47	5	.252
2003 Pittsburgh	558	58	9	62	5	.256

WILSON, PRESTON - OF - BR - b: 7/19/74 $26

The centerpiece of the Mike Hampton trade at the 2002 winter meetings, Wilson became an All-Star center fielder in Colorado in 2003. He had 91 runs batted in at the All-Star break, the most by any player in NL history at that point and the fifth-most in major league history, and was the quickest Rocky to reach 100 in franchise history, doing that in 107 games. Wilson is a fastball hitter who likes the ball middle-out, the better to extend his arms, and is a dead pull hitter. He still has trouble with breaking pitches away, refusing to shorten his big swing when he behind in counts, although it was hard to complain with his results in 2003. He has good speed, although with the big-boppin' Rockies was not asked to steal bases as before, missing out on a fourth straight 20-20 season. Although Wilson is not a classic center fielder because of his occasional misreads and poor routes, he has enough speed to outrun a lot of his mistakes. His arm is above average. Wilson was expected to remain the regular center fielder and No. 4 hitter, and is fully capable of providing the 30-100 numbers expected of a Coors Field cleanup man.

	AB	R	HR	RBI	SB	BA
2001 Florida	468	70	23	71	20	.274
2002 Florida	510	80	23	65	20	.243
2003 Colorado	600	94	36	141	14	.282

WILSON, TOM - C - BR - b: 12/19/70 $2

With one of the more open stances in baseball, Wilson is a decent but unexceptional hitter who can take a walk and whose statistical totals don't do justice to his gap power. While not the sort of bat likely to get an everyday playing time and slowed enough that he saw less time behind the plate, he can contribute as a second or third catcher who is comfortable backing up at first base. He didn't look like an outfielder when the Blue Jays tried him there early last year. This season, he's fighting in the spring to win a second or third catching spot.

	AB	R	HR	RBI	SB	BA
2002 Toronto	265	33	8	37	0	.257
2003 Toronto	256	37	5	35	0	.258

WILSON, VANCE - C - BR - b: 3/17/73 $2

Wilson played far more in 2003 than he expected because Mike Piazza was injured. As the regular catcher, Wilson's biggest problem was that he wasn't Piazza. In addition to less power, New York got help for its pitching staff and defense, for Wilson threw out 45 per cent of those trying to steal against him. His offense was in line with what he had done in Triple-A and in his earlier major league exposure, except that he stole a few more bases in the minors. He has shown that he is good enough to be a regular major league catcher.

	AB	R	HR	RBI	SB	BA
2001 New York - NL	57	3	0	6	0	.298
2002 New York - NL	163	19	5	26	0	.245
2003 New York - NL	268	28	8	39	1	.243

WINN, RANDY - OF - BR - b: 6/9/74 $25

Winn was given to Seattle prior to the 2003 season, in compensation for the Mariners letting the Devil Rays have manager Lou Piniella. A switch-hitter, Winn has learned how to drive the ball in gaps as he has matured, although Safeco Field cut down on his home runs production. Winn has exceptional speed and is a good bunter; he can lay down bunts for hits and also turn gap-singles into doubles and doubles into triples. He steals 20 bases a year, although he has the speed for many more. A fleet outfielder, his arm is only so-so and he is best-suited for left. Winn was expected to be the regular in left and near the top of the batting order.

	AB	R	HR	RBI	SB	BA
2001 Tampa Bay	429	54	6	50	12	.273
2002 Tampa Bay	607	87	14	75	27	.298
2003 Seattle	600	103	11	75	23	.295

WITT, KEVIN - 1B/DH - BL - b: 1/5/76 $2

A utility player (first base, third base and left field) Witt 28, gave the Tigers, his third team, a live left handed bat and his performance enhances his chances to stay in the majors. He opened some eyes and he could have a career similar to Matt Stairs.

	AB	R	HR	RBI	SB	BA
2003 Detroit	270	25	10	26	1	.263

WOMACK, TONY - 2B/SS - BL - b: 9/25/69 $6

Womack has no patience at the plate and no power, making him one of the least valuable regulars in baseball. He was truly woeful at the plate in 2003 and not even his speed could keep him in the starting lineup. Although he once stole more than 200 bases in a four year span while with Pittsburgh and Arizona, he can't come close to getting on base enough to take advantage of his wonderful basestealing ability. He is a dependable fielder, capable of playing second, short and third. Because of his experience, there is a chance that Womack will land a spot at second or short this season. However, he doesn't get on base enough, nor does he hit for nearly enough power for him to keep it. More likely, he'll wind up as a utility player and pinch hitter this year.

	AB	R	HR	RBI	SB	BA
2001 Arizona	481	66	3	30	28	.266
2002 Arizona	590	90	5	57	29	.271
2003 AZ/COL/CHI - NL	349	43	2	22	13	.226

WOODWARD, CHRIS - SS - BR - b: 6/27/76 $5

A decent-hitting shortstop with underrated power, Woodward started last year as the regular shortstop but had lost his job mid-season to the veteran Mike Bordick. Woodward has multiple problems that have held him back from graduating to the ranks of true full-timer, not the least of which are his limited fielding range and confidence and that he doesn't take walks. Probably better suited to be a third baseman, Woodward start s this season as a contender for an everyday spot as the shortstop but will have to hit as he did in 2002 if he's to maintain a full-season spot.

	AB	R	HR	RBI	SB	BA
2001 Toronto	63	9	2	5	0	.190
2002 Toronto	312	48	13	45	3	.276
2003 Toronto	349	43	2	22	13	.226

WOOTEN, SHAWN - 1B/DH - BR - b: 7/24/72 $3

A utility player who can hit for average, Wooten has played a variety of positions in parts of three major league seasons. He is not an accomplished defensive player, which might suggest first base as an option, but Wooten doesn't hit with the kind of power a team would like at that position. He was tried at third base last season, and was planning to work on his defense at the hot corner in the offseason. Wooten also can serve as a catcher, which makes him more versatile than the average utility player. He is a slow runner. Expect Wooten to hit well in occasional duty as a pinch hitter and injury replacement.

	AB	R	HR	RBI	SB	BA
2001 Anaheim	221	24	8	32	2	.312
2002 Anaheim	113	13	3	19	2	.292
2003 Anaheim	272	25	7	32	0	.243

YOUNG, DMITRI - OF/DH - BB - b: 10/11/73 $18

After a hernia shelved Young for most of 2002, he returned to have the best year of his career in 2003. Young plays an adequate left field and he is sure handed but he doesn't cover a lot of ground. He can also fill in at first base but not well enough to displace Carlos Pena. The Tigers continue to try to clear their house of average outfielders and as soon as they have more reliable talent, Young will become a full time designated hitter.

	AB	R	HR	RBI	SB	BA
2001 Cincinnati	540	68	21	69	8	.302
2002 Detroit	201	25	7	27	2	.284
2003 Detroit	562	78	29	85	2	.297

YOUNG, ERIC - 2B - BR - b: 5/18/67 $20

Young has never had anything to offer offensively except stolen bases, which makes one wonder how he has managed to be a starter for the last seven seasons. He does not hit for average, draw walks or hit for any power at all. And although Young still has some speed and will steal a lot of bases, his poor instincts mean he winds up being thrown out more than a quarter of time he tries to run. Defensively, he can cover enough ground to look good, but his arm is weak and he has trouble turning the double play. Young's only value is as a bench player at this point. Anybody who thinks about making him a starter is in for a long season.

	AB	R	HR	RBI	SB	BA
2001 Chicago - NL	603	98	6	42	31	.279
2002 Milwaukee	496	57	3	28	31	.280
2003 MIL/SF	475	80	15	34	28	.251

YOUNG, MICHAEL - 2B - BR - b: 10/19/76 $20

Young has always been a superb fielder, and last season he came into his own as a hitter as well. He has only modest power, but is capable of hitting for a high average. Young has good speed on the bases, which translates into double-digit steals and lots of triples. His defense is Gold Glove-caliber. Young will be 27 at the beginning of this season, and should be primed for a strong year as an everyday second baseman.

	AB	R	HR	RBI	SB	BA
2001 Texas	386	57	11	49	3	.249
2002 Texas	573	77	9	62	6	.262
2003 Texas	666	106	14	72	13	.306

ZAUN, GREGG - C - BB - b: 4/14/71 $0

Zaun, a nephew of former Gold Glover Rick Dempsey, has made a solid career as a switch-hitting reserve. He has a gap power with a little pop, and the fact that he can hit from both sides makes him a valuable bench asset. Zaun does not have a particularly strong arm and had surgery to repair a torn tendon in his throwing elbow after the 2002 season. He was released by Houston in August but made a good first impression after being signed by Colorado later that month and was expected to open spring training as a candidate for a reserve catcher spot.

	AB	R	HR	RBI	SB	BA
2001 Kansas City	125	15	6	18	1	.320
2002 Houston	185	18	3	24	1	.222
2003 HOU/COL	166	15	4	21	1	.229

ZEILE, TODD - 1B/3B - BR - b: 9/9/65 $4

Zeile joined Montreal in August after his release from the Yankees. Montreal is his eleventh stop in the majors and while he'll turn 39 in September, he still has some pop in his bat and he won't embarrass himself on defense.

	AB	R	HR	RBI	SB	BA
2001 New York - NL	531	66	10	62	1	.266
2002 Colorado	506	61	18	87	1	.273
2003 NY - AL/MON	299	40	11	42	1	.227

ON THE MOUND

ABBOTT, PAUL - TR - b: 9/15/67 $0

A former 17-game winner for Seattle, Paul Abbott spent most of 2003 mired at Triple-A Tucson before he was acquired by the Royals in August. Abbott made eight starts for Kansas City before missing his last start due to a strained right quadricep. He had a couple of excellent outings mixed in with mostly mediocre results as he filled a gap for the pitching-starved Royals. Abbott's 90-MPH fastball, often thrown off the plate, sets up a plus straight change which he can spot to the corners of the strikezone. He tends to work long counts and give up a lot of fly balls, especially when he works behind in the count. He has not seen much success out of the bullpen and has often had trouble working deep into his starts. Abbott will vary his delivery to prevent baserunners from getting a good jump and he's a good fielder. In 2004, Abbott will have to work hard to earn a spot at the back of a rotation, or spend most of the year, again, in the high minors.

	W	SV	ERA	IP	H	BB	SO	B / I
2001 Seattle	17	0	4.25	163	145	87	118	1.42
2002 Seattle	1	0	11.98	26	40	20	22	2.28
2003 Kansas City	1	0	5.28	48	47	26	32	1.53

ACEVEDO, JOSE - TR - b: 12/18/77 $1

Acevedo has had his share of personal and professional explosions but his outlook has grown more mature and professional and he can pitch. The Reds have jerked him around a little too much and he did not always deserve it.

	W	SV	ERA	IP	H	BB	SO	B / I
2001 Cincinnati	5	0	5.44	96	101	34	68	1.41
2002 Cincinnati	4	0	7.23	24	28	12	14	1.69
2003 Cincinnati	2	0	2.67	27	17	6	23	0.85

ADAMS, TERRY - TR - b: 3/6/73 $1

The Phillies rotation is so solid now that Adams should no longer be given consideration to be part of it. Adams is a very effective righthanded reliever and it was no coincidence that the Phillies struggled and faded when he went on the DL in late August with a strained oblique muscle. Adams came off the DL but he was able to pitch onlyonce and that was it for the year, and for the Phillies. Adams is expected to be one hundred percent by spring training.

	W	SV	ERA	IP	H	BB	SO	B / I
2001 Los Angeles	12	0	4.33	166	172	54	141	1.36
2002 Philadelphia	7	0	4.35	137	132	58	96	1.39
2003 Phildelphia	1	0	2.65	68	68	23	51	1.34

AFFELDT, JEREMY - TL - b: 6/6/79 $7

Jeremy Affeldt lost a coin flip to Runelvys Hernandez to determine the club's opening day starter, but it was a persistent blister that knocked him out of the rotation for good. The Royals refined Affeldt's grip to move his fingers off the seams in an effort to avoid the blistering, but he made a trip to the DL early in the year and eventually had to turn to short relief work to keep the problem under control. The bullpen move, and changed grip, seemed to add even more life to his already strong fastball. While Affeldt was a good starter, he became an excellent short reliever who soon won an important role and closed out some games late in the year. Affeldt can be effective with just two pitches if his mid-90s four-seam fastball is working along with his big 12-to-6 curve; Affeldt will also throw sliders to keep hitters off-balance, although they are rarely needed if his other two pitches are sharp. Part of what makes him so effective is the vast difference in velocity on his two primary pitches. He can run the heater at 95 MPH, good enough to throw past hitters high in the strikezone, then come back at them with a big curve thrown in the low 70s, down and to the opposite corner of the plate. Even if hitters can catch up with the fastball or wait out the curve, they often just hit them foul. Affeldt has the stuff to be effective in short relief; stamina over the long haul is the only unproven component.

	W	SV	ERA	IP	H	BB	SO	B / I
2002 Kansas City	3	0	4.63	78	85	37	67	1.57
2003 Kansas City	7	4	3.93	126	126	38	98	1.30

AINSWORTH, KURT - TR - b: 9/9/78 $1

The Orioles have had a history of trading for pitchers who turned out to be damaged goods, and Ainsworth appeared to be one of them. When they obtained him in the Sidney Ponson trade, Ainsworth had a broken shoulder blade. He had pitched well in the Giants' rotation during the season's first two months. He had been their first-round draft pick in 1999 and an Olympian the next year. Ainsworth recovered in time to pitch for Baltimore during the season's last week, but was hit hard. He's best when his off-speed pitches are working to complement a low-to-mid-90s fastball. If his shoulder recovers, he has a bright future.

	W	SV	ERA	IP	H	BB	SO	B / I
2002 San Francisco	1	0	2.10	26	22	12	15	1.32
2003 SF/BAL	5	0	4.08	68	72	27	52	1.45

ALFONSECA, ANTONIO - TR - b: 4/16/72 $0

The Cubs went into the 2003 campaign hoping that being in better shape would do wonders for Alfonseca's velocity, however it didn't work out that way. Hitters have learned to lay off his sinker and wait to pounce on a better offering. Alfonseca always has allowed a lot of baserunners, even when he saved more than 70 games in a three-year span for the Marlins, meaning he is one of the most overrated closers in the game. Even though he will get another chance to be the man based on his reputation, don't look for him to keep that role for the entire season. He is far too inconsistent at this point in his career for that to happen.

	W	SV	ERA	IP	H	BB	SO	B / I
2001 Florida	4	28	3.06	61	68	15	40	1.35
2002 Chicago - NL	2	19	4.00	74	73	36	61	1.47
2003 Chicago - NL	3	0	5.84	66	76	27	51	1.55

ALMANZA, ARMANDO - TL - b: 10/26/72 $0

Prior to 2003, Almanza was known to be tough on lefthanded hitters who struggled with control. Last season, his control did not improve and hitters hit almost .300 against him, and he didn't have the same success against lefties. He has a live arm and a good breaking pitch, but he's merely a situational reliever at this point. He was out for the season in August because he required surgery for a bone spur in his pitching elbow.

	W	SV	ERA	IP	H	BB	SO	B / I
2001 Florida	2	0	4.83	41	34	26	45	1.46
2002 Florida	3	2	4.33	46	36	23	57	1.29
2003 Florida	4	0	6.08	50	59	25	49	1.67

ALVAREZ, WILSON - TL - b: 3/24/70 $13

Alvarez became a valuable addition to the Los Angeles starting rotation after injuries KO'd Andy Ashby and Darren Dreifort in 2003. He had a 25-inning scoreless streak in September, keeping the Dodgers in wildcard race until the final days. Alvarez missed the 2000 and 2001 seasons after undergoing surgery on the rotator cuff in his left shoulder, although he has maintained his stuff which consists of a low-90s fastball that he complements with a changeup and a curve. He is a big man and not as agile in the field as he could be, although his move to first is above average and he does a good job controlling the running game. The further he gets from surgery, the more likely he is to claim a starter's role, although he was expected to be in the bullpen when the season starts.

	W	SV	ERA	IP	H	BB	SO	B / I
2002 Tampa Bay	2	1	5.28	75	80	36	56	1.55
2003 Los Angeles	6	1	2.37	95	80	23	82	1.08

ANDERSON, BRIAN - TL - b: 4/26/72 $15

An important trade-deadline acquisition from Cleveland, Brian Anderson gave the Royals several outstanding starts in September and they won six of his seven outings as Anderson earned pitcher of the month honors from the club. For Anderson, it was his best season ever as he set career marks in wins and ERA. He started slowly, winning just twice in his first ten starts, and was bothered by a sore hamstring in April. From June through September, though, Anderson posted a 3.30 ERA and won 12 of 21 starts, including two complete game victories in September. Anderson works primarily with two pitches: a low-90s fastball and a good changeup. He'll throw a cutter or slider to righthanders to give them another look, but rarely locates them in hittable locations. Anderson can throw either the fastball or changeup to any spot. He has remarkable control; Anderson regularly works ahead of hitters and has averaged fewer than two walks per nine innings throughout his career. A good fielder, Anderson has a strong pickoff move; baserunners succeeded just once in nine steal attempts last year. Anderson became a free agent at the end of 2003 and was looking for a long-term deal. He can be a decent number two man in a rotation for a non-contender, or drop lower in the rotation on a stronger staff.

	W	SV	ERA	IP	H	BB	SO	B / I
2001 Arizona	4	0	5.20	133	156	30	55	1.40
2002 Arizona	6	0	4.79	156	174	32	81	1.32
2003 CLE/KC	14	0	3.78	198	212	43	87	1.29

ANDERSON, JASON - TR - b: 6/9/79 $0

Even though Anderson moved from high Class A through Triple-A in 2002, he still surprised the Yankees by pitching well enough in spring training to go north with the major league team. He was up and down between the majors and Triple-A (1-3, 2.03, 7 saves) after that, even after he went to the Mets in the Armando Benitez deal. Anderson had some lapses in concentration that caused him to give up runs in bunches. He can throw a mid-90s fastball to go with passable offspeed pitches. Though he's being groomed as a closer, he didn't pitch in any save situations last season. That could be the move he makes in 2004.

	W	SV	ERA	IP	H	BB	SO	B / I
2003 NY-AL/NY-NL	1	0	4.88	31	33	19	16	1.66

ANDERSON, MATT - TR - b: 8/17/76 $1

Anderson was blessed with a fastball that, until he was injured in early 2002, was one of the fastest in the history of the game and it earned for him a place among the elite closers in the game. His velocity has not been the same since and he no longer closes.

	W	SV	ERA	IP	H	BB	SO	B / I
2001 Detroit	3	22	4.82	56	56	18	52	1.32
2002 Detroit	2	0	9.00	11	17	8	8	2.27
2003 Detroit	0	3	5.41	23	25	9	13	1.46

APPIER, KEVIN - TR - b: 12/6/67 $0

Kevin Appier originally left the Royals in 1999 because he wanted a shot at postseason play; how ironic that he'd return to Kansas City trying to help them reach the playoffs for the first time in 18 years. In 2003, Appier was bothered by a sore right elbow while pitching poorly for four months prior to his July release from Anaheim. The sore elbow prevented Appier from throwing his devastating splitter which moves down and away from righthanded hitters. No longer a power pitcher, Appier will now work his high-80s fastball at the corners and mix in curves to set up the splitter and hard slider. His exaggerated delivery often leaves him out of position to field grounders and he doesn't hold baserunners especially well. Appier made four starts for Kansas City before his elbow gave out for good, requiring season-ending surgery to repair a partially-torn ligament. Appier pitched well in his short stint, including six innings of shutout ball in an inspirational win against the Yankees. He expressed a desire to return to Kansas City in 2004 which may suit the Royals well considering his expensive contract would still be the responsibility of the Angels.

	W	SV	ERA	IP	H	BB	SO	B/I
2001 New York - NL	11	0	3.57	206	181	64	172	1.19
2002 Anaheim	14	0	3.92	188	191	64	132	1.35
2003 ANA/KC	8	0	5.40	112	120	43	55	1.46

ARMAS JR., TONY - TR - b: 4/29/78 $3

Last year's entry in Armas' profile ended with, "He's ready for a break out year." The way he began 2003 indicated that 2003 would be just that but it turned out that it was another break down year for the talented but injury-riddled Armas. He was disabled in mid May by a torn rotator cuff but in the few games that he pitched, Armas was dominant. Now the question is what will Armas have when he returns. Will he have his mid-90s fastball and will his great breaking pitches still be tight? Spring training began with the expectation that he would answer those questions.

	W	SV	ERA	IP	H	BB	SO	B/I
2001 Montreal	9	0	4.03	196	180	91	176	1.38
2002 Montreal	12	0	4.44	164	149	78	131	1.38
2003 Montreal	2	0	2.61	31	25	8	23	1.06

ARROYO, BRONSON - TR - b: 2/24/77 $0

A former Pirate and a parrothead from Key West, Arroyo gained attention by pitching the fourth nine-inning perfect game in the Triple-A International League's 120 seasons. That earned him a promotion from Pawtucket to the Boston bullpen late in August. In his first appearance for the Bosox, he earned his first major league save with three scoreless innings against Seattle. His role became that of an infrequent long reliever. Because his fastball hovers only on either side of 90 MPH and he has an excellent curve, he's the kind of pitcher who would be effective in Triple-A but have difficulty in the majors. Long relief or setup work appears to be his best bet.

	W	SV	ERA	IP	H	BB	SO	B/I
2001 Pittsburgh	5	0	5.09	88	99	34	39	1.51
2002 Pittsburgh	2	0	4.00	27	30	15	22	1.67
2003 Boston	0	1	2.08	17	10	4	14	0.81

ASENCIO, MIGUEL - TR - b: 9/29/80 $0

Miguel Asencio made just eight starts for Kansas City in 2003 before a sore elbow sent him to the disabled list in May; he had surgery to remove bone chips in June but his rehab effort went poorly and he was finally shut down for the year in September. It was a disappointing season for Asencio as he was expected to become a regular member of the Royals starting rotation a year after coming to the club as a Rule 5 pick from the Phillies. He has always had good stuff; when his hard sinker is working Asencio will induce many grounders. He works with a straight low-90s fastball and his above-average changeup complements his heater well. Unfortunately, Asencio often has poor command of his pitches and ends up having to work strictly with his fastball, and his command often escapes him from one inning to the next turning a good outing bad in a matter of a few pitches. Asencio has had more success the first time through a batting order as hitters refuse to swing at the off-speed stuff the second time around. Still, he'll remain a starting pitcher because his unpredictable command prevents his use in short relief. Asencio is expected to fully recover by spring training in 2004 and be ready to compete for a rotation spot.

	W	SV	ERA	IP	H	BB	SO	B/I
2002 Kansas City	4	0	5.11	123	136	64	58	1.62
2003 Kansas City	2	0	5.22	48	54	21	27	1.55

ASHBY, ANDY - TR - b: 7/11/67 $0

Ashby's career was threatened by his latest right elbow injury, which required Tommy John ligament replacement surgery late last summer. Ashby made only two starts in 2002 before requiring season-ending surgery to repair a torn flexor muscle in the same elbow. When right, Ashby throws a hard, sinking fastball that he can also cut, giving him a pitch that breaks down to hitters on both sides. Ashby was expected to miss the majority of the 2004 season after his surgery.

	W	SV	ERA	IP	H	BB	SO	B/I
2001 Los Angeles	2	0	3.86	11	14	1	7	1.17
2002 Los Angeles	9	0	3.91	182	179	65	107	1.34
2003 Los Angeles	3	0	5.18	73	90	17	41	1.47

ASTACIO, PEDRO - TR - b: 11/28/69 $0

Astacio was among the group of ailing Mets in 2003. He began the season on the disabled list because of biceps tendinitis, then underwent shoulder surgery in June after trying to pitch through his pain. Somehow, he managed a winning record even though he didn't go more than six innings and gave up multiple runs in every start. When he's right, Astacio gets batters out with a low-90s fastball, sharp-breaking curve and changeup. He gets so many batters out on ground balls that he was even the most effective pitcher in the Rockies' history. His status for 2004 depends entirely on his injury situation; watch spring training reports carefully.

	W	SV	ERA	IP	H	BB	SO	B/I
2001 COL/HOU	8	0	5.09	169	181	54	144	1.39
2002 New York - NL	12	0	4.79	192	192	63	152	1.33
2003 New York - NL	3	0	7.36	37	47	18	20	1.77

AVERY, STEVE - TL - b: 4/14/70 $0

A decade ago Avery had a bright future but now all he has just enough left to cling to a nondescript relief role for one of the worst teams in the history of baseball. Detroit will get better but Avery won't.

	W	SV	ERA	IP	H	BB	SO	B/I
2003 Detoit	2	0	5.63	16	19	7	6	1.63

AYALA, LUIS - TR - b: 1/12/78 $9

Ayala was effective in setup work for the Expos, typically pitching the seventh or eighth inning and then handing off to Biddle. Ayala might be in line for saves in 2004 if the Expos follow their recent pattern of rotating closers every year so one doesn't get so successful that he can demand a closer's salary. It should be noted however that while Ayala kept righty hitters below a .200 batting average, he struggled with great difficulty against lefty hitters, which would indicate he is best suited to be a righty setup man.

	W	SV	ERA	IP	H	BB	SO	B/I
2003 Montreal	10	5	2.92	71	65	13	46	1.10

BAEZ, DANYS - TR - b: 9/10/77 $10

Baez flopped as a starter and then he got a shot at closing and lost that job, too. Baez has a big, heavy fastball that can reach the high 90s, but his only other reliable pitch is an average curve. Baez allegedly throws a splitter but it's more "eau de splitter" in that it behaves more like a moderately sinking fastball than a real, killer, die-at-the-plate splitter that he badly needs to improve his chances at becoming the pitcher Cleveland hoped that he'd be by now. The 2003 season ended with Baez as the highest paid middle reliever in baseball and on a cost conscious team.

	W	SV	ERA	IP	H	BB	SO	B / I
2001 Cleveland	5	0	2.50	50	34	20	52	1.07
2002 Cleveland	10	6	4.41	165	160	82	130	1.46
2003 Cleveland	2	25	3.80	76	65	23	66	1.16

BALE, JOHN - TL - b: 5/22/74 $1

Bale was part of the call to arms for the Reds who tried to fill the void created by the total physical breakdown of their starting rotation. A career minor league reliever, Bale made his first major league start in August, but being 30 years old, short on big league experience and very hittable suggests that unless he improves in the winter, Bale has a slim chance to see much action in the majors in 2004.

	W	SV	ERA	IP	H	BB	SO	B / I
2001 Baltimore	1	0	3.04	27	18	17	21	1.31
2003 Cincinnati	1	0	4.47	46	50	12	37	1.34

BALFOUR, GRANT - TR - b: 12/30/77 $0

Balfour has emerged as a prospect thanks to a 94 MPH fastball that moves down in the zone and causes a lot of ground balls. He came up through the Twins minor league system as a relief prospect, but has developed a good enough change up to complement his fastball. Throw in a good curve and slider, and Balfour now is viewed as a starter of the near future. Like many prospects, Balfour is learning what happens when he uses his fastball too much or gets pitches too far up in the zone. He's maturing and has gotten physically stronger in recent years, but still needs a little polish before he enters the rotation.

	W	SV	ERA	IP	H	BB	SO	B / I
2003 Minnesota	1	0	4.15	26	23	14	30	1.42

BATISTA, MIGUEL - TR - b: 2/19/71 $10

Batista has some of the wickedest stuff, outside Randy Johnson, on the Arizona staff. His fastball touches the mid-90s consistently and has a nasty down-and-in break that makes him not only difficult to hit but also difficult to catch. With a hard slider that moves away to righthanders, batters have a hard time centering the ball. His consistent success the past three years has come with control; he has learned to throw the ball over the plate and let the movement do the work. He is a poor hitter and only an average fielder, and opponents can take advantage of his slow delivery to the plate. For all his success as a starter, he never has entered spring training with a spot in the rotation locked up because his resilient arm also is suited for relief. Expect more of the same this year, although Batista should end up in the rotation.

	W	SV	ERA	IP	H	BB	SO	B / I
2001 Arizona	11	0	3.36	139	113	60	90	1.24
2002 Arizona	8	0	4.29	185	172	70	112	1.31
2003 Arizona	10	0	3.54	193	197	60	142	1.33

BAUER, RICK - TR - b: 1/10/77 $0

Bauer was considered a marginal prospect before winning 12 games in Double-A and Triple-A in 2001, then earning his first shot at the majors. He has been back and forth between major league meal money and eating at Denny's since. Now he's a marginal major leaguer, a midrange power pitcher (fastball/slider) without enough power to call up strikeout pitches at will. Bauer arrived in the majors as a starter, had some save opportunities beginning in 2002 and has settled into no better than a middle-relief role. He has average stuff, throwing a 92 MPH fastball and a slider.

	W	SV	ERA	IP	H	BB	SO	B/I
2001 Baltimore	0	0	4.64	33	35	9	16	1.33
2002 Baltimore	6	1	3.98	84	84	36	45	1.43
2003 Baltimore	0	0	4.55	61	58	24	43	1.34

BECK, ROD - TR - b: 8/3/68 $11

Beck, affectionately in baseball circles as "Shooter," was out of work last spring, hoping to catch on as a minor league invitee in the Cubs' organization after missing the 2002 season following Tommy John surgery. He did more the catch on. After San Diego lost Trevor Hoffman for most of the season, Beck returned to his form as a closer par excellence with the Padres. Beck seems to do it with mirrors - slow, slower, slowest. Just when you think you have seen his slow curve, he slows it down some more. Beck is the perfect example of control and intelligence can accomplish on the mound. He understands the value of keeping runners close. Beck showed there is a lot of life left in his reconstructed arm, and was expected to open the season as a viable bullpen member who could save games in a pinch.

	W	SV	ERA	IP	H	BB	SO	B/I
2001 Boston	6	6	3.90	81	77	28	63	1.30
2003 San Diego	3	20	1.78	35	25	11	32	1.02

BECKETT, JOSH - TR - b: 5/15/80 $15

Beckett is made out by some to be an injury risk. Twice, blisters on his throwing hand forced him to the DL in 2002, and in 2003 he was laid up with a sprained elbow. To fill his spot, the Marlins called up little known Dontrelle Willis and when Becket returned to the rotation, the Marlins took off. Despite Willis' flashy debut, Beckett was and is the ace of the staff and he will improve this year and remain one of the top pitchers in baseball for years.

	W	SV	ERA	IP	H	BB	SO	B/I
2001 Florida	2	0	1.50	24	14	11	24	1.04
2002 Florida	6	0	4.09	108	93	44	113	1.27
2003 Florida	9	0	3.04	142	132	56	152	1.32

BEIMEL, JOE - TL - b: 4/19/77 $0

He received a slight bullpen promotion when he assumed the role held by Scott Sauerbeck, who was traded to Boston. He's been used in the past as a starter, but he's best suited as a reliever. Beimel is a lefty relivar with a four-pitch arsenal but he struggled with his command, and actually did worse against lefthanded batters, who hit .311 against him. He had a horrible second-half last season, and his spring training performance will indicate whether or not he can get it together.

	W	SV	ERA	IP	H	BB	SO	B/I
2001 Pittsburgh	7	0	5.23	115	131	49	58	1.56
2002 Pittsburgh	2	0	4.64	85	88	45	53	1.56
2003 Pittsburgh	1	0	5.06	62	69	33	42	1.64

BELL, ROB - TR - b: 1/17/77 $0

Rob Bell Scouts have been attracted to Bell's stuff — a first-rate fastball and curveball. When he gets his curveball over for strikes, his fastball can be an effective out pitch. Consistency within individual games has been a problem for Bell, and he struggled with walks last year. After more than 85 major league starts, Bell has not made much concrete progress. He was called up by the Devil Rays in mid June last year and by July had earned himself an extended stay on the Devil Rays, and finished the season with a winning record. Bell began spring training trying to win himself a spot on the rotation for this year.

	W	SV	ERA	IP	H	BB	SO	B/I
2001 CIN/TEX	5	0	6.67	149	176	64	97	1.61
2002 Texas	4	0	6.22	94	113	35	70	1.57
2003 Tampa Bay	5	0	5.52	101	103	39	44	1.41

BENITEZ, ARMANDO - TR - b: 11/3/72 $7

Benitez has the stuff to be one of the dominant closers in the game. His fastball regularly registers at 97-98 MPH, and he complements that with a hard slider and a newly developed split-finger fastball that works as a changeup. With that repertoire he has averaged 12 strikeouts per nine innings during his career, and he is just as successful against lefties as righties. At the same time, he occasionally loses location, especially when he is used several games in a row. He fields his position adequately for a big man, although he often loses track of baserunners and can be run against. While Benitez bounced to three different teams the final year of his contract in 2003, he was expected to be a firmly ensconced as a closer again this season.

	W	SV	ERA	IP	H	BB	SO	B/I
2001 New York - NL	6	43	3.77	76	59	40	93	1.30
2002 New York - NL	1	33	2.27	67	46	25	79	1.06
2003 NYM/NYY/SEA	4	21	2.96	73	59	41	75	1.37

BENOIT, JOAQUIN - TR - b: 7/26/78 $0

Benoit pitched his way out of the rotation last season with inconsistency and wildness. He pitched somewhat better in long relief, and is young with a high enough ceiling to be given additional opportunities to break through. Benoit has a plus fastball with good movement and can be dominant at times. Health has been a recurring problem, and he struggled with tendinitis in his pitching elbow last season.

	W	SV	ERA	IP	H	BB	SO	B/I
2002 Texas	4	1	5.31	85	91	58	59	1.76
2003 Texas	8	0	5.49	105	99	51	87	1.43

BENSON, KRIS - TR - b: 11/7/74 $3

Benson hit a wall early in the 2003 season and by July he was put on the DL and went on an exercise rehab program but he was finally shut down for the year in August. His problem was diagnosed as shoulder irritation and surgery was not deemed necessary at the end of last season. When healthy, he has a good fastball, curve and slider.

	W	SV	ERA	IP	H	BB	SO	B/I
2002 Pittsburgh	9	0	4.70	130	152	50	79	1.55
2003 Pittsburgh	5	0	4.97	105	127	36	68	1.55

BERNERO, ADAM - TR - b: 11/28/76 $0

Bernero may have been the happiest man in the Motor City on July 13, when he was traded from Detroit to Colorado. While Bernero did not have great success with the Rockies, he does have the stuff to make an impact at the major league level. His fastball hits 92 MPH and has good sink, and he also has a good breaking pitch. His inconsistent location works against him, although at 27 he is not too old to improve. Bernero had the worst run support in baseball while starting for the Tigers. Altough Bernero was a starter when he arrived in the majors, he was used out of the bullpen in Colorado and was expected to remain in that role for the foreseeable future.

	W	SV	ERA	IP	H	BB	SO	B/I
2002 Detroit	4	0	6.20	102	128	31	69	1.56
2003DET/COL	1	0	5.87	133	137	54	80	1.43

BETANCOURT, RAFAEL - TR - b: 4/29/75 $0

At age 29, Betancourt is a bit old to be starting his major league career. He pitched well in relief but he will have to fight hard in spring for another year in the majors in 2004.

	W	SV	ERA	IP	H	BB	SO	B / I
2003 Cleveland	2	1	2.13	38	27	13	36	1.05

BIDDLE, ROCKY - TR - b: 5/21/76 $17

Easy saves came early in the season but Biddle wore down by the end of the year. It's hard to say what the Expos have in mind for him. Based on his performance in 2003, he should be their closer this year but what did the Expos see in him when they got him in the Colon trade with the White Sox? As a member of the Sox in 2002, Biddle was put back in the starting rotation at the end of the year and didn't show much potential to be a closer. He's not a hard thrower, and his lack of control is the main reason why he has not had more success at the major league level. He needs to throw a lot of strikes to be succesful - he gets hit hard when he misses his spots.

	W	SV	ERA	IP	H	BB	SO	B / I
2001 Chicago - AL	7	0	5.39	128	137	52	85	1.47
2002 Chicago - AL	3	1	4.05	78	72	39	64	1.43
2003 Montreal	5	34	4.64	72	71	40	54	1.55

BOEHRINGER, BRIAN - TR - b: 1/8/70 $0

Boehringer's job is to come in late in the game and retire righthanded hitters then give the ball to the closer. He was up to the task in 2002 as he kept righties to a composite .218 batting average. Last year it turned sour and righties hit .309 against him and took him deep eight times. Boehringer has a decent fastball that can reach 92 MPH and to keep hitters honest, he will show them a curve and a slider.

	W	SV	ERA	IP	H	BB	SO	B / I
2001 NY - AL/SF	0	2	3.65	69	67	29	60	1.39
2002 Pittsburgh	4	1	3.39	80	65	33	65	1.23
2003 Pittsburgh	5	0	5.49	62	64	30	47	1.51

BONDERMAN, JEREMY - TR - b: 10/28/82 $0

Just a puppy at age 21, Bonderman was Oakland's first round pick in 2001. Bonderman has guts, a good fastball, curve and slider although he was thrust into the utter chaos and oblivion of the Tigers when he should have been in the minors. Bonderman was removed from the rotation to protect him after he lost his nineteenth game late in September but he will improve faster than the Tigers so his work will often be in vain again this year. Once the team stabilizes, Bonderman will be a solid number one or two starter for the next decade.

	W	SV	ERA	IP	H	BB	SO	B / I
2003 Detroit	6	0	5.56	162	193	58	108	1.55

BONG, JUNG - TL - b: 7/15/80 $0

Jung Bong works mostly with a fastball that touches 90 MPH and an excellent changeup. His fastball doesn't overpower hitters, but it has good movement, making it a difficult pitch to drive. Although Bong worked most commonly as a starter in the minors, he is seen as a reliever by the Braves because he lacks a useful breaking pitch and because his method of pitching often results in high pitch counts, limiting the number of innings Bong can go in a starting role. He's a good bullpen fit for a team with a strong rotation, as Bong can come in and throw his fastball to setup the changeup without having to go to his weaker breaking pitches. If forced into the rotation he'd be a five or six-inning pitcher who would have trouble the second and subsequent times through a batting order.

	W	SV	ERA	IP	H	BB	SO	B/I
2003 Atlanta	6	1	5.05	57	56	31	47	1.53

BOOTCHECK, CHRIS - TR - b: 10/24/78 $0

A first round pick out of Auburn in the 2000 draft, Bootcheck has worked his way up the minor league ladder and got his first major league experience late last season. A power pitcher, Bootcheck had mixed results in his Triple-A stint last year, posting an 8-9 record and a 4.25 ERA with 82 strikeouts and 43 walks in 171 innings. Bootcheck throws a two-seam fastball and a cut fastball, as well as a slider and changeup. He has a good work ethic, but has to fight perfectionist tendencies. Bootcheck was expected to begin this season in the minors but could graduate to the majors at some point, either in relief or as an injury replacement for a starting pitcher.

	W	SV	ERA	IP	H	BB	SO	B/I
2003 Anaheim	0	0	9.61	10	16	6	7	2.14

BOROWSKI, JOE - TR - b: 5/4/71 $30

Borowski is living proof that you don't have to be a particularly good pitcher to rack up a lot of saves. Unlike many of the successful closers, he doesn't have any one pitch that is dominating. Instead he does his job by keeping the ball down, throwing strikes, and relying on his defense to help him get hitters out. Since Borowski isn't a hard thrower, he will be on a short leash in his life as a closer. If he is on a team with a more established reliever, he will be back pitching in the seventh and eighth innings. If he gets an opportunity to be the primary closer again, there is no reason why he can't wind up with 30 saves for a winning ballclub.

	W	SV	ERA	IP	H	BB	SO	B/I
2002 Chicago - NL	4	2	2.73	96	84	29	97	1.18
2003 Chicago - NL	2	33	2.64	68	53	19	66	1.05

BOYD, JASON - TR - b: 2/23/73 $0

At age 31 and with the vast majority of his baseball career spent in the minor leagues, Boyd's eye-popping "stuff" will always tantalize big league scouts who think that a couple of adjustments are all that Boyd needs to become an effective major league reliever. His stuff works great in the minors but so far, it hasn't worked at the major league level.

	W	SV	ERA	IP	H	BB	SO	B/I
2002 San Diego	1	0	7.94	28	33	15	18	1.70
2003 Cleveland	3	0	4.30	52	38	26	31	1.22

BRADFORD, CHAD - TR - b: 9/14/74 $7

Bradford, one of the featured players in last summer's controversial Moneyball book, is almost unhittable when facing righthanded batters. A true submariner, Bradford's motion is so severe that during his delivery his right hand sometimes scrapes the dirt on the front edge of the mound. That, combined with his big sinker and sweeping breaking ball, keeps righthanders praying for rain every time they face him. However, that same motion gives lefties a great look at the pitch, and Bradford has a whale of a time getting them out (lefties have batted nearly .300 against him over the past three seasons). Because he is so effective against righthanders, Bradford will have no trouble keeping his role as a situational reliever.

	W	SV	ERA	IP	H	BB	SO	B/I
2001 Oakland	2	1	2.70	36	41	6	34	1.28
2002 Oakland	4	2	3.11	75	73	14	56	1.16
2003 Oakland	7	2	3.04	77	67	30	62	1.26

BRAZELTON, DEWON - TR - b: 6/16/80 $0

Brazelton did a fine job in his first full professional season in 2002, posting a solid 3.33 ERA in 26 starts at Double-A. After he was the Devil Rays' number one pick in 2001 he's been on the fast track in the Tampa Bay system. He began last season at Triple-A Durham, but was called up to the majors in early May to replace Victor Zambrano on the rotation. By late June it was obvious that Brazelton had been too rushed and wasn't ready for the majors yet. He was sent back to Single-A Bakersfield instead of Triple-A in the hopes that he could focus on pitching development rather than have him worry about getting back into the majors. Brazelton will be competing for a major league job this spring training.

	W	SV	ERA	IP	H	BB	SO	B/I
2002 Tampa Bay	0	0	4.85	13	12	6	5	1.38
2003 Tampa Bay	1	0	6.89	48	57	23	24	1.66

BROWER, JIM - TR - b: 12/29/72 $4

Brower doesn't have a dominant pitch, instead relying on location and his defense to get hitters out. His best pitch is his slider, which he uses frequently when he's pitching in relief. As a starter he throws more fastballs and changeups, though neither pitch is good enough to keep him in the rotation. Brower's strength is his flexibility to spend a month or two in the bullpen and still have enough to throw five or six innings if called upon to start the occasional game. He will certainly find a spot on somebody's roster as a long reliever and spot starter.

	W	SV	ERA	IP	H	BB	SO	B/I
2001 Cincinnati	7	1	3.97	129	119	60	94	1.38
2002 CIN/MONI	3	0	4.37	80	77	32	57	1.36
2003 San Francisco	8	2	3.96	100	90	39	65	1.29

BROWN, KEVIN - TR - b: 3/14/65 $22

Brown, in his first full season since 2000, was his same dominating self while anchoring the Los Angeles starting rotation and finished No. 2 in the NL with a 2.39 ERA. After fighting elbow and back problems the last two seasons, Brown returned with command of his low-90s, two-seam fastball (which sinks) and a hard slider. He keeps the ball down and on the black and gives lefties almost as much problems as righties; in 2003, he did not give up a home run to a lefthanded batter in 97 innings. Amazing. A fierce competitor, Brown fields his position well and has an adequate move to first. While the wear has affected his body, Brown was expected to head the starting rotation again this season at the ripe age of 39.

	W	SV	ERA	IP	H	BB	SO	B/I
2001 Los Angeles	10	0	2.65	115	94	38	104	1.14
2002 Los Angeles	3	0	4.80	64	68	23	58	1.43
2003 Los Angeles	14	0	2.39	211	184	56	185	1.14

BUEHRLE, MARK - TL - b: 3/23/79 $16

Buehrle hadn't come close to a losing record in his first two full seasons in the big leagues, but he fell victim to the White Sox offensive struggles in the first half of the season. It's true that he wasn't quite as dominant as in previous years, as he gave up more hits while striking out fewer batters than before. Buehrle's best pitch is his curve, which he throws at any time in the count to hitters from both sides of the plate. His fastball is barely average, though he has outstanding control. Expect Buehrle to bounce back this season and lower his ERA back under 4.00 and win 15 to 18 games.

	W	SV	ERA	IP	H	BB	SO	B/I
2001 Chicago - AL	16	0	3.29	221	188	48	126	1.07
2002 Chicago - AL	19	0	3.58	239	236	61	134	1.24
2003 Chicago - AL	14	0	4.14	230	250	61	119	1.35

BUMP, NATE - TR - b: 7/24/76 $0

Bump was only in the majors for half the season last year and he was exclusively used in relief after being a starter in the minors. Bump relies on control, rather than power but he was plagued by walks. Bump walked 20 in 34 innings but he only allowed 21 hits which is an indication that he has the stuff to deal with major leaguers but he doesn't have enough faith in his stuff.

	W	SV	ERA	IP	H	BB	SO	B/I
2003 Florida	4	0	4.71	36	34	20	17	1.49

BURBA, DAVE - TR - b: 7/7/66 $0

Still pitching after all these years, Burba claimed a spot in the Milwaukee bullpen in the second half of 2003 after spending most of the year as a Triple-A starter. Burba, 37, gets by with a variety of pitches that he can tweak to fit the situation, and his arm recovers quickly. He can get his fastball into the lower 90s when used out of the bullpen and also throws a slider, a curve and split-finger pitch. He is susceptible to the long ball. He moves well for a big man, fields his position adroitly and keeps runners close with a quick move to the plate. While in the twilight of a career in which he was a three-time 15-game winner, Burba still can help a team, although he is now best suited as a reliever.

	W	SV	ERA	IP	H	BB	SO	B/I
2001 Cleveland	10	0	6.21	150	188	54	118	1.61
2002 TEX/CLE	5	0	5.20	145	155	57	95	1.46
2003 Milwaukee	1	0	3.53	43	42	19	35	1.41

BURKETT, JOHN - TR - b: 11/28/64 $4

On an aging Boston staff in 2003, Burkett literally was the graybeard. He's like a nutty professor on the mound - trying to find new ways to make his fastball sink, cut in on lefthanders or sneak over a corner of the plate. Burkett's curve is his out pitch, and his changeup can make his below-average fastball more effective. When runners reach base against him, that's the time to go out for a hot dog. By the time you return, he might have thrown over to first base three times without throwing a pitch. However, very few runners steal against Burkett. He would seem more effective following the hard-throwing Pedro Martinez in the rotation, but that wasn't the case in 2003.

	W	SV	ERA	IP	H	BB	SO	B/I
2001 Atlanta	12	0	3.04	219	187	70	187	1.17
2002 Boston	13	0	4.53	173	199	50	124	1.44
2003 Boston	12	0	5.15	182	202	47	107	1.37

BURNETT, A.J. - TR - b: 1/3/77 $2

After four starts, Burnett's elbow let go and he required an operation to put it all back in order. Originally expected to miss the 2004 season, Burnett was throwing lightly in September and barring complications, he may be ready to go in May. A high octane strikeout artist before his injury, all he has to do is gaze upon teammate Carl Pavano, and try not to scream as if he's just seen the ghost of his pitching future.

	W	SV	ERA	IP	H	BB	SO	B/I
2001 Florida	11	0	4.05	173	145	83	128	1.32
2002 Florida	12	0	3.30	204	153	90	203	1.19
2003 Florida	0	0	4.70	23	18	18	21	1.57

BYNUM, MIKE - TL - b: 3/20/78 $0

Bynum has put up solid numbers in his minor league career with a slider that compares to some of the best around. At the same time, he occasionally falls in love with the pitch at the expense of his fastball and changeup, which he needs to throw for strikes. He has a herky-jerky delivery that is difficult to read but also difficult to manage in times of stress. He was used as a starter and reliever in 2003 but was expected to open this season as a relief candidate.

	W	SV	ERA	IP	H	BB	SO	B/I
2002 San Diego	1	0	5.27	27	33	15	17	1.76
2003 San Diego	1	0	8.75	36	44	15	35	1.64

CALERO, KIKO - TR - b: 1/9/75 $1

2003 was his first season in the majors, with the Cardinals calling him up from Triple-A Memphis to fill a spot in their bullpen. He was an increasingly dominating reliever for the Cardinals until the end of June, when he ruptured a tendon in his right knee, requiring season-ending surgery. When healthy,Calero works off a low-90s fastball that has good movement and he also throws a good curveball, slurve and forkball.He has been working on developing his changeup and cut fastball. Durability has long been a question for Calero.

	W	SV	ERA	IP	H	BB	SO	B/I
2003 St. Louis	1	1	2.82	38	29	20	51	1.28

CALLAWAY, MICKEY - TR - b: 5/13/75 $0

Callaway is a control-type pitcher who can be successful when he keeps the ball down in the strike zone. Lacking an overpowering out- pitch, Callaway needs to have good command of his pitches to get hitters out. Last season, he was used irregularly early in the season and then missed time with shoulder tendinitis. As a result, he never got into a groove. Callaway can be a serviceable fifth starter or middle reliever at the major league level.

	W	SV	ERA	IP	H	BB	SO	B/I
2002 Anaheim	2	0	4.19	34	31	11	23	1.22
2003 ANA/TEX	1	0	6.67	61	84	24	41	1.78

CAPUANO, CHRIS - TL - b: 8/19/78 $2

Capuano may make it into some medical journals after recovering so rapidly from Tommy John surgery that he was able to join the Arizona rotation down the stretch in 2003. Capuano was off to a stellar start at Triple-A Tucson in 2002 before undergoing ligament replacement surgery on May 17. Not only was he back pitching in spring training, 2003, he also was recalled early in the season by the parent Diamondbacks to fill a vacany in the rotation caused by injuries. Capuano throws in the low-90s and spots his fastball well, mixing in an above-average curveball with an improving changeup. He threw seven shutout innings against Los Angeles in a start down the stretch. Capuano, 25, has the stuff to qualify as a candidate for the starting rotation, but a logjam ahead of him may force him to open the season at Triple-A.

	W	SV	ERA	IP	H	BB	SO	B/I
2003 Arizona	2	0	4.64	33	27	11	23	1.15

CARRARA, GIOVANNI - TR - b: 3/4/68 $0

Carrara had stretches of quality work undone by command problems before being designated for assignment in Seattle in 2003. He backs a 92 MPH fastball with two varieties of curve ball, the slower of which he uses as a changeup. He must locate well to be effective. He is not a nimble athlete, although he has a good move to first base to slow down the running game. He was expected to compete for a job in the bullpen.

	W	SV	ERA	IP	H	BB	SO	B/I
2001 Los Angeles	6	0	3.16	85	73	24	70	1.14
2002 Los Angeles	6	1	3.27	91	83	32	56	1.27
2003 Seattle	2	0	6.83	29	40	14	13	1.86

CARRASCO, HECTOR - TR - b: 10/22/69 $0

The Twins released Carrasco after the 2001 season, and he sat out the next year. The

---

Orioles signed him as a free agent and sent him to Triple-A Ottawa, where he pitched well enough as the closer to earn a return trip to the majors at the end of June. Carrasco throws hard stuff with a downward movement, allowing him to get runners out on ground balls. But his pitches don't have the power they had in the mid 1990s, when the Reds thought he could be their closer. Now he's more like a hanger-on as one of the last options on a pitching staff.

	W	SV	ERA	IP	H	BB	SO	B/I
2001 Minnesota	4	1	4.64	74	77	30	70	1.45
2003 Baltimore	2	1	4.93	38	40	20	27	1.57

CARTER, LANCE - TR - b: 12/18/74 $24
Devil Rays Manager Lou Pinealla is a hitter's manager and he likes his pitchers to throw strikes and not give up walks. Thats just what Lance Carter did to maintain the job of closer for Tampa Bay in 2003, challenging hitters with his low-90s fastball which is his best pitch, and his breaking stuff which he sometimes gets over the plate too much. While at times during the 2003 season he was considered merely the head of the closer committee, the 2003 season ended with Carter entrenched in that job. He has undergone two Tommy John surgeries, one in 1996 and the other in 2000. Coming into the 2003 season, he was a relatively obscure pitcher, having only pitched a total of 25 major league innings and was expected at the end of spring training to be a middle reliever and setup man, but he established himself as a capable closer last year. He was streaky in 2003, having good months when he's unhittable but also having the occasional bad outing when he gets clobbered. He should get another opportunity to get saves this year.

	W	SV	ERA	IP	H	BB	SO	B/I
2002 Tampa Bay	2	2	1.33	20	15	5	14	0.99
2003 Tampa Bay	7	26	4.33	79	72	19	47	1.15

CERDA, JAIME - TL - b: 10/26/78 $0
The Mets last season crowded their bullpen with more lefthanders than most teams. Cerda was at the back of that line, despite a promising major league debut in 2002. His biggest problem was that he walked more major league batters than he struck out. Cerda can throw strikes; his minor league K:W ratios have uniformly been good, and it was 3.5:1 last year during his time at Triple-A Norfolk. In his four minor league seasons, with just one start, he has a 15-3 won-lost record. Cerda's primary asset is a moving fastball thrown out of a funky delivery.

	W	SV	ERA	IP	H	BB	SO	B/I
2002 New York - NL	0	0	2.45	26	22	14	21	1.40
2003 New York - NL	1	0	5.85	32	32	20	19	1.61

CHACON, SHAWN - TR - b: 12/23/77 $0
Chacon missed three weeks in July with tendinitis in his right elbow but still finished among the leaders in most pitching categories for Colorado, which needs all the pitching it can get. Chacon rediscovered the fastball he seemingly lost in 2002, when he missed time with a strained pectoral muscle and was never the same. His velocity again topped 90 MPH, and so he was able to challenge hitters and pitch inside, a practice he got away from the year before. A Colorado native, Chacon has found a breaking ball that works at altitude, a plus for a franchise that saw the late Darryl Kile and Mike Hampton mysteriously lose their breaking pitches in the rare air. Chacon dabbles with a slider. He hit his first major league homer in 2003, although he is a poor bunter, a skill he should be working on. He was expected to maintain his spot near the top of the starting rotation this year.

	W	SV	ERA	IP	H	BB	SO	B/I
2001 Colorado	6	0	5.06	160	157	87	134	1.52
2002 Colorado	5	0	5.73	119	122	60	67	1.53
2003 Colorado	11	0	4.60	137	124	58	93	1.33

CHEN, BRUCE - TL - b: 6/19/77 $0

Although Bruce Chen is moderately talented, he tends to overanalyze things when he pitches. He has average stuff and must hit spots to be effective, particularly with his fastball and offspeed pitches. The lefthander could be a fourth or fifth starter if he gets his act together. He's got a long way to go, and needs to work on both his stamina and strength.

	W	SV	ERA	IP	H	BB	SO	B/I
2001 PHI/NY - NL	7	0	4.87	146	146	59	126	1.40
2002 NYM/MON/CIN	2	0	5.56	78	85	43	80	1.65
2003 HOU/BOS	0	0	5.56	24	26	10	20	1.48

CHULK, VINNIE - TR - b: 12/19/78 $0

Already capable of reaching the mid 90s with his fastball, Chulk has a biting sinker to go with a pretty good slider and occasional changeup. It was a bit of a surprise that Toronto called him up last year as he was having a mediocre season with Triple-A Syracuse, particularly because he still walks way too many hitters. He has a remote chance to crack the roster in the spring as a starter but more likely is headed back to the minors for another year.

	W	SV	ERA	IP	H	BB	SO	B/I
2003 Toronto	0	0	5.09	5	6	3	2	1.70

CLAUSSEN, BRANDON - TL - b: 5/1/79 $6

The highly touted Claussen appears to be fully recovered from his 2002 Tommy John surgery. He made one start and pitched beautifully for the Yankees, who then had to trade him to the Reds to get Aaron Boone. It remains to be seen what Claussen has left. Prior to the surgery Claussen had a live, moving fastball that topped out at about 93 mph. He also had an effective slider and a fair changeup. After the trade the Reds wisely did not use him which will help to ensure that he is ready to go in 2004.

	W	SV	ERA	IP	H	BB	SO	B/I
2003 NY - AL/CIN	1	0	1.43	6	8	1	5	1.43

CLEMENS, ROGER - TR - b: 8/4/62 $0

Clemens' 2003 season took on the appearance of a farewell tour, though as he pitched into the postseason speculation was that instead of leading to retirement it might be like one of the Rolling Stones' incessant "last" concerts. Little wonder, for The Rocket hasn't lost it any more quickly than Mick Jagger has. Clemens, however, reached the milestones of 300 victories and 4,000 strikeouts last season, when he still was successful with his mid-90s fastball and splitter. Surprisingly, he has been more effective against lefthanded batters than righthanders. He reversed his home/road tendency in 2003 by going 10-2 away from Yankee Stadium.

	W	SV	ERA	IP	H	BB	SO	B/I
2001 New York - AL	20	0	3.51	220	205	72	213	1.26
2002 New York - AL	13	0	4.35	180	172	63	192	1.31
2003 New York - AL	17	0	3.91	212	199	58	190	1.21

CLEMENT, MATT - TR - b: 8/12/74 $12

Clement's numbers last season were down just a bit from 2002 primarily because his slider wasn't quite as sharp. While it was an overpowering pitch in 2002, he didn't have the control over it he had during that season, and as a result he got a few less strikeouts. One possible explanation might be a slight back problem which dogged him most of the first half of the year. Clement needs his slider to be effective because he has only an average fastball and doesn't have another reliable out pitch. Even at his 2003 level, Clement will be an effective starter and will win more games than he loses, especially if he gets rewarded by pitching for a better than average offensive club.

	W	SV	ERA	IP	H	BB	SO	B/I
2001 Florida	9	0	5.05	169	172	85	134	1.52
2002 Chicago - NL	12	0	3.60	205	162	85	215	1.20
2003 Chicago - NL	14	0	4.11	202	169	79	171	1.23

COLOME, JESUS - TR - b: 6/2/80 $0

Colome started the 2003 season as the closer for the Devil Rays but lost that job within the first week of April after several bad outings. Although Colome has a great arm he's still a thrower and not a pitcher. He had some success against major league hitters in 2001, but fell flat on his face in 2002, and again struggled with his control in 2003, at one point getting ejected from a game for throwing a pitch behind the batter's back. Colome succeeds when he can harness his upper 90's fastball, and while he did cut down his walk rate last year, he still wasn't good enough to keep a job in a late-inning setup role for the Devil Rays.

	W	SV	ERA	IP	H	BB	SO	B/I
2001 Tampa Bay	2	0	3.40	48	37	25	31	1.27
2002 Tampa Bay	2	0	8.28	41	56	33	33	2.15
2003 Tampa Bay	3	2	4.50	74	69	46	69	1.55

COLON, BARTOLO - TR - b: 5/24/75 $19

A true workhorse, Colon is a dominating pitcher who doesn't throw a consistently overpowering fastball. Although he can get his heater up above 95 MPH when he wants, he is much more content to throw 90 to 93 MPH and get hitters out with his big overhand curve and filthy change. He has the arm strength to consistently throw more than 100 pitches a start, meaning high pitch counts shouldn't be a concern. Colon is one of the best and most consistent pitchers in the game who will have many, many more outstanding seasons before his career is over. Paired with a good offense, he will come close to 20 wins this season.

	W	SV	ERA	IP	H	BB	SO	B/I
2001 Cleveland	14	0	4.09	222	220	90	201	1.39
2002 CLE/MONI	20	0	2.93	233	219	70	149	1.24
2003 Chicago -AL	15	0	3.87	242	223	67	173	1.20

COLYER, STEVE - TL - b: 4/2/78 $0

The Dodgers moved Colyer to the bullpen in 2002 after he had spent the two previous years as a starter. Last season, he shuttled back and forth between the Dodgers and Triple-A Las Vegas. He throws very hard, in the mid 90's, yet his control has been inconsistent. Hard-throwing lefties never get overlooked, so he could have an impact in the majors before long.

	W	SV	ERA	IP	H	BB	SO	B/I
2003 Los Angeles	0	0	2.74	20	22	9	16	1.57

CONDREY, CLAY - TR - b: 11/19/75 $0

Condrey got the decision on Opening Day, 2003, and was in the rotation for the rest of April before suffering a strained left oblique muscle, missing two months, and then returning to Triple-A. He has a low-90s fastball and a good breaking pitch that enabled him to make the transition from reliever to starter at the Triple-A level in 2002. He was expected to open the season with a shot at the starting rotation, although another turn at Triple-A was a distinct possibility.

	W	SV	ERA	IP	H	BB	SO	B/I
2002 San Diego	1	0	1.69	27	20	8	16	1.05
2003 San Diego	1	0	8.47	34	43	21	25	1.88

CONTRERAS, JOSE - TR - b: 12/12/71   **$7**

The Yankees won a bidding war for the right to pay Contreras, a Cuban defector, $32 million for four years. For part of the year, he was more hype than hope. Pitching exclusively out of the bullpen, he was 1-1 with an 8.74 ERA on Memorial Day. After that, all but one appearance was as a starter, and he went 6-1 with a 2.26 ERA. Contreras also had extended time on the disabled list because of a shoulder problem and in various minor league venues. He arrived in the States with a reputation for throwing a mid-90s fastball, but more often worked as a finesse pitcher last season. He's likely to be a rotation starter this year.

	W	SV	ERA	IP	H	BB	SO	B/I
2003 New York - AL	7	0	3.30	71	52	30	72	1.15

COOK, AARON - TR - b: 2/8/79   **$0**

After blossoming in his sixth season at the minor league level in 2002, Cook stumbled when thrust into the starting rotation in 2003 and spent the second half of the season in the bullpen. Cook has the tools to be a quality starter in the big leagues, and more particularly, at Coors Field. He throws a hard, sinking fastball that is regularly clocked in the mid-90s, a pitch that hitters have trouble lifting. Cook gave up a homer every 17 innings in 2003, by far the best ratio on the Colorado staff. At the same time, he did not develop a quality breaking pitch, giving hitters a leg up on what to expect. Moreover, Cook, like many rookies, had a tendency to give hitters too much credit and try to be too fine with his pitches. He nibbled instead of challenged, and the resulting walks led to his undoing. Cook settled into a good routine during his time in the bullpen in 2003 and was expected to use that experience as a springboard to a spot in the starting rotation this season.

	W	SV	ERA	IP	H	BB	SO	B/I
2002 Colorado	2	0	4.54	36	41	13	14	1.51
2003 Colorado	4	0	6.02	124	160	57	43	1.75

CORDERO, FRANCISCO - TR - b: 8/11/77   **$25**

Installed as the closer at mid-season, Cordero once again demonstrated that he has the stuff to close out games. He established a career high in games pitched last year, and there was some concern about overworking him, particularly given his track record of frequent injuries. Cordero can be useful to a major league team as a setup man or closer, and should be expected to succeed in either role if he remains healthy.

	W	SV	ERA	IP	H	BB	SO	B/I
2002 Texas	2	10	1.79	45	33	13	41	1.02
2003 Texas	5	15	2.94	83	70	38	90	1.31

CORMIER, RHEAL - TL - b: 4/23/67   **$10**

Cormier has had many problems in his career, but last year he was brilliant in middle relief. Overall, he was one of the top three middle relievers in the National League. The Canadian reliever throws a sinking fastball and splitter that make him a groundball, finesse pitcher. However, he has trouble getting the radar gun over 90 MPH.

	W	SV	ERA	IP	H	BB	SO	B/I
2001 Philadelphia	5	1	4.21	51	49	17	37	1.29
2002 Philadelphia	5	0	5.25	60	61	32	49	1.55
2003 Philadelphia	8	1	1.70	85	54	25	67	0.93

CORNEJO, NATE - TR - b: 9/24/79   **$0**

Cornejo has good control and he works on the black but he doesn't walk many batters because they are eager to hack away at him. Hitters usually get the bat on the ball and Cornejo racks up very few strikeouts. In one five game stretch in May, Cornejo pitched 31 innings and he struck out one hitter. When he's got his good sinking fastball, hitters pound the ball into the ground and Cornejo can cruise along for six or seven innings. When his fastball does not move enough, Cornejo gives up a lot of hits but most of them stay in the park. He was the Tigers best pitcher in 2003.

	W	SV	ERA	IP	H	BB	SO	B/I
2001 Detroit	4	0	7.38	42	63	28	22	2.13
2002 Detroit	1	0	5.04	50	63	18	23	1.62
2003 Detroit	6	0	4.67	195	236	58	46	1.51

CRESSEND, JACK - TR - b: 5/13/75 $3

Cressend was called up in July and he pitched well in relief in July and August. He started to run into trouble in September however, as he got into some jams and gave up multiple runs in some of his appearances on the mound. Cressend is not a hard thrower but he's suffered from bouts of poor control throughout his career. Based on last year's effort, Cressend has harnessed his control and figured out how to pitch.

	W	SV	ERA	IP	H	BB	SO	B/I
2001 Minnesota	3	0	3.67	56	50	16	40	1.17
2002 Minnesota	0	0	5.91	32	40	19	22	1.84
2003 Cleveland	2	0	2.51	43	40	9	28	1.14

CRUDALE, MIKE - TR - b: 1/3/77 $1

Sent to Milwaukee for closer Mike DeJean late in 2003, Crudale was a pleasant addition to the Brewers' bullpen. His fastball is in the low 90s, and his best pitch is a biting slider with a late break that he can spot on the outside part of the plate. That combination makes him very tough on righties. He challenges hitters and does not mess around when ahead in the count, although he had trouble with location late in the year. He is a good athlete who fields his position well, although his high leg kick does not impede the running game. He was expected to be a mainstay in the bullpen as a setup man.

	W	SV	ERA	IP	H	BB	SO	B/I
2002 St. Louis	3	0	1.88	53	43	14	47	1.08
2003 STL/MIL	0	0	2.61	21	12	18	13	1.45

CRUZ, JUAN - TR - b: 10/15/80 $0

Cruz can bring it despite his slender frame. His fastball, which can reach the mid 90s on occasion, has plenty of movement and he also has a top notch slider that is close to unhittable when he's on. The Cubs shuttled Cruz back and forth between Chicago and Iowa last year, and Cruz wasn't very happy about it. To his credit, he didn't lose his cool and took advantage of the opportunities he was given late in the season, when he pitched extremely well in what proved to be a tough pennant race. While he would be a successful relief pitcher, and has the ability to save plenty of games, he deserves to be a starter. Given an opportunity, he would be a consistent performer in either role.

	W	SV	ERA	IP	H	BB	SO	B/I
2001 Chicago - NL	3	0	3.22	44	40	17	39	1.28
2002 Chicago - NL	3	1	3.98	97	84	59	81	1.47
2003 Chicago - NL	2	0	6.05	61	66	28	65	1.54

CRUZ, NELSON - TR - b: 9/13/72 $0

Cruz has played for four major league teams in his six year career. Traded to Houston after the 2000 season, he was a key member of the Astro bullpen in 2001 as a middle reliever and could pitch effectively for two or three innings. He was not as successful in 2002, finishing the season as a mop-up man. He struggled last year with Coloradoand was sent to the minors in September. He began the winter looking for a team to sign him.His pitch repertoire includes a fastball in the low 90's, an effective slider and an excellent changeup,

---

his best pitch. His biggest weakness has been a tendency to give up home runs. The fact that he wasn't able to improve in 2003 could mean his career is in jepeoardy.

	W	SV	ERA	IP	H	BB	SO	B/I
2001 Houston	3	2	4.15	82	72	24	75	1.17
2002 Houston	2	0	4.48	78	90	29	61	1.52
2003 Colorado	3	0	7.21	54	65	11	38	1.42

CUNNANE, WILL - TR - b: 4/24/74 $0

Journeyman reliever Will Cunnane was not given a contract by the Cubs after the 2002 season and lingered unsigned until July when the Braves gave him a chance at Triple-A Richmond. A month later, Cunnane was called up to replace injured Darren Holmes and gave the Braves 19 useful innings, initially in a mop up role, but later as a closer replacing John Smoltz. He converted all three save opportunities. His fastball hits 92 MPH on the radar gun, but is rather straight so he has to work with a slow curve and a changeup. None are especially top-quality pitches, but can be used effectively if mixed and thrown to the corners. Despite the chance to close a few September games for Atlanta, Cunnane remains a replacement-level righthanded reliever who is likely in 2004 to move on to his fifth team in as many years.

	W	SV	ERA	IP	H	BB	SO	B/I
2001 Milwaukee	0	0	5.40	52	66	22	37	1.70
2002 Chicago - NL	1	0	5.47	26	27	13	30	1.52
2003 Atlanta	2	3	2.70	20	14	6	20	1.00

DAAL, OMAR - TL - b: 3/1/72 $7

Pitchers are a frustrating breed, and few are as frustrating as Daal. In a five-year stretch he posted a 2.88 ERA, then won 16 games, then lost 19, then came back with 13-7 and 11-9 seasons. And then the Orioles signed him as a free agent before last season. They were expecting Dr. Jekyll to fit in their rotation, but instead got Mr. Daal. An 0-5 June signaled that something was wrong, and he went on the disabled list because of tendinitis in his shoulder. Though Daal is 6'3", he throws like a little lefty with a mid-80s fastball, roundhouse curve and changeup.

	W	SV	ERA	IP	H	BB	SO	B/I
2001 Philadelphia	13	0	4.46	185	199	56	107	1.37
2002 Los Angeles	11	0	3.91	161	142	54	105	1.22
2003 Baltimore	4	0	6.34	94	134	30	53	1.75

D'AMICO, JEFF - TR - b: 11/9/74 $1

Over his first six years, D'Amico broke down every year but in 2003 he started 29 games and while that's not exactly a regular five day workload, it is still the most that he's ever pitched in any season. D'Amico may be ready to become the pitcher that he was supposed to be when he broke into the majors at age 21 with the Brewers, who made him their number one draft pick at age 18. Although he was out of gas in August and September, D'Amico continued to pitch and that's good news. He made a career high 29 starts and he pitched two complete games, also a seasonal high. It's impossible to know how he will hold up in 2004 but the Pirates did the right thing by keeping him in the rotation and working him regularly, unlike the Mets, his team in 2002 that sent him to the bullpen after he's made 22 starts. If he has turned the corner on his injury filled career, remember that he is still just age 28 and worth watching.

	W	SV	ERA	IP	H	BB	SO	B/I
2001 Milwaukee	2	0	6.08	47	60	16	32	1.61
2002 New York - NL	6	0	4.94	146	152	37	101	1.30
2003 Pittsburgh	9	0	4.77	175	204	42	100	1.40

DAVIS, DOUG - TL - b: 9/21/75 $0

Davis, a one-time up-and-comer in the Texas organization, started for three teams and was released by two before ending a topsy-turvy season with a spot in the Milwaukee starting rotation. Davis has bounced around in part because of a reputation as not wanting to challenge hitters. His fastball is in the low 90s and he can cut it well, although he is still struggling to find a suitable offspeed complement. Hitters have a hard time picking up the ball out of his jerky delivery, although he ends off-balance and is not a good fielder. He was expected to contend for a spot in a starting rotation, although he needs to make the most of his next opportunity.

	W	SV	ERA	IP	H	BB	SO	B/I
2001 Texas	11	0	4.45	186	220	69	115	1.55
2002 Texas	3	0	4.97	60	67	22	28	1.49
2003 TEX/TOR/MIL	7	0	4.03	109	123	51	62	1.59

DAVIS, JASON - TR - b: 5/8/80 $2

Davis had a pretty heavy workload and he was briefly shut down with fatigue in his shoulder in early August. No damage was found and Davis returned to the rotation three weeks later and he pitched well. Victories are hard to come by on a weak rebuilding team and Davis had his share of frustration. While his win total was not good, he showed up and pitched well against playoff contenders in the stretch. He allowed seven runs to the Twins on September 15 but the Twins were fortunate to convert a few bloops and bleeders into runs to chase Davis from the mound. Davis has a good moving fastball that he can crank up to about 93 MPH and even though he is 6'6", Davis is agile and a good athlete.

	W	SV	ERA	IP	H	BB	SO	B/I
2002 Cleveland	1	0	1.84	15	12	4	11	1.09
2003 Cleveland	8	0	4.68	165	172	47	85	1.32

DAY, ZACH - TR - b: 6/15/78 $2

In 2003, Day, a former reliever, took a step forward as a starter, but not without trouble. He was suspended in May for using glue to mend his blistered finger. He then missed nearly two months with an inflamed shoulder, allegedly caused in a collision with teammate Wil Cordero. All told, Day didn't pitch a lot of innings for a starter, but that might be to his benefit in 2004. Day has a decent fastball that he uses to set up his excellent sinker, which is a tough pitch to drive. Being a ground ball pitcher, Day takes advantage of the Expos solid middle infield defense. He has the stuff to be a strikeout pitcher but that has not been the case yet. The thing to watch with Day is his strikeout rate. If his K's per inning improve, he will continue to do well. If his Ks don't pick up he will be hit harder and he'll suffer a downturn in 2004 similar to Ohka's in 2003.

	W	SV	ERA	IP	H	BB	SO	B/I
2002 Montreal	4	1	3.62	37	28	15	25	1.15
2003 Montreal	9	0	4.18	131	132	59	61	1.45

DeJEAN, MIKE - TR - b: 9/28/70 $7

Despite having only moderate success as a setup man in Colorado, DeJean fell into the closer's role in Milwaukee almost by accident, and proved that you don't have to be particularly good to get saves. Like most closers, he throws mostly fastballs and sliders, though neither of his offerings is a dominating pitch. Overall in 2003, DeJean blew nearly half of his save opportunities, though he was perfect in five such situations after his trade to St. Louis. His career numbers suggest that he is best suited to pitch in middle and long relief. However, since he has 46 saves over the past two seasons it is reasonable to believe that someone will give him a shot at being a closer this year. Don't expect him to improve much at all.

	W	SV	ERA	IP	H	BB	SO	B/I
2001 Milwaukee	4	2	2.77	84	79	39	68	1.35
2002 Milwaukee	1	27	3.12	75	66	39	65	1.40
2003 MIL/STL	5	19	4.68	83	86	39	71	1.51

DE LOS SANTOS, VALERIO - TL - b: 10/6/75 $0

De Los Santos had Tommy John surgery in 2001 but he's fine now and he's posted two good seasons since. He's not flashy but he is a solid middle reliever. He throws a 94 MPH fastball and a splitter.

	W	SV	ERA	IP	H	BB	SO	B/I
2002 Milwaukee	2	0	3.12	58	42	26	38	1.18
2003 MIL/PHI	4	1	4.50	52	45	25	39	1.35

DEMPSTER, RYAN - TR - b: 5/3/77 $0

Counted on to be the Reds number one starter, Dempster pitched well only a few times but the questions about his diminished ability were answered when it was revealed that Dempster's arm was injured. He was finally disabled and required Tommy John surgery, which will shelve him until 2005.

	W	SV	ERA	IP	H	BB	SO	B/I
2001 Florida	15	0	4.94	211	218	112	171	1.56
2002 FLA/CIN	10	0	5.38	209	228	93	153	1.54
2003 Cincinnati	3	0	6.53	116	134	70	84	1.76

DESSENS, ELMER - TR - b: 1/13/72 $0

Expected to be a quality No. 3 starter in Arizona in 2003, Dessens had an abysmal year after being obtained in a four-team trade at the winter meetings that cost the Diamondbacks power hitting first baseman Erubiel Durazo. Dessens, a finesse pitcher who finished No. 6 in the NL in ERA with Cincinnati in 2002, suffered through poor location. Dessens' best pitch is a sinking fastball, and when he is able to deliver that at shin level, he can be difficult to hit. When he does not ... well, he has given up 80 homers in his three full years as a starter. He helps himself by holding runners, and he bunts well, so much so that he was used several times as a pinch-bunter. He was expected to maintain his spot in the starting rotation, although No. 5 is more likely than No. 3.

	W	SV	ERA	IP	H	BB	SO	B/I
2001 Cincinnati	10	0	4.48	205	221	56	128	1.35
2002 Cincinnati	7	0	3.03	178	173	49	93	1.25
2003 Arizona	8	0	5.07	176	212	57	113	1.53

DICKEY, R.A. - TR - b: 10/29/74 $0

Dickey does not have great stuff, but over his seven seasons as a professional he has learned to pitch. His greatest assets are not physical; the attributes of tenacity, determination and competitiveness are key elements of Dickey's approach. His performance over the last half of 2003 cemented his place as a member of a major league pitching staff. Able to start or relieve, his role will likely depend on the needs of his team. Dickey has the tools to be a dependable fourth or fifth starter on a major league team.

	W	SV	ERA	IP	H	BB	SO	B/I
2003 Texas	9	1	5.09	117	135	38	94	1.48

DOMINGUEZ, JUAN - TR - b: 5/18/80 $0

Formerly and erroneously known as 20-year old Jose Dominguez, 23-year old Juan Dominguez had a whirlwind trip through the minors last season, going 10-0 with a 2.87 ERA in Single-, Double- and Triple-A. He then capped the year with a brief appearance in the big leagues last season in which he had some good moments and some trouble keeping the ball down. His best pitch at this point is a terrific changeup, which complements a good fastball. Dominguez was expected to work in winter ball on his slider and on holding runners. He was expected to compete for a roster spot this spring, but is more likely to open the season in the minors.

	W	SV	ERA	IP	H	BB	SO	B/I
2003 Texas	0	0	7.18	16	16	12	13	1.72

DONNELLY, BRENDAN -TR - b: 7/4/71 $6

Donnelly throws a sidearm fastball that registers in the low 90s and has good movement. He thrives on keeping the ball down and hitting the corners. Donnelly has good control and keeps the ball in the park, qualities that have made him an effective setup reliever over the past two seasons. He was scored on in only 10 of 63 games last year. Minor surgery to remove bone chips from his pitching elbow was scheduled for the offseason and was not expected to keep Donnelly from being fully ready for spring training.

	W	SV	ERA	IP	H	BB	SO	B/I
2002 Anaheim	1	1	2.17	50	32	19	54	1.03
2003 Anaheim	2	3	1.58	74	55	24	79	1.07

DOTEL, OCTAVIO - TR - b: 11/25/75 $18

Dotel has established himself as one of the top setup men in the major leagues. He has a live arm with a fastball that consistently reaches the 95 to 97 MPH range and he has an effective slider in the mid 80s. Command of both pitches has improved significantly. Without an effective offspeed pitch, he has not been successful as a starter but he did pitch effectively as a closer in 2000 when Billy Wagner was injured. Originally unhappy about his conversion from a starter to a reliever, he took to the role in 2001 and was even better as a bullpen force in 2002 and 2003. He could close now that an opportunity is available.

	W	SV	ERA	IP	H	BB	SO	B/I
2001 Houston	7	2	2.66	105	79	47	145	1.20
2002 Houston	6	6	1.85	97	58	27	118	0.87
2003 Houston	6	4	2.48	87	53	31	97	0.97

DREIFORT, DARREN - TR - b: 5/18/72 $0

Dreifort signed a $50 million contract three years ago but has yet to play a full season since because of right elbow and right knee injuries. Dreifort struggled in the bullpen in 2003 while attempting to return from Tommy John ligament replacement surgery in July 2001, (the second of his career) and arthroscopic knee surgery in July 2002. He was forced to return to the disabled list with a sprained medial collateral ligament in the knee last summer and did not pitch the rest of the season. Although Dreifort is only 31, his body appears to have broken down irreparably and he was not expected to contribute this season.

	W	SV	ERA	IP	H	BB	SO	B/I
2001 Los Angeles	4	0	5.13	94	89	47	91	1.44
2003 Los Angeles	4	0	4.03	60	58	25	67	1.38

DRESE, RYAN - TR - b: 4/5/76 $0

Drese has been up and down between the big leagues and minors during the last two years. He has a starter's repertoire of pitches (fastball, slider, curve and change) but his command is often lacking, leading to wildness inside the strike zone and out. Drese has had elbow and knee problems in the past and missed time last year with a pulled ribcage muscle. Late in the 2003 Triple-A season, Drese was pitching better and he will be in the mix for a big league roster spot this year.

	W	SV	ERA	IP	H	BB	SO	B/I
2001 Cleveland	1	0	3.43	37	32	15	24	1.28
2002 Cleveland	10	0	6.55	137	176	62	102	1.73
2003 Texas	2	0	6.85	46	61	24	26	1.85

DuBOSE, ERIC - TL - b: 5/15/76 $9

DuBose took a long and winding road to arrive in Baltimore's rotation last August. He was in three different organizations, then missed all of 2001 after rotator cuff surgery. He really opened the Orioles' eyes when brought up from Triple-A Ottawa for an emergency start in May. They recalled him again two months later, and he pitched his way into a starting job. DuBose reached his low point by giving up six earned runs in 2 1/3 innings against the Yankees, but bounced back to frustrate the Mariners in consecutive starts with a big-breaking curveball and changeup. His strong finish in 2003 could put him back into the lower end of a big-league rotation this season.

	W	SV	ERA	IP	H	BB	SO	B/I
2003 Baltimore	3	0	3.79	74	60	25	44	1.15

DUCHSCHERER, JUSTIN - TR - b: 11/19/77 $0

Duchscherer's stock has shot way, way up ever since he was traded from Texas to Oakland in the middle of the 2002 season. He went 14-2 for Triple-A Sacramento in 2003 in large part because he walked only 18 hitters in 155 innings. He pitches a lot like Brian Lawrence or Derek Lowe, getting a lot of movement on his pitches and letting the hitters get themselves out. Duchscherer was set to play for the U.S. Olympic qualifying team in the fall. Had he not been awarded that honor, there was a chance he could have made Oakland's postseason roster. He certainly has done enough in the past year to prove that he belongs in the big leagues. Even if he doesn't make the starting staff out of spring training, with his control he can provide a lot of help pitching in middle innings as a setup man.

	W	SV	ERA	IP	H	BB	SO	B/I
2001 Texas	1	0	12.24	15	24	4	11	1.90
2003 Oakland	1	0	3.31	16	17	3	15	1.23

DUCKWORTH, BRANDON - TR - b: 1/23/76 $0

Duckworth has enormous potential and talent but he's been inconsistent. To be fair, Duckworth fought tendinitis in his elbow all last year and he was never right. Health is critical but it's not the only drag on his career. Such inconsistency is disturbing for a pitcher of his ability, age and experience but there is just so much to like about him. He could "arrive" at any time.

	W	SV	ERA	IP	H	BB	SO	B/I
2001 Philadelphia	3	0	3.52	69	57	29	40	1.25
2002 Philadelphia	8	0	5.41	163	167	69	167	1.45
2003 Philadelphia	4	0	4.94	93	98	44	68	1.53

EATON, ADAM - TR - b: 11/23/77 $10

Eaton had a decent season in his first full year back after undergoing ligament replacement surgery on July 5, 2001, and should only get stronger the further removed from the operation. Eaton has a moving fastball that can hit 93-94 MPH and complements that with a full repertoire - a hard slider, a looping curve and a changeup that is his second-best pitch. He has a terrific mound presence and does not get rattled, having the ability to come up with the right pitch at the right time. He is quick off the mound and fields his position well, and holds runners well. He is a big plus at the plate, hitting his first two major league homers last year. Eaton, only 26, was expected to be a front-of-the-rotation starter capable of a breakout, 12-15 win season.

	W	SV	ERA	IP	H	BB	SO	B / I
2001 San Diego	8	0	4.32	116	108	40	109	1.27
2002 San Diego	1	0	5.41	33	28	17	25	1.35
2003 San Diego	9	0	4.08	183	173	68	146	1.32

EISCHEN, JOEY - TL - b: 5/25/70 $2

Eischen has been around the block and he's old enough and has traveled enough to appreciate having a steady job in the major leagues. While middle reliever is the least glamorous job in the game, Eischen does it very well and he was the most reliable pitcher in the Expos bullpen. Any team could benefit by having him, because he throws lefthanded and has good control over a mild arsenal of pitches, consistently dominating lefthanded hitters.

	W	SV	ERA	IP	H	BB	SO	B / I
2001 Montreal	0	0	4.85	29	29	16	19	1.52
2002 Montreal	6	2	1.34	54	43	18	51	1.14
2003 Montreal	2	1	3.06	53	57	13	40	1.32

ELARTON, SCOTT - TR - b: 2/23/76 $0

Elarton, attempting to come back after missing the 2002 season with a torn labrum, was knocked around in his eight starts and spent the majority of the season at Triple-A Colorado Springs. Elarton won 17 games with Houston in 2002, combining a major league average fastball with a big-time curveball. He has been unable to find a similar groove since his operation. The league hit .351 against him in 2003, when he gave up 12 home runs in just over 40 innings. Although Elarton will be only 28 when the 2004 season starts, he does not have a future as a major league starter unless he can improve his numbers. His last victory in the big leagues was May 6, 2001.

	W	SV	ERA	IP	H	BB	SO	B / I
2001 HOU/COL	4	0	7.06	132	146	59	87	1.53
2003 Colorado	4	0	6.27	52	73	20	20	1.80

ELDRED, CAL - TR - b: 11/24/67 $3

Eldred rebounded from injuries to have a decent year for the Cardinals. He pitched exclusively in relief for the first time in his career, and even saved a handful of games early in the year when Jason Isringhausen was on the disabled list. A true finesse pitcher at this point in his career, Eldred needs to stay ahead of hitters to be effective. Because he lacks a good fastball, he tries to consistently paint the corners, and can get himself in real trouble when he is not sharp. Eldred is a middle reliever at this point in his career. He could get some saves, as he proved in 2003, though he likely won't get many opportunities at all.

	W	SV	ERA	IP	H	BB	SO	B / I
2003 St. Louis	7	8	3.74	67	62	31	67	1.38

EMBREE, ALAN - TL - b: 1/23/70 $1

If there was a preseason favorite to chair Boston's bullpen committee, it was Embree, even though he rarely had closed games. Instead, he missed three weeks in April because of a shoulder injury, typical of those that have limited Embree's production throughout his career. Batters know pretty much what they're getting with Embree: hard stuff, a straight-as-a-string mid-90s fastball and a slider. He throws strikes, which sometimes are too good and easy to belt out of the park. Embree seems limited to no more than a setup lefthander's role.

	W	SV	ERA	IP	H	BB	SO	B / I
2001 SF/CHI - AL	1	0	7.33	54	65	17	59	1.52
2002 Boston	4	2	2.03	62	47	20	81	1.08
2003 Boston	4	1	4.25	55	49	16	45	1.18

ESCOBAR, KELVIM - TR - b: 4/11/76 $7

With a dominating mid-90s fastball with great movement and an overpowering and animated presence on the mound, Escobar has the tools to graduate to a whole new level but hasn't. Largely because of control problems, particularly with his breaking stuff that tends to settle too high in the strike zone, Escobar has been inconsistent at best and for this reason, was moved from the closer's role to the starting rotation early last season. His potential remains high and he goes into this season as a starting pitcher, his first full season as a starter since 1999. If he ever gains control, he's going to be a number one starter.

	W	SV	ERA	IP	H	BB	SO	B/I
2001 Toronto	6	0	3.50	126	93	52	121	3.50
2002 Toronto	5	38	4.27	78	75	44	85	1.53
2003 Toronto	13	4	4.29	180	189	78	159	1.48

ESTES, SHAWN - TL - b: 2/18/73 $0

Whatever ability Estes once had earlier in his career is long gone. He has been a failure each of the last two seasons with the Mets, Reds and Cubs. He can still get his fastball up to the high 80s, though he has to overthrow to do it, which results in a total loss of control. He has a big, breaking curve, though it is ineffective because he can't keep hitters off balance with his fastball. Estes, who stayed in the rotation in Chicago in 2003 because the Cubs didn't want to go with a young pitcher down the stretch, also blamed everybody but himself for his failures. While he will get another chance because he is lefthanded and reasonably healthy, he will not be a reliable option and will struggle just to keep a spot in even a weak starting rotation.

	W	SV	ERA	IP	H	BB	SO	B/I
2001 San Francisco	9	0	4.02	159	151	77	109	1.43
2002 NY - AL/CIN	5	0	5.10	161	171	83	109	1.58
2003 Chicago - NL	8	0	5.73	152	182	83	103	1.74

ESTRELLA, LEO - TR - b: 2/20/75 $2

After bouncing around the minor leagues for nine seasons, Estrella got his chance in the Milwaukee bullpen in 2003, spending the final five months of the season in the majors when his contract was purchased April 29. He is not overpowering, a command-and-control type, and his success comes when he spots his 88-89 MPH fastball and breaking pitches. He did a good job early, although he tired as the season went on and did not handle a brief stint as closer, converting three of eight save opportunities. He was expected to be used in middle relief if he stuck in the majors.

	W	SV	ERA	IP	H	BB	SO	B/I
2003 Milwaukee	7	3	4.36	66	75	21	25	1.45

ETHERTON, SETH - TR - b: 10/17/76 $0

In the 1998 draft, Etherton then 22, was Anaheim's number one pick. He wrecked his shoulder in 2000 and he rehabbed in the minors until he finally made it back to the majors in August 2003, with Cincinnati. Before his injury Etherton was a finesse pitcher with decent control but he has had very little major league experience or success. That he was not a flamethrower prior to his injury, improves his chance for a comeback at age 28.

	W	SV	ERA	IP	H	BB	SO	B/I
2003 Cincinnati	2	0	6.90	30	39	15	17	1.80

EYRE, SCOTT - TL - b: 5/30/72 $0

A well-traveled journeyman, Eyre is evidence of the truism that lefties who can throw strikes will always be able to find work. The Giants got Eyre on waivers from the Blue Jays in early August of 2002. Eyre's fastball is in the mid to high 80's at best. His out pitch is a straight change which can be quite deceptive. The problem is that he doesn't have good command of the offspeed pitch, and therefore can't rely on it when he's behind in the count. In the past he tried to develop a slider and a curve (and actually worked in a starting role in 1998, going 1-7). These extra pitches never worked well for him. Eyre is, at best, a lefty-lefty matchup specialist, and he is not a premier performer within that job description.

	W	SV	ERA	IP	H	BB	SO	B/I
2001 Toronto	1	2	3.45	16	15	7	16	1.40
2002 TOR/SF	2	0	4.46	75	80	36	58	1.55
2003 San Francisco	2	1	3.32	57	60	26	35	1.51

FARNSWORTH, KYLE - TR - b: 4/14/76 $3

The Cubs stressed to Farnsworth during the winter before last season the importance of taking care of his body, and were expecting big things from him. He was successful in the first half of the season, though he slipped badly after the All-Star break and was relieved of his setup duties by his irritated skipper Dusty Baker. Farnsworth can throw the ball as hard as anybody, though he often has little idea of where it is going. Those control problems have dogged him ever since he came to the big leagues, and are threatening to turn him into just another long reliever. It's beginning to look as if Farnsworth, who was a complete and total failure as a starting pitcher, is never going to be able to turn into a dominating reliever. While he throws hard enough to get at least a few more chances, he has done little to make anyone think he is going to take advantage of them.

	W	SV	ERA	IP	H	BB	SO	B/I
2001 Chicago - NL	4	2	2.74	82	65	29	107	1.15
2002 Chicago - NL	4	1	7.32	47	53	24	46	1.65
2003 Chicago - NL	3	0	3.30	76	53	36	92	1.17

FASSERO, JEFF - TL - b: 1/5/63 $0

Fassero has had a long career, one that has been prolonged because of his durable arm and his willingness to accept a reduced role in recent years. He never was an overpowering pitcher, even when he was younger and in the starting rotation. Now he rarely throws a fastball, instead trying to get hitters to chase a curve ball out of the strike zone. Fassero is about done. He could get another opportunity, but only because he throws lefthanded. He cannot be counted on to get the job done and will not pitch with the game on the line very often.

	W	SV	ERA	IP	H	BB	SO	B/I
2001 Chicago - NL	4	12	3.42	73	66	23	79	1.21
2002 St. Louis	8	0	5.35	69	81	27	56	1.57
2003 St. Louis	1	3	5.68	78	93	34	55	1.63

FELICIANO, PEDRO - TL - b: 8/25/76 $0

Feliciano, who began his pro career in the Dodgers' organization in 1995, pitched well last season while splitting time between Triple-A Norfolk (3-2, 3.97, 1 save) and the Mets. He didn't exactly light their fire, but he didn't pour fuel on it either. He has shown good control and enough speed on his fastball to strike out batters, even at the major league level. With a bad team, he frequently pitched multiple innings in long relief in losing games. Feliciano was shut down late in the season because of a blister on his middle finger that made it difficult for him to throw breaking pitches.

	W	SV	ERA	IP	H	BB	SO	B/I
2003 New York - NL	0	0	3.35	48	52	21	43	1.51

FERNANDEZ, JARED - TR - b: 2/2/72 $1

Fernandez is strictly a knuckleball pitcher who throws what passes for a fastball only when he is behind in the count 3-0 or 3-1. He was signed as a non-drafted free agent by Boston in 1994 and bounced around the minor leagues until he made brief appearances with Cincinnati in 2001 and 2002. He spent most of the 2003 season at Triple-A New Orleans (7-10, 3.81) before being called up to Houston where he started six games with mixed results before finishing the year pitching effectively in the bullpen. His best hope is to find a spot as a middle reliever in a major league bullpen in 2004.

	W	SV	ERA	IP	H	BB	SO	B / I
2003 Houston	3	0	3.99	38	37	12	19	1.28

FETTERS, MIKE - TR - b: 12/19/64 $0

Fetters entered 2003 as a key setup man in Minnesota's bullpen. But the years of wear and tear on his elbow limited him to all of six innings. "(The surgeon) has been expecting my elbow for quite some time," Fetters admitted. He ended up having Tommy John surgery, one in which a ligament is taken from his wrist and placed in his elbow. He has a decent fastball, good split-fingered pitch and a curveball he's developed in recent years. But he'll be lucky to pitch again in 2004, let alone ever again.

	W	SV	ERA	IP	H	BB	SO	B / I
2001 Pittsburgh	3	9	5.51	47	49	26	37	1.64
2002 Arizona	3	0	4.09	55	53	37	53	1.64
2003 Minnesota	0	0	0.00	6	2	1	1	0.50

FIELD, NATE - TR - b: 12/11/75 $0

Nate Field is your basic garden-variety, hard-throwing short reliever. He has a moving low-90s fastball but little else to go with it. He will throw a curve and a slider, although neither pitch has been reliable. When Field comes into the game without his good fastball, he has little to work with and often ends up running long counts and walking too many batters. Field spent the first half of the season, and much of August, at Triple-A Omaha where he got a handful of saves and fanned 17 in 22.2 innings against only four walks, but even in the minors he was stung by occasional lack of command; he allowed seven homers in just 42.1 combined innings between Omaha and Kansas City. In Kansas City, Field was rarely used in "game" situations, usually entering the game wielding a mop. To earn a more important role, Field will have to have much better command of his fastball and possibly add an effective off-speed pitch, and he'll have to handle righthanded hitters better if he's to remain a short reliever.

	W	SV	ERA	IP	H	BB	SO	B / I
2003 Kansas City	1	0	4.15	22	19	14	19	1.52

FIGUEROA, NELSON - TR - b: 5/18/74 $1

Figueroa had some major league success with the Phillies in 2001 but not much since and he's bounced between the major and minors. He has a miniscule chance to hook on as a fifth starter/long relief swingman. He's not a hard thrower and there's not much movement on his pitches so, he has to live on the corners to survive which he's been able to do in the minors (12-5 .2.79 ERA at Triple A Nashville) but it's been a struggle for him in the majors.

	W	SV	ERA	IP	H	BB	SO	B / I
2001 Philadelphia	4	0	3.94	89	95	37	61	1.48
2002 Milwaukee	1	0	5.03	93	96	37	51	1.43
2003 Pittsburgh	2	0	3.31	35	28	13	23	1.16

FOGG, JOSH - TR - b: 12/13/76 $0

Fogg continued to struggle with lefthanded hitters, who hit better than .300 against him last year. Fogg lasted into the eighth inning only twice and he had one complete game against a zombified Cincinnati Reds squad in September. Unless he sharpens up against lefties, he runs the risk of losing his spot in the rotation.

	W	SV	ERA	IP	H	BB	SO	B/I
2002 Pittsburgh	12	0	4.35	194	199	69	113	1.38
2003 Pittsburgh	10	0	5.26	142	166	40	71	1.45

FOPPERT, JESSE - TR - b: 7/10/80 $0

Foppert didn't live up to his promise in 2003, though much of his ineffectiveness can be explained by his elbow problems. Foppert, who never was able to pitch consistently, finally was diagnosed with a torn ligament in this throwing elbow and had the "Tommy John" surgery in mid-September. While he likely won't pitch at all this season, his long term prognosis is good. These days, pitchers who have elbow reconstructions are able to bounce back and regain their velocity, often in as little as 18 months. That would put him on track to be ready for the start of the 2005 campaign.

	W	SV	ERA	IP	H	BB	SO	B/I
2003 San Francisco	8	0	5.03	111	103	69	101	1.55

FORD, MATT - TL - b: 4/8/81 $0

Ford, acquired as a Rule 5 pick from Toronto prior to the 2003 season, was forced to remain in the majors last year at age 21 and acquitted himself well before missing the second half of the season with a left elbow sprain. A bone spur was removed in September surgery. A third-round pick in 1999, Ford touches the low 90s with his fastball and mixes in a good breaking pitch. He spent most of his time with Milwaukee in the bullpen, although he was an accomplished starter in the minor leagues and probably will end up in that role in the majors. He was expected to be returned to the minors for additional seasoning this season.

	W	SV	ERA	IP	H	BB	SO	B/I
2003 Milwaukee	0	0	4.32	44	46	21	26	1.52

FOSSUM, CASEY - TL - b: 1/9/78 $1

Smaller lefthanders should be soft-tossing control artists, like Jamie Moyer. Fossum tries to be more of a power pitcher, with a cut fastball and curve in his repertoire with just a low-90s fastball. Because he throws almost from a sidearm delivery, his curve tends to slide across the strike zone on a level plane, making it easier to hit. A shoulder injury put him on the disabled list last June. Fossum's slight build limits his stamina and could make him better suited for relief than the starting role the Red Sox envisioned for him in 2003.

	W	SV	ERA	IP	H	BB	SO	B/I
2001 Boston	3	0	4.87	44	44	20	26	1.44
2002 Boston	5	1	3.46	107	113	30	101	1.34
2003 Boston	6	1	5.47	79	82	34	63	1.47

FOULKE, KEITH - TR - b: 10/19/72 $40

For whatever reason, Foulke fell out of favor with the White Sox and the Athletics were only too happy to take him off their hands. The trade (Foulke for Billy Koch) was a total disaster for the White Sox. While Koch was hurt much of the season, Foulke was outstanding, saving a career high 43 games while allowing precious few baserunners. Foulke has outstanding control. He gets good movement on all his pitches and gets a lot of easy outs on weak broken bat grounders. Foulke has saved at least 42 games in two of the last three seasons (and both years when he was the full-time closer). If he is pitching for a contending team there is no reason why he won't break the 40-save mark once again.

	W	SV	ERA	IP	H	BB	SO	B/I
2001 Chicago - AL	4	42	2.33	81	57	22	75	0.98
2002 Chicago - AL	2	11	2.90	78	65	13	58	1.00
2003 Oakland	9	43	2.08	87	57	20	88	0.89

FOX, CHAD - TR - b: 9/3/70 $2

There's not much in Fox's right elbow that look the way an elbow is supposed to look, and his career has been a series of brutal physical setbacks and improbable comebacks but Fox keeps bouncing back. It's hard to give up on a pitcher who, despite such physical difficulty, still has brutal stuff and can mow down batters. A former closer, Fox is for the moment a setup guy, but it would be no surprise to see him get another shot at closing.

	W	SV	ERA	IP	H	BB	SO	B / I
2001 Milwaukee	5	2	1.89	67	44	36	80	1.20
2003 BOS/FLA	3	3	3.12	43	35	31	46	1.52

FRANCO, JOHN - TL - b: 9/17/60 $2

Franco made it back from some 20 months of rehab following elbow surgery to pitch against lefthanded batters and in setup, mopup and even closer roles for the 2003 Mets. He also offered veteran leadership as the team captain. Clearly, he didn't throw as hard as he did before the surgery; he had difficulty putting hitters away but got by pretty much on guile. Franco has 424 career saves, but his streak of 15 consecutive years in double figures ended in 1999. He's not baseball's oldest lefthander or even its oldest player named Franco, but John is nearly at the end of his line.

	W	SV	ERA	IP	H	BB	SO	B / I
2001 New York - NL	6	2	4.05	53	55	19	50	1.38
2003 New York - NL	0	2	2.62	34	35	13	16	1.40

FRANKLIN, RYAN - TR - b: 3/5/73 $13

A long-time apprentice, Franklin made the most of his first full season in a starting rotation in Seattle, setting career records in virtually every category when the Mariners tied a major league record by using only five starters all year. Franklin's fastball barely touches 90 MPH, so he must spot the ball to be effective. He is prone to giving up the long ball, although he is a gutsy competitor who does not let it rattle him. Franklin, 31, holds runners well and is agile on the mound. He was expected to maintain his spot at the lower end of the starting rotation.

	W	SV	ERA	IP	H	BB	SO	B / I
2001 Seattle	5	0	3.56	78	76	24	60	1.28
2002 Seattle	7	0	4.02	119	117	22	65	1.17
2003 Seattle	11	0	3.57	212	199	61	99	1.23

FRANKLIN, WAYNE - TL - b: 3/9/74 $0

Franklin's conversion to a starter was complete in 2003, when he was given a spot in the Milwaukee rotation out of spring training and held it throughout the season. A reliever in his first six seasons in the minors, Franklin had marginal success, leading major league hurlers in home runs allowed (36). His fastball/changeup repertoire is only average, and he gets himself in trouble when he remembers that and tries to be too fine. For a finesse pitcher, he walks way too many. He holds runners well and is a decent fielder. He was expected to again contend for a spot at the bottom of the starting rotation.

	W	SV	ERA	IP	H	BB	SO	B / I
2003 Milwaukee	2	0	2.63	24	16	17	17	1.38
2003 Milwaukee	10	0	5.50	195	201	94	116	1.52

FUENTES, BRIAN - TL - b: 8/9/75 $11

Fuentes has funky motion that he likens to throwing a Frisbee, and it serves him well. While his fastball is just a tick above major league average at 91-92 MPH, the ball seems to get on hitters much quicker than they anticipate, often leaving them swinging at air. Fuentes has averaged more than a strikeout an inning. He has good command and can spot the ball on the outside corner

---

to righties. His fastball is his only consistent pitch, and he needs to refine his slider. His jerky delivery is long, giving baserunners a chance to steal a bag. Fuentes found himself in a few save situations as Colorado searched for consistency in the bullpen and converted, cementing his role. Fuentes was expected to be a middle-inning reliever/setup type this season.

	W	SV	ERA	IP	H	BB	SO	B / I
2002 Colorado	2	0	4.72	27	25	13	38	1.42
2003 Colorado	3	4	2.75	75	64	34	82	1.30

FULTZ, AARON - TL - b: 9/4/73 $0

Fultz is a lefty matchup reliever, pure and simple. He has never started a big league game, and has averaged around an inning per appearance in the majors. Fultz has not often been used in save situations. Righthanders hit 100 points higher against Fultz than lefties, and with better power, so he is much better off in strict matchup situations. He should have that setup role in a major league bullpen this season.

	W	SV	ERA	IP	H	BB	SO	B / I
2001 San Francisco	3	1	4.56	71	70	21	67	1.28
2003 San Francisco	2	0	4.79	41	47	19	31	1.60
2003 Texas	1	0	5.22	67	75	27	53	1.52

GAGNE, ERIC - TR - b: 1/7/76 $44

Gagne had the best season in major league history for closers, converting all 55 of his save opportunities and won the Cy Young award. His 55-for-55 season is a major league record, and he will enter 2004 with 62 straight save conversions, another major league record. He is the first major league with two 50-save seasons, doing it in both seasons since moving to the bullpen in 2002. Gagne has a fastball that touches 98 MPH and a devastating changeup that gets to the plate at 87 MPH. Opponents hit .133 against him last year, when he averaged 15 strikeouts per nine innings. His strikeout to walk ratio was a sensational 7:1. A native of Montreal who grew up on hockey, Gagne is an agile athlete who despite his size fields his position well. He does not need a pickoff move, although he has a good one anyway. He has taken his place as the top closer in the major leagues after two short seasons in the role, and has the stuff to continue apace.

	W	SV	ERA	IP	H	BB	SO	B / I
2001 Los Angeles	6	0	4.75	151	144	46	130	1.25
2002 Los Angeles	4	52	1.97	82	55	16	114	0.86
2003 Los Angeles	2	55	1.20	82	37	20	137	0.69

GALLO, MIKE - TR - b: 12/19/64 $0

Gallo signed with Houston as a fifth round draft choice in 1999. He was not considered a strong prospect, spending over three years at the Low Class A level. He started the 2003 season at Double-A (1-1, 1.37), with a stop at Triple-A (3-0, 2.08) before being promoted to Houston in mid-season. He has found a niche as a left-handed relief specialist and is likely to remain in that role. His fastball tops out at 91MPH and his breaking ball is effective against left handed batters. He needs to find ways to get righthanded hitters out to enhance his career.

	W	SV	ERA	IP	H	BB	SO	B / I
2003 Houston	1	0	3.00	30	28	10	16	1.27

GARCIA, FREDDY - TR - b: 10/6/76 $11

Garcia, the most prominent name on the other side of the Randy Johnson trading deadline deal in 1998, has turned into a Johnson-esque workhorse while anchoring the Seattle rotation, having thrown at least 210 innings in each of the last three years. He has a quality repertoire which includes a fastball in the low 90s, a big-time curve and a changeup. His wicked curve ball is his out pitch, although his others are above-average major league pitches. Garcia gets in trouble when he loses command of the breaking ball and is up in the zone; he has given up at least 30 homers in each of the last two seasons. He is an average defender at best, and his long motion gives runners a chance to steal a base. Strong and durable, Garcia was expected to remain at the head of the rotation in 2004.

	W	SV	ERA	IP	H	BB	SO	B / I
2001 Seattle	18	0	3.05	238	199	69	163	1.12
2002 Seattle	16	0	4.39	224	227	63	181	1.30
2003 Seattle	12	0	4.52	201	196	71	144	1.33

GARLAND, JON - TR - b: 9/27/79 $7

Garland continued to show steady improvement and development last season, peaking in the second half of the season. Despite being tall, he isn't overpowering. His fastball peaks in the low 90s, meaning he must rely on his strong command to get the job done. It doesn't appear that Garland is ever going to strike out a lot of hitters, though that doesn't mean he can't be effective. Garland still has tremendous upside. It is going to take him a few more years of learning, but he could be a staff ace down the road. Meanwhile, look for him to be a solid contributor who will win 12-14 games a year.

	W	SV	ERA	IP	H	BB	SO	B / I
2001 Chicago - AL	6	1	3.69	117	123	55	61	1.52
2002 Chicago - AL	12	0	4.58	193	188	88	112	1.41
2003 Chicago - AL	12	0	4.51	192	188	74	108	1.37

GEORGE, CHRIS - TL - b: 9/16/79 $0

Chris George's 2003 season can be used as a case study about the influence of run support is in determining a pitcher's won-lost record. George had the second-most wins for the Royals despite an ERA two runs higher than league average, largely due to receiving almost six runs per start from the Royals offense. George was repeatedly hammered over his last starts and he was demoted to Triple-A Omaha at mid-season. He continued his struggles at Omaha and was not recalled during September roster expansion. At his best George works his moving, low-90s fastball to the corners of the plate and keeps hitters honest with a deceptive changeup. All too often, however, George gets his fastball up in the strike zone where batters can take a ferocious rip. Lack of a consistent off-speed pitch lets hitters time George's fastball. Despite constantly pitching in trouble most of the season, George has shown excellent poise on the mound and he fields his position well. George has the stuff to be a successful starter, especially if he can regain command of his off-speed repertoire, but he has a great deal to prove after such a disappointing 2003 campaign.

	W	SV	ERA	IP	H	BB	SO	B / I
2001 Kansas City	4	0	5.59	74	83	18	32	1.36
2002 Kansas City	0	0	5.60	27	37	8	13	1.65
2003 Kansas City	9	0	7.11	94	120	44	39	1.75

GERMAN, FRANKLYN - TR - b: 1/20/80 $4

A hard thrower with a live arm and a football lineman's build, German was part of the Jeff Weaver for Carlos Pena trade with Athletics and Yankees. In 2002, he accumulated 30 saves in three levels with two organizations. He started the 2003 season as one of the rookie pitchers to watch and while German has the big heater that managers want on their closer, his control is poor. German should get another shot at closing and when he harnesses his control he will be a good one.

	W	SV	ERA	IP	H	BB	SO	B / I
2003 Detroit	2	5	6.04	45	47	45	41	2.06

GLAVINE, TOM - TL - b: 3/25/66 $5

Glavine might not have wanted to remember what it was like pitching for a losing team, but 2003 was nearly as bad as his first four major league seasons. He was 33-41 for losing Braves teams from 1987 to '90. Glavine signed a free-agent deal with the Mets before last season, figuring it would take him four years to reach 300 career wins, but he remains 49 short. His high-80s fastball and changeup weren't getting it done last year against righthanded or lefthanded batters, who both averaged in the .280s against Glavine. He had career-low strikeouts for a full season, and received team-low support at 3.41 runs per game.

	W	SV	ERA	IP	H	BB	SO	B/I
2001 Atlanta	16	0	3.57	219	213	97	116	1.41
2002 Atlanta	18	0	2.96	225	210	78	127	1.28
2003 Atlanta	9	0	4.52	183	205	66	82	1.48

GLOVER, GARY - TR - b: 12/3/76　　　　　　　　$0

Basically a fastball/slider pitcher, Glover has made the transition from starting to relief work fairly well. His fastball tops out in the low 90s, and it can be an effective pitch when he throws it for strikes. Three bad outings late last season added over a run to his ERA, but he was generally effective for most of the season. Glover has improved his control and has cut down on the number of home runs he allows. In the upcoming season, Glover was expected to find most of his work in the middle innings.

	W	SV	ERA	IP	H	BB	SO	B/I
2001 Chicago - AL	5	0	4.93	100	98	32	63	1.30
2002 Chicago - AL	7	1	5.21	138	136	52	70	1.36
2003 CHI - AL/ANA	2	0	4.74	63	77	22	37	1.58

GOBBLE, JIMMY - TL - b: 7/19/81　　　　　　　　$1

A supplemental first-round draft pick in 1999, Jimmy Gobble found few challenges as he quickly advanced through the Royals farm system. He was the club's minor-league pitcher of the year as he finished among league leaders while still just a teenager pitching for Single-A Wilmington in 2001. A sore shoulder and a groin strain limited his 2002 campaign at Double-A Wichita, but he picked up where he left off with a strong showing at Wichita in 2003, earning an August callup to the majors where he held his own at the tender age of 21. Because lefty Gobble works primarily with a low-90s fastball, he has been compared to Tom Glavine, but it is his plus curveball and well-disguised changeup that fools more hitters; he has excellent command of all three pitches. Gobble stood up well to the pressures of being thrown into the fire of a pennant race. He still has a lot to learn, but he projects as a solid number two or three starter in the majors leagues. Gobble will need to gain strength and build his stamina and continue to make adjustments as he challenges for a full-season starter role with the Royals in 2004.

	W	SV	ERA	IP	H	BB	SO	B/I
2003 Kansas City	4	0	4.61	53	56	15	31	1.35

GONZALEZ, JEREMI - TR - b: 1/8/75　　　　　　　　$9

Gonzalez entered the 2003 season not having pitched in the majors since 1998, almost five years, because of injury to his pitching elbow and a torn ACL in his left knee both of which required surgery. He was called up to the majors in May after a strong start at Triple-A. Before his major elbow surgery in 1999, Gonzalez was a promising talent. Gonzalez has a good fastball and breaking pitch to go along with his bulldog mentality. He showed in 2003 that he has what it takes to be a good middle-of-the-rotation pitcher for most teams, but his performances are inconsistent and gives up too many walks.

	W	SV	ERA	IP	H	BB	SO	B/I
2003 Tampa Bay	6	0	3.92	156	131	69	97	1.28

GOOD, ANDREW - TR - b: 9/19/79　　　　　　　　$0

Good opened the 2003 season at Triple-A before being recalled early in the season to fill

---

a hole in the Arizona rotation. He does not have overpowering stuff but understands his craft well. His fastball tops outs in the low 90s, although he spots it well. Good is at his best when he is living on the corners. He has two breaking pitches and is not afraid to throw any pitch in any count. He throws strikes and does not beat himself. He was expected to open the season in the starting rotation at Triple-A Tucson.

	W	SV	ERA	IP	H	BB	SO	B/I
2003 Arizona	4	0	5.29	66	74	16	42	1.36

GORDON, TOM - TR - b: 11/18/67 $15

Gordon's velocity was back last season and he responded with another decent, if unspectacular, season. After having his 2002 campaign end prematurely with yet another arm injury, Gordon threw the ball well for the White Sox, eventually regaining the closer's role he held so long throughout his career. Gordon has been remarkably consistent the last three years, so expect pretty much the same this year, assuming that he remains healthy. He will pick up a few saves along the way, though he won't be consistent enough to keep the closer's role for the entire season. He should be considered a high injury risk, given his past history. He's managed more than 45 innings only twice in the last six seasons.

	W	SV	ERA	IP	H	BB	SO	B/I
2001 Chicago - NL	1	27	3.38	45	32	16	67	1.06
2002 CHI - NL/HOU	1	0	3.37	43	42	16	48	1.36
2003 Chicago - AL	7	12	3.16	74	57	31	91	1.19

GRAVES, DANNY - TR - b: 8/7/73 $1

The former stopper entered the Reds starting rotation in September 2002 and he pitched well but his conversion proved to be a disaster in 2003. The problem was that Graves often got clobbered in the first inning as the opposition batted over .300. The other problem was that the Reds let Graves stay in the game and continue to get beaten to a pulp. He gave up a boatload of homers and too often they came in the first inning. Factor in his inability to strike out hitters and he was the biggest bust the Cincinnati Shreds had in 2003. They let him close a couple of games and he got saves and maybe a pleasant warm feeling that he used to be pretty good at something. The workload led to shoulder trouble that eventually sidelined Graves before the year was over. If this is all that Graves has, he won't be a starter very long.

	W	SV	ERA	IP	H	BB	SO	B/I
2001 Cincinnati	6	32	4.15	80	83	18	49	1.26
2002 Cincinnati	7	32	3.19	99	99	25	58	1.26
2003 Cincinnati	4	2	5.33	169	204	41	60	1.45

GREGG, KEVIN - TR - b: 6/20/78 $0

Gregg got a cup of coffee late last season and pitched well in the big leagues. Despite his 6-foot-6 stature, Gregg is a control pitcher rather than a fireballer. At Triple-A last season, he went 7-4 with a 4.03 ERA and better than a four-to-one ratio of strikeouts to walks. His 2003 performance puts him in the hunt for a roster spot this year, either as a starter at the end of the rotation or, more likely, a long reliever. Like most rookie finesse pitchers, Gregg had a little more difficulty throwing strikes after his promotion to the majors, and improvement in that area will be a key to his future success as a big leaguer.

	W	SV	ERA	IP	H	BB	SO	B/I
2003 Anaheim	2	0	3.28	25	18	8	14	1.05

GRIFFITHS, JEREMY - TR - b: 3/22/78 $0

Griffiths was lightly regarded before last season, even though a strong finish had made him the Double-A Eastern League's Pitcher of the Year in 2002 at Binghamton. Then he pitched so well at Triple-A Norfolk (7-6, 2.74 ERA) that the Mets brought him up to their rotation on three separate occasions. Griffiths had a 3:1 strikeout/walk ratio in the minors in '03, but he struck out just 78 batters in 115 innings because he doesn't throw very hard. That was a bigger problem in the majors, where his walk rate was up and he gave up a .328 batting average.

	W	SV	ERA	IP	H	BB	SO	B/I
2003 New York - NL	1	0	7.02	41	57	19	25	1.85

GRIMSLEY, JASON - TR - b: 8/7/67 $0

The Royals placed a heavy burden on Jason Grimsley in 2003 and he was all too often found wanting. Despite finishing second in the league in holds, Grimsley was usually unable to maintain a lead or keep a game close; his seven blown saves are a more accurate guage. He was at his worst when the pennant race reached it's most critical point; Grimsley was scored upon in ten of his final 13 outings, yet manager Tony Pena kept relying on Grimsley's experience when the game was on the line. Grimsley throws hard, usually hitting 95 MPH with his fastball, but he is more effective pitching in the low-90s when his heater has better movement. Grimsley claims he has too much strength on his fastball when he isn't used regularly, but his record when pitching on consecutive days is poor as he often has trouble throwing strikes when overused. At his best, Grimsley throws a good fastball with movement, then uses his sinker to get grounders; that kind of pitching was in short supply from Grimsley over the second half of 2003 however, as he allowed far too many long fly balls, often in critical situations. He doesn't help himself with the glove and doesn't hold runners well. A hard-nosed combatant, Grimsley should expect his role as primary setup man to diminish as he finds work elsewhere in 2004.

	W	SV	ERA	IP	H	BB	SO	B/I
2001 Kansas City	1	0	3.02	80	71	28	61	1.23
2002 Kansas City	4	1	3.91	71	64	37	59	1.42
2003 Kansas City	2	0	5.16	75	88	36	58	1.65

GROOM, BUDDY - TL - b: 7/10/65 $0

Groom is on his way to becoming one of those lefthanders who hangs on in the majors until he receives his A.A.R.P. card. His workload diminished considerably last season, the first since 1995 when he didn't pitch in at least 70 games. That's because both the sharp-breaking curve he used to get lefthanders out and the cut fastball he used against righties both deserted Groom. A setup man and occasional closer in years past, he was used more in a one-lefty-batter role in 2003. If he can get his curve back, he can do more.

	W	SV	ERA	IP	H	BB	SO	B/I
2001 Baltimore	1	11	3.55	66	64	9	54	1.11
2002 Baltimore	3	2	1.60	62	44	12	48	0.90
2003 Baltimore	1	1	5.36	45	58	14	34	1.59

GRYBOSKI, KEVIN - TR - b: 11/15/73 $0

With another team, Kevin Gryboski might be closer material; with the Braves, he must remain content setting up John Smoltz. Gryboski jumped to the head of the class among Atlanta setup men with an outstanding second half before missing almost a month due to a partially torn labrum; he returned in time to be ready for post-season play. Gryboski works with a strong, mid-90s fastball and uses a sharp split-fingered pitch to generate numerous ground balls. The splitter makes him especially effective against lefty hitters whom he has limited to a .191 batting average over the first two years of his career. Gryboski has shown little ill effect from use on consecutive days, although he was rarely used in that situation in the second half of 2003. He has closer stuff but Gryboski will need a change of venue before he gets a chance at that role.

	W	SV	ERA	IP	H	BB	SO	B/I
2002 Atlanta	2	0	3.48	52	50	37	33	1.68
2003 Atlanta	6	0	3.86	44	44	23	32	1.51

GUARDADO, EDDIE - TL - b: 10/2/70 $36

Guardado is one of the game's great competitors. He doesn't throw over 91 MPH and really doesn't have an outstanding second pitch. But he has excellent control and tenacity. He's developed a split-fingered fastball to use against righthanded hitters. Other than that, it's the fastball-slider. It doesn't matter who's in the batter's box, Guardado is going after him. His career as a closer underscores the importance of mental toughness in late-game situations. He shakes off bad outings and hasn't shown any signs of slowing down as he enters free agency.

	W	SV	ERA	IP	H	BB	SO	B/I
2001 Minnesota	7	12	3.51	19	27	23	67	1.05
2002 Minnesota	1	45	2.92	68	53	18	70	1.05
2003 Minnesota	3	41	2.89	65	50	14	60	0.98

GUTHRIE, MARK - TL - b: 9/22/65 $1

Guthrie has nothing on his fastball anymore, meaning he is forced to throw that big, spinning curve ball time and time again. He can locate that pitch well enough to get out enough lefthanded hitters to stay in the big leagues, though he is virtually useless against any of the better hitters in the league. He started off strong in 2003, but fell off drastically late in the season as he was called on to try and get out of tougher and tougher situations. He doesn't have much hope of being anything more than a situational lefty in the bullpen this year. He certainly won't get any save opportunities.

	W	SV	ERA	IP	H	BB	SO	B/I
2001 Oakland	5	1	2.44	48	35	19	44	1.13
2002 New York - NL	5	1	2.44	48	35	19	44	1.13
2003 Chicago - NL	2	0	2.74	43	40	22	24	1.45

HACKMAN, LUTHER - TR - b: 10/10/74 $0

Hackman has two fastballs, one that sinks and one that cuts, and can be effective in keeping the ball down and in the park. He has command issues that undermine his effectiveness, however, as he walks too many. He has a complicated delivery and is slow to plate, making him easy to run on. While Hackman was used a spot starter in both Colorado and St. Louis, he was exclusively a reliever in 2003 and was expected to remain in the bullpen.

	W	SV	ERA	IP	H	BB	SO	B/I
2001 St. Louis	1	1	4.29	36	28	14	21	1.18
2002 St. Louis	5	0	4.11	81	90	39	46	1.59
2003 San Diego	2	0	5.16	77	78	36	48	1.49

HALAMA, JOHN - TL - b: 2/22/72 $1

Halama has spent the past three seasons going back and forth between the starting rotation and the bullpen. The biggest reason he cannot keep a starting spot is that he can't throw his fastball hard enough to keep hitters off balance. His breaking pitches aren't special, either, meaning if his control is off just a little bit he is easy to hit. Halama can stick around a little while longer as a middle reliever and a spot starter. He is not good enough, however, to pitch in the late innings in relief or to keep a spot in the starting rotation.

	W	SV	ERA	IP	H	BB	SO	B/I
2001 Seattle	10	0	4.73	110	132	26	50	1.43
2002 Seattle	6	0	3.56	101	112	33	70	1.44
2003 Oakland	3	0	4.22	1.09	117	36	51	1.41

HALL, JOSH - TR - b: 12/16/80 $0

Healthy now after suffering career threatening arm and shoulder problems, it's not out of the question that the 23 year old Hall could be on the Reds opening day roster. He is a ground ball pitcher which is especially important in the GAB. His money pitch is a fall-off-the-table curve that is a fine complement to his good, sinking fastball.

	W	SV	ERA	IP	H	BB	SO	B/I
2003 Cincinnati	0	0	6.56	25	33	15	18	1.94

HALLADAY, ROY - TR - b: 5/14/77 $23

With a superb moving fastball that peaks in the mid-90s and newly-developed pinpoint control, Halladay is among the elite pitchers in the league. Efficient with his pitches, he goes late into games and mixes in a good assortment of off-speed pitches to complement his hard stuff. Easily one of the most poised pitchers in baseball, Halladay occasionally leaves the ball up in the zone but it usually doesn't burn him because he allows so few baserunners that extra base hits turn into solo home runs or stranded doubles. He is easily the number one starter on any staff.

	W	SV	ERA	IP	H	BB	SO	B/I
2001 Toronto	5	0	3.16	105	97	25	96	3.16
2002 Toronto	19	0	2.93	239	223	62	168	1.19
2003 Toronto	22	0	3.25	266	253	32	204	1.07

HAMMOND, CHRIS - TR - b: 1/21/66 $5

Hammond parlayed what certainly was a career year for just about any pitcher as an Atlanta setup man in 2002 (7-2, 0.95 ERA, 1.11 WHIP in 76 innings) into a two-year contract with the Yankees. It was inevitable that he couldn't match that, but 2003 was the second or third best of his 11 major league seasons. Because his best pitch is a changeup, he's as effective against lefthanded batters as against righties. He had to throw his 85-MPH fastball enough last season that opponents' batting average went up 75 points to .270. He has excellent control and prevented runners from stealing any bases. He'll be back in a setup role this year.

	W	SV	ERA	IP	H	BB	SO	B/I
2002 Atlanta	7	0	0.95	76	53	31	63	1.11
2003 New York - AL	3	1	2.86	63	65	11	45	1.21

HAMPTON, MIKE - TL - b: 9/9/72 $8

Mike Hampton's first year with the Braves saw a positive turnaround in a career that had gone south since his first season in Colorado in 2001. He led the impressive Atlanta starting rotation in ERA as he returned to working mostly with an upper-80s hard sinker which induces grounders, a pitch that worked intermittently in Colorado. Hampton gets most of his strikeouts with a four-seam fastball that can reach 94 MPH. To keep hitters honest, he'll mix in a slider, curveball or changeup, all of which he can throw to edges of the strikezone. Hampton works deep into most games and has never shown much ill effect from overuse despite averaging more than 200 innings per season for almost a decade. For a pitcher, Hampton is an outstanding hitter who has enough power to hit an occasional homer, and he has even been used as a pinch-hitter. He's also a superior fielder who moves quickly to field bunts. Hampton has a quick delivery and above-average pickoff move which helps control the running game. Overall, Hampton is a strong competitor and one of the most complete players in the game.

	W	SV	ERA	IP	H	BB	SO	B/I
2001 Colorado	14	0	5.41	203	236	85	122	1.58
2002 Colorado	7	0	6.14	179	228	91	74	1.79
2003 Atlanta	14	0	3.84	190	186	78	110	1.39

HARANG, AARON - TR - b: 5/19/78 $0

Despite being 6'7", Harang is not a power pitcher and for so large a man, that's not bad because tall pitchers often lack control and lose their release point. Harang was good enough to be Oakland's fifth starter before he was traded to Cincinnati, although he is not a product of the A's brilliant pitching rich farm system. It is reasonable to expect Harang to be number a four or five starter for a lesser team and he can improve.

	W	SV	ERA	IP	H	BB	SO	B/I
2002 Oakland	5	0	4.83	78	78	45	64	1.57
2003 OAK/CIN	5	0	5.31	76	89	19	42	1.42

HARDEN, RICH - TR - b: 11/30/81 $0

Harden was so impressive at Triple-A at the start of last season that many observers wondered what took the Athletics so long to finally bring him to Oakland. Harden has a power fastball, one that he can throw consistently in the mid-90s. When he has good location, it is hard for even the best hitters to touch. Harden also has an outstanding splitter, which he uses often in tough situations. There is no reason to think that Harden won't develop into a quality big league starter. He's had success at every level in the minors and needs just a little more experience in the majors.

	W	SV	ERA	IP	H	BB	SO	B/I
2003 Oakland	5	0	4.46	75	72	40	67	1.50

HAREN, DANNY - TR - b: 9/17/80 $0

Haren hadn't pitched above Single-A before last season, though he was so dominating at the start of the season that he earned a shot with the Cardinals by midseason. Like many young and inexperienced starters, Haren looked outstanding at times and struggled badly at times. He never lost his command, however, and that should be a good sign for his future development. Haren isn't a particularly hard thrower. He succeeds when he is able to keep the ball down and fool hitters with the late movement on his sinker. He likely will open the season as the fourth or fifth starter, though it is possible he would begin the year in the minors.

	W	SV	ERA	IP	H	BB	SO	B/I
2003 St. Louis	3	0	5.08	73	84	22	43	1.46

HARPER, TRAVIS - TR - b: 5/21/76 $2

Harper was one of the few pleasant surprises for Tampa Bay last year. Although Harper has been used as both a starter and a reliever during his time in the majors, he proved in 2003 that he is most effective as a reliever and that is likely where his future will be. Harper doesn't have great stuff; he mixes his fastball, curve and changeup reasonably well and throws strikes, making him an effective setup man, although he does have difficulties against lefties. The save opportunities he got in 2003 indicates that he could get some saves this year in a setup role.

	W	SV	ERA	IP	H	BB	SO	B/I
2002 Tampa Bay	5	1	5.46	86	101	27	60	1.49
2003 Tampa Bay	4	1	3.77	93	86	31	64	1.26

HASEGAWA, SHIGETOSHI - TR - b: 8/1/68 $18

Hasegawa elevated himself to the closer's role in the second half of the 2003 season with Seattle while flirting with history. Hasegawa's ERA was under 1.00 much of the year, as he made a run at Dennis Eckersley's major league record 0.61 ERA (for pitchers with at least 55 innings). Hasegawa has a 90 MPH fastball, a forkball and a slider and can throw all three for strikes in almost any count. He keeps the ball down and induces groundball after groundball. He does all the little things, too. He fields his position with grace and virtually shuts off the running game with his attention to baserunners and his quick delivery. He was expected to be at least a top setup man this season, and he could continue to close.

	W	SV	ERA	IP	H	BB	SO	B/I
2001 Anaheim	5	0	4.04	55	52	20	41	1.29
2002 Seattle	8	1	3.20	70	60	30	39	1.28
2003 Seattle	2	16	1.48	73	62	18	32	1.10

HAWKINS, LaTROY - TR - b: 12/21/72   **$11**

Hawkins is one of the best setup men in the league and, since he's eligible for free agency, perhaps a closer-in-waiting. After several years of trying, Hawkins has finally controlled his great 95 MPH fastball. In a league in which most hitters cheat on anything over 92 MPH, that's a big factor. He can be used to match up with other teams' power hitters, or he can pitch two innings if needed. He'll throw over a curve, slider or even a change just to keep hitters from digging in, but it's his fastball that makes him tough.

	W	SV	ERA	IP	H	BB	SO	B/I
2001 Minnesota	1	28	5.96	51	59	39	36	1.91
2002 Minnesota	6	0	2.13	80	63	15	63	0.97
2003 Minnesota	9	2	1.86	77	69	15	75	1.09

HAYNES, JIMMY - TR - b: 9/5/72   **$0**

Durability has been Haynes' calling card but he suffered with back trouble all last year and he was shut down in early August. If healthy Haynes can be decent as a third or fourth starter.

	W	SV	ERA	IP	H	BB	SO	B/I
2001 Milwaukee	8	0	4.85	172	182	78	112	1.51
2002 Cincinnati	15	0	4.12	197	210	81	126	1.48
2003 Cincinnati	2	0	6.30	94	118	57	49	1.86

HEILMAN, AARON - TR - b: 11/12/78   **$0**

Heilman began last season 6-4 with a 3.24 ERA for Triple-A Norfolk. Injuries to Mets starters moved him up into their rotation in late June. Heilman, a Notre Dame graduate and 2001 draft choice, wasn't up to the task in the majors. In only one of his 13 starts did he pitch longer than six innings. Big-league hitters batted .300 and hit a home run every five innings against him. His best pitch is a sinking fastball. Unless he can refine his slider and changeup, Heilman could end up as no more than a reliever.

	W	SV	ERA	IP	H	BB	SO	B/I
2003 New York - NL	2	0	6.75	65	79	41	51	1.84

HELLING, RICK - TR - b: 12/15/70   **$2**

Helling will find work somewhere as a back-of-the-rotation starter. His 20 win season in 1998 may or may not have been a fluke but if he hooks on with a team that allows him to start and he wins 10 games – well, that will be a fluke. A flyball pitcher, Helling gives up a lot of homeruns but also understands how to pitch in situations, minimizing their effects. He has a sparkling curve that keeps hitters guessing and because of his quick delivery from the stretch, is almost steal-proof.

	W	SV	ERA	IP	H	BB	SO	B/I
2001 Texas	12	0	5.17	215	256	63	154	1.48
2002 Arizona	10	0	4.51	176	180	48	120	1.30
2003 BAL/FLA	8	0	5.17	155	167	45	98	1.37

HENDRICKSON, MARK - TL - b: 6/23/74   **$0**

The former NBA player who stands 6'9", Hendrickson peaks in the low 90s and he mixes in a looping curve and a still-unfinished changeup. While the movement on his fastball is decent, making it appear a bit faster than it is, his curve is ordinary by major league standards and he was knocked around often last year. He goes into spring training as the favorite to be a fourth or fifth starter but will need to show early improvement if he's to hang on to a starting rotation spot for another full season. He would be interesting as a situational guy. His basketball career held back his start in baseball and so he is older than most players who are as inexperienced as he is.

	W	SV	ERA	IP	H	BB	SO	B/I
2002 Toronto	3	0	2.45	37	25	12	21	1.01
2003 Toronto	9	0	5.51	158	207	40	76	1.56

HENTGEN, PAT - TR - b: 11/13/68 $8

The 1996 American League Cy Young Award winner seemed to thrive on a diet of lots of work, going all the way back to when he pitched 188 innings as an 18-year-old in the Sally League. After eight seasons of 174-265 major league innings, along came Tommy John surgery. Last season, he threw more innings than in the previous two years combined. And he pitched as well as anyone wearing a Baltimore uniform after Sidney Ponson was traded. Poor run support held down Hentgen's winning percentage. Never a big strikeout pitcher, he has to get by on guile more than ever now. But he showed signs last season that he can do that, with the savvy we'd expect from a veteran pitcher who has known how to win.

	W	SV	ERA	IP	H	BB	SO	B/I
2001 Baltimore	2	0	3.47	62	51	19	33	1.12
2002 Baltimore	0	0	7.77	22	31	10	11	1.86
2003 Baltimore	7	1	4.09	161	150	58	100	1.29

HEREDIA, FELIX - TL - b: 6/18/75 $5

Fans of the Marlins and Cubs, with whom Heredia had marginal success, were wondering what the Yankees were doing picking him up from the Reds last season. Somebody in New York must have scouted him with the Reds or remembered how he pitched late in 2002 and foreseen that Heredia could pitch more than a month without allowing an inherited runner to score. Though the Yankees used him as a situational specialist against lefthanded batters, he's effective against righthanded because his changeup is his best pitch. Heredia's fastball hovers only about 90 MPH. He has earned another year in a major league bullpen.

	W	SV	ERA	IP	H	BB	SO	B/I
2001 Chicago - NL	2	0	6.17	35	45	16	28	1.74
2002 Toronto	1	0	3.61	52	51	26	31	1.47
2003 CIN/NY-AL	5	1	2.69	87	74	33	45	1.23

HERGES, MATT - TR - b: 4/1/70 $4

Herges served as a setup man for Padres and Giants last season, and dramatically improved over his 2002 performance. Herges throws a 90 MPH fastball, a curve, a slider and a changeup. Although he has confidence in his pitches, he has in the past been too hittable to be a closer, but in 2003 was one of the best setup men in the game, dominating against both righthanded and lefthanded batters. As a premium setup man, he should also get some save opportunities.

	W	SV	ERA	IP	H	BB	SO	B/I
2001 Los Angeles	9	1	3.44	99	97	46	76	1.44
2002 Montreal	2	6	4.03	65	80	26	50	1.64
2003 SD/SF	3	3	2.62	79	68	29	68	1.23

HERMANSON, DUSTIN - TR - b: 12/21/72 $0

Hermanson's herky-jerky windup and delivery might help confuse hitters, though it likely also robs Hermanson of some much-needed command. He was an innings eater, if nothing else, until a couple of years ago, when injuries began to take their toll. His best pitches are his low-90s fastball and his splitter. Hermanson isn't nearly consistent enough to be counted on to be a consistent winner. Even when he was posting a good ERA he was no better than a .500 pitcher. He won't win more than 10-12 games this year, assuming he is able to stay in the starting rotation all season.

	W	SV	ERA	IP	H	BB	SO	B/I
2001 St. Louis	14	0	4.45	192	195	73	123	1.39
2002 Boston	1	0	7.77	22	35	7	13	1.91
2003 STL/SF	3	1	4.06	69	70	24	39	1.37

HERNANDEZ, CARLOS - TL - b: 4/22/80 $0

Hernandez is a small lefthander who broke into the majors with a bang in August 2001 with three strong starts in which he allowed only two runs in 17 innings. He opened the 2002 season as Houston's number five starter after skipping the Triple-A level but was hampered by a lingering shoulder problem which eventually required surgery. He missed the entire 2003 season but should be ready for the 2004 campaign. If he can regain his arm strength, he can be a solid mid-rotation starter. His fastball reaches 91 to 93 MPH and he has an excellent curve and changeup. However, he needs to improve the command of all of his pitches to be a consistent winner.

	W	SV	ERA	IP	H	BB	SO	B/I
2001 Houston	1	0	1.02	17	11	7	17	1.02
2002 Houston	7	0	4.38	111	112	61	93	1.56

HERNANDEZ, LIVAN - TR - b: 2/20/75 $14

Every pitcher is erratic to some degree but few have the ability of Hernandez, so, when he goes south, baseball Egberts smirk and knowingly shake their heads, haul out their penny arcane stats, frown, roll their rheumy eyes and do whatever cipherin' geeks do to make sure that the breathing world understands that they view Livan Hernandez with great disdain. With all that, what are we to say of Hernandez for 2004? Look out? He stinks? He's been lucky? No, no. Just this: He just had his finest year in 2003 and with his experience, talent and durability; the still-youthful Hernandez has no reason not to turn in another stellar year, depending on whether or not he is joined by more than a handful of certified major league teammates.

	W	SV	ERA	IP	H	BB	SO	B/I
2001 San Francisco	13	0	5.24	226	266	85	138	1.55
2002 San Francisco	12	0	4.38	216	233	71	134	1.41
2003 Montreal	15	0	3.20	233	225	57	178	1.21

HERNANDEZ, ORLANDO - TR - b: 10/11/65 $0

Hernandez' exact age is unknown as the Carbon-14 method yields only an approximation. The nitty-gritty here is that the Prince of the Pleistocene is a terrific pitcher and he just had a whole year off. His ailing right shoulder was cleaned up and repaired in May 2003 so, if he's throwing his maddening array of pitches with velocity by spring training, he will be a mighty help to any team and odds-on to be the Comeback Player of the Year.

	W	SV	ERA	IP	H	BB	SO	B/I
2001 New York - AL	4	0	4.85	94	90	42	77	1.39
2002 New York - AL	8	1	3.64	146	131	36	113	1.14

HERNANDEZ, ROBERTO - TR - b: 11/11/64 $0

After spending a decade as a closer, Roberto Hernandez accepted a setup role when he Joined the Braves in 2003. Although he was a paler version of his formerly high-powered self, Hernandez managed to lead the Braves in holds. His fastball no longer reaches 100 MPH, but it is still strong enough for him to work up in the strike zone. Hernandez also works with a slider and a sharp-breaking splitter that is difficult to hit but even more difficult for Hernandez to throw for strikes in recent years. He loves the challenge of power pitching to top power hitters and rises to the challenge of pitching out of jams, even those he creates himself through his often poor control against first batters faced. Hernandez has been one of the most durable short relievers in the game and has made at least 53 appearances every year except the '94 strike season. His focus on blowing away hitters sometimes detracts from holding baserunners close; he forgets about them and they can take advantage.

Hernandez wants to win a World Series ring before his career is over, so he'd rather be a setup man for a contender than a closer for a second-division team.

	W	SV	ERA	IP	H	BB	SO	B / I
2001 Kansas City	5	28	4.12	67	69	26	46	1.40
2002 Kansas City	1	26	4.33	52	62	12	39	1.42
2003 Atlanta	5	0	4.35	60	61	43	45	1.73

HERNANDEZ, RUNELVYS - TR - b: 4/27/78 $0

Hernandez began the season as one of baseball's best starters, winning four of his first five starts; his sudden emergence as an ace made a large contribution to the Royals overall hot start. Development of more consistent sinking action on his fastball has dropped his top speed into the low-90s, but makes it a difficult pitch for hitters to drive. It is his primary pitch and he succeeds best when throwing it to either corner of the plate. Powerfully built, Hernandez keeps the hitters honest with a deceptive changeup thrown out of his palm; his slider is mostly for show, although he has improved his command of an average curveball. Not playing winter ball prior to the 2003 season was intended to help Hernandez keep his stamina throughout the season and avoid the tired arm he'd developed during his rookie campaign. However, elbow problems cost him two months at mid-season and he was later sidelined for good due to a torn elbow ligament which required "Tommy John" surgery and is expected to keep him on the shelf until late in 2004.

	W	SV	ERA	IP	H	BB	SO	B / I
2002 Kansas City	4	0	4.36	74	79	22	45	1.36
2003 Kansas City	7	0	4.61	92	87	37	48	1.35

HITCHCOCK, STERLING - TL - b: 4/29/71 $0

Hitchcock is a typical southpaw starter. His fastball barely gets into the 90s and he throws many more curve balls, especially to lefthanded hitters. He spent the first half of last season pitching in relief for the Yankees, but immediately became a starter after he was traded to St. Louis. He was very hittable at both places, and suffered through some control problems. He also didn't have much success except in his two starts against the hapless Reds. Hitchcock has never been a big winner, despite pitching for some very good teams in New York and San Diego, and has spent considerable time on the disabled list in the last four seasons. Even with a contending team, he couldn't be expected to be much more than a .500 pitcher.

	W	SV	ERA	IP	H	BB	SO	B / I
2001 SD/NY - AL	6	0	5.63	70	89	21	43	1.57
2002 New York - AL	1	0	5.50	39	57	15	31	1.83
2003 NY - AL/STL	6	0	4.72	88	91	32	68	1.40

HODGES, TREY - TR - b: 6/29/78 $0

A great knowledge of how to pitch has helped Trey Hodges advance more than a blazing fastball. Hodges has fine command as he pitches to the corners, throwing strikes with his 90-MPH fastball and a fairly good changeup and slow curve to set up his out pitch, a sharp-breaking slider. Although his role with Atlanta was almost exclusively in relief, he has shown durability as a minor league starter. Hodges was named 2001 Carolina League Pitcher of the Year and then led the International League in victories in 2002. He works quickly, throws strikes with a complete repertoire and is durable, so he could still reclaim the starting role he enjoyed in the minors. Despite a brief stint on the DL at mid-season due to an elbow strain, Hodges' first full season in the majors was a success.

	W	SV	ERA	IP	H	BB	SO	B / I
2003 Atlanta	3	0	4.66	66	69	31	66	1.52

HOFFMAN, TREVOR - TR - b: 10/13/67 $4

Hoffman, who has the best career save percentage in major league history, missed the first five months of the season after undergoing right shoulder surgery after 2002. He returned in September, when he was used in a setup role. Hoffman has one of the best changeups in baseball. Like Tom Glavine's, it is a pitch batters know is coming but still cannot put into play. Hoffman's fastball is no longer 90-plus MPH, but with his location and his changeup major league average is better than good enough. Hoffman, a former college shortstop, is a tremendous athlete and a gamer. He fields his position well, holds runners, and handles the bat in the infrequent opportunities. A Hall of Famer-in-waiting, Hoffman was expected to reclaim his closer's role this season.

	W	SV	ERA	IP	H	BB	SO	B/I
2001 San Diego	3	43	3.43	60	48	21	63	1.14
2002 San Diego	2	38	2.73	59	52	18	69	1.18
2003 San Diego	0	0	2.00	9	7	3	11	1.11

HOLMES, DARREN - TR - b: 4/25/66 $0

The Braves expected Darren Holmes to be an important element in their bullpen in 2003, and despite battling repeated shoulder woes, he served those expectations well enough. His overall results paled in comparison to 2002, although the poor ERA was primarily due to a handful of bad early outings. Later, he missed more than a month after going on the disabled list with a strained right shoulder. Later diagnosed with shoulder tendinitis, he pitched gingerly until season's end when it was revealed he had a torn rotator cuff that caused him to miss the playoffs entirely. When healthy, Holmes will work with a wider repertoire and sharper command than most short relievers, mixing a 90-MPH fastball with a slider and changeup, setting up a sharp-breaking curveball that he uses as an out pitch, thrown to either corner. Holmes has had a lot of success against righthanders with that curveball and is able to get a strikeout when he needs one. Holmes will be 38 in April, 2004, and coming off a season filled with shoulder problems. A reduced workload might be in order for Holmes, if he is able to fully recover.

	W	SV	ERA	IP	H	BB	SO	B/I
2002 Atlanta	2	1	1.81	55	41	12	47	0.97
2003 Atlanta	1	0	4.29	42	47	11	46	1.38

HOWARD, BEN - TR - b: 1/15/79 $1

Howard has one of the best arms in the Padres farm system. He's not as refined as some of their other young guns, but his fastball can reach the mid-90s and has the ability to rack up strikeouts. His control can be erratic however, and he is still developing his secondary pitches. He had a surprisingly good stint with the Padres last season when he was called up from Triple-A Portland in late August to replace Oliver Perez. Prior to being promoted, he had a 4.55 ERA, with a 7-9 record in 22 starts for Portland. He started six games for San Diego, and began spring training hoping to win himself a full-time role as either the number four or five starter in the rotation.

	W	SV	ERA	IP	H	BB	SO	B/I
2003 San Diego	1	0	3.63	35	31	15	24	1.33

HUDSON, TIM - TR - b: 7/14/75 $27

Hudson, though sometimes considered the No. 3 pitcher on Oakland's staff, is more than good enough to be the marquee name in most big league rotations. He has good sink on his fastball, and throws a nasty splitter, which allows him to keep the ball down and get a ton of groundball outs. Even though he doesn't strike out a lot of hitters, he has impeccable control and is willing to use a minimum of pitches. That lets him throw a ton of innings, even though the Athletics always kept a close watch on his pitch counts. Hudson, nearly 50 games over .500 in his five seasons, has won at least 15 games each of the past four years. There is no reason to expect that to change. With a little luck, he could wind up winning the Cy Young award.

	W	SV	ERA	IP	H	BB	SO	B/I
2001 Oakland	18	0	3.37	235	216	71	181	1.22
2002 Oakland	15	0	2.98	238	237	62	152	1.25
2003 Oakland	16	0	2.70	240	197	61	162	1.08

ISHII, KAZUHISA - TL - b: 9/9/73 $1

Ishii has good stuff, but a lack of command works to limit his effectiveness and shorten his outings. Ishii leads with a fastball in the low 90s and complements that with a big, roundhouse curve and a quality changeup. His trouble is putting the ball where he wants it - he has been among the NL leaders in walks in his two seasons since coming over from the Yakult Swallows. Consequently, Ishii runs up deep pitch counts early and is seldom around past the sixth inning. He does not help himself in the field either because of his slow reaction time to come-backers and his so-so move to first. He just cannot hit. He was expected to be in the lower reaches of the starting rotation.

	W	SV	ERA	IP	H	BB	SO	B/I
2002 Los Angeles	14	0	4.27	154	137	106	143	1.58
2003 Los Angeles	9	0	3.86	147	129	101	140	1.56

ISRINGHAUSEN, JASON - TR - b: 9/7/72 $30

Isringhausen has proven to be a reliable and dependable closer over the past three seasons. He fought through a tough rehab period from shoulder surgery early last year and came back strong in the second half. He still can get the ball into the mid 90s consistently, though his slider was a little less consistent last season than it had been previously The fact that Isringhausen got as many saves as he did last year, despite missing close to half the season because of injury and suffering through the Cardinals' second half struggles, shows that he is capable of saving a lot of games. Even though he is not nearly as dominating as Eric Gagne or John Smoltz, he could save around 40 games if pitching for a contender. He'll get at least 30 anyway.

	W	SV	ERA	IP	H	BB	SO	B/I
2001 Oakland	4	34	2.65	71	54	23	74	1.08
2002 St. Louis	3	32	2.48	65	46	18	68	0.98
2003 St. Louis	0	22	2.36	42	31	18	41	1.17

JACKSON, EDWIN - TR - b: 9/9/83 $7

Jackson is a high impact pitching prospect . The 6'3", 190, righthander leans heavily on his low-90s fastball, but is getting a progressively better feel for his curve and changeup. He has surprisingly advanced command and mechanical consistency for his age. He jumped from Double-A to the majors last year to fill in for an injured Hideo Nomo succefully, and made himself a serious candidate for the starting rotation in 2004.

	W	SV	ERA	IP	H	BB	SO	B/I
2003 Los Angeles	2	0	2.45	22	17	11	19	1.27

JARVIS, KEVIN - TR - b: 8/1/69 $0

After establishing himself as a starter in 2001, Jarvis was San Digeo's Opening Day starter in 2002 before missing the second half of that season and first half of 2003 because of surgery to repair a torn flexor tendon in his right elbow. Jarvis is a plucky sort of journeyman who gets by with an assortment of pitches - fastball, curve, slider and change - that he must locate to be effective. He is not overpowering and is prone to giving up home runs when his ball catches too much of the plate. He works quickly and holds runners well. He is a good hitter who can put the ball in play. He was a candidate for one of the final spots in the starting rotation, although the San Diego youth movement may catch him in the near future.

	W	SV	ERA	IP	H	BB	SO	B/I
2001 San Diego	12	0	4.79	193	189	49	133	1.23
2002 San Diego	2	0	4.37	35	36	10	24	1.31
2003 San Diego	4	0	5.87	92	113	32	49	1.58

JENNINGS, JASON - TR - b:7/17/78 $0

Jennings, the 2002 NL Rookie of Year, had another strong season, and if he continues to develop and maintain his residency, he will be the best pitcher in Colorado franchise history by the time the decade ends. Jennings is a great athlete and a consummate pitcher. He is not overpowering (neither is Greg Maddux) but has command of a sinking fastball, a slider and a changeup. He understands the art, mixes his pitches well and throws quality strikes. He walked a few more hitters in 2003 than previously after they began to recognize his pitching pattern, although Jennings is smart enough to make his own adjustments as he gets older. Do not be deceived by his 240 pounds - Jennings is an agile, quick athlete, polished enough to be the cleanup hitter in college at Baylor. He homered and threw a shutout in his first major league start for Colorado, a tipoff to his natural ability. He is quick off the mound and fields his position well while also demonstrating an ability to keep runners close. He will be the No. 1 starter in the rotation, and he has the potential to win 15-18 games.

	W	SV	ERA	IP	H	BB	SO	B/I
2001 Colorado	2	0	4.58	39	42	19	26	1.55
2002 Colorado	16	0	4.52	185	201	70	127	1.46
2003 Colorado	12	0	5.11	181	212	88	119	1.65

JIMENEZ, JOSE - TR - b: 7/7/73 $2

Despite his 20 saves, Jimenez was brutal as a closer, and Colorado decided to put him out of his (and its) misery by moving him into the starting rotation in early August. Jimenez won two games in the rotation, one against old pal Arizona, and looked like he belonged. Jimenez, who threw a no-hitter in beating Randy Johnson, 1-0, on June 25, 1999, features a fastball that explodes down in the strike zone when he is throwing it right, leaving batters unable to center it up. He also has a plus-slider that gives him two power pitches that move down; thus he gives up few home runs, even in Coors Field. He does not have an off-speed pitch, however, the reason he was moved to the bullpen when he was traded to Colorado in 2000. His trouble in 2003 came when he lost his command and left pitches up. Jimenez is an aggressive defender but is awfully slow to the plate, leaving his catcher at the mercy of opposing baserunners. Jimenez set the franchise record with 41 saves in 2002 and is best-suited for the closer's role. He entered spring training ready to anwer the question whether he could reclaim that job or whether the Rockies wanted to see more of him in the starting rotation.

	W	SV	ERA	IP	H	BB	SO	B/I
2001 Colorado	6	17	4.09	55	56	22	37	1.42
2002 Colorado	2	41	3.56	73	76	11	47	1.19
2003 Colorado	2	20	5.22	102	137	32	45	1.66

JOHNSON, ADAM - TR - b: 7/12/79 $0

Four pitches. None of them exceptional. And not great control. That has added up to stunted growth for Adam Johnson, a former first-round pick who's had a couple of brief flings in the majors. His fastball can hit 91-92 MPH but he still throws it up in the strike zone too much. His other pitches are decent, but he lacks the precision needed to make them effective. Johnson lost his minor league starting role in 2003 and now is being considered a relief prospect. He'll be hard-pressed to land such a role in 2004.

	W	SV	ERA	IP	H	BB	SO	B/I
2001 Minnesota	1	0	8.28	25	32	13	17	1.80

JOHNSON, JASON - TR - b: 10/27/73 $0

Johnson had the best year of his career in 2003, and signs point to ways that he can improve on that. One statistic that jumps out from Johnson's career is that he averages about six innings per start, low even by today's standards. For some pitchers, that means a lack of stamina — and for Johnson, a diabetic, that would seem likely. His real problem is that he's throwing too many pitches. One reason Roy Halladay could average 7 1/3 innings per start last season was an economy of pitches. He averaged less than 14 pitches per inning; Johnson's average was nearly 17. That's because he walked more than 3 1/2 batters per nine innings. If he can trust his outstanding curve when behind in the count, Johnson's walks and pitches would drop and he could ascend toward the level of the majors' ace pitchers.

	W	SV	ERA	IP	H	BB	SO	B/I
2001 Baltimore	10	0	4.09	196	194	77	114	1.38
2002 Baltimore	5	0	4.59	131	141	41	97	1.39
2003 Baltimore	10	0	4.18	190	216	80	118	1.56

JOHNSON, RANDY - TL - b: 9/10/63 $13

During his four-year dominance from 1999-2002, Johnson always cautioned that trouble was only an injury away, and in 2003 he suffered his first major injury since undergoing back surgery while with Seattle that cost him most of the 1996 season. Johnson missed two months with torn cartilage in his right knee and never regained his Cy Young form after returning in June. His right knee joint has worn pretty much to the point that it is basically bone on bone, and the medical staff hopes that does not become an ongoing concern. Johnson still has his 100 MPH fastball, although he was not able to unleash it as much. His slider still starts outside the plate and ends at a righthanded hitters shoetops. Some feel his subpar 2003 will only spur him to greater heights; after missing his back problems in 1996, he was 20-4 with a 2.28 ERA in 1997. Johnson is the unquestioned No. 1 starter in this rotation.

	W	SV	ERA	IP	H	BB	SO	B/I
2001 Arizona	21	0	2.49	249	181	71	372	1.01
2002 Arizona	24	0	2.32	260	197	71	334	1.03
2003 Arizona	6	0	4.26	114	125	27	125	1.33

JONES, TODD - TR - b: 4/24/68 $0

The Red Sox acquired Jones during last season in one of several moves designed to shore up their ailing bullpen. Though he pitched better than he had for Colorado, he didn't help Boston much. Since posting a career-high 42 saves in 2000, Jones has converted less than half of his opportunities, with four different teams. His fastball barely clears 90 MPH these days, making his changeup less effective, and his curve doesn't have the bite of his earlier years. A free agent after last season, Jones seemed likely to have difficulty finding a new employer.

	W	SV	ERA	IP	H	BB	SO	B/I
2001 DET/MIN	5	13	4.24	68	87	29	54	1.87
2002 Colorado	1	1	4.70	82	84	28	73	1.36
2003 COL/BOS	3	0	7.07	69	93	31	59	1.80

JULIO, JORGE - TR - b: 3/3/79 $26

On the surface, Julio seems like a somewhat smaller, Venezuelan Armando Benitez. Julio can throw almost as hard; he has been clocked at 98 mph. He can be dominating, as some 60 saves in his first two major league seasons would attest. He also can blow up — and blow saves — at inopportune times. However, despite feeding batters a steady diet of hard stuff (four-seam fastball and high-80s slider), Julio has not been a big strikeout pitcher. He's young enough that he could improve, but he won't unless he can find a way to blow hitters away.

	W	SV	ERA	IP	H	BB	SO	B/I
2001 Baltimore	1	0	3.80	21	25	9	22	1.52
2002 Baltimore	5	25	1.99	68	55	27	55	1.21
2003 Baltimore	0	36	4.38	62	60	34	52	1.52

KARSAY, STEVE - TR - b: 3/24/72 $0

In 2002, Karsay was the Yankees' closer while Mariano Rivera was sidelined. Even though Karsay wasn't pitching well by the time of the Championship Series, he worked in every game and received New York's only win in that series. His workload — more than 70 games in each of the first three years beginning with 2 — apparently made an impact on him. Karsay underwent back surgery in November 2002 and shoulder surgery last May, and missed the entire 2003 season. If he's back with something resembling his mid-90s fastball and big-breaking curve, he'll be an effective setup man again.

	W	SV	ERA	IP	H	BB	SO	B/I
2001 CLE/ATL	3	8	2.35	88	73	25	83	1.11
2002 New York - AL	6	12	3.26	88	87	30	65	1.33

KENNEDY, JOE - TL - b: 1/11/78 $0

Kennedy began the 2003 season looking like he was on his way to becoming a workhorse, being named as the opening day starter for the Devil Rays but the season ended up being a dissapointing one for Kennedy, losing his spot on the rotation at the end of August and getting moved to the bullpen. Righthanded batters hit over .320 against him. He's not overpowering, though his fastball is generally in the low 90's, and he's not a strikeout pitcher, though he throws strikes. He began spring training ready to fight to win himself a spot on the rotation.

	W	SV	ERA	IP	H	BB	SO	B/I
2001 Tampa Bay	7	0	4.44	117	122	34	78	1.33
2002 Tampa Bay	8	0	4.53	197	204	55	109	1.32
2003 Tampa Bay	3	1	6.13	134	167	47	77	1.60

KERSHNER, JASON - TL - b: 12/19/76 $10

He's essentially become a two-pitch pitcher who now varies the speed of his fastball and changeup and only rarely mixes in a slider as a third pitch. He throws two types of changeup, largely because he has abandoned his curve almost completely and because each change has a different tailing action, it gives the illusion of having an extra pitch in his repertoire. Kershner was fantastic last year and will start the season as a primary lefthanded specialist who is also comfortable and effective in longer outings. It's unlikely he'll post as good results but he's going to pitch a lot more this year than he did last year.

	W	SV	ERA	IP	H	BB	SO	B/I
2002 SD/TOR	0	1	4.88	24	20	14	18	1.42
2003 Toronto	3	0	3.17	54	43	15	32	1.07

KIESCHNICK, BROOKS - TR - b: 6/6/72 $0

A No. 1 pick of the Chicago Cubs out of the University of Texas in 1993, Kieschnick reprised his college role as a pitcher/hitter when he did both with Milwaukee in 2003. He became the only player in major league history to homer as a pitcher, pinch-hitter and a designated hitter when he homered as a reliever on May 12. Drafted as a first baseman/left fielder Kieschnick, had four 20-home run seasons in the minors before getting back into pitching at Triple-A Charlotte in 2002. He made the Brewers' roster as a reliever and had his major league pitching debut May 2. His fastball touches 90 MPH and he features a hard slider. He displayed a nice touch and command on the mound, considering his long absence. He was expected to continue his role as a pitcher-first this season.

	W	SV	ERA	IP	H	BB	SO	B/I
2003 Milwaukee	1	0	5.26	53	66	13	39	1.49

KIM, BYUNG-HYUN - TR - b: 1/21/79 $19

During a season when he changed leagues, and from starter back to closer, one thing remained constant for Kim: The Yankees gave him trouble. He was 1-2 with a blown save against the Bombers, who batted .300 against the sidearming righthander. Kim throws a low-90s fastball, a changeup that can be effective because it's some 25 mph slower and a slider. He had more success against lefthanded batters as a starter for Arizona, but the scouting consensus still seems to be that Kim has a brighter future as a reliever.

	W	SV	ERA	IP	H	BB	SO	B/I
2001 Arizona	5	19	2.94	98	58	44	113	1.04
2002 Arizona	8	36	2.04	84	64	26	92	1.07
2003 AZ/BOS	9	16	3.31	122	104	33	102	1.12

KIM, SUN WOO - TR - b: 9/4/77 $0

Kim was obtained by the Expos in a June, 2002 trade, because he had a live arm, and had strikeout pitcher written all over him. He has quality stuff and at times good control, but he is very inconsistent and easily rattled. The Expos want to get Kim ready for their rotation but he was 10-8 with a 5.03 ERA in Edmonton and despite his 94 MPH fastball and a sharp breaking curve, Kim can't figure out how to get through a lineup more than twice.

	W	SV	ERA	IP	H	BB	SO	B/I
2001 Boston	0	0	5.83	41	54	21	27	1.80
2002 BOS/MON	3	0	4.75	49	52	14	29	1.34
2003 Montreal	0	0	8.36	14	24	8	5	2.29

KING, RAY - TL - b: 1/15/74 $1

King throws a mid-90's fastball that moves as well as a slider, curve and changeup. He was extremely effective as a lefty setup man and middle reliever for Atlanta last year, keeping lefthanded and righthanded batters to .200 and .223 batting averages, respectively. He's been effective against both lefty and righties for a while and he'll be valuable again this season as a one-man gang in relief.

	W	SV	ERA	IP	H	BB	SO	B/I
2001 Milwaukee	0	1	3.60	55	49	25	49	1.35
2002 Milwaukee	3	0	3.05	65	61	24	50	1.31
2003 Atlanta	3	0	3.51	59	46	27	43	1.24

KINNEY, MATT - TR - b: 12/16/76 $0

Kinney spent his first full season in a major league starting rotation in Milwaukee, and while he did post double-digit victories he was roughed up. A former sixth-round draft choice, Kinney is a big man with a power arm. His fastball gets into the mid-90s and he can blow it by some hitters. He took a step in the right direction with location and command in 2003, although he still walks too many and is especially loath to challenge lefties. Still only 27, Kinney was expected to retain a spot in the starting rotation.

	W	SV	ERA	IP	H	BB	SO	B/I
2002 Minnesota	2	0	4.64	66	78	33	45	1.68
2003 Milwaukee	10	0	5.19	191	201	80	152	1.47

KLINE, STEVE - TL - b: 8/22/72 $4

Although he is often used strictly as a situational lefty, facing just one or two lefthanded hitters at a time, he has moderate success against righthanders as well. Normally he spins curve ball after curve ball at hitters, hoping that he will get them to chase one down in the dirt with two strikes. He does not have a fastball that is capable of getting major league hitters out so he has to rely on his offspeed stuff. Kline is a fairly dependable veteran arm and will be counted on to pitch in key situations in the seventh and eighth innings again this season. While it isn't likely he will be the full-time closer, he has the ability to pick up a save every now and then. He has averaged about seven saves a year for the past four seasons, so expect a few more this year.

	W	SV	ERA	IP	H	BB	SO	B/I
2001 St. Louis	3	9	1.80	75	53	29	54	1.09
2002 St. Louis	2	6	3.40	58	54	21	41	1.29
2003 St. Louis	5	3	3.81	64	56	30	31	1.35

KNOTTS, GARY - TR - b: 2/12/77 $0

Knotts was acquired by the Tigers from Florida along with Rob Henkel and Nate Robertson for Jerrod Fuell and Mark Redman prior to the 2003 season. Knotts has a live fastball but his control deserts him at times. His stint as a Tigers starter was an experiment in the midst of their nightmare season. Granted, he built stamina, but he belongs in the bullpen. In June of last year, he had to be moved from the starting rotation to the bullpen, then to the minors because in six of the previous starts he had failed to make it past the fifth inning in four of them. He got called up again to the majors in September.

	W	SV	ERA	IP	H	BB	SO	B/I
2002 Florida	3	0	4.40	31	21	16	21	1.21
2003 Detroit	3	0	6.04	95	111	47	51	1.66

KOCH, BILLY - TR - b: 12/14/74 $3

The White Sox acquisition of Billy Koch wound up being a complete disaster. Not only did Koch struggle all season while he was troubled by elbow soreness, but Keith Foulke, the closer the Sox dealt to Oakland for Koch, wound up having a career year with the Athletics. Although Koch is a bulldog and one of the toughest competitors around, he throws a lot of pitches in each outing, and that appeared to have taken its toll last season. He appeared in more than half of Oakland's contests in 2002, and was used almost as heavily in the first half of 2003 in Chicago. Koch is going to have to earn his way back to the closer's role. However, if he is healthy that shouldn't be much of a concern. He has proven that he can be a reliable closer, so if his arm is sound he'll wind up being the man once again.

	W	SV	ERA	IP	H	BB	SO	B/I
2001 Toronto	2	36	4.80	69	69	33	55	1.47
2002 Oakland	11	44	3.27	94	73	46	93	1.27
2003 Chicago - AL	5	11	5.77	53	59	28	42	1.64

KOLB, DANNY - TR - b: 3/29/75 $31

Kolb, claimed by Milwaukee when Texas let him go in the spring of 2003, became a dominant closer in the second half of last season. Kolb missed most of the 2000 season after undergoing Tommy John surgery and parts of the next two seasons with rotator cuff problems, although he showed no hint of trouble last year. Kolb's fastball was timed at 98 MPH in a late-season appearance against Arizona, and he also features a respectable slider and split-fingered pitch. He improved his effectiveness against lefties by using the sinking fastball. A big man, Kolb has a long delivery to the plate and can be run on. He was expected to lay claim to the closer's role out of spring training this year.

	W	SV	ERA	IP	H	BB	SO	B/I
2001 Texas	0	0	4.70	15	15	10	15	1.63
2002 Texas	3	1	4.22	32	27	22	20	1.53
2003 Milwaukee	1	21	1.96	31	34	19	39	1.28

KOPLOVE, MIKE - TR - b: 8/30/76 $0

Koplove's career parallels that of former Arizona reliever Bret Prinz, traded to the New York Yankees at the 2003 trading deadline with David Dellucci for Raul Mondesi - he was worked hard, then broke down. Koplove was too good for his own good in 2002, when he emerged as the top setup man in the bullpen and was overused. He appeared in 31 games through June, 2003 before being shut down for the rest of the season with a shoulder injury. Koplove does not have overpowering stuff but keeps his fastball down and has a slow, looping breaking ball that freezes batters. A former college shortstop, he may be the best fielding pitcher in baseball although no one outside of Arizona has seen enough to judge. He has a quick release and holds runners well. Health permitting, he was expected to open the season as a top setup man.

	W	SV	ERA	IP	H	BB	SO	B/I
2002 Arizona	6	0	3.35	62	47	23	46	1.13
2003 Arizona	3	0	2.15	38	31	10	27	1.09

LACKEY, JOHN - TR - b: 10/23/78 $6

The lanky Texan throws a sinking fastball in the low 90s as well as a curve and slider. His breaking pitches lack consistency, sometimes forcing him to rely excessively on the fastball. Lackey has continued to struggle with high pitch counts that have prevented him from pitching deeper into games. After a meteoric rise to the majors in 2002, Lackey had trouble achieving any consistency in his sophomore season. Home runs, in particular, were a problem when his fastball didn't sink quite enough. Lackey's future is still bright, especially if he can learn to throw his off-speed stuff consistently for strikes.

	W	SV	ERA	IP	H	BB	SO	B/I
2002 Anaheim	9	0	3.66	108	113	33	69	1.35
2003 Anaheim	10	0	4.63	204	223	66	151	1.42

LAWRENCE, BRIAN - TR - b: 5/14/76 $11

San Diego's Opening Day starter in 2003, Lawrence has a fastball that may not light up scouts' eyes but is effective because he can move it down and in with good command. He has a hard-breaking slider that breaks the other way and complements both power pitches with a good changeup. He throws a lot of groundballs, although he had location lapses in 2003. He tied a major league record by hitting three batters in one inning on April 26. Hitters caught up to him a bit last season when they learned to lay off the low stuff sinking out of the zone, and he must make the next adjustment. He is a capable fielder and has worked hard on keeping runners close. He developed at the plate and had his first major league homer last year. He was expected to be a top-of-the-rotation starter again this season.

	W	SV	ERA	IP	H	BB	SO	B/I
2001 San Diego	5	0	3.45	114	107	34	84	1.23
2002 San Diego	12	0	3.69	210	230	52	149	1.34
2003 San Diego	10	0	4.19	211	206	57	116	1.25

LEE, CLIFF - TL - b: 8/30/78 $4

Lee is a pitcher to watch. The lefty began the season at Triple-A Buffalo where he was 7-1 with a 2.82 ERA. He moved into the Cleveland rotation in August when Jason Boyd went on the DL and Lee continued to pitch well for the rest of the year. He can bring his fastball in at about 92 MPH and he can change arm angles to keep hitters from locking onto his release point. Lee also throws a nice curve, slider and a tricky changeup, all with good control.

	W	SV	ERA	IP	H	BB	SO	B/I
2003 Cleveland	3	0	3.61	52	41	20	44	1.17

LEITER, AL - TL - b: 10/23/65 $9

Leiter earned nearly a fourth of the Mets' victories even though there were danger signs in his season. His strikeouts were down, his walks were up, baserunners took liberties with Leiter and lefthanders batted .299 against him. He's better against righthanders anyway, because his out pitch is a low-90s cut fastball. Last season was his ninth in a row with 11 or more victories. After starting the season 8-5 with a 5.57 ERA, he went on the disabled list because of an inflamed right knee, then went 7-4 with a 2.15 ERA the rest of the way. Leiter's work on postseason telecasts augured well for a broadcasting career when his playing days end.

	W	SV	ERA	IP	H	BB	SO	B/I
2001 New York - NL	11	0	3.31	187	178	46	142	1.20
2002 New York - NL	13	0	3.48	204	194	69	172	1.29
2003 New York - NL	15	0	3.98	181	176	94	139	1.49

LESKANIC, CURTIS - TR - b: 4/2/68 $5

The most successful of several pennant drive bullpen acquisitions for Kansas City, Curtis Leskanic was at his best with the game on the line; he went almost three months without giving up a run and eventually worked his way into sharing the closer job with Mike MacDougal by season's end. Leskanic works with a moving, low-90s fastball and a hard slider. He sometimes has control difficulty and will give up too many fly balls when he doesn't keep the ball down. Leskanic lacks the bounce-back arm required to be effective on consecutive days, although he isn't bothered by frequent use. He can get a strikeout when needed and has had sufficient success against both left and righthanded batters that he can be used in a late-inning, short-relief role. Leskanic is a below-average fielder with an average move to first. Following one of his better seasons, Leskanic talked of retirement, although he would still be interested in pitching short relief for another season if the circumstances were right.

	W	SV	ERA	IP	H	BB	SO	B/I
2001 Milwaukee	2	17	3.64	69	63	31	64	1.36
2003 MIL/KC	5	2	2.22	53	38	29	50	1.27

LEVINE, ALAN - TR - b: 5/22/68 $3

In 2003, Al Levine made a roundabout trek from the Anaheim Angels to Kansas City. He was not offered a contract by Anaheim over the winter and got a chance with the Cardinals in spring training. Levine pitched poorly for St. Louis before getting released in March and hooking on with Tampa Bay. The Royals, desperate for bullpen help down the stretch, acquired Levine at the trade deadline and he worked well as one of several short-relief pitchers used in non-save situations. Levine's fastball reaches only into the upper-80s so he must rely heavily on his mid-80s sinker and a sweeping slider which is especially useful against lefties. Levine is a durable pitcher who can pitch on short rest although he works better with more than a day's rest. Levine has a few years left as a short-reliever who can pick up an occasional multi-inning save, or be used in situational settings to setup a closer.

	W	SV	ERA	IP	H	BB	SO	B/I
2001 Anaheim	8	2	2.38	75	71	28	40	1.31
2002 Anaheim	4	5	4.24	64	61	34	40	1.49
2003 TB/KC	3	1	2.79	71	67	29	30	1.35

LEWIS, COLBY - TR - b: 8/2/79 $0

A supplemental first-round pick in the 1999 draft, Lewis throws a low-90s fastball, a plus slider and a splitter. Scouts have been impressed with Lewis' ability, but he has yet to translate that into any consistent success in the majors. Lack of control and susceptibility to the home run have been two major problems for Lewis. He is still maturing as a pitcher, so there is a chance that things will fall into place for him within the next couple of seasons, although additional time in the minor leagues may be needed. A good showing in the spring could still land him a rotation spot this year.

	W	SV	ERA	IP	H	BB	SO	B/I
2002 Texas	1	0	6.30	34	42	26	28	1.98
2003 Texas	10	0	7.30	127	163	70	88	1.83

LIDGE, BRAD - TR - b: 12/23/76 $4
Lidge was a number one draft choice by Houston in 1998 but suffered through 4 injury-filled seasons when he pitched a total of only 100 innings. He finally remained healthy in 2002 at Double-A Round Rock and Triple-A New Orleans and was promoted to Houston late in the year. He became a strong part of the Astros bullpen in 2003, usually pitching the seventh inning ahead of Octavio Dotel and Billy Wagner. His fastball reaches 96 to 97 MPH but his most effective pitch is a hard, knee-buckling slider. While he was a starter through his minor league career, his success in 2003, especially in remaining healthy, has solidified his status as a reliever who should assume increasingly more important roles in the future.

	W	SV	ERA	IP	H	BB	SO	B/I
2003 Houston	6	1	3.60	85	60	42	97	1.20

LIDLE, CORY - TR - b: 3/22/72 $0
After starting last season 8-2, Lidle collapsed in the second half. He throws a pretty good moving fastball that peaks, at best, in the low-90s with a good assortment of off-speed pitches and decent control. The movement on his pitches was noticeably off for most of last year and he will not only have to recover but he suffered through ongoing groin problems for most of the first half of last year and when the groin problems were corrected, that's when he stopped pitching well. He will be battling to make it as a bottom-of-the-rotation starter and needs to get off to a quick start this season to stick.

	W	SV	ERA	IP	H	BB	SO	B/I
2001 Oakland	13	0	3.59	188	170	47	118	1.15
2002 Oakland	8	0	3.89	192	191	39	111	1.20
2003 Toronto	12	0	5.74	193	216	60	112	1.43

LIEBER, JON - TR - b: 4/2/70 $0
The Yankees knew Lieber wouldn't be able to pitch for them in 2003, but they signed the free agent before that season knowing that their rotation was aging. He had undergone Tommy John surgery in August 2002, and didn't return to the mound until a year later. In eight innings at the Rookie and high Single-A levels, Lieber gave up 11 hits in 37 at-bats (.297). We'll see in the spring whether he again has the sharp-breaking slider that has helped him hold righthanded batters to a .239 average against him. Lieber might not be ready to take a regular turn in the rotation at the beginning of 2004, but he should eventually contribute this season.

	W	SV	ERA	IP	H	BB	SO	B/I
2001 Chicago - NL	20	0	3.80	232	226	41	148	1.15
2002 Chicago - NL	6	0	3.70	141	153	12	87	1.17

LIGTENBERG, KERRY - TR - b: 5/11/71 $4
Ligtenberg has led an interesting, if nomadic, baseball life. The former independent leaguer became the Braves' closer, then underwent elbow surgery and later signed as a free agent with Baltimore. For the Orioles last year, Ligtenberg was a middle reliever sometimes used as a situational specialist against righthanded batters. That's because lefty hitters have begun to crush his offerings — a splitter as an out pitch, with a fastball at about 90 mph and a hard slider. Home runs have created problems for him. Though Ligtenberg avoided his customary slow start during the 2003 season, Ligtenberg struggled down the stretch. His future is cloudy.

	W	SV	ERA	IP	H	BB	SO	B / I
2001 Atlanta	3	1	3.02	59	50	30	56	1.34
2002 Atlanta	3	0	2.97	67	52	33	51	1.27
2003 Baltimore	4	1	3.34	59	60	14	47	1.25

LILLY, TED - TL - b: 1/4/76 $7

Lilly's season, and possibly his career, turned around in the middle of last season when the Athletics banned him from shaking off the pitches his catcher was calling. When that happened, Lilly went from a guy who constantly nibbled at the edges of the strike zone and was simply struggling to keep his spot in the rotation, to a consistent winner. Even though Lilly has an ordinary fastball, one which gets in the low 90s but no higher, he is able to get both lefthanded and righthanded hitters out with his slider and curve. Lilly, now that he has figured things out, has established him as a quality member of the starting rotation, and can be expected to win 12 to 15 games this season.

	W	SV	ERA	IP	H	BB	SO	B / I
2001 New York - AL	5	0	5.37	120	126	51	112	1.47
2002 NY - AL/OAK	5	0	3.69	100	80	31	77	1.11
2003 Oakland	12	0	4.34	178	179	58	147	1.33

LIMA, JOSE - TR - b: 9/30/75 $0

It's not often that you can find a potential eight-game winner pitching in an independent league, but that's exactly what happened with Jose Lima and the Royals in 2003. Discovered pitching for the Newark Bears, Lima came to Kansas City and was an immediate sensation as the club won his first eight starts. Lima suffered a groin strain in a start August 1st against Tampa Bay and missed his next two starts. He returned too early and the strained groin reduced the velocity on his fastball to barely topping 80 MPH. After one more poor start, Lima went on the DL for a month, returning in mid-September to pick up his eighth win. When Lima can't throw his fastball at 90 MPH, he won't be effective with his out pitch - an upper-70s changeup - because their velocities are too similar to fool hitters. In 2003, he showed a more effective breaking ball, but it was still a secondary pitch to the change. Lima is no more than a six-inning pitcher at this point; he loses effectiveness after two times through a batting order. An animated personality, he is quick to ire when calls don't go his way, but the fun-loving Lima always keeps teammates on their toes in the dugout. Lima appears to have re-learned his craft when relegated to the independent league. If he can maintain sufficient velocity on his fastball, he can again be a mildly successful big-league pitcher.

	W	SV	ERA	IP	H	BB	SO	B / I
2001 HOU/DET	6	0	5.54	166	197	38	84	1.42
2002 Detroit	4	0	7.77	68	86	21	33	1.57
2003 Kansas City	8	0	4.91	73	80	26	32	1.45

LINCOLN, MIKE - TR - b: 4/10/75 $5

Lincoln was injured and unable to pitch for the Pirates until July. Oddly, he was selected to replace the traded Mike Williams as the Pirates closer but he just doesn't have the gas to do the job and the experiment ended quickly and Lincoln returned to middle relief, a role he is decent in filling. His fastball is average, and he mixes in a nice curve and a deceptive changeup.

	W	SV	ERA	IP	H	BB	SO	B / I
2001 Pittsburgh	2	0	2.68	40	34	11	24	1.12
2002 Pittsburgh	2	0	3.11	72	80	27	50	1.48
2003 Pittsburgh	3	5	5.21	36	38	13	28	1.40

LINEBRINK, SCOTT - TR - b: 7/4/76 $2

Linebrink had success in the bullpen after moving from Houston to San Diego in early 2003, although his season was cut short by a shoulder injury in September. He missed a month in 2002 with an elbow strain, so injuries are a concern. He will not overpower hitters, although he can be effective when spotting fastball and good breaking ball. He was expected to be in the mix for a bullpen role.

	W	SV	ERA	IP	H	BB	SO	B / I
2001 Houston	0	0	2.62	10	6	6	9	1.17
2002 Houston	0	0	7.04	24	31	13	24	1.81
2003 HOU/SD	3	0	3.32	92	93	36	68	1.40

LLOYD, GRAEME - TL - b: 4/9/67 $0

Not every pennant-race move by Royals GM Allard Baird was a success. Graeme Lloyd was supposed to give Kansas City an effective lefty setup man in the bullpen but he was an unmitigated disaster, posting a double-digit ERA and failing to hold important leads. Opposing hitters bashed Lloyd at a .439 clip in the second half as he allowed 44 baserunners in 15.2 innings. Even more telling was his lack of success against lefthanders, who hit .338 against him in 2003, the second straight year in which Lloyd has been ineffective against lefties. Lloyd can be effective when he keeps his two-seam, 90-MPH fastball and upper-80s cut fastball down. All too often though, he missed with his slider, then got far too much of the plate with his hittable fastballs. Being lefthanded will help Lloyd get another chance in the majors in 2004, but he'll have to show a lot more ability to retire lefties in a short relief role if his career is to continue.

	W	SV	ERA	IP	H	BB	SO	B / I
2001 Montreal	9	1	4.35	70	74	21	44	1.35
2002 MON/FLA	4	5	5.21	57	67	19	37	1.51
2003 NY - NL/KC	1	0	5.28	48	68	14	25	1.72

LOAIZA, ESTEBAN - TR - b: 12/31/71 $16

There wasn't much doubt that Loaiza was the surprise of the 2003 season. After seeing his ERA rise for five of the previous six seasons, Loaiza put together the kind of year most pitchers only dream of having. He was a dominant pitcher from the start of the season, fading only slightly in the last month of the season. What turned Loaiza around? In 2003 he moved the ball around more in the strike zone, mixing in his two- and four-seam fastballs with a very good change and a cut fastball he began throwing the year before. He finally realized he doesn't have the stuff to blow the ball by hitters every time and began to trust his stuff more. There is virtually no chance of Loazia coming close to 20 victories this year. Still, he has learned enough to win more than he loses, while keeping his ERA at respectable levels.

	W	SV	ERA	IP	H	BB	SO	B / I
2001 Toronto	11	0	5.02	190	239	40	110	1.47
2002 Toronto	9	0	5.71	151	192	38	87	1.52
2003 Chicago - AL	21	0	2.90	226	196	56	207	1.11

LOEWER, CARLTON - TR - b: 9/24/73 $0

Loewer was pounded in five starts with San Diego in 2003, although just getting back on the mound was a step in the right direction. He was expected to join the San Diego rotation after being acquired in 2000 but fell out of a duck blind while hunting in the offseason and suffered a fractured left ankle. After recovering, he underwent surgery on his rotator cuff to tighten ligaments in his right shoulder. After a brief return in 2001, he missed all of the 2002 season with arm injuries. Loewer has a low-90s fastball and a good slider, although he has not been on the field long enough to master them. He has enough tools to make a major league roster, but time and rust are catching up to him.

	W	SV	ERA	IP	H	BB	SO	B / I
2003 San Diego	1	0	6.64	22	35	8	11	1.98

LOHSE, KYLE - TR - b: 10/4/78 $8

Good command of four pitches has made Kyle Lohse an up and coming starter. Blessed with a 94 MPH fastball, Lohse has learned to throw it on the corners rather than challenge hitters over the middle of the plate with it. He also has a quality slider, curve and change up. Lohse is learning his limitations. When his fastball is sailing high in the strike zone, he'll go with the slider because the delivery for that pitch helps him with his fastball. Lohse is entering an arbitration year and could get a nice boost in salary.

	W	SV	ERA	IP	H	BB	SO	B/I
2001 Minnesota	4	0	5.68	90	102	29	64	1.45
2002 Minnesota	13	0	4.23	181	181	70	124	1.39
2003 Minnesota	14	0	4.61	201	211	45	130	1.27

LOOPER, BRADEN - TR - b: 10/28/74 $8

Looper was effective as a closer for the Marlins but after two blown saves in a row against the Braves in the Marlins frenetic wild card chase, the Marlins acquired Ugueth Urbina and said that Looper had a tired arm while Urbina took over as the closer. There is no doubt that Urbina is still a better closer than Looper and while the change to Urbina was perfectly justified in a playoff race, it was also a vote of no-confidence in Looper's ability. His fastball can reach the upper 90's with some movement, but he's not a strikeout pitcher.

	W	SV	ERA	IP	H	BB	SO	B/I
2001 Florida	3	3	3.55	71	63	30	52	1.31
2002 Florida	2	13	3.14	86	73	28	55	1.17
2003 Florida	6	28	3.68	81	82	29	56	1.38

LOPEZ, AQUILINO- TR - b: 4/21/75 $21

Left unprotected by the Mariners after the 2002 season because his true age was revealed to be much older than he claimed, Lopez was snatched up by Toronto in the Rule Five draft and by season's end last year, he had emerged as the team's de factor closer. Lopez throws a low to mid-90s fastball, throws two different style sliders depending on the situation and has developed an ordinary and still unfinished split finger pitch which he has tried to incorporate as an extra weapon against lefties. His poise and confidence is that of a veteran and as well as he pitched last year, he projects to have a significant role in the bullpen this season from day one.

	W	SV	ERA	IP	H	BB	SO	B/I
2003 Toronto	1	14	3.42	74	58	34	64	1.25

LOPEZ, JAVIER - TL - b: 7/11/77 $3

Lopez was a nondescript lefthander in the minor leagues until he met Mike Myers when the two played for the Diamondbacks in 2002. Myers, who throws with a radical sidearm motion, taught Lopez the delivery, and Lopez has been on the rise ever since. After being claimed in the 2002 Rule 5 draft, Lopez had a successful rookie season at the major league level in Colorado, becoming an effective presence out of the bullpen against lefthanders. Lopez's fastball touches 90 MPH and he has a good slider, and with that delivery can be murder, since it seems his pitches are being delivered from somewhere near Todd Helton. Lopez allowed only two earned runs in his first 30 appearances, the first major leaguer since 1980 to accomplish that. He set a Colorado rookie record for appearances in 2003 and has established himself as a solid situational specialist in the bullpen. It would not be a surprise for Lopez to get a few save opportunities against some particular lefthanders.

	W	SV	ERA	IP	H	BB	SO	B/I
2003 Colorado	4	1	3.70	58	58	12	40	1.20

LOPEZ, RODRIGO - TR - b: 12/14/75   **$2**

Lopez was a surprise as the runner-up in Rookie of the Year voting in 2002, and a disappointment last year. Sophomore jinx? Perhaps partially, but his decline began during the second half of '02, when American League batters figured out Lopez's limited repertoire that includes just a high-80s fastball. An injury to an oblique muscle limited him early last season, but he came back and at times could be dominating. At other times, hitters found him comfortable enough that they averaged better than .300 against him for the season. Lopez can't be a major league ace, but can fit in the middle of a rotation.

	W	SV	ERA	IP	H	BB	SO	B/I
2002 Baltimore	15	0	3.57	197	172	62	136	1.19
2003 Baltimore	7	0	5.82	147	188	43	103	1.57

LOWE, DEREK - TR - b: 6/1/73   **$8**

Lowe has been Boston's biggest winner the last two seasons, but without being considered the Sox ace. What's more, he dropped off in virtually every statistical category in 2003, including an increase of about two runs in his ERA. Aside from his won-lost record, last year's performance was closer to his 5-10 season in 2001 than to his career-best 21-8 the next year. Lowe had skin cancer before the season, and had a benign growth removed from his nose during June. The sinker specialist struggled as a starter early in his career before becoming the closer during 1999. He still can start, so he doesn't need to return to the bullpen full time, but that could be his ultimate destination.

	W	SV	ERA	IP	H	BB	SO	B/I
2001 Boston	5	24	3.53	91	103	29	82	1.44
2002 Boston	21	0	2.58	220	166	48	127	0.97
2003 Boston	17	0	4.47	203	216	72	110	1.42

LOWE, SEAN - TR - b: 3/29/71   **$0**

Sean Lowe got off to a good start for Triple-A Omaha in 2003, earning a recall to the Royals in May. In Kansas City, Lowe enjoyed only sporadic success out of the bullpen before falling apart at the end of July; he was demoted to Omaha after allowing eleven runs in his last four outings. Lowe had more success in the Omaha rotation, although Kansas City saw him strictly as a reliever. Although his fastball barely tops 90 MPH, Lowe is unafraid to pitch inside, which especially helps against righthanded hitters. He has an effective curveball, but uneven command. Lowe has pitched for four different organizations in the last three years; his nomadic movements are likely to continue in 2004.

	W	SV	ERA	IP	H	BB	SO	B/I
2001 Chicago - AL	9	3	3.61	127	123	32	71	1.22
2002 PIT/COL	5	0	5.79	79	101	41	64	1.79
2003 Kansas City	1	0	6.24	45	55	21	28	1.70

LOWRY, NOAH - TL - b: 10/10/81   **$0**

Lowry shot through San Francisco's farm system after being taken 30th overall in the 2001 draft. Despite not having pitched above Single-A, he made it all the way to the big leagues at the end of last season, impressing nearly everybody with his stuff and his presence on the mound. As a reliever, he can get his fastball up to the mid 90s. He also features a good change and is working to improve his curve. With all the other pitching prospects that the Giants have, Lowry isn't likely to get a shot in the starting rotation this season. However, he could make a difference this year in the big leagues as a lefthanded reliever.

	W	SV	ERA	IP	H	BB	SO	B/I
2003 San Francisco	0	0	0.00	6	1	2	5	0.48

LYON, BRANDON - TR - b: 8/10/79   **$0**

Lyon rose from Boston's bullpen committee to become its closer early last season, when he converted his first nine save opportunities. That streak blew up June 28, when the Marlins touched him for four runs. During the next month, Lyon was traded to Pittsburgh and returned because the Pirates said he had a bum elbow, then put on the disabled list. Lyon didn't have another save, even failing an audition to recapture the closer's job in the regular-season finale. A failed starter with the Blue Jays, he throws a low-90s sinking fastball and a changeup.

	W	SV	ERA	IP	H	BB	SO	B / I
2001 Toronto	5	0	4.29	63	63	15	35	1.24
2002 Toronto	1	0	6.53	62	78	19	30	1.56
2003 Boston	4	9	4.12	59	73	19	50	1.56

MacDOUGAL, MIKE - TR - b: 1/8/75 $11

A career starter who was converted to short relief late in 2002, Mike MacDougal had an outstanding first half and became known as "Mac the Ninth" before earning an All-Star berth as a rookie closer. The second half was less kind to MacDougal as he converted just three save opportunities and lost his closer job. The wild extremes over the course of the season are representative of MacDougal's pitching style as he has outstanding stuff but unpredict-able control. MacDougal's best fastball flirts with the 100 MPH barrier, strong enough for him to challenge even the best fastball hitters up in the strikezone. He has a nasty hard slider that can buckle a righthanded hitter's knees and a decent changeup, but he tends to get caught up in the excitement of the moment and overthrows, sailing his fastball and burying his slider in the dirt. When MacDougal grooved pitches to get a strike hitters teed off, hitting 100 points higher against him in the second half. Much like a young Randy Johnson, MacDougal's control woes come from unwinding his lanky body during his delivery. To succeed in the future, MacDougal needs to maintain his composure in tense situations and simplify his delivery, letting his natual ability take over. The Royals will give MacDougal another shot at the closer job in 2004.

	W	SV	ERA	IP	H	BB	SO	B / I
2003 Kansas City	3	27	4.08	64	64	32	57	1.50

MADDUX, GREG - TR - b: 4/14/66 $19

The master of the art of making batters mis-hit the ball, Greg Maddux has pinpoint control with a wide repertoire of pitches. His fastball barely reaches 90 MPH, so it is location that breeds success for Maddux. He goes right after the hitters, primarily with a cut fastball kept low in the strikezone to induce grounders, mixing the cutter with high four-seam fastballs, sinkers, sliders, curves and changeups; no batter sees the same pitch in the same location and he can use any of them as an out pitch at any time. Maddux is an above-average athlete in other respects; he's won 13 consecutive Gold Gloves and also handles the bat well. His primary flaw is an inability to hold baserunners. Maddux, a four-time Cy Young award winner, surpassed even old Cy himself in 2003 by winning at least 15 games for the 16th straight year. As usual, Maddux finished among league leaders in many pitching categories and was the Braves' leader in many other categories. Another 15-win season in 2004 will put this future Hall of Famer into the elite class of 300-game winners.

	W	SV	ERA	IP	H	BB	SO	B / I
2001 Atlanta	17	0	3.05	233	220	27	173	1.05
2002 Atlanta	16	0	2.62	199	194	45	118	1.20
2003 Atlanta	16	0	3.96	218	225	33	124	1.18

MAHAY, RON - TL - b: 6/28/71 $4

A converted outfielder, Mahay has developed into a serviceable lefty reliever. He is a hard thrower who prefers to challenge hitters. Last season, he spent half the year at Triple-A, compiling a 4-2 record with three saves and a 4.22 ERA. In his big league stint, he was as effective against lefties as righties, and began to see some setup work. Mahay is unlikely to be used in save situations.

	W	SV	ERA	IP	H	BB	SO	B/I
2001 Chicago - NL	0	0	2.61	21	14	15	24	1.40
2002 Chicago - NL	2	0	8.57	15	13	8	14	1.43
2003 Texas	3	0	3.18	45	33	20	38	1.17

MANTEI, MATT - TR - b: 7/7/73 $31

Closer Mantei returned to his dominating form in 2003 despite missing time with yet another injury, this time a balky shoulder that caused him to miss three weeks. Mantei throws hard enough - he tops out at 98-99 MPH - to get his fastball by any, and he became even harder to handle after mastering a curve ball that he was able to spot well. After alternating between the curve and his slider since coming to Arizona in 1999, Mantei finally committed on the curve and let it work for him. He often started hitters with his curve, sneaking a first strike while causing them to wonder what was coming next. Less able to cheat on his fastball, hitters were less often able to catch up with it. Mantei tinkered with his mechanics in an attempt to stay away from arm injuries that have plagued him during his career, although he always seem to need a little time in the training room each year. He will remain the closer after exercising a player option worth $8 million.

	W	SV	ERA	IP	H	BB	SO	B/I
2001 Arizona	0	2	2.57	7	6	4	12	1.43
2002 Arizona	2	0	4.72	27	28	12	26	1.50
2003 Arizona	5	29	2.62	55	37	18	68	1.00

MAROTH, MIKE - TL - b: 8/17/77 $0

Too much was made of hard luck Maroth losing over 20 games. Well, he was not a hard luck loser and his record is an accurate reflection of how he pitched last year. Maroth should try a more aggressive approach and if he can move his money pitch, a sinker, in on righthanded hitters he'll improve. If he keeps trying to fool them he's going to lose a lot of games again.

	W	SV	ERA	IP	H	BB	SO	B/I
2002 Detroit	6	0	4.48	129	136	36	58	1.34
2003 Detroit	9	0	5.73	193	231	50	87	1.45

MARQUIS, JASON - TR - b: 8/21/78 $0

An heir-apparent to a Braves' rotation job, Marquis instead spent a large portion of 2003 at Triple-A Richmond. He pitched well enough there, but had little to prove at that level. Overall, Marquis made just two starts for Atlanta, although he finished the year getting a save in the Braves last game of the season. At his best, Marquis has a fine mid-90s, four-seam fastball thrown with excellent movement and he also owns an above-average slider and changeup. However, he has never had good command of any pitch. Marquis lacks the other non-pitching qualities often possessed by Braves pitchers; he's a poor fielder and hitter, and doesn't adjust to meet game situations. Marquis didn't endear himself to Braves management with public comments made about not getting a chance to start and scouts have been critical of his poise on the mound. Marquis has all the tools to succeed but before he'll get a lengthy chance in Atlanta he'll need much better command of those tools, and of himself.

	W	SV	ERA	IP	H	BB	SO	B/I
2001 Atlanta	5	0	3.48	129	113	59	98	1.33
2002 Atlanta	8	0	5.04	114	127	49	84	1.54
2003 Atlanta	0	1	5.53	41	43	18	19	1.50

MARTE, DAMASO - TL - b: 2/14/75 $15

Last season Marte wound up taking the closer's role from a more experienced righthander for the second straight year. Marte began the year pitching as a setup man for Billy Koch. However, shortly after the All-Star break, Marte emerged as the top guy in the bullpen. Marte throws very hard and has a sharp-breaking slider. He also has outstanding control, especially for guy with only two full seasons in the big leagues. Marte likely will start this season as he has the last two, pitching in the eighth inning or sharing the closer's role with a more experienced righthander. However, Marte has what it takes to finish games, and he will get his share of saves once again.

	W	SV	ERA	IP	H	BB	SO	B/I
2001 Pittsburgh	0	0	4.71	36	34	12	39	1.27
2002 Chicago - AL	1	10	2.84	60	44	18	72	1.03
2003 Chicago - AL	4	11	1.58	80	50	34	87	1.05

MARTIN, TOM - TL - b: 5/21/70 $0

Martin missed most of the 2002 season with a strained rotator cuff, although he suffered no ill effects as an integral situational reliever last year. Martin has a major league average fastball that he couples with a curve that he uses effectively against lefties, who hit only .189 against him in 2003. Since he is not overpowering, he must locate to be effective. He holds runners well although he is no threat at the plate. He appears to have found his niche as a situational setup man.

	W	SV	ERA	IP	H	BB	SO	B/I
2001 New York - NL	1	0	10.06	17	23	10	12	1.94
2003 Los Angeles	1	0	3.53	51	36	24	51	1.18

MARTINEZ, PEDRO - TR - b: 10/25/71 $28

Martinez still can pitch very effectively. Every year since 1998, he has won at least 70 per cent of his games, with ERAs under 3.00 and WHIPs hovering on either side of 1.00. What he can't do is stay in the rotation all season. Last year, he went on the disabled list in May because of a back injury, and missed a start during an important September series against the Yankees. Before that, though, Pedro made the Red Sox blink and pick up a $17.5-million option for 2004. When he does pitch, he can mix a low-90s fastball with an assortment of curves, circle changes and cut fastballs that he can move in or out on righthanded or lefthanded batters.

	W	SV	ERA	IP	H	BB	SO	B/I
2001 Boston	7	0	2.39	116	84	25	163	0.93
2002 Boston	20	0	2.26	199	144	40	239	0.92
2003 Boston	14	0	2.22	187	147	47	206	1.04

MATEO, JULIO - TR - b: 8/22/78 $10

Mateo, one of the top young arms in the Seattle chain, shined in his first extended visit to the major leagues in 2003 as a middle reliever/setup man. He is the second Mariner (and first reliever) to begin his career 4-0; starter Joel Piniero was 4-0 in 2001. Mateo has a fastball in the mid 90s that he locates well, complementing that with a slider. He challenges hitters with his good command, although he is susceptible to the home run. He is an OK fielder, although he needs to pay a little more attention to the running game. He was expected to be a fixture in the bullpen after earning his stripes in 2003.

	W	SV	ERA	IP	H	BB	SO	B/I
2002 Seattle	0	0	4.29	21	20	12	15	1.52
2003 Seattle	4	1	3.15	86	69	13	71	0.96

MATTHEWS, MIKE - TL - b: 10/24/79 $0

A late bloomer without overpowering stuff, Matthews had recent success out of the bullpen but appears to be suited to either relief or starting. He has command of an average fastball and good breaking pitch and is not afraid of challenging righthanded hitters inside. His splits indicate he is as successful against righties as he is against lefties. A long-time starter in the minors, Matthews was expected to enter camp as a reliever but could start in the right spot.

	W	SV	ERA	IP	H	BB	SO	B/I
2001 St. Louis	3	1	4.30	38	38	12	29	1.35
2002 STL/MIL	2	0	3.94	46	43	29	34	1.58
2003 San Diego	6	0	4.45	65	65	29	44	1.45

MAY, DARRELL - TL - b: 6/13/72 $16

As the most consistent starter throughout the 2003 season, Darrell May gave the Royals a lot more than his season-opening fifth starter role would have indicated. As every other starter fell to injury, or became ineffective, May continued to give the Royals one quality start after another, eventually becoming the ace of the staff. Never one to overpower hitters, May works the corners with his upper-80s fastball and slider thrown away from hitters, then looks to get them out with his changeup. In 2003, May began to add an effective cut fastball to the mix more often, and his changeup improved as he used fingertip pressure to get more movement on the pitch. May is susceptible to the long ball and has not shown the stamina to consistently pitch deep into ballgames. He was able to work longer outings in 2003 because he kept his pitch counts down and, especially, avoided the long innings that plagued his earlier attempts as a starter. To continue succeeding in the future, May will have to continue making adjustments, especially adding movement to his pitches without losing the control which allows him to hit spots. May is an average fielder who has begun to vary his delivery to better control baserunners.

	W	SV	ERA	IP	H	BB	SO	B/I
2002 Kansas City	4	0	5.35	131	144	50	95	1.48
2003 Kansas City	10	0	3.77	210	197	53	115	1.19

MAYS, JOE - TR - b: 12/10/75 $0

Joe Mays' career is in jeopardy and he should not be counted on for 2004. After struggling for much of the 2003 season, Mays elected to have ulnar collateral ligament reconstruction (Tommy John surgery). A ligament was taken out of his leg (the one in his wrist was too small) and placed in his elbow. Mays was unable to get that extra snap on his pitches because of an elbow that had been operated on in each of the two previous seasons. The former All-Star and 17-game winner is not expected back until 2005.

	W	SV	ERA	IP	H	BB	SO	B/I
2001 Minnesota	17	0	3.16	233	205	64	123	1.15
2002 Minnesota	4	0	5.38	95	113	25	38	1.45
2003 Minnesota	8	0	6.30	130	159	39	50	1.52

McCLUNG, SETH - TR - b: 2/7/81 $0

McClung, 23, made his major league debut last year with a great start on April 26, giving up one run in over six innings to get the win. Last season started well for him, but he injured his elbow in late May, and it was later discovered to be tendinitis and he was out for the remainder of 2003 and the beginning of 2004. He underwent Tommy John surgery at the end June. The 6'6", 235, righthander featured a heavy mid-90s fastball and was developing his curve and changeup, prior to his injury. He still needs improvement on his breaking pitches. McClung is still young, and while he needs more time in the minors, he could start helping his team in the big leagues not-too-far into 2004.

	W	SV	ERA	IP	H	BB	SO	B/I
2003 Tampa Bay	4	0	5.35	39	33	25	25	1.50

MEADOWS, BRIAN - TR - b: 11/21/75 $1

Meadows career went backwards in 2003. In 2002 he was used quite a bit for spot starting and relief but last year, between trips to the minors, Meadows did the same job last year but he didn't get as much work. He relies on an average fastball and a decent curve and while he can throw a slider, he's never gotten much out of it.

	W	SV	ERA	IP	H	BB	SO	B/I
2001 Kansas City	1	0	6.97	50	73	12	21	1.69
2002 Pittsburgh	1	0	3.88	63	62	14	31	1.21
2003 Pittsburgh	2	1	4.72	76	91	11	38	1.34

MECHE, GIL - TR - b: 9/8/78 $5

A former No.1 draftee out of high school in 1996, Meche returned to form after surgery on his right rotator cuff cost him the 2002 season, setting career highs in virtually every category while spending the season in the Seattle starting rotation. Meche has a fastball that reaches the mid 90s and complements that with a slider that can be downright nasty. His change can be effective, and he has an idea of what he is doing on the mound. Meche is athletic for a big man and understands the importance of holding runners close. His future is all ahead of him, as Yogi might say, and he was expected to be a solid member of the starting rotation.

	W	SV	ERA	IP	H	BB	SO	B/I
2003 Seattle	15	0	4.59	186	187	63	130	1.34

MECIR, JIM - TR - b: 5/16/70 $0

A durable reliever in the past, Mecir's best pitch is his screwball, which he used to stay effective against lefthanded hitters. However, he struggled throughout last season, and lefthanded hitters hit over .300 against him. Prior to the 2003 season, he had surgery on his left knee and was on the DL through April, and in August was placed on the DL again because of inflammation in his right knee. When healthy, Mecir throws his fastball in the low 90's, and also features a slider and a splitter. He is also versatile, and is capable of pitching on consecutive days, or pitching more than one inning at a time. His performance has deteriorated for three consecutive years so he's going to have to battle for a full-time relief role.

	W	SV	ERA	IP	H	BB	SO	B/I
2001 Oakland	2	3	3.43	63	54	26	61	1.27
2002 Oakland	6	1	4.25	68	68	29	53	1.43

MENDOZA, RAMIRO - TR - b: 6/15/72 $0

Mendoza had great success swinging between starting, long relief and setting up Mariano Rivera with the Yankees. He signed as a free agent before last season with the Red Sox, who tried him in similar roles. Boston fans seemed to think he still was pitching for the Yankees, who batted .400 against him. The sinkerballer had trouble throwing strikes and gave up home runs at an unprecedented rate in the worst of his eight major league seasons. He missed more than a month while on the disabled list. The silver lining there was that it was his right knee and not his arm that caused him trouble.

	W	SV	ERA	IP	H	BB	SO	B/I
2001 New York - AL	8	6	3.75	100	89	23	70	1.11
2002 New York - AL	8	4	3.44	92	102	16	61	1.29
2003 Boston	3	0	6.75	67	98	20	36	1.77

MERCKER, KENT - TL - b: 2/1/68 $2

Former Braves star Kent Mercker spent most of the season in Cincinnati, before the Braves re-acquired him in an August trade. Mercker did a fine job out of the bullpen for both clubs and set career bests in holds and ERA. It was quite a turnaround for Mercker, who had posted an ERA over 6.00 in his previous two seasons, had suffered a brain hemorrhage in 2000 and missed the entire 2001 season. His fastball velocity has returned to the low-90s and he'll vary speeds by throwing a sinker or cut fastball. He has battled control problems for much of his career and is prone to grooving a hittable fastball when he is struggling to find the strikezone. Mercker will be 36 before opening day, and his future depends upon his ability to get out lefties, which he has done well enough since moving to the bullpen in 2000.

	W	SV	ERA	IP	H	BB	SO	B / I
2002 Colorado	3	0	6.14	44	55	22	37	1.75
2003 CIN/ATL	0	1	1.95	55	46	32	48	1.41

MESA, JOSE - TR - b: 5/22/66 $1

Rumors that he shaved a few years off his true age are not so important because he admits to being 38 and that's old, too old for a power closer. It's hard to envision a team letting him close. He just can't find the plate anymore.

	W	SV	ERA	IP	H	BB	SO	B / I
2001 Philadelphia	3	42	2.34	69	65	20	59	1.23
2002 Philadelphia	4	45	2.97	76	65	39	64	1.37
2003 Philadelphia	5	24	6.52	58	71	31	45	1.76

MICELI, DANNY - TR - b: 9/9/70 $4

Miceli is a journeyman who pitched for four different major league teams in 2003. He was originally signed as a non-drafted free agent in 1990 by Kansas City. He has been almost exclusively a reliever, including a season (1995) as a closer with Pittsburgh. Miceli has a mid-90s fastball, a curve ball and a split-finger pitch which are good enough to hang on for an eleven year major league career. He pitched surprisingly well in middle relief after joining Houston in mid-season in 2003 and will be seeking a similar role with upward possibilties in 2004.

	W	SV	ERA	IP	H	BB	SO	B / I
2001 FLA/COL	2	1	4.80	45	47	16	48	1.40
2003 4 TEAMS	2	1	3.20	70	59	25	58	1.19

MIDDLEBROOK, JASON - TR - b: 6/26/75 $0

Jason Middlebrook is a talented righthander whose best pitch is a good moving fastball. Once considered a great prospect, his progress has been limited by various elbow and shoulder injuries going back to his Stanford days. He also needs to learn to become a pitcher rather than a thrower who tries to blow fastballs past Barry Bonds. He was sharp in Triple-A and his brief stint with the Mets last year indicated he still has upward potential. If healthy, Middlebrook can be a solid number two or three starter in the majors.

	W	SV	ERA	IP	H	BB	SO	B / I
2001 San Diego	2	0	5.12	19	18	10	10	1.45
2002 New York - NL	2	0	4.74	51	44	22	42	1.29

MILLER, JUSTIN - TR - b: 8/27/77 $0

Miller has a mediocre fastball which he can cut or sink, and he can throw a slider, curve and change. Unfortunately he doesn't have consistent command of any of these pitches and can't rely on them, and thus finds himself frequently behind in the count and needing to throw a fat pitch over the plate (or, almost as often, giving up a walk). Control is the main issue. When he stays ahead in the count, his unpredictable location becomes an asset. He was hoping to win himself a starter's role in 2003, but was out for the season. He was expected to be ready for spring training and try to win himself a spot in the rotaion.

MILLER, TREVER - TL - b: 5/29/73 $4

A first round pick of the Tigers way back more than ten years ago, Miller brought a bit of stability to the Blue Jays' bullpen last year, leading the American League in appearances. Not a particularly hard thrower, Miller's control can be erratic and that's why he's often limited to facing one or two batters as a situational lefty. He tends to pitch up in the strike zone too often and he'll have to improve on that if he's to stick around for a few years. He'll resume his situational lefty role this year and should expect similar results as last season.

	W	SV	ERA	IP	H	BB	SO	B/I
2003 Toronto	2	4	4.61	53	46	28	44	1.40

MILLER, WADE - TR - b: 9/13/76 $12

Miller showed promise when he arrived in the major leagues to stay during the 2000 season and became the workhorse of the Houston staff in his first full major league season in 2001. After a strong season in 2002, great things were expected in 2003. It didn't happen as he was inconsistent and occasionally struggled with his command. He has a fastball in the mid 90s, which he mixes well with a slider, curveball and changeup. Miller has a strong presence on the mound and can be dominant at times. After finishing strong in 2003, he has a chance to be one of the premier pitchers in the major leagues in 2004.

	W	SV	ERA	IP	H	BB	SO	B/I
2001 Houston	16	0	3.40	212	183	76	183	1.22
2002 Houston	15	0	3.28	165	151	62	144	1.29
2003 Houston	14	0	4.13	187	168	77	161	1.31

MILLWOOD, KEVIN - TR - b: 12/24/74 $15

Millwood was supposed to propel the Phillies to a division title but he has to bear some responsibility for the club not even winning a wild card spot. With the Braves, he was a money pitcher in the second half but last year his post All-Star break numbers were poor at 4-6 with a 4.58 ERA and especially damaging was his 2-4 record with a 4.68 ERA from late August on, which is not what the Phillies had in mind when they signed him and atypical of his past performance.

	W	SV	ERA	IP	H	BB	SO	B/I
2001 Atlanta	7	0	4.31	121	121	40	84	1.33
2002 Atlanta	18	0	3.24	217	186	65	178	1.16
2003 Philadelphia	14	0	4.01	222	210	68	169	1.25

MILTON, ERIC - TL - b: 8/4/75 $8

Eric Milton's 2003 season was nearly wiped out by extensive knee surgery, but he came back to contribute late in the year. When right, Milton throws plenty of strikes and bears down with runners in scoring position. He has a fastball that hits 94 mph when he's in midseason form, a good curveball, solid cut fastball and tough change up. Surgery in March removed 30 particles from his left knee and cleaned up inflamed areas. He was ordered to drop about 20 pounds to take the weight off his knees. Look for him to be one of the better lefthanders in the league in 2004.

	W	SV	ERA	IP	H	BB	SO	B/I
2001 Minnesota	15	0	4.32	220	222	61	157	1.28
2002 Minnesota	13	0	4.84	171	173	30	121	1.19
2003 Minnesota	1	0	2.65	17	15	1	7	0.94

MORRIS, MATT - TR - b: 8/9/74 $11

Over the past few seasons Morris has gone from a hard thrower who struck out a lot of hitters to one who has much more command of his pitches. Though he can still get his fastball to the plate in the low 90s consistently, his control has improved tremendously. He can throw his breaking pitches for strikes at any time in the count, and with maturity he has learned to challenge even the best hitters. Morris, who sat out all of 1999 after having reconstructive elbow surgery, missed nearly a month last season, though it was because of a badly sprained ankle and not from any arm problems. Morris is a big-game pitcher and, if healthy, should be counted on to win at least 15 to 18 games this season. He is one of the best pitchers around and has the potential to put together a season dominating enough to win the Cy Young award.

	W	SV	ERA	IP	H	BB	SO	B/I
2001 St. Louis	22	0	3.16	216	218	54	185	1.26
2002 St. Louis	17	0	3.42	210	210	64	171	1.30
2003 St. Louis	11	0	3.76	172	164	39	120	1.18

MOSS, DAMIAN - TL - b: 11/24/76 $0

Moss' 2003 season will be remembered more for what his former teams acquired for him in trades than for what Moss himself accomplished. The Braves received 20-game winner Russ Ortiz from the Giants, then San Francisco obtained Sidney Ponson to help them to a pennant. Moss' problem is simply that he doesn't throw enough strikes. The Australian doesn't seem to have enough confidence that he can get out major league batters with a high-80s fastball, changeup and curve. The change really seemed to desert him; lefthanders couldn't seem to get a hit against him two years ago; he didn't seem able to get them out last season. Instead of challenging hitters, Moss tries to nibble at the corners, then falls behind batters and either walks them or throws a fat pitch they can hit easily.

	W	SV	ERA	IP	H	BB	SO	B/I
2002 Atlanta	12	0	3.42	179	140	89	111	1.28
2003 SF/BAL	10	0	5.16	166	184	92	79	1.67

MOTA, GUILLERMO - TR - b: 7/25/73 $10

Mota has exceptional stuff. A consummate power pitcher, he features a fastball that routinely reaches the mid 90s and a biting slider, a package that keeps him just as effective against lefties as against righties. Mota, a converted shortstop from the breeding ground of shortstops, San Pedro de Macoris, D.R., is still refining his art. He still attempts to overthrow at times, which leads to his fastball flattening out, although he is working through that. He is a good fielder, though opponents can take advantage of his long delivery in the running game. He was expected to remain a solid setup man.

	W	SV	ERA	IP	H	BB	SO	B/I
2001 Montreal	1	0	5.26	49	51	18	31	1.39
2002 Los Angeles	1	0	4.15	61	45	27	49	1.19
2003 Los Angeles	6	1	1.97	105	78	26	99	0.99

MOUNCE, TONY - TL - b: 2/8/75 $0

Mounce is a soft-tossing lefty who relies on location and changing speeds to get batters out. Thus far, he has been able to do so at Triple-A but has been cuffed around in his brief major league trial. Like many rookie pitchers, Mounce's control deserted him at the big league level last season. At best, Mounce could develop into a Jamie Moyer-type pitcher, but it took Moyer years to get it right. Mounce is likely to see some time in the majors this season.

	W	SV	ERA	IP	H	BB	SO	B/I
2003 Texas	1	0	7.10	51	65	25	30	1.78

MOYER, JAMIE - TL - b: 11/18/62 $22

Moyer has the best winning percentage in the major leagues over the last eight years, although that number seems to have sneaked in under the radar gun, exactly as his fastball does. Moyer, to use the old line, has three speeds: slow, slower and slowest, while relying on pinpoint control and a changeup that is one of the best in the game - a late-breaker that heads down and away to righties. Hitters cannot cheat on Moyer, either, because he is not afraid to zip his fastball in on the hands. As might be expected of a finesse guy, Moyer does all the little things well. He fields his position with aplomb and has a good move to first. A late-bloomer, he won 20 for the first time at age 40 and is still going strong. Moyer was expected to again be near the top of the starting rotation.

	W	SV	ERA	IP	H	BB	SO	B/I
2001 Seattle	20	0	3.43	209	187	44	119	1.10
2002 Seattle	13	0	3.32	231	198	50	147	1.08
2003 Seattle	21	0	3.27	215	199	66	129	1.23

MULDER, MARK - TL - b: 8/5/77 $20

The fact that Mulder was able to pitch until August, and pitch as well as he did, with a stress fracture in his right hip shows what a competitor he really is. The hip had bothered him since early in the season, though that didn't stop him from posting the lowest ERA of his still brief career and completing a career high nine games. Part of the reason he was able to pitch as long as he did was because he doesn't rely on his fastball, which usually is in the upper-80s. He throws his big-breaking curve a lot and tries to sneak the fastball by hitters when they're expecting another offspeed offering. Mulder was expected to be fully healed by the start of the season. Assuming he doesn't suffer any setbacks, expect him to win 18-20 games and be one of the best pitchers in the league once again.

	W	SV	ERA	IP	H	BB	SO	B/I
2001 Oakland	21	0	3.45	229	214	51	153	1.16
2002 Oakland	19	0	3.47	207	182	55	159	1.14
2003 Oakland	15	0	3.13	187	180	40	128	1.18

MULHOLLAND, TERRY - TL - b: 3/9/63 $0

At age 41, Mullholland knows the art of being a major league pitcher and while his best years are long over, he is a virtual pitching coach for strong armed young moundsmen. Mullholland hits spots and changes speed with a mild assortment of curve, change, and fastball and if he feels confident, he might throws his slider a little.

	W	SV	ERA	IP	H	BB	SO	B/I
2001 PIT/LA	1	0	5.08	65	79	19	42	1.49
2002 LA/CLE	3	0	5.70	79	101	21	38	1.54
2003 Cleveland	3	0	4.91	99	117	37	42	1.56

MUNRO, PETE - TR - b: 6/14/75 $0

Munro was a pleasant surprise in 2002, but was very ineffective in 2003. Munro has good enough command of his marginal major league stuff to keep the ball away from the middle of the plate. His fastball reaches 90 MPH, and his breaking pitches and changeup keep hitters off balance. He managed to break into the Astros rotation in May after making 21 appearances as a reliever, but was sent to the minors in early August because of his struggles. He'll begin the spring trying to win a job as a reliever or number four or five starter.

	W	SV	ERA	IP	H	BB	SO	B/I
2002 Houston	5	0	3.57	81	89	23	45	1.39
2003 Houston	3	0	4.67	54	63	26	27	1.65

MUSSINA, MIKE - TR - b: 12/8/68 $22

Mussina was the hottest pitcher in baseball early last season, when he won his first seven starts. He was just two games over .500 the rest of the way, but he now has won at least 11 games for the 12th consecutive season, seven of those with 17 or more. Only once did he fail to pitch at least five innings. Moose features a low-90s fastball, a knuckle curve and a changeup that makes him unusually tough against lefthanded batters. Mussina, who helps himself with his defense and holds runners well, will begin this season one short of 200 career wins.

	W	SV	ERA	IP	H	BB	SO	B/I
2001 New York - AL	17	0	3.15	228	202	42	214	1.07
2002 New York - AL	18	0	4.05	216	208	48	182	1.19
2003 New York - AL	17	0	3.40	215	192	40	195	1.08

MYERS, BRETT - TR - b: 8/17/80 $5

Myers has brutal stuff. He throws a hopping fastball and a fall-off-the-table curve. If he has a downside it's his inexperience which makes him vulnerable when he gets in trouble. Every pitcher has tough times in almost every game but the successful pitchers know how to work out of trouble. Once Myers acquires this ability, he'll take off.

	W	SV	ERA	IP	H	BB	SO	B/I
2002 Philadelphia	4	0	4.25	72	73	29	34	1.42
2003 Philadelphia	14	0	4.43	193	205	76	143	1.46

MYERS, MIKE - TL - b: 6/26/69 $0

A fan at Bank One Ballpark dons the Mike Myers mask - you know, the scary guy from the horror movie series - every time lefthander Mike Myers has entered the game the last two seasons in Arizona. Neither scared anyone in 2003, when Myers had the worst season of his pro career as his control and confidence seemed to desert him. A situational sidearmer, Myers always had been more effective against lefthanded hitters than righties throughout his career, although both battered him last year. He lost his job as a late-inning specialist and spent the final two months of the season deep in the bullpen. He needs to return to previous form to regain his spot.

	W	SV	ERA	IP	H	BB	SO	B/I
2001 Colorado	2	0	3.60	40	32	24	36	1.40
2002 Arizona	4	4	4.38	37	39	17	31	1.51
2003 Arizona	0	0	5.70	36	38	21	21	1.63

NANCE, SHANE - TL - b: 9/7/77 $0

Nance is a hard-thrower acquired by Milwaukee with another top prospect, Ben Diggins, from Los Angeles at the 2002 trading deadline. Nance gets his fastball up over 90 MPH and has a sharp breaking pitch that can be murder of lefties. Righties ate him up in his first trip to the majors, however. Nance threw 34.2 consecutive scoreless innings at Triple-A Indianapolis in 2003, the longest scoreless streak in the minors last year. If Nance can develop a pitch to counter lefties, he'll have the other qualities necessary to remain in a major league bullpen.

	W	SV	ERA	IP	H	BB	SO	B/I
2003 Milwaukee	0	0	4.81	24	34	10	25	1.81

NATHAN, JOE - TR - b: 11/22/74 $7

A converted starter, Nathan was a reliable late-inning reliever in 2003. His velocity was back after missing almost two full seasons because of major shoulder surgery, and he managed an outstanding record because he was able to keep the Giants close enough for their potent offense to score the winning runs. He didn't give up many hits last year and had enough command so that he wasn't walking the bases loaded every other appearance. Nathan never was considered a top-flight prospect as a starter, though he has enough to be a solid guy in the late innings. After all, if Tim Worrell can save 38 games in one season, Nathan can too.

	W	SV	ERA	IP	H	BB	SO	B/I
2003 San Francisco	12	0	2.96	79	51	33	83	1.06

NEAGLE, DENNY - TL - b: 9/13/68 $0

Neagle's disjointed season ended for good in late July when he was placed on the disabled list with inflammation in his left elbow, but he never really had much of a season. After suffering elbow tightness during spring training, Neagle opened the 2003 season on the disabled list and was not activated until late May. He made seven forgettable starts - giving up 12 homers in 35 innings - before being shut down for good. Although Neagle was paid $55 million to join Mike Hampton as Colorado's one and two starters in 2001, he has never

---

pitched up to his 20-win 1997 form. He has been awful, and was demoted to the bullpen in July of 2002. Neagle' best pitch is a changeup he spots on the outside part of the plate, although he has not been able to command the pitch with any regularity recently. His fastball tops out in the high 80s, so he is not going to throw it by anyone. He must locate. He excels at the peripherals - he fields his position well and holds runners on, although he is not particularly quick to the plate and can be run on. Neagle is a good hitter; not only can he bunt, he puts the bat on the ball well enough to be asked to hit-and-run. Injuries and inexact location have sent his career into a downward spiral, and Neagle was expected to enter spring training on the outside of the rotation looking in.

	W	SV	ERA	IP	H	BB	SO	B / I
2001 Colorado	9	0	5.38	170	192	60	139	1.48
2002 Colorado	8	0	5.26	164	170	63	111	1.42
2003 Colorado	2	0	7.90	35	47	12	21	1.67

NEAL, BLAINE - TR - b: 4/6/78 $0

Neal is a big righthander with a strong arm who bounced between the majors and minors when Marlins regular got hurt. Neal was a succesful minor league closer and he lives or dies with a mid-90s fastball and a decent curve.

	W	SV	ERA	IP	H	BB	SO	B / I
2001 Florida	0	0	6.75	5	7	5	3	2.25
2002 Florida	3	0	2.73	33	32	14	33	1.39
2003 Florida	0	0	8.14	21	38	9	10	2.24

NELSON, JEFF - TR - b: 11/17/66 $4

When the Yankees' bullpen was struggling last season, the call went out: "Get me a Jeff Nelson type." Instead, GM Brian Cashman got the original Jeff Nelson, only a little the worse for wear after 2 1/2 years in Seattle. He reached a major league-career high in saves for the Mariners while Kazuhiro Sasaki was out, but returned to his accustomed setup role in New York. He wasn't as successful as he had been between 1996 and 2000. The best way to get to the 6'8" Nelson is to wait him out and hope he misses the plate instead of throwing his sweeping sidearm slider for nearly unhittable strikes.

	W	SV	ERA	IP	H	BB	SO	B / I
2001 Seattle	4	4	2.76	65	30	44	88	1.13
2002 Seattle	3	2	3.94	46	36	27	55	1.38
2003 SEA/NY - AL	4	8	3.74	55	51	24	68	1.36

NEN, ROBB - TR - b: 11/28/69 $10

Nen missed all of last season after having surgery to fix a partially torn rotator cuff on his throwing shoulder. While it is never good news to have that kind of surgery, especially at Nen's age, his surgeon performed the same procedure on Curt Schilling in 1999 and he was able to come back to full strength. Even if he loses a couple of miles off his fastball because of the surgery, he still will have plenty left to go with his outstanding slider. Assuming Nen is healthy, and he was expected to be ready for the start of the season, he should have no problem getting saves.

	W	SV	ERA	IP	H	BB	SO	B / I
2001 San Francisco	4	45	3.01	77	58	22	93	1.01
2002 San Francisco	6	43	2.20	74	64	20	81	1.14

NEU, MIKE - TR - b: 3/9/78 $0

A Rule Five selection before the 2003 season, the Athletics kept Neu at the back of their bullpen all year, pitching him only in mop-up roles during games that had already been decided. In spite of that, Neu had a successful rookie season and showed a lot of promise. Although he has only an average fastball, one that rarely tops 90 MPH, he features a devastating changeup. He had some control problems last year, likely due to some rookie jitters, yet he rebounded in the second half of the season to post an ERA of around 2.00. Neu was a dominating closer in college with Miami, and he could succeed in that role if given a chance. That is likely a couple years down the road, however, as he will have to prove himself pitching in the seventh and eighth innings first.

	W	SV	ERA	IP	H	BB	SO	B/I
2003 Oakland	0	1	3.64	42	43	26	20	1.64

NEUGEBAUER, NICK - TR - b: 7/15/80 $0

Highly regarded Nick Neugebauer was just not ready in 2002. He struggled to control an explosive combination of power pitches, featuring a fastball that approaches 100 MPH. After Neugebauer was bothered by shoulder trouble he went to the minors and didn't return to the Brewers until September roster expansion. Although he started again the Brewers limited his innings to protect his arm and shoulder. Aside from the big fastball, Neugebauer has a great slider, a strong curve and a good changeup. He missed all of 2003 because of shoulder surgery. If he can show he's healthy, it's just a matter of time before he puts it together.

	W	SV	ERA	IP	H	BB	SO	B/I
2001 Milwaukee	1	0	7.50	6	6	6	11	2.00
2002 Milwaukee	1	0	4.72	55	56	44	47	1.81

NOMO, HIDEO - TR - b: 8/31/68 $17

Nomo equaled his career high with 16 victories in 2003 when hitters again were troubled by his unqiue, stop-and-go delivery that catches them off-balance. Nomo is a two-pitch pitcher, working the top of the zone with a four-seam fastball in the low 90s and balancing that with a diving split-finger pitch in the mid-80s. He is deadly when ahead in the count. His twisting motion leaves him in poor fielding position, and his long delivery does little to deter the running game. He has allowed more stolen bases than any pitcher in the major leagues since he arrived in the U.S. in 1995. Yikes. He gets his hacks at the plate and can surprise with some power. He was expected to be near the top of the starting rotation again this season.

	W	SV	ERA	IP	H	BB	SO	B/I
2001 Boston	13	0	4.50	198	171	96	220	1.35
2002 Los Angeles	16	0	3.39	220	189	101	193	1.32
2003 Los Angeles	16	0	3.09	218	175	98	177	1.25

OBERMUELLER, WES - TR - b: 12/22/76 $0

Obermueller had a cup of coffee with Kansas City in 2002 and a spot in the Milwaukee rotation late in 2003 after injuries struck the team. Obermueller has a major league average fastball and breaking pitch, although location was an issue. A second-round draftee in 1999, he must start to get ahead of hitters or his stay in the majors will be a short one. He was expected to open the season in Triple-A, where he belongs at this point in his career.

	W	SV	ERA	IP	H	BB	SO	B/I
2003 Milwaukee	2	0	5.07	66	81	25	34	1.61

OHKA, TOMOKAZU - TR - b: 3/18/76 $8

Ohka was not as consistent as he had been in 2002. Only once in 2002 did his monthly earned run average exceed 5.00. In 2003 his monthly earned run average topped the 5.00 mark three times and he never brought it lower than 3.18 (April). What caused the downturn and what can be expected of Ohka now? The simple answer is Ohka is an average pitcher with average stuff and decent control. Average pitchers should get hit harder by above average teams and Ohka was often battered by good teams. Collectively, Atlanta, St. Louis, Houston and Florida beat him like a rented mule and that trend is likely to continue in 2004. Against weaker teams, Ohka held together somewhat better but he is not a power pitcher and more teams will get to him this year.

He really doesn't match up well against righthanded batters or left and it would be no surprise to see Ohka permanently banished to the bullpen at some point in 2004.

	W	SV	ERA	IP	H	BB	SO	B / I
2001 BOS/MON	3	0	5.47	107	134	29	68	1.52
2002 Montreal	13	0	3.18	193	194	45	118	1.24
2003 Montreal	10	0	4.16	199	233	45	118	1.40

OLIVER, DARREN - TL - b: 10/6/70 $0

Oliver was a quality starter in the middle 1990s, but lately has been one of those patch-the-cracks-in-the rotation guys who latches on with a team that a) suffers excessive injuries or b) does not get the production expected from an up-and-comer. In 2002, that was Boston. Last year, it was Colorado, where Oliver was a season-long member of the starting rotation because of injuries to Denny Neagle and Denny Stark and the slow development of Aaron Cook. Oliver showed he could still do a job, too, posting double-digit victories for the first time since 1997, when he was 13-12 in Texas after winning 14 games the year before. Oliver has a tremendous curveball and a fastball that touches the low 90s, so he has the stuff to win. He is durable and a proven an innings-eater, a top commodity in Coors Field. Oliver, the son of former major league outfielder Bob Oliver, is only 33 and could be catching his second wind. At the same time, he was expected to enter spring training once again having to battle for a job in the starting rotation.

	W	SV	ERA	IP	H	BB	SO	B / I
2001 Texas	11	0	6.02	154	189	65	104	1.65
2002 Boston	4	0	4.66	58	70	27	32	1.67
2003 Colorado	13	0	5.04	180	201	61	88	1.45

OLSEN, KEVIN - TR - b: 7/26/76 $0

Olsen had a bigger relief role in 2002 than in 2003, but he was DL'd when he was hit in the head by a line drive in June and he didn't return until September. He will vie for a middle relief spot in 2004. His stuff is alright and he's got a good approach to pitching, but he doesn't project as more than a middle reliever and spot starter.

	W	SV	ERA	IP	H	BB	SO	B / I
2001 Florida	0	0	1.20	15	11	2	13	0.87
2002 Florida	0	0	4.52	56	57	31	38	1.58
2003 Florida	0	0	12.75	12	25	4	12	2.42

OROPESA, EDDIE - TL - b: 11/23/71 $0

Oropesa celebrated his first year as a naturalized citizen with his best year on the mound, ascending to the role of situational specialist in Arizona after Mike Myers' decline. Oropesa, a native of Cuba who emigrated in 1993 and was naturalized during a spring training ceremony in Miami, has a moving fastball that while not overpowering is spotted well. He also features a big breaking ball that is particularly difficult for lefthanded hitters to hang in against. Oropesa has a good move to first base and is difficult to run against. He was expected to inherit the role of lefty specialist in the bullpen.

	W	SV	ERA	IP	H	BB	SO	B / I
2001 Philadelphia	1	0	4.74	19	16	17	15	1.74
2002 Arizona	2	0	10.32	25	39	15	18	2.13
2003 Arizona	3	0	5.81	39	38	27	39	1.68

OROSCO, JESSE - TL - b: 4/21/57 $0

Although Orosco will be 47 this season, he could probably still find a job. He's not the pitcher he once was, and struggled terribly in 2003 but he's capable of getting a tough lefthanded hitter or two out in tight situations. The problem last season was that righties hit almost .400 against him, and got on base almost half the time they came to the plate. He's appeared in more games than any pitcher in the history of baseball, and given the fact that teams are always searching for lefthanded relievers, Orosco always finds a taker. While Orosco's not in a position to put up numbers, he's still capable.

	W	SV	ERA	IP	H	BB	SO	B / I
2001 Los Angeles	0	0	3.94	16	17	7	21	1.50
2002 Los Angeles	1	1	3.00	27	24	12	22	1.33
2003 SD/NYY/MIN	2	2	7.68	34	41	21	29	1.82

ORTIZ, RAMON - TR - b: 5/23/76 $6

Ortiz has great stuff: a mid-90s fastball, an effective changeup and a slider. Historically a strikeout pitcher, Ortiz has recently become more of a finesse pitcher, relying on his defense to make the outs. Ortiz likes to challenge hitters, and has been homer-prone at times during his career, especially against lefthanded hitters. Ortiz followed up a solid 2002 with a disappointing season last year; in particular, Ortiz struggled after the All-Star break. Still a quality pitcher, Ortiz needs to improve his game-to-game consistency in order to take the next step into the top ranks of starters.

	W	SV	ERA	IP	H	BB	SO	B / I
2001 Anaheim	13	0	4.36	208	223	76	135	1.43
2002 Anaheim	15	0	3.77	217	188	68	162	1.18
2003 Anaheim	16	0	5.20	180	209	63	94	1.51

ORTIZ, RUSS - TR - b: 6/5/74 $12

As the Braves designated winning pitcher, Russ Ortiz cracked the 20-win plateau and led the league in victories as he put together a Cy Young-type campaign in his first year in Atlanta. Still, despite the sparkling won-lost record, he didn't pitch any better than he had in winning 67 games for the Giants the previous five years; having a powerhouse Braves offense behind him surely made a big difference. Ortiz's fastball is described as "heavy" by opposition hitters; it seems harder than it is, even at its 93 MPH top speed. Ortiz's low-90s cut fastball can be even more effective than the four-seam heater; however, Ortiz has trouble controlling it, likewise for his hard curveball which can be very difficult to hit, but even more difficult for Ortiz to throw in the strikezone. Despite putting a lot of batters on base via the walk, Ortiz refuses to give in and groove a pitch. He stays out of the hitter's zones — and away from home runs — by keeping his pitches down and working on the hitters' hands; he's one of the more uncomfortable at-bats in the big leagues. Ortiz is a good fielder who works hard to control the running game. Big and burly, Ortiz often works deep into the ballgame, just as expected of the ace of the staff. He's a big league ace in the prime of his career; Ortiz should expect to succeed at the top of the rotation for the foreseeable future.

	W	SV	ERA	IP	H	BB	SO	B / I
2001 San Francisco	17	0	3.29	218	187	91	169	1.27
2002 San Francisco	14	0	3.61	214	191	94	137	1.33
2003 Atlanta	21	0	3.82	212	177	102	149	1.31

OSUNA, ANTONIO - TR - b: 4/12/73 $1

After he had closed part time for the 2002 White Sox, the Yankees hoped Osuna could be part of their bullpen solution last season. Instead, he was a bit of the problem. He was hit fairly hard (.282 average), didn't do a good job keeping inherited runners from scoring and blew his only save opportunity. By rehabbing from shoulder surgery in 2001, Osuna has his fastball up near the mid-90s to go with a slider and screwball. Because of a groin injury, he was twice on the disabled list last season, bringing his career total of stints on the DL to nine.

	W	SV	ERA	IP	H	BB	SO	B / I
2002 Chicago - AL	8	11	3.86	68	64	28	66	1.36
2003 New York - AL	2	0	3.73	51	58	20	47	1.54

OSWALT, ROY - TR - b: 8/29/77 $14

Oswalt made a sensational major league debut in 2001 after being recalled from Triple-A in May. He was even better in 2002, as he established himself as one of the top pitchers in baseball. His 2003 season was a disappointment as he had three stints on the disabled list with a recurring groin injury. When healthy, he was effective with outstanding command of a fastball in the 94 to 96 MPH range and a knee-buckling curve. He effectively mixes in an occasional slider and change-up, and when all pitches are working, he is dominant. He has exceptional poise on the mound, works quickly and goes right after the hitters. Oswalt is expected to be fully recovered in 2004 and should regain his status as one of the top pitchers in the major leagues.

		W	SV	ERA	IP	H	BB	SO	B / I
2001	Houston	14	0	2.73	141	126	24	144	1.06
2002	Houston	19	0	3.01	233	215	62	208	1.19
2003	Houston	10	0	2.97	127	116	29	108	1.14

PADILLA, VICENTE - TR - b: 9/27/77 $16

Padilla's record was identical to Millwood's but Padilla seems to have more of an upside while Millwood has peaked. Padilla should move his game up another notch in 2004. If he does, he will become the Phillies ace. He has incredible stuff and he varies his delivery to keep hitters from locking on. He's confident enough to work his plan and let the opposition hack away because it's tough to make solid contact and batters tend to beat balls into the ground. With his stuff, there is no need to try to blow everyone away. Unlike Millwood, Wolf and Myers, Padilla got tougher down the stretch.

		W	SV	ERA	IP	H	BB	SO	B / I
2001	Philadelphia	3	0	4.24	34	36	12	29	1.41
2002	Philadelphia	14	0	3.28	206	198	53	128	1.22
2003	Philadelphia	14	0	3.62	209	196	62	133	1.24

PARK, CHAN HO - TR - b: 6/30/73 $0

Park lost most of the 2003 season to back problems that surfaced during spring training and then flared up again early in the season. Even more troubling was a seemingly total loss of confidence that may or may not improve with Park's physical soundness. Park has had little, if any, success in his two American League seasons and must be considered a major risk for the upcoming campaign. If Park is healthy and can string together a few good outings, he could return to something approaching his previous levels of performance.

		W	SV	ERA	IP	H	BB	SO	B / I
2001	Los Angeles	15	0	3.50	234	183	91	218	1.17
2002	Texas	9	0	5.74	146	154	78	121	1.59
2003	Texas	1	0	7.58	30	34	25	16	1.99

PARRIS, STEVE - TR - b: 12/17/67 $0

In the winter prior to the 2003 season, Parris signed a minor league contract with Triple-A Durham, then was called up the the Devil Rays at the end of March, but lost his job on the rotation by early May, getting sent to the bullpen. He released by the team in June. He ended last season like he did at the end of 2002, looking to sign with a team that could use him as a fifth starter. He still has sharp action on his breaking ball but his velocity has been off, and basically gave up too many hits and walks to look appealing to almost any team.

		W	SV	ERA	IP	H	BB	SO	B / I
2001	Toronto	4	0	4.60	105	126	41	49	1.57
2002	Toronto	5	0	5.98	75	96	35	48	1.74
2003	Tampa Bay	0	0	6.18	44	60	13	14	1.67

PARRISH, JOHN - TL - b: 11/26/77 $1

Parrish missed all of 2002 after suffering a torn right knee ligament during a rundown in an exhibition game. On one level, it's conceivable that Parrish could mess up a rundown because he has established a record as a poor fielder. On a more important level, it's important that his injury wasn't to his arm. He had been a starter, mostly in the minors, before then, but the Orioles brought him along slowly as a reliever this season. He gained confidence as a closer at Double-A Bowie before Baltimore recalled him in mid-August. Pitching mostly against contending teams, Parrish proved very difficult to hit for either lefthanded or righthanded batters. The smallish (5'11", 180) pitcher doesn't throw hard, but got outs last season by spotting his fastball better and changing speeds to keep batters off balance.

	W	SV	ERA	IP	H	BB	SO	B / I
2001 Baltimore	1	0	6.14	22	22	17	20	1.77
2003 Baltimore	0	0	1.90	24	17	8	15	1.05

PATTERSON, JOHN - TR - b: 1/30/78 $0

A funny thing happened on Patterson's seemingly certain inclusion in the 2003 Arizona starting rotation. He never got there. Patterson struggled with his breaking ball in spring training and despite the fact that he entered camp with a virtual lock on a starting spot, he broke camp with Triple-A Tucson, where he again dominated. Patterson, all the way back from Tommy John surgery in 2000, has a mid-90s fastball. What made Patterson the fifth overall selection in the 1996 draft, however, is his 12-to-6 curve ball that was above major league average the day he signed as a loophole free agent with Arizona. Patterson again appears as a solid contender for a spot in the major league starting rotation, although he struggled in brief stints with the parent club in 2003 and may again be on the outside looking in.

	W	SV	ERA	IP	H	BB	SO	B / I
2002 Arizona	2	0	3.22	31	27	7	31	1.11
2003 Arizona	1	1	6.05	55	61	30	43	1.65

PAVANO, CARL - TR - b: 1/8/76 $9

The past two years have gone relatively well for Pavano in that he didn't break down. He built up his arm by relieving and starting in 2002 and he cracked the 200 inning mark as a starter for the first time in his career in 2003. Look at Mark Prior, Kerry Wood and all the other young studs in the game. That was supposed to Pavano's career path before he destroyed his elbow in 2000. Pavano was once a coddled prospect but now he is a 28-year-old project and he has to deliver or he will follow the same paths traveled by once-heralded prospects such as Steve Karsay, Todd Van Poppel and Jeff D'Amico.

	W	SV	ERA	IP	H	BB	SO	B / I
2001 Montreal	8	0	6.33	42	59	16	36	1.76
2002 MON/FLA	6	0	5.16	136	174	45	92	1.61
2003 Florida	12	0	4.30	201	204	49	133	1.26

PEAVY, JAKE - TR - b: 5/31/81 $7

Peavy made a strong impression in his first full season in the major leagues in 2003, winning in double-digits while limiting opponents to fewer hits than innings. He has a fastball that touches the low 90s, although his success is more the result of his ability to spot three pitches - his changeup and slider are above average. He has a good feel for his craft and is not afraid to throw any pitch in any count. He helps himself in the field and at the plate, too. He is agile on the mound, although he must work to hold runners close. Although he struggled with the bat in 2003, his first career hit was a bases-clearing double against Randy Johnson in 2003. Although only 22, Peavy was expected to open the season as the No. 1 or No. 2 starter in the rotation.

	W	SV	ERA	IP	H	BB	SO	B/I
2002 San Diego	6	0	4.51	98	106	33	90	1.42
2003 San Diego	12	0	4.11	195	173	82	156	1.31

PENNY, BRAD - TR - b: 5/24/78 $13

Penny can pitch but in years that he's pitched a lot, he's broken down the next year. He made 32 starts and threw 196 innings over the 2003 season and then he threw more in the playoffs but, fears that he will break down again should be lessened somewhat by the fact that his arm is as seasoned as it will ever get. Frequently, when pitchers go through physical ups and downs early in their career, they get into a nice groove for the rest of their career. Penny is a good bet to improve in 2004.

	W	SV	ERA	IP	H	BB	SO	B/I
2001 Florida	10	0	3.69	205	183	54	154	1.16
2002 Florida	8	0	4.66	129	148	50	93	1.53
2003 Florida	14	0	4.13	196	195	56	138	1.28

PERCIVAL, TROY - TR - b: 8/9/69 $26

A pure power pitcher, Percival can overpower the opposition with his high-90s fastball, while mixing in an outstanding curve for called third strikes. As he enters his mid-30s, Percival will need to rely more on location and pitch selection than pure heat, and indications last season were that he is making the transition successfully. Injuries have been a persistent problem for Percival, who has had shoulder, back, neck, elbow and hip problems during his career. Last year, Percival missed time with a degenerative hip condition that caused him to lower his leg kick. By the end of the season, however, he was pretty much unhittable again. Percival has a tendency to go through short streaks of wildness, but can still be a dominant closer when fully healthy.

	W	SV	ERA	IP	H	BB	SO	B/I
2001 Anaheim	4	39	2.65	57	39	18	71	0.99
2002 Anaheim	4	40	1.92	56	38	25	68	1.12
2003 Anaheim	0	33	3.47	49	33	23	48	1.14

PEREZ, ODALIS - TL - b: 6/7/78 $10

Perez has blossomed in his two seasons in the Los Angeles rotation, although he struggled at times with location in 2003. He has a quality repertoire that begins with a moving fastball in the low 90s and includes a curveball and a change. Perez understands his art and does not walk batters. When he misses with his location, however, he can give up the long ball, as he did 28 times in 2003. Perez helps himself in other areas, too. He is quick off the mound to field bunts and has one of the best pickoff moves in the majors. He is a good bunter and usually puts the ball in play when asked to swing away. He was expected to be in the upper tier of the starting rotation this season.

	W	SV	ERA	IP	H	BB	SO	B/I
2001 Atlanta	7	0	4.91	95	108	39	71	1.54
2002 Los Angeles	15	0	3.00	222	182	38	155	0.99
2003 Los Angeles	12	0	4.52	185	191	46	141	1.28

PEREZ, OLIVER - TL - b: 8/15/81 $0

Still very raw and when you review his stats there is little to like — until you get to his strikeouts – 141 in only 126 innings. It gets more interesting when you see him pitch because hitters have no clue when he's on and they miss his offerings by a foot. Perez was very inconsistent but he also had a few outings when he showed incredible stuff and gave evidence of what he might become when he develops some consistency and the know-how to get out of a jam. As nasty as he can be, he can blow up just as fast when he walks a couple of hitters and then he tends to over throw, his mechanics desert him, and he's in the shower.

He fanned 11 batters in a six inning stint and lost. He fanned 10 and 13 in seven innings and didn't figure in the decision and he nailed seven guys in four innings. Filthy, filthy stuff.

	W	SV	ERA	IP	H	BB	SO	B/I
2002 San Diego	4	0	3.50	90	71	48	94	1.32
2003 SD/PIT	4	0	5.47	127	129	77	141	1.63

PERSON, ROBERT - TR - b: 10/6/69 $0

Person won 34 games as a Phillies starter between 1999 and 2001, but the strain of pitching more than 200 innings in his 15-7 season as their ace in '01 resulted in August 2002 shoulder surgery. He has been mostly on the disabled list, pitching less than 100 innings, the last two years. Boston signed Person before last season, hoping he could help its bullpen. But after seven mostly unsuccessful appearances in May and June, the Sox shut him down because of an inflamed hip. Before the surgery, Person threw hard but was held back by erratic control. Now he can't throw as hard, and his career is in jeopardy.

	W	SV	ERA	IP	H	BB	SO	B/I
2001 Philadelphia	15	0	4.19	208	179	80	183	1.24
2002 Philadelphia	4	0	5.44	88	79	51	61	1.48
2003 Boston	0	1	7.69	12	11	8	10	1.62

PETTITTE, ANDY - TL - b: 6/15/72 $15

We have become accustomed to seeing Pettitte peering intently over his glove while pitching during the postseason. Last year, he finished the regular season strong, with 16 victories in his final 18 decisions for his first 20-win season since 1996. Still, lefthanders hit him surprisingly well (.321 average). An intense competitor, Pettitte gets batters out with a four-seam fastball, cut fastball and changeup that he can work up or down in the strike zone. Most of his outs, however, come on the ground. He's regarded as so good at holding runners that he didn't even have to pick off any in 2003. Pettitte picked a good year to become a free agent.

	W	SV	ERA	IP	H	BB	SO	B/I
2001 New York - AL	15	0	3.99	200	224	41	164	1.32
2002 New York - AL	13	0	3.27	135	144	32	97	1.31
2003 New York - AL	21	0	4.02	208	227	50	180	1.33

PINEIRO, JOEL - TR - b: 9/25/78 $14

Piniero has been a quality starter since bursting onto the scene at the midway point of the 2001 season. Piniero has a full complement in his repertoire — he throws a four-seam and a two-seam fastball, a slider, a curve and a changeup. He locates well and while not overpowering keeps hitters off balance. He helps himself as a fielder, although he must work on holding runners closer at first base. Nevertheless, Piniero's star is still rising and he was expected to be a fixture in the starting rotation.

	W	SV	ERA	IP	H	BB	SO	B/I
2001 Seattle	6	0	2.03	75	50	21	56	0.94
2002 Seattle	14	0	3.24	194	189	54	136	1.25
2003 Seattle	16	0	3.78	212	192	76	151	1.27

PLESAC, DAN - TL - b: 2/4/62 $2

Old rubber arm. Plesac's vital stats: Age 42 - Games: 58 - Innings pitched: 33 – Ks: 37. Once a hard thrower, the Sac-man now has just a low-90s fastball and is more likely to retire batters by making them chase junk pitches or his slider. He's an excellent fielder. He was last a full-time closer in 1990, and has been good at coming in troublesome spots; in recent years he has stranded about 80 per cent of his inherited runners.

	W	SV	ERA	IP	H	BB	SO	B/I
2001 Toronto	4	1	3.57	45	34	24	68	3.57
2002 TOR/PHI	3	1	4.21	36	27	18	41	1.24
2003 Philadelphia	2	2	2.70	33	29	11	37	1.20

POLITTE, CLIFF - TR - b: 2/27/74 $0

A mid to high-90s thrower who has good movement on his pitches and better control than his walks totals would imply, Politte appeared every bit the closer-in-waiting at the start of last season but after being handed the job when Kelvim Escobar was moved to the starting rotation, he failed miserably. After spending much of the season on the shelf with a shoulder injury, Politte came back to find a much less important role waiting for him in the Toronto bullpen. Neither as bad as he looked last year nor as good as he looked in 2002, Politte will start the season in a middle relief role with an eye on regaining at least the setup sort of role he had two years ago but he faces an uphill battle and must demonstrate that last season was simply an off-year. He's a longshot, at best, to end up back in a closer's role and the 12 saves of last year will likely end up being an eventual career-high.

	W	SV	ERA	IP	H	BB	SO	B/I
2001 Philadelphia	2	0	2.42	26	24	8	23	1.23
2002 Toronto	3	1	3.66	74	57	28	72	1.15
2003 Toronto	1	12	5.66	49	52	17	40	1.40

PONSON, SIDNEY - TR - b: 11/2/76 $12

Ponson rebounded in a big way in 2003 after missing good chunks of the previous two seasons with arm and shoulder problems. When he's healthy, he mixes in all four of his pitches, fastball, curve, slider and splitter, well. He has improved in the last couple of years primarily because he has improved his command. It will be very interesting to see how Ponson responds after signing the big-money deal he was expected to ink after becoming a free agent for the first time. Even if he doesn't get any better, or even takes a small step back, he still will be a pretty good pitcher. He should be good for 15 wins and an ERA of a little less than 4.00.

	W	SV	ERA	IP	H	BB	SO	B/I
2001 Baltimore	5	0	4.94	138	161	37	84	1.43
2002 Baltimore	7	0	4.09	176	172	63	120	1.34
2003 BAL/SF	17	0	3.75	216	211	61	134	1.26

POWELL, JAY - TR - b: 1/9/72 $5

Powell throws a hard, sinking fastball that helps him against lefthanded hitters, and a slider. Late last season, he was working on a sidearm delivery to help him against righthanded hitters, and the early results were promising. Powell generally keeps the ball in the park, and good infield defense behind him is an important ingredient to his success. Powell has never started a game in the big leagues, and he should continue as a setup man in the majors this year.

	W	SV	ERA	IP	H	BB	SO	B/I
2001 HOU/COL	5	7	3.24	75	75	31	54	1.41
2002 Texas	3	0	3.44	50	50	24	35	1.49
2003 Texas	3	0	7.82	59	75	34	40	1.86

PRIOR, MARK - TR - b: 9/7/80 $25

Prior has an immense amount of talent in his powerful right arm and has had seemingly little trouble adjusting to being in a big league starting rotation. Prior was almost an instant success when first called up to the big leagues in 2002, and absolutely dominated NL hitters over the last two months of last season. He has an overpowering fastball which he throws consistently in the low 90s, and supplements that pitch with a good curve, which he can throw at any time in the count. Many think Prior has the best mechanics of any pitcher in baseball, meaning the odds of him having arm problems are far lower than other hurlers. Assuming he stays healthy, he is going to be one of the top pitchers in the game for many, many years to come.

	W	SV	ERA	IP	H	BB	SO	B/I
2002 Chicago - NL	6	0	3.32	117	98	38	147	1.17
2003 Chicago - NL	18	0	2.43	211	183	50	245	1.10

QUANTRILL, PAUL - TR - b: 11/3/68 $7

Quantrill had a quietly phenomenal season as a setup man/situational specialist in Los Angeles, posting a career-low ERA while giving up only two home runs in 77.1 innings. He is not overpowering with a fastball that tops out at 90 MPH, although he keeps that at calf-level while mixing in a slider. He has a quirky delivery that gets batters out in front. He has appeared in 80 or more games in each of the last three seasons, although instead of tiring him out that seems to lend more break to his sinking fastball. He is a good fielder and works to hold runners. He has earned his spurs as a quality setup man and will continue in that role.

	W	SV	ERA	IP	H	BB	SO	B/I
2001 Toronto	11	2	3.04	83	86	12	58	1.18
2002 Los Angeles	5	1	2.70	77	80	25	53	1.37
2003 Los Angeles	2	1	1.75	77	61	15	44	0.98

QUEVEDO, RUBEN - TR - b: 1/5/79 $0

Quevedo was removed from the Milwaukee rotation in late June, after he gave up five runs (and two home runs) while getting two outs. He really was awful, giving up at least one home run in each of his eight 2003 starts while at times completely losing the plate, giving up five walks per nine innings. His lack of success is no mystery. His fastball tops out in the high 80s, yet he continues to work high in the zone. He throws a slider, curve and change, although all are just average. He weighs too much to move well enough to help himself on the mound and does not have an extra-base hit in 98 major league at-bats. If he makes the rotation, that team is reaching.

	W	SV	ERA	IP	H	BB	SO	B/I
2001 San Diego	4	0	4.61	56	56	30	60	1.52
2002 Milwaukee	6	0	5.76	139	159	68	93	1.63
2003 Milwaukee	1	0	6.74	43	53	23	19	1.78

RADKE, BRAD - TR - b: 10/27/72 $15

Still one of the game's best control pitchers, Radke is a credit to any staff. His change up is excellent and he really dominates when he sets it up by pounding his 91 MPH fastball in on hitters. Consistency was a problem in 2003, as Radke uncharacteristically laid many pitches over the plate. But he recovered late to pitch his team into a playoff race. He also used his curveball more, with positive results. He's not among the upper echelon starters in baseball, but can win 15 games a year and throw 200 innings.

	W	SV	ERA	IP	H	BB	SO	B/I
2001 Minnesota	15	0	3.94	226	235	26	137	1.15
2002 Minnesota	9	0	4.72	118	124	20	62	1.22
2003 Minnesota	14	0	4.49	212	242	28	120	1.27

RAMIREZ, ERASMO - TL - b: 4/29/76 $2

Ramirez made his major league debut last season, getting called up from the minors three times. He was effective in his role as a setup man, pitching equally well against lefties and righties. He is not particularly overpowering with his high-80s fastball, but his best pitch is his curve, which he supplements with a changeup. He posted ERAs under 2.00 as a reliever the last couple of seasons at Triple-A Oklahoma. He'll enter spring training, ready to fight for a full-time reliever role with the Rangers.

	W	SV	ERA	IP	H	BB	SO	B / I
2003 Texas	3	0	3.86	49	46	9	28	1.12

RAMIREZ, HORACIO - TL - b: 11/24/79 $9

Horacio Ramirez has come a long way from missing almost the entire 2001 season after having Tommy John surgery. After a strong rebound in 2002, spent mostly at Double-A Greenville, Ramirez skipped Triple-A and jumped straight into the Braves rotation out of spring training in 2003. Despite a few rough outings early in the year, Ramirez persevered and finished strong, winning his last four decisions to finish among league leaders in winning percentage. He was relegated to a bullpen role for the post-season as the Braves deferred to experience. Ramirez doesn't throw especially hard - his fastball barely touches 90 MPH - but he throws with such an easy delivery that hitters don't get a good read against him and are often fooled when he switches to the cut fastball or changeup. He showed a severe platoon advantage against lefties, who batted just .206 with only two homers against him. Righthanded hitters get a better look and connected for most of the extra-base hits Ramirez surrendered in 2003. He keeps the ball down and induces many grounders, especially with his cut fastball. While he lacks the raw stuff to be a staff ace, Ramirez has a bright future. His biggest challenges in 2004 will be to make the necessary adjustments required of a sophomore pitcher, and to find a more effective pitch to show righthanders.

	W	SV	ERA	IP	H	BB	SO	B / I
2003 Atlanta	12	0	4.00	182	181	72	100	1.39

RANDOLPH, STEPHEN - TL - b: 5/1/74 $0

After toiling for eight years in the minor leagues, Randolph made Arizona's Opening Day roster in 2003 for his first taste of the majors. While Randolph had been a starter throughout his minor league career, he spent the entire season in the bullpen, with so-so results. His fastball touches the low 90s and he has a sharp breaking slider, although control continued to be an issue as it was during his long minor league stretch. He walks too many batters to stay out of trouble. He was expected to be a candidate for a mid-level bullpen job, but his control must improve for him to have a secure future.

	W	SV	ERA	IP	H	BB	SO	B / I
2003 Arizona	8	0	4.05	60	50	43	50	1.55

RAUCH, JON - TL - b: 9/27/78 $0

Shoulder problems again plagued Rauch in 2003. The White Sox were planning on him making a contribution to the big league team last year, though the acquisition of some veteran pitchers and shoulder soreness combined to keep him in the minors all season. Rauch, at 6-foot-11, is the tallest player in professional baseball history and his a truly imposing presence on the mound. While his fastball gets only into the low 90s, he changes arm angles frequently and relies a lot on a good curve and slider. Rauch finished the season strong, winning his last five decisions for Triple-A Charlotte and posting a 2.17 ERA in his final six starts of the season. If nothing else, Rauch could wind up being a fine closer. Moving to the bullpen also might be the way to help ease the stress on his right shoulder.

	W	SV	ERA	IP	H	BB	SO	B / I
2002 Chicago - AL	2	0	6.59	29	28	14	19	1.46

REDDING, TIM - TR - b: 2/12/78 $9

Redding had a promising season in 2003 as he gained better command of his breaking balls and off-speed pitches to mix with his low-90s fastball. He was in and out of the major leagues in 2002 after being named the top pitcher in Single-A Florida State League in 2000 and the top pitcher in the Double-A Texas league in 2001. Another factor in his success in 2003 was in dealing with adversity. He still needs to improve his ability to go deeper into games. Redding was in the Astros rotation all year and is establishing himself as a solid mid-rotation starter.

	W	SV	ERA	IP	H	BB	SO	B/I
2001 Houston	3	0	5.50	55	62	24	55	1.54
2002 Houston	3	0	5.40	73	78	35	63	1.54
2003 Houston	10	0	3.68	176	179	65	116	1.39

REDMAN, MARK - TL - b: 1/5/74 $14

Redman does not have lights-out power stuff but, he does have good control and he knows how to set up hitters. While Redman seemed to be a big surprise, he was no different last year than he had been with the Tigers in 2002. The difference in teams, run support and bullpen were the reasons the reliable Redman emerged in 2003. He is similar to Kenny Rogers and that's not bad at all.

	W	SV	ERA	IP	H	BB	SO	B/I
2001 MIN/DET	2	0	4.50	58	68	23	33	1.57
2002 Detroit	8	0	4.21	203	211	51	109	1.29
2003 Florida	14	0	3.59	191	172	61	151	1.22

REED, RICK - TR - b: 8/16/65 $2

Reed is getting along in years, and his pitching is starting to show it. Once considered a control artist, Reed couldn't hit his spots in 2003 and gave up plenty of hits. He admitted several times during the season that he wasn't doing his job. Reed can touch 90 MPH on the radar, throws a decent curveball and has a nice fastball that runs back in on righthanded hitters. Age and nagging injuries seem to be taking their toll, which is dangerous when you're without a contract and looking for work.

	W	SV	ERA	IP	H	BB	SO	B/I
2001 NY - NL/MIN	12	0	4.05	202	211	31	142	1.20
2002 Minnesota	15	0	3.78	188	192	26	121	1.16
2003 Minnesota	6	0	5.07	135	155	29	71	1.36

REED, STEVE - TR - b: 3/11/65 $1

Reed is the consummate journeyman, in the best sense of the word. Need a middle-inning relief man? He's your guy. Reed is not overpowering with a fastball that struggles to reach 90 MPH, but he has command of three pitches and keeps hitters off balance. He paints the corners with his fastball and slider and gets hitters lunging after a quality changeup. He features a sidearm style that hitters do not see every day, another angle he works well. Reed is as consistent as the sun, the only righthanded reliever to appear in 50 games in each of the last 11 seasons. Although Reed will turn 39 in spring training, he does not appear to be slowing down and was expected to be a mainstay in middle reliever or as a setup man out of the bullpen.

	W	SV	ERA	IP	H	BB	SO	B/I
2002 New York - NL	2	1	2.01	67	56	14	50	1.04
2003 Colorado	5	0	3.27	63	59	26	39	1.34

REICHERT, DAN - TR - b: 7/12/76 $0

Once a top prospect for Kansas City, Reichert has fallen all the way from being near the top of KC's rotation two years ago to being a guy who is fighting to stick in the majors. His fastball has a mind of its own, which can be a good thing if he could become effective at keeping the ball down a bit more than he does. Reichert is a diabetic who has to have four shots of insulin each day but it apparently hasn't interfered with his pitching. Ineffective after his recall to Toronto last year, Reichert will fight for another minor league contract this spring and will try to make an impression at Triple-A for a midseason recall in the event of a major league injury. It's unlikely he'll start this year in the big leagues.

	W	SV	ERA	IP	H	BB	SO	B/I
2001 Kansas City	8	0	5.63	123	131	67	77	1.61
2002 Kansas City	3	0	5.32	66	77	25	36	1.55
2003 Toronto	0	0	6.07	16	28	8	13	2.21

REITH, BRIAN - TR - b: 2/28/78 $0
Of the nearly five dozen pitchers the desperate Reds used in 2003, Reith is one of the few that never started a game or got a chance to save a game. He walks far too many hitters.

	W	SV	ERA	IP	H	BB	SO	B/I
2001 Cincinnati	0	0	7.81	40	56	16	22	1.79
2003 Cincinnati	2	1	4.11	61	61	36	39	1.58

REITSMA, CHRIS - TR - b: 12/31/77 $12
One look at Reitsma's blown saves in 2003 suggests that he is not cut out to be a closer. However, some of his failed opportunities happened when he filled in for Scott Williamson. When he assumed the job of closer after Williamson was traded, Reitsma was better at it and ended the 2003 season as the odds-on-favortite to assume that role in 2004.

	W	SV	ERA	IP	H	BB	SO	B/I
2001 Cincinnati	7	0	5.29	182	209	49	96	1.42
2002 Cincinnati	6	0	3.64	138	144	45	84	1.37
2003 Cincinnati	9	12	4.29	84	92	19	53	1.32

REMLINGER, MIKE - TL - b: 3/23/66 $3
Remlinger's ERA predictably went way up last season, mostly the result of allowing many more home runs than he did in 2002 with the Braves. He now throws nearly as many breaking balls as fastballs and is the kind of pitcher who can have real trouble pitching in a small ballpark like Wrigley Field. He now uses his curve almost exclusively against lefthanded hitters and will try to spot that pitch on the outside corner to righthanded swingers rather than challenge them with a fastball. Since he has been reasonably healthy the last few years, and can still throw in the upper 80s, he likely will have a few more years left before the end of his career. He had precious few save opportunities in 2003 with the Cubs, and won't get many more this season either.

	W	SV	ERA	IP	H	BB	SO	B/I
2001 Atlanta	3	1	2.76	75	67	23	93	1.20
2002 Atlanta	7	0	1.99	68	48	28	69	1.12
2003 Chicago - NL	6	0	3.65	69	54	39	83	1.35

REYES, CARLOS - TR - b: 4/4/69 $0
Last May, Reyes was called up from Triple-A Durham to make his first major league start since 1997 - that's a long time. He saw limited playing time last year as a spot starter and as a reliever for the struggling Devil Rays, bouncing between the minors and the majors. One of his biggest problems was that he was prone to giving up the homer. Reyes began spring training on the outside looking in, most likely starting the season in the minors.

	W	SV	ERA	IP	H	BB	SO	B/I
2003 Tampa Bay	0	0	5.21	40	40	5	13	1.13

REYNOLDS, SHANE - TR - b: 3/26/68 $0
Shane Reynolds was very disappointed that his Astros released their former ace starter the last week of spring training. He'd had season-ending surgery in June the previous year and had worked very hard to return to full health for spring training. Reynolds felt betrayed by his former

team, but recovered nicely by signing with the Braves in April and posting a winning record, and his sixth season of double-digit wins. Although he needed a lot of help from the powerful Braves offense, Reynolds made the most of his opportunities. Alas, he suffered the same fate as with the Astros as he wasn't kept for the Braves post-season roster. Reynolds must have sharp command to succeed; he throws an upper-80s sinking fastball to each side of the plate and uses an occasional curveball to set up a splitter thrown with unusually low velocity; he keeps the ball down in the strikezone at all times. Reynolds holds runners well and fields his position adequately. Until the latter part of his career he displayed good durability although that is, obviously, in question for a 36-year-old who is still recovering from serious back surgery. Reynolds may have proven his point in 2003, showing that he was still able to pitch in the majors, but he'll be hard-pressed to find willing takers in 2004.

	W	SV	ERA	IP	H	BB	SO	B/I
2001 Houston	14	0	4.34	182	208	36	102	1.34
2002 Houston	3	0	4.86	74	80	26	47	1.43
2003 Atlanta	11	0	5.43	167	191	59	94	1.49

RHODES, ARTHUR - TL - b: 10/24/69 $1
Rhodes remains one of the most powerful setup men in the game, although he was used in a slightly different manner in 2003, when he was more of a situational guy than a one-inning guy. Perhaps because of that his numbers slipped slightly. Rhodes has the classic 1-2 power punch, a mid-90s fastball and a hard slider with a lot of late break. He locates his fastball well and is adept at climbing the ladder when he has a count in his favor. He also features a changeup that he can use with runners on base to get ground balls. His control is outstanding for such a hard thrower. He negates the running game with a good move to first and a quick delivery home. Rhodes had an occasional save opportunity in the jumbled Seattle bullpen in 2003, although he was expected to be used in his typical eighth-inning setup role again.

	W	SV	ERA	IP	H	BB	SO	B/I
2001 Seattle	8	3	1.72	68	46	12	83	0.85
2002 Seattle	10	2	2.32	70	45	13	81	0.83
2003 Seattle	3	3	4.17	54	53	18	48	1.31

RIEDLING, JOHN - TR - b: 8/29/75 $0
Riedling began the 2003 season as a reliever but like most of all the Reds pitchers, he got an audition as a starter. He made seven starts but he lasted more than six innings just twice. He returned to the bullpen and he was an effective setup man.

	W	SV	ERA	IP	H	BB	SO	B/I
2001 Cincinnati	1	1	2.41	33	22	14	23	1.07
2002 Cincinnati	2	0	2.70	47	39	26	30	1.39
2003 Cincinnati	2	1	4.90	101	107	47	65	1.52

RINCON, JUAN - TR - b: 1/23/79 $2
Rincon began 2003 in the minors, earned a callup to the majors then pitched his way into meaningful relief work. He's never been able to develop a changeup that would make him a starter, but he's quite a reliever with a 95 MPH fastball and excellent slider. He still has his moments when he can't find the plate, but pitching coach Rick Anderson has helped him with his control. As a result, Rincon moved ahead of veterans in the pecking order and was trusted with holding late leads. Look for him to continue to emerge as a key setup man.

	W	SV	ERA	IP	H	BB	SO	B/I
2002 Minnesota	0	0	6.27	29	44	9	21	1.85
2003 Minnesota	5	0	3.68	86	74	38	63	1.31

RINCON, RICARDO - TL - b: 4/13/70 $2
Rincon took several steps back in 2003. Where the previous year he displayed outstanding

control, he had all kinds of trouble throwing strikes last season. As a result, he went from being a true setup guy to being much more of a situational lefthander, facing one or two hitters at a time. His fastball and slider are good enough to get most guys out, and he is able to keep runners close at first with an outstanding pickoff move. He'll be around for another few years, if for no other reason than he is lefthanded. If he can avoid the wildness he displayed last year he will be a valuable setup man. Even if he can't, he still will be called upon to get the big lefties out. Either way, don't expect any saves.

	W	SV	ERA	IP	H	BB	SO	B / I
2001 Cleveland	2	2	2.83	54	44	21	50	1.20
2002 Oakland	1	1	4.18	56	47	11	49	1.04
2003 Oakland	8	0	3.25	55	45	32	40	1.39

RISKE, DAVID - TR - b: 10/23/76　　　　　　　　　　$14

Riske took over as the Indians closer in mid August. He didn't get a lot of save chances but he was effective when he did and he should continue in that role this season. Riske is always trying to learn another pitch to set up his fastball, but his heater is truly Gossage-like and he'd help a hitter by not throwing his fastball. He's come back from a torn labrum and he really didn't endure the grind of closing for the whole year so some caution is advised there but, Riske can flat bring it.

	W	SV	ERA	IP	H	BB	SO	B / I
2001 Cleveland	2	1	1.98	27	20	18	29	1.39
2002 Cleveland	2	1	5.26	51	49	35	65	1.64
2003 Cleveland	2	8	2.29	75	52	20	82	0.96

RITCHIE, TODD - TR - b: 11/7/71　　　　　　　　　　$0

Milwaukee signed Ritchie prior to the 2003 season as a rotation anchor and innings-eater, but Ritchie made only five starts before undergoing season-ending arthroscopic surgery to repair a torn rotator cuff. He missed five weeks late in the 2002 season with shoulder inflammation, so maybe the Brewers should have seen it coming. Ritchie is a power pitcher who can carry a load (and a staff) when he is right. His fastball is in the low to mid 90s and he comes equipped with a power slider. He needs something to throw to lefties, who battered him for a .409 average in his limited time last year. Ritchie is a good athlete who fields his position well, although his long delivery does little to hinder the running game. When healthy, and he should be, he is a solid rotation member.

	W	SV	ERA	IP	H	BB	SO	B / I
2001 Pittsburgh	11	0	4.47	207	211	52	124	1.27
2002 Chicago - AL	5	0	6.06	134	176	52	77	1.71
2003 Milwaukee	1	0	5.09	28	36	10	15	1.63

RIVERA, MARIANO - TR - b: 11/29/69　　　　　　　　　　$40

Since closers were invented, none has been more effective in the postseason than Rivera. His cut fastball is so effective against lefthanders that they batted just .199 against him last year. Rivera also throws a mid-to-high-90s four-seam fastball. He has excellent control over both pitches. When they're working well, opponents tend to hit the ball into the ground, if they hit it at all. Rivera has recovered so well from his 2002 shoulder injury that his ERA was the best of his nine-year career. The Yankees also could call on him for 10 saves when he pitched more than one inning.

	W	SV	ERA	IP	H	BB	SO	B / I
2001 New York - AL	4	50	2.34	80	61	12	83	0.90
2002 New York - AL	1	28	2.74	46	35	11	41	1.00
2003 New York - AL	5	40	1.65	71	61	10	63	1.00

ROBERTS, GRANT - TR - b: 9/13/77 $0

Roberts was a highly touted prospect after going 20-4 in the lower minors in 1996 and '97. His reputation went up in smoke late in the 2002 season. Roberts has been bothered the last two years by biceps tendinitis, which kept him on the disabled list until August. He made 13 minor league rehab appearances before returning to the Mets' bullpen. If his arm is right, Roberts can throw a low-to-mid-90s fastball, but he needs a better breaking pitch. To that end, Tom Seaver has taken on Roberts as a personal project. Expect him to pitch in a major league bullpen this season.

	W	SV	ERA	IP	H	BB	SO	B/I
2001 New York - NL	1	0	3.81	26	24	8	29	1.23
2002 New York - NL	3	0	2.20	45	43	16	31	1.31
2003 New York - NL	0	1	3.79	19	19	3	10	1.16

ROBERTS, WILLIS - TR - b: 6/19/75 $0

The Orioles thought they really had a promising pitcher after Roberts broke in with them in 2001, showing low-to-mid-90s two- and four-seam fastballs and moving into their rotation. When he failed to throw his slider for strikes, he moved to the bullpen and showed some success as a closer. The next year, he lost that job to Jorge Julio. Roberts became a middle reliever manager Mike Hargrove really couldn't trust in a tight game. Then in late June, Roberts went on the disabled list because of a partially torn ligament in his elbow. That's an injury that spells potential career-ending disaster.

	W	SV	ERA	IP	H	BB	SO	B/I
2001 Baltimore	9	6	4.91	132	142	55	95	1.49
2002 Baltimore	5	1	3.36	75	79	32	51	1.48
2003 Baltimore	3	0	5.73	39	41	16	26	1.45

ROBERTSON, JERIOME - TL - b: 3/30/77 $0

Robertson has been in the Houston organization since 1996. While he was not considered a top prospect, he compiled a 63-47 record over the years before getting his first major league opportunity late in 2002. He opened the 2003 season in Houston's starting rotation and, except for a brief trip back to the minors, remained there all year. He was inconsistent but managed a nine game winning streak despite an unimpressive earned run average. Robertson does not throw hard but has consistently recorded impressive strikeout to walk ratios in the minors. He will be competing for a spot as a bottom-of-the-rotation major league starting pitcher in 2004.

	W	SV	ERA	IP	H	BB	SO	B/I
2003 Houston	15	0	5.10	161	180	64	99	1.52

ROBERTSON, NATE - TL - b: 9/3/77 $0

Robertson was called up to Detroit from Triple-A Toledo, where he generally pitched well as a starter. In Detroit, Robertson started and he was unimpressive. He should be allotted some more time in the minors but he's just a strong spring away from earning a spot in the Tigers rotation.

	W	SV	ERA	IP	H	BB	SO	B/I
2003 Detroit	1	0	5.44	45	55	23	33	1.74

RODRIGUEZ, FELIX - TR - b: 12/5/72 $4

Rodriguez doesn't strike out nearly as many hitters as he used to, however in his case, it's a good thing. Rodriguez cut a few miles an hour off his fastball, which not only cut down his walk total, but it also reduced the number of 2-0 and 3-0 meatball pitches he had to throw. Rodriguez has an outstanding slider, which he uses as often as he can with two strikes. Rodriguez still hasn't earned the complete trust of management, which means he won't get many save opportunities. If he can continue to progress and come closer to being a true "pitcher," then he will earn more of those chances.

	W	SV	ERA	IP	H	BB	SO	B / I
2001 San Francisco	9	0	1.68	80	53	27	91	1.00
2002 San Francisco	8	0	4.17	69	53	29	58	1.19
2003 San Francisco	8	2	3.10	61	59	29	46	1.44

RODRIGUEZ, FRANCISCO - TR - b: 1/7/82 $11

Rodriguez is basically a two-pitch pitcher: a mid-90s fastball that explodes at the last moment, and a sharply-breaking slider. Since being converted to relief, Rodriguez has been able to concentrate on his best two pitches and when he is on his game, he is nearly unhittable. He arrived suddenly late in 2002 and starred in the post-season. Then, after a slow start to the 2003 season, Rodriguez rounded into form and was a dominant force in the bullpen by early summer. Rodriguez is still seen as a closer in waiting, and the only question now is how long he will have to wait.

	W	SV	ERA	IP	H	BB	SO	B / I
2003 Anaheim	8	2	3.03	86	50	35	95	0.99

RODRIGUEZ, RICARDO - TR - b: 5/18/79 $0

An aggressive pitcher, Rodriguez has a mid-90s fastball along with a curve and changeup. He is not afraid to throw inside and sometimes irritates opponents with his actions on the mound. Rodriguez started out strongly last season, but ran into trouble with the longball his second time around the league. Shortly thereafter, he suffered a hip injury and was lost for the season. Scouts are split on Rodriguez: some still regard him as highly as he was during his days as a top Dodger prospect, while others believe that he was over-hyped. He was traded twice in a year, for what it's worth. He was expected to be healthy for spring training, and to compete for a rotation spot.

	W	SV	ERA	IP	H	BB	SO	B / I
2002 Cleveland	2	0	5.67	41	40	18	24	1.40
2003 Cleveland	3	0	5.73	82	89	28	41	1.43

ROGERS, KENNY - TL - b: 11/10/64 $6

Deception. Guile. Confusion. Those are good words to describe Kenny Rogers, who, if he really rears back and lets it loose may touch 88 MPH on the radar gun. The veteran lefthander was at his finest in 2003, when he was one of the key pitchers on the Twins starting rotation. Rogers throws a 86 MPH sinking fastball with incredible accuracy. He's able to throw it on both corners, especially inside, where it surprises hitters with its bite. He also had a slider, curve and changeup he'll use to baffle hitters. Even has he nears 40, Rogers can still get hitters out and pitch nearly 200 innings. A free agent, he surely will be pitching for someone in 2004.

	W	SV	ERA	IP	H	BB	SO	B / I
2001 Texas	5	0	6.19	120	150	49	74	6.19
2002 Texas	13	0	3.84	211	212	70	107	1.34
2003 Minnesota	13	0	4.57	195	227	50	116	1.42

ROMERO, J.C. - TL - b: 6/4/76 $0

Romero is an example of a player who was concerned with heading into his first year of salary arbitration. He tried to do too much at times, fell behind hitters and got into jams. The 2003 season was a letdown for him because he was so dominant the year before. He has a good sinking fastball and very good slider. When he's on, he can get lefties and righties out. He was once considered a closer-in-waiting, and is still good. But he now must regain his reputation for being one of the better lefthanded setup men in baseball.

	W	SV	ERA	IP	H	BB	SO	B/I
2001 Minnesota	1	0	6.23	65	71	24	39	1.46
2002 Minnesota	9	1	1.89	81	62	36	76	1.21
2003 Minnesota	2	0	5.00	63	66	42	50	1.71

ROSARIO, RODRIGO - TR - b: 3/14/78 $0

Rosario made his major league debut in 2003 with a promising start before incurring a shoulder injury in his second start which required surgery and put him out for the season. He is a product of Houston's Dominican Academy, originally signed in 1996. Rosario made steady progress through the organization being named to league All-Star teams at low Single-A in 2001 and Double-A in 2002. He was 5-7, 4.03 with Triple-A New Orleans before being recalled to Houston in June 2003. He has good command of his low nineties fastball, off speed pitches and breaking balls. If his shoulder is recovered, he will be competing for a spot in a major league starting rotation in 2004.

	W	SV	ERA	IP	H	BB	SO	B/I
2003 Houston	1	0	1.13	8	5	3	6	1.00

RUETER, KIRK - TL - b: 12/1/70 $0

Rueter struggled through an injury-plagued 2003 season, though he finished strong by allowing only five earned runs in his final four starts. Rueter throws a veritable boatload of curveballs because his fastball isn't going to get big league hitters out by itself. He has been as successful because, when healthy, his command is very good and he doesn't put a lot of extra runners on base. Rueter is at the age where losing even a couple of miles an hour off can be deadly. He will be helped by the fact he never threw hard, though. The fact that he missed several starts with shoulder soreness is another concern. He shouldn't be expected to make a strong comeback. He will be good enough to be a .500 pitcher and keep his spot in the rotation, though he won't be much better.

	W	SV	ERA	IP	H	BB	SO	B/I
2001 San Francisco	14	0	4.42	195	213	66	83	1.43
2002 San Francisco	14	0	3.23	204	204	54	76	1.27
2003 San Francisco	10	0	4.53	147	170	47	41	1.48

RUSCH, GLENDON - TL - b: 11/7/74 $0

After three quality seasons as a middle-of-the-rotation starter, Rusch took a step backward in Milwaukee in 2003 in a disjointed season that included time the disabled list because of a groin injury and more time in the minors because of ineffectiveness. He ended the season in the bullpen. Rusch does not have overpowering stuff; his fastball tops out in the high-80s, and relies on location and mixing in his changeup and curve. He has lost some command the last two years, something he cannot do with his repertoire. Rusch does all the other things that can keep him in a game. He is a very good hitter and helps himself with a good move to first. Not only does he hold runners well, but also his slide step grinds the opposing running game to a half. If he recovers his command, he could again challenge for a middle spot in the starting rotation. If ...

	W	SV	ERA	IP	H	BB	SO	B/I
2001 New York - NL	8	0	4.63	179	216	43	156	1.45
2002 Milwaukee	10	0	4.70	211	227	76	140	1.44
2003 Milwaukee	1	1	6.42	123	171	45	93	1.75

RYAN, B.J. - TL - b: 12/28/75 $2

The lanky (6'6") Ryan has tantalized scouts, managers, pitching coaches, media and fans with some obvious talents that haven't translated into great success in the majors. Because his stock in trade is just a low-90s fastball, made more difficult against lefthanded batters because of a funky motion, Ryan has become increasing vulnerable against righthanded bats. His number of appearances has increased in each of his five seasons, but his innings were down in 2003 as he increasingly was used as a specialist against lefty swingers. And a darn good one at that. He has been strong enough to shoulder a busy workload, and has traditionally pitched better late in seasons. The best he could hope for would be to become a lefthanded setup man occasionally called on for saves.

	W	SV	ERA	IP	H	BB	SO	B/I
2001 Baltimore	2	2	4.25	53	47	30	54	1.45
2002 Baltimore	2	1	4.68	58	51	33	56	1.46
2003 Baltimore	4	0	3.40	50	42	27	63	1.37

SAARLOOS, KIRK - TR - b: 5/23/79 $0

Saarloos reached the majors in midseason in 2002 in only his second professional season after compiling a 10-1, 1.40 record at Double-A Round Rock. He failed to stick in the majors out of spring training in 2003, spending the season bouncing between Triple-A and the majors and pitching both as a starter and a reliever. He relies on a changeup and a sinking two-seam fastball that rarely exceeds 86. He must have pinpoint control and keep the ball low to be effective. It has worked well in the minors where he has compiled excellent numbers but he has had trouble getting major league batters out. His future is cloudy as he could be a journeyman middle reliever or he could develop into an effective sinker ball pitcher in the mold of Brandon Webb.

	W	SV	ERA	IP	H	BB	SO	B/I
2003 Houston	2	0	4.93	49	55	17	43	1.46

SABATHIA, C.C. - TL - b: 7/21/80 $12

Sabathia is the ace of the Cleveland staff and he seems to be headed in the right direction now. In past seasons, Sabathia was well on his way to establishing himself as a guy with a million-dollar-arm and a not-so-valuable brain, and while he doesn't have the intensity and focus of Bob Gibson or Roger Clemens, now he's become more professional in his approach and he is as tough as any lefty in the game. Had the Indians of the late 1990s been behind him, instead of the punchless wonders that surrounded him, Sabathia would have won 20 games last year.

	W	SV	ERA	IP	H	BB	SO	B/I
2001 Cleveland	17	0	4.39	180	149	95	171	1.35
2002 Cleveland	13	0	4.37	210	198	88	149	1.36
2003 Cleveland	13	0	3.60	198	190	66	141	1.29

SANCHEZ, DUANER - TR - b: 10/14/79 $0

Sanchez was signed by Arizona at the age of 16, then came to the Pirates in the Mike Fetters trade. Young but slow to develop, Sanchez closed in the low minors and he was brought to Pittsburgh twice in 2003 but he's far from ready to pitch in the major leagues in any capacity. He is still more a thrower than a pitcher and relies heavily on a live fastball which he often can't control.

	W	SV	ERA	IP	H	BB	SO	B/I
2003 Pittsburgh	1	0	6.50	6	15	1	3	2.67

SANTANA, ERVIN - TR - b: 1/10/83 $0

Formerly known as the other Johan Santana, Ervin Santana is a top power pitching prospect who could be in the big leagues by late this season. At Single-A last season, Santana went 10-2 with a 2.53 ERA and 130 strikeouts in 20 starts, then followed that with a 1-1, 3.94 performance at Double-A. Santana is still very young, but continued progress through the minors and good health could get him to the majors very quickly.

SANTANA, JOHAN - TL - b: 3/13/79 $19

Santana had a breakout year in 2003, pitching his way out of the bullpen and into a playoff race. He throws 93 MPH and mixes in a nice slider. His big pitches are two amazing changeups - one straight, the other breaks away from righties - that made him one of the top strikeout artists in the American League. After a controversial decision landed him in the bullpen in spring training. Santana became a starter shortly before the All-Star break and won seven straight starts at one point. Look for a big year from him.

	W	SV	ERA	IP	H	BB	SO	B/I
2001 Minnesota	1	0	4.74	43	50	16	28	1.51
2002 Minnesota	8	1	2.99	108	84	49	137	1.23
2003 Minnesota	12	0	3.07	158	127	47	169	1.10

SANTIAGO, JOSE - TR - b: 11/5/74 $0

Santiago has shown flashes of competence as a reliever but he lacks focus and consistency. He's Jose Mesa without the notoriety.

	W	SV	ERA	IP	H	BB	SO	B/I
2001 KC/PHI	4	0	4.61	92	106	22	43	1.40
2002 Philadelphia	1	0	6.70	47	56	15	30	1.51
2003 Cleveland	1	0	2.84	32	37	14	15	1.61

SASAKI, KAZUHIRO - TR - b: 2/22/68 $7

Sasaki had the worst season of his four in the American majors in 2003 after returning from offseason surgery to remove bone chips in his right wrist. Beginning June 6, he missed 10 weeks with fractured ribs and did not have a save the rest of the season. The Japanese career save leader after a 10-year career in Yokahama, Suzuki has a style not often featured in the U.S. He likes to spot his 95-mph fastball high in the zone to set up his dramatic split-finger, which has one of the largest downward breaks in the game. His command suffered a times in 2003, however, resulting in an inordinate amount of walks. He has become gradually more difficult to run on as his time in the majors has increased. He was expected to enter spring training as the nominal closer, with a final decision to be made after he demonstrated a full return to health.

	W	SV	ERA	IP	H	BB	SO	B/I
2001 Seattle	0	45	3.24	66	48	11	62	0.89
2002 Seattle	4	37	2.52	61	44	20	73	1.05
2003 Seattle	1	10	4.05	33	31	15	29	1.38

SAUERBECK, SCOTT - TL - b: 11/9/71 $0

In 2003, Sauerbeck went from a career in Pittsburgh without any thought of postseason play to the heat of the Yankees-Red Sox rivalry and pennant race. The Sox traded for him because of his ability to get out lefthanded batters with a big-breaking curve. In the American League, the control problems that hampered him early in his career returned and he could hardly get out righthanded batters. Sauerbeck's fastball reaches only the high 80s, so if his curve isn't working, he's in trouble. He didn't arrive in the majors until he was 27, and he has had a heavy work load (averaging 70-plus appearances), so he could be expected to make an early exit if he weren't lefthanded. At this point, he'll probably be used mostly as a one-lefthanded-batter reliever.

	W	SV	ERA	IP	H	BB	SO	B/I
2001 Pittsburgh	2	2	5.60	62	61	40	79	5.60
2002 Pittsburgh	5	0	2.30	63	50	27	70	1.23
2003 PIT/BOS	3	0	4.76	57	47	43	50	1.59

SCHILLING, CURT - TR - b: 11/14/66 $24

Between his appendectomy and other assorted minor ailments, Schilling got in only two-thirds of a season in 2003, although when healthy he was as dominant as ever. For all his strengths,

---

Schilling is primarily a fastball pitcher, and that is the key to his success. He can locate with any pitcher in the major leagues, and he has taken advantage of the slightly higher strike zone by learning to climb the ladder, especially when ahead in the count. At the same time, his split-fingered pitch dives into the dirt and he is able to command both a slider and a curveball, usually using whichever is working best that night. He keeps a computer page on each opponent that charts every pitch ever thrown, and also takes a notebook to the bench during games to jot down thoughts while his team is hitting. Schilling is a better-than-average bunter and usually can put the bat on the ball. He is a solid No. 2 in the starting rotation, and would be No. 1 on all but a handful of major league teams.

	W	SV	ERA	IP	H	BB	SO	B/I
2001 Arizona	22	0	2.98	256	237	39	293	1.08
2002 Arizona	23	0	3.23	259	218	33	316	0.97
2003 Arizona	8	0	2.95	168	144	32	194	1.05

SCHMACK, BRIAN - TR - b: 12/7/73 $0
A 30-year-old rookie, Schmack was called up to the Tigers to shore up an exhausted bullpen. He had been in Double-A with the Erie Sea Wolves where he was their best reliever. He's been an effective minor league reliever, for a long time, but has never been considered a top prospect.

	W	SV	ERA	IP	H	BB	SO	B/I
2003 Detroit	1	0	3.46	13	14	4	4	1.38

SCHMIDT, JASON - TR - b: 1/29/73 $25
Schmidt is one of the hardest throwers around, and combines his mid-90s fastball with an outstanding slider. He was arguably the top pitcher in the National League last season, even though he pitched the final two months of the season with a torn tendon in his right elbow, an injury the Giants never revealed until after their Division Series loss to the Marlins. He was scheduled to have surgery shortly after the Giants were eliminated from the postseason, though it was not known if he would be ready to go by Opening Day. Schmidt will be fine once his elbow is repaired and healthy again. If he could pitch as well as he did down the stretch last season throwing only fastballs and changeups, then there should be little concern about his ability to get hitters out when he gets his slider and curve back.

	W	SV	ERA	IP	H	BB	SO	B/I
2001 PIT/SF	13	0	4.07	150	138	61	142	1.33
2002 San Francisco	13	0	3.45	185	148	73	196	1.19
2003 San Francisco	17	0	2.34	208	152	46	208	0.95

SCHOENEWEIS, SCOTT - TL - b: 10/2/73 $1
While Schoeneweis was a failure as a starter, he has carved something of a niche out for himself pitching in relief. He has only an average fastball, one that tops out in the low 90s, so he relies primarily on his sinker to get outs. He also throws a change, though he hasn't quite mastered that pitch yet and leaves it up in the strike zone much too often. Lefthanders have hit only .212 against him over the past three seasons, meaning he will get to stick around as a lefthanded relief specialist. He has been easy for righthanders to hit, so it will be very hard for him to earn a less restrictive role.

	W	SV	ERA	IP	H	BB	SO	B/I
2001 Anaheim	10	0	5.08	205	227	77	104	1.48
2002 Anaheim	9	1	4.88	118	119	49	65	1.42
2003 ANA/CHI - AL	3	0	4.17	65	63	19	56	1.27

SEDLACEK, SHAWN - TR - b: 6/29/77 $0
In many respects, Shawn Sedlacek is representative of the Royals' pitching staff: he's had a modicum of minor league success, doesn't throw especially hard (upper-80's fastball, at best), and relies on sharp control while spotting his straight-breaking curve

and mixing in some changeups to keep hitters off balance. When he can't hit the edges of the strike zone, Sedlacek is an easy mark for major league hitters. Fairly tall and thin, Sedlacek might be able to add a few more MPH to his otherwise unremarkable heater; he'll need it if he hopes to stay in the bigs. His best hope is with a poorer major league staff. Otherwise, he'll have to settle for a job in the high minors as injury insurance.

	W	SV	ERA	IP	H	BB	SO	B/I
2002 Kansas City	3	0	6.73	84	99	36	52	1.60

SELE, AARON - TR - b: 6/25/70 $0

Aaron Sele's claim to fame has been a big, sweeping curveball; when he has been able to throw it for strikes, it sets up an average fastball. Since Sele's rotator cuff surgery following the 2002 season, he has struggled with his location and been hit hard by the righthanded hitters he once dominated. Before his shoulder injury, Sele's best role was as an inning-eating middle-of-the-rotation starter; if he can return to health and regain his sharpness, he could resume that role.

	W	SV	ERA	IP	H	BB	SO	B/I
2001 Seattle	15	0	3.60	215	216	51	114	1.24
2002 Anaheim	8	0	4.89	160	190	49	82	1.49
2003 Anaheim	7	0	5.77	122	135	58	53	1.59

SEO, JAE WEONG - TR - b: 5/24/77 $7

Seo had a roller coaster rookie season. He was 5-2 with a 2.66 ERA on June 26, then lost six consecutive decisions, won three in a row, lost four and beat the Marlins in his final start. He has battled back after a reconstructive elbow surgery in 1999 stole about 5 MPH from his fastball, which now registers about 90. Seo has worked on a slider to help make his changeup more effective. And it seemed to work well, for lefthanders batted just .223 against him. Seo is a fly-ball pitcher, but although Shea Stadium is a pitchers' park, he gave up a home run every seven innings there and one every 19 innings on the road.

	W	SV	ERA	IP	H	BB	SO	B/I
2003 New York - NL	9	0	3.82	188	193	46	110	1.27

SHEETS, BEN - TR - b: 7/18/78 $8

Sheets, the 10th player taken in the 1999 draft, had his third straight 11-victory, workhorse season at the head of the Milwaukee rotation. He is the mold of an old-time starter, with a mid-90s fastball and a hard overhand curveball as his breaking pitch. He challenges hitters and has learned to climb the ladder when ahead, although because he comes right after opponents will give up his share of home runs. He was much more effective against lefthanded hitters in 2003, a key to his continued development, and was very economical with his pitches, averaging only 99 a start, a low number for a staff horse. He is a good athlete, and not only fields his position well but has a top pickoff move. He was expected to be the No. 1 man in the rotation again.

	W	SV	ERA	IP	H	BB	SO	B/I
2001 Milwaukee	11	0	4.76	151	166	48	94	1.41
2002 Milwaukee	11	0	4.15	217	237	70	170	1.42
2003 Milwaukee	11	0	4.44	221	232	43	157	1.25

SHIELDS, SCOT - TR - b: 7/22/75 $12

Shields has two plus pitches, a low-90s fastball and a sharp slider. He has been used both as a starter and reliever, and has pitched well in both roles. Shields is a groundball pitcher, relying on his defense to make plays behind him. Toward the end of last season, he seemed to tire a little. Shields was also noticeably less effective after throwing around 75 pitches in a game; additional experience with a heavier workload could lead to further improvement. He was expected to be in the mix for a rotation spot this season, with a setup role also an option.

	W	SV	ERA	IP	H	BB	SO	B/I
2001 Anaheim	0	0	0.00	11	8	7	7	1.36
2002 Anaheim	5	0	2.20	49	31	21	30	1.06
2003 Anaheim	5	1	2.85	148	138	38	111	1.19

SHOUSE, BRIAN - TL - b: 9/26/68 $2

The term "crafty lefty" applies to Shouse. He makes good use of his assortment of offspeed pitches but has been pounded in brief major league trials in the past. 2003 was his first extended stay in the majors, when he was called up from Triple-A Oklahoma to replace C.J. Nitkowski. He struggled a little in July, but was finished the season with a strong August and September. He kept lefties hitting under .200 with only two walks, but righthanded hitters batted .364 against him. This spring training, he'll try to hold onto his job as a situational lefty and setup man, and if he does, he'll get a save or two.

	W	SV	ERA	IP	H	BB	SO	B/I
2003 Texas	0	1	3.10	61	62	14	40	1.25

SHUEY, PAUL - TR - b: 9/16/70 $3

Shuey still has the stuff that made him a closer-in-waiting in Cleveland — a mid-90 MPH fastball and a big-time changeup that is his strikeout pitch. He can throw in a curve, too. Control has always been his issue, and he will go through stretches where he cannot find the plate. Shuey does not do the little things particularly well, either. He finishes his delivery off balance, hurting his glove work. He does not have a good move, and he compounds the problem with a slow delivery home. He is easy to run on. He was expected to remain a setup man.

	W	SV	ERA	IP	H	BB	SO	B/I
2001 Cleveland	5	2	2.82	54	53	26	70	1.45
2002 CLE/LA	8	1	3.31	68	56	31	63	1.28
2003 Los Angeles	6	0	3.00	69	50	33	60	1.20

SILVA, CARLOS - TR - b: 5/23/79 $1

A big, strong youngster with mid-90's velocity,Silva mixes in his curve and change effectively. He has the potential to be more of strikeout pitcher. Meanwhile he is content to let the batters get themselves out by putting the ball in play. He jumped from Double-A in 2001 to the majors in 2002 without missing a beat; the only noticeable difference was that major league batters got a few more walks because they know the strike zone better. In the minors Silva was among the best for not issuing walks. Silva is often mentioned as a potential starting pitcher, which he was in the minors but there are no openings in Philadelphia and Silva probably is a pitch or two short of being able to start and last more than a few innings. If given the chance, he has a shot to solve the Phillies closer queston.

	W	SV	ERA	IP	H	BB	SO	B/I
2002 Philadelphia	5	1	3.21	84	88	22	41	1.31
2003 Philadelphia	3	1	4.43	87	92	37	48	1.48

SIMONTACCHI, JASON - TR - b: 11/13/73 $1

While Simontacchi has gone 20-10 the past two seasons for St. Louis, he has been largely ineffective. A pitcher for the Italian Olympic team in the 2000 games, Simontacchi's claim to fame was his 7-1 start for the Cardinals in 2002. Once the scouting reports caught up to him, he has struggled to get hitters out. His fastball doesn't regularly get into the 90s on the radar gun, and his breaking pitches are only adequate. He can be a long reliever and a spot starter for many clubs. He will not, however, be able to keep a spot on the starting staff. He simply isn't good enough for that.

	W	SV	ERA	IP	H	BB	SO	B/I
2002 St. Louis	11	0	4.02	143	134	54	72	1.31
2003 St. Louis	9	1	5.56	126	153	41	74	1.54

SMOLTZ, JOHN - TR - b: 5/15/67 $35

Only elbow tendinitis prevented John Smoltz from having a record-setting season in 2003. As the closer behind an outstanding Braves starting rotation and solid setup corps, Smoltz quickly amassed 44 saves through late-August before missing games in the last month. Moving to the bullpen has permitted Smoltz to focus primarily on his hard stuff; his upper-90s fastball keeps hitters back on their heels enough they can't reach his upper-80s slider or sharp-breaking splitter. Batters have to hit their way on against Smoltz; he walked fewer than one batter per seven outings. Hitters fare best against Smoltz by looking fastball early in the count; the deeper the count gets, however, the more Smoltz begins to dominate. A past history as a starter helps Smoltz maintain his stuff in those rare outings when he has to go more than a handful of pitches. Smoltz is an above-average fielder and a good-hitting pitcher, although he's now rarely called upon to bat. There are few closers in Smoltz's class, and none better.

	W	SV	ERA	IP	H	BB	SO	B/I
2001 Atlanta	3	10	3.36	59	53	10	57	1.07
2002 Atlanta	3	55	3.25	80	59	24	85	1.03
2003 Atlanta	0	45	1.12	64	48	8	73	0.87

SNYDER, KYLE - TR - b: 9/9/77 $0

Smyth wasn't as good in 2002 (at any level) as he was the year before when he lead the Double-A Southern League in ERA. Smyth, not a hard thrower at all, relies on a big breaking curve and change to get hitters out. When his control is on, he can have a very easy time on the mound. When he is missing his spots, however, it can be a quick night for the young southpaw. Smyth wasn't good enough in his late-season starts to solidify a spot on the Opening Day roster, so he will need to have a little bit of success in Triple-A before getting the call.

	W	SV	ERA	IP	H	BB	SO	B/I
2003 Kansas City	1	0	5.17	85	94	21	39	1.35

SORIANO, RAFAEL - TR - b: 12/19/79 $9

After converting from the outfield in 1999, Soriano has made tremendous strides in his development on the mound and is one of the rising stars of the Seattle staff. Soriano's best pitch is a moving fastball that clocks in at 95 mph, and he took the next step with a hard slider he can throw for strikes. He is not afraid to pitch inside to power hitters, and also can spot his fastball on the outer half, a wicked approach that keeps hitters constantly off-balance. He has a viable changeup that remains a work in progress. Soriano was expected to open the season in the bullpen, although he has the repertoire and command to be a starter in the future.

	W	SV	ERA	IP	H	BB	SO	B/I
2002 Seattle	0	1	4.57	47	45	16	32	1.29
2003 Seattle	3	1	1.53	53	30	12	68	0.79

SOSA, JORGE - TR - b: 4/28/77 $2

Sosa was a Rule 5 draft pick by the Devil Rays before 2002 and he stuck with the Devil Rays since then, seeing time as both a starter and a reliever. He has a history of being erratic most of his outings, but that's understandable considering he's been a pitcher for only a three years. He got his first shutout in September of 2003, and his strong second-half last year indicates he's ready to stay in the majors for good. The question at the end of the 2003 season was if he was going to stay in the majors as a starter, reliever, or continue as he has since 2002, pitching in both roles. Part of the problem for him as a starter is that he struggles terribly against lefty hitters who not only hit over .300 with power against him in 2003, but he also walked them more than he struck them out. This year he will most likely continue as a spot starter/ relief pitcher.

	W	SV	ERA	IP	H	BB	SO	B/I
2002 Tampa Bay	2	0	5.53	99	88	54	48	1.43
2003 Tampa Bay	5	0	4.62	129	137	60	72	1.53

SPARKS, STEVE - TR - b: 7/2/65 $0

Steve Sparks is 38 and a pure knuckleball pitcher. After he couldn't make it work as a starter, the Tigers pulled him out of the rotation in May, 2002. It was a brief respite — they put him back in June and Sparks was hit hard the rest of the season. In 2003, he was used exclusively as a reliever, but was dumped by the Tigers in late August. He was picked up by Oakland in September. He's a typical innings eater and mop-up man. If he does manage to spend significant time in a major league bullpen this year, it will be an insignificant role.

	W	SV	ERA	IP	H	BB	SO	B/I
2001 Detroit	14	0	3.65	232	244	64	116	1.33
2002 Detroit	8	0	5.52	189	238	67	98	1.61
2003 DET/OAK	0	2	4.88	107	114	37	54	1.41

SPEIER, JUSTIN - TR - b: 11/6/73 $12

When Jose Jimenez failed, Colorado turned to Speier to close games the final two months of the season. While the Rockies did not win enough games to get Speier consistent work, he appears to have a future in that role. Speier, the son of long-time major league shortstop Chris Speier, has a nice one-two punch with a fastball that reaches the mid-90s and a drop-off-the-table split-finger pitch. He sets up batters with the fastball and gets them swinging over the top at the splitty, made even harder to hit because of a jerky delivery. He does not have command of a slider, although he has not needed a third pitch yet. Speier is a good athlete, as you might expect given the gene pool, and fields his position well. He is slow to the plate, however, and runners can take advantage. Speier was expected to open the season assured of a spot in the bullpen, with the closer's role to be determined.

	W	SV	ERA	IP	H	BB	SO	B/I
2001 CLE/COL	6	0	4.58	76	71	20	62	1.13
2002 Colorado	5	1	4.33	62	51	19	47	1.12
2003 Colorado	3	9	4.05	73	73	23	66	1.31

SPOONEYBARGER, TIM - TR - b: 10/21/79 $1

Spooneybarger was expected to miss the entire 2004 season after having reconstructive elbow surgery in September. In June, he had been battling tendinitis and was placed on the DL, then later in the month felt pain in his pitching elbow. When healthy, Spooneybarger relies on a two and four seam fastball that he can bring in at 96 MPH. Although Spooneybarger is still a little wild he's equally hard to hit. He may have a future as a major league closer.

	W	SV	ERA	IP	H	BB	SO	B/I
2002 Atlanta	1	1	2.63	51	38	26	33	1.25
2003 Florida	1	0	4.07	42	27	11	32	0.90

SPRINGER, RUSS - TR - b: 11/7/68 $0

Springer missed almost four months last season due to elbow problems. He wasn't good before he went on the disabled list and was even worse in September when he returned to the active roster. His body simply won't let him throw with enough velocity to be an effective pitcher. Springer has nothing left to offer at this point in his career, so beware of a promising performance in exhibition games. Although he is experienced enough to look impressive while pitching against mostly minor leaguers in spring training, he has proven over the last three seasons that he simply can't get major league hitters out.

	W	SV	ERA	IP	H	BB	SO	B / I
2001 Arizona	0	1	7.13	18	20	4	12	1.36
2003 St. Louis	1	0	8.32	17	19	6	11	1.45

SPURLING, CHRIS - TR - b: 6/28/77 $1

Spurling had minor league experience as a closer and the Tigers briefly tried him there last year. He lacks the big fastball that most closers have. Spurling was dominating against righty hitters, but lefty hitters dominated him, hitting over .350 with power against him.

	W	SV	ERA	IP	H	BB	SO	B / I
2003 Detroit	1	3	4.68	77	78	22	38	1.30

STANFORD, JASON - TL - b: 1/27/77 $3

After posting an 8-3 record with a 3.18 ERA in 16 starts with Triple-A Buffalo, Stanford was called up by the Indians in early July. During the rest of the season, he was shuttled back and forth between the majors and Triple-A. Stanford is yet another in the Indians stockpile of young lefthanded starters. Of all the young southpaws in Cleveland, Stanford needs the most work and he won't be a regular in the majors for a while.

	W	SV	ERA	IP	H	BB	SO	B / I
2003 Cleveland	1	0	3.60	50	48	16	30	1.28

STANTON, MIKE - TL - b: 6/2/67 $7

Stanton has gone from closer with the Braves to setup stud with the Yankees to not-very-good lefty with the Mets. Time will do that do a pitcher, just as surely as it will reduce his strikeout/walk ratio from 3.28 to 1.79 in four years. Stanton's 50 appearances and 45.1 innings pitched were his lowest totals since 1995. Stanton's low-90s fastball, slider and splitter still are hard to hit, but increased walk and home run rates got him in trouble last season. He's a terrible fielder, but on his return to the National League going 0-for-1 lowered his career batting average to .412.

	W	SV	ERA	IP	H	BB	SO	B / I
2001 New York - AL	9	0	2.58	80	80	29	78	1.36
2002 New York - AL	7	6	3.00	78	73	28	44	1.29
2003 New York - NL	2	5	4.57	45	37	19	34	1.24

STARK, DENNY - TR - b: 10/27/74 $0

Stark missed the first half of the 2003 season because of a back injury suffered late in spring trianing and never returned to the form he displayed with Colorado in 2002, when he won 11 games as a rookie after being obtained from Seattle for Jeff Cirillo. Stark made 12 starts before finishing 2003 in the bullpen. Stark has a nice repertoire, beginning with a sinking fastball that touches 91 MPH and is complemented by a slider and a changeup. He has an unorthodox delivery, reworked after shoulder surgery cost him most of the 2000 season, and gets late movement on his pitches. Stark is not afraid to challenge hitters and has the command to make it work. He is a fluid fielder and uses a slide step to make it harder on opposing baserunners. After spending his entire career in the Seattle organization before 2002, he was learning to handle the bat. Stark is the kind of competitor you want in the starting rotation, and he was expected to enter spring training with a spot in the lower part of the rotation.

	W	SV	ERA	IP	H	BB	SO	B / I
2002 Colorado	11	0	4.00	128	108	64	64	1.34
2003 Colorado	3	0	5.83	79	98	33	30	1.66

STECHSCHULTE, GENE - TR - b: 8/12/73 $0

Stechschulte missed all of last season after having shoulder surgery and faces a tough road back to the big leagues. While he was a successful closer in the minors, he lacks the overpowering fastball or offspeed pitch required to pitch in the late innings in the big leagues. Stechschulte can provide inexpensive bullpen help to a lot of clubs, though he will have to start the season in the minor leagues to prove that he is fully recovered from shoulder surgery. If he can stay healthy, look for him to re-emerge in the second half of the season, pitching in the sixth and seventh innings.

	W	SV	ERA	IP	H	BB	SO	B/I
2001 St. Louis	1	6	3.86	70	71	30	51	1.44
2002 St.Louis	6	0	4.78	32	27	17	21	1.38

STEPHENSON, GARRETT - TR - b: 1/2/72 $3

Stephenson strikes out far fewer hitters per game than he did four and five seasons ago, which is a sure sign that his elbow has never fully recovered from the injury that caused him to miss all of the 2001 campaign. He was a decent pitcher in the first half of 2003, though he struggled mightily in the second half and after being banished to the bullpen, was taken off the active roster at the end of August, meaning he would have been ineligible to pitch in the postseason had the Cardinals made the playoffs. Given his age, and previous elbow injuries, it's not reasonable to believe that Stephenson has another 16 win season in him. He is experienced enough to win a spot in the rotation out of spring training, though he isn't likely to keep it for more than a couple of months.

	W	SV	ERA	IP	H	BB	SO	B/I
2001 St. Louis	0	0	6.00	0	0	0	0	2.00
2002 St. Louis	2	0	5.40	45	48	25	34	1.62
2003 St. Louis	7	0	4.60	174	167	60	91	1.30

STEWART, SCOTT - TL - b: 8/14/75 $2

Stewart was removed from the closers role and replaced by Rocky Biddle. On the surface it seems to be a demotion but it's really not. It demonstrates the need for cash strapped teams to have effective, well-rounded pitchers in the bullpen. Relievers are always under pressure and maybe closing is more pressure than protecting a lead, but there's not all that much difference. Losing the closers job is no slam at Stewart's ability. As a reliever, his job is to get hitters out and the Expos now know that he can close. Now they also know that Rocky Biddle can close and maybe by the end of 2004, they will know that some other reliever can close. A relief generalist like Stewart gives his manager the confidence to bring him into any situation and this approach helps to create a cheap, flexible and effective bullpen.

	W	SV	ERA	IP	H	BB	SO	B/I
2001 Montreal	3	3	3.78	47	43	13	39	1.17
2002 Montreal	4	17	3.09	64	49	22	67	1.11
2003 Montreal	3	0	3.98	43	52	13	29	1.51

STONE, RICKY - TR - b: 2/28/75 $3

Stone toiled in the minor leagues for 8 years before getting a late-season opportunity with Houston in 2001. He made the most of the chance and stayed with the Astros all year in both 2002 and 2003. Stone is not overpowering, with a sinking fastball that reaches 90 and good command of an assortment of offspeed and breaking pitches. He has never been a closer and is not likely to get that opportunity in the future. He is expected to continue to pitch in middle relief in 2004.

	W	SV	ERA	IP	H	BB	SO	B/I
2002 Houston	3	1	3.61	77	78	34	63	1.45
2003 Houston	6	1	3.69	83	76	31	47	1.29

STRICKLAND, SCOTT - TR - b: 4/26/76 $0

The Mets obtained Strickland from the Expos in April 2002 to be a setup man. He brought

---

a strong repertoire — low-to-mid-90s fastball, slider and changeup — that made him seem also to be a closer candidate. Twice in the past he had nine saves in a season for Montreal. Last season, he was pitching effectively but had some control problems. Then he went on the disabled list in May, underwent Tommy John surgery and was out the rest of the year. Strickland is not likely to be ready by the beginning of this season, but should be back sometime in '04.

	W	SV	ERA	IP	H	BB	SO	B / I
2001 Montreal	2	9	3.21	81	67	41	85	1.33
2002 New York - NL	6	2	3.54	69	61	33	69	1.37
2003 New York - NL	0	0	2.25	20	16	10	16	1.30

STURTZE, TANYON - TR - b: 10/12/70 $0

Sturtze is essentially a fastball/slider pitcher who mixes in a decent occasional and apparently uncontrollable splitter. He peaks in the low 90s and he leaves far too many balls up in the strike zone. Sturtze went into last season looking to be a number four starter but by midseason he was relegated to the bullpen and by September, he was performing mop-up duty. He does have a certain intensity about his pitching but it hasn't been backed up by his results and he'll be looking to battle for a job in someone's bullpen this spring as a long reliever. It's unlikely that he's going to return to the starting rotation unless injuries force him there and even at that, he hasn't shown any sign that he would stick.

	W	SV	ERA	IP	H	BB	SO	B / I
2001 Tampa Bay	11	1	4.42	195	200	79	110	1.43
2002 Tampa Bay	4	0	5.18	224	271	89	137	1.61
2003 Toronto	7	0	5.95	89	107	43	54	1.68

SULLIVAN, SCOTT - TR - b: 3/13/71 $2

Sullivan has been a real workhorse of a relief pitcher the last several seasons, and it is apparent that throwing all those innings has finally caught up to him. Sullivan threw more than 100 innings (counting his work in the minor leagues) from 1996 to 2001, and he simply hasn't been the same the last two seasons. He suffered all kinds of injuries, from his back to his elbow to his knee, and his pitching hasn't been nearly as good. He's a sidearmer who can throw in the low 90s. He throws his curve a lot and he will sometimes throw with a higher arm angle to certain lefthanded hitters. Sullivan can be quite valuable, though he doesn't have good enough stuff to pitch in the eighth and ninth innings.

	W	SV	ERA	IP	H	BB	SO	B / I
2001 Cincinnati	7	0	3.31	103	94	36	82	1.26
2002 Cincinnati	6	1	6.06	79	93	31	78	1.58
2003 CIN/CHI - AL	6	0	3.66	64	48	32	56	1.25

SUPPAN, JEFF - TR - b: 1/2/75 $7

Despite an influx of young pitching talent in the majors, there's still a feeding frenzy at the trade deadline for any starting pitcher doing well with a poor team. Last year's prize on the market was Suppan. By throwing strikes with regularity unprecedented in his career, he had won five consecutive decisions (including two shutouts) with Pittsburgh to match his career high in wins by the end of July. The Red Sox traded for him, his control suffered and he won just one of his first seven starts back in the American League. Suppan uses a curve as his out pitch, and to allow him to spot a low-90s fastball. He's a consistent 200-innings workhorse best suited for the back of a rotation.

	W	SV	ERA	IP	H	BB	SO	B / I
2001 Kansas City	10	0	4.37	218	227	74	120	1.38
2002 Kansas City	9	0	5.32	208	229	68	109	1.43
2003 PIT/BOS	13	0	4.19	204	217	51	110	1.31

TAM, JEFF - TR - b: 8/19/70 $0

A basic fastball/curve type with a below average slider, Tam had a history of throwing strikes before last year, which wasn't necessarily an advantage given that he doesn't throw that hard. Now, newfound control problems the past two years have essentially erased what once was his biggest asset. An intense competitor, Tam spent all of last season bouncing between Triple-A and the majors before being released by Toronto in September. He's facing a spring training battle to catch on somewhere and looks to be a middle reliever, at best. His problems of last year don't offer much hope for a turnaround.

	W	SV	ERA	IP	H	BB	SO	B/I
2001 Oakland	2	3	3.01	74	68	29	44	1.30
2002 Oakland	1	0	5.14	40	56	13	14	1.71
2003 Toronto	0	1	5.64	45	58	25	26	1.86

TANKERSLEY, DENNIS - TR - b: 2/24/79 $0

Tankersley is one of the top pitching prospects in the San Diego organization, although it is hard to tell that from his 2003 stats. He gave up three hits and four walks in his one start after being recalled on April 9 and was returned to the minors for the rest of the season the next day. Tankersley has a fastball that reaches the mid-90s and a hard slider that scouts consider his best pitch. He has had trouble with location in two major league stints, perhaps a function of age. He is adequate defensively although he must learn to pay attention to the running game. He has had success in very limited trials at the plate. He was expected to spend another year in the minors for seasoning purposes, although he has the arm to make a major league rotation.

	W	SV	ERA	IP	H	BB	SO	B/I
2002 San Diego	1	0	8.07	51	59	40	39	1.93

TAVAREZ, JULIAN - TR - b: 5/22/73 $5

Tavarez is a sinker/slider pitcher and many thought he would develop into a star. That hasn't happened, primarily because he has trouble getting lefthanded hitters out. Over the last five years, lefty swingers have batted well .300 against Tavarez. He will have to come up with another pitch to continue dominating lefthanders like he did in September with 8 saves.

	W	SV	ERA	IP	H	BB	SO	B/I
2001 Chicago - NL	10	0	4.52	161	172	69	107	1.49
2002 Florida	10	0	5.39	154	188	74	67	1.70
2003 Pittsburgh	3	11	3.66	84	75	27	39	1.22

TAYLOR, AARON - TR - b: 8/20/77 $0

Taylor had poor numbers in a brief trial with Seattle in 2003, although he seems to have the stuff to be a successful major leaguer. He combines a fastball in the mid 90s with a slider and a split-finger pitch. A former starter who was converted to the bullpen in 2001, Taylor has had command issues, although he had a dominant season at Double-A San Antonio in 2002, when he had 24 saves and averaged 10.9 strikeouts per nine innings. He was expected to compete for a job in the major league bullpen.

	W	SV	ERA	IP	H	BB	SO	B/I
2003 Seattle	0	0	8.50	13	17	6	9	1.81

TEJERA, MICHAEL - TL - b: 10/18/76 $2

In 2000, Tejera had his elbow rebuilt after rupturing a ligament. He was a solid performer for the Marlins in 2002, but faltered in the second half of that year. His struggles continued into 2003 in his role as a spot starter and reliever. Lefthanded batters hit almost .400 against him. He's a little guy and he doesn't throw hard so he has to hit spots to stay in the game.

To date he's losing that battle. On the positive side, he had a very strong July and August last year, and may again have extended streaks when he's effective.

	W	SV	ERA	IP	H	BB	SO	B/I
2002 Florida	8	1	4.45	140	144	60	95	1.46
2003 Florida	3	2	4.67	81	82	36	58	1.46

TELEMACO, AMAURY - TR - b: 1/19/74 $3

To say that Telemaco has been a fringe player is an understatement. Since 1996 he's shuttled between the majors and minors ten times but he's hung in there with the Phillies organization when he could have played for a weaker team. His reward will be no doubt be an eleventh trip to the minors. His 2003 tour with the Phillies came about because the Phillies had to play frequently with no days off and they needed an arm.

	W	SV	ERA	IP	H	BB	SO	B/I
2001 Philadelphia	5	0	5.54	89	93	32	59	1.40
2003 Philadelphia	1	0	3.87	45	41	11	29	1.15

THOMSON, JOHN - TR - b: 10/1/73 $11

After missing much of the 2000 and 2001 seasons with injuries, Thomson has returned as a durable inning-eater kind of starting pitcher. On a good day, his fastball can reach the mid-90s, and he mixes in a hard sinker and a changeup. Usually around the plate, Thomson doesn't walk many, but can be homer-prone. Thomson does not hold runners well and is not a good fielder. He was expected to be a middle-of-the-rotation starter once again this season.

	W	SV	ERA	IP	H	BB	SO	B/I
2001 Colorado	4	0	4.04	93	84	25	68	1.16
2002 COL/NY - NL	9	0	4.71	182	201	44	107	1.35
2003 Texas	13	0	4.85	217	234	49	136	1.30

THURMAN, COREY - TR - b: 11/5/78 $0

After Thurman met the Rule 5 requirements of remaining on the roster for all of 2002, the Blue Jays were able to send him back to the minors to work on his mechanics. Thurman incorporated an excellent slider into an arsenal that already included a good fastball, a deceptive changeup and a subpar and still uncontrollable curve. He did get a brief chance to impress as a starter with the major league team but didn't stick and his statistical results with Toronto didn't reflect the tremendous progress he made in his development. He'll be auditioning in spring training for a long relief or back-of-the-rotation type starting spot and barring a dominating spring, is headed back to the minors to start the season.

	W	SV	ERA	IP	H	BB	SO	B/I
2002 Toronto	2	0	4.37	68	65	45	56	1.62
2003 Toronto	1	0	6.47	15	21	9	11	1.96

TIMLIN, MIKE - TR - b: 3/10/66 $8

Timlin had planned to retire before last season if he couldn't get a job closer to his home in Texas, but the Red Sox offer was good enough to keep him in the Northeast. He throws a low-90s sinking fastball and a downward-breaking slider that enable him to get a lot of ground-ball outs. Timlin has impeccable control that even extends to the occasional hit batter because he's not afraid to pitch inside. Though lefthanded batters gave him more trouble than usual in 2003, he still has enough left to be able to help a major league bullpen.

	W	SV	ERA	IP	H	BB	SO	B/I
2001 St. Louis	4	3	4.09	73	38	19	47	1.33
2002 STL/PHI	4	0	2.98	97	75	14	50	0.92
2003 Boston	6	2	3.55	84	77	9	65	1.03

TOLLBERG, BRIAN - TR - b: 9/16/72 $0

Tollberg tried to return from Tommy John ligament replacement surgery in 2003 but managed only three ineffective starts before being shut down again. He is a feel and finesse pitcher who gets by on location. It will be hard to count on him in 2004 until he shows he has recovered from injury.

	W	SV	ERA	IP	H	BB	SO	B/I
2001 San Diego	10	0	4.30	117	133	25	71	1.35
2002 San Diego	1	0	6.13	62	88	19	33	1.73
2003 San Diego	0	0	6.99	10	9	4	2	1.26

TOMKO, BRETT - TR - b: 4/7/73 $2

Tomko has the ability to throw the ball hard, and his arm is durable enough to log a ton of innings, so it has been a big mystery to many observers why he doesn't win more games. It's because Tomko pitches like he thinks he is simply better than he is. Rather than take a few miles an hour off his pitches to get more movement, he throws as hard as he can. That flattens out his pitches and makes them much more easier to hit. Tomko is one of the most stubborn players around and has butted heads with the coaching staff of every team he has been with in his career. While he can throw a lot of innings, and look very impressive every now and then, he is not going to be a big winner, even on a pennant contender. He will have trouble maintaining his spot in the starting rotation.

	W	SV	ERA	IP	H	BB	SO	B/I
2001 Seattle	3	0	5.19	34	42	15	22	1.43
2002 San Diego	10	0	4.49	204	212	60	126	1.33
2003 St. Louis	13	0	5.28	203	252	57	114	1.52

TORRES, SALOMON - TR - b: 3/11/72 $1

After being out of baseball from 1998-2001, the comeback of the 32-year-old Torres is still in progress but, he may be running out of time. He was just fair in middle relief but he made spots starts all year and by September, he was in the starting rotation so, it appears as if the Pirates may have him on an up or out plan and they'll keep him if he wins a spot in the rotation. If he's only able to pass muster as a reliever, what's the point of continuing the experiment? Torres was hit pretty hard last year.

	W	SV	ERA	IP	H	BB	SO	B/I
2002 Pittsburgh	2	0	2.70	30	28	13	12	1.37
2003 Pittsburgh	7	2	4.76	121	128	42	84	1.41

TOWERS, JOSH - TL - b: 2/26/77 $4

After getting banged around in the Orioles system a couple of years ago, Towers caught on with the Blue Jays by midseason last year and was solid enough that by season's end he had joined the starting rotation. He doesn't throw particularly hard and his pitch location is somewhat predictable which means he has to rely on his control and mixing up his pitch speeds along with a good game plan to execute a performance. A control pitcher, Towers goes into spring training as a front-runner for a low spot in the starting rotation and has a shot to be a decent fourth or fifth starter over a full season.

	W	SV	ERA	IP	H	BB	SO	B/I
2001 Baltimore	8	0	4.49	140	165	16	58	1.29
2002 Baltimore	0	0	7.90	27	42	5	13	1.72
2003 Toronto	8	1	4.48	64	67	7	42	1.15

TRABER, BILLY - TL - b: 9/18/79 $0

Traber is a highly intelligent and professional young pitcher and he had some strong outings in 2003. Unfortunately, in September Traber had to have Tommy John surgery to replace a ligament

---

in his left elbow. While the rehabilitation period after this operation has been significantly reduced, Traber will be hard pressed to produce much in 2004.

	W	SV	ERA	IP	H	BB	SO	B/I
2003 Cleveland	6	0	5.24	112	132	40	88	1.54

TRACHSEL, STEVE - TR - b: 10/31/70 $12

How would you figure that Trachsel would have the best year of his career with the worst team he has pitched for in his 11 seasons? The 2003 Mets were even worse than the '99 Cubs, for whom Trachsel led the league with 18 losses. His career was in such disarray in 2001 that he was optioned to the minors for three starts, but he has posted ERAs under 4.00 the last two seasons. With a fastball that barely reaches 90 mph, Trachsel is like a batting practice pitcher when he's off (26 homers allowed). But his changeup is devastating to lefthanded batters. He had another year remaining on his contract with New York.

	W	SV	ERA	IP	H	BB	SO	B/I
2001 New York - NL	11	0	4.46	173	168	47	144	1.24
2002 New York - NL	11	0	3.37	174	170	69	105	1.38
2003 New York - NL	16	0	3.78	205	204	65	111	1.31

TSAO, CHIN-HUI - TR - b: 6/2/81 $2

The first native of Taiwan to pitch in the major leagues, Tsao is considered the best young pitching prospect in the Colorado organization. Long and lean, Tsao gets natural leverage on a fastball that averages 93 MPH and can touch 96. He also has good command of a curveball and a changeup and knows how to set up hitters. His control is a big asset. Although Tsao missed most of the 2001 season after undergoing reconstructive elbow surgery, he has not missed a beat the last two years and got his first taste of the majors last July, when he won his first start, 7-3, against Milwaukee. Before his recall, Tsao dominated the Texas League, going 11-4 with a 2.46 ERA in 18 starts. He struck out 125 and gave up only 88 hits and 26 walks in 113 innings. Tsao has moved up the organizational ladder at an accelerated pace, and it would not be a big shock to see him in the Colorado starting rotation this season. He was expected to open the season at Triple-A Colorado Springs, however.

	W	SV	ERA	IP	H	BB	SO	B/I
2003 Colorado	3	0	6.03	43	48	20	29	1.57

TUCKER, T.J. - TR - b: 8/20/78 $0

Tucker shuttled between Montreal and Triple-A Edmonton working in short relief and blowing two saves. Tucker has good control of an often outstanding curve and he can hit spots with a 92 MPH fastball. Tucker will get more save opportunities in the future because he is righthanded, has control of two very good pitches, and is also more effective against lefthanded batters than righthanded batters.

	W	SV	ERA	IP	H	BB	SO	B/I
2002 Montreal	6	4	4.11	61	69	31	42	1.63
2003 Montreal	2	0	4.73	80	90	20	47	1.38

TURNBOW, DERRICK - TR - b: 1/25/78 $0

The hard-throwing Turnbow features a low- to mid-90s fastball, curve and changeup. A former Rule V pick in 2000, Turnbow suffered a broken bone in his arm in 2001 and missed most of the 2001 and 2002 seasons. A successful Arizona Fall League stint in 2002 was an encouraging sign and Turnbow spent most of last season at Triple-A, where he went 1-2 with a 5.73 ERA and 63 strikeouts in 55 relief innings before getting a September callup. Expectations are high for Turnbow and he was expected to compete for a roster spot out of spring training this season. Eventually, Turnbow projects as a starting pitcher, but his short-term future is more likely in middle relief.

	W	SV	ERA	IP	H	BB	SO	B / I
2003 Anaheim	2	0	0.59	15	7	3	15	0.65

URBAN, JEFF - TL - b: 1/25/77 $0

Urban came out of nowhere to become a star at Ball State University and a sandwich pick between the first and second rounds of the 1998 draft. His progress was slowed because of a dislocated shoulder suffered playing pickup basketball before the 2000 season. He doesn't throw particularly hard, and his best pitch at this point is his curve. Urban fell behind some of the other pitching prospects in San Francisco with a disappointing year at Fresno, although he can help at the big league level in long relief, or as a lefthanded bullpen specialist.

URBINA, UGUETH - TR - b: 2/15/74 $20

Urbina saved 32 games last year and that's fine but, 26 saves came before the All Star break. Urbina was then traded to the Marlins who used Urbina in setup work while they continued to go with Braden Looper as the stopper. When the chips were on the table late in the wild card race, Looper blew a couple of saves and McKeon quickly installed Urbina as the closer. There should be no more bullpen shuttling for Urbina but it was another point made by management that the day of the highly paid closer is about over.

	W	SV	ERA	IP	H	BB	SO	B / I
2001 MON/BOS	2	24	3.65	66	58	24	89	1.23
2002 Boston	1	40	3.00	60	44	20	71	1.07
2003 TEX/FLA	3	32	2.81	77	56	31	78	1.13

VALDES, ISMAEL - TR - b: 8/21/73 $0

The well-traveled Valdes always seems to be in demand at trade-deadline time as a dependable end-of-the-rotation starter at a reasonable price. When he can locate his 90 MPH fastball, Valdes can get people out, but if his command is off, he doesn't have much to fall back on. Valdes has a decent curve, but relies very little on his other two pitches, a slider and change. Last season, Valdes was sidelined by patella tendinitis, and he has had recurring blisters on his pitching hand throughout his career. When healthy, he's a serviceable #4 starter for a big league team.

	W	SV	ERA	IP	H	BB	SO	B / I
2001 Anaheim	9	0	4.45	163	177	50	100	1.39
2002 TEX/SEA	8	0	4.18	196	194	47	102	1.23
2003 Texas	8	0	6.10	115	148	29	47	1.54

VALVERDE, JOSE - TR - b: 7/24/79 $9

After two seasons' worth of teasing, Valverde finally delivered on his terrific upside with Arizona in 2003, his first season in the major leagues. Valverde's fastball was once timed at 102 MPH in the minor leagues, and he was able to pitch at near that velocity while adding a slider to keep hitters off-balance. Valverde learned the pitch from cousin Jose Mercedes, a former major leaguer who provided counsel in the offseason. Valverde has a sneaky delivery in which the ball seems to jump at the hitters. While control remains an issue, Valverde, 24, is the kind of guy who can walk the bases loaded and then strike out the side. He was expected to open the season as the principal setup man, although he was used as a closer when Matt Mantei was hurt last year and projects as the closer of the future.

	W	SV	ERA	IP	H	BB	SO	B / I
2003 Arizona	2	10	2.15	50	24	26	71	0.99

VAN POPPEL, TODD - TR - b: 12/9/71 $0

A journeyman most recently with Cincinnati, Van Poppel will pop up sometime, somewhere in the majors. How long he'll stay in the majors is the question. He's a swingman that can go 5-6 innings in a spot start or relieve. He made his major league debut as a golden armed 19- year-old in 1991 and he's still relatively young at age 32, but his arm lost its shine long ago.

	W	SV	ERA	IP	H	BB	SO	B/I
2001 Chicago - NL	4	0	2.52	75	63	38	90	1.35
2002 Texas	3	1	5.45	73	80	29	85	1.50
2003 TEX/CIN	3	0	5.59	48	51	15	34	1.37

VARGAS, CLAUDIO - TR - b: 6/19/78 $0

Vargas is a big kid at 6'3", 210 with a low-90s fastball that has excellent movement. He also throws a hard slider and has a very smooth throwing motion that should help him avoid injuries. Last year was his first season in the majors, when he was called up by the Expos from Triple-A Edmonton to become their fifth starter. He missed more than five weeks to tendinitis in his rotator cuff but came back in September and pitched six scoreless innings. He didn't disappoint, and should find himself at the low-end to middle of the rotation for a major league team this season.

	W	SV	ERA	IP	H	BB	SO	B/I
2003 Montreal	6	0	4.34	114	111	41	62	1.33

VASQUEZ, JAVIER - TR - b: 6/25/76 $20

Javier Vazquez is as good as any pitcher yet he doesn't have the terrific high win / low loss record of better pitchers. A more discriminating manager than Old School Frank Robinson would have protected Vazquez and watched his innings more carefully but Robinson can be cranky and he knows that the free agent Vazquez would seek greener pastures and, well, if he's going to leave, why not use him up? Not to take tissue with Robinson, but when Vazquez made his final start against the Braves in late September, he cruised through seven inning scattering three hits and walking none but the Expos couldn't get him a run. His opponent was Shane Reynolds, who was also shutting out the Expos, indicating that the Expos hitters had packed it in for the year. Bobby Cox pulled Reynolds after seven innings but Robinson sent Vazquez out and the Braves got to him in the eighth for a couple of runs and the Expos never crossed the plate. Aside from games affected by bad weather, Vazquez pitched at least five innings every time that he started and he averaged nearly seven innings per start. Vazquez throws an excellent changeup and curveball to set up his 94 MPH fastball and he can knock a flea off a fence post with any pitch. Of concern is his workload. In the last four years Vazquez has pitched over 900 innings.

	W	SV	ERA	IP	H	BB	SO	B/I
2001 Montreal	16	0	3.42	223	197	44	208	1.08
2002 Montreal	10	0	3.91	230	243	49	179	1.27
2003 Montreal	13	0	3.24	231	198	57	241	1.11

VERES, DAVE - TR - b: 10/19/66 $3

Veres battled shoulder problems most of last season, twice spending significant stints on the disabled list. Overall his numbers were pretty bad in 2003, though he was much improved in the last month of the season after returning from his second trip to the DL. Veres, a former closer with St. Louis and Colorado, has one of the better split-finger offerings around. He has lost some of his velocity on his fastball in recent years because of injuries, meaning he will be relegated to setup duties despite his experience. While he can have success in that role if he stays healthy, don't expect him to get any save opportunities.

	W	SV	ERA	IP	H	BB	SO	B/I
2001 St. Louis	3	15	3.70	66	57	28	61	1.29
2002 St. Louis	5	4	3.48	83	67	39	68	1.28
2003 Chicago - NL	2	1	4.68	33	36	5	26	1.25

VILLAFUERTE, BRANDON - TR - b: 12/17/75 $0

Villafuerte had a career year in 2002 and was expected to be a mainstay in the San Diego bullpen before losing his command and being outrighted to Portland in midseason. After putting up stellar numbers there, the Padres purchased his contract and put him back on the 40-man roster. Villafuerte's best pitch is a 91-92 MPH fastball that cuts in on the hands of righthanded hitters, and he also throws a slider. His delivery leaves him off-balance and out of fielding position. He was expected to compete for a bullpen position that would be his with control.

	W	SV	ERA	IP	H	BB	SO	B/I
2002 San Diego	1	1	1.41	32	29	12	25	1.28
2003 San Diego	0	2	4.20	41	39	26	34	1.60

VILLARREAL, OSCAR - TR - b: 11/22/81 $8

A long-shot to make the Arizona roster in spring training, Villarreal became a valuable middle-inning reliever while setting a major league record for appearances by a rookie at the tender after of 21. Villarreal pitches way beyond his years, using a deceptive delivery that enables him to hide the ball well before delivery. He has good command of four pitches and is not afraid to pitch inside, a trait some believe is the key to good pitching. A native of Mexico who signed as a free agent at 17, Villarreal was a starter all through his minor league career but proved well-suited to the bullpen. He was expected to be ensconced in the bullpen again this season, although he has the repertoire to develop into a quality starter in the future.

	W	SV	ERA	IP	H	BB	SO	B/I
2003 Arizona	10	0	2.57	98	80	46	80	1.29

VILLONE, RON - TL - b: 1/16/70 $3

Villone is a veteran who has pitched for seven different major league teams. He was a first round pick by Seattle in 1992. Primarily a reliever through most of his career, he pitched effectively in his second stint with Houston as a starter after being signed as a free agent in May. Villone's fastball is in the 90-93 MPH range but it appears faster because of his imposing presence on the mound. He mixes in an effective slider and curve ball but has not had good enough command of his pitches throughout his career to be a consistent winner in the major leagues. His versatility will allow him to compete for a job in a major league rotation or bullpen in 2004.

	W	SV	ERA	IP	H	BB	SO	B/I
2001 HOU/COL	6	0	5.89	115	133	53	113	1.62
2002 Pittsburgh	4	0	5.81	93	95	34	55	1.39
2003 Houston	6	0	4.13	107	91	48	91	1.30

VIZCAINO, LUIS - TR - b: 6/1/77 $2

Vizcaino regressed after his stellar major league debut in 2002, falling from primary setup man to mopup guy when his command failed him. Vizcaino has a fastball that touches 97 MPHand is a consistent 94 to 95 MPH, more than enough to keep major league hitters at bay, although he has yet to perfect a second pitch. His slider, so effective in 2002, was problematic last year, leading to big problems. He gave up 15 home runs in just more than 60 innings. He likes to work up in the zone and pays the price when he does not locate. He does little to hinder the running game. With his stuff, Vizcaino was expected to be given every opportunity to reclaim a setup role in the bullpen.

	W	SV	ERA	IP	H	BB	SO	B/I
2001 Oakland	2	1	4.66	36	38	12	31	1.36
2002 Milwaukee	5	5	2.99	81	55	30	79	1.05
2003 Milwaukee	4	0	6.39	62	64	25	61	1.44

VOGELSONG, RYAN - TR - b: 7/22/77 $0

It's been a long journey back from a torn elbow ligament that occurred two years ago but Vogelsong finally took the mound for the Pirates. It's much too soon to speculate on what he might do in a full season. The first thing is, of course, to pitch a full season and if he can throw the way he did before he blew out his elbow, Vogelsong will come up big.

	W	SV	ERA	IP	H	BB	SO	B / I
2001 SF/PIT	0	0	6.75	35	39	20	24	1.70
2003 Pittsburgh	2	0	6.55	22	30	9	15	1.77

VOYLES, BRAD - TR - b: 12/30/76 $0

After seeing strictly bullpen use in his first five pro seasons, Brad Voyles was gradually converted to the starting rotation by the Royals in 2003. He made nine starts for Triple-A Omaha and had fine results. Voyles was recalled by Kansas City on three separate occasions, with disappointing results. The switch to rotation work was prompted by Voyles having a deeper repertoire than most relievers; his low-90s fastball and curve have superior movement and he owns a better changeup than most righthanded bullpen denizens. Unfortunately, Voyles had poor command of his pitches during his short big-league stints in 2003. Still, the Royals are encouraged by his Triple-A success and plan to again try him as a starter in 2004.

	W	SV	ERA	IP	H	BB	SO	B / I
2002 Kansas City	0	1	6.51	28	31	18	26	1.77
2003 Kansas City	0	0	7.19	31	47	18	24	2.08

WAECHTER, DOUG - TR - b: 1/28/81 $4

Waechter was called up from the minors at the end of August and soon became the first Devil Rays pitcher to ever get a shutout in his first major league start. At 6'4". 210, the 23-year-old Waechter definitely looks the part of a major league pitcher. He has a low-90s fastball and excellent control and put it to good use the last couple of seasons in the minors. In 2002, he advanced all the way from Single-A to Triple-A and showed last September that he was ready for the majors. He may not be superstar material, but has what it takes to fill a role from the mid to bottom in the rotation.

	W	SV	ERA	IP	H	BB	SO	B / I
2003 Tampa Bay	3	0	3.31	35	29	15	29	1.25

WAGNER, BILLY - TL - b: 6/25/71 $41

Wagner was the top closer in the National League in 1999 when he won the Rolaids Relief Man Award. After suffering a setback in 2000 with an elbow injury, which required surgery, he has regained his position as one of the top closers in baseball. In 2003, he set the Houston Club records for both career saves and single season saves. The lefthander is one of the hardest throwers in baseball, consistently working in the 97 MPH range and occasionally hitting 100 on the radar gun. He mixes in a slider, which has become more reliable as he has used it more. He has struck out over 12 batters per 9 innings in his career. Wagner should remain as a top closer for the foreseeable future.

	W	SV	ERA	IP	H	BB	SO	B / I
2001 Houston	2	39	2.73	62	44	20	79	1.02
2002 Houston	4	35	2.52	75	51	22	88	0.97
2003 Houston	1	44	1.78	86	52	23	105	0.87

WAGNER, RYAN - TR - b: 7/15/82 $5

The Reds made Wagner their number one pick in the 2003 draft and after just nine minor league games he was called up to Cincinnati in July. The Reds didn't want to risk overworking Wagner after he'd pitched college and minor league ball, so he worked in relief and he pitched very well.

Wagner averaged more than a strikeout per inning and batters who didn't whiff usually beat balls into the ground; a great asset for a pitcher who works in the Great American Ball Park.

	W	SV	ERA	IP	H	BB	SO	B / I
2003 Cincinnati	2	0	1.66	22	13	12	25	1.15

WAKEFIELD, TIM - TR - b: 8/2/66 $15

Lefthanders are the only pitchers who have more lives than knuckleballers. Wakefield has been from minor league first baseman to surprise star of Pittsburgh's most recent playoff team (in 1992) to leading two leagues in losses to being better than mediocre in multiple roles for the Red Sox. He was more effective as a spot starter/reliever/sometime starter in 2001 and '02 than he was as a starter last season. For a flutterball pitcher, Wakefield has developed exceptional control, with K/W ratios better than 2:1 the last three years. It is very easy for baserunners to steal against Wakefield's slow offerings.

	W	SV	ERA	IP	H	BB	SO	B / I
2001 Boston	9	3	3.90	168	156	73	148	1.36
2002 Boston	11	3	2.81	163	121	51	134	1.05
2003 Boston	11	1	4.09	202	193	71	169	1.31

WALKER, JAMIE - TL - b: 7/1/71 $7

Walker was used as a situational lefty, but he's also good against righties and ended up being the Tigers most effective reliever and their only regular pitcher with an ERA under 4.00. He tends to hang curves and he is vulnerable to the long ball. He has two good consecutive seasons under his belt, though.

	W	SV	ERA	IP	H	BB	SO	B / I
2002 Detroit	1	1	3.71	44	32	9	40	0.94
2003 Detroit	4	3	3.32	65	61	17	45	1.20

WALKER, KEVIN - TL - b: 9/20/76 $0

Walker missed the first half of the season with a left elbow strain suffered in spring training and spent most of the second half in Triple-A before earning a late promotion. He had Tommy John surgery in August, 2001 and had not regained his former 95 MPH velocity, topping out in the low 90s. Control is an issue. If he can get back to form, he would be a quality lefthander in the bullpen.

	W	SV	ERA	IP	H	BB	SO	B / I
2003 San Diego	0	0	5.37	7	5	5	5	1.49

WALKER, PETE - TR - b: 4/8/69 $0

A pitcher with a fastball that peaks in the low 90s, at best, Walker was expected to battle for the fifth starter's job last year but suffered through a miserable first half as he battled both shoulder and knee problems for the first few months of the season. He wastes a lot of pitches and though he showed he could stretch out to being a starter in 2002, he was used as a swing man last year and looks destined for a long relief role this season. Barring a spring collapse, he'll spend all of this season in the majors though his starting opportunities will be few and far between.

	W	SV	ERA	IP	H	BB	SO	B / I
2002 NY - NL/TOR	10	1	4.36	140	145	51	80	1.40
2003 Toronto	2	0	4.88	55	59	24	29	1.50

WASHBURN, JARROD - TL - b: 8/13/74 $14

Washburn thrives by changing speeds on his low-90s fastball, which has good late movement. His breaking pitches are unexceptional. Washburn has developed into a dependable and durable starter, taking the ball every fifth day and turning in a quality start about two-thirds of the time. Washburn likes to challenge hitters with high fastballs, so he gets a lot of fly balls and is susceptible to the long ball. He holds runners very well and is a good fielder.

	W	SV	ERA	IP	H	BB	SO	B / I
2001 Anaheim	11	0	1.93	193	196	54	126	1.29
2002 Anaheim	18	0	3.15	206	183	59	139	1.17
2003 Anaheim	10	0	4.43	207	205	54	118	1.25

WEATHERS, DAVID - TR - b: 9/25/69 $7

Weathers had just 7 saves in 30 opportunities before last season, when he found himself in the role of Mets closer after they traded Armando Benitez. Weathers didn't have many games to save with a bad team, but he pitched well. Though he allowed plenty of baserunners, only 27 percent of his inherited runners scored. A low-90s fastball and a slider are his out pitches. Weathers' double-chinned visage has become a familiar sight in New York, where he has worked 148 games the last two seasons. He will be in the final year of a three-year, $9.4-million contract this year.

	W	SV	ERA	IP	H	BB	SO	B / I
2001 MIL/CHI - NL	4	4	2.41	86	65	34	66	1.14
2002 New York - NL	6	0	2.91	77	69	36	61	1.36
2003 New York - NL	1	7	3.08	88	87	40	75	1.45

WEAVER, JEFF - TR - b: 8/22/76 $1

Call him a 21st-century Ed Whitson. When the Yankees obtained Weaver in July 2002 from the Tigers, where he had pitched well with a team that made his record look bad, they thought they were acquiring a future staff ace. It hasn't worked that way at all. Perhaps because of the pressure to perform in big games in the bright lights of the big city, Weaver has been just a .500 pitcher with an escalating ERA for New York. He was in and out of the rotation last season, when lefthanders smacked him around at a .342 rate. If Weaver is right, he can get batters out with hard stuff — a mid-90s fastball and slider.

	W	SV	ERA	IP	H	BB	SO	B / I
2001 Detroit	13	0	4.08	229	235	68	152	1.32
2002 New York - AL	11	2	3.52	200	193	48	132	1.21
2003 New York - AL	7	0	5.99	159	211	47	93	1.62

WEBB, BRANDON - TR - b: 5/9/79 $15

Webb was a darkhorse candidate for NL Rookie of the Year in 2003 after blossoming in his first shot at the big time. Webb, recalled from Triple-A early in the season to replace an injured Randy Johnson in the starting rotation, did a very passable Johnson, arguably becoming the dominant horse on a staff that included Curt Schilling. Webb, a 2000 eighth-round draft choice out of the University of Kentucky, relies on a star-quality sinking fastball that batters can not seem to put into play. The ball breaks down and in to righthanded hitters and is almost impossible to center. He combines that with a late, hard slider that has the same movement to the opposite side of the plate. Webb, 24, holds runners well and is quick to the plate, which impedes the running game. He was expected to enter spring training as the No. 3 starter in the rotation, and with his stuff and mental approach has the makings of becoming a No. 1 or 2 starter in years to come.

	W	SV	ERA	IP	H	BB	SO	B / I
2003 Arizona	10	0	2.84	181	140	68	172	1.15

WEBER, BEN - TR - b: 11/17/69 $15

A finesse righthander, Weber keeps hitters off balance with a funky delivery and a sinking fastball that reaches the low 90s. Weber generally has excellent control and hitters find it hard to get the ball into the air against him with any regularity. He can be used frequently without a noticeable decline in his effectiveness. Weber is not often used in save situations, and generally pitches in the seventh and eighth innings. His delivery makes it difficult for him to control the running game. Weber was expected to continue in his role as a big league set-up man this year.

	W	SV	ERA	IP	H	BB	SO	B / I
2001 Anaheim	6	0	3.42	68	66	31	40	1.42
2002 Anaheim	7	7	2.54	78	70	22	43	1.18
2003 Anaheim	5	0	2.69	80	84	22	46	1.32

WELLEMEYER, TODD - TR - b: 8/30/78 $0

Wellemeyer features a blazing fastball, one he can throw close to 100 MPH on occasion, and a devastating changeup that can fool even the best big league hitters. He spent the second half of 2003 working on improving his curve, something that would go a long way toward ensuring his success at the big league level. His command suffered last season, as he had real problems throwing strikes at all three levels he pitched during the season. Though Wellemeyer has the stuff to be a successful starter, he likely will spend at least some of this season pitching out of the bullpen. If turned into a closer, a la Eric Gagne, Wellemeyer could be equally as dominating.

	W	SV	ERA	IP	H	BB	SO	B / I
2003 Chicago - NL	1	1	6.50	28	25	19	30	1.59

WELLS, DAVID - TL - b: 5/20/63 $14

Wells has always had excellent control, and it was better than ever in 2003, when his 20 walks were his lowest total in a season with 100 innings pitched. The downside was that too many of the strikes he threw were more hittable; opponents batted .286 with 24 homers against him. Despite a spring flap over uncomplimentary comments in a book he "wrote," he seems to be a good teammate who gets good run support from his offense. Wells throws mainly a high-80s fastball and a curve, but he's a fierce competitor who gets by with his limited arsenal.

	W	SV	ERA	IP	H	BB	SO	B / I
2001 Chicago - AL	5	0	4.47	100	120	21	59	1.40
2002 New York - AL	19	0	3.75	206	210	45	137	1.24
2003 New York - AL	15	0	4.14	213	242	20	101	1.23

WELLS, KIP - TR - b: 4/21/77 $14

Wells has been the Pirates best starting pitcher for the two years he has been in Pittsburgh. He has no particular killer pitch but he spots his fastball, curve and sinker very well and his results are far better than any other Pirates pitcher. He'll probably never be an impressive pitcher but he's good enough to win 14 games every year.

	W	SV	ERA	IP	H	BB	SO	B / I
2001 Chicago - AL	10	0	4.79	133	145	61	99	1.55
2002 Pittsburgh	12	0	3.59	198	197	71	134	1.35
2003 Pittsburgh	10	0	3.28	197	171	76	147	1.25

WENDELL, TURK - TR - b: 5/19/67 $1

Wendell blew out his elbow and he missed the entire 2002 season but he came back and was one of eight Phillies relievers to pitch in 50 games, or more, in 2003. In the early going he was effective but the bullpen was overworked and Wendell could have used a little more rest which led to a bad second half.

	W	SV	ERA	IP	H	BB	SO	B / I
2001 NY - NL/PHI	4	1	4.43	67	63	34	56	1.45
2003 Philadelphia	3	1	3.38	64	54	28	27	1.28

WESTBROOK, JAKE - TR - b: 9/29/77 $1

The highly regarded Westbrook should be ready to step forward. In a career plagued by health problems, Westbrook was injury free last year and the Indians threw him into the rotation when Jason Bere went on the DL early in the year. Westbrook responded with six consecutive decent starts in a row, averaging about six innings a game and allowing 12 earned runs in 36 innings. After Bere returned, Westbrook went to the bullpen but he'd made his case and after the All Star break Westbrook was in the rotation to stay and he pitched well. The Indians were careful to limit him to about six innings a game. He'll improve even more this year.

	W	SV	ERA	IP	H	BB	SO	B/I
2001 Cleveland	4	0	5.85	65	79	22	48	1.56
2002 Cleveland	1	0	5.83	42	50	12	20	1.49
2003 Cleveland	7	0	4.33	133	142	56	58	1.49

WHEELER, DAN - TR - b: 12/10/77 $1

The Mets' pitching staff, once loaded with prospects, has come down to players cast off by poor teams — such as Wheeler, formerly with Tampa Bay. The funny thing was that he pitched pretty well, both at Triple-A Norfolk (4-2, 3.94) and after his promotion to New York. Wheeler gave up less than one hit per inning and struck out more than twice as many as he walked. He doesn't throw hard, but his offspeed pitches made him very difficult for lefthanded batters to hit. Wheeler has earned another chance at a middle relief job this season.

	W	SV	ERA	IP	H	BB	SO	B/I
2001 Tampa Bay	1	0	8.64	18	30	5	12	1.98
2003 New York - NL	1	2	3.71	51	49	17	35	1.29

WHITE, GABE - TL - b: 11/20/71 $0

White was minding his own business on the Reds' disabled list, trying to figure out what to do in October, when the Yankees traded for him. He recovered from his groin injury in late August to help the Yankees get out lefthanders down the stretch. He's actually more effective against righthanders because he can mix up his changeup away with an average fastball in on their hands. White has exceptional control, which works well for him unless he's pitching in Colorado. An exceptional fielder, he committed the first error of his career last season. He'll be back as a setup man in 2004.

	W	SV	ERA	IP	H	BB	SO	B/I
2001 Colorado	1	0	6.25	67	70	26	47	1.42
2002 Cincinnati	6	0	2.98	54	49	10	41	1.09
2003 CIN/NY-AL	5	0	4.05	47	44	8	29	1.11

WHITE, RICK - TR - b: 12/23/68 $0

White is a veteran relief pitcher who tends to bounce from team to team each year. Originally signed by Pittsburgh in 1990 as a fifteenth round draft choice, he was viewed as a potential closer when he arrived in the majors in 1994. However, a series of injuries over the years have relegated him to a role in middle relief. White has a fastball in the 93 MPH range and an effective breaking pitch. He pitched well for Houston after being picked up in mid-August in 2003 and will compete for a job in a major league bullpen in 2004.

	W	SV	ERA	IP	H	BB	SO	B/I
2001 New York - NL	4	2	3.88	69	71	17	51	1.26
2002 COL/STL	5	0	4.31	63	62	21	41	1.32
2003 CHI - AL/HOU	1	1	5.78	67	74	21	54	1.42

WICKMAN, BOB - TR - b: 2/6/69 $0

Wickman had surgery to replace his right elbow ligament in 2002 but he was pitching again before

---

the end of the 2003 season and he and hopes to return to the majors in 2004. When healthy, he was the Rodney Dangerfield of major league closers. Wickman always seemed in danger of losing his job. As an atypical closer, he put a fair number of runners on base, didn't blow hitters away, and often had to pitch out of trouble. A fully recovered Wickman generally gets the job done. His out pitch is a good sinker, which is set up by his low-90s fastball and a slider.

	W	SV	ERA	IP	H	BB	SO	B/I
2001 Cleveland	5	32	2.39	67	61	14	66	1.11
2002 Cleveland	1	20	4.46	34	42	10	36	1.52

WILLIAMS, JEROME - TR - b: 12/4/81 $9

Williams' rapid development was one of the main reasons the Giants were able to trade Kurt Ainsworth for Sidney Ponson during the pennant chase last year. It was somewhat of a surprise that Williams made a significant contribution in San Francisco last year, considering he had to quit pitching in the Arizona Fall League after experiencing soreness in his right elbow. Still, once he proved in Triple-A that he was healthy, it was only a matter of time before he earned a promotion to San Francisco. Williams is a hard thrower who complements his fastball with a changeup that already is capable of making even experienced big league hitters look silly. Williams is a solid pitcher and will only continue to get better. Now that he's firmly established in the rotation, expect 12 to 15 wins this season.

	W	SV	ERA	IP	H	BB	SO	B/I
2003 San Francisco	7	0	3.30	131	116	49	88	1.26

WILLIAMS, MIKE - TR - b: 7/29/68 $0

Williams was a closer with the Pirates but when they traded him to Philadelphia, Bowa used him as a setup guy for the incendiary Jose Mesa, whose inconsistency gave Williams a lot of chances to take the job and when he did, Williams would promptly boot the job back to Mesa, who would then fumble it back to….

	W	S	ERA	IP	H	BB	SO	B/I
2001 PIT/HOU	6	22	3.80	64	60	35	59	1.48
2002 Pittsburgh	2	46	2.94	61	54	21	43	1.22
2003 PIT/PHI	1	28	6.14	63	66	41	39	1.70

WILLIAMS, WOODY - TR - b: 8/19/66 $10

A Cy Young candidate at the All-Star break, Williams, like many of the St. Louis pitchers, faltered down the stretch. He struggled with his command and his breaking pitches didn't have the bite they had earlier in the season, which hurt since he throws his fastball only in the low 90s. That meant his ERA for the second half of the season was well over 5.00, while opposing hitters batted nearly .300 against him. All of this is of great concern given his age and the number of innings he has thrown in recent years. Last year's total was the second highest of his career, and he has logged more than 200 innings in four of the last six seasons. Still, he should be good enough, and his arm should be healthy enough, to win 12 to15 games this season.

	W	SV	ERA	IP	H	BB	SO	B/I
2001 SD/STL	15	0	4.05	220	224	56	154	1.27
2002 St. Louis	9	0	2.53	103	84	25	76	1.06
2003 St. Louis	18	0	3.87	221	220	55	153	1.25

WILLIAMSON, SCOTT - TR - b: 2/17/76 $12

Williamson was part of the infusion of talent into Boston's bullpen. A closer in Cincinnati, he didn't have great success as a Red Sox setup man. Williamson throws a mid-90s fastball and hard slider that help him average about a strikeout an inning. Reconstructive elbow surgery cost him almost all of the 2001 season, but he didn't seem to have arm trouble last year. He tended to pitch carefully to lefthanded batters, resulting in a low strikeout/walk ratio, but challenged righties, who hit for a much higher average against him. Williamson still could be in the running for a major league closer's job.

	W	SV	ERA	IP	H	BB	SO	B/I
2001 Cincinnati	0	0	0.00	0	1	2	0	4.50
2002 Cincinnati	3	8	2.92	74	46	36	84	1.11
2003 CIN/BOS	5	21	4.16	63	54	34	74	1.40

WILLIS, DONTRELLE - TL - b: 1/12/82 $11

Willis had a tremendous debut in 2003. In addition to his funky leg kick and Luis Tiant motion, Willis is a fantastic athlete. Just having the coordination and balance to deliver his pitches from an uncoiling position is example enough of his physical talent but then you look at his results and throw in incidentals like his getting three hits in a playoff game and he's off the charts. The only concern from this vantage point is his motion. How much does he stress his shoulder, arm and elbow — and will it get to him? Also, factor in that Willis tossed over 200 innings at age 21 and, he warmed up, sat down and warmed up to relieve in postseason action — between starts.

	W	SV	ERA	IP	H	BB	SO	B/I
2003 Florida	14	0	3.30	161	148	58	142	1.28

WILSON, KRIS - TR - b: 8/6/76 $0

Kris Wilson spent another sporadic season with the Royals in 2003. Used infrequently out of the bullpen and for an occasional spot start, Wilson had some good moments, but more often was hit hard. He primarily throws a 90-MPH fastball, mixing in adequate changeups and curveballs. Wilson is not a strikeout pitcher, so he must hit the corners, but uneven use in 2003 impinged his ability to have good command. All too often Wilson would follow a good inning with a disastrous inning. Wilson is a superior athlete who was once a Georgia Tech quarterback prospect. He has major league stuff, but has had a hard time finding his proper role. Wilson has had especially poor results in short relief, yet as a starter he can barely go five innings. His future would seem to be as a long man out of the bullpen although his ability to make a start on short notice is a plus.

	W	SV	ERA	IP	H	BB	SO	B/I
2003 Kansas City	6	0	5.32	73	92	16	42	1.49

WILSON, PAUL - TR - b: 3/28/73 $1

Wilson was a faint glimmer of hope and the Reds most effective starter last year. A one time a flame throwing phenom, Wilson's injuries have sapped his power and he now exists by spotting a slider, curve and low octane fastball. Wilson's fiery personality is intact but his competitiveness led him to charge Cubs reliever Kyle Farnsworth, who brutally pancaked Wilson onto the ground which certainly did his fragile arm no good and predictably, Wilson had to be shut down before the year ended.

	W	SV	ERA	IP	H	BB	SO	B/I
2001 Tampa Bay	8	0	4.88	151	165	52	119	4.88
2002 Tampa Bay	6	0	4.83	194	219	67	111	1.48
2003 Cincinnati	8	0	4.64	167	190	50	93	1.44

WISE, MATT - TR - b: 11/18/75 $0

Wise is a tall finesse righthander whose fastball tops out in the high-80s. He also throws a changeup and slurve. He survives by moving the ball around and getting lefty hitters to chase the offspeed stuff. Wise has generally had excellent control in the high minors and in two brief major league trials. He missed all of last season with a ruptured elbow ligament that necessitated Tommy John surgery. Wise was expected to be ready for spring training, and will likely begin this season getting his innings in at Triple-A, with a promotion to the majors sometime in the season a possibility.

	W	SV	ERA	IP	H	BB	SO	B/I
2001 Anaheim	1	0	4.38	49	47	18	50	1.32

WITASICK, JAY - TR - b: 8/28/72 $0

Witasick was the designated San Diego closer when 2003 spring training opened in Trevor Hoffman's absence, but Witasick also got hurt, missing more than two months with a strained right flexor tendon. His second-half was strong when his 92-94 MPH fastball returned, although his command and defense was an issue. He was expected to open the season as a setup man.

	W	SV	ERA	IP	H	BB	SO	B/I
2001 SD/NY - AL	8	1	3.30	79	78	33	106	1.41
2002 San Francisco	1	0	2.37	68	58	21	54	1.16
2003 San Diego	3	2	4.53	46	42	25	42	1.47

WOHLERS, MARK - TR - b: 1/23/70 $0

Wohlers was an ace closer for the Braves from 1995-97, but then struggled with wildness and arm surgery. In 2002, he overcame all that and became a valuable part of the Indians bullpen, where his role was a setup man, middle reliever, and occasional closer. Wohlers had a bone chip removed in March 2003, and his recovery stalled when ligament damage to his elbow was discovered later in the year. He did not pitch at all in 2003. With a full recovery, Wohlers relies on a low 90s fastball and a splitter in his role as a middle reliever and setup man.

	W	SV	ERA	IP	H	BB	SO	B/I
2001 CIN/NY - AL	4	0	4.26	67	69	25	54	1.39
2002 Cleveland	3	7	4.80	71	71	26	46	1.36

WOLF, RANDY - TL - b: 8/22/76 $14

Wolf is a low octane control specialist and the closest thing that the National League has to Jaime Moyer. The soft tossing Moyer won 20 games at age 40 and Wolf is only 27 so, barring an injury, Wolf will maintain his performance level for a few more years. Wolf has a 90 MPH fastball, but because of his changeup, he is just as tough against righty batters as lefties.

	W	SV	ERA	IP	H	BB	SO	B/I
2001 Philadelphia	10	0	3.70	163	150	51	152	1.23
2002 Philadelphia	11	0	3.20	211	172	63	172	1.12
2003 Philadelphia	16	0	4.23	200	176	78	177	1.27

WOOD, KERRY - TR - b: 6/16/77 $17

Wood is blessed with some of the greatest physical attributes of any pitcher in baseball. He has one of the strongest arms around and can consistently throw the ball in the mid 90s, even late in the game. He also can throw a devastating curve that is nearly impossible to hit when thrown across the plate. However, the thing that is keeping him from being truly great is his lack of control. Wood has been in the big leagues since 1998, yet hasn't been able to learn to let hitters get themselves out every now and then. He consistently overthrows, trying to get a strikeout all the time, which leads to high pitch counts and likely costs him several wins a year. Wood will never be anything more than a number three or four starter, despite his gifts, until he figures out how to keep his pitch count down. Given his age, experience and apparent stubbornness, that is unlikely to happen.

	W	SV	ERA	IP	H	BB	SO	B/I
2001 Chicago - NL	12	6	3.36	174	127	92	217	1.26
2002 Chicago - NL	12	0	3.66	214	169	97	217	1.24
2003 Chicago - NL	14	0	3.20	211	152	100	266	1.19

WOOD, MIKE - TR - b: 4/26/80 $0

The Athletics groomed Wood much as they did with their big three starters, Barry Zito, Mark Mulder and Tim Hudson. Like those three, Wood doesn't have an overpowering fastball that lights up the radar guns. He just throws a lot of strikes and keeps getting batters out. Wood could be the fourth or fifth starter on most big league ballclubs. Like Rich Harden, he has some learning to do before he becomes a consistent winner. He won't be a big winner this season, even if he spends the whole year in the major leagues. More likely he will start the season in Triple-A to get just a little more experience.

	W	SV	ERA	IP	H	BB	SO	B/I
2003 Oakland	2	0	10.51	14	24	7	15	2.26

WORRELL, TIM - TR - b: 7/5/67 $32

Going into last season, Worrell was about the last guy anybody would have expected to save 38 games. He was in his mid 30s, had 10 career saves in 10 seasons, didn't throw very hard (and never did), and was never really considered to be a closer for any of the seven clubs for which he had pitched. Yet, Worrell filled in for the injured Robb Nen as well as could be expected. He was consistent, dependable and reliable, despite not having overpowering stuff. His fastball doesn't get out of the low 90s and he doesn't possess an outstanding breaking pitch. Worrell is a competent reliever, though he should not be considered an exceptional one. A lot of big league relievers are capable of saving 30 games. If he gets a shot at being the closer again this year, there is no reason why Worrell can't do that as well.

	W	SV	ERA	IP	H	BB	SO	B/I
2001 San Francisco	2	0	3.45	78	71	33	63	1.33
2002 San Francisco	8	0	2.25	72	55	30	55	1.18
2003 San Francisco	4	38	2.87	78	74	28	65	1.30

WRIGHT, DAN - TR - b: 12/14/77 $0

Wright's disappointing season was yet another reason why the White Sox weren't able to put up much of a fight in the AL Central last year. Wright, a former second round draft pick, was expected to use his sinker to get plenty of easy outs. However, he had trouble getting that sinker in the strike zone and gave up a ton of home runs. He finally was pulled from the rotation early in September as the White Sox were desperate for consistent pitching. The fact that Wright threw more than six innings only four times last season means that he likely is better suited to being a long reliever and spot starter than a regular member of the rotation. Starting pitchers are hard to find, however, so Wright will get another try or two before he gets banished to the bullpen for good. Don't expect him to last long in the rotation, however.

	W	SV	ERA	IP	H	BB	SO	B/I
2001 Chicago - AL	5	0	5.70	66	78	39	36	1.76
2002 Chicago - AL	14	0	5.18	196	200	71	136	1.38
2003 Chicago - AL	1	1	6.15	86	91	46	47	1.59

WRIGHT, JAMEY - TR - b: 12/24/74 $0

Journeyman Jamey Wright made a particularly long journey in 2003, belonging to the Seattle, Milwaukee, and Texas organizations before joining the Royals at Triple-A Omaha in mid-season. Wright surprised even the most optimistic Royals coaches as he refined his curveball to become a viable big league starter who was especially sharp during the Royals September pennant push. Wright has outstanding natural movement on his pitches, including a fastball that reaches 94 MPH and an upper 80s sinker. The Royals tinkered with his mechanics, straightening him into a more upright delivery, and it worked wonders as he found the strikezone with more consistency and his pitches regained their movement. Wright is still capable of following long stretches of being unhittable with fatal mistakes which let the opposition post a crooked number on the scoreboard. Wright owns an outstanding pickoff move and he moves well to field his position. As one of several successful reclamation projects for the Royals in 2003, Wright will have a chance to win a rotation job in spring training, 2004. To win the job he'll need to maintain and improve his stamina within the ballgame; he regularly runs into difficulty when going past the fifth inning.

	W	SV	ERA	IP	H	BB	SO	B/I
2001 Milwaukee	11	0	4.90	194	201	98	129	1.54
2002 MIL/STL	7	0	5.29	129	130	75	77	1.59
2003 Kansas City	1	0	4.27	25	23	11	19	1.34

WRIGHT, JARET - TR - b: 12/29/75 $0

Jaret Wright's star has fallen considerably since his 1997 World Series Game Seven start. Shoulder surgery forced him from the Indians rotation for the first time in 2000 and he struggled to get back to previous form before ending up in the Padres bullpen in 2003. The Braves claimed him off waivers August 30th and he made ten scoreless appearances in eleven outings down the stretch. Wright throws two different hard fastballs in the mid-90s, as well as a hard curve and deceptive changeup. Late in 2003 Wright appeared to be regaining some of his previous velocity, although command remained a problem; he managed to place among league leaders in wild pitches despite throwing just 55.1 innings. If he can pitch with more consistency, Wright could again become a solid addition to any big-league staff, either in the bullpen or in the starting rotation.

	W	SV	ERA	IP	H	BB	SO	B/I
2001 Cleveland	2	0	6.52	29	36	22	18	2.00
2002 Cleveland	2	0	15.71	18	40	19	12	3.20
2003 Atlanta	2	2	7.35	56	76	31	50	1.90

WUNSCH, KELLY - TL - b: 7/12/72 $0

Wunsch was so thoroughly dominating last year that it's hard to believe that he didn't escape his somewhat limited role. Wunsch, always tough against lefthanded hitters, was nearly as dominant against righthanded swingers. Overall, opponents batted only .139 against him, primarily because his sharp breaking curve was nearly unhittable. His other best asset is his ability to keep the ball in the ballpark. He allowed only one home run last year, and has given up but four long balls in the past two seasons. Given a chance, Wunsch could be an effective closer. However, given his age he is unlikely to get that opportunity. He'll pitch effectively in middle relief again this year.

	W	SV	ERA	IP	H	BB	SO	B/I
2001 Chicago - AL	2	0	7.66	22	21	9	16	1.35
2002 Chicago - AL	2	0	3.41	32	26	19	22	1.42
2003 Chicago - AL	0	0	2.75	36	17	25	33	1.17

YOUNG, JASON - TR - b: 9/28/79 $0

Young proudly featured a pitch he claimed to invent last season - the "Vulcan changeup," thrown with the ball placed between the middle and third finger, as Mr. Spock might grip it. But that is not what gives him the best chance at the Colorado starting rotation. Young, a second round draft choice out of Stanford in 2000, has a fastball in the low-90s and also features a hard slider. After missing half the 2001 season with elbow soreness, he won 13 games at two levels in 2002 and got his first taste of the majors in 2003. Although he was battered around, he is a player the Rockies feel has a solid future. Young was expected to open the season at Triple-A Colorado Springs in order to work every fifth day, although it would not be a surprise to see him in the majors early this season.

	W	SV	ERA	IP	H	BB	SO	B/I
2003 Colorado	0	0	8.45	21	34	9	18	2.02

ZAMBRANO, CARLOS - TR - b: 6/1/81 $14

An imposing figure on the mound, Zambrano combines a power arm with a knowledge of how to pitch rarely seen in such a young hurler. He throws consistently in the mid-90s and could challenge guys like Kerry Wood or Curt Schilling for the league lead in strikeouts if he wanted. However, Zambrano pounds hitters with his heavy sinker and is content to use a minimum of pitches and let hitters get themselves out. His second-half performance from last season, where he was one of the most consistent winners the Cubs had, is an indication he is ready to move up into the elite class of pitchers in all of baseball. Barring a major injury, he will be a consistent winner for many years to come.

	W	SV	ERA	IP	H	BB	SO	B/I
2001 Chicago - NL	1	0	15.26	7	11	8	4	2.48
2002 Chicago - NL	4	0	3.66	108	94	63	93	1.45
2003 Chicago - NL	13	0	3.11	214	188	94	168	1.32

ZAMBRANO, VICTOR - TR - b: 8/6/75 $5

Zambrano had more success as a starter than he did as a reliever in 2002, and in 2003 he was used even more so as a starter, proving very effective in that capacity for the Devil Rays, and also posting the only winning record of their starters. He started the season on the rotation, but after difficulties in April was sent to the bullpen, then to the minors for 2 weeks in May. Upon returning from Triple-A Durham, he had several good pitching performances during the season, finishing the season as Tampa Bay's de facto ace. When Zambrano's fastball and changeup's location is good, he pitches effectively. When it's not, he gets pounded.

	W	SV	ERA	IP	H	BB	SO	B/I
2001 Tampa Bay	6	2	3.16	51	38	18	58	1.09
2002 Tampa bay	8	1	5.53	114	120	68	73	1.65
2003 Tampa Bay	12	0	4.21	188	165	106	132	1.44

ZIMMERMAN, JEFF - TR - b: 8/9/72 $0

Zimmerman has missed the last two seasons due to Tommy John surgery, but was tentatively expected to be ready for spring training. Some pitchers are more effective after the surgery than they were before it, so there is a chance that Zimmerman could be quite good in 2004. His out pitch is a devastating slider that is almost unhittable when Zimmerman has his "A" game. When he was healthy, Zimmerman was an effective closer, although he could be used initially for setup work this season.

	W	SV	ERA	IP	H	BB	SO	B/I
2001 Texas	3	28	2.40	71	48	16	72	0.90

ZITO, BARRY - TL - b: 5/13/78 $24

For the first time in his career last year, Zito wasn't a big winner, for a couple of reasons. It's true that he wasn't quite as sharp in 2003; he struck out fewer hitters and walked more than he did the previous two seasons. He also was a victim of Oakland's somewhat weak offense, especially in the first half of the season. He was the loser, or got a no-decisions, ten times last year when he still threw a "quality start" (pitching six innings or more while allowing three runs or less. Zito's curve ball is perhaps the best in the big leagues, and is nearly impossible for lefthanded swingers to hit. He also is able to run his fastball in to righthanded hitters to keep them off balance. Zito is one of the top pitchers in the game and it will be a surprise if he doesn't rebound to contend for the Cy Young award.

	W	SV	ERA	IP	H	BB	SO	B/I
2001 Oakland	17	0	3.49	214	184	80	205	1.23
2002 Oakland	23	0	2.75	229	182	78	182	1.13
2003 Oakland	14	0	3.30	232	186	88	146	1.18

4

Down on the Farm

Down on the Farm
By Lary Bump

The 2004 Minor League Report

John Benson posed the question this way: "If you could have picked anyone in the minor leagues on August 31, and draft him for 2004, who would it be?" Uh, let's see ... Perhaps we'll get back to you on that one. John was making a point. There didn't seem to be any sure-fire, can't-miss prospects for 2004 who weren't already in the majors. And going back a year the same phenomenon was visible for 2003, although less pronounced.

On August 31, 2002, Miguel Cabrera wouldn't have been predicted to have the impact he would have in 2003. Hell, he wouldn't have been projected on March 31 to have any big impact. And that was even though plenty of managers, scouts and writers (myself included) had seen him have an impressive spring.

Scott Podsednik was an aging ex-prospect. He was already 27 years old on opening day, with 26 major league at-bats and a .192 average through 2002. Really, who could have seen him coming? Even Milwaukee manager Ned Yost didn't until he was up to here with Alex Sanchez.

Dontrelle Willis? Oh, yeah, we heard about him as the Sports Weekly Minor League Pitcher of the Year, but that was in A ball. He did some nice pitching in spring training, but so did others who went to Double-A for opening day - and stayed there.

Brandon Webb? Baseball America headlined the cover proclaiming him as its Rookie of the Year this way: "Brandon Webb emerges from obscurity."

That brings up another point. The top rookies of 2004 might not have been in the minor leagues last season for very long, if at all. The rookie talent these days might not seem as exciting as in the days when we heard hype about the top players in Triple-A, but it might be more important. And clearly, it's coming from deeper in the minors. Two pitchers who were drafted last June - the Reds' Ryan Wagner and the Expos' Chad Cordero - were contributing to major league bullpens within a few weeks.

It seems likely that the best rookie pitchers of 2004 - like Willis and Webb last year - will rise from Class A or Double-A. In 2003, the Triple-A level was woefully short of hard-throwing prospects, but the high-A Carolina and Florida State leagues and the low-A Midwest League (where Willis began a year earlier) were heavy on pitching studs.

This season's top rookie might have been in the majors last year - but in another country. In August of '02, Hideki Matsui was more rumor than reality on these shores, like his namesake was a rumor in August '03. During the past off-season, one of the most highly sought free agents was first baseman Lee Seung-yeop, who set the Asian season record of 56 home runs in the Korean Baseball Organization. Major league teams were bidding for another Korean slugger, Shim Jong-soo, as well as Japanese shortstop Kazuo Matsui and second baseman Tadahita Iguchi. Rookie talent is coming from less traditional sources in part because the job description for major league general managers has swung from scout more toward bean counter. Of course they're supposed to put a competitive team on the field, but they're also supposed to save money, or spend it wisely.

With a new generation of GMs comes a new realization, one of the basic baseball truths of the 21st century, one we have been telling you about for years. These GMs know that

Triple-A baseball is an extension of the major league bench, and that at any time there are a couple of highly professional first basemen in the minors. Thus, the Tigers could bring up Kevin Witt to replace slumping "prospect" Carlos Pena. It seems as if Phil Hiatt, David McCarty and Alan Zinter are always available, as they were last season. The GMs know they could bring one of those first basemen up to the majors and pay him a few hundred thousand dollars - and that there wouldn't be much difference at bat between him and the guy who was a $5-million disappointment. If the truth hurts, so be it. Another money-driven trend in the majors is diverting money and attention toward pitching and away from the sluggers who dominated the '90s as if the '30s had come back to roost.

Pitching, pitching and pitching: three things no major league team can get enough of. Remember how last spring the Yankees didn't think they had enough starting pitchers with Roger Clemens, Mike Mussina, Andy Pettitte, David Wells, Jeff Weaver and possibly even Sterling Hitchcock? Remember, too, how the Bronx Bombers went out and got "rookie" Jose Contreras from Cuba? That tells you about the value of pitching today. So does the fact that the Yanks discarded and picked up relief pitchers as if they were so many cards in a rummy game. College students are well aware of where jobs are available or scarce, and they tend to gravitate toward professions where there are openings. "There's a shortage of teachers? Then, by golly, I'm an education major." Young athletes are taking the same tack. All they had to do was pick up a newspaper - no, pardon me, this is the 21st century, so they looked at a web site - to see that run production was up, there was a glut of hitters and a shortage of pitching. "By golly, I'm a pitcher."

The old model used to be that if a good amateur pitching prospect could hit, it wouldn't matter how well he threw. He'd become a position player only as a pro. For examples, think of Dave Winfield, Cal Ripken Jr. and John Olerud. Now the state of pitching need has meant that some prospects who became position players have been turned back into pitchers - for example, Ron Mahay and Brooks Kieschnick, who first made it to the majors as outfielders. It's almost as if anybody, especially a lefthanded thrower, has a pitching background to go along with his everyday position, he'll become a pro pitcher. Organizations are even looking at catchers, right fielders and shortstops with really strong arms and trying to see whether they can pitch. Woody Williams was a shortstop at the University of Houston. Trevor Hoffman was drafted as a shortstop. Troy Percival began his pro career as a catcher. Stephen Randolph was a college first baseman. In 2003, he was doing his on-the-job pitching training not in the minors, but in the Diamondbacks' bullpen. Rafael Soriano started his baseball career as an outfielder. Dodgers pitching prospect Edwin Jackson is another who switched to pitching after becoming a pro player. Pitchers today can hit and field - because they are good athletes. Today's up-and-coming pitchers are looking more like Roger Clemens than like David Wells or Randy Johnson. Look at the world-champion Marlins' starting rotation, with pitchers who look more like linebackers than baseball players. Brad Penny played a big role in the first World Series victory by driving in two runs with a single and setting up another with a sacrifice bunt. Kerry Wood might have had a better postseason with his bat than with his arm.

A side effect of having more top athletes turning to pitching is that the state of hitting, so high a decade ago, is in decline. The batting champions in the Double-A Texas League and high Class A Florida State League barely broke .300. It certainly was exciting to have nine players finish within three points in the Texas League batting race, but it doesn't look very impressive on the resume of Arkansas outfielder Jake Weber (Angels organization) that he led the league at .302. Also, power still sells tickets, so minor league power hitters don't stick around long enough to accumulate high home run totals. They either earn a promotion to a higher minor league or the big-league club, or have their contract sold to a Japanese team. The highest home run total by a minor league leader last season was 34 by first baseman Graham Koonce. At 28, he's too old to be a viable long-term prospect.

In preparing for your auction or draft, keep these ideas in mind, and read on for some tips on what to look for in young players. But don't stop here. Continue your research through spring training and even into the regular season, so you don't miss a Rocco Baldelli or Mark Teixeira or Jody Gerut. Equally important, you don't want to jump on this year's version of a bust such as Bobby Hill, Joe Thurston or Joe Borchard.

John Benson's Forecast Draft Software and internet Private Pages, along with baseballnotebook.com, stats.com, and fantasybaseballscout.com, are our favorite sources of information, but we always advise you to look at whatever you think can help you. There is a lot of useful information in print, on the air waves and online. Your challenge is to be able to separate the substance from the hype.

Who are the hottest rookies? Although the answers can't be "known" until mid 2004, there are some methods that will work immediately. We can tell you what types of players to look for and where to look for them. You should start your search with the majors' worst teams, the ones that need the most help. They have the most openings and opportunity - a word that means playing time. You'll also need to follow free agency effects, trades and other changes of scenery that could affect the chances of both existing major leaguers and prospects.

What have we learned? Some of the basic truths that we have held self-evident still apply. And believe me, even though those truths are self-evident, they are not inalienable. We examine them regularly to make sure they still apply. Let's examine some of those tried-and-true truths to see if they're still true.

Ask three questions about minor league pitchers. Can he get a strikeout when he needs it? Does he have control? Is it hard to hit his pitches? If the answer to those three questions is yes, then you will usually have a good pitching prospect. He won't give up a lot of hits or walks, so he'll have a good ratio. Without a lot of runners cluttering up the basepaths, he isn't likely to give up a lot of runs. Ergo, a relatively low ERA. Combining those factors with other variables, primarily how good his team is, he could rack up high numbers of wins or saves.

Good minor league statistics, even in Rotisserie categories, don't necessarily correlate to major league success. There are differences in ballparks and leagues. Another factor is that breaking-ball pitchers who excel in the upper minors usually won't be successful in the majors unless they can blow away a big-league batter now and again. Pitchers with good curves, sinkers, and sliders can be outstanding in the minors, because batters will swing at low-moving pitches that aren't strikes. In the majors, those low offerings become ball one, ball two, ball three, and then a fastball up in the zone, easy to hit.

We want our pitching prospects to have a strikeout/walk ratio of 2.5:1 or better, and an opponents' batting average lower than .250. We call that the Rule of 25, because both 2.5 and .250 can be expressed by mathematicians better than we are as 25 to some kind of power of 10. And 25 is easier to remember than 2.5 or .250. We took a list of 106 of today's minor league prospects and chopped it up into fourths. The 13 pitchers listed below came out in the top one-quarter in both K/W ratio and opponents' batting average. You should consider them the best of the best prospects. They might not all make it this season, but you should file away the names of those from the lower minors. One or more of them could be this year's Dontrelle Willis.

Triple-A relievers: Fernando Rodney, Tigers, and Jesse Crain, Twins. Relievers naturally have better raw statistics than starters because they are used in more optimum situations. However, these two were exceptional, holding opponents to averages in the .150s and striking out about 4 ½ batters for every one they walked. Minor league starters who reached the majors briefly during 2003: Rafael Soriano, Mariners; Juan Dominguez, Rangers; Chin-hui Tsao, Rockies; Chad Gaudin, Devil Rays.

From Double-A: Joe Blanton, Athletics.

Class A pitchers: Kameron Loe, Rangers; John Maine, Orioles; Cole Hamels, Phillies; Blake Hawksworth, Cardinals; Matthew Cain and Merkin Valdez, Giants.

1-2-3 strikes, and young batters are out at the old ballgame. Just as it's important for young pitchers to make batters miss the strikes that they throw, it's important for young hitters to be able to make consistent contact. Just as it's important for pitchers to be able to blow away a hitter, it's important for those hitters to show some power when they make contact. Think of it this way. Has Barry Bonds hit so many runs the last few years because he's a wild swinger? Of course not. He is so selective at the plate that he forces pitchers either to throw strikes he can hit hard or to walk him. Either option can cause pitchers problems, and work to Bonds' and the Giants' advantage. Don't get the wrong idea. There isn't a Barry Bonds in this year's group of prospects. No one hit more than 34 homers in the minors last season. But you want to look first for a batter who makes contact, with a good walk/strikeout ratio.

A quick way to try to find contact hitters, and those who walk frequently, is to look at league leaders in on-base percentage. We compared the 48 leaders in the 10 top minor leagues in both walk/strikeout ratio (to determine their ability as contact hitters) and slugging percentage (to learn which of those also had some pop in their bats). Again, that group was divided into four groups in each category. Three of the 48 players were in the top one-quarter in both BB/K ratio and slugging percentage. All reached Double-A ball last season, and bear watching this spring and summer. They are third baseman/second baseman Brian Myrow from the Yankees organization; first baseman/catcher Chris Shelton, Pirates; and outfielder Greg Jacobs, Mariners.

Avoid over-aged rookies. Despite what Podsednik did last year, it's best not to gamble on players several years beyond the optimum age for prospects. In nine years in the minors, his best average was .290 in 269 at-bats in the hitter-friendly Pacific Coast League, and his highest stolen base total was 35. It's anybody's guess how he batted .314 with 43 steals for the Brewers. He was age 27 and had only 26 major-league at-bats.

What is a "good" age for a prospect? Easy to remember, and useful, are: 23 for a player coming out of Triple-A, 22 for a player in Double-A, 21 for high Class A, and 20 for low Class A.

Give extra credit for well organized scouting and player development. Some major league organizations just seem to get it. So it's good to recognize which organizations those are, and figure that the prospects they favor could really pay off. The elements that define a scouting and minor league system as a winner are talented scouts, a commitment to player development, organized instruction, an organizational focus on unified methods for playing the game and - not least of all - a commitment of money. There's a history behind this, going back to the 1930s when Branch Rickey established the best-organized farm system.

When the free-agency era began, some organizations tried unsuccessfully to take the quick and easy road to success by spending money on established stars. The smarter teams went back toward growing their own talent. Compare, for example, the Yankees of 1985-1995 with the more recent vintages that brought Derek Jeter, Bernie Williams, Andy Pettitte et al. through their farm system. Our picks for best systems right now appear on page 337.

Why should you listen to us? The simple answer to this question is "Because we're good." We have been formulating and refining methods for identifying the top prospects for years. As we just showed above, we test and re-examine old truths. Just because they've worked for a long time doesn't mean conditions can't change. If you go back and look at the profiles of our top 100 in last year's book, you'll see that it was heavy with long-range prospects from the lower minors. Even so, half of those players were in the major leagues during 2003. Our rookie all-star teams included Hank Blalock, Carl Crawford, Sean Burroughs, Marlon Byrd and Brett Myers. And you would have found Miguel Cabrera, Jeremy Bonderman, Rocco Baldelli and Mark Teixeira on lists compiled well before those players had been able to show anything in spring training. In 2001, we identified Juan Pierre, Doug Mientkiewicz, Jimmy Rollins, Ben Sheets and Barry Zito as ready for immediate success. A year later, Josh Beckett, Vernon Wells and Nick Johnson were among the names on our list. We said, nearly a year before his World Series success, that Francisco Rodriguez was the best AL pitching prospect for the long term. He was included on our list of players who were "good bets for 2003 or 2004" - along with Jose Reyes and Miguel Cabrera. So, you see? We do have an eye for talent. Actually, several eyes. And we know what we're talking about.

Pages 338-344 include our latest cut at identifying the best long-term prospects. We use methods developed by Tony Blengino, who got a job as a major league scout and so cannot write and analyze for us any longer. Fortunately for us and for you, Tony left his methods behind. The basic concept is that a year of age is worth one standard deviation in total offensive performance (a refined version of on-base plus slugging percentages, with a similar measure for pitchers) compared to league median performance. Just be clear that we are focused on long-term potential, not this-year likelihood of a callup. That is why you see some low Class A players ranked higher than Triple-A players. The question is how well they perform when they get to the majors, not how soon they will arrive. There is a tendency for top players to rise quickly, however, as evidenced by the ranking of players like Miguel Cabrera for what they did in the minors in 2003. We look at quality of performance, not quantity of performance. The measures for hitters and pitchers are both called "RPP" - relative production potential and relative pitching potential. The emphasis is on potential. ("If you see it, it's real.")

Just remember that one unit is worth one year of age or one standard deviation in total performance compared to league median. A score of +2.0 means a player performed at the league median while two years younger than the "good" age (identified above) or had the "good" age and performed two standard deviations above the league median, for example.

Note: Lary Bump is the President of Fantasy Baseball Scout (fantasybaseballscout.com) and the Commissioner of the World Championship of Fantasy Baseball. He once was described as "John Benson's minor league wizard."

Best Organizations for 2003 Minor League Talent

	Quantity of Good Prospects			Intensity of Top Talent		
	Overall	Offense	Pitching	Overall	Offense	Pitching
1	Cubs	Indians	Cubs	Dodgers	Indians	Cubs
2	Braves	Twins	Braves	Braves	Dodgers	Dodgers
3	Indians	D-Backs	Angels	Cubs	Braves	Braves
4	D-Backs	Dodgers	D-Backs	Angels	D-Rays	Angels
5	Dodgers	Yankees	Indians	Marlins	Brewers	Marlins
6	Angels	D-Rays	Dodgers	Indians	Royals	Giants
7	Marlins	Brewers	Marlins	Tigers	Angels	Phillies
8	ChiSox	Blue Jays	Giants	Royals	Yankees	D-Backs
9	Blue Jays	Cubs	Mariners	D-Rays	Tigers	Mariners
10	(tie) Athletics Rangers Rangers White Sox	(tie) Braves Royals	(tie) Athletics Pirates	D-Backs	Twins	Rangers

Leaders by League

Relative Production Potential and Relative Pitching Potential

International League

RANK	NAME	LEV	TM	ML	POS	RPP
1	Infante, Omar	AAA	TOL	DET	SS	2.906
2	Betemit, Wilson	AAA	RIC	ATL	3B	2.880
3	Martinez, Victor	AAA	BUF	CLE	C	2.761
4	Morneau, Justin	AAA	ROC	MIN	1B	2.555
5	Rodney, Fernando	AAA	TOL	DET	P	2.437
6	Moseley, Dustin	AAA	LOU	CIN	P	2.303
7	Ross, Cody	AAA	TOL	DET	OF	2.177
8	Crain, Jesse	AAA	ROC	MIN	P	2.097
9	Cantu, Jorge	AAA	DUR	TB	SS	2.087
10	Martinez, Luis	AAA	IND	MIL	P	1.895
11	Madson, Ryan	AAA	SWB	PHI	P	1.833
12	De La Rosa, Jorge	AAA	PAW	BOS	P	1.811
13	Sequea, Jorge	AAA	SYR	TOR	2B	1.770
14	Izturis, Maicer	AAA	BUF	CLE	SS	1.677
15	Waechter, Doug	AAA	DUR	TB	P	1.349
16	Crisp, Coco	AAA	BUF	CLE	OF	1.236
17	Calzado, Napoleon	AAA	OTT	BAL	3B	1.157
18	Henson, Drew	AAA	COL	NYY	3B	1.141

19	Brazelton, Dewon	AAA	DUR	TB	P	1.139
20	LaRoche, Adam	AAA	RIC	ATL	1B	0.977
21	Hall, Bill	AAA	IND	MIL	2B	0.965
22	Belisle, Matt	AAA	LOU	CIN	P	0.905
23	Raines Jr, Tim	AAA	OTT	BAL	OF	0.874
24	Riley, Matt	AAA	OTT	BAL	P	0.869
25	Diaz, Felix	AAA	CHL	CHW	P	0.812

Pacific Coast League

RANK	NAME	LEV	TM	ML	POS	RPP
1	Gonzalez, Edgar	AAA	TUS	AZ	P	4.196
2	Harden, Rich	AAA	SAC	OAK	P	3.219
3	Bonser, Boof	AAA	FRS	SF	P	3.172
4	Williams, Jerome	AAA	FRS	SF	P	3.047
5	Perez, Oliver	AAA	POR	SD	P	2.876
6	Bruney, Brian	AAA	TUS	AZ	P	2.528
7	Crosby, Bobby	AAA	SAC	OAK	SS	2.270
8	Soriano, Rafael	AAA	TAC	SEA	P	2.119
9	Fernandez, Alex	AAA	POR	SD	OF	1.674
10	Haren, Dan	AAA	MEM	STL	P	1.370
11	Bay, Jason	AAA	POR	SD	OF	1.349
12	Cormier, Lance	AAA	TUS	AZ	P	1.268
13	Wood, Mike	AAA	SAC	OAK	P	1.200
14	DeJesus, David	AAA	OMA	KC	OF	1.133
15	Edwards, Mike	AAA	SAC	OAK	OF	0.997
16	Johnson, Rett	AAA	TAC	SEA	P	0.924
17	Davis, J.J.	AAA	NAS	PIT	OF	0.899
18	Cruz, Juan	AAA	IWA	CHC	P	0.807
19	Lewis, Colby	AAA	OKL	TEX	P	0.735
20	Song, Seung	AAA	EDM	MON	P	0.549
21	Atkins, Garrett	AAA	COS	COL	3B	0.530
22	Young, Jason	AAA	COS	COL	P	0.489
23	Terrero, Luis	AAA	TUS	AZ	OF	0.429
24	Tracy, Chad	AAA	TUS	AZ	3B	0.423
25	Linden, Todd	AAA	FRS	SF	OF	0.346

Eastern League

RANK	NAME	LEV	TM	ML	POS	RPP
1	Navarro, Dioner	AA	TRE	NYY	C	3.938
2	Crain, Jesse	AA	NB	MIN	P	2.862
3	McGowan, Dustin	AA	NH	TOR	P	2.860
4	Burnett, Sean	AA	ALT	PIT	P	2.741
5	Mauer, Joe	AA	NB	MIN	C	2.734
6	Sizemore, Grady	AA	AKR	CLE	OF	2.729
7	Quiroz, Guillermo	AA	NH	TOR	C	2.392
8	Connolly, Mike	AA	ALT	PIT	P	2.017
9	Rios, Alexis	AA	NH	TOR	OF	1.748
10	Cruceta, Francisco	AA	AKR	CLE	P	1.713
11	Durbin, J.D.	AA	NB	MIN	P	1.707
12	Buchholz, Taylor	AA	REA	PHI	P	1.678
13	Huber, Justin	AA	BNG	NYM	C	1.638
14	Keppel, Bob	AA	BNG	NYM	P	1.628
15	Oquendo, Ian	AA	ALT	PIT	P	1.569
16	Cabrera, Fernando	AA	AKR	CLE	P	1.526
17	De La Rosa, Jorge	AA	PRT	BOS	P	1.439

18	Peterson, Matt	AA	BNG	NYM	P	1.318
19	Smith, Corey	AA	AKR	CLE	3B	1.273
20	Bonser, Boof	AA	NOR	SF	P	1.212

Southern League

RANK	NAME	LEV	TM	ML	POS	RPP
1	Miller, Greg	AA	JAC	LA	P	7.581
2	Cabrera, Miguel	AA	CAR	FLA	3B	5.292
3	Jackson, Edwin	AA	JAC	LA	P	4.148
4	Reed, Jeremy	AA	BIR	CHW	OF	3.750
5	Pilkington, Brian	AA	JAC	LA	P	2.732
6	Willis, Dontrelle	AA	CAR	FLA	P	2.670
7	Ryu, Jae-kuk	AA	WTE	CHC	P	2.637
8	Jones, Mike	AA	HVL	MIL	P	2.600
9	Haren, Dan	AA	TEN	STL	P	2.235
10	Bautista, Denny	AA	CAR	FLA	P	2.232
11	Hardy, J.J.	AA	HVL	MIL	SS	2.210
12	Germano, Justin	AA	MOB	SD	P	2.163
13	Hanrahan, Joel	AA	JAC	LA	P	2.076
14	Encarnacion, Edwin	AA	CHT	CIN	3B	2.038
15	Guzman, Angel	AA	WTE	CHC	P	1.953
16	Diaz, Victor	AA	JAC	LA	2B	1.773
17	Johnson, Kelly	AA	GRV	ATL	SS	1.677
18	Wainwright, Adam	AA	GRV	ATL	P	1.673
19	Krynzel, Dave	AA	HVL	MIL	OF	1.506
20	Moseley, Dustin	AA	CHT	BOS	P	1.242

Texas League

RANK	NAME	LEV	TM	ML	POS	RPP
1	Dominguez, Juan	AA	FRI	TEX	P	3.563
2	Greinke, Zack	AA	WIC	KC	P	3.312
3	Gonzalez, Edgar	AA	ELP	AZ	P	3.242
4	Blackley, Travis	AA	SAN	SEA	P	3.091
5	Lopez, Jose	AA	SAN	SEA	SS	2.653
6	Tsao, Chin-hui	AA	TUL	COL	P	2.603
7	Santana, Ervin	AA	ARK	ANA	P	2.341
8	Jenks, Bobby	AA	ARK	ANA	P	1.994
9	Blanton, Joe	AA	MID	OAK	P	1.774
10	Machado, Alejandro	AA	WIC	KC	2B	1.767
11	Nageotte, Clint	AA	SAN	SEA	P	1.313
12	Gobble, Jimmy	AA	WIC	KC	P	1.281
13	Murray, A.J.	AA	FRI	TEX	P	1.242
14	Nix, Laynce	AA	FRI	TEX	OF	1.240
15	Ansman, Craig	AA	ELP	AZ	C	1.032
16	Hart, Corey	AA	WIC	KC	SS	0.838
17	Baek, Cha Seung	AA	SAN	SEA	P	0.773
18	Daigle, Casey	AA	ELP	AZ	P	0.756
19	Kroeger, Josh	AA	ELP	AZ	OF	0.641
20	Murphy, Bill	AA	MID	OAK	P	0.590

California League

RANK	NAME	LEV	TM	ML	POS	RPP
1	Santana, Ervin	HI A	RC	ANA	P	2.706
2	Gaudin, Chad	HI A	BAK	TB	P	2.637

3	Kotchman, Casey	HI A	RC	ANA	1B	2.593
4	Barfield, Josh	HI A	LKE	SD	2B	2.429
5	Mathis, Jeff	HI A	RC	ANA	C	2.174
6	Kroeger, Josh	HI A	LNC	AZ	OF	2.085
7	Shell, Steven	HI A	RC	ANA	P	2.050
8	Martinez, Javier	HI A	LKE	SD	P	1.777
9	Nix, Jayson	HI A	VIS	COL	2B	1.646
10	Ketchner, Ryan	HI A	INL	SEA	P	1.630
11	Santos, Sergio	HI A	LNC	AZ	SS	1.590
12	Gathright, Joey	HI A	BAK	TB	OF	1.550
13	Choo, Shin-soo	HI A	INL	SEA	OF	1.442
14	Germano, Justin	HI A	LKE	SD	P	1.417
15	Bourgeois, Jason	HI A	STO	TEX	2B	1.403
16	McPherson, Dallas	HI A	RC	ANA	3B	1.249
17	Thompson, Erik	HI A	STO	TEX	P	1.145
18	Loe, Kameron x	HI A	STO	TEX	P	1.020
19	Swisher, Nick	HI A	MOD	OAK	OF	0.793
20	Castro, Ismael	HI A	INL	SEA	2B	0.715

Carolina League

RANK	NAME	LEV	TM	ML	POS	RPP
1	Greinke, Zack	HI A	WIL	KC	P	3.828
2	Marte, Andy	HI A	MYR	ATL	3B	3.169
3	Reed, Jeremy	HI A	W-S	CHW	OF	2.807
4	Encarnacion, Edwin	HI A	POT	CIN	3B	2.778
5	Blanco, Gregor	HI A	MYR	ATL	OF	2.681
6	Shelton, Chris	HI A	LYN	PIT	C/1B	2.581
7	McBride, Macay	HI A	MYR	ATL	P	1.961
8	Honel, Kris	HI A	W-S	CHW	P	1.953
9	Foley, Travis	HI A	KIN	CLE	P	1.630
10	Oquendo, Ian	HI A	LYN	PIT	P	1.549
11	Bass, Brian	HI A	WIL	KC	P	1.466
12	Taveras, Willy	HI A	KIN	CLE	OF	1.447
13	Rodriguez, Mike	HI A	SLM	HOU	OF	1.382
14	McLouth, Nathan	HI A	LYN	PIT	OF	1.376
15	Spidale, Mike	HI A	W-S	CHW	OF	1.342
16	Bergolla, William	HI A	POT	CIN	2B	1.278
17	Tierney, Chris	HI A	WIL	KC	P	1.257
18	Maine, John	HI A	FRE	BAL	P	1.238
19	Martin, J.D.	HI A	KIN	CLE	P	1.120
20	Cooper, Jason	HI A	KIN	CLE	OF	1.056

Florida State League

RANK	NAME	LEV	TM	ML	POS	RPP
1	Miller, Greg	HI A	VB	LA	P	3.997
2	Gutierrez, Franklin	HI A	VB	LA	OF	3.771
3	Kazmir, Scott	HI A	SLU	NYM	P	3.581
4	Navarro, Dioner	HI A	TAM	NYY	C	3.444
5	Hamels, Cole	HI A	CLR	PHI	P	3.167
6	Wright, David	HI A	SLU	NYM	3B	3.162
7	Loney, James	HI A	VB	LA	1B	2.881
8	Diaz, Joselo	HI A	VB	LA	P	2.844
9	Aybar, Willy	HI A	VB	LA	3B	2.174
10	Bautista, Denny	HI A	JUP	FLA	P	2.157
11	Nolasco, Ricky	HI A	DAY	CHC	P	2.156

12	Mauer, Joe	HI A	FTM	MIN	C	1.990
13	Floyd, Gavin	HI A	CLR	PHI	P	1.821
14	Pinto, Renyel	HI A	DAY	CHC	P	1.800
15	Peterson, Matt	HI A	SLU	NYM	P	1.623
16	Ramirez, Elizardo	HI A	CLR	PHI	P	1.617
17	McGowan, Dustin	HI A	DUN	TOR	P	1.602
18	Pignatiello, Carmen	HI A	DAY	CHC	P	1.571
19	Durbin, J.D.	HI A	FTM	MIN	P	1.496
20	Greenberg, Adam	HI A	DAY	CHC	OF	1.352

Midwest League

RANK	NAME	LEV	TM	ML	POS	RPP
1	Fielder, Prince	LO A	BEL	MIL	1B	4.207
2	Zumaya, Joel	LO A	WMI	DET	P	3.766
3	Rosario, Adriano	LO A	SBN	AZ	P	3.611
4	Jones, Justin	LO A	LAN	CHC	P	3.241
5	Aybar, Erick	LO A	CR	ANA	SS	2.657
6	Pie, Felix	LO A	LAN	CHC	OF	2.595
7	Jepsen, Kevin	LO A	CR	ANA	P	2.486
8	Rodriguez, Rafael	LO A	CR	ANA	P	2.424
9	Hawksworth, Blake	LO A	PEO	STL	P	2.180
10	Ryu, Jae-kuk	LO A	LAN	CHC	P	1.830
11	Clevlen, Brent	LO A	WMI	DET	OF	1.800
12	Kaaihue, Kila	LO A	BUR	KC	1B	1.734
13	Sardinha, Bronson	LO A	BC	NYY	OF	1.664
14	Pauley, David	LO A	FTW	SD	P	1.658
15	Murphy, Donald	LO A	BUR	KC	2B	1.626
16	Callaspo, Alberto	LO A	CR	ANA	2B	1.517
17	Sisco, Andy	LO A	LAN	CHC	P	1.516
18	Guillen, Rudy	LO A	BC	NYY	OF	1.423
19	Parra, Manny	LO A	BEL	MIL	P	1.052
20	Sanchez, Humberto	LO A	WMI	DET	P	1.014

South Atlantic League

RANK	NAME	LEV	TM	ML	POS	RPP
1	Hamels, Cole	LO A	LKW	PHI	P	4.305
2	Upton, B.J.	LO A	CHS	TB	SS	3.655
3	Cain, Matthew	LO A	HAG	SF	P	3.480
4	Everts, Clint	LO A	SAV	MON	P	2.494
5	Dukes, Elijah	LO A	CHS	TB	OF	2.326
6	Olsen, Scott	LO A	GBO	FLA	P	2.247
7	Hermida, Jeremy	LO A	GBO	FLA	OF	2.219
8	Ramirez, Hanley	LO A	AUG	BOS	SS	1.991
9	McCann, Brian	LO A	ROM	ATL	C	1.973
10	Bazardo, Yorman	LO A	GBO	FLA	P	1.964
11	Guzman, Joel	LO A	SGA	LA	SS	1.947
12	Broxton, Jonathan	LO A	SGA	LA	P	1.872
13	Jimenez, Ubaldo	LO A	ASH	COL	P	1.864
14	Davies, Kyle	LO A	ROM	ATL	P	1.843
15	Francoeur, Jeff	LO A	ROM	ATL	OF	1.809
16	League, Brandon	LO A	CWV	TOR	P	1.738
17	Johnson, Josh	LO A	GBO	FLA	P	1.595
18	Bankston, Wes	LO A	CHS	TB	OF	1.405
19	Humphries, Justin	LO A	LEX	HOU	1B	1.398
20	Wright, Matt	LO A	ROM	ATL	P	1.357

Top Pitching Performances of 2003

RANK	NAME	LEV	TM	LG	ML	RPP
1	Miller, Greg	AA	JAC	SOU	LA	7.581
2	Hamels, Cole	LO A	LKW	SAL	PHI	4.305
3	Gonzalez, Edgar	AAA	TUS	PCL	AZ	4.196
4	Jackson, Edwin	AA	JAC	SOU	LA	4.148
5	Miller, Greg	HI A	VB	FSL	LA	3.997
6	Greinke, Zack	HI A	WIL	CAR	KC	3.828
7	Zumaya, Joel	LO A	WMI	MID	DET	3.766
8	Rosario, Adriano	LO A	SBN	MID	AZ	3.611
9	Kazmir, Scott	HI A	SLU	FSL	NYM	3.581
10	Dominguez, Juan	AA	FRI	TXL	TEX	3.563
11	Cain, Matthew	LO A	HAG	SAL	SF	3.480
12	Greinke, Zack	AA	WIC	TXL	KC	3.312
13	Gonzalez, Edgar	AA	ELP	TXL	AZ	3.242
14	Jones, Justin	LO A	LAN	MID	CHC	3.241
15	Harden, Rich	AAA	SAC	PCL	OAK	3.219
16	Bonser, Boof	AAA	FRS	PCL	SF	3.172
17	Hamels, Cole	HI A	CLR	FSL	PHI	3.167
18	Blackley, Travis	AA	SAN	TXL	SEA	3.091
19	Williams, Jerome	AAA	FRS	PCL	SF	3.047
20	Perez, Oliver	AAA	POR	PCL	SD	2.876
21	Crain, Jesse	AA	NB	EAS	MIN	2.862
22	McGowan, Dustin	AA	NH	EAS	TOR	2.860
23	Diaz, Joselo	HI A	VB	FSL	LA	2.844
24	Burnett, Sean	AA	ALT	EAS	PIT	2.741
25	Pilkington, Brian	AA	JAC	SOU	LA	2.732
26	Santana, Ervin	HI A	RC	CAL	ANA	2.706
27	Willis, Dontrelle	AA	CAR	SOU	FLA	2.670
28	Gaudin, Chad	HI A	BAK	CAL	TB	2.637
29	Ryu, Jae-kuk	AA	WTE	SOU	CHC	2.637
30	Tsao, Chin-hui	AA	TUL	TXL	COL	2.603
31	Jones, Mike	AA	HVL	SOU	MIL	2.600
32	Bruney, Brian	AAA	TUS	PCL	AZ	2.528
33	Everts, Clint	LO A	SAV	SAL	MON	2.494
34	Jepsen, Kevin	LO A	CR	MID	ANA	2.486
35	Rodney, Fernando	AAA	TOL	INT	DET	2.437
36	Rodriguez, Rafael	LO A	CR	MID	ANA	2.424
37	Santana, Ervin	AA	ARK	TXL	ANA	2.341
38	Moseley, Dustin	AAA	LOU	INT	CIN	2.303
39	Olsen, Scott	LO A	GBO	SAL	FLA	2.247
40	Haren, Dan	AA	TEN	SOU	STL	2.235

Top 2003 Offensive Performances by Position

Catcher

1	Navarro, Dioner	AA	TRE	EAS	NYY	3.938
2	Navarro, Dioner	HI A	TAM	FSL	NYY	3.444
3	Martinez, Victor	AAA	BUF	INT	CLE	2.761
4	Mauer, Joe	AA	NB	EAS	MIN	2.734
5	Shelton, Chris	HI A	LYN	CAR	PIT	2.581
6	Quiroz, Guillermo	AA	NH	EAS	TOR	2.392
7	Mathis, Jeff	HI A	RC	CAL	ANA	2.174
8	Mauer, Joe	HI A	FTM	FSL	MIN	1.990
9	McCann, Brian	LO A	ROM	SAL	ATL	1.973
10	Huber, Justin	AA	BNG	EAS	NYM	1.638

11	Willingham, Josh	HI A	JUP	FSL	FLA	1.193
12	Ansman, Craig	AA	ELP	TXL	AZ	1.032

First Base

1	Fielder, Prince	LO A	BEL	MID	MIL	4.207
2	Loney, James	HI A	VB	FSL	LA	2.881
3	Kotchman, Casey	HI A	RC	CAL	ANA	2.593
4	Morneau, Justin	AAA	ROC	INT	MIN	2.555
5	Kaaihue, Kila	LO A	BUR	MID	KC	1.734
6	Humphries, Justin	LO A	LEX	SAL	HOU	1.398
7	Stokes, Jason	HI A	JUP	FSL	FLA	1.121
8	Tejeda, Juan	HI A	LAK	FSL	DET	1.071
9	LaRoche, Adam	AAA	RIC	INT	ATL	0.977
10	Blanco, Tony	HI A	POT	CAR	CIN	0.959

Second Base

1	Barfield, Josh	HI A	LKE	CAL	SD	2.429
2	Diaz, Victor	AA	JAC	SOU	LA	1.773
3	Sequea, Jorge	AAA	SYR	INT	TOR	1.770
4	Machado, Alejandro	AA	WIC	TXL	KC	1.767
5	Nix, Jayson	HI A	VIS	CAL	COL	1.646
6	Murphy, Donald	LO A	BUR	MID	KC	1.626
7	Callaspo, Alberto	LO A	CR	MID	ANA	1.517
8	Bourgeois, Jason	HI A	STO	CAL	TEX	1.403
9	Young, Delwyn	LO A	SGA	SAL	LA	1.289
10	Bergolla, William	HI A	POT	CAR	CIN	1.278
11	Lopez, Pedro	LO A	KAN	SAL	CHW	1.096
12	Yan, Ruddy	HI A	W-S	CAR	CHW	1.019

Third Base

1	Cabrera, Miguel	AA	CAR	SOU	FLA	5.292
2	Marte, Andy	HI A	MYR	CAR	ATL	3.169
3	Wright, David	HI A	SLU	FSL	NYM	3.162
4	Betemit, Wilson	AAA	RIC	INT	ATL	2.880
5	Encarnacion, Edwin	HI A	POT	CAR	CIN	2.778
6	Aybar, Willy	HI A	VB	FSL	LA	2.174
7	Encarnacion, Edwin	AA	CHT	SOU	CIN	2.038
8	Spann, Chad	LO A	AUG	SAL	BOS	1.337
9	Smith, Corey	AA	AKR	EAS	CLE	1.273
10	McPherson, Dallas	HI A	RC	CAL	ANA	1.249
11	Calzado, Napoleon	AAA	OTT	INT	BAL	1.157
12	Henson, Drew	AAA	COL	INT	NYY	1.141

Shortstop

1	Upton, B.J.	LO A	CHS	SAL	TB	3.655
2	Infante, Omar	AAA	TOL	INT	DET	2.906
3	Aybar, Erick	LO A	CR	MID	ANA	2.657
4	Lopez, Jose	AA	SAN	TXL	SEA	2.653
5	Crosby, Bobby	AAA	SAC	PCL	OAK	2.270
6	Hardy, J.J.	AA	HVL	SOU	MIL	2.210
7	Cantu, Jorge	AAA	DUR	INT	TB	2.087
8	Ramirez, Hanley	LO A	AUG	SAL	BOS	1.991
9	Guzman, Joel	LO A	SGA	SAL	LA	1.947

10	Johnson, Kelly	AA	GRV	SOU	ATL	1.677
11	Izturis, Maicer	AAA	BUF	INT	CLE	1.677
12	Santos, Sergio	HI A	LNC	CAL	AZ	1.590
13	Machado, Andy	AA	REA	EAS	PHI	0.995
14	Ochoa, Ivan	HI A	KIN	CAR	CLE	0.974
15	Hart, Corey	AA	WIC	TXL	KC	0.838

Outfield

1	Gutierrez, Franklin	HI A	VB	FSL	LA	3.771
2	Reed, Jeremy	AA	BIR	SOU	CHW	3.750
3	Reed, Jeremy	HI A	W-S	CAR	CHW	2.807
4	Sizemore, Grady	AA	AKR	EAS	CLE	2.729
5	Blanco, Gregor	HI A	MYR	CAR	ATL	2.681
6	Pie, Felix	LO A	LAN	MID	CHC	2.595
7	Dukes, Elijah	LO A	CHS	SAL	TB	2.326
8	Hermida, Jeremy	LO A	GBO	SAL	FLA	2.219
9	Ross, Cody	AAA	TOL	INT	DET	2.177
10	Kroeger, Josh	HI A	LNC	CAL	AZ	2.085
11	Francoeur, Jeff	LO A	ROM	SAL	ATL	1.809
12	Clevlen, Brent	LO A	WMI	MID	DET	1.800
13	Rios, Alexis	AA	NH	EAS	TOR	1.748
14	Fernandez, Alex	AAA	POR	PCL	SD	1.674
15	Sardinha, Bronson	LO A	BC	MID	NYY	1.664
16	Gathright, Joey	HI A	BAK	CAL	TB	1.550
17	Krynzel, Dave	AA	HVL	SOU	MIL	1.506
18	Taveras, Willy	HI A	KIN	CAR	CLE	1.447
19	Choo, Shin-soo	HI A	INL	CAL	SEA	1.442
20	Guillen, Rudy	LO A	BC	MID	NYY	1.423
21	Bankston, Wes	LO A	CHS	SAL	TB	1.405
22	Rodriguez, Mike	HI A	SLM	CAR	HOU	1.382
23	McLouth, Nathan	HI A	LYN	CAR	PIT	1.376
24	Greenberg, Adam	HI A	DAY	FSL	CHC	1.352
25	Bay, Jason	AAA	POR	PCL	SD	1.349
26	Spidale, Mike	HI A	W-S	CAR	CHW	1.342
27	Nix, Laynce	AA	FRI	TXL	TEX	1.240
28	Crisp, Coco	AAA	BUF	INT	CLE	1.236
29	Lydon, Wayne	HI A	SLU	FSL	NYM	1.196
30	Pridie, Jason	LO A	CHS	SAL	TB	1.151
31	DeJesus, David	AAA	OMA	PCL	KC	1.133
32	Espinosa, David	HI A	LAK	FSL	DET	1.088
33	Majewski, Val	LO A	DEL	SAL	BAL	1.058
34	Cooper, Jason	HI A	KIN	CAR	CLE	1.056
35	Edwards, Mike	AAA	SAC	PCL	OAK	0.997
36	Ball, Jarred	LO A	SBN	MID	AZ	0.979
37	Gomes, Jonny	AA	ORL	SOU	TB	0.973
38	Oeltjen, Trent	LO A	QC	MID	MIN	0.957
39	Kubel, Jason	HI A	FTM	FSL	MIN	0.922
40	Romero, Alex	LO A	QC	MID	MIN	0.920

THE 2003 AMATEUR DRAFT REPORT

By John Manuel

For once, Major League Baseball's first-year player draft provided little drama in 2003.

The top talents went at the top of the draft. No holdouts lasting into the winter—and lots of players signing for reasonable amounts of money. Even the top unsigned player of 2002, Canadian lefthander Adam Loewen, joined the bandwagon and signed as a draft-and-follow with the Orioles.

It was the first draft ever (meaning since 1965) in which every pick in the first two rounds signed, and just 16 players in the first 10 rounds failed to sign, also the lowest such rate ever. Signing bonuses in the first round averaged $1.757 million, down more than 16 percent from the $2.106 million average in 2002.

Three players drafted in 2003—righthanders Chad Cordero (Expos) and Ryan Wagner (Reds) and second baseman Rickie Weeks (Brewers)—already debuted in the major leagues. Weeks was the second overall pick, following California high school outfielder Delmon Young, the younger brother of Detroit Tigers outfielder Dmitri Young. The Devil Rays had the No. 1 pick for the second time and followed the same formula they did in 1999, when they took prep outfielder Josh Hamilton. They certainly hope Delmon's big league bloodlines help him avoid the injuries and personal problems that have shelved Hamilton for most of the last two seasons. Young eventually signed a major league contract worth a guaranteed $5.8 million, shortly after Weeks signed for $5.3 million on a major league deal.

Weeks was the first college player drafted and certainly not the last. The draft takes two days, with 22 rounds on the first day and the last 28 on day two. About 70 percent of the players taken on day one were college or junior-college players as the draft continued to trend toward older players. Clubs take college players for several reasons. College pitchers are considered less of an injury risk; college hitters take less time to reach the majors; and college draftees involve less projection (what you see if often what you get) and have trade value sooner than high school picks. Plus, they can be a lot cheaper—teams don't have to buy those college years away. The Kansas City Royals, for example, drafted college seniors in rounds five through nine and signed each one for a $1,000 bonus.

Two first-round picks had intriguing injury sagas. Richmond righthander Tim Stauffer injured his shoulder in his last start, during the NCAA tournament, and the San Diego Padres signed him for a bargain $750,000. Of course, it will only be a bargain if Stauffer returns to health. The other injured first-rounder was Stanford right fielder Carlos Quentin, who signed for $1.1 million with the Arizona Diamondbacks despite an elbow injury that necessitated Tommy John surgery.

Here's an All-Star team of the players drafted and signed in 2003, organized by the league of their parent organization. It's coupled with grades for the first 30 overall picks of 2002 and 2001.

AMERICAN LEAGUE

C: Mitch Maier, Kansas City Royals
The Royals goofed last offseason and were stuck with two teams in the Rookie-level Arizona League, rather than having a club in a more advanced league like the Pioneer, Northwest or New York-Penn. In other words, college draftees like Maier, who was the last pick of the first round, should dominate the AZL. Maier did, hitting .350-2-45, smacking 14 double (and six triples) and controlling the strike zone adequately. His athleticism and solid bat give Maiaer a chance to eventually become the third Toledo Rocket in the big leagues (joining Mets RHP Jeremy Griffiths and Rockies RHP Denny Stark).

1B: Vito Chiaravallotti, Toronto Blue Jay
It was a tough choice between Chiaravallotti (can we just say Vito on second reference?) and Indians first-rounder Michael Aubrey, who hit .348 in low Class A. But Vito, a three-year starter at Richmond, dominated the New York-Penn League. The __th-round pick doesn't have great tools or athletic ability. What he has is raw power, a decent swing and hitting aptitude. He won the triple crown in the New York-Penn League for short-season Auburn, hitting .351-12-67, adding 20 doubles and walking (47) as often as he struck out (48).

2B: Eric Rodland, Detroit Tigers.
Teamed with shortstop Tony Giarratano (a runner-up at that position), Rodland helped form one of the minors' more dynamic middle-infield combos. The Alaska League batting champion in 2002 after his junior season at Gonzaga, Rodland struggled in the spring of 2003 with the Bulldogs and fell in the draft to the ninth round. He has a smooth lefthanded stroke and runs well (eight triples, 13-for-15 SBs), and could be a solid No. 2 hitter down the line.

3B: Eric Duncan, New York Yankees.
Despite their prodigious resources, the Yankees have drafted conservatively in recent years. Duncan, out of Seton Hall Prep School in Florham Park, N.J., is one of the higher-ceiling picks the organization has made of late. He had a splendid debut, hitting a combined .301-4-41 with 27 extra-base hits between the Rookie-level Gulf Coast League and short-season Staten Island and got better as the year went on. He ranked as the GCL's No. 1 prospect. His offense inspires comparisons to Chipper Jones, though his body, which has just average athleticism, does not.

SS: Aaron Hill, Toronto Blue Jays.
The epitome of what teams like the Blue Jays, who now emphasize college players, want in a draft pick is Hill, who has athletic ability combined with baseball savvy and polished hitting skills. The Louisiana State product was a seventh-round pick out of high school, and a stellar college career made improved his stock to the first round after three seasons. He takes walks, runs adequately and wisely, has gap power for now and may develop more in the future. The only downside: He may end up at second or third base thanks to Toronto's artificial turf.

OF: Jeremy Cleveland, Texas Rangers
After two years as a part-time player for North Carolina, Cleveland blossomed in 2003 and led the Atlantic Coast Conference in hitting as a junior. Another hitter with an advanced approach at the plate, Cleveland uses an open stance to see the ball well, command the strike zone and generate good power. He fell to the eighth round over concerns about his position, but he showed more than enough arm and athletic ability for right field. Now he'll have to keep hitting like he did at short-season Spokane (.322-7-53, 20 doubles).

OF: Ricardo Nanita, White Sox.
Just a 14th-round pick out of Florida International, Nanita led the Golden Panthers in the triple-crown categories, his 6-foot, 180-pound package didn't make him a high draft possibility. Nevertheless, he had one of the best debuts in the minors, hitting .384-5-37 for Rookie-level Great Falls. Nanita ranked second the Pioneer League in batting. His lefthanded stroke was consistently lethal, leading to a 30-game hitting streak for the Dominican Republic native that set a new league record. His season ended early because of a wrist injury, which shouldn't short-circuit his rising prospect status in an organization suddenly flush with outfield prospects.

OF: Ryan Goleski, Indians
Goleski's spring at Central Michigan was interrupted by an injury suffered when he went to help a teammate during a mugging. Goleski showed he had recovered his power stroke quickly in his pro debut, slugging nearly .500 while making the transition from metal to wood bats. He hit .296-8-37 and added 15 doubles. Goleski has sufficient power to stay in a corner outfield spot; the big question is whether he can make consistent-enough contact (66 strikeouts in 243 at-bats) to be an everyday player.

RHP: Wes Littleton, Texas Rangers
Littleton was one of the more highly touted college pitchers in the nation entering 2003, then had an unusual spring season for Cal State Fullerton. He began the year as the ace, then was suspended for a month for an undisclosed violation of team rules. When he returned, the Titans had found new starters, and Littleton didn't return as an important contributor until the College World Series. Consequently, he fell to the fourth round and became a coup for the Rangers, as he returned to having the kind of stuff that made him so touted in the first place. He's a power sinker-slider pitcher with a low three-quarters arm angle who is athletic enough and polished enough to move quickly through the pitching-starved system.

LHP: Kurt Isenburg, Toronto Blue Jays.

Isenburg is part of the Blue Jays' newfound emphasis on drafting college players, which came to the organization with general manager J.P. Ricciardi from the Oakland organization. Isenburg wasn't necessarily a stats-based pick, though, because he had an ERA of almost 6.00 as a junior at James Madison. However, the Blue Jays saw an athletic lefthander who played both ways in college and had some power in his arm. He went 7-2, 1.63 and allowed just 40 hits in 60 2/3 innings, using superior command of his fastball, slider and changeup to keep New York-Penn League hitters off balance. The best lefthander the Jays have developed of late might be Mark Hendrickson, so if they get Isenburg to the big leagues, it will be news.

CL: Shaun Marcum, RHP, Toronto Blue Jays.

Another member of Auburn's ridiculously good 56-28 team, Marcum and Bubbie Buzachero teamed to give the Doubledays one of the minors' best bullpens. Buzachero was a 2002 draftee who had 13 saves; Marcum was a 2003 pick who joined the Jays after helping lead Southwest Missouri State to its first College World Series. Marcum was a shortstop and closer at SMS but will just pitch in the pros, thanks to a lively fastball in the 90-91 mph range that consistently misses bats. He gave up just 15 hits in 34 innings while posting an impressive 47-7 strikeout-to-walk ratio. He could get to Toronto quickly thanks to his athleticism, command and fresh arm.

NATIONAL LEAGUE

C: Todd Jennings, San Francisco Giants.

The Giants are desperate for catching help in their minor league system, what with Benito Santiago pushing 40. Jennings could be the answer in a hurry, having emerged as a prospect behind the plate after spending much of his college career at third base. Long Beach State put Jennings behind the plate last year, and his athleticism and arm strength played well back there. He also has a solid line-drive bat, batting .296-3-32 for short-season Salem-Keizer. Better yet, he ranked first in the Northwest League among regulars by throwing out 39 percent of opposing baserunners.

1B: Jamie D'Antona, Arizona Diamondbacks

D'Antona played 58 of his 65 games at third base, but his 18 errors at third and erratic, though powerful, arm profile D'Antona better as a first baseman down the line. He's got the power bat for it, thanks to a strong frame and exceptional bat speed. He showed off his power stroke at short-season Yakima, hitting .277-15-57, adding 18 doubles and posting a robust .517 slugging percentage. D'Antona was a three-year starter at Wake Forest and the Atlantic Coast Conference player of the year as a junior, and his offensive polish could help him advance quickly.

2B: Rickie Weeks, Milwaukee Brewers.

The draft's second overall pick, Weeks held out for more than a month, but his brief professional appearance was impressive enough to merit mention here. Weeks made it to the big leagues for a pair of reasons—his contract requires him already to be on the 40-man roster, and it eased his transition to the Arizona Fall League. However, Weeks really impressed the Brewers by teaming with Prince Fielder and Anthony Gwynn to help low Class A Beloit to a deep run in the Midwest League playoffs, where the Snappers lost in the finals. He hit .349-1-16 in 63 at-bats and had more walks (15) than strikeouts (nine).

3B: Ian Stewart, Colorado Rockies.

Just what the Rockies need—another power bat. The organization has had surprising success drafting pitchers highly, including picks like 1999 first-rounder and 2002 N.L. Rookie of the Year Jason Jennings, but decided Stewart was too good a hitter to pass up. He earned comparisons to Jim Thome while earning top prospect recognition in the Pioneer League. Stewart hit .317-10-43, tying for fifth in the league in homers and slugging a healthy .558. Stewart, like D'Antona, may profile best as a first baseman, but the bottom line is his bat will play.

SS: Jose Ronda, Cincinnati Reds

He's not ready to take over for Barry Larkin yet, but Ronda was the best of a bad lot of NL shortstops picked in 2003; the top three AL-drafted picks (Hill, Tony Giarratano and Oakland's Omar

Quintanilla) all project as better prospects. Ronda, a Puerto Rican drafted in the third round, signed for $440,000 and had a successful debut. He hit .301-2-26 in the Rookie-level Gulf Coast League and switch-hits for good measure. It's too early to get too excited, but Ronda got off to a good start.

OF: Josh Anderson, Houston Astros.
While productive in Latin America, the Astros have had success with college draft picks of late as well, developing regulars like Keith Ginter (now with the Brewers), Lance Berkman and Morgan Ensberg as well as pitchers like Brad Lidge. Anderson's speed helped make him one of the top hitters in college baseball, as he hit .447 with 57 stolen bases. The Astros plucked him in the fourth round out of Eastern Michigan, and he had a solid debut. Anderson will have to be more selective (16-53 walk-to-strikeout ratio), but he showed surprising pop and stole 26 more bags, and could be a leadoff candidate.

OF: Anthony Gwynn, Milwaukee Brewers.
Everyone knows the name—Gwynn is the son of future Hall of Famer Tony Gwynn, and played for his father in his last season at San Diego State, where Tony is now the head coach. Anthony has his father's early 1980s build, but doesn't quite have dad's tools or gift for putting the bat on the ball. He does make solid, consistent contact, though, and is an excellent defensive center fielder, one claim his father never could make. Anthony Gwynn could be the perfect No. 2 hitter thanks to his good speed and excellent bat control.

OF: Conor Jackson, Arizona Diamondbacks.
Jackson was one of the most-watched players in college baseball this season, after a solid summer with the bat for USA Baseball's college national team. He sprained his ankle in the California Bears' first game, though, and his defensive shortcomings continued to be exposed. Once considered a possible third baseman, he's now thought of as a corner outfielder or first baseman. The bat should carry him, though, and the early returns on his power were good. He slugged a Northwest League-best 35 doubles in just 257 at-bats, added six homers and drove in 60 runs while hitting .319. He also showed good plate discipline with 36 walks and 41 strikeouts.

RHP: Paul Bacot, Atlanta Braves.
No organization has the proclivity or the success for drafting high school righthanders, and the Braves especially like to stay close to home in recent drafts. On both counts, Bacot, out of Atlanta's Lakeside High, fits the bill. He signed for $550,000 and instantly made an impact, helping the organization win its first Rookie-level Gulf Coast League title since 197_. He went 4-0, 0.95 and showed exceptional command for his age, with just four walks in 38 innings. He has size (6-foot-6, 200 pounds), athletic ability (high school basketball star) and plenty of projection left on his 87-91 mph fastball. He's one to watch intently.

LHP: Tom Gorzelanny, Pittsburgh Pirates.
Gorzelanny started his college career at Kansas, but after two nondescript years (one a redshirt), he transferred to Triton (Ill.) Junior College, the same school that produced Kirby Puckett. While he won't be slamming home runs in the World Series, he has a chance to join Triton's big league tradition. He throws an 88-91 mph fastball with good life as well as a plus breaking ball. Both were on display at short-season Williamsport, where he only went 1-2 but posted a 1.78 ERA over his eight starts. He also pitched well in the playoffs, helping lead Williamsport to the New York-Penn League championship.

CL: Ryan Wagner, Cincinnati Reds; Chad Cordero, Montreal Expos (tie)
It's a wimpy way to go out, but it's impossible to choose between the two relievers who jumped from college to the big leagues in the same season. Wagner got there first and came the furthest—a draft-eligible sophomore out of Houston, he wasn't on many draft boards last year. His funky delivery may not hold up forever, but his low-to-mid 90s power sinking fastball and incredible downer slider is as nasty a two-pitch combination as this draft had. Cordero has a similar combo, though his stuff doesn't have as much life. He has better command, though, and attitude to spare. He helped lead Cal State Fullerton to a pair of College World Series trips in his career.

2002 Draft Grades

1. Pirates: Bryan Bullington, RHP: C. Middle-of-the-rotation ceiling, not what you want for No. 1 pick.

2. Devil Rays: B.J. Upton, SS: A. Fabulous debut season, prep talent showed plate discipline and tools.

3. Reds: Chris Gruler, RHP: D. It's early, but he's already injured, like many pitching picks.

4. Orioles: Adam Loewen, LHP: B+. Not an A because he didn't sign until this year, but he's a top talent.

5. Expos: Clint Everts, RHP: C. Athletic, talented but still a ways away, and initial pro action was modest.

6. Royals: Zack Greinke, RHP: A+. Had as good a year in 2003 as any minor leaguer, regardless of age.

7. Brewers: Prince Fielder, 1B: A. His name is Prince, and he looks funky, but he rakes (.313-27-112).

8. Tigers: Scott Moore, SS: D. Maybe he'll come around, but was drafted for the bat and has struggled.

9. Rockies: Jeff Francis, LHP: B. Started slow, but finished very strong; not far away from Coors Field.

10. Rangers: Drew Meyer, SS: C. Has performed fine, but move to center field will determine his future.

11. Marlins: Jeremy Hermida, OF: B. Developing power soon will complement smooth stroke, speed (28-for-30 SBs).

12. Angels: Joe Saunders, LHP: D. Shoulder injury clouds future, helped cause scouting director Danny Rowland his job.

13. Padres: Khalil Greene, SS: B. Already reached the majors; greater selectivity would help productivity.

14. Blue Jays: Russ Adams, SS: C. Move to 2B isn't far away; should be big leaguer, though not an all-star.

15. Mets: Scott Kazmir, LHP: A. Power arm, electric stuff and still healthy; one of baseball's best prospects.

16. Athletics: Nick Swisher, OF: C. Showing modest offensive potential, and that he's not a center fielder.

17. Phillies: Cole Hamels, LHP: A. Rivals Kazmir for top lefty in minors; possible Team USA ace as well.

18. White Sox: Royce Ring, LHP: B. Projects as setup reliever; dealt to Mets in Roberto Alomar trade.

19. Dodgers: James Loney, 1B: B. Injured for part of 2003; LA's supplemental pick, Greg Miller, a better prospect.

20. Twins: Denard Span, OF: C. Tools are there (mostly speed, athleticism), and Twins have depth to wait.

21. Cubs: Bobby Brownlie, RHP: B. If he stays healthy (just so-so so far), he could be best RHP of the 2002 class.

22. Indians: Jeremy Guthrie, RHP: B. Rocked in Triple-A after solid Double-A start; strikeout rate a concern.

23. Braves: Jeff Francoeur, OF: A-. Swing, hitting skills starting to catch up to prodigious raw talent.

24. Athletics: Joe Blanton, RHP: A. Dominated low Class A, then handled Double-A. Best pick of A's litter.

25. Giants: Matt Cain, RHP: B. Dominated for half a season in 2003; injuries again the concern for young power arm.

26. Athletics: John McCurdy, SS: C. A's refuse to admit defensive shortcomings of bat-first infielder.

27. Diamondbacks: Sergio Santos, SS: B. Also a bat-first guy, maybe not a shortstop; solid, not spectacular, debut.

28. Mariners: John Mayberry Jr., 1B: F. Didn't sign, now at Stanford; Seattle drafted RHP

Adam Jones with supplemental pick this season.

29. Astros: Derick Grigsby, RHP: D. Not much idea of how to use his power stuff to miss bats.

30. Athletics: Ben Fritz, RHP: C. Arm injury limited him to 77 ineffective innings at Class A Modesto.

2001 Draft Grades

1. Twins: Joe Mauer, C. A. Baseball America's Minor League Player of the Year.

2. Cubs: Mark Prior, RHP. A+. Best draft pick since Alex Rodriguez? He's that good.

3. Devil Rays: Dewon Brazelton, RHP. D. He's not done, but he struggled mightily in 2003.

4. Phillies: Gavin Floyd, RHP: B. Power righty has stayed healthy and performed well.

5. Rangers: Mark Teixeira, 3B: A. Moved to 1B, led major league rookies in HRs with 26.

6. Expos: Josh Karp, RHP. C. Expos say he was better than Double-A numbers indicate.

7. Orioles: Chris Smith, LHP: F. Still hurt; no team has gotten as little from a signed '01 pick.

8. Pirates: John VanBenschoten, RHP. B. Dominated high Class A; some scouts consider him a No. 3 starter at best.

9. Royals: Colt Griffin, RHP: C. Coming along, though slowly; not throwing 100 mph anymore, though.

10. Astros: Chris Burke, 2B: B. Astros wised up by moving him to second base; leadoff skills showed up again.

11. Tigers: Kenny Baugh, RHP: C. Back after injury-plagued 2002; Tigers need more good news, though.

12. Brewers: Mike Jones, RHP: B. Grade will fall in elbow woes that cut season short requires surgery.

13. Angels: Casey Kotchman, 1B: B. Great hitter (.326 so far) can't seem to avoid nagging injuries.

14. Padres: Jake Gautreau, 2B: C. Intestinal malady has sapped power; defense has been better than expected.

15. Blue Jays: Gabe Gross, OF: B. Improved plate approach restored luster for solid lefthanded hitter.

16. White Sox: Kris Honel, RHP: B. Illinois product showing better than expected feel for strike zone, less velocity.

17. Indians: Dan Denham, RHP: C. Has been passed by other power arms in the organization from same draft class.

18. Mets: Aaron Heilman, RHP. D. Reached majors, where Mets discovered his stuff is fringy; middle reliever?

19. Orioles: Mike Fontenot, 2B: C. Restored prospect status with good Double-A year, but still just 5-foot-8.

20. Reds: Jeremy Sowers, LHP: F. Didn't sign; Vanderbilt pitcher a top prospect for 2004 draft.

21. Giants: Brad Hennessey, RHP: D. Hard to grade so tough for a guy who had cancer, but he's behind.

22. Diamondbacks: Jason Bulger, RHP: F. Budget pick (less than $1 million bonus) hasn't panned out.

23. Yankees: John-Ford Griffin: C. Long-since traded (Ted Lilly deal), now a DH-LF in Blue Jays system.

24. Braves: Macay McBride, LHP: B. Solid outlook, though he didn't dominate like many have at Class A Myrtle Beach.

25. Athletics: Bobby Crosby, SS: A. No Tejada, but Crosby fields adequately and has good power for the position.

26. Athletics: Jeremy Bonderman, RHP: B. Stuff was worthy of big leagues; will all the losses affect his future?

27. Indians: Alan Horne, RHP: F. Didn't sign, and has had Tommy John surgery interrupt Mississippi career.

---

28. Cardinals: Justin Pope, RHP: D. Career has stalled at Class A; traded to Yankees for Sterling Hitchcock.

29. Braves: Josh Burrus, 3B: D. Bat was supposed to be the best tool; he hit .254 in Rookie ball this year.

30. Giants: Noah Lowry, LHP: C. Made it to major leagues after having mediocre Double-A season.

Note: John Manuel writes for Baseball America.

5

Front Office

Keeping Score

(Or How I Learned to Stop Worrying and Love the Stat Service)

Once upon a time, the entire front office complex of Rotisserie League Baseball consisted of Beloved Founder and Former Commissioner-for-Life Daniel Okrent. There is a fading daguerreotype of Marse Dan, one hand clinching an unfiltered Camel, the other slowly stroking his abacus, sitting alone in his Berkshire woodshed, from which post he spewed out — we use the word advisedly — our fledging league's biweekly standings every third fortnight or so. We were having too much fun to know any better that first season, but eventually we got smart and figured that the BFFCL would never compile and distribute the standings in a timely fashion until his team, the hapless Fenokees, got themselves in a pennant race and gave him something to crow about. Not willing to wait 'til the end of time or hell froze over, whichever came first, we fired him.

That single, surgical act marked the yawning of a new Rotisserie Era.

You can still do your league's stats by hand, of course — if the task required a mathematical genius, we'd still be waiting for our first standings report for the 1980 season. All you need is a calculator and about four hours of free time a week, every week of the season (you're going to want weekly standings, whether you know it or not). But it's tiresome, tedious work, the only thing about Rotisserie League Baseball that isn't a whole lot of fun. We don't recommend it.

You can hire someone to do the stats by hand for you. We did that from 1981 through 1983, and our first (and only) Director of Statistical Services, Sandra Krempasky, is enshrined in the Rotisserie Hall of Fame. Problem is, Sandra retired (actually, she was phased out by a computer), and you're never going to find anyone as good as she was.

You can develop your own computer program for crunching Rotisserie stats and put the family computer to better use than prepping for the SATs, keeping track of the family fortune, or playing "Jeopardy." At least we think you can. When it comes to computers, the Founding Fathers are still trying to figure out why the light in the refrigerator comes on when you open the door. Other people say it can be done, though - something about spreading sheets, we think.

The best thing you can do, of course, is to do what the Founding Fathers have done, which is to use **USA Stats** to do your stat-keeping. **USA Stats** is the exclusive, Official Stat Service for Rotisserie League Baseball and the only stat service sanctioned by the Founding Fathers of the game. Most important for you, they're the best.

We know. Back in the Jurassic Era of rotisserie baseball, we were in the stat service game ourselves, and **USA Stats** was always the class of the league. They're one of the old timers in the business (they've been around since 1988), and really know the game. They take care of thousands of Rotisserians around the country (and even a fair number of expatriate Rotisserians living abroad), and they'll take good care of you. Call them at **1-800-USA-1980** (that's **1-800-872-1980** for those of who don't like to spell and dial at the same time).

For the more technologically inclined, USA Stats runs the Official Web Site of Rotisserie League Baseball(at www.usastats.com or www.rotisserie.com where you can buy the Official Rule Book, purchase great baseball memorabilia and other great stuff at the official Roto Store, and, most importantly, get detailed stat reports for your league that are updated each day! Even the Founding Fathers are learning how to point and click. Check it out yourself!

USA STATS!
(You play. They do the work.)

It's easy to work with USA Stats. Follow these simple rules: (1) Have your draft. (2) Send **USA Stats** the rosters. (3) Report roster moves to them regularly. (4) Enjoy the season. That's it — **USA Stats** does the rest. They keep track of your rosters, process your league's transactions, compute the stats for the entire league, provide complete, detailed, and updated stat reports all season long, and in general, provide reliable, outstanding customer service.

Reports are also available at no extra charge on the Web, updated daily with the latest stats. You can also get weekly reports by mail or fax. Here is some of what you get:

*__Outstanding personal service__ - We've built our business by providing the best customer service in the business. It's a free phone call to report transactions, ask questions, and get you what you need. We'll take care to make sure your league has the ultimate Rotisserie experience!

*__Detailed Stat Reports__ - Your daily and weekly stat reports show all your players (active and inactive), their stats, league transactions, major league activity, free agents and their stats, games played by position, and more. Everything's available on the Web - updated daily!

*__The Official Rotisserie Web Site__ - Get your league's stats off our Web site. Check the latest player stats or latest trade news. Go shopping for Roto-gear in the RotoStore. It's where to go for cyber-satisfaction, Rotisserie style. The address: www.usastats.com or www.rotisserie.com.

*__Your league's own Web message board__ - Your league gets its own password-protected message board on the Web. Great for leaving trade proposals, league announcements, or challenges!

*__Mail and Fax Service__ - We can mail or fax out complete stat reports to anyone in your league on Mondays or Tuesdays. Customized stat packages also available (call for details).

*__Salaries and Contracts__ - Player salaries and contracts tracked and displayed on your stat reports - no extra charge!

*__Unlimited Transactions__ - Make as many or as few transactions - there's no limit or extra charge. Report roster changes on our toll-free 800 number, our 24-hour-a-day fax line, or e-mail (usastats@aol.com). There are no player ID numbers to use or confusing forms to fill out.

*__Weekly or daily transactions__ - Your choice of effective dates for your roster changes: Once a week (traditional style) or "daily transactions" (roster changes can be effective 7 days a week). It's up to you.

THE USA STATS "SELF-SERVE" OPTION

If you prefer to make your own transactions, or if your league secretary was forced to resign in a money laundering scandal, try the **USA Stats'** "self-serve" option. With the "self-serve" option, your commissioner or any team owner can set up team rosters and make roster moves directly over the website. It's fast and easy! Check it out yourself. Go to the Web site at **www.usastats.com** and enter TEST as the league ID and TEST as the password. You'll see how easy it is to manage your league over the Web.

For complete information about **USA Stats**, visit their web site at **www.usastats.com** or **www.rotisserie.com**. Or call them at **1-800-872-1980**.

THE RLBA WANTS YOU

You've collared a roomful of other baseball fanatics, memorized this book, subscribed to *Baseball America, USA Today Baseball Weekly,* and *ESPN Magazine,* bought every pre-season baseball magazine on the racks, and appointed someone to bring the chow for the Auction Draft Day. What's next? Membership in the **Rotisserie League Baseball Association** makes a lot of sense from where we sit. Join now and miss the Christmas rush. Here's what your league gets with membership in the **RLBA:**

1.*Commissioner's Services.* No need for your league to be rent asunder by rules disputes and internecine fighting. One Civil War was quite enough, thank you. For members of the **RLBA,** we adjudicate disputes, interpret rules, issue Solomonic judgments, and otherwise maintain law and order in the Rotisserie world.

2.*Position Eligibility List.* Complete and up-to-date. Sent via mail as soon as receive your membership info.

3.*Player Stats.* A complete list of player stats from last season. Everything you need for quick reference at the Auction.

4.*Regular Updates.* We send you regular updates on rule changes, player values, baseball gossip and happenings from around the Rotisseworld.

5.*Championship Certificate.* Signed by Beloved Founder and Former Commissioner-for-Life Daniel Okrent and Honorary Clubhouse Attendant Glen Waggoner, this suitable-for-framing certificate is the perfect grace note for your pennant winner's rec room wall.

6.*Company Store.*The right to purchase an astonishing range of Rotisserie products at full retail price. Check out our Web site at wwww.rotisserie.com.

7.*Yoo-Hoo.* We'll send you a bottle of the precious nectar to pour over your pennant winner's head, in solemn observance of that most sacred of Rotisserituals.

How does your league join? Simple. Just fill out the form on the next page and send it with league dues of $50 or $25 for renewal leagues (check or money order please) to the **Rotisserie League Baseball Association, c/o USA Stats, 408 Allegheny Avenue, Baltimore MD 21204**

Check out

The official Web Site
of
Rotisserie League Baseball

Stats, Player Info, Rules Questions, Roto Gear,
and more!

www.rotisserie.com

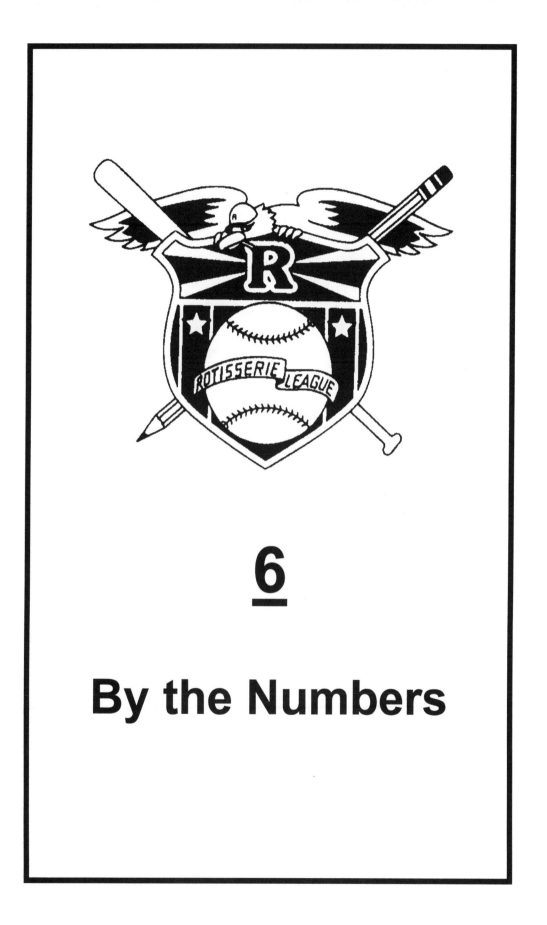

6

By the Numbers

Actual "Earned" 2003 Dollar Values

American League Hitters

NAME	TEAM	$Val	NAME	TEAM	$Val
Andy Abad	BOS	-$3	Frank Catalanotto	TOR	$14
Brent Abernathy	KC	-$3	Eric Chavez	OAK	$22
Benny Agbayani	KC	-$2	Ryan Christenson	TEX	-$2
Erick Almonte	NYY	$0	Jeff Cirillo	SEA	-$2
Roberto Alomar	CHW	$11	Howie Clark	TOR	$0
Sandy Alomar	CHW	$2	Mike Colangelo	TOR	-$2
Alfredo Amezaga	ANA	-$1	Greg Colbrunn	SEA	-$1
Garret Anderson	ANA	$26	Lou Collier	BOS	-$2
Marlon Anderson	TB	$16	Marty Cordova	BAL	-$1
Bruce Aven	TOR	-$2	Carl Crawford	TB	$33
Rocco Baldelli	TB	$26	Joe Crede	CHW	$11
Josh Bard	CLE	$2	Cesar Crespo	BOS	-$2
Tony Batista	BAL	$12	Coco Crisp	CLE	$10
Justin Baughman	TB	-$2	Bobby Crosby	OAK	-$3
Albert Belle	BAL	-$2	Deivi Cruz	BAL	$8
Carlos Beltran	KC	$38	Mike Cuddyer	MIN	$0
Dave Berg	TOR	$1	Jack Cust	BAL	$0
Brandon Berger	KC	-$2	Johnny Damon	BOS	$25
Angel Berroa	KC	$23	Brian Daubach	CHW	$1
Larry Bigbie	BAL	$10	Jeff Davanon	ANA	$15
Casey Blake	CLE	$13	Ben Davis	SEA	$2
Hank Blalock	TEX	$20	Travis Dawkins	KC	-$3
Willie Bloomquist	SEA	$2	David Dejesus	KC	-$2
Hiram Bocachica	DET	-$3	Carlos Delgado	TOR	$27
Aaron Boone	NYY	$25	Wilson Delgado	ANA	-$2
Bret Boone	SEA	$30	Dave Dellucci	NYY	$5
Joe Borchard	CHW	-$2	Einar Diaz	TEX	$4
Pat Borders	SEA	-$3	Matt Diaz	TB	-$3
Mike Bordick	TOR	$7	Mike Difelice	KC	$2
Rob Bowen	MIN	-$3	Rube Durazo	OAK	$13
Milton Bradley	CLE	$19	Trent Durrington	ANA	-$2
Juan Brito	KC	-$2	Jermaine Dye	OAK	-$2
Ben Broussard	CLE	$9	Damion Easley	TB	-$3
Adrian Brown	BOS	-$2	David Eckstein	ANA	$10
Dee Brown	KC	-$1	Mike Edwards	OAK	-$2
Cliff Brumbaugh	CHW	-$2	Mark Ellis	OAK	$9
Jamie Burke	CHW	-$2	Darin Erstad	ANA	$5
Morgan Burkhart	KC	-$2	Felix Escalona	TB	-$2
Ellis Burks	CLE	$3	Alex Escobar	CLE	$1
Eric Byrnes	OAK	$12	Tom Evans	DET	-$2
Alex Cabrera	BAL	-$2	Carl Everett	CHW	$21
Mike Cameron	SEA	$17	Jorge Fabregas	TB	-$2
Robinson Cancel	DET	-$2	Carlos Febles	KC	$3
Jay Canizaro	TB	-$2	Chone Figgins	ANA	$9
Mike Caruso	KC	-$2	Luis Figueroa	SEA	-$2
Kevin Cash	TOR	-$4	John Flaherty	NYY	$0

Actual "Earned" 2003 Dollar Values

NAME	TEAM	$Val	NAME	TEAM	$Val
Jose Flores	OAK	-$2	Ken Huckaby	TOR	-$2
Lew Ford	MIN	$2	Orlando Hudson	TOR	$9
Brook Fordyce	BAL	$5	Aubrey Huff	TB	$25
Brad Fullmer	ANA	$8	Torii Hunter	MIN	$16
Ron Gant	OAK	-$3	Raul Ibanez	KC	$21
Karim Garcia	NYY	$4	Omar Infante	DET	$0
Nomar Garciaparra	BOS	$31	Brandon Inge	DET	$1
Esteban German	OAK	-$2	Damian Jackson	BOS	$7
Jody Gerut	CLE	$15	Ryan Jackson	TB	-$2
Jason Giambi	NYY	$18	Derek Jeter	NYY	$20
Jeremy Giambi	BOS	-$1	Gary Johnson	ANA	-$2
Jay Gibbons	BAL	$16	Mark Johnson	OAK	-$3
Benji Gil	ANA	-$1	Nick Johnson	NYY	$11
Geronimo Gil	BAL	$0	Reed Johnson	TOR	$13
Charles Gipson	NYY	-$1	Rontrez Johnson	KC	-$2
Troy Glaus	ANA	$9	Jacque Jones	MIN	$20
Ross Gload	CHW	-$2	Jason Jones	TEX	-$1
Jonny Gomes	TB	-$3	Gabe Kapler	BOS	$5
Alexis Gomez	KC	-$2	Kenny Kelly	SEA	-$2
Chris Gomez	MIN	$0	Adam Kennedy	ANA	$18
Juan Gonzalez	TEX	$13	Bobby Kielty	TOR	$10
Jason Grabowski	OAK	-$3	Gene Kingsale	DET	-$2
Tony Graffanino	CHW	$7	Danny Klassen	DET	-$1
Todd Greene	TEX	$1	Paul Konerko	CHW	$6
Rusty Greer	TEX	-$2	Graham Koonce	OAK	-$3
Tom Gregorio	ANA	-$3	Corey Koskie	MIN	$17
Ben Grieve	TB	$0	Chad Kreuter	TEX	-$3
Aaron Guiel	KC	$10	Pete Laforest	TB	-$3
Carlos Guillen	SEA	$9	Gerald Laird	TEX	-$1
Jose Guillen	OAK	$20	Tim Laker	CLE	$1
Ricky Gutierrez	CLE	-$2	David Lamb	MIN	-$2
Cristian Guzman	MIN	$15	Mike Lamb	TEX	-$3
Travis Hafner	CLE	$6	Greg Larocca	CLE	-$2
Jerry Hairston	BAL	$7	Chris Latham	NYY	-$2
Toby Hall	TB	$6	Matt Lawton	CLE	$11
Shane Halter	DET	$2	Matt Lecroy	MIN	$10
Willie Harris	CHW	$3	Carlos Lee	CHW	$29
Jason Hart	TEX	-$2	Travis Lee	TB	$15
Ken Harvey	KC	$9	Jose Leon	BAL	-$2
Bill Haselman	BOS	-$3	Brian Lesher	TB	-$2
Scott Hatteberg	OAK	$7	Jeff Liefer	TB	-$2
Drew Henson	NYY	-$3	Mark Little	CLE	-$2
Michel Hernandez	NYY	-$2	Steve Lomasney	BAL	-$2
Ramon Hernandez	OAK	$12	George Lombard	TB	-$1
Bob Higginson	DET	$8	Terrence Long	OAK	$8
A.J. Hinch	DET	-$2	Luis Lopez	BAL	-$2
Eric Hinske	TOR	$12	Mendy Lopez	KC	$1
Denny Hocking	MIN	$0	Ryan Ludwick	CLE	$2

Actual "Earned" 2003 Dollar Values

NAME	TEAM	$Val	NAME	TEAM	$Val
Julio Lugo	TB	$15	Luis Ordaz	KC	-$2
Fernando Lunar	TEX	-$2	Magglio Ordonez	CHW	$27
John Mabry	SEA	-$1	Rey Ordonez	TB	$2
Robert Machado	BAL	-$1	David Ortiz	BOS	$18
Chris Magruder	CLE	-$1	Hector Ortiz	TB	-$2
Al Martin	TB	$2	Eric Owens	ANA	$6
Edgar Martinez	SEA	$17	Rafael Palmeiro	TEX	$19
Victor Martinez	CLE	$1	Dean Palmer	DET	-$4
Julius Matos	KC	-$1	Craig Paquette	DET	-$3
Luis Matos	BAL	$18	Jarrod Patterson	KC	-$3
Hideki Matsui	NYY	$17	Carlos Pena	DET	$8
Brent Mayne	KC	$3	Elvis Pena	KC	-$2
David McCarty	BOS	$0	Jhonny Peralta	CLE	$0
John McDonald	CLE	-$1	Antonio Perez	TB	$1
Ryan McGuire	NYY	-$2	Herbert Perry	TEX	-$3
Mark McLemore	SEA	$3	Ben Petrick	DET	-$1
Billy McMillon	OAK	$2	Josh Phelps	TOR	$10
Adam Melhuse	OAK	$1	Brandon Phillips	CLE	$1
Kevin Mench	TEX	$2	Adam Piatt	TB	$0
Carlos Mendez	BAL	-$2	A.J. Pierzynski	MIN	$15
Frankie Menechino	OAK	-$2	Jorge Posada	NYY	$18
Lou Merloni	BOS	$1	Curtis Pride	NYY	-$3
Chad Meyers	SEA	-$2	Alex Prieto	MIN	-$3
Doug Mientkiewicz	MIN	$14	Tom Prince	KC	-$1
Aaron Miles	CHW	-$2	Robb Quinlan	ANA	$0
Kevin Millar	BOS	$17	Tim Raines Jr.	BAL	-$3
Doug Mirabelli	BOS	$1	Julio Ramirez	ANA	-$2
Dustan Mohr	MIN	$6	Manny Ramirez	BOS	$28
Ben Molina	ANA	$10	Joe Randa	KC	$14
Izzy Molina	BAL	-$2	Desi Relaford	KC	$15
Jose Molina	ANA	-$3	Michael Restovich	MIN	-$1
Craig Monroe	DET	$10	Adam Riggs	ANA	$0
Melvin Mora	BAL	$15	Armando Rios	CHW	-$2
Jose Morban	BAL	$1	Luis Rivas	MIN	$13
Mike Moriarty	TOR	-$2	Juan Rivera	NYY	$2
Justin Morneau	MIN	-$1	Brian Roberts	BAL	$16
Warren Morris	DET	$6	Alex Rodriguez	TEX	$34
Chad Mottola	TB	-$2	Eddie Rogers	BAL	-$2
Lyle Mouton	CLE	-$2	Damian Rolls	TB	$9
Bill Mueller	BOS	$20	Cody Ross	DET	-$2
Eric Munson	DET	$6	Aaron Rowand	CHW	$3
Greg Myers	TOR	$10	Michael Ryan	MIN	$3
Wil Nieves	ANA	-$2	Rob Ryan	TOR	-$2
Ramon Nivar	TEX	-$1	Donnie Sadler	TEX	$0
Laynce Nix	TEX	$4	Olmedo Saenz	OAK	-$2
Trot Nixon	BOS	$20	Oscar Salazar	ANA	-$2
John Olerud	SEA	$10	Tim Salmon	ANA	$14
Miguel Olivo	CHW	$4	Alex Sanchez	DET	$29

Actual "Earned" 2003 Dollar Values

NAME	TEAM	$Val
Freddy Sanchez	BOS	-$2
Rey Sanchez	SEA	$1
Jared Sandberg	TB	$0
Anthony Sanders	CHW	-$2
Ramon Santiago	DET	$4
Angel Santos	CLE	-$1
David Segui	BAL	$2
Fernando Seguignol	NYY	-$3
Bill Selby	CLE	-$3
Terry Shumpert	TB	-$2
Ruben Sierra	NYY	$6
Chris Singleton	OAK	$4
Jason Smith	TB	-$2
Chris Snelling	SEA	-$2
Earl Snyder	BOS	-$2
Luis Sojo	NYY	-$3
Zach Sorensen	CLE	-$3
Alfonso Soriano	NYY	$37
Shane Spencer	TEX	$6
Scott Spiezio	ANA	$13
Shannon Stewart	MIN	$18
Jamal Strong	SEA	-$2
BJ Surhoff	BAL	$7
Larry Sutton	BOS	-$2
Ichiro Suzuki	SEA	$33
Pedro Swann	BAL	-$2
Mike Sweeney	KC	$14
Mark Teixeira	TEX	$13
Miguel Tejada	OAK	$22
Marcus Thames	TEX	-$2
Frank Thomas	CHW	$19
Andres Torres	DET	$1
Bubba Trammell	NYY	-$3
Chris Truby	TB	-$2
Michael Tucker	KC	$11
Jason Tyner	TB	$0
Luis Ugueto	SEA	-$1
Javier Valentin	TB	-$1
Jose Valentin	CHW	$14
Jason Varitek	BOS	$14
Omar Vizquel	CLE	$4
Matt Walbeck	DET	-$4
Todd Walker	BOS	$14
Dusty Wathan	CLE	-$2
Vernon Wells	TOR	$29
Jayson Werth	TOR	-$1
Barry Wesson	ANA	-$2
Rondell White	KC	$15

NAME	TEAM	$Val
Bernie Williams	NYY	$12
Dan Wilson	SEA	$2
Enrique Wilson	NYY	$1
Tom Wilson	TOR	$3
Randy Winn	SEA	$25
Dewayne Wise	TOR	-$2
Kevin Witt	DET	$4
Chris Woodward	TOR	$5
Shawn Wooten	ANA	$2
Ron Wright	CLE	-$2
Dmitri Young	DET	$19
Ernie Young	DET	-$3
Mike Young	TEX	$24
Julio Zuleta	BOS	-$2

National League Hitters

NAME	TEAM	$Val
Bob Abreu	PHI	$31
Edgardo Alfonzo	SF	$11
Chad Allen	FLA	-$4
Luke Allen	COL	-$4
Moises Alou	CHC	$18
Tony Alvarez	PIT	-$4
Garrett Atkins	COL	-$5
Rich Aurilia	SF	$11
Brad Ausmus	HOU	$4
Carlos Baerga	AZ	$5
Jeff Bagwell	HOU	$26
Paul Bako	CHC	-$1
Brian Banks	FLA	$0
Rod Barajas	AZ	-$1
Clint Barmes	COL	-$3
John Barnes	COL	-$4
Larry Barnes	LA	-$5
Michael Barrett	MON	$1
Danny Bautista	AZ	$4
Jason Bay	PIT	$1
David Bell	PHI	-$3
Jay Bell	NYM	-$5
Mike Bell	AZ	-$4
Mark Bellhorn	COL	$1
Ron Belliard	COL	$12
Adrian Beltre	LA	$9
Marvin Benard	SF	-$4
Gary Bennett	SD	$3
Peter Bergeron	MON	-$4
Lance Berkman	HOU	$22
Wilson Betemit	ATL	-$4

Actual "Earned" 2003 Dollar Values

NAME	TEAM	$Val	NAME	TEAM	$Val
Craig Biggio	HOU	$16	Ron Coomer	LA	-$3
Henry Blanco	ATL	-$3	Alex Cora	LA	$4
Geoff Blum	HOU	$6	Wil Cordero	MON	$10
Barry Bonds	SF	$30	Humberto Cota	PIT	-$3
Darren Bragg	ATL	-$1	Craig Counsell	AZ	$5
Russ Branyan	CIN	-$1	Felipe Crespo	CIN	-$4
Emil Brown	CIN	-$4	Tripp Cromer	HOU	-$4
Kevin L. Brown	STL	-$4	Bubba Crosby	LA	-$4
Eric Bruntlett	HOU	-$3	Enrique Cruz	MIL	-$6
Brian Buchanan	SD	$5	Jose Cruz	SF	$13
Mark Budzinski	CIN	-$4	Midre Cummings	CHC	-$4
Damon Buford	MON	-$4	J.J. Davis	PIT	-$4
Jeromy Burnitz	LA	$14	Kory Dehaan	SD	-$4
Pat Burrell	PHI	$4	Tom Delarosa	PIT	-$4
Sean Burroughs	SD	$12	Joe Depastino	NYM	-$3
Brent Butler	COL	-$3	Mark Derosa	ATL	$3
Marlon Byrd	PHI	$17	Chris Donnels	CHC	-$4
Jolbert Cabrera	LA	$8	Kelly Dransfeldt	CIN	-$4
Miguel Cabrera	FLA	$6	J.D. Drew	STL	$9
Orlando Cabrera	MON	$30	Jeff Duncan	NYM	-$2
Miguel Cairo	STL	$4	Adam Dunn	CIN	$12
Ron Calloway	MON	$8	Todd Dunwoody	STL	-$4
Jamey Carroll	MON	$1	Ray Durham	SF	$11
Raul Casanova	COL	-$4	Jim Edmonds	STL	$19
Sean Casey	CIN	$15	Jason Ellison	SF	-$4
Vinny Castilla	ATL	$13	Juan Encarnacion	FLA	$24
Alberto Castillo	SF	-$2	Mario Encarnacion	STL	-$4
Luis Castillo	FLA	$25	Morgan Ensberg	HOU	$16
Juan Castro	CIN	$4	Bobby Estalella	COL	$1
Ramon Castro	FLA	$0	Johnny Estrada	ATL	-$2
Roger Cedeno	NYM	$13	Tony Eusebio	MON	-$4
Matt Cepicky	MON	-$4	Adam Everett	HOU	$9
Jim Chamblee	CIN	-$5	Pedro Feliz	SF	$5
Travis Chapman	PHI	-$5	Robert Fick	ATL	$8
Endy Chavez	MON	$14	Steve Finley	AZ	$23
Raul Chavez	HOU	-$2	Cliff Floyd	NYM	$13
Chin-feng Chen	LA	-$4	Andy Fox	FLA	-$3
Hee Choi	CHC	-$1	Julio Franco	ATL	$2
McKay Christensen	PHI	-$4	Matt Franco	ATL	-$3
Alex Cintron	AZ	$15	Ryan Freel	CIN	$5
Chris Clapinski	LA	-$4	Rafael Furcal	ATL	$31
Brady Clark	MIL	$10	Andres Galarraga	SF	$6
Jermaine Clark	SD	-$3	Danny Garcia	NYM	-$3
Tony Clark	NYM	$2	Jesse Garcia	ATL	-$3
Royce Clayton	MIL	$5	Luis Garcia	AZ	-$4
Ivanon Coffie	STL	-$4	Brian Giles	SD	$19
Jeff Conine	FLA	$19	Marcus Giles	ATL	$27
Jason Conti	MIL	-$3	Keith Ginter	MIL	$7

Actual "Earned" 2003 Dollar Values

NAME	TEAM	$Val	NAME	TEAM	$Val
Joe Girardi	STL	-$3	Marcus Jensen	PHI	-$4
Doug Glanville	CHC	$3	Dangelo Jimenez	CIN	$16
Mike Glavine	NYM	-$5	Charles Johnson	COL	$8
Alex Gonzalez	FLA	$10	Andruw Jones	ATL	$24
Alex S. Gonzalez	CHC	$8	Chipper Jones	ATL	$23
Luis Gonzalez	AZ	$24	Brian Jordan	LA	$4
Raul Gonzalez	NYM	$0	Felix Jose	AZ	-$3
Wiki Gonzalez	SD	-$3	Eric Karros	CHC	$6
Tom Goodwin	CHC	$10	Matt Kata	AZ	$4
Mark Grace	AZ	-$4	Austin Kearns	CIN	$9
Shawn Green	LA	$18	David Kelton	CHC	-$4
Khalil Greene	SD	-$3	Jason Kendall	PIT	$21
Ken Griffey	CIN	$3	Jeff Kent	HOU	$20
Marquis Grissom	SF	$23	Mike Kinkade	LA	-$1
Mark Grudzielanek	CHC	$14	Ryan Klesko	SD	$8
Vladimir Guerrero	MON	$23	Randy Knorr	MON	-$4
Wilton Guerrero	CIN	-$4	Mark Kotsay	SD	$9
Mike Gulan	PIT	-$4	Jason Lane	HOU	-$2
Edwards Guzman	MON	-$3	Ryan Langerhans	ATL	-$4
Bill Hall	MIL	$1	Barry Larkin	CIN	$3
Robby Hammock	AZ	$6	Brandon Larson	CIN	-$5
Jeffrey Hammonds	SF	-$1	Jason Larue	CIN	$7
Dave Hansen	SD	-$3	Joe Lawrence	MIL	-$4
Lenny Harris	FLA	-$4	Ricky Ledee	PHI	$4
Bo Hart	STL	$5	Derrek Lee	FLA	$27
Wes Helms	MIL	$10	Jessie Levis	PHI	-$4
Todd Helton	COL	$32	Mike Lieberthal	PHI	$17
Rickey Henderson	LA	-$2	Todd Linden	SF	-$3
Chad Hermansen	LA	-$4	Keith Lockhart	SD	-$2
Jose Hernandez	PIT	$5	Paul Loduca	LA	$9
Mike Hessman	ATL	-$3	Kenny Lofton	CHC	$29
Phil Hiatt	CHC	-$4	Felipe Lopez	CIN	$2
Richard Hidalgo	HOU	$25	Javy Lopez	ATL	$28
Bobby Hill	PIT	-$4	Mark Loretta	SD	$19
Koyie Hill	LA	-$4	Mike Lowell	FLA	$19
Shea Hillenbrand	AZ	$14	Trey Lunsford	SF	-$3
Todd Hollandsworth	FLA	$1	Andy Machado	PHI	-$3
Dave Hollins	PHI	-$4	Jose Macias	MON	$1
Paul Hoover	FLA	-$4	Rob Mackowiak	PIT	$4
J.R. House	PIT	-$4	Wendell Magee	PHI	-$4
Tyler Houston	PHI	-$2	Mike Mahoney	CHC	-$4
Trenidad Hubbard	CHC	-$3	Eli Marrero	STL	-$2
Tim Hummel	CIN	-$3	Ramon E. Martinez	CHC	$3
Todd Hundley	LA	-$2	Tino Martinez	STL	$10
Brian L. Hunter	HOU	-$3	Henry Mateo	MON	$4
Adam Hyzdu	PIT	-$3	Ruben Mateo	CIN	-$1
Cesar Izturis	LA	$8	Mike Matheny	STL	$6
Geoff Jenkins	MIL	$19	Dave Matranga	HOU	-$3

Actual "Earned" 2003 Dollar Values

NAME	TEAM	$Val	NAME	TEAM	$Val
Gary Matthews	SD	$11	Mike Piazza	NYM	$6
Jason Maxwell	CIN	-$4	Juan Pierre	FLA	$46
Quinton McCracken	AZ	$0	Scott Podsednik	MIL	$38
Donzell McDonald	ATL	-$4	Placido Polanco	PHI	$20
Keith McDonald	CHC	-$4	Bo Porter	ATL	-$4
Joe McEwing	NYM	$1	Colin Porter	HOU	-$4
Fred McGriff	LA	$2	Todd Pratt	PHI	$1
Cody McKay	MIL	-$4	Albert Pujols	STL	$39
Walt McKeel	COL	-$4	Nick Punto	PHI	-$2
Pat Meares	PIT	-$4	Mark Quinn	SD	-$4
Mitch Meluskey	HOU	-$4	Humberto Quintero	SD	-$3
Donaldo Mendez	SD	-$2	Aramis Ramirez	CHC	$17
Carlos Mendoza	SF	-$4	Cody Ransom	SF	-$3
Orlando Merced	HOU	$0	Jeff Reboulet	PIT	$1
Jason Michaels	PHI	$1	Prentice Redman	NYM	-$3
Corky Miller	CIN	-$2	Tike Redman	PIT	$8
Damian Miller	CHC	$3	Mike Redmond	FLA	-$2
Damon Minor	PHI	-$4	Pokey Reese	PIT	$0
Chad Moeller	AZ	$4	Edgar Renteria	STL	$39
Raul Mondesi	AZ	$25	Jose Reyes	NYM	$12
Mike Mordecai	FLA	-$1	Rene Reyes	COL	-$1
Calvin Murray	LA	-$4	Chris Richard	COL	-$3
Xavier Nady	SD	$8	Carlos Rivera	PIT	-$4
Phil Nevin	SD	$6	Mike Rivera	SD	-$3
Lance Niekro	SF	-$5	Ruben Rivera	SF	-$3
Greg Norton	COL	$1	Dave Roberts	LA	$22
Abraham Nunez	FLA	-$4	Kerry Robinson	STL	$2
Abraham O. Nunez	PIT	$6	Ivan Rodriguez	FLA	$22
Jonathan Nunnally	STL	-$4	Scott Rolen	STL	$26
Troy O'Leary	CHC	$1	Jimmy Rollins	PHI	$20
Augie Ojeda	CHC	-$4	Jason Romano	LA	-$4
Miguel Ojeda	SD	$1	Mandy Romero	COL	-$2
Ray Olmedo	CIN	-$1	Dave Ross	LA	$2
Keith Osik	MIL	$1	Wilkin Ruan	LA	-$3
Lyle Overbay	AZ	$1	Jim Rushford	MIL	-$4
Pablo Ozuna	COL	-$2	Reggie Sanders	PIT	$25
Orlando Palmeiro	STL	$4	Benito Santiago	SF	$9
Corey Patterson	CHC	$17	Francisco Santos	SF	-$4
Josh Paul	CHC	-$2	Dane Sardinha	CIN	-$3
Jay Payton	COL	$24	Brian Schneider	MON	$3
Kit Pellow	COL	-$1	Marco Scutaro	NYM	-$2
Wily Pena	CIN	$0	Scott Seabol	MIL	-$4
Eddie Perez	MIL	$6	Todd Sears	SD	-$4
Eduardo Perez	STL	$9	Richie Sexson	MIL	$23
Neifi Perez	SF	$2	Chris Sexton	SD	-$4
Timoniel Perez	NYM	$6	Gary Sheffield	ATL	$41
Tomas Perez	PHI	$3	Tsuyoshi Shinjo	NYM	-$4
Jason Phillips	NYM	$11	Brian Simmons	SF	-$4

Actual "Earned" 2003 Dollar Values

NAME	TEAM	$Val
Randall Simon	CHC	$8
Mark Smith	MIL	-$2
Stephen Smitherman	CIN	-$3
Esix Snead	NYM	-$4
J.T. Snow	SF	$5
Sammy Sosa	CHC	$21
Junior Spivey	AZ	$8
Matt Stairs	PIT	$10
Dernell Stenson	CIN	-$2
Lee Stevens	MIL	-$4
Kelly Stinnett	PHI	$0
Chris Stynes	COL	$9
Mark Sweeney	COL	-$2
So Taguchi	STL	-$2
Fernando Tatis	MON	-$3
Reggie Taylor	CIN	$2
Luis Terrero	AZ	-$4
Jim Thome	PHI	$23
Joe Thurston	LA	-$4
Jorge Toca	NYM	-$4
Tony Torcato	SF	-$4
Steve Torrealba	STL	-$4
Yorvit Torrealba	SF	$2
Juan Uribe	COL	$7
Chase Utley	PHI	$0
Carlos Valderrama	SF	-$4
Mario Valdez	SD	-$4
Eric Valent	CIN	-$4
Yohanny Valera	PIT	-$4
John Vanderwal	MIL	$6
Greg Vaughn	COL	-$3
Mo Vaughn	NYM	-$4
Ramon Vazquez	SD	$9
Jorge Velandia	NYM	-$4
Robin Ventura	LA	$4
Wilton Veras	MIL	-$4
Shane Victorino	SD	-$1
Jose Vidro	MON	$17
Fernando Vina	STL	$3
Joe Vitiello	MON	$0
Jose Vizcaino	HOU	$0
Chris Wakeland	FLA	-$4
Larry Walker	COL	$17
Daryle Ward	LA	-$6
Matt Watson	NYM	-$4
Rickie Weeks	MIL	-$4
Chris Widger	STL	-$2
Ty Wigginton	NYM	$14

NAME	TEAM	$Val
Brad Wilkerson	MON	$19
Gerald Williams	FLA	-$3
Matt Williams	AZ	-$2
Craig Wilson	PIT	$10
Jack Wilson	PIT	$10
Preston Wilson	COL	$31
Vance Wilson	NYM	$3
Tony Womack	CHC	$6
Eric Young	SF	$21
Kevin Young	PIT	-$4
Gregg Zaun	COL	$0
Todd Zeile	MON	$2
Alan Zinter	HOU	-$4
Pete Zoccolillo	MIL	-$5

American League Pitchers

NAME	TEAM	$Val
Paul Abbott	KC	-$3
Juan Acevedo	TOR	$0
Jon Adkins	CHW	-$3
Jeremy Affeldt	KC	$9
Kurt Ainsworth	BAL	$1
Brian Anderson	KC	$13
Matt Anderson	DET	-$1
Kevin Appier	KC	$0
Bronson Arroyo	BOS	$0
Miguel Asencio	KC	-$3
Steve Avery	DET	-$3
Brandon Backe	TB	-$3
Danys Baez	CLE	$22
James Baldwin	MIN	-$2
Grant Balfour	MIN	-$2
Willie Banks	NYY	-$3
Rick Bauer	BAL	-$1
Erik Bedard	BAL	-$3
Rob Bell	TB	-$1
Alan Benes	TEX	-$5
Armando Benitez	SEA	$19
Joaquin Benoit	TEX	$0
Jason Bere	CLE	-$3
Rafael Betancourt	CLE	$3
Nick Bierbrodt	CLE	-$9
Jeremy Bonderman	DET	-$3
Chris Bootcheck	ANA	-$5
Micah Bowie	OAK	-$4
Brian Bowles	TOR	-$3
Jason Boyd	CLE	$1
Chad Bradford	OAK	$7

Actual "Earned" 2003 Dollar Values

NAME	TEAM	$Val	NAME	TEAM	$Val
Dewon Brazelton	TB	-$5	Scott Erickson	BAL	-$3
Mark Buehrle	CHW	$11	Kelvim Escobar	TOR	$9
Ryan Bukvich	KC	-$4	Brian Falkenborg	SEA	-$3
John Burkett	BOS	$4	Mike Fetters	MIN	-$2
Mickey Callaway	TEX	-$6	Nate Field	KC	-$2
Buddy Carlyle	KC	-$3	Jeremy Fikac	OAK	-$3
Giovanni Carrara	SEA	-$4	Bob File	TOR	-$3
D.J. Carrasco	KC	$1	Tony Fiore	MIN	-$3
Hector Carrasco	BAL	-$1	Brian Fitzgerald	TB	-$3
Lance Carter	TB	$24	Ben Ford	MIN	-$3
Bruce Chen	BOS	-$3	Casey Fossum	BOS	$0
Randy Choate	NYY	-$3	Keith Foulke	OAK	$45
Vinnie Chulk	TOR	-$3	Ryan Franklin	SEA	$15
Roger Clemens	NYY	$16	Kevin Frederick	TOR	-$3
Ken Cloude	SEA	-$3	Aaron Fultz	TEX	-$3
Jesus Colome	TB	$0	Mike Fyhrie	CLE	-$3
Bartolo Colon	CHW	$17	Freddy Garcia	SEA	$8
Jose Contreras	NYY	$5	Reynaldo Garcia	TEX	-$5
Dennis Cook	ANA	-$3	Rosman Garcia	TEX	-$5
Brian Cooper	CHW	-$3	Jon Garland	CHW	$7
Francisco Cordero	TEX	$16	Chad Gaudin	TB	$0
Nate Cornejo	DET	$1	Chris George	KC	-$6
David Cortes	CLE	-$4	Franklyn German	DET	-$2
Neal Cotts	CHW	-$5	Jason Gilfillan	KC	-$4
Tim Crabtree	CLE	-$3	Matt Ginter	CHW	-$3
Doug Creek	TOR	-$3	Gary Glover	ANA	-$2
Jack Cressend	CLE	$2	Jimmy Gobble	KC	$0
Darwin Cubillan	BAL	-$3	Dicky Gonzalez	BOS	-$3
Eric Cyr	ANA	-$3	Jeremi Gonzalez	TB	$7
Omar Daal	BAL	-$6	Tom Gordon	CHW	$14
Tom Davey	BOS	-$3	Kevin Gregg	ANA	$0
Jason Davis	CLE	$5	Seth Greisinger	DET	-$3
Rick Dehart	KC	-$4	Jason Grimsley	KC	-$3
Luis De Los Santos	TB	-$3	Buddy Groom	BAL	-$2
Jorge Depaula	NYY	-$1	Eddie Guardado	MIN	$36
R.A. Dickey	TEX	$2	John Halama	OAK	$1
Juan Dominguez	TEX	-$4	Roy Halladay	TOR	$29
Brendan Donnelly	ANA	$9	Chris Hammond	NYY	$4
Sean Douglass	BAL	-$5	Rich Harden	OAK	$0
Ryan Drese	TEX	-$6	Travis Harper	TB	$4
Travis Driskill	BAL	-$2	Chad Harville	OAK	-$3
Eric Dubose	BAL	$3	Shigetoshi Hasegawa	SEA	$19
Justin Duchscherer	OAK	-$1	La Troy Hawkins	MIN	$11
Chad Durbin	CLE	-$4	Mark Hendrickson	TOR	-$2
Eric Eckenstahler	DET	-$2	Pat Hentgen	BAL	$8
Dave Elder	CLE	-$4	Felix Heredia	NYY	$7
Robert Ellis	TEX	-$5	Gil Heredia	CHW	-$3
Alan Embree	BOS	$2	Adrian Hernandez	NYY	-$3

Actual "Earned" 2003 Dollar Values

NAME	TEAM	$Val	NAME	TEAM	$Val
Runelvys Hernandez	KC	$2	Brandon Lyon	BOS	$6
Alex Herrera	CLE	-$4	Mike Macdougal	KC	$20
Erik Hiljus	OAK	-$3	Ron Mahay	TEX	$2
Jeremy Hill	KC	-$3	Mark Malaska	TB	-$2
Bob Howry	BOS	-$4	Mike Maroth	DET	$0
Tim Hudson	OAK	$26	Damaso Marte	CHW	$17
Hansel Izquierdo	BOS	-$3	Pedro Martinez	BOS	$23
Delvin James	TB	-$3	Julio Mateo	SEA	$8
Jason Jimenez	DET	-$3	Darrell May	KC	$14
Adam Johnson	MIN	-$4	Joe Mays	MIN	-$3
Jason Johnson	BAL	$3	Seth McClung	TB	-$2
Greg Jones	ANA	-$3	Kevin McGlinchy	TB	-$3
Todd Jones	BOS	-$7	Chris Mears	DET	$1
Jorge Julio	BAL	$26	Gil Meche	SEA	$8
Steve Karsay	NYY	-$3	Jim Mecir	OAK	-$2
Justin Kaye	BOS	-$3	Ramiro Mendoza	BOS	-$6
Joe Kennedy	TB	-$5	Bart Miadich	ANA	-$4
Jason Kershner	TOR	$3	Justin Miller	TOR	-$3
Byung Kim	BOS	$23	Trever Miller	TOR	$2
Gary Knotts	DET	-$5	Eric Milton	MIN	-$1
Billy Koch	CHW	$6	Mike Mohler	BAL	-$3
Ryan Kohlmeier	CHW	-$3	Damian Moss	BAL	-$2
Ben Kozlowski	TEX	-$3	Tony Mounce	TEX	-$6
John Lackey	ANA	$5	Jamie Moyer	SEA	$20
Wilfredo Ledezma	DET	-$4	Mark Mulder	OAK	$17
Cliff Lee	CLE	$2	Terry Mulholland	CLE	-$2
Corey Lee	NYY	-$3	Mike Mussina	NYY	$21
David Lee	CLE	-$2	Aaron Myette	CLE	-$4
Curt Leskanic	KC	$5	Mike Nakamura	MIN	-$3
Al Levine	KC	$3	Jeff Nelson	NYY	$7
Colby Lewis	TEX	-$9	Mike Neu	OAK	-$2
Cory Lidle	TOR	$1	Doug Nickle	ANA	-$3
Jon Lieber	NYY	-$3	C.J. Nitkowski	TEX	-$5
Kerry Ligtenberg	BAL	$3	Jesse Orosco	MIN	-$4
Ted Lilly	OAK	$8	Ramon Ortiz	ANA	$3
Jose Lima	KC	$1	Jimmy Osting	KC	-$3
Doug Linton	TOR	-$2	Antonio Osuna	NYY	-$1
Graeme Lloyd	KC	-$4	Jose Paniagua	CHW	-$3
Esteban Loaiza	CHW	$25	Chan Ho Park	TEX	-$6
Kyle Lohse	MIN	$10	Christian Parker	NYY	-$3
Aaron Looper	SEA	-$3	Chad Paronto	CLE	-$3
Albie Lopez	KC	-$8	Jim Parque	TB	-$7
Aquilino Lopez	TOR	$13	John Parrish	BAL	$0
Rodrigo Lopez	BAL	-$3	Danny Patterson	DET	$1
Shane Loux	DET	-$4	Troy Percival	ANA	$26
Derek Lowe	BOS	$8	Matt Perisho	TB	-$3
Sean Lowe	KC	-$5	Robert Person	BOS	-$3
Mark Lukasiewicz	ANA	-$3	Andy Pettitte	NYY	$14

Actual "Earned" 2003 Dollar Values

NAME	TEAM	$Val	NAME	TEAM	$Val
Travis Phelps	TB	-$3	Brian Schmack	DET	-$2
Jason C. Phillips	CLE	-$4	Scott Schoeneweis	CHW	$1
Joel Pineiro	SEA	$14	Rudy Seanez	BOS	-$4
Cliff Politte	TOR	$7	Bobby Seay	TB	-$3
Mike Porzio	CHW	-$3	Shawn Sedlacek	KC	-$3
Jay Powell	TEX	-$7	Aaron Sele	ANA	-$3
Bret Prinz	NYY	-$4	Wascar Serrano	SEA	-$3
Carlos Pulido	MIN	-$2	Scott Service	TOR	-$1
Bill Pulsipher	BAL	-$3	Scot Shields	ANA	$12
J.J. Putz	SEA	-$3	Jason Shiell	BOS	-$2
Brad Radke	MIN	$11	Brian Shouse	TEX	$2
Erasmo Ramirez	TEX	$2	Jose Silva	OAK	-$3
Mario Ramos	TEX	-$3	Mike Smith	TOR	-$3
Jon Rauch	CHW	-$3	Roy Smith	OAK	-$3
Rick Reed	MIN	$2	Kyle Snyder	KC	-$1
Dan Reichert	TOR	-$4	Rafael Soriano	SEA	$7
Alberto Reyes	NYY	-$2	Jorge Sosa	TB	$0
Carlos Reyes	TB	-$1	Steve W. Sparks	OAK	$0
Arthur Rhodes	SEA	$3	Chris Spurling	DET	$2
Jerrod Riggan	CLE	-$3	Jason Standridge	TB	-$4
Matt Riley	BAL	-$2	Jason Stanford	CLE	$0
Juan Rincon	MIN	$3	Blake Stein	TB	-$3
Ricardo Rincon	OAK	$3	John Stephens	BAL	-$3
David Riske	CLE	$13	Josh Stewart	CHW	-$4
Mariano Rivera	NYY	$39	Everett Stull	MIN	-$3
Willis Roberts	BAL	-$2	Tanyon Sturtze	TOR	-$4
Nate Robertson	DET	-$4	Scott Sullivan	CHW	$3
John Rocker	TB	-$3	Jeff Suppan	BOS	$10
Fernando Rodney	DET	-$2	Brian Sweeney	SEA	-$2
Francisco Rodriguez	ANA	$10	Jon Switzer	TB	-$4
Jose Rodriguez	MIN	-$3	Brian Tallet	CLE	-$3
Ricardo Rodriguez	CLE	-$2	Jeff Tam	TOR	-$4
Rich Rodriguez	ANA	-$3	Aaron Taylor	SEA	-$4
Kenny Rogers	MIN	$6	Brad Thomas	MIN	-$3
J.C. Romero	MIN	-$3	Justin Thompson	TEX	-$3
Matt Roney	DET	-$3	John Thomson	TEX	$8
Brian Rose	KC	-$3	Corey Thurman	TOR	-$4
Ryan Rupe	BOS	-$3	Mike Timlin	BOS	$8
B.J. Ryan	BAL	$1	Kevin Tolar	BOS	-$3
C.C. Sabathia	CLE	$13	Josh Towers	TOR	$4
Erik Sabel	TB	-$3	Billy Traber	CLE	-$1
Carl Sadler	CLE	-$2	Derrick Turnbow	ANA	$1
David Sanders	CHW	-$4	Ismael Valdes	TEX	-$3
Johan Santana	MIN	$15	Andy Van Hekken	DET	-$3
Jose Santiago	CLE	-$2	Mike Venafro	TB	-$2
Victor Santos	TEX	-$5	Brad Voyles	KC	-$6
Kazuhiro Sasaki	SEA	$6	Doug Waechter	TB	$0
Scott Sauerbeck	BOS	-$2	Tim Wakefield	BOS	$11

Actual "Earned" 2003 Dollar Values

NAME	TEAM	$Val	NAME	TEAM	$Val
Jamie Walker	DET	$5	Manny Aybar	SF	-$3
Pete Walker	TOR	-$2	Mike Bacsik	NYM	-$5
Tyler Walker	DET	-$3	John Bale	CIN	-$1
Les Walrond	KC	-$4	Miguel Batista	AZ	$10
John Wasdin	TOR	-$6	Rod Beck	SD	$16
Jarrod Washburn	ANA	$10	Josh Beckett	FLA	$9
Jeff Weaver	NYY	-$5	Joe Beimel	PIT	-$3
Ben Weber	ANA	$5	Matt Belisle	CIN	-$3
David Wells	NYY	$14	Todd Belitz	COL	-$3
Jake Westbrook	CLE	$2	Francis Beltran	CHC	-$3
Gabe White	NYY	$2	Kris Benson	PIT	-$1
Matt White	SEA	-$6	Adam Bernero	COL	-$3
Bob Wickman	CLE	-$3	Rocky Biddle	MON	$23
Scott Wiggins	TOR	-$3	Nate Bland	HOU	-$3
Scott Williamson	BOS	$17	Brian Boehringer	PIT	-$1
Kris Wilson	KC	-$1	Jung Bong	ATL	$0
Matt Wise	ANA	-$3	Pedro Borbon	STL	-$5
Mark Wohlers	CLE	-$3	Toby Borland	FLA	-$2
Mike Wood	OAK	-$5	Joe Borowski	CHC	$27
Steve Woodard	BOS	-$3	Ricky Bottalico	AZ	-$3
Dan Wright	CHW	-$4	Troy Brohawn	LA	-$2
Jamey Wright	KC	-$2	Jim Brower	SF	$6
Kelly Wunsch	CHW	$0	Kevin Brown	LA	$21
Ed Yarnall	OAK	-$3	Mike Buddie	MIL	-$3
Victor Zambrano	TB	$7	Kirk Bullinger	HOU	-$3
Jeff Zimmerman	TEX	-$3	Nate Bump	FLA	-$1
Barry Zito	OAK	$19	Dave Burba	MIL	-$1
			A.J. Burnett	FLA	-$3
			Mike Bynum	SD	-$5
			Paul Byrd	ATL	-$3

National League Pitchers

NAME	TEAM	$Val	NAME	TEAM	$Val
Jose Acevedo	CIN	$1	Kiko Calero	STL	$1
Terry Adams	PHI	$2	Chris Capuano	AZ	-$1
Antonio Alfonseca	CHC	-$3	Chris Carpenter	STL	-$3
Armando Almanza	FLA	-$3	Jaime Cerda	NYM	-$3
Edwin Almonte	NYM	-$5	Juan Cerros	CIN	-$3
Hector Almonte	MON	-$5	Shawn Chacon	COL	$5
Juan Alvarez	FLA	-$2	Scott Chiasson	CHC	-$3
Victor Alvarez	LA	-$4	Matt Childers	MIL	-$3
Wilson Alvarez	LA	$9	Jason Christiansen	SF	-$3
Jason Anderson	NYM	-$3	Brandon Claussen	CIN	-$2
Jimmy Anderson	CIN	-$7	Matt Clement	CHC	$12
Clayton Andrews	CIN	-$3	Brad Clontz	COL	-$3
Rick Ankiel	STL	-$3	Pasqual Coco	MIL	-$3
Tony Armas	MON	$1	Dave Coggin	PHI	-$3
Andy Ashby	LA	-$1	Steve Colyer	LA	-$2
Pedro Astacio	NYM	-$4	Clay Condrey	SD	-$6
Jeff Austin	CIN	-$5	David Cone	NYM	-$4
Luis Ayala	MON	$10	Aaron Cook	COL	-$6

Actual "Earned" 2003 Dollar Values

NAME	TEAM	$Val	NAME	TEAM	$Val
Roy Corcoran	MON	-$2	Jesse Foppert	SF	$0
Chad Cordero	MON	$0	Matt Ford	MIL	-$2
Bryan Corey	LA	-$3	John Foster	MIL	-$3
Mark Corey	PIT	-$2	Chad Fox	FLA	$2
Rheal Cormier	PHI	$11	John Franco	NYM	$0
Kevin Correia	SF	-$1	Wayne Franklin	MIL	$0
Rich Croushore	FLA	-$3	Brian Fuentes	COL	$6
Mike Crudale	MIL	-$2	Chris Fussell	ATL	-$3
Juan Cruz	CHC	-$3	Eric Gagne	LA	$49
Nelson Cruz	COL	-$3	Mike Gallo	HOU	-$1
Will Cunnane	ATL	$2	Geoff Geary	PHI	-$3
Jeff C. Damico	PIT	$4	Tom Glavine	NYM	$3
Vic Darensbourg	MON	-$4	Ryan Glynn	FLA	-$3
Doug Davis	MIL	$1	Edgar Gonzalez	AZ	-$3
Lance Davis	CIN	-$3	Mike Gonzalez	PIT	-$3
Joey Dawley	ATL	-$5	Andrew Good	AZ	-$1
Zach Day	MON	$4	John Grabow	PIT	-$3
Roger Deago	SD	-$4	Danny Graves	CIN	$1
Mike Dejean	STL	$13	Jeremy Griffiths	NYM	-$5
Valerio De Los Santos	PHI	$1	Jason Grilli	FLA	-$3
Ryan Dempster	CIN	-$8	Kevin Gryboski	ATL	$0
Sean Depaula	CIN	-$3	Mark Guthrie	CHC	$0
Elmer Dessens	AZ	$0	Luther Hackman	SD	-$2
Ben Diggins	MIL	-$3	Josh Hall	CIN	-$5
Octavio Dotel	HOU	$11	Joey Hamilton	CIN	-$5
Scott Downs	MON	-$4	Mike Hampton	ATL	$9
Darren Dreifort	LA	$1	Josh Hancock	PHI	-$3
Tim Drew	MON	-$5	Chris Haney	ATL	-$3
Brandon Duckworth	PHI	-$1	Aaron Harang	CIN	-$1
Matt Duff	STL	-$3	Danny Haren	STL	-$1
Jayson Durocher	MIL	-$3	Pete Harnisch	CIN	-$3
Adam Eaton	SD	$8	Jimmy Haynes	CIN	-$7
Joey Eischen	MON	$2	Bryan Hebson	MON	-$3
Scott Elarton	COL	-$4	Aaron Heilman	NYM	-$6
Cal Eldred	STL	$8	Rick Helling	FLA	$2
John Ennis	ATL	-$3	Matt Herges	SF	$6
Todd Erdos	STL	-$3	Dustin Hermanson	SF	$1
Shawn Estes	CHC	-$5	Carlos Hernandez	HOU	-$3
Leo Estrella	MIL	$3	Livan Hernandez	MON	$18
Seth Etherton	CIN	-$4	Orlando Hernandez	MON	-$3
Scott Eyre	SF	$0	Roberto Hernandez	ATL	-$2
Kyle Farnsworth	CHC	$4	Sterling Hitchcock	STL	$1
Jeff Fassero	STL	-$2	Trey Hodges	ATL	-$1
Pedro Feliciano	NYM	-$1	Trevor Hoffman	SD	-$2
Jared Fernandez	HOU	$0	Darren Holmes	ATL	-$1
Anthony Ferrari	MON	-$3	Mike Holtz	PIT	-$3
Nelson Figueroa	PIT	$0	Ben Howard	SD	-$1
Josh Fogg	PIT	$1	Luke Hudson	CIN	-$3

Actual "Earned" 2003 Dollar Values

NAME	TEAM	$Val	NAME	TEAM	$Val
Kazuhisa Ishii	LA	$3	Tom Martin	LA	$1
Jason Isringhausen	STL	$16	Luis Martinez	MIL	-$6
Edwin Jackson	LA	-$1	TJ Mathews	STL	-$3
Kevin Jarvis	SD	-$3	Mike Matthews	SD	$0
Jason Jennings	COL	-$1	Brian Meadows	PIT	$1
Ryan Jensen	SF	-$5	Hector Mercado	PHI	-$3
Jose Jimenez	COL	$10	Jose Mercedes	MON	-$2
Jonathan Johnson	HOU	-$4	Kent Mercker	ATL	$2
Randy Johnson	AZ	$3	Jose Mesa	PHI	$13
Kevin Joseph	STL	-$3	Danny Miceli	HOU	$3
Jimmy Journell	STL	-$4	Chris Michalak	COL	-$3
Mike Judd	FLA	-$3	Jason Middlebrook	NYM	-$4
Eric Junge	PHI	-$2	Matt Miller	COL	-$3
Randy Keisler	SD	-$4	Matt Miller	COL	-$3
Kris Keller	SD	-$3	Travis Miller	CIN	-$3
Steve Kent	FLA	-$3	Wade Miller	HOU	$10
Masao Kida	LA	-$2	Kevin Millwood	PHI	$13
Brooks Kieschnick	MIL	-$2	Sergio Mitre	CHC	-$4
Sun-Woo Kim	MON	-$5	Brian Moehler	HOU	-$4
Ray King	ATL	$2	Gabe Molina	STL	-$4
Matt Kinney	MIL	$2	Orber Moreno	NYM	-$3
Steve Kline	STL	$4	Matt Morris	STL	$12
Eric Knott	MON	-$2	Guillermo Mota	LA	$12
Dan Kolb	MIL	$15	Scott Mullen	LA	-$5
Mike Koplove	AZ	$2	Bobby Munoz	NYM	-$3
Brian Lawrence	SD	$11	Peter Munro	HOU	-$2
Al Leiter	NYM	$7	Heath Murray	CHC	-$3
Allen Levrault	FLA	-$3	Brett Myers	PHI	$6
Brad Lidge	HOU	$5	Mike Myers	AZ	-$4
Mike Lincoln	PIT	$2	Rodney Myers	LA	-$3
Scott Linebrink	SD	$2	Charles Nagy	SD	-$3
Carlton Loewer	SD	-$4	Shane Nance	MIL	-$3
Braden Looper	FLA	$22	Joe Nathan	SF	$8
Javier Lopez	COL	$3	Denny Neagle	COL	-$4
Noah Lowry	SF	-$2	Blaine Neal	FLA	-$6
David Lundquist	SD	-$3	Robb Nen	SF	-$3
Greg Maddux	ATL	$15	Nick Neugebauer	MIL	-$3
Ryan Madson	PHI	-$3	Hideo Nomo	LA	$17
Cal Maduro	LA	-$3	Phil Norton	CIN	-$1
Pat Mahomes	PIT	-$3	Jose Nunez	SD	-$3
Oswaldo Mairena	FLA	-$3	Vladimir Nunez	FLA	-$6
Brian Mallette	LA	-$3	Wes Obermueller	MIL	-$3
Jim Mann	PIT	-$3	Tomokazu Ohka	MON	$7
David Manning	MIL	-$5	Will Ohman	CHC	-$3
Julio Manon	MON	-$1	Kevin Ohme	STL	-$2
Matt Mantei	AZ	$24	Darren Oliver	COL	$4
Josias Manzanillo	CIN	-$5	Kevin Olsen	FLA	-$6
Jason Marquis	ATL	-$2	Eddie Oropesa	AZ	-$3

Actual "Earned" 2003 Dollar Values

NAME	TEAM	$Val	NAME	TEAM	$Val
Russ Ortiz	ATL	$14	Kirk Rueter	SF	$3
Roy Oswalt	HOU	$11	Glendon Rusch	MIL	-$8
Vicente Padilla	PHI	$14	Kirk Saarloos	HOU	-$2
Lance Painter	STL	-$3	Duaner Sanchez	PIT	-$5
John Patterson	AZ	-$4	Felix Sanchez	CHC	-$3
Carl Pavano	FLA	$10	Jesus Sanchez	COL	-$4
Josh Pearce	STL	-$3	Curt Schilling	AZ	$15
Jason Pearson	STL	-$4	Jason Schmidt	SF	$26
Jake Peavy	SD	$9	Jae Seo	NYM	$10
Brad Penny	FLA	$11	Dan Serafini	CIN	-$4
Odalis Perez	LA	$8	Ben Sheets	MIL	$10
Oliver Perez	PIT	-$4	Paul Shuey	LA	$4
Tommy Phelps	FLA	$0	Carlos Silva	PHI	$0
Dan Plesac	PHI	$2	Bill Simas	LA	-$3
Sidney Ponson	SF	$15	Jason Simontacchi	STL	$0
Brian Powell	SF	-$4	Mike Sirotka	CHC	-$3
Andy Pratt	ATL	-$3	Aaron Small	CHC	-$3
Ariel Prieto	PIT	-$3	Bud Smith	PHI	-$3
Mark Prior	CHC	$23	Chuck Smith	MIL	-$3
Luke Prokopec	CIN	-$3	Dan Smith	MON	-$3
Brandon Puffer	HOU	-$4	John Smoltz	ATL	$37
Paul Quantrill	LA	$8	Steve Smyth	CHC	-$3
Ruben Quevedo	MIL	-$5	John Snyder	STL	-$3
Brady Raggio	AZ	-$3	Justin Speier	COL	$7
Horacio Ramirez	ATL	$8	Tim Spooneybarger	FLA	$1
Robert Ramsay	SD	-$3	Russ Springer	STL	-$3
Scott Randall	CIN	-$3	Mike Stanton	NYM	$3
Stephen Randolph	AZ	$1	Denny Stark	COL	-$4
Britt Reames	MON	-$4	Gene Stechschulte	STL	-$3
Tim Redding	HOU	$8	Garrett Stephenson	STL	$6
Mark Redman	FLA	$14	Scott Stewart	MON	-$1
Steve Reed	COL	$2	Ricky Stone	HOU	$4
Brian Reith	CIN	-$1	Pat Strange	NYM	-$5
Chris Reitsma	CIN	$12	Scott Strickland	NYM	-$1
Mike Remlinger	CHC	$2	Dennis Tankersley	SD	-$3
Dennis Reyes	AZ	-$5	Julian Tavarez	PIT	$11
Shane Reynolds	ATL	$1	Michael Tejera	FLA	$1
Armando Reynoso	AZ	-$3	Amaury Telemaco	PHI	$0
John Riedling	CIN	-$1	Anthony Telford	HOU	-$3
Jose Rijo	CIN	-$3	Brian Tollberg	SD	-$3
Todd Ritchie	MIL	-$3	Brett Tomko	STL	$1
Joe Roa	SD	-$4	Salomon Torres	PIT	$3
Jason Roach	NYM	-$4	Steve Trachsel	NYM	$12
Grant Roberts	NYM	-$1	J.J. Trujillo	SD	-$3
Jeriome Robertson	HOU	$3	Chin-hui Tsao	COL	-$3
Felix Rodriguez	SF	$4	T.J. Tucker	MON	$0
Nerio Rodriguez	STL	-$3	Ugueth Urbina	FLA	$27
Rodrigo Rosario	HOU	-$2	Joe Valentine	CIN	-$4

Actual "Earned" 2003 Dollar Values

A.L. Catchers

NAME	TEAM	$Val	NAME	TEAM	$Val
Jose Valverde	AZ	$10	Jorge Posada	NYY	$19
Cory Vance	COL	-$3	A.J. Pierzynski	MIN	$16
Todd Van Poppel	CIN	-$2	Jason Varitek	BOS	$15
Claudio Vargas	MON	$3	Ramon Hernandez	OAK	$13
Javier Vazquez	MON	$20	Greg Myers	TOR	$11
Dave Veres	CHC	$0	Ben Molina	ANA	$10
Brandon Villafuerte	SD	-$1	Matt Lecroy	MIN	$10
Oscar Villarreal	AZ	$7	Toby Hall	TB	$6
Ron Villone	HOU	$4	Brook Fordyce	BAL	$5
Ken Vining	HOU	-$3	Miguel Olivo	CHW	$4
Luis Vizcaino	MIL	-$2	Einar Diaz	TEX	$4
Ryan Vogelsong	PIT	-$3	Tom Wilson	TOR	$3
Billy Wagner	HOU	$39	Brent Mayne	KC	$3
Ryan Wagner	CIN	$0	Josh Bard	CLE	$3
Kevin Walker	SD	-$3	Sandy Alomar	CHW	$2
Mark Watson	CIN	-$3	Dan Wilson	SEA	$2
Justin Wayne	FLA	-$4	Ben Davis	SEA	$2
Dave Weathers	NYM	$6	Mike Difelice	KC	$2
Brandon Webb	AZ	$15	Victor Martinez	CLE	$2
Todd Wellemeyer	CHC	-$3	Doug Mirabelli	BOS	$2
Kip Wells	PIT	$13	Todd Greene	TEX	$1
Turk Wendell	PHI	$2	Brandon Inge	DET	$1
Dan Wheeler	NYM	$1	Adam Melhuse	OAK	$1
Rick White	HOU	-$2	Tim Laker	CLE	$1
Marc Wilkins	CHC	-$3	John Flaherty	NYY	$1
Dave Williams	PIT	-$3	Geronimo Gil	BAL	$0
Jerome Williams	SF	$8	Javier Valentin	TB	-$1
Mike Williams	PHI	$15	Gerald Laird	TEX	-$1
Woody Williams	STL	$15	Tom Prince	KC	-$1
Dontrelle Willis	FLA	$12	Robert Machado	BAL	-$1
Paul Wilson	CIN	$3	A.J. Hinch	DET	-$1
Jay Witasick	SD	$0			
Randy Wolf	PHI	$12			
Kerry Wood	CHC	$17	**A.L. First Basemen**		
Tim Worrell	SF	$30	Carlos Delgado	TOR	$28
Jaret Wright	ATL	-$5	Aubrey Huff	TB	$26
Estaban Yan	STL	-$3	Raul Ibanez	KC	$21
Jason Young	COL	-$5	Frank Thomas	CHW	$19
Tim Young	COL	-$3	Rafael Palmeiro	TEX	$19
Carlos Zambrano	CHC	$14	Jason Giambi	NYY	$18
Chad Zerbe	SF	-$2	David Ortiz	BOS	$18
			Kevin Millar	BOS	$17
			Travis Lee	TB	$15
			Doug Mientkiewicz	MIN	$14
			Mike Sweeney	KC	$13
			Scott Spiezio	ANA	$13
			Mark Teixeira	TEX	$13
			Casey Blake	CLE	$13

NAME	TEAM	$Val
Rube Durazo	OAK	$12
Nick Johnson	NYY	$10
John Olerud	SEA	$9
Ken Harvey	KC	$9
Ben Broussard	CLE	$8
Carlos Pena	DET	$8
Scott Hatteberg	OAK	$7
BJ Surhoff	BAL	$6
Paul Konerko	CHW	$5
Travis Hafner	CLE	$5
Kevin Witt	DET	$3
Shawn Wooten	ANA	$1
Brian Daubach	CHW	$0
Mendy Lopez	KC	$0

A.L. Second Basemen

NAME	TEAM	$Val
Alfonso Soriano	NYY	$38
Bret Boone	SEA	$30
Mike Young	TEX	$23
Adam Kennedy	ANA	$17
Brian Roberts	BAL	$15
Marlon Anderson	TB	$15
Desi Relaford	KC	$14
Todd Walker	BOS	$14
Luis Rivas	MIN	$13
Roberto Alomar	CHW	$10
Orlando Hudson	TOR	$8
Mark Ellis	OAK	$8
Tony Graffanino	CHW	$7
Jerry Hairston	BAL	$6
Damian Jackson	BOS	$6
Warren Morris	DET	$5
Ramon Santiago	DET	$3
Shane Halter	DET	$1
Carlos Febles	KC	$1
Antonio Perez	TB	$0

A.L. Third Basemen

NAME	TEAM	$Val
Aaron Boone	NYY	$25
Eric Chavez	OAK	$22
Hank Blalock	TEX	$21
Bill Mueller	BOS	$20
Corey Koskie	MIN	$17
Desi Relaford	KC	$14
Joe Randa	KC	$14
Scott Spiezio	ANA	$13
Casey Blake	CLE	$13

NAME	TEAM	$Val
Tony Batista	BAL	$12
Eric Hinske	TOR	$11
Joe Crede	CHW	$11
Carlos Guillen	SEA	$9
Troy Glaus	ANA	$9
Damian Rolls	TB	$8
Tony Graffanino	CHW	$7
Mike Bordick	TOR	$6
Eric Munson	DET	$6
Mark McLemore	SEA	$2
Shane Halter	DET	$1
Willie Bloomquist	SEA	$1
Lou Merloni	BOS	$1

A.L. Third Basemen

NAME	TEAM	$Val
Aaron Boone	NYY	$25
Eric Chavez	OAK	$22
Hank Blalock	TEX	$21
Bill Mueller	BOS	$20
Corey Koskie	MIN	$17
Desi Relaford	KC	$14
Joe Randa	KC	$14
Scott Spiezio	ANA	$13
Casey Blake	CLE	$13
Tony Batista	BAL	$12
Eric Hinske	TOR	$11
Joe Crede	CHW	$11
Carlos Guillen	SEA	$9
Troy Glaus	ANA	$9
Damian Rolls	TB	$8
Tony Graffanino	CHW	$7
Mike Bordick	TOR	$6
Eric Munson	DET	$6
Mark McLemore	SEA	$2
Shane Halter	DET	$1
Willie Bloomquist	SEA	$1
Lou Merloni	BOS	$1

A.L. Shortstops

NAME	TEAM	$Val
Alex Rodriguez	TEX	$35
Nomar Garciaparra	BOS	$32
Angel Berroa	KC	$24
Miguel Tejada	OAK	$23
Derek Jeter	NYY	$20
Cristian Guzman	MIN	$15
Julio Lugo	TB	$15
Jose Valentin	CHW	$14

NAME	TEAM	$Val
David Eckstein	ANA	$10
Carlos Guillen	SEA	$9
Deivi Cruz	BAL	$8
Tony Graffanino	CHW	$7
Mike Bordick	TOR	$6
Chris Woodward	TOR	$5
Omar Vizquel	CLE	$4
Ramon Santiago	DET	$3
Mark McLemore	SEA	$2
Shane Halter	DET	$1
Rey Ordonez	TB	$1
Lou Merloni	BOS	$1
Rey Sanchez	SEA	$1

A.L. Outfielders

NAME	TEAM	$Val
Carlos Beltran	KC	$39
Carl Crawford	TB	$35
Ichiro Suzuki	SEA	$34
Alex Sanchez	DET	$30
Carlos Lee	CHW	$30
Vernon Wells	TOR	$30
Manny Ramirez	BOS	$29
Magglio Ordonez	CHW	$28
Garret Anderson	ANA	$27
Rocco Baldelli	TB	$27
Randy Winn	SEA	$26
Johnny Damon	BOS	$26
Aubrey Huff	TB	$26
Carl Everett	CHW	$22
Raul Ibanez	KC	$21
Jacque Jones	MIN	$21
Jose Guillen	OAK	$20
Trot Nixon	BOS	$20
Dmitri Young	DET	$20
Milton Bradley	CLE	$19
Luis Matos	BAL	$18
Shannon Stewart	MIN	$18
Mike Cameron	SEA	$17
Hideki Matsui	NYY	$17
Kevin Millar	BOS	$17
Jay Gibbons	BAL	$16
Torii Hunter	MIN	$16
Jeff Davanon	ANA	$15
Rondell White	KC	$15
Jody Gerut	CLE	$15
Melvin Mora	BAL	$15
Desi Relaford	KC	$14

NAME	TEAM	$Val
Frank Catalanotto	TOR	$14
Tim Salmon	ANA	$14
Juan Gonzalez	TEX	$13
Reed Johnson	TOR	$13
Mark Teixeira	TEX	$13
Eric Byrnes	OAK	$12
Bernie Williams	NYY	$12
Michael Tucker	KC	$11
Matt Lawton	CLE	$11
Coco Crisp	CLE	$10
Aaron Guiel	KC	$10
Bobby Kielty	TOR	$10
Larry Bigbie	BAL	$10
Craig Monroe	DET	$10
Chone Figgins	ANA	$9
Bob Higginson	DET	$8
Terrence Long	OAK	$8
Damian Rolls	TB	$8
Damian Jackson	BOS	$6
BJ Surhoff	BAL	$6
Dustan Mohr	MIN	$6
Eric Owens	ANA	$6
Shane Spencer	TEX	$6
Ruben Sierra	NYY	$5
Gabe Kapler	BOS	$5
Darin Erstad	ANA	$5
Dave Dellucci	NYY	$4
Chris Singleton	OAK	$4
Karim Garcia	NYY	$3
Laynce Nix	TEX	$3
Michael Ryan	MIN	$2
Aaron Rowand	CHW	$2
Willie Harris	CHW	$2
Juan Rivera	NYY	$2
Ryan Ludwick	CLE	$2
Lew Ford	MIN	$1
Billy McMillon	OAK	$1
Kevin Mench	TEX	$1
Alex Escobar	CLE	$1

Designated Hitters

NAME	TEAM	$Val
Manny Ramirez	BOS	$29
Aubrey Huff	TB	$26
Jacque Jones	MIN	$21
Dmitri Young	DET	$20
Frank Thomas	CHW	$19
Rafael Palmeiro	TEX	$19

Actual "Earned" 2003 Dollar Values By Postiion

NAME	TEAM	$Val
Jason Giambi	NYY	$18
David Ortiz	BOS	$18
Edgar Martinez	SEA	$17
Frank Catalanotto	TOR	$14
Tim Salmon	ANA	$14
Mike Sweeney	KC	$13
Juan Gonzalez	TEX	$13
Rube Durazo	OAK	$12
Greg Myers	TOR	$11
Matt Lawton	CLE	$11
Nick Johnson	NYY	$10
Josh Phelps	TOR	$10
Matt Lecroy	MIN	$10
Bobby Kielty	TOR	$10
Ken Harvey	KC	$9
Brad Fullmer	ANA	$8
BJ Surhoff	BAL	$6
Ruben Sierra	NYY	$5
Travis Hafner	CLE	$5
Kevin Witt	DET	$3
Ellis Burks	CLE	$2
David Segui	BAL	$2
Al Martin	TB	$1
Shawn Wooten	ANA	$1

A.L. Pitchers

NAME	TEAM	$Val
Keith Foulke	OAK	$45
Mariano Rivera	NYY	$39
Eddie Guardado	MIN	$36
Roy Halladay	TOR	$29
Tim Hudson	OAK	$26
Troy Percival	ANA	$26
Jorge Julio	BAL	$26
Esteban Loaiza	CHW	$25
Lance Carter	TB	$24
Pedro Martinez	BOS	$23
Byung Kim	BOS	$23
Danys Baez	CLE	$22
Mike Mussina	NYY	$21
Mike Macdougal	KC	$20
Jamie Moyer	SEA	$20
Barry Zito	OAK	$19
Armando Benitez	SEA	$19
Shigetoshi Hasegawa	SEA	$19
Bartolo Colon	CHW	$17
Mark Mulder	OAK	$17
Scott Williamson	BOS	$17

NAME	TEAM	$Val
Damaso Marte	CHW	$17
Francisco Cordero	TEX	$16
Roger Clemens	NYY	$16
Johan Santana	MIN	$15
Ryan Franklin	SEA	$15
Tom Gordon	CHW	$14
Joel Pineiro	SEA	$14
Darrell May	KC	$14
Andy Pettitte	NYY	$14
David Wells	NYY	$14
Aquilino Lopez	TOR	$13
David Riske	CLE	$13
C.C. Sabathia	CLE	$13
Brian Anderson	KC	$13
Scot Shields	ANA	$12
Mark Buehrle	CHW	$11
Brad Radke	MIN	$11
Tim Wakefield	BOS	$11
Latroy Hawkins	MIN	$11
Jeff Suppan	BOS	$10
Francisco Rodriguez	ANA	$10
Kyle Lohse	MIN	$10
Jarrod Washburn	ANA	$10
Brendan Donnelly	ANA	$9
Jeremy Affeldt	KC	$9
Kelvim Escobar	TOR	$9
John Thomson	TEX	$8
Freddy Garcia	SEA	$8
Derek Lowe	BOS	$8
Gil Meche	SEA	$8
Ted Lilly	OAK	$8
Julio Mateo	SEA	$8
Mike Timlin	BOS	$8
Pat Hentgen	BAL	$8
Jeff Nelson	NYY	$7
Jeremi Gonzalez	TB	$7
Rafael Soriano	SEA	$7
Jon Garland	CHW	$7
Felix Heredia	NYY	$7
Cliff Politte	TOR	$7
Chad Bradford	OAK	$7
Victor Zambrano	TB	$7
Brandon Lyon	BOS	$6
Kazuhiro Sasaki	SEA	$6
Kenny Rogers	MIN	$6
Billy Koch	CHW	$6
Jamie Walker	DET	$5
Jose Contreras	NYY	$5

Actual "Earned" 2003 Dollar Values By Position

NAME	TEAM	$Val
Jason Davis	CLE	$5
John Lackey	ANA	$5
Curt Leskanic	KC	$5
Ben Weber	ANA	$5
John Burkett	BOS	$4
Travis Harper	TB	$4
Josh Towers	TOR	$4
Chris Hammond	NYY	$4
Al Levine	KC	$3
Jason Johnson	BAL	$3
Juan Rincon	MIN	$3
Kerry Ligtenberg	BAL	$3
Eric Dubose	BAL	$3
Scott Sullivan	CHW	$3
Rafael Betancourt	CLE	$3
Jason Kershner	TOR	$3
Ramon Ortiz	ANA	$3
Ricardo Rincon	OAK	$3
Arthur Rhodes	SEA	$3
Alan Embree	BOS	$2
Runelvys Hernandez	KC	$2
Chris Spurling	DET	$2
Jake Westbrook	CLE	$2
Trever Miller	TOR	$2
Brian Shouse	TEX	$2
Gabe White	NYY	$2
Jack Cressend	CLE	$2
Cliff Lee	CLE	$2
Rick Reed	MIN	$2
R.A. Dickey	TEX	$2
Ron Mahay	TEX	$2
Erasmo Ramirez	TEX	$2
John Halama	OAK	$1
D.J. Carrasco	KC	$1
Nate Cornejo	DET	$1
Chris Mears	DET	$1
Cory Lidle	TOR	$1
B.J. Ryan	BAL	$1
Scott Schoeneweis	CHW	$1
Jose Lima	KC	$1
Kurt Ainsworth	BAL	$1
Jason Boyd	CLE	$1
Danny Patterson	DET	$1
Derrick Turnbow	ANA	$1
Doug Waechter	TB	$0
Jesus Colome	TB	$0
Steve W. Sparks	OAK	$0
Joaquin Benoit	TEX	$0

NAME	TEAM	$Val
Jason Stanford	CLE	$0
Kevin Appier	KC	$0
Bronson Arroyo	BOS	$0
Kelly Wunsch	CHW	$0
Casey Fossum	BOS	$0
Jimmy Gobble	KC	$0
Kevin Gregg	ANA	$0
Rich Harden	OAK	$0
Jorge Sosa	TB	$0
John Parrish	BAL	$0
Chad Gaudin	TB	$0
Mike Maroth	DET	$0
Juan Acevedo	TOR	$0

N.L. Catchers

NAME	TEAM	$Val
Javy Lopez	ATL	$28
Ivan Rodriguez	FLA	$22
Jason Kendall	PIT	$21
Mike Lieberthal	PHI	$17
Jason Phillips	NYM	$11
Craig Wilson	PIT	$10
Paul Loduca	LA	$9
Benito Santiago	SF	$9
Charles Johnson	COL	$8
Jason Larue	CIN	$7
Eddie Perez	MIL	$6
Mike Piazza	NYM	$6
Robby Hammock	AZ	$6
Mike Matheny	STL	$6
Brad Ausmus	HOU	$4
Chad Moeller	AZ	$4
Vance Wilson	NYM	$3
Damian Miller	CHC	$3
Brian Schneider	MON	$3
Gary Bennett	SD	$3
Yorvit Torrealba	SF	$2
Dave Ross	LA	$2
Michael Barrett	MON	$1
Todd Pratt	PHI	$1
Bobby Estalella	COL	$1
Miguel Ojeda	SD	$1
Keith Osik	MIL	$1
Gregg Zaun	COL	$0
Ramon Castro	FLA	$0
Kelly Stinnett	PHI	$0

Actual "Earned" 2003 Dollar Values By Position

N.L. First Basemen

NAME	TEAM	$Val
Albert Pujols	STL	$39
Todd Helton	COL	$32
Derrek Lee	FLA	$27
Jeff Bagwell	HOU	$26
Richie Sexson	MIL	$23
Jim Thome	PHI	$23
Brad Wilkerson	MON	$19
Jeff Conine	FLA	$19
Sean Casey	CIN	$15
Shea Hillenbrand	AZ	$14
Jason Phillips	NYM	$11
Matt Stairs	PIT	$10
Craig Wilson	PIT	$10
Wil Cordero	MON	$10
Tino Martinez	STL	$10
Paul Loduca	LA	$9
Randall Simon	CHC	$8
Ryan Klesko	SD	$8
Robert Fick	ATL	$8
Phil Nevin	SD	$6
Andres Galarraga	SF	$6
Eric Karros	CHC	$6
Brian Buchanan	SD	$5
J.T. Snow	SF	$5
Carlos Baerga	AZ	$5
Robin Ventura	LA	$4
Fred McGriff	LA	$2
Tony Clark	NYM	$2
Todd Zeile	MON	$2
Julio Franco	ATL	$2
Lyle Overbay	AZ	$1

N.L. Second Basemen

Marcus Giles	ATL	$27
Luis Castillo	FLA	$25
Eric Young	SF	$21
Jeff Kent	HOU	$20
Placido Polanco	PHI	$20
Mark Loretta	SD	$19
Jose Vidro	MON	$17
Dangelo Jimenez	CIN	$16
Mark Grudzielanek	CHC	$14
Ron Belliard	COL	$12
Ray Durham	SF	$11
Jolbert Cabrera	LA	$8
Junior Spivey	AZ	$8
Keith Ginter	MIL	$7

NAME	TEAM	$Val
Abraham O. Nunez	PIT	$6
Geoff Blum	HOU	$6
Tony Womack	CHC	$6
Bo Hart	STL	$5
Matt Kata	AZ	$4
Alex Cora	LA	$4
Juan Castro	CIN	$4
Miguel Cairo	STL	$4
Henry Mateo	MON	$4
Ramon E. Martinez	CHC	$3
Mark Derosa	ATL	$3
Tomas Perez	PHI	$3
Fernando Vina	STL	$3
Neifi Perez	SF	$2
Jeff Reboulet	PIT	$1
Mark Bellhorn	COL	$1
Bill Hall	MIL	$1
Joe McEwing	NYM	$1

N.L. Third Basemen

Scott Rolen	STL	$26
Placido Polanco	PHI	$20
Mike Lowell	FLA	$19
Aramis Ramirez	CHC	$17
Morgan Ensberg	HOU	$16
Shea Hillenbrand	AZ	$14
Ty Wigginton	NYM	$14
Vinny Castilla	ATL	$13
Sean Burroughs	SD	$12
Edgardo Alfonzo	SF	$11
Wes Helms	MIL	$10
Adrian Beltre	LA	$9
Chris Stynes	COL	$9
Keith Ginter	MIL	$7
Geoff Blum	HOU	$6
Miguel Cabrera	FLA	$6
Craig Counsell	AZ	$5
Pedro Feliz	SF	$5
Jose Hernandez	PIT	$5
Matt Kata	AZ	$4
Robin Ventura	LA	$4
Juan Castro	CIN	$4
Ramon E. Martinez	CHC	$3
Mark Derosa	ATL	$3
Tomas Perez	PHI	$3
Todd Zeile	MON	$2
Greg Norton	COL	$1

Actual "Earned" 2003 Dollar Values By Position

NAME	TEAM	$Val
Jamey Carroll	MON	$1
Mark Bellhorn	COL	$1
Jose Macias	MON	$1

N.L. Shortstops

NAME	TEAM	$Val
Edgar Renteria	STL	$39
Rafael Furcal	ATL	$31
Orlando Cabrera	MON	$30
Jimmy Rollins	PHI	$20
Alex Cintron	AZ	$15
Jose Reyes	NYM	$12
Rich Aurilia	SF	$11
Alex Gonzalez	FLA	$10
Jack Wilson	PIT	$10
Adam Everett	HOU	$9
Ramon Vazquez	SD	$9
Alex S. Gonzalez	CHC	$8
Cesar Izturis	LA	$8
Juan Uribe	COL	$7
Abraham O. Nunez	PIT	$6
Tony Womack	CHC	$6
Craig Counsell	AZ	$5
Royce Clayton	MIL	$5
Jose Hernandez	PIT	$5
Juan Castro	CIN	$4
Ramon E. Martinez	CHC	$3
Barry Larkin	CIN	$3
Mark Derosa	ATL	$3
Neifi Perez	SF	$2
Felipe Lopez	CIN	$2
Bill Hall	MIL	$1
Joe McEwing	NYM	$1

N.L. Outfielders

NAME	TEAM	$Val
Juan Pierre	FLA	$46
Gary Sheffield	ATL	$41
Albert Pujols	STL	$39
Scott Podsednik	MIL	$38
Bob Abreu	PHI	$31
Preston Wilson	COL	$31
Barry Bonds	SF	$30
Kenny Lofton	CHC	$29
Richard Hidalgo	HOU	$25
Raul Mondesi	AZ	$25
Reggie Sanders	PIT	$25
Jay Payton	COL	$24
Juan Encarnacion	FLA	$24

NAME	TEAM	$Val
Luis Gonzalez	AZ	$24
Andruw Jones	ATL	$24
Chipper Jones	ATL	$23
Marquis Grissom	SF	$23
Vladimir Guerrero	MON	$23
Steve Finley	AZ	$23
Lance Berkman	HOU	$22
Dave Roberts	LA	$22
Sammy Sosa	CHC	$21
Jim Edmonds	STL	$19
Brian Giles	SD	$19
Brad Wilkerson	MON	$19
Jeff Conine	FLA	$19
Geoff Jenkins	MIL	$19
Shawn Green	LA	$18
Moises Alou	CHC	$18
Marlon Byrd	PHI	$17
Corey Patterson	CHC	$17
Larry Walker	COL	$17
Craig Biggio	HOU	$16
Jeromy Burnitz	LA	$14
Endy Chavez	MON	$14
Roger Cedeno	NYM	$13
Jose Cruz	SF	$13
Cliff Floyd	NYM	$13
Adam Dunn	CIN	$12
Gary Matthews	SD	$11
Brady Clark	MIL	$10
Matt Stairs	PIT	$10
Craig Wilson	PIT	$10
Tom Goodwin	CHC	$10
J.D. Drew	STL	$9
Austin Kearns	CIN	$9
Mark Kotsay	SD	$9
Eduardo Perez	STL	$9
Jolbert Cabrera	LA	$8
Xavier Nady	SD	$8
Tike Redman	PIT	$8
Ron Calloway	MON	$8
Phil Nevin	SD	$6
John Vanderwal	MIL	$6
Miguel Cabrera	FLA	$6
Timoniel Perez	NYM	$6
Brian Buchanan	SD	$5
Ryan Freel	CIN	$5
Danny Bautista	AZ	$4
Ricky Ledee	PHI	$4
Orlando Palmeiro	STL	$4

Actual "Earned" 2003 Dollar Values By Position

NAME	TEAM	$Val	NAME	TEAM	$Val
Pat Burrell	PHI	$4	Steve Trachsel	NYM	$12
Brian Jordan	LA	$4	Matt Clement	CHC	$12
Rob Mackowiak	PIT	$4	Guillermo Mota	LA	$12
Miguel Cairo	STL	$4	Matt Morris	STL	$12
Ken Griffey	CIN	$3	Chris Reitsma	CIN	$12
Doug Glanville	CHC	$3	Dontrelle Willis	FLA	$12
Reggie Taylor	CIN	$2	Randy Wolf	PHI	$12
Kerry Robinson	STL	$2	Rheal Cormier	PHI	$11
Jason Michaels	PHI	$1	Octavio Dotel	HOU	$11
Todd Hollandsworth	FLA	$1	Roy Oswalt	HOU	$11
Jason Bay	PIT	$1	Brad Penny	FLA	$11
Jose Macias	MON	$1	Julian Tavarez	PIT	$11
Troy O'Leary	CHC	$1	Brian Lawrence	SD	$11
			Ben Sheets	MIL	$10
N.L. Pitchers			Miguel Batista	AZ	$10
			Jose Valverde	AZ	$10
Eric Gagne	LA	$49	Carl Pavano	FLA	$10
Billy Wagner	HOU	$39	Luis Ayala	MON	$10
John Smoltz	ATL	$37	Jose Jimenez	COL	$10
Tim Worrell	SF	$30	Jae Seo	NYM	$10
Joe Borowski	CHC	$27	Wade Miller	HOU	$10
Ugueth Urbina	FLA	$27	Jake Peavy	SD	$9
Jason Schmidt	SF	$26	Mike Hampton	ATL	$9
Matt Mantei	AZ	$24	Wilson Alvarez	LA	$9
Mark Prior	CHC	$23	Josh Beckett	FLA	$9
Rocky Biddle	MON	$23	Odalis Perez	LA	$8
Braden Looper	FLA	$22	Joe Nathan	SF	$8
Kevin Brown	LA	$21	Adam Eaton	SD	$8
Javier Vazquez	MON	$20	Tim Redding	HOU	$8
Livan Hernandez	MON	$18	Cal Eldred	STL	$8
Hideo Nomo	LA	$17	Paul Quantrill	LA	$8
Kerry Wood	CHC	$17	Horacio Ramirez	ATL	$8
Rod Beck	SD	$16	Jerome Williams	SF	$8
Jason Isringhausen	STL	$16	Justin Speier	COL	$7
Greg Maddux	ATL	$15	Oscar Villarreal	AZ	$7
Brandon Webb	AZ	$15	Al Leiter	NYM	$7
Dan Kolb	MIL	$15	Tomokazu Ohka	MON	$7
Curt Schilling	AZ	$15	Matt Herges	SF	$6
Woody Williams	STL	$15	Dave Weathers	NYM	$6
Sidney Ponson	SF	$15	Jim Brower	SF	$6
Mike Williams	PHI	$15	Brian Fuentes	COL	$6
Russ Ortiz	ATL	$14	Brett Myers	PHI	$6
Vicente Padilla	PHI	$14	Garrett Stephenson	STL	$6
Carlos Zambrano	CHC	$14	Shawn Chacon	COL	$5
Mark Redman	FLA	$14	Brad Lidge	HOU	$5
Kevin Millwood	PHI	$13	Paul Shuey	LA	$4
Kip Wells	PIT	$13	Ricky Stone	HOU	$4
Mike Dejean	STL	$13	Felix Rodriguez	SF	$4
Jose Mesa	PHI	$13			

Actual "Earned" 2003 Dollar Values By Position

NAME	TEAM	$Val	NAME	TEAM	$Val
Jeff C. Damico	PIT	$4	Kiko Calero	STL	$1
Ron Villone	HOU	$4	Darren Dreifort	LA	$1
Zach Day	MON	$4	Brian Meadows	PIT	$1
Kyle Farnsworth	CHC	$4			
Steve Kline	STL	$4			
Darren Oliver	COL	$4			
Danny Miceli	HOU	$3			
Tom Glavine	NYM	$3			
Randy Johnson	AZ	$3			
Salomon Torres	PIT	$3			
Claudio Vargas	MON	$3			
Leo Estrella	MIL	$3			
Kazuhisa Ishii	LA	$3			
Kirk Rueter	SF	$3			
Mike Stanton	NYM	$3			
Paul Wilson	CIN	$3			
Javier Lopez	COL	$3			
Jeriome Robertson	HOU	$3			
Rick Helling	FLA	$2			
Turk Wendell	PHI	$2			
Scott Linebrink	SD	$2			
Mike Remlinger	CHC	$2			
Steve Reed	COL	$2			
Mike Lincoln	PIT	$2			
Will Cunnane	ATL	$2			
Mike Koplove	AZ	$2			
Terry Adams	PHI	$2			
Chad Fox	FLA	$2			
Matt Kinney	MIL	$2			
Dan Plesac	PHI	$2			
Ray King	ATL	$2			
Joey Eischen	MON	$2			
Kent Mercker	ATL	$2			
Josh Fogg	PIT	$1			
Brett Tomko	STL	$1			
Dan Wheeler	NYM	$1			
Dustin Hermanson	SF	$1			
Sterling Hitchcock	STL	$1			
Tim Spooneybarger	FLA	$1			
Doug Davis	MIL	$1			
Jose Acevedo	CIN	$1			
Stephen Randolph	AZ	$1			
Shane Reynolds	ATL	$1			
Michael Tejera	FLA	$1			
Valerio Delossantos	PHI	$1			
Danny Graves	CIN	$1			
Tom Martin	LA	$1			
Tony Armas	MON	$1			

3-Year Average Lists

Top 3-yr Batting Average

NAME	TEAM	Avg.	NAME	TEAM	Avg.
Barry Bonds	SF	.345	Placido Polanco	PHI	.295
Joe Vitiello	MON	.342	Carlos Beltran	KC	.294
Todd Helton	COL	.341	Aubrey Huff	TB	.294
Albert Pujols	STL	.334	Reed Johnson	TOR	.294
Ichiro Suzuki	SEA	.328	Jacque Jones	MIN	.294
Manny Ramirez	BOS	.325	Edgar Martinez	SEA	.294
Larry Walker	COL	.325	Phil Nevin	SD	.294
Vladimir Guerrero	MON	.324	Randall Simon	CHC	.293
Chipper Jones	ATL	.321	Todd Walker	BOS	.293
Gary Sheffield	ATL	.317	Brian Jordan	LA	.292
Carlos Baerga	AZ	.316	Raul Ibanez	KC	.291
Jose Vidro	MON	.315	Jason Kendall	PIT	.291
Magglio Ordonez	CHW	.314	John Olerud	SEA	.291
Mike Sweeney	KC	.313	Doug Mientkiewicz	MIN	.290
Greg Colbrunn	SEA	.310	Jay Payton	COL	.290
Derek Jeter	NYY	.309	Randy Winn	SEA	.290
Shannon Stewart	MIN	.309	Sean Casey	CIN	.289
Luis Gonzalez	AZ	.307	Jeff Conine	FLA	.289
Juan Pierre	FLA	.307	Julio Franco	ATL	.289
Jose Reyes	NYM	.307	Mike Lieberthal	PHI	.289
Frank Catalanotto	TOR	.306	Paul Loduca	LA	.289
Juan Gonzalez	TEX	.306	Mike Piazza	NYM	.289
Ivan Rodriguez	FLA	.306	Rich Aurilia	SF	.288
Alex Rodriguez	TEX	.305	Todd Hollandsworth	FLA	.288
Bernie Williams	NYY	.305	Roberto Alomar	CHW	.287
Lance Berkman	HOU	.304	Shawn Green	LA	.287
Juan Brito	KC	.304	Alfonso Soriano	NYY	.287
Nomar Garciaparra	BOS	.304	Jeff Bagwell	HOU	.286
Mark Loretta	SD	.304	Ellis Burks	CLE	.286
Garret Anderson	ANA	.303	Carlos Delgado	TOR	.286
Jeff Kent	HOU	.303	J.D. Drew	STL	.286
Alex Cintron	AZ	.302	Jim Thome	PHI	.286
Jason Giambi	NYY	.302	Brad Fullmer	ANA	.285
Brian Giles	SD	.302	Marcus Giles	ATL	.285
Bret Boone	SEA	.301	Jose Guillen	OAK	.285
A.J. Pierzynski	MIN	.301	Miguel Tejada	OAK	.285
Cliff Floyd	NYM	.300	Mark Grudzielanek	CHC	.284
Edgar Renteria	STL	.300	Adam Kennedy	ANA	.284
Bob Abreu	PHI	.299	Steve Finley	AZ	.283
Bill Mueller	BOS	.299	Ricky Gutierrez	CLE	.283
Sammy Sosa	CHC	.299	Mark Kotsay	SD	.283
Vernon Wells	TOR	.298	Jose Vizcaino	HOU	.283
Jim Edmonds	STL	.297	Eric Chavez	OAK	.282
Kevin Millar	BOS	.297	Rafael Furcal	ATL	.282
Dmitri Young	DET	.297	Ryan Klesko	SD	.282
Danny Bautista	AZ	.296	Alex Sanchez	DET	.282
Moises Alou	CHC	.295	BJ Surhoff	BAL	.282
Luis Castillo	FLA	.295	Fernando Vina	STL	.281

Top 3-yr HR Average

NAME	TEAM	HR	NAME	TEAM	HR
Barry Bonds	SF	55	Mike Lowell	FLA	25
Alex Rodriguez	TEX	52	Fred McGriff	LA	25
Sammy Sosa	CHC	51	Frank Thomas	CHW	25
Jim Thome	PHI	49	Bob Abreu	PHI	24
Rafael Palmeiro	TEX	43	Jose Cruz	SF	24
Jason Giambi	NYY	40	Adam Dunn	CIN	24
Richie Sexson	MIL	40	Javy Lopez	ATL	24
Carlos Delgado	TOR	38	Jorge Posada	NYY	24
Albert Pujols	STL	38	Mike Cameron	SEA	23
Luis Gonzalez	AZ	37	Tino Martinez	STL	23
Shawn Green	LA	37	David Ortiz	BOS	23
Todd Helton	COL	37	Mike Sweeney	KC	23
Manny Ramirez	BOS	37	Rich Aurilia	SF	22
Jeff Bagwell	HOU	36	Ellis Burks	CLE	22
Andruw Jones	ATL	35	Jay Gibbons	BAL	22
Lance Berkman	HOU	34	Juan Gonzalez	TEX	22
Vladimir Guerrero	MON	33	Aubrey Huff	TB	22
Magglio Ordonez	CHW	33	Phil Nevin	SD	22
Gary Sheffield	ATL	33	Moises Alou	CHC	21
Bret Boone	SEA	32	Aaron Boone	NYY	21
Eric Chavez	OAK	32	Jose Hernandez	PIT	21
Jim Edmonds	STL	32	Richard Hidalgo	HOU	21
Brian Giles	SD	32	Edgar Martinez	SEA	21
Alfonso Soriano	NYY	32	Robin Ventura	LA	21
Miguel Tejada	OAK	31	Vinny Castilla	ATL	20
Chipper Jones	ATL	30	J.D. Drew	STL	20
Garret Anderson	ANA	29	Steve Finley	AZ	20
Troy Glaus	ANA	29	Kevin Millar	BOS	20
Reggie Sanders	PIT	29	Ivan Rodriguez	FLA	20
Jeromy Burnitz	LA	28	Bernie Williams	NYY	20
Pat Burrell	PHI	28	Adrian Beltre	LA	19
Scott Rolen	STL	28	Carl Everett	CHW	19
Tony Batista	BAL	27	Nomar Garciaparra	BOS	19
Torii Hunter	MIN	27	Marquis Grissom	SF	19
Jeff Kent	HOU	27	Geoff Jenkins	MIL	19
Ryan Klesko	SD	27	Jacque Jones	MIN	19
Carlos Lee	CHW	27	Tim Salmon	ANA	19
Mike Piazza	NYM	27	Vernon Wells	TOR	19
Jose Valentin	CHW	27	Dmitri Young	DET	19
Larry Walker	COL	27			
Preston Wilson	COL	27			
Carlos Beltran	KC	26			
Cliff Floyd	NYM	26			
Paul Konerko	CHW	26			
Derrek Lee	FLA	26			
Raul Mondesi	AZ	26			
Trot Nixon	BOS	26			
Aramis Ramirez	CHC	26			

3-Year Average Lists

Top 3-yr RBI Average

NAME	TEAM	RBI	NAME	TEAM	RBI
Alex Rodriguez	TEX	132	Moises Alou	CHC	87
Albert Pujols	STL	127	Reggie Sanders	PIT	87
Todd Helton	COL	124	Bernie Williams	NYY	87
Sammy Sosa	CHC	124	Tino Martinez	STL	86
Jim Thome	PHI	124	Jeff Conine	FLA	85
Bret Boone	SEA	122	Derrek Lee	FLA	84
Garret Anderson	ANA	121	Cliff Floyd	NYM	83
Carlos Delgado	TOR	118	Aaron Boone	NYY	82
Richie Sexson	MIL	117	Juan Gonzalez	TEX	82
Miguel Tejada	OAK	117	Raul Ibanez	KC	82
Lance Berkman	HOU	116	Fred McGriff	LA	82
Jason Giambi	NYY	116	Raul Mondesi	AZ	81
Luis Gonzalez	AZ	116	Corey Koskie	MIN	80
Magglio Ordonez	CHW	116	Edgar Renteria	STL	80
Rafael Palmeiro	TEX	113	Kevin Millar	BOS	79
Barry Bonds	SF	112	Nomar Garciaparra	BOS	78
Manny Ramirez	BOS	112	Joe Randa	KC	78
Jeff Bagwell	HOU	109	Jeromy Burnitz	LA	77
Eric Chavez	OAK	108	Orlando Cabrera	MON	77
Shawn Green	LA	108	Juan Encarnacion	FLA	77
Scott Rolen	STL	107	Steve Finley	AZ	77
Andruw Jones	ATL	105	Travis Lee	TB	77
Gary Sheffield	ATL	105	Vinny Castilla	ATL	76
Chipper Jones	ATL	103	Shea Hillenbrand	AZ	76
Carlos Beltran	KC	102	Javy Lopez	ATL	76
Jeff Kent	HOU	102	Phil Nevin	SD	76
Larry Walker	COL	102	Jose Cruz	SF	75
Bob Abreu	PHI	99	David Ortiz	BOS	75
Vladimir Guerrero	MON	99	Mike Piazza	NYM	75
Mike Lowell	FLA	99	Todd Walker	BOS	75
Jorge Posada	NYY	98	Vernon Wells	TOR	74
Torii Hunter	MIN	96	Scott Spiezio	ANA	73
Aramis Ramirez	CHC	96	Jose Vidro	MON	73
Brian Giles	SD	95	Rich Aurilia	SF	72
Jim Edmonds	STL	94	Adrian Beltre	LA	72
John Olerud	SEA	93	Richard Hidalgo	HOU	72
Ryan Klesko	SD	92	Jose Valentin	CHW	72
Carlos Lee	CHW	92	Jermaine Dye	OAK	71
Preston Wilson	COL	92	Carl Everett	CHW	71
Tony Batista	BAL	91	Terrence Long	OAK	71
Edgar Martinez	SEA	91	Sean Casey	CIN	70
Pat Burrell	PHI	90	Aubrey Huff	TB	70
Troy Glaus	ANA	90	Ivan Rodriguez	FLA	70
Trot Nixon	BOS	90	Tim Salmon	ANA	70
Mike Cameron	SEA	89	Robin Ventura	LA	70
Paul Konerko	CHW	89			
Alfonso Soriano	NYY	89			
Mike Sweeney	KC	89			

3-Year Average Lists

Top 3-yr SB Average

NAME	TEAM	SB
Juan Pierre	FLA	53
Alfonso Soriano	NYY	40
Ichiro Suzuki	SEA	40
Carlos Beltran	KC	36
Luis Castillo	FLA	34
Jimmy Rollins	PHI	32
Alex Sanchez	DET	32
Roger Cedeno	NYM	31
Bob Abreu	PHI	30
Eric Young	SF	30
Johnny Damon	BOS	29
Vladimir Guerrero	MON	29
Dave Roberts	LA	28
Mike Cameron	SEA	27
Rafael Furcal	ATL	25
Kenny Lofton	CHC	25
Edgar Renteria	STL	24
Orlando Cabrera	MON	23
Derek Jeter	NYY	23
Tony Womack	CHC	23
David Eckstein	ANA	22
Raul Mondesi	AZ	22
Carl Crawford	TB	21
Jerry Hairston	BAL	21
Mark McLemore	SEA	21
Randy Winn	SEA	21
Aaron Boone	NYY	20
Roberto Alomar	CHW	19
Ray Durham	SF	19
Darin Erstad	ANA	19
Tom Goodwin	CHC	19
Luis Rivas	MIN	19
Cristian Guzman	MIN	18
Preston Wilson	COL	18
Doug Glanville	CHC	17
Damian Jackson	BOS	17
Adam Kennedy	ANA	17
Juan Encarnacion	FLA	16
Corey Koskie	MIN	16
Matt Lawton	CLE	16
Reggie Sanders	PIT	16
Michael Tucker	KC	16

Top 3-yr Runs Average

NAME	TEAM	Runs
Alex Rodriguez	TEX	127
Todd Helton	COL	125
Albert Pujols	STL	122
Sammy Sosa	CHC	122
Barry Bonds	SF	119
Ichiro Suzuki	SEA	116
Jeff Bagwell	HOU	110
Johnny Damon	BOS	110
Lance Berkman	HOU	109
Jason Giambi	NYY	109
Carlos Beltran	KC	107
Carlos Delgado	TOR	107
Derek Jeter	NYY	107
Bob Abreu	PHI	106
Bret Boone	SEA	106
Alfonso Soriano	NYY	106
Craig Biggio	HOU	105
Shawn Green	LA	105
Miguel Tejada	OAK	104
Jim Thome	PHI	104
Luis Gonzalez	AZ	103
Magglio Ordonez	CHW	103
Chipper Jones	ATL	102
Gary Sheffield	ATL	102
Brian Giles	SD	101
Andruw Jones	ATL	99
Juan Pierre	FLA	99
Shannon Stewart	MIN	99
Manny Ramirez	BOS	98
Rafael Palmeiro	TEX	96
Larry Walker	COL	96
Vladimir Guerrero	MON	95
Kenny Lofton	CHC	95
Scott Rolen	STL	94
Bernie Williams	NYY	94
Ray Durham	SF	93
Jim Edmonds	STL	93
Richie Sexson	MIL	92
Eric Chavez	OAK	91
Derrek Lee	FLA	90
Cliff Floyd	NYM	89
Rafael Furcal	ATL	88
Jeff Kent	HOU	88
Jimmy Rollins	PHI	88
Todd Walker	BOS	88

3-Year Average Lists

Top 3-yr OBP+SLG

NAME	TEAM	OPS	NAME	TEAM	OPS
Barry Bonds	SF	1.350	Adam Dunn	CIN	.863
Todd Helton	COL	1.072	Fred McGriff	LA	.862
Manny Ramirez	BOS	1.038	Derrek Lee	FLA	.860
Jim Thome	PHI	1.035	Dmitri Young	DET	.859
Jason Giambi	NYY	1.035	Craig Wilson	PIT	.859
Sammy Sosa	CHC	1.031	Bill Mueller	BOS	.857
Albert Pujols	STL	1.025	Reggie Sanders	PIT	.856
Larry Walker	COL	1.014	Garret Anderson	ANA	.849
Alex Rodriguez	TEX	1.011	Geoff Jenkins	MIL	.844
Brian Giles	SD	1.003	John Olerud	SEA	.843
Lance Berkman	HOU	.988	Javy Lopez	ATL	.843
Luis Gonzalez	AZ	.987	Richard Hidalgo	HOU	.843
Vladimir Guerrero	MON	.986	Frank Catalanotto	TOR	.843
Jim Edmonds	STL	.986	Moises Alou	CHC	.843
Gary Sheffield	ATL	.983	Troy Glaus	ANA	.842
Carlos Delgado	TOR	.975	Raul Ibanez	KC	.839
Chipper Jones	ATL	.974	Aubrey Huff	TB	.839
Magglio Ordonez	CHW	.939	Corey Koskie	MIN	.838
Cliff Floyd	NYM	.933	Marcus Giles	ATL	.838
Jeff Bagwell	HOU	.927	Vernon Wells	TOR	.836
Rafael Palmeiro	TEX	.924	Steve Finley	AZ	.834
Mike Sweeney	KC	.921	Andruw Jones	ATL	.833
Edgar Martinez	SEA	.919	Alfonso Soriano	NYY	.832
Mike Piazza	NYM	.917	Derek Jeter	NYY	.830
Bob Abreu	PHI	.916	Mike Lowell	FLA	.826
Shawn Green	LA	.910	Todd Hollandsworth	FLA	.826
Juan Gonzalez	TEX	.899	Miguel Tejada	OAK	.825
Richie Sexson	MIL	.896	Preston Wilson	COL	.824
Ryan Klesko	SD	.893	Shannon Stewart	MIN	.824
J.D. Drew	STL	.892	Tim Salmon	ANA	.824
Jeff Kent	HOU	.891	Karim Garcia	NYY	.823
Frank Thomas	CHW	.885	Brad Wilkerson	MON	.820
Bret Boone	SEA	.885	Carlos Lee	CHW	.820
Ellis Burks	CLE	.884	Pat Burrell	PHI	.820
Trot Nixon	BOS	.883	Doug Mientkiewicz	MIN	.819
Scott Rolen	STL	.882	Brian Daubach	CHW	.818
David Ortiz	BOS	.876	Junior Spivey	AZ	.816
Ken Griffey	CIN	.876	Brian Jordan	LA	.815
Carlos Beltran	KC	.876	Ichiro Suzuki	SEA	.814
Bernie Williams	NYY	.875	Paul Konerko	CHW	.814
Ivan Rodriguez	FLA	.873	Ray Durham	SF	.812
Phil Nevin	SD	.872	Eric Hinske	TOR	.811
Kevin Millar	BOS	.872	Carl Everett	CHW	.810
Nomar Garciaparra	BOS	.872	Matt Franco	ATL	.809
Eric Chavez	OAK	.868	Jay Payton	COL	.807
Jorge Posada	NYY	.867	Rich Aurilia	SF	.807
Matt Stairs	PIT	.866	Jacque Jones	MIN	.804
Jose Vidro	MON	.864	Marty Cordova	BAL	.804

3-Year Average Lists

Top 3-yr Wins Average

NAME	TEAM	W
Jamie Moyer	SEA	18
Mark Mulder	OAK	18
Curt Schilling	AZ	18
Barry Zito	OAK	18
Roger Clemens	NYY	17
Randy Johnson	AZ	17
Matt Morris	STL	17
Mike Mussina	NYY	17
Russ Ortiz	ATL	17
Mark Buehrle	CHW	16
Bartolo Colon	CHW	16
Tim Hudson	OAK	16
Greg Maddux	ATL	16
Andy Pettitte	NYY	16
Freddy Garcia	SEA	15
Roy Halladay	TOR	15
Wade Miller	HOU	15
Hideo Nomo	LA	15
Ramon Ortiz	ANA	15
Tom Glavine	NYM	14
Esteban Loaiza	CHW	14
Derek Lowe	BOS	14
Pedro Martinez	BOS	14
Roy Oswalt	HOU	14
C.C. Sabathia	CLE	14
Jason Schmidt	SF	14
Woody Williams	STL	14
Livan Hernandez	MON	13
Al Leiter	NYM	13
Kevin Millwood	PHI	13
Brad Radke	MIN	13
Kirk Rueter	SF	13
Steve Trachsel	NYM	13
Javier Vazquez	MON	13
Jarrod Washburn	ANA	13
David Wells	NYY	13
Kerry Wood	CHC	13
John Burkett	BOS	12
Matt Clement	CHC	12
Mike Hampton	ATL	12
Joel Pineiro	SEA	12
Randy Wolf	PHI	12
Kevin Appier	KC	11
Jason Jennings	COL	11
Cory Lidle	TOR	11
Brad Penny	FLA	11
Odalis Perez	LA	11
Rick Reed	MIN	11

Top 3-yr Saves Average

NAME	TEAM	Sv
Mariano Rivera	NYY	39
Billy Wagner	HOU	39
Jose Mesa	PHI	37
Troy Percival	ANA	37
John Smoltz	ATL	37
Eric Gagne	LA	36
Eddie Guardado	MIN	33
Armando Benitez	SEA	32
Keith Foulke	OAK	32
Ugueth Urbina	FLA	32
Mike Williams	PHI	32
Kazuhiro Sasaki	SEA	31
Billy Koch	CHW	30
Jason Isringhausen	STL	29
Robb Nen	SF	29
Trevor Hoffman	SD	27
Jose Jimenez	COL	26
Byung Kim	BOS	24
Danny Graves	CIN	22
Jorge Julio	BAL	20
Roberto Hernandez	ATL	18
Bob Wickman	CLE	17
Antonio Alfonseca	CHC	16
Mike Dejean	STL	16
Braden Looper	FLA	15
Kelvim Escobar	TOR	14
Estaban Yan	STL	14
Tom Gordon	CHW	13
Tim Worrell	SF	13
Rocky Biddle	MON	12
Joe Borowski	CHC	12
Juan Acevedo	TOR	11
Danys Baez	CLE	10
Latroy Hawkins	MIN	10
Matt Mantei	AZ	10
Scott Williamson	BOS	10
Rod Beck	SD	9
Lance Carter	TB	9
Mike Macdougal	KC	9
Jeff Zimmerman	TEX	9
Matt Anderson	DET	8
Francisco Cordero	TEX	8
Derek Lowe	BOS	8
John Rocker	TB	8
Steve Karsay	NYY	7
Dan Kolb	MIL	7
Damaso Marte	CHW	7
Vladimir Nunez	FLA	7

3-Year Average Lists

Top 3-yr Ratio Av. (Starters)

NAME	TEAM	Rat.	NAME	TEAM	Rat.
Pedro Martinez	BOS	0.96	John Thomson	TEX	1.29
Curt Schilling	AZ	1.03	Kevin Appier	KC	1.30
Randy Johnson	AZ	1.07	Matt Clement	CHC	1.30
Mike Mussina	NYY	1.11	Adam Eaton	SD	1.30
Mark Prior	CHC	1.12	Darrell May	KC	1.30
Roy Halladay	TOR	1.13	Hideo Nomo	LA	1.30
Jamie Moyer	SEA	1.13	Russ Ortiz	ATL	1.30
Jason Schmidt	SF	1.13	John Burkett	BOS	1.31
Greg Maddux	ATL	1.14	Ted Lilly	OAK	1.31
Roy Oswalt	HOU	1.14	Joe Mays	MIN	1.31
Jon Lieber	NYY	1.15	Steve Trachsel	NYM	1.31
Mark Mulder	OAK	1.15	Brian Anderson	KC	1.32
Javier Vazquez	MON	1.15	Al Leiter	NYM	1.32
Barry Zito	OAK	1.17	Robert Person	BOS	1.32
Kevin Brown	LA	1.18	Andy Pettitte	NYY	1.32
Tim Hudson	OAK	1.18	Kevin Jarvis	SD	1.33
Odalis Perez	LA	1.20	Esteban Loaiza	CHW	1.33
Johan Santana	MIN	1.20	Sidney Ponson	SF	1.33
Randy Wolf	PHI	1.20	C.C. Sabathia	CLE	1.33
Joel Pineiro	SEA	1.21	Jake Peavy	SD	1.34
Brad Radke	MIN	1.21	Tony Armas	MON	1.35
Mark Buehrle	CHW	1.22	Jason Bere	CLE	1.35
Ryan Franklin	SEA	1.22	Kyle Lohse	MIN	1.35
Eric Milton	MIN	1.22	Rodrigo Lopez	BAL	1.35
Rick Reed	MIN	1.22	Ben Sheets	MIL	1.35
Woody Williams	STL	1.22	Tomokazu Ohka	MON	1.36
Kerry Wood	CHC	1.22	Ramon Ortiz	ANA	1.36
Paul Byrd	ATL	1.23	Garrett Stephenson	STL	1.36
Orlando Hernandez	MON	1.23	Ismael Valdes	TEX	1.36
Derek Lowe	BOS	1.23	Jeff Weaver	NYY	1.36
Kevin Millwood	PHI	1.23	Kip Wells	PIT	1.36
Jarrod Washburn	ANA	1.23	Andy Ashby	LA	1.37
Freddy Garcia	SEA	1.24	Elmer Dessens	AZ	1.37
Vicente Padilla	PHI	1.24	Chan Ho Park	TEX	1.37
Tim Wakefield	BOS	1.24	Jeff Suppan	BOS	1.37
Roger Clemens	NYY	1.25	Jeff C. Damico	PIT	1.38
Matt Morris	STL	1.25	Tom Glavine	NYM	1.38
A.J. Burnett	FLA	1.26	Livan Hernandez	MON	1.38
Cory Lidle	TOR	1.26	Brian Meadows	PIT	1.38
David Wells	NYY	1.26	Chris Reitsma	CIN	1.38
Josh Beckett	FLA	1.27	Kirk Rueter	SF	1.38
Bartolo Colon	CHW	1.27	Carlos Zambrano	CHC	1.38
Wade Miller	HOU	1.27	Pedro Astacio	NYM	1.39
Brian Lawrence	SD	1.28	Omar Daal	BAL	1.39
Miguel Batista	AZ	1.29	Josh Fogg	PIT	1.39
Pat Hentgen	BAL	1.29	Rick Helling	FLA	1.39
Brad Penny	FLA	1.29	John Lackey	ANA	1.39
Mark Redman	FLA	1.29	Casey Fossum	BOS	1.40

3-Year Average Lists

Top 3-yr Ratio Av.(Relievers)

NAME	TEAM	Rat.	NAME	TEAM	Rat.
Billy Wagner	HOU	0.94	Armando Benitez	SEA	1.24
Keith Foulke	OAK	0.95	Latroy Hawkins	MIN	1.24
Mariano Rivera	NYY	0.95	Dan Plesac	PHI	1.24
Arthur Rhodes	SEA	0.97	Cliff Politte	TOR	1.24
Francisco Rodriguez	ANA	0.98	Luis Vizcaino	MIL	1.24
John Smoltz	ATL	0.99	Bob Wickman	CLE	1.24
Eric Gagne	LA	1.00	Alan Embree	BOS	1.25
Octavio Dotel	HOU	1.01	Grant Roberts	NYM	1.25
Eddie Guardado	MIN	1.02	Scott Williamson	BOS	1.25
Joe Nathan	SF	1.02	Valerio Delossantos	PHI	1.26
Rafael Soriano	SEA	1.02	Vladimir Nunez	FLA	1.26
Kazuhiro Sasaki	SEA	1.04	David Riske	CLE	1.26
Brendan Donnelly	ANA	1.05	Kyle Farnsworth	CHC	1.27
Jason Isringhausen	STL	1.06	Jeff Nelson	NYY	1.27
Julio Mateo	SEA	1.06	Dave Veres	CHC	1.27
Mike Timlin	BOS	1.07	Tim Worrell	SF	1.27
Byung Kim	BOS	1.08	Jeremi Gonzalez	TB	1.28
Damaso Marte	CHW	1.08	Brian Lawrence	SD	1.28
Robb Nen	SF	1.08	Kerry Ligtenberg	BAL	1.28
Troy Percival	ANA	1.08	Braden Looper	FLA	1.28
Jamie Walker	DET	1.09	Dontrelle Willis	FLA	1.28
Lance Carter	TB	1.11	Miguel Batista	AZ	1.29
Tim Spooneybarger	FLA	1.11	Giovanni Carrara	SEA	1.29
Guillermo Mota	LA	1.13	Joey Eischen	MON	1.29
Joe Borowski	CHC	1.14	Mark Guthrie	CHC	1.29
Darren Holmes	ATL	1.14	Pat Hentgen	BAL	1.29
Ugueth Urbina	FLA	1.14	Ray King	ATL	1.29
Chris Hammond	NYY	1.15	Paul Shuey	LA	1.29
Trevor Hoffman	SD	1.15	Mike Jackson	FA	1.30
Buddy Groom	BAL	1.16	Mike Stanton	NYM	1.30
Paul Quantrill	LA	1.17	Ben Weber	ANA	1.30
Matt Mantei	AZ	1.18	Danys Baez	CLE	1.31
Tom Gordon	CHW	1.19	Brian Fuentes	COL	1.31
Felix Rodriguez	SF	1.19	Danny Miceli	HOU	1.31
Ricardo Rincon	OAK	1.20	Dave Weathers	NYM	1.31
Rod Beck	SD	1.21	Jack Cressend	CLE	1.32
Rheal Cormier	PHI	1.21	Curt Leskanic	KC	1.32
Shigetoshi Hasegawa	SEA	1.21	Jim Mann	PIT	1.32
Steve Reed	COL	1.21	Tony Fiore	MIN	1.33
Justin Speier	COL	1.21	Rick White	HOU	1.33
Chad Bradford	OAK	1.22	Jay Witasick	SD	1.33
Francisco Cordero	TEX	1.22	Jim Brower	SF	1.34
Steve Karsay	NYY	1.22	Mike Fyhrie	CLE	1.34
Doug Linton	TOR	1.22	Matt Ginter	CHW	1.34
Mike Remlinger	CHC	1.22	Ramiro Mendoza	BOS	1.34
Gabe White	NYY	1.22	Travis Phelps	TB	1.34
Steve Kline	STL	1.23	Scott Strickland	NYM	1.34
Scott Stewart	MON	1.23	Danny Graves	CIN	1.35

3-Year Average Lists

Top 3-yr ERA Av. (Starters)

NAME	TEAM	ERA	NAME	TEAM	ERA
Pedro Martinez	BOS	2.27	John Thomson	TEX	4.64
Randy Johnson	AZ	2.74	Omar Daal	BAL	4.65
Mark Prior	CHC	2.74	Oliver Perez	PIT	4.65
Kevin Brown	LA	2.85	Kyle Lohse	MIN	4.66
Roy Oswalt	HOU	2.92	Robert Person	BOS	4.67
Tim Hudson	OAK	3.01	Jason Bere	CLE	4.71
Curt Schilling	AZ	3.06	Ismael Valdes	TEX	4.73
Roy Halladay	TOR	3.10	Jason Simontacchi	STL	4.74
Barry Zito	OAK	3.17	Garrett Stephenson	STL	4.76
Jason Schmidt	SF	3.19	Jason Jennings	COL	4.78
Greg Maddux	ATL	3.22			
Johan Santana	MIN	3.27			
Joel Pineiro	SEA	3.28			
Josh Beckett	FLA	3.31			
Jamie Moyer	SEA	3.33			
Mark Mulder	OAK	3.36			
Kerry Wood	CHC	3.41			
Matt Morris	STL	3.42			
Derek Lowe	BOS	3.49			
Vicente Padilla	PHI	3.51			
Mike Mussina	NYY	3.52			
Javier Vazquez	MON	3.52			
Russ Ortiz	ATL	3.57			
Carlos Zambrano	CHC	3.57			
Al Leiter	NYM	3.58			
Wade Miller	HOU	3.60			
Bartolo Colon	CHW	3.62			
Tom Glavine	NYM	3.62			
Hideo Nomo	LA	3.63			
Tim Wakefield	BOS	3.63			
Mark Buehrle	CHW	3.67			
Woody Williams	STL	3.68			
Ryan Franklin	SEA	3.69			
A.J. Burnett	FLA	3.70			
Randy Wolf	PHI	3.70			
Miguel Batista	AZ	3.75			
Jon Lieber	NYY	3.76			
Kevin Millwood	PHI	3.77			
Kip Wells	PIT	3.77			
Jarrod Washburn	ANA	3.78			
Andy Pettitte	NYY	3.82			
Brian Lawrence	SD	3.83			
Steve Trachsel	NYM	3.86			
Roger Clemens	NYY	3.89			
Odalis Perez	LA	3.92			
Freddy Garcia	SEA	3.94			
Mark Redman	FLA	3.98			
Horacio Ramirez	ATL	4.00			

3-Year Average Lists

Top 3-yr ERA Av. (Relievers)

NAME	TEAM	ERA	NAME	TEAM	ERA
Brendan Donnelly	ANA	1.81	Tim Spooneybarger	FLA	3.23
Chris Hammond	NYY	1.81	Scott Strickland	NYM	3.23
Mariano Rivera	NYY	2.18	Dan Kolb	MIL	3.24
Billy Wagner	HOU	2.29	Matt Mantei	AZ	3.24
Octavio Dotel	HOU	2.33	Rod Beck	SD	3.25
Keith Foulke	OAK	2.42	Jay Witasick	SD	3.26
Paul Quantrill	LA	2.50	Tom Gordon	CHW	3.27
Chad Fox	FLA	2.51	Mark Guthrie	CHC	3.27
Jason Isringhausen	STL	2.51	Buddy Groom	BAL	3.32
Francisco Cordero	TEX	2.55	Matt Herges	SF	3.32
John Smoltz	ATL	2.60	Guillermo Mota	LA	3.33
Robb Nen	SF	2.61	Ray King	ATL	3.37
Arthur Rhodes	SEA	2.62	Julio Mateo	SEA	3.37
Troy Percival	ANA	2.64	Brian Fuentes	COL	3.40
Damaso Marte	CHW	2.65	Jeff Nelson	NYY	3.41
Joey Eischen	MON	2.77	Ricardo Rincon	OAK	3.42
Dave Weathers	NYM	2.79	Rheal Cormier	PHI	3.44
Shigetoshi Hasegawa	SEA	2.80	Braden Looper	FLA	3.44
Steve Karsay	NYY	2.80	Jamie Walker	DET	3.47
Mike Remlinger	CHC	2.80	Scott Williamson	BOS	3.47
Joe Nathan	SF	2.82	John Franco	NYM	3.48
Byung Kim	BOS	2.84	Mike Timlin	BOS	3.48
Francisco Rodriguez	ANA	2.84	Mike Lincoln	PIT	3.50
Ben Weber	ANA	2.86	Dan Plesac	PHI	3.52
Tim Worrell	SF	2.87	Mike Dejean	STL	3.53
Darren Holmes	ATL	2.88	Scott Stewart	MON	3.54
Steve Reed	COL	2.90	Ricky Stone	HOU	3.59
Felix Rodriguez	SF	2.90	Kevin Gryboski	ATL	3.65
Steve Kline	STL	2.92	Felix Heredia	NYY	3.66
Latroy Hawkins	MIN	2.96	Lance Carter	TB	3.71
Rafael Soriano	SEA	2.96	Giovanni Carrara	SEA	3.73
Joe Borowski	CHC	2.99	Jose Mesa	PHI	3.77
Chad Bradford	OAK	3.00	Vladimir Nunez	FLA	3.77
Trevor Hoffman	SD	3.00	Dave Veres	CHC	3.77
Grant Roberts	NYM	3.00	Brandon Villafuerte	SD	3.78
Curt Leskanic	KC	3.02	Mike Matthews	SD	3.79
Armando Benitez	SEA	3.03	Kent Mercker	ATL	3.80
Paul Shuey	LA	3.05	Valerio De Los Santos	PHI	3.82
Al Levine	KC	3.08	Jack Cressend	CLE	3.83
Bob Wickman	CLE	3.08	David Lee	CLE	3.83
Eric Gagne	LA	3.10	Carlos Silva	PHI	3.83
Eddie Guardado	MIN	3.10	Chad Zerbe	SF	3.84
Kerry Ligtenberg	BAL	3.10	John Riedling	CIN	3.87
Kazuhiro Sasaki	SEA	3.13	Scott Eyre	SF	3.90
Ugueth Urbina	FLA	3.13	Turk Wendell	PHI	3.91
Mike Stanton	NYM	3.18	Danys Baez	CLE	3.92
Jorge Julio	BAL	3.22	John Parrish	BAL	3.93
David Riske	CLE	3.22	Tony Fiore	MIN	3.94

3-Year Average Lists

Top 3-yr Strikeouts Av.

NAME	TEAM	K	NAME	TEAM	K
Randy Johnson	AZ	277	Steve Trachsel	NYM	120
Curt Schilling	AZ	268	Chanho Park	TEX	118
Kerry Wood	CHC	233	A.J. Burnett	FLA	117
Javier Vazquez	MON	209	Kevin Brown	LA	116
Pedro Martinez	BOS	203	Brian Lawrence	SD	116
Roger Clemens	NYY	198	Miguel Batista	AZ	115
Mike Mussina	NYY	197	Cory Lidle	TOR	114
Hideo Nomo	LA	197	Joel Pineiro	SEA	114
Jason Schmidt	SF	182	Sidney Ponson	SF	113
Barry Zito	OAK	178	Jeff Suppan	BOS	113
Bartolo Colon	CHW	174	Ted Lilly	OAK	112
Matt Clement	CHC	173	Elmer Dessens	AZ	111
Randy Wolf	PHI	167	Rick Reed	MIN	111
Tim Hudson	OAK	165	Johan Santana	MIN	111
Freddy Garcia	SEA	163	Tony Armas	MON	110
Wade Miller	HOU	163	Jason Johnson	BAL	110
Matt Morris	STL	159	Tom Glavine	NYM	108
Roy Halladay	TOR	156	Paul Wilson	CIN	108
C.C. Sabathia	CLE	154	Shawn Estes	CHC	107
Roy Oswalt	HOU	153	Kyle Lohse	MIN	106
Russ Ortiz	ATL	152	Derek Lowe	BOS	106
Al Leiter	NYM	151	Brad Radke	MIN	106
Livan Hernandez	MON	150	Pedro Astacio	NYM	105
Tim Wakefield	BOS	150	John Thomson	TEX	104
Mark Mulder	OAK	147	Mike Hampton	ATL	102
Andy Pettitte	NYY	147	Byung Kim	BOS	102
Kevin Millwood	PHI	144	Tomokazu Ohka	MON	101
Ben Sheets	MIL	140	Tanyon Sturtze	TOR	100
John Burkett	BOS	139	Kenny Rogers	MIN	99
Greg Maddux	ATL	138	David Wells	NYY	99
Ryan Dempster	CIN	136	Shawn Chacon	COL	98
Esteban Loaiza	CHW	135	Mark Redman	FLA	98
Jamie Moyer	SEA	132	Vicente Padilla	PHI	97
Mark Prior	CHC	131	Terry Adams	PHI	96
Ramon Ortiz	ANA	130	Josh Beckett	FLA	96
Glendon Rusch	MIL	130	Jimmy Haynes	CIN	96
Brad Penny	FLA	128	Eric Milton	MIN	95
Jarrod Washburn	ANA	128	Jon Garland	CHW	94
Woody Williams	STL	128	Kazuhisa Ishii	LA	94
Eric Gagne	LA	127	Adam Eaton	SD	93
Kip Wells	PIT	127	Brandon Duckworth	PHI	92
Mark Buehrle	CHW	126	Jason Jennings	COL	91
Jeff Weaver	NYY	126	Billy Wagner	HOU	91
Rick Helling	FLA	124	Denny Neagle	COL	90
Kelvim Escobar	TOR	122	Steve W. Sparks	OAK	89
Odalis Perez	LA	122	Omar Daal	BAL	88
Kevin Appier	KC	120	Joe Kennedy	TB	88
Octavio Dotel	HOU	120	Carlos Zambrano	CHC	88

3-Year Average Lists

Top 3-yr K/9 Av. (Starters)

NAME	TEAM	K/9
Randy Johnson	AZ	12.00
Pedro Martinez	BOS	10.90
Mark Prior	CHC	10.78
Curt Schilling	AZ	10.58
Kerry Wood	CHC	10.50
Johan Santana	MIN	9.65
Josh Beckett	FLA	9.46
Jason Schmidt	SF	9.04
Roger Clemens	NYY	8.74
Kazuhisa Ishii	LA	8.43
Hideo Nomo	LA	8.36
Jesse Foppert	SF	8.25
Javier Vazquez	MON	8.24
Roy Oswalt	HOU	8.23
Matt Clement	CHC	8.11
Mike Mussina	NYY	8.07
Kevin Brown	LA	8.02
John Stephens	BAL	7.92
A.J. Burnett	FLA	7.89
Randy Wolf	PHI	7.86
Wade Miller	HOU	7.80
Chanho Park	TEX	7.79
Jason Bere	CLE	7.71
Brandon Duckworth	PHI	7.65
Tim Wakefield	BOS	7.58
Ted Lilly	OAK	7.58
Tony Armas	MON	7.58
Jake Peavy	SD	7.56
Adam Eaton	SD	7.53
Robert Person	BOS	7.46
Ryan Rupe	BOS	7.33
Andy Pettitte	NYY	7.30
Nick Bierbrodt	CLE	7.20
Carlos Zambrano	CHC	7.19
Matt Morris	STL	7.17
Pedro Astacio	NYM	7.13
Barry Zito	OAK	7.12
Al Leiter	NYM	7.12
C.C. Sabathia	CLE	7.07
Orlando Hernandez	MON	7.07

Top 3-yr K/9 Av. (Relievers)

NAME	TEAM	K/9
Dan Plesac	PHI	11.51
Tom Gordon	CHW	11.50
Jeff Nelson	NYY	11.37
Octavio Dotel	HOU	11.20
Billy Wagner	HOU	10.98
Eric Gagne	LA	10.84
Kyle Farnsworth	CHC	10.81
Matt Mantei	AZ	10.64
Francisco Rodriguez	ANA	10.59
John Rocker	TB	10.59
Ugueth Urbina	FLA	10.47
Mike Remlinger	CHC	10.44
Rudy Seanez	BOS	10.42
Scott Williamson	BOS	10.41
David Riske	CLE	10.39
Robb Nen	SF	10.36
Troy Percival	ANA	10.26
Armando Benitez	SEA	10.22
Brian Fuentes	COL	10.21
Chad Fox	FLA	10.13
Damaso Marte	CHW	10.10
Trevor Hoffman	SD	10.09
Arthur Rhodes	SEA	10.00
Armando Almanza	FLA	9.85
Scott Sauerbeck	BOS	9.79
Alan Embree	BOS	9.79
B.j. Ryan	BAL	9.72
Oliver Perez	PIT	9.71
Todd Vanpoppel	CIN	9.65
Brendan Donnelly	ANA	9.59
John Smoltz	ATL	9.54
Jay Witasick	SD	9.38
Hector Mercado	PHI	9.27
Kazuhiro Sasaki	SEA	9.25
Jason Isringhausen	STL	9.23
Darren Dreifort	LA	9.23
Joe Nathan	SF	9.13
Francisco Cordero	TEX	9.10
Scott Strickland	NYM	9.06
Byung Kim	BOS	9.04
Paul Shuey	LA	9.03
Bob Wickman	CLE	9.00
Doug Creek	TOR	9.00
Joe Borowski	CHC	8.97
Eddie Guardado	MIN	8.92
Britt Reames	MON	8.88
Rafael Soriano	SEA	8.87
Antonio Osuna	NYY	8.80

Second Half Lists

Second Half Batting Avg.

NAME	TEAM	AVG	NAME	TEAM	AVG
Barry Bonds	SF	.393	Ivan Rodriguez	FLA	.304
Todd Helton	COL	.384	Vinny Castilla	ATL	.303
Derek Jeter	NYY	.354	Richard Hidalgo	HOU	.303
Vladimir Guerrero	MON	.353	Scott Podsednik	MIL	.303
Jason Kendall	PIT	.351	Alex Sanchez	DET	.303
Magglio Ordonez	CHW	.347	Raul Ibanez	KC	.302
Joe Randa	KC	.346	Carl Everett	CHW	.301
Jose Reyes	NYM	.343	Alex Rodriguez	TEX	.301
Marcus Giles	ATL	.342	Dmitri Young	DET	.300
Javy Lopez	ATL	.342	Carlos Delgado	TOR	.298
Mark Grudzielanek	CHC	.341	Brian Giles	SD	.298
Gary Sheffield	ATL	.337	Mike Lieberthal	PHI	.298
Cliff Floyd	NYM	.333	Doug Mientkiewicz	MIN	.298
A.J. Pierzynski	MIN	.332	Danny Bautista	AZ	.297
Manny Ramirez	BOS	.331	Mike Young	TEX	.297
Albert Pujols	STL	.330	Mike Bordick	TOR	.296
Tike Redman	PIT	.330	Orlando Cabrera	MON	.296
Randy Winn	SEA	.330	Lance Berkman	HOU	.295
Doug Glanville	CHC	.328	Trot Nixon	BOS	.295
Mark Loretta	SD	.327	Jose Vidro	MON	.295
Carlos Beltran	KC	.326	Edgardo Alfonzo	SF	.294
Bill Mueller	BOS	.325	Jeff Conine	FLA	.293
Vernon Wells	TOR	.325	Joe Crede	CHW	.293
Bob Abreu	PHI	.323	Travis Lee	TB	.293
Larry Bigbie	BAL	.323	Ramon E. Martinez	CHC	.293
Alex Cintron	AZ	.323	Jason Phillips	NYM	.293
Edgar Renteria	STL	.321	Angel Berroa	KC	.292
Aubrey Huff	TB	.320	Jolbert Cabrera	LA	.292
Placido Polanco	PHI	.320	Frank Catalanotto	TOR	.292
Luis Castillo	FLA	.319	Marquis Grissom	SF	.292
Marlon Byrd	PHI	.318	Chone Figgins	ANA	.291
Garret Anderson	ANA	.315	Rafael Furcal	ATL	.291
Geoff Jenkins	MIL	.315	Karim Garcia	NYY	.291
Jorge Posada	NYY	.315	Barry Larkin	CIN	.291
Juan Pierre	FLA	.313	Brady Clark	MIL	.290
Kenny Lofton	CHC	.312	Dangelo Jimenez	CIN	.290
Miguel Tejada	OAK	.312	Alfonso Soriano	NYY	.290
Chipper Jones	ATL	.311	Mark Derosa	ATL	.289
Eric Owens	ANA	.310	Andres Galarraga	SF	.288
Jay Payton	COL	.310	Jose Guillen	OAK	.288
Shawn Green	LA	.309	Julio Lugo	TB	.288
Jacque Jones	MIN	.309	Edgar Martinez	SEA	.288
Carlos Lee	CHW	.309	Johnny Damon	BOS	.287
Matt Stairs	PIT	.309	Luis Gonzalez	AZ	.287
Shannon Stewart	MIN	.309	Victor Martinez	CLE	.286
Eric Chavez	OAK	.306	Richie Sexson	MIL	.286
Carl Crawford	TB	.305	Rondell White	KC	.286
Reggie Sanders	PIT	.305	Wes Helms	MIL	.284

Second Half Lists

Second Half Home Runs

NAME	TEAM	HR
Sammy Sosa	CHC	30
David Ortiz	BOS	27
Alex Rodriguez	TEX	27
Jim Thome	PHI	26
Jeff Bagwell	HOU	25
Frank Thomas	CHW	25
Barry Bonds	SF	23
Richie Sexson	MIL	23
Javy Lopez	ATL	20
Albert Pujols	STL	20
Aramis Ramirez	CHC	20
Manny Ramirez	BOS	20
Jason Giambi	NYY	19
Todd Helton	COL	19
Aubrey Huff	TB	19
Rafael Palmeiro	TEX	19
Reggie Sanders	PIT	19
Preston Wilson	COL	19
Carlos Lee	CHW	18
Trot Nixon	BOS	18
Adrian Beltre	LA	17
Hank Blalock	TEX	17
Jeromy Burnitz	LA	17
Vladimir Guerrero	MON	17
Jose Guillen	OAK	17
Richard Hidalgo	HOU	17
Craig Monroe	DET	17
Jay Payton	COL	17
Gary Sheffield	ATL	17
Alfonso Soriano	NYY	17
Carlos Delgado	TOR	16
Nomar Garciaparra	BOS	16
Shea Hillenbrand	AZ	16
Andruw Jones	ATL	16
Jose Valentin	CHW	16
Carlos Beltran	KC	15
Torii Hunter	MIN	15
Paul Konerko	CHW	15
Derrek Lee	FLA	15
Magglio Ordonez	CHW	15
Mark Teixeira	TEX	15
Craig Wilson	PIT	15
Jim Edmonds	STL	14
Jody Gerut	CLE	14
Chipper Jones	ATL	14
Bill Mueller	BOS	14
Jorge Posada	NYY	14
Matt Stairs	PIT	14

Second Half RBI

NAME	TEAM	RBI
Jim Thome	PHI	73
Preston Wilson	COL	71
Richie Sexson	MIL	69
Gary Sheffield	ATL	68
Alex Rodriguez	TEX	67
Sammy Sosa	CHC	67
Frank Thomas	CHW	66
David Ortiz	BOS	65
Carlos Lee	CHW	64
Chipper Jones	ATL	63
Jeff Bagwell	HOU	62
Aubrey Huff	TB	62
Javy Lopez	ATL	61
Rafael Palmeiro	TEX	60
Carlos Beltran	KC	59
Andruw Jones	ATL	59
Aramis Ramirez	CHC	59
Scott Spiezio	ANA	59
Miguel Cabrera	FLA	56
Carlos Delgado	TOR	56
Jay Payton	COL	56
Eric Chavez	OAK	55
Bob Abreu	PHI	54
Brian Giles	SD	53
Todd Helton	COL	53
Shea Hillenbrand	AZ	53
Magglio Ordonez	CHW	53
Reggie Sanders	PIT	53
Edgardo Alfonzo	SF	52
Adrian Beltre	LA	52
Richard Hidalgo	HOU	52
Torii Hunter	MIN	52
Jorge Posada	NYY	52
Albert Pujols	STL	52
Bret Boone	SEA	51
Bill Mueller	BOS	51
Miguel Tejada	OAK	51
Aaron Boone	NYY	49
Nomar Garciaparra	BOS	49
Garret Anderson	ANA	48
Paul Konerko	CHW	48
Derrek Lee	FLA	48
Scott Rolen	STL	48
Jose Guillen	OAK	47
Mike Lieberthal	PHI	47
Randy Winn	SEA	47
Lance Berkman	HOU	46
Shawn Green	LA	46

Second Half Lists

Second Half Stolen Bases

NAME	TEAM	SB
Carl Crawford	TB	36
Alex Sanchez	DET	30
Juan Pierre	FLA	27
Scott Podsednik	MIL	27
Carlos Beltran	KC	22
Angel Berroa	KC	18
Edgar Renteria	STL	17
Johnny Damon	BOS	16
Kenny Lofton	CHC	16
Dave Roberts	LA	16
Orlando Cabrera	MON	14
Brian Roberts	BAL	14
Bob Abreu	PHI	13
Rocco Baldelli	TB	13
Ichiro Suzuki	SEA	13
Aaron Boone	NYY	12
Jose Reyes	NYM	12
Coco Crisp	CLE	11
Rafael Furcal	ATL	11
Nomar Garciaparra	BOS	11
Cristian Guzman	MIN	11
Adam Kennedy	ANA	11
Luis Rivas	MIN	11
Jimmy Rollins	PHI	11
Alfonso Soriano	NYY	11
Eric Young	SF	11
Bret Boone	SEA	10
Mike Cameron	SEA	10
Chone Figgins	ANA	10
Steve Finley	AZ	10
Eric Hinske	TOR	10
Carlos Lee	CHW	10
Alex Rodriguez	TEX	10
Marlon Byrd	PHI	9
Brady Clark	MIL	9
Jeff Davanon	ANA	9
Desi Relaford	KC	9
Reggie Sanders	PIT	9
Randy Winn	SEA	9
Marlon Anderson	TB	8
Jeff Bagwell	HOU	8
Tom Goodwin	CHC	8
Willie Harris	CHW	8
Gary Matthews	SD	8
Scott Rolen	STL	8
Preston Wilson	COL	8

Second Half Runs

NAME	TEAM	Runs
Alex Rodriguez	TEX	70
Rafael Furcal	ATL	67
Marlon Byrd	PHI	65
Todd Helton	COL	64
Albert Pujols	STL	63
Jeff Bagwell	HOU	60
Carlos Beltran	KC	60
Gary Sheffield	ATL	60
Carlos Lee	CHW	59
Mike Young	TEX	59
Chipper Jones	ATL	58
Scott Podsednik	MIL	58
Randy Winn	SEA	58
Barry Bonds	SF	57
Sammy Sosa	CHC	57
Jim Thome	PHI	57
Lance Berkman	HOU	56
Brian Giles	SD	55
Angel Berroa	KC	54
Marcus Giles	ATL	54
Miguel Tejada	OAK	54
Craig Biggio	HOU	52
Eric Chavez	OAK	52
Derek Jeter	NYY	52
Ichiro Suzuki	SEA	52
Vernon Wells	TOR	52
Aaron Guiel	KC	51
Juan Pierre	FLA	51
Manny Ramirez	BOS	51
Bret Boone	SEA	50
Nomar Garciaparra	BOS	50
Richard Hidalgo	HOU	50
Magglio Ordonez	CHW	50
Rocco Baldelli	TB	49
Carlos Delgado	TOR	49
Andruw Jones	ATL	49
Javy Lopez	ATL	49
Placido Polanco	PHI	49
Bob Abreu	PHI	48
Luis Castillo	FLA	48
Rube Durazo	OAK	48
Shawn Green	LA	48
Eric Hinske	TOR	48
David Ortiz	BOS	48
Edgar Renteria	STL	48
Scott Rolen	STL	48
Shannon Stewart	MIN	48

Second Half Lists

Second Half OBP+SLG

NAME	TEAM	OPS	NAME	TEAM	OPS
Barry Bonds	SF	1.460	Miguel Tejada	OAK	.873
Todd Helton	COL	1.175	Travis Lee	TB	.871
Vladimir Guerrero	MON	1.095	Carlos Lee	CHW	.871
Javy Lopez	ATL	1.072	Alfonso Soriano	NYY	.869
Manny Ramirez	BOS	1.057	Danny Bautista	AZ	.868
Albert Pujols	STL	1.055	Paul Konerko	CHW	.865
Alex Rodriguez	TEX	1.051	Jim Edmonds	STL	.865
Matt Stairs	PIT	1.043	Joe Crede	CHW	.864
David Ortiz	BOS	1.023	Tim Salmon	ANA	.861
Gary Sheffield	ATL	1.015	Placido Polanco	PHI	.860
Trot Nixon	BOS	1.015	Edgar Renteria	STL	.859
Reggie Sanders	PIT	1.012	Tike Redman	PIT	.857
Rob Mackowiak	PIT	1.009	Mark Grudzielanek	CHC	.857
Marcus Giles	ATL	.991	Matt Lecroy	MIN	.856
Jim Thome	PHI	.987	Milton Bradley	CLE	.856
Magglio Ordonez	CHW	.987	Jose Guillen	OAK	.855
Richie Sexson	MIL	.985	Josh Phelps	TOR	.852
Jeff Bagwell	HOU	.979	Jason Kendall	PIT	.851
Richard Hidalgo	HOU	.961	Edgar Martinez	SEA	.850
Carlos Delgado	TOR	.961	Carl Everett	CHW	.850
Lance Berkman	HOU	.957	Nick Johnson	NYY	.848
Carlos Beltran	KC	.957	Preston Wilson	COL	.847
Jorge Posada	NYY	.956	Jose Reyes	NYM	.847
Bill Mueller	BOS	.951	Larry Walker	COL	.844
Brian Giles	SD	.948	Aaron Guiel	KC	.843
Craig Wilson	PIT	.940	Doug Mientkiewicz	MIN	.841
Chipper Jones	ATL	.937	Steve Finley	AZ	.840
Aubrey Huff	TB	.936	Rafael Palmeiro	TEX	.838
Geoff Jenkins	MIL	.930	Ricky Ledee	PHI	.838
Frank Thomas	CHW	.924	A.J. Pierzynski	MIN	.836
Eric Chavez	OAK	.924	Alex Cintron	AZ	.836
Joe Randa	KC	.922	Bret Boone	SEA	.836
Jay Payton	COL	.920	J.D. Drew	STL	.830
Derrek Lee	FLA	.918	Edgardo Alfonzo	SF	.830
Cliff Floyd	NYM	.915	Mark Loretta	SD	.828
Jason Giambi	NYY	.907	Jeff Conine	FLA	.828
Bob Abreu	PHI	.905	Shannon Stewart	MIN	.827
Dmitri Young	DET	.904	Miguel Cabrera	FLA	.827
Vernon Wells	TOR	.899	Phil Nevin	SD	.826
Sammy Sosa	CHC	.899	Raul Mondesi	AZ	.825
Shawn Green	LA	.898	Billy McMillon	OAK	.825
Derek Jeter	NYY	.895	Jason Varitek	BOS	.823
Luis Gonzalez	AZ	.889	Jeff Kent	HOU	.823
Eduardo Perez	STL	.883	Garret Anderson	ANA	.823
Travis Hafner	CLE	.881	Ivan Rodriguez	FLA	.822
Scott Rolen	STL	.878	Craig Monroe	DET	.822
Larry Bigbie	BAL	.875	Kenny Lofton	CHC	.822
Randy Winn	SEA	.874	Hank Blalock	TEX	.822

Second Half Lists

Second Half Wins

NAME	TEAM	WINS
Andy Pettitte	NYY	12
Roy Halladay	TOR	11
Mike Hampton	ATL	11
Russ Ortiz	ATL	11
Tim Hudson	OAK	10
Esteban Loaiza	CHW	10
Greg Maddux	ATL	10
Jamie Moyer	SEA	10
Mark Prior	CHC	10
Brian Anderson	KC	9
Mark Buehrle	CHW	9
Roger Clemens	NYY	9
Matt Clement	CHC	9
Bartolo Colon	CHW	9
Livan Hernandez	MON	9
Pedro Martinez	BOS	9
Darrell May	KC	9
Wade Miller	HOU	9
Brad Radke	MIN	9
Jeriome Robertson	HOU	9
Jason Schmidt	SF	9
Brett Tomko	STL	9
Steve Trachsel	NYM	9
Kelvim Escobar	TOR	8
Kyle Lohse	MIN	8
Derek Lowe	BOS	8
Darren Oliver	COL	8
Brad Penny	FLA	8
Odalis Perez	FLA	8
Joel Pineiro	SEA	8
Mark Redman	FLA	8
Johan Santana	MIN	8
John Thomson	TEX	8
Kip Wells	PIT	8
Woody Williams	STL	8
Josh Beckett	FLA	7
Adam Eaton	SD	7
Al Leiter	NYM	7
Ted Lilly	OAK	7
Mike Mussina	NYY	7
Brett Myers	PHI	7
Hideo Nomo	LA	7
Ramon Ortiz	ANA	7
Vicente Padilla	PHI	7
Sidney Ponson	SF	7
Jeff Suppan	BOS	7
Josh Towers	TOR	7
Javier Vazquez	MON	7

Second Half Saves

NAME	TEAM	SV
Eric Gagne	LA	26
Mariano Rivera	NYY	25
Keith Foulke	OAK	22
Matt Mantei	AZ	22
Billy Wagner	HOU	22
Eddie Guardado	MIN	21
Dan Kolb	MIL	21
Tim Worrell	SF	21
Jason Isringhausen	STL	20
Jorge Julio	BAL	20
Joe Borowski	CHC	18
Troy Percival	ANA	17
Rod Beck	SD	16
Byung Kim	BOS	16
John Smoltz	ATL	16
Shigetoshi Hasegawa	SEA	14
Braden Looper	FLA	14
Lance Carter	TB	13
Francisco Cordero	TEX	13
Rocky Biddle	MON	12
Aquilino Lopez	TOR	12
Chris Reitsma	CIN	12
Tom Gordon	CHW	11
Julian Tavarez	PIT	11
Ugueth Urbina	FLA	10
Justin Speier	COL	8
Mike Macdougal	KC	7
Damaso Marte	CHW	7
David Riske	CLE	7
Dave Weathers	NYM	7
Mike Williams	PHI	7
Danys Baez	CLE	6
Jose Mesa	PHI	6
Mike Lincoln	PIT	5
Chris Mears	DET	5
Mike Stanton	NYM	5
Jeremy Affeldt	KC	4
Brian Fuentes	COL	4
Trever Miller	TOR	4
Luis Ayala	MON	3
Will Cunnane	ATL	3
Mike Dejean	STL	3
Leo Estrella	MIL	3
Danny Patterson	DET	3
Fernando Rodney	DET	3
Jamie Walker	DET	3
Scott Williamson	BOS	3

Second Half Lists

Second Half Strikeouts

NAME	TEAM	K
Kerry Wood	CHC	123
Pedro Martinez	BOS	120
Mark Prior	CHC	118
Livan Hernandez	MON	115
Javier Vazquez	MON	114
Brandon Webb	AZ	114
Esteban Loaiza	CHW	113
Curt Schilling	AZ	112
Josh Beckett	FLA	107
Roy Halladay	TOR	104
Johan Santana	MIN	101
Oliver Perez	PIT	99
Matt Clement	CHC	94
Randy Johnson	AZ	94
Andy Pettitte	NYY	94
Tim Hudson	OAK	92
Mike Mussina	NYY	91
Kevin Brown	LA	88
Mark Redman	FLA	87
Bartolo Colon	CHW	86
Jason Schmidt	SF	86
Tim Wakefield	BOS	85
Carlos Zambrano	CHC	85
Wade Miller	HOU	84
Randy Wolf	PHI	84
Kelvim Escobar	TOR	82
Russ Ortiz	ATL	81
Kip Wells	PIT	81
Rodrigo Lopez	BAL	80
Dontrelle Willis	FLA	80
Victor Zambrano	TB	80
John Lackey	ANA	77
Ted Lilly	OAK	77
Barry Zito	OAK	77
Kevin Millwood	PHI	76
Woody Williams	STL	76
Miguel Batista	AZ	75
Freddy Garcia	SEA	75
Joel Pineiro	SEA	75
Ron Villone	HOU	75
Hideo Nomo	LA	74
Jake Peavy	SD	74
C.C. Sabathia	CLE	74
Matt Kinney	MIL	73
Brett Myers	PHI	73
John Thomson	TEX	72
Roger Clemens	NYY	71
Mike Hampton	ATL	70

Second Half Innings Pitched

NAME	TEAM	IP
Roy Halladay	TOR	137
Livan Hernandez	MON	130
Tim Hudson	OAK	121
Bartolo Colon	CHW	120
Darrell May	KC	119
Barry Zito	OAK	118
Javier Vazquez	MON	117
Mike Hampton	ATL	117
Mark Buehrle	CHW	117
John Thomson	TEX	113
Brad Radke	MIN	113
Kip Wells	PIT	112
Esteban Loaiza	CHW	111
Matt Clement	CHC	110
Carlos Zambrano	CHC	110
Kevin Millwood	PHI	110
Woody Williams	STL	109
Kelvim Escobar	TOR	109
Mike Mussina	NYY	108
Jamie Moyer	SEA	107
Tim Wakefield	BOS	107
Sidney Ponson	SF	107
John Lackey	ANA	107
Tomokazu Ohka	MON	107
Jason Johnson	BAL	107
Andy Pettitte	NYY	107
Ryan Franklin	SEA	106
Vicente Padilla	PHI	106
Greg Maddux	ATL	105
Brian Anderson	KC	105
Pedro Martinez	BOS	105
Brandon Webb	AZ	104
Joel Pineiro	SEA	104
Victor Zambrano	TB	104
Mark Redman	FLA	103
Rodrigo Lopez	BAL	103
Horacio Ramirez	ATL	103
Nate Cornejo	DET	102
Jeremi Gonzalez	TB	102
Jeff Suppan	BOS	102
Josh Beckett	FLA	101
Steve Trachsel	NYM	101
Mark Prior	CHC	101
Brian Lawrence	SD	101
Jarrod Washburn	ANA	100
Kenny Rogers	MIN	100
Derek Lowe	BOS	100

Second Half Lists

Second Half ERA

NAME	TEAM	ERA	NAME	TEAM	ERA
Eric Gagne	LA	0.42	Aquilino Lopez	TOR	2.61
B.J. Ryan	BAL	1.02	Jason Schmidt	SF	2.61
Damaso Marte	CHW	1.19	Francisco Rodriguez	ANA	2.64
Billy Wagner	HOU	1.33	Jose Acevedo	CIN	2.67
Rafael Soriano	SEA	1.39	Julio Mateo	SEA	2.68
Rod Beck	SD	1.42	Joe Borowski	CHC	2.74
Matt Mantei	AZ	1.42	Dave Weathers	NYM	2.74
David Riske	CLE	1.46	Luis Ayala	MON	2.75
Joe Nathan	SF	1.50	Josh Beckett	FLA	2.75
Kent Mercker	ATL	1.52	Felix Heredia	NYY	2.75
Mariano Rivera	NYY	1.56	Armando Benitez	SEA	2.76
Brian Bowles	TOR	1.58	Chris Hammond	NYY	2.77
Keith Foulke	OAK	1.62	Jeremy Affeldt	KC	2.78
Chad Cordero	MON	1.64	Roy Halladay	TOR	2.82
Ugueth Urbina	FLA	1.67	Cal Eldred	STL	2.83
Rheal Cormier	PHI	1.76	Jason Isringhausen	STL	2.85
Dan Kolb	MIL	1.80	Roy Oswalt	HOU	2.85
Matt Riley	BAL	1.80	Glendon Rusch	MIL	2.87
Pedro Martinez	BOS	1.81	Chris Capuano	AZ	2.88
Paul Quantrill	LA	1.88	Doug Davis	MIL	2.88
Francisco Cordero	TEX	1.89	Curt Schilling	AZ	2.88
Latroy Hawkins	MIN	1.95	Chad Fox	FLA	2.91
Oscar Villarreal	AZ	1.98	Mark Mulder	OAK	2.91
Chad Bradford	OAK	2.00	Octavio Dotel	HOU	2.93
Guillermo Mota	LA	2.01	John Franco	NYM	2.93
Ricardo Rincon	OAK	2.08	Brian Fuentes	COL	2.98
Rafael Betancourt	CLE	2.13	Mike Gallo	HOU	3.00
Al Leiter	NYM	2.15	Dustin Hermanson	SF	3.00
Felix Rodriguez	SF	2.19	Greg Maddux	ATL	3.00
Mark Prior	CHC	2.23	John Riedling	CIN	3.02
Shigetoshi Hasegawa	SEA	2.27	Michael Tejera	FLA	3.03
Byung Kim	BOS	2.28	Eddie Guardado	MIN	3.04
Tim Hudson	OAK	2.31	Kip Wells	PIT	3.05
Ben Weber	ANA	2.35	Brendan Donnelly	ANA	3.07
Terry Adams	PHI	2.36	Jamie Walker	DET	3.08
Tom Gordon	CHW	2.36	Carlos Zambrano	CHC	3.10
Jason Kershner	TOR	2.40	Pat Hentgen	BAL	3.16
Livan Hernandez	MON	2.42	Scott Linebrink	SD	3.16
Danny Miceli	HOU	2.45	Jerome Williams	SF	3.16
Javier Vazquez	MON	2.45	Jeff Nelson	NYY	3.21
Matt Herges	SF	2.46	Erasmo Ramirez	TEX	3.21
Jose Valverde	AZ	2.48	Steve Trachsel	NYM	3.21
Brian Shouse	TEX	2.49	Scott Eyre	SF	3.24
Jack Cressend	CLE	2.51	Kevin Gregg	ANA	3.28
Scott Sullivan	CHW	2.52	Andy Pettitte	NYY	3.29
Wilson Alvarez	LA	2.55	Steve Reed	COL	3.30
Kevin Brown	LA	2.55	Nelson Figueroa	PIT	3.31
Jose Contreras	NYY	2.56	Doug Waechter	TB	3.31

Second Half Lists

Second Half Ratio

NAME	TEAM	RAT	NAME	TEAM	RAT
Eric Gagne	LA	0.67	Rod Beck	SD	1.07
Rafael Soriano	SEA	0.71	Joe Borowski	CHC	1.08
Keith Foulke	OAK	0.77	Latroy Hawkins	MIN	1.08
Julio Mateo	SEA	0.78	Greg Maddux	ATL	1.08
Billy Wagner	HOU	0.81	Mark Mulder	OAK	1.08
Matt Mantei	AZ	0.82	Johan Santana	MIN	1.08
David Riske	CLE	0.84	Lance Carter	TB	1.09
Jose Acevedo	CIN	0.85	Brad Penny	FLA	1.09
Rheal Cormier	PHI	0.91	Curt Schilling	AZ	1.09
Byung Kim	BOS	0.91	Mark Prior	CHC	1.10
Joe Nathan	SF	0.94	Francisco Cordero	TEX	1.11
Eddie Guardado	MIN	0.95	Wilson Alvarez	LA	1.12
Tom Gordon	CHW	0.96	Michael Tejera	FLA	1.12
Roy Halladay	TOR	0.96	Jim Brower	SF	1.13
Guillermo Mota	LA	0.96	Matt Clement	CHC	1.13
Scott Sullivan	CHW	0.96	Steve Kline	STL	1.13
Roy Oswalt	HOU	0.97	Darrell May	KC	1.13
Francisco Rodriguez	ANA	0.97	Jack Cressend	CLE	1.14
Jason Schmidt	SF	0.98	Dustin Hermanson	SF	1.15
Jason Kershner	TOR	0.99	Ray King	ATL	1.15
Damaso Marte	CHW	0.99	Amaury Telemaco	PHI	1.15
Jose Valverde	AZ	0.99	Josh Towers	TOR	1.15
Kirk Bullinger	HOU	1.00	Nelson Figueroa	PIT	1.16
Chris Capuano	AZ	1.00	Brad Radke	MIN	1.16
Will Cunnane	ATL	1.00	Julian Tavarez	PIT	1.16
Ugueth Urbina	FLA	1.00	Jamie Walker	DET	1.16
Tim Hudson	OAK	1.01	Dan Kolb	MIL	1.17
Luis Vizcaino	MIL	1.01	Al Leiter	NYM	1.17
Jeremy Affeldt	KC	1.02	Mike Mussina	NYY	1.17
Pedro Martinez	BOS	1.02	John Riedling	CIN	1.17
Paul Quantrill	LA	1.02	B.J. Ryan	BAL	1.17
Javier Vazquez	MON	1.02	Tim Wakefield	BOS	1.17
Oscar Villarreal	AZ	1.02	Bartolo Colon	CHW	1.18
Jose Contreras	NYY	1.03	Matt Morris	STL	1.18
Mike Crudale	MIL	1.03	Eric Dubose	BAL	1.19
Octavio Dotel	HOU	1.03	Chris Hammond	NYY	1.19
Danny Miceli	HOU	1.03	Cliff Lee	CLE	1.19
Cliff Politte	TOR	1.03	Esteban Loaiza	CHW	1.19
Matt Herges	SF	1.04	Sidney Ponson	SF	1.19
Curt Leskanic	KC	1.04	Dave Veres	CHC	1.19
Erasmo Ramirez	TEX	1.04	Scott Schoeneweis	CHW	1.20
Mike Timlin	BOS	1.04	Steve Trachsel	NYM	1.20
Todd Vanpoppel	CIN	1.04	Barry Zito	OAK	1.20
Rafael Betancourt	CLE	1.05	Brad Lidge	HOU	1.21
Kevin Gregg	ANA	1.05	Tom Martin	LA	1.21
Livan Hernandez	MON	1.05	Jose Santiago	CLE	1.21
Pat Hentgen	BAL	1.06	Jerome Williams	SF	1.21
Mariano Rivera	NYY	1.06	Brian Anderson	KC	1.22

Second Half Dollar Values - A.L. Hitters

NAME	TEAM	$VAL	AB	RUN	HR	RBI	SB	AVG	OBA	SLG
Carl Crawford	TB	$45	341	46	4	32	36	.305	.325	.396
Carlos Beltran	KC	$44	291	60	15	59	22	.326	.390	.567
Alex Rodriguez	TEX	$38	296	70	27	67	10	.301	.409	.642
Carlos Lee	CHW	$35	327	59	18	64	10	.309	.336	.535
Alex Sanchez	DET	$34	271	33	1	17	30	.303	.333	.373
Angel Berroa	KC	$32	298	54	9	44	18	.292	.331	.446
Randy Winn	SEA	$30	306	58	9	47	9	.330	.377	.497
Magglio Ordonez	CHW	$29	308	50	15	53	3	.347	.399	.588
Miguel Tejada	OAK	$27	308	54	12	51	7	.312	.370	.503
Aubrey Huff	TB	$27	325	46	19	62	1	.320	.373	.563
Nomar Garciaparra	BOS	$26	321	50	16	49	11	.262	.315	.461
Manny Ramirez	BOS	$26	275	51	20	43	2	.331	.439	.618
Johnny Damon	BOS	$26	286	46	6	31	16	.287	.362	.399
Alfonso Soriano	NYY	$26	317	46	17	43	11	.290	.330	.539
Derek Jeter	NYY	$26	288	52	5	33	7	.354	.426	.469
Ichiro Suzuki	SEA	$26	341	52	6	36	13	.284	.325	.408
Vernon Wells	TOR	$25	326	52	13	41	3	.325	.368	.531
David Ortiz	BOS	$25	271	48	27	65	0	.284	.362	.661
Rocco Baldelli	TB	$23	328	49	6	39	13	.265	.309	.375
Bret Boone	SEA	$23	303	50	13	51	10	.274	.361	.475
Aaron Boone	NYY	$22	294	47	9	49	12	.269	.326	.425
Jorge Posada	NYY	$22	238	38	14	52	1	.315	.414	.542
Julio Lugo	TB	$22	288	46	13	40	6	.288	.349	.465
Raul Ibanez	KC	$22	298	44	8	45	6	.302	.350	.446
Mike Young	TEX	$22	350	59	9	40	7	.297	.325	.454
Travis Lee	TB	$22	294	41	13	45	5	.293	.374	.497
Frank Thomas	CHW	$22	290	46	25	66	0	.255	.355	.569
Garret Anderson	ANA	$21	314	36	10	48	2	.315	.345	.478
Carlos Delgado	TOR	$21	272	49	16	56	0	.298	.424	.537
Shannon Stewart	MIN	$21	320	48	8	42	3	.309	.371	.456
Eric Chavez	OAK	$20	294	52	13	55	2	.306	.376	.548
Jose Guillen	OAK	$20	285	46	17	47	1	.288	.329	.526
Bill Mueller	BOS	$20	280	46	14	51	0	.325	.408	.543
Aaron Guiel	KC	$19	284	51	13	43	3	.278	.347	.496
Coco Crisp	CLE	$19	338	41	3	23	11	.278	.304	.364
Carl Everett	CHW	$19	256	40	10	41	4	.301	.377	.473
Jody Gerut	CLE	$19	298	40	14	44	3	.279	.337	.483
Rafael Palmeiro	TEX	$19	294	42	19	60	1	.259	.341	.497
Dmitri Young	DET	$19	280	41	14	40	1	.300	.375	.529
Trot Nixon	BOS	$18	210	38	18	40	1	.295	.391	.624
Cristian Guzman	MIN	$18	225	34	3	34	11	.280	.340	.391
Eric Hinske	TOR	$18	275	48	10	41	10	.251	.340	.473
Adam Kennedy	ANA	$18	251	43	10	28	11	.271	.347	.442
Larry Bigbie	BAL	$18	220	34	8	26	5	.323	.380	.495

Second Half Dollar Values - A.L. Hitters

NAME	TEAM	$VAL	AB	RUN	HR	RBI	SB	AVG	OBA	SLG
Jacque Jones	MIN	$18	217	30	6	34	7	.309	.356	.452
Luis Matos	BAL	$18	301	42	8	28	6	.282	.341	.415
Torii Hunter	MIN	$17	286	44	15	52	3	.245	.294	.465
Craig Monroe	DET	$17	245	35	17	45	2	.265	.300	.522
Scott Spiezio	ANA	$17	284	35	9	59	5	.278	.323	.479
A.J. Pierzynski	MIN	$17	253	37	2	27	2	.332	.389	.447
Mark Teixeira	TEX	$17	307	39	15	45	1	.267	.325	.489
Hank Blalock	TEX	$16	293	43	17	44	2	.270	.313	.509
Brian Roberts	BAL	$16	302	38	2	24	14	.262	.329	.344
Paul Konerko	CHW	$15	233	33	15	48	0	.279	.346	.519
Luis Rivas	MIN	$15	265	42	7	29	11	.253	.295	.400
Jose Valentin	CHW	$15	241	41	16	39	4	.232	.299	.469
Joe Crede	CHW	$15	266	44	12	43	1	.293	.345	.519
Ramon Hernandez	OAK	$15	239	34	11	43	0	.276	.337	.452
Joe Randa	KC	$15	228	38	7	42	0	.346	.404	.518
Reed Johnson	TOR	$15	271	44	4	32	5	.277	.336	.376
Jason Giambi	NYY	$15	258	45	19	44	1	.229	.399	.508
Chone Figgins	ANA	$14	199	25	0	24	10	.291	.342	.367
Edgar Martinez	SEA	$14	264	36	9	43	0	.288	.403	.447
Hideki Matsui	NYY	$14	290	38	7	44	2	.272	.338	.407
Jason Varitek	BOS	$14	235	24	12	40	1	.260	.346	.477
Matt Lecroy	MIN	$14	199	26	11	36	0	.281	.353	.503
Mike Cameron	SEA	$13	268	30	6	26	10	.231	.317	.362
Tim Salmon	ANA	$13	250	39	9	36	1	.276	.385	.476
Ben Broussard	CLE	$13	246	34	11	37	4	.244	.306	.451
Jay Gibbons	BAL	$13	319	38	9	41	0	.270	.310	.423
Kevin Millar	BOS	$13	290	41	13	39	2	.238	.316	.400
Bernie Williams	NYY	$12	270	45	8	33	3	.248	.346	.381
Casey Blake	CLE	$12	313	44	9	39	4	.249	.293	.396
Nick Johnson	NYY	$12	204	31	9	29	3	.270	.402	.446
Doug Mientkiewicz	MIN	$12	245	35	4	33	1	.298	.421	.420
Rube Durazo	OAK	$11	274	48	12	34	1	.237	.344	.401
Rondell White	KC	$11	220	25	7	41	0	.286	.338	.473
Travis Hafner	CLE	$11	194	27	10	29	1	.278	.350	.531
Carlos Pena	DET	$11	277	36	12	30	1	.245	.338	.462
Marlon Anderson	TB	$10	238	32	2	25	8	.269	.319	.370
Jeff Davanon	ANA	$10	193	27	2	18	9	.238	.345	.342
Laynce Nix	TEX	$10	184	25	8	30	3	.255	.289	.440
Damian Rolls	TB	$10	284	28	4	33	7	.250	.287	.345
Brook Fordyce	BAL	$10	217	18	5	25	1	.276	.316	.396
Josh Phelps	TOR	$9	156	19	10	34	1	.263	.358	.494
Brandon Inge	DET	$9	163	19	4	19	4	.258	.309	.405
Ben Molina	ANA	$9	171	14	8	31	0	.269	.276	.474
Carlos Guillen	SEA	$9	151	24	4	27	4	.265	.369	.391

Second Half Dollar Values - A.L. Hitters

NAME	TEAM	$VAL	AB	RUN	HR	RBI	SB	AVG	OBA	SLG
Frank Catalanotto	TOR	$9	185	26	6	18	1	.292	.361	.459
Bobby Kielty	TOR	$9	234	38	4	26	4	.235	.345	.363
Terrence Long	OAK	$9	228	28	6	30	3	.241	.281	.377
John Olerud	SEA	$9	271	31	6	44	0	.251	.354	.376
Mike Bordick	TOR	$9	199	24	3	27	1	.296	.371	.382
David Eckstein	ANA	$8	168	18	0	12	7	.280	.341	.345
Tony Graffanino	CHW	$8	130	27	3	13	5	.277	.326	.446
Ken Harvey	KC	$8	252	22	5	28	1	.274	.316	.393
Milton Bradley	CLE	$8	131	19	4	19	4	.282	.383	.473
Shane Spencer	TEX	$8	221	24	9	33	0	.253	.341	.430
Mark Ellis	OAK	$8	278	41	4	29	5	.245	.293	.360
Roberto Alomar	CHW	$8	253	42	3	17	6	.253	.330	.340
Tony Batista	BAL	$8	322	32	11	45	4	.211	.246	.345
Toby Hall	TB	$8	241	28	7	24	0	.237	.273	.382
Warren Morris	DET	$8	271	28	3	28	4	.269	.314	.354
Greg Myers	TOR	$8	156	22	7	21	0	.256	.296	.429
Bob Higginson	DET	$7	201	25	9	29	1	.234	.308	.418
Miguel Olivo	CHW	$7	145	16	1	11	5	.248	.295	.338
Michael Ryan	MIN	$7	61	13	5	13	2	.393	.441	.754
Gabe Kapler	BOS	$7	149	25	2	16	4	.262	.325	.362
Ryan Ludwick	CLE	$7	162	17	7	26	2	.247	.299	.438
Desi Relaford	KC	$7	250	30	2	26	9	.220	.286	.312
Corey Koskie	MIN	$7	187	30	2	19	5	.267	.382	.369
Mike Sweeney	KC	$7	177	22	4	33	1	.260	.325	.379
Ramon Santiago	DET	$6	242	22	2	23	6	.223	.281	.289
Josh Bard	CLE	$6	97	14	5	20	0	.278	.320	.495
Sandy Alomar	CHW	$6	114	13	4	18	0	.281	.284	.456
Victor Martinez	CLE	$6	147	14	1	15	1	.286	.346	.320
Dan Wilson	SEA	$6	164	21	3	23	0	.250	.276	.378
Karim Garcia	NYY	$6	141	15	5	19	0	.291	.327	.433
Todd Greene	TEX	$5	120	15	7	15	0	.242	.246	.467
Adam Melhuse	OAK	$5	52	9	4	12	0	.365	.441	.692
Deivi Cruz	BAL	$5	287	29	4	28	0	.240	.268	.338
Willie Harris	CHW	$5	45	12	0	2	8	.222	.340	.267
Scott Hatteberg	OAK	$5	256	28	6	23	0	.238	.334	.375
Matt Lawton	CLE	$5	88	18	4	13	2	.273	.354	.443
Billy McMillon	OAK	$5	120	13	6	24	0	.267	.350	.475
Eric Owens	ANA	$5	116	14	0	8	3	.310	.341	.336
Todd Walker	BOS	$5	275	34	5	39	0	.247	.298	.385
Einar Diaz	TEX	$5	143	14	2	15	1	.252	.285	.322
Alex Escobar	CLE	$5	99	16	5	14	1	.273	.324	.444
Juan Gonzalez	TEX	$4	53	10	6	18	0	.321	.351	.717
Aaron Rowand	CHW	$4	65	13	3	11	0	.385	.397	.585
Brent Mayne	KC	$4	188	23	2	16	0	.239	.304	.324

Second Half Dollar Values - A.L. Hitters

NAME	TEAM	$VAL	AB	RUN	HR	RBI	SB	AVG	OBA	SLG
Juan Rivera	NYY	$4	60	11	6	15	0	.317	.339	.683
Jhonny Peralta	CLE	$4	218	22	4	20	1	.234	.302	.344
Rey Sanchez	SEA	$4	215	23	0	13	1	.265	.297	.298
Kevin Witt	DET	$4	160	17	5	12	1	.250	.292	.375
BJ Surhoff	BAL	$3	164	16	3	18	0	.262	.335	.378
Enrique Wilson	NYY	$3	82	14	2	9	3	.256	.299	.402
Melvin Mora	BAL	$3	114	20	4	10	1	.246	.338	.360
Doug Mirabelli	BOS	$3	67	9	4	9	0	.254	.342	.522
Damian Jackson	BOS	$3	97	22	1	9	5	.268	.290	.351
Shane Halter	DET	$3	182	17	7	15	1	.214	.275	.335
Mark McLemore	SEA	$3	154	14	0	18	2	.253	.329	.299
Willie Bloomquist	SEA	$3	129	19	1	11	3	.279	.338	.364
John Flaherty	NYY	$3	49	7	3	9	0	.265	.288	.531
Adam Riggs	ANA	$3	61	11	3	5	3	.246	.343	.492
Michael Tucker	KC	$2	116	17	3	14	1	.233	.310	.371
Mike Difelice	KC	$2	80	12	1	10	1	.225	.281	.350
Ruben Sierra	NYY	$2	125	12	3	18	1	.232	.267	.352
Chris Singleton	OAK	$2	137	12	0	15	6	.175	.245	.241
Darin Erstad	ANA	$2	117	13	1	5	4	.214	.276	.299
Adam Piatt	TB	$2	72	9	4	10	1	.236	.263	.514
Dave Dellucci	NYY	$2	89	10	1	4	6	.157	.250	.202
Antonio Perez	TB	$2	111	17	2	12	4	.243	.351	.360
Lou Merloni	BOS	$1	88	13	1	11	1	.261	.337	.364
Ben Petrick	DET	$1	120	18	4	12	0	.225	.273	.375
Jack Cust	BAL	$1	73	7	4	11	0	.260	.357	.521
Lew Ford	MIN	$1	31	8	1	6	2	.290	.371	.581
Tim Laker	CLE	$1	78	7	1	8	1	.218	.265	.308
Dustan Mohr	MIN	$1	142	17	2	14	2	.204	.294	.310
Ramon Nivar	TEX	$1	90	9	0	7	4	.211	.253	.267
Chris Woodward	TOR	$1	117	13	2	15	0	.248	.295	.376
Alfredo Amezaga	ANA	$1	105	15	2	7	2	.210	.278	.333
Orlando Hudson	TOR	$1	219	21	4	21	1	.237	.306	.352
Robert Machado	BAL	$1	45	7	1	3	0	.267	.353	.356
Eric Munson	DET	$1	96	11	8	19	0	.229	.309	.479
Robb Quinlan	ANA	$1	94	13	0	4	1	.287	.330	.372
Andres Torres	DET	$1	63	11	1	5	3	.206	.261	.317
Al Martin	TB	$1	99	8	3	17	0	.232	.294	.394
David McCarty	BOS	$1	53	6	1	8	0	.340	.368	.491
Gerald Laird	TEX	$1	38	8	1	4	0	.237	.326	.395
A.j. Hinch	DET	$1	43	5	2	6	0	.209	.271	.395
Brian Daubach	CHW	$1	78	13	4	10	0	.218	.354	.410
Mendy Lopez	KC	$1	51	8	3	8	0	.275	.315	.529

Second Half Dollar Values - N.L. Hitters

NAME	TEAM	$VAL	AB	RUN	HR	RBI	SB	AVG	OBA	SLG
Scott Podsednik	MIL	$45	330	58	6	34	27	.303	.359	.439
Juan Pierre	FLA	$41	320	51	1	19	27	.313	.370	.384
Gary Sheffield	ATL	$36	294	60	17	68	7	.337	.427	.588
Jeff Bagwell	HOU	$34	289	60	25	62	8	.280	.394	.585
Edgar Renteria	STL	$34	280	48	6	44	17	.321	.398	.461
Bob Abreu	PHI	$34	291	48	8	54	13	.323	.427	.478
Albert Pujols	STL	$33	288	63	20	52	5	.330	.433	.622
Todd Helton	COL	$32	276	64	19	53	0	.384	.487	.688
Reggie Sanders	PIT	$31	239	43	19	53	9	.305	.372	.640
Marlon Byrd	PHI	$29	346	65	6	34	9	.318	.375	.442
Kenny Lofton	CHC	$29	266	46	4	21	16	.312	.363	.459
Marcus Giles	ATL	$29	275	54	13	33	7	.342	.416	.575
Preston Wilson	COL	$29	278	44	19	71	8	.259	.325	.522
Sammy Sosa	CHC	$28	312	57	30	67	0	.266	.319	.580
Orlando Cabrera	MON	$28	314	43	6	35	14	.296	.338	.439
Richard Hidalgo	HOU	$28	287	50	17	52	5	.303	.372	.589
Barry Bonds	SF	$28	168	57	23	43	0	.393	.579	.881
Javy Lopez	ATL	$27	240	49	20	61	0	.342	.393	.679
Vladimir Guerrero	MON	$27	218	40	17	46	4	.353	.434	.661
Jim Thome	PHI	$27	292	57	26	73	0	.271	.384	.603
Rafael Furcal	ATL	$27	337	67	5	33	11	.291	.347	.398
Jay Payton	COL	$26	294	36	17	56	3	.310	.359	.561
Richie Sexson	MIL	$25	301	45	23	69	0	.286	.390	.595
Brian Giles	SD	$25	292	55	13	53	4	.298	.414	.534
Chipper Jones	ATL	$25	286	58	14	63	1	.311	.402	.535
Steve Finley	AZ	$25	279	39	12	36	10	.280	.345	.495
Derrek Lee	FLA	$25	246	45	15	48	7	.280	.381	.537
Scott Rolen	STL	$25	286	48	13	48	8	.283	.364	.514
Shawn Green	LA	$24	301	48	11	46	4	.309	.396	.502
Jose Reyes	NYM	$23	201	38	4	17	12	.343	.379	.468
Lance Berkman	HOU	$23	271	56	11	46	4	.295	.422	.535
Placido Polanco	PHI	$22	244	49	8	37	5	.320	.372	.488
Andruw Jones	ATL	$22	301	49	16	59	2	.266	.316	.485
Jason Kendall	PIT	$21	308	42	2	26	3	.351	.413	.438
Mark Loretta	SD	$20	306	40	7	43	2	.327	.377	.451
Marquis Grissom	SF	$20	284	43	9	41	4	.292	.306	.447
Dangelo Jimenez	CIN	$19	290	34	7	31	7	.290	.365	.421
Luis Castillo	FLA	$19	282	48	1	16	7	.319	.392	.390
Aramis Ramirez	CHC	$19	308	39	20	59	1	.256	.303	.497
Raul Mondesi	AZ	$19	209	35	10	28	7	.278	.347	.478
Tike Redman	PIT	$19	230	36	3	19	7	.330	.374	.483
Jimmy Rollins	PHI	$18	286	37	4	27	11	.259	.331	.392
Jeff Conine	FLA	$18	266	42	11	42	1	.293	.347	.481
Dave Roberts	LA	$17	170	24	1	6	16	.247	.340	.312

Second Half Dollar Values - N.L. Hitters

NAME	TEAM	$VAL	AB	RUN	HR	RBI	SB	AVG	OBA	SLG
Brady Clark	MIL	$17	200	25	5	21	9	.290	.359	.455
Juan Encarnacion	FLA	$17	282	36	8	42	6	.252	.295	.411
Brad Wilkerson	MON	$17	272	43	10	34	6	.243	.347	.423
Phil Nevin	SD	$17	226	30	13	46	2	.279	.339	.487
Ivan Rodriguez	FLA	$17	263	46	6	41	1	.304	.362	.460
Matt Stairs	PIT	$16	178	37	14	40	0	.309	.419	.624
Luis Gonzalez	AZ	$16	272	38	9	44	1	.287	.411	.478
Shea Hillenbrand	AZ	$16	296	36	16	53	0	.267	.302	.480
Jeff Kent	HOU	$16	240	35	11	43	2	.279	.327	.496
Eric Young	SF	$16	215	31	6	14	11	.242	.336	.349
Mike Lieberthal	PHI	$16	265	36	8	47	0	.298	.353	.453
Adrian Beltre	LA	$16	295	28	17	52	1	.258	.297	.488
Roger Cedeno	NYM	$15	261	42	4	19	7	.268	.308	.391
Alex Cintron	AZ	$15	291	38	6	27	1	.323	.365	.471
Jeromy Burnitz	LA	$15	274	34	17	42	4	.212	.272	.423
Craig Wilson	PIT	$15	197	37	15	33	1	.269	.366	.574
Moises Alou	CHC	$15	266	41	12	41	1	.263	.350	.462
Miguel Cabrera	FLA	$15	276	35	11	56	0	.283	.341	.486
Vinny Castilla	ATL	$15	267	29	10	41	1	.303	.325	.491
Ron Belliard	COL	$15	232	41	7	30	6	.246	.311	.414
Jason Phillips	NYM	$14	263	30	8	44	0	.293	.362	.449
Craig Biggio	HOU	$14	303	52	6	31	3	.257	.355	.393
Edgardo Alfonzo	SF	$14	238	30	8	52	1	.294	.368	.462
Gary Matthews	SD	$14	196	34	3	13	8	.270	.356	.398
Geoff Jenkins	MIL	$14	200	30	9	34	0	.315	.405	.525
Morgan Ensberg	HOU	$13	233	33	11	23	3	.279	.351	.468
Mark Grudzielanek	CHC	$13	185	29	1	23	4	.341	.392	.465
Wil Cordero	MON	$13	219	34	9	40	0	.283	.354	.466
Jose Vidro	MON	$12	234	34	7	27	1	.295	.377	.440
Timoniel Perez	NYM	$12	227	21	3	28	5	.278	.299	.388
Juan Uribe	COL	$12	200	27	6	20	7	.250	.294	.440
Abraham O. Nunez	PIT	$12	181	26	4	24	6	.276	.343	.442
Larry Walker	COL	$12	207	34	8	29	2	.266	.400	.444
Mark Kotsay	SD	$12	265	35	4	25	2	.283	.346	.419
Sean Burroughs	SD	$11	268	37	3	29	4	.272	.343	.377
Sean Casey	CIN	$11	265	27	6	41	0	.283	.350	.389
Ty Wigginton	NYM	$11	274	27	5	33	7	.234	.307	.358
Rob Mackowiak	PIT	$11	92	13	5	17	5	.348	.400	.609
Eduardo Perez	STL	$11	118	21	7	24	4	.280	.358	.525
Jack Wilson	PIT	$11	281	30	5	34	2	.270	.318	.363
Cliff Floyd	NYM	$10	108	19	4	25	3	.333	.406	.509
Jim Edmonds	STL	$10	185	36	14	30	0	.222	.357	.508
Keith Ginter	MIL	$10	222	36	12	29	0	.243	.349	.468
Tino Martinez	STL	$10	223	30	6	31	1	.269	.358	.386

Second Half Dollar Values - N.L. Hitters

NAME	TEAM	$VAL	AB	RUN	HR	RBI	SB	AVG	OBA	SLG
Rich Aurilia	SF	$10	231	24	6	31	0	.299	.335	.424
Jose Cruz	SF	$10	258	41	8	35	0	.244	.362	.384
Ryan Freel	CIN	$10	96	17	4	10	6	.292	.343	.490
Tom Goodwin	CHC	$10	79	14	0	6	8	.329	.379	.418
Randall Simon	CHC	$10	188	24	9	32	0	.271	.310	.441
Alex S. Gonzalez	CHC	$9	235	28	11	30	3	.209	.289	.413
Wes Helms	MIL	$9	211	22	10	24	0	.284	.348	.469
Cesar Izturis	LA	$9	289	25	1	23	5	.253	.278	.336
Charles Johnson	COL	$8	161	26	11	24	1	.224	.315	.491
Andres Galarraga	SF	$8	156	21	6	22	1	.288	.339	.455
Jolbert Cabrera	LA	$8	209	22	2	20	2	.292	.321	.411
Bo Hart	STL	$8	242	34	3	22	3	.244	.290	.347
Brad Ausmus	HOU	$8	225	24	2	23	3	.253	.332	.311
Adam Everett	HOU	$8	236	26	4	32	2	.254	.328	.364
Alex Cora	LA	$7	235	20	4	17	2	.272	.304	.374
Mike Lowell	FLA	$7	175	21	7	37	1	.257	.342	.406
Gary Bennett	SD	$7	165	14	1	30	3	.267	.326	.339
Matt Kata	AZ	$7	240	33	4	22	3	.233	.286	.371
J.T. Snow	SF	$7	142	30	5	21	1	.268	.392	.408
Junior Spivey	AZ	$7	161	22	4	20	3	.255	.330	.422
Ron Calloway	MON	$7	183	16	2	21	5	.235	.266	.322
Pat Burrell	PHI	$7	246	23	10	35	0	.220	.309	.411
Eric Karros	CHC	$7	171	21	5	22	1	.269	.308	.409
Endy Chavez	MON	$7	181	25	1	20	4	.238	.302	.343
Geoff Blum	HOU	$6	202	26	4	28	0	.262	.284	.351
J.D. Drew	STL	$6	138	27	6	17	0	.268	.373	.457
Doug Glanville	CHC	$6	122	15	3	12	1	.328	.341	.434
Ryan Klesko	SD	$6	159	15	6	24	1	.252	.346	.403
Ray Durham	SF	$6	181	28	5	18	1	.249	.310	.442
Jason Bay	PIT	$6	79	13	3	12	3	.291	.423	.506
Bill Hall	MIL	$5	142	23	5	20	1	.261	.298	.458
Kerry Robinson	STL	$5	130	11	1	11	4	.269	.307	.369
Danny Bautista	AZ	$5	111	15	3	18	1	.297	.373	.495
Pedro Feliz	SF	$5	126	12	8	23	2	.238	.263	.492
Juan Castro	CIN	$5	148	15	5	20	1	.270	.325	.419
Craig Counsell	AZ	$5	187	22	2	11	6	.209	.289	.273
Wily Pena	CIN	$5	131	12	5	14	2	.252	.324	.412
Ricky Ledee	PHI	$5	104	15	6	23	0	.260	.328	.510
Michael Barrett	MON	$5	79	14	5	19	0	.291	.371	.608
Robert Fick	ATL	$5	205	24	4	36	0	.224	.305	.337
Robby Hammock	AZ	$5	114	15	4	11	2	.254	.338	.404
Miguel Cairo	STL	$5	100	17	3	17	3	.230	.279	.360
Ramon Vazquez	SD	$5	212	27	0	10	3	.255	.335	.316
Tony Clark	NYM	$4	127	14	7	18	0	.252	.324	.472

Second Half Dollar Values - N.L. Hitters

NAME	TEAM	$VAL	AB	RUN	HR	RBI	SB	AVG	OBA	SLG
Orlando Palmeiro	STL	$4	142	15	2	15	2	.261	.314	.338
Royce Clayton	MIL	$4	223	21	3	15	3	.233	.291	.300
Mark Derosa	ATL	$4	159	22	2	10	1	.289	.339	.390
Jason Larue	CIN	$4	175	27	6	22	0	.211	.299	.366
Paul Loduca	LA	$4	288	34	2	24	0	.229	.297	.302
Joe McEwing	NYM	$4	167	21	1	10	3	.257	.332	.317
Yorvit Torrealba	SF	$4	122	15	3	15	1	.262	.326	.385
Julio Franco	ATL	$4	90	14	4	16	0	.300	.379	.511
Jeffrey Hammonds	SF	$4	94	20	3	10	1	.277	.370	.479
Chris Stynes	COL	$4	217	35	3	24	1	.230	.300	.350
Jose Hernandez	PIT	$4	246	24	4	29	1	.224	.273	.337
Mike Matheny	STL	$4	188	17	4	21	1	.223	.310	.319
Xavier Nady	SD	$4	86	12	2	10	3	.244	.305	.337
Todd Zeile	MON	$4	142	15	5	20	1	.254	.325	.408
Tomas Perez	PHI	$3	195	26	4	21	0	.231	.291	.359
Mike Piazza	NYM	$3	123	16	4	19	0	.244	.338	.366
Damian Miller	CHC	$3	167	14	4	12	1	.240	.308	.371
Dave Ross	LA	$3	89	12	7	11	0	.236	.330	.539
Benito Santiago	SF	$3	158	22	1	16	0	.259	.318	.373
John Vanderwal	MIL	$3	146	17	6	20	0	.219	.321	.425
Joe Vitiello	MON	$3	70	11	3	12	0	.329	.392	.529
Russ Branyan	CIN	$3	145	18	8	22	0	.221	.313	.455
Rene Reyes	COL	$3	116	13	2	7	2	.259	.287	.388
Adam Dunn	CIN	$3	140	19	4	11	1	.229	.363	.371
Barry Larkin	CIN	$3	127	18	1	9	1	.291	.338	.386
Henry Mateo	MON	$3	78	14	0	4	5	.205	.295	.244
Miguel Ojeda	SD	$3	99	11	3	12	1	.253	.380	.394
Carlos Baerga	AZ	$2	62	8	1	11	0	.387	.479	.435
Chase Utley	PHI	$2	119	11	1	17	2	.244	.336	.361
Jason Michaels	PHI	$2	56	11	2	8	0	.357	.438	.571
Darren Bragg	ATL	$2	77	16	0	6	0	.338	.414	.416
Ramon.e. Martinez	CHC	$2	150	15	0	14	0	.293	.331	.353
Ruben Mateo	CIN	$2	157	14	2	14	0	.255	.296	.344
Greg Norton	COL	$2	62	8	4	16	1	.290	.357	.581
Tony Womack	CHC	$2	130	13	0	7	5	.208	.220	.254
Keith Osik	MIL	$2	122	15	1	13	0	.262	.357	.344
Brian Schneider	MON	$2	195	16	3	25	0	.215	.270	.354
Jeff Duncan	NYM	$2	134	12	1	10	4	.187	.288	.239
Rickey Henderson	LA	$2	72	7	2	5	3	.208	.321	.306
Todd Pratt	PHI	$2	72	11	3	7	0	.278	.391	.458
Jamey Carroll	MON	$1	136	19	1	6	2	.250	.318	.287
Quinton McCracken	AZ	$1	98	9	0	7	2	.255	.302	.296
Brian Buchanan	SD	$1	80	12	1	7	2	.225	.333	.338
Alex Gonzalez	FLA	$1	249	19	6	26	0	.201	.271	.325

Rotisserie League Baseball • **BY THE NUMBERS**

Second Half Dollar Values - N.L. Hitters

NAME	TEAM	$VAL	AB	RUN	HR	RBI	SB	AVG	OBA	SLG
Ken Griffey	CIN	$1	35	8	5	6	0	.257	.409	.800
Jason Lane	HOU	$1	27	5	4	10	0	.296	.296	.815
Eddie Perez	MIL	$1	170	8	3	11	0	.241	.280	.371
Marco Scutaro	NYM	$1	58	7	2	6	2	.241	.375	.414
Robin Ventura	LA	$1	161	16	5	19	0	.224	.335	.373
Ramon Castro	FLA	$1	22	5	4	6	0	.318	.318	.955
Reggie Taylor	CIN	$1	93	9	3	10	1	.215	.277	.355
Gregg Zaun	COL	$1	85	9	4	12	0	.212	.299	.376
Fred McGriff	LA	$1	70	9	3	5	0	.271	.346	.429
So Taguchi	STL	$1	51	7	3	11	0	.255	.296	.510
Paul Bako	CHC	$1	104	16	0	9	0	.250	.339	.375
Troy O'Leary	CHC	$1	53	3	2	9	2	.189	.267	.377

Second Half Dollar Values - A.L. Pitchers

NAME	TEAM	$VAL	W	SV	ERA	IP	H	BB	K	RATIO
Keith Foulke	OAK	$46	5	22	1.62	44	24	10	43	0.77
Mariano Rivera	NYY	$45	3	25	1.56	40	37	6	34	1.06
Eddie Guardado	MIN	$36	2	21	3.04	33	23	8	31	0.95
Byung Kim	BOS	$36	6	16	2.28	47	33	10	50	0.91
Roy Halladay	TOR	$30	11	0	2.82	137	119	12	104	0.96
Jorge Julio	BAL	$28	0	20	4.69	31	32	16	24	1.56
Tim Hudson	OAK	$27	10	0	2.31	121	92	30	92	1.01
Francisco Cordero	TEX	$25	2	13	1.89	38	28	14	43	1.11
Troy Percival	ANA	$25	0	17	3.91	25	20	15	24	1.38
Pedro Martinez	BOS	$25	9	0	1.81	105	83	24	120	1.02
Shigetoshi Hasegawa	SEA	$24	1	14	2.27	32	28	12	12	1.26
Tom Gordon	CHW	$23	3	11	2.36	34	22	11	41	0.96
Lance Carter	TB	$22	3	13	5.01	38	34	7	21	1.09
Damaso Marte	CHW	$20	2	7	1.19	45	26	19	51	0.99
Aquilino Lopez	TOR	$19	0	12	2.61	31	26	14	21	1.29
Darrell May	KC	$18	9	0	3.55	119	105	29	62	1.13
David Riske	CLE	$18	1	7	1.46	37	20	11	41	0.84
Bartolo Colon	CHW	$18	9	0	3.53	120	113	28	86	1.18
Andy Pettitte	NYY	$18	12	0	3.29	107	109	23	94	1.24
Brad Radke	MIN	$17	9	0	3.50	113	121	10	68	1.16
Esteban Loaiza	CHW	$17	10	0	3.65	111	103	29	113	1.19
Johan Santana	MIN	$16	8	0	3.47	99	81	25	101	1.08
Pat Hentgen	BAL	$16	6	0	3.16	94	72	28	60	1.06
Barry Zito	OAK	$16	7	0	3.43	118	100	42	77	1.20
Brian Anderson	KC	$15	9	0	3.34	105	104	24	55	1.22
Jeremy Affeldt	KC	$15	3	4	2.78	55	42	14	46	1.02
Jamie Moyer	SEA	$14	10	0	3.52	107	110	29	56	1.30
Mark Buehrle	CHW	$14	9	0	3.70	117	128	22	61	1.29
Mike Mussina	NYY	$14	7	0	3.83	108	103	23	91	1.17
Rafael Soriano	SEA	$13	3	1	1.39	45	23	9	58	0.71
Tim Wakefield	BOS	$13	5	0	3.53	107	97	28	85	1.17
John Thomson	TEX	$13	8	0	3.89	113	112	28	72	1.24
Julio Mateo	SEA	$13	3	1	2.68	54	38	4	46	0.78
Joel Pineiro	SEA	$11	8	0	3.91	104	99	35	75	1.29
Danys Baez	CLE	$10	2	6	4.15	35	34	10	33	1.27
Ryan Franklin	SEA	$10	5	0	3.64	106	105	32	48	1.29
C.c. Sabathia	CLE	$10	6	0	3.72	97	92	31	74	1.27
Latroy Hawkins	MIN	$10	4	2	1.95	37	34	6	27	1.08
Mark Mulder	OAK	$10	4	0	2.91	65	59	11	54	1.08
Francisco Rodriguez	ANA	$10	4	1	2.64	44	25	18	54	0.97
Roger Clemens	NYY	$10	9	0	4.53	99	101	27	71	1.29
Josh Towers	TOR	$10	7	1	4.20	60	62	7	39	1.15
John Lackey	ANA	$9	5	0	3.87	107	106	36	77	1.33

Second Half Dollar Values - A.L. Pitchers

NAME	TEAM	$VAL	W	SV	ERA	IP	H	BB	K	RATIO
Jason Kershner	TOR	$9	3	0	2.40	49	36	12	30	0.99
Jamie Walker	DET	$8	2	3	3.08	38	36	8	26	1.16
Ted Lilly	OAK	$8	7	0	3.78	83	87	26	77	1.36
Jose Contreras	NYY	$8	4	0	2.56	46	31	16	46	1.03
Scot Shields	ANA	$8	3	0	3.68	88	90	20	62	1.25
Derek Lowe	BOS	$7	8	0	4.43	100	107	33	52	1.41
Mike Macdougal	KC	$7	0	7	5.60	27	31	12	27	1.58
Rafael Betancourt	CLE	$7	2	1	2.13	38	27	13	36	1.05
Kenny Rogers	MIN	$7	6	0	4.23	100	110	27	56	1.37
Jeff Suppan	BOS	$7	7	0	4.60	102	112	25	53	1.35
Jeremi Gonzalez	TB	$7	3	0	3.96	102	94	41	55	1.32
Kelvim Escobar	TOR	$7	8	0	4.31	109	113	48	82	1.48
Jon Garland	CHW	$6	6	0	4.38	99	94	41	54	1.37
Eric Dubose	BAL	$6	3	0	3.87	67	57	23	39	1.19
Curt Leskanic	KC	$6	1	2	1.73	26	16	11	22	1.04
Jarrod Washburn	ANA	$6	4	0	4.68	100	100	28	63	1.28
Trever Miller	TOR	$6	1	4	3.90	25	20	14	23	1.34
R.a. Dickey	TEX	$6	6	1	5.02	81	89	20	62	1.35
Chad Bradford	OAK	$6	2	1	2.00	36	32	13	28	1.25
Armando Benitez	SEA	$6	3	2	2.76	29	23	18	32	1.40
Erasmo Ramirez	TEX	$6	3	0	3.21	39	34	7	22	1.04
John Burkett	BOS	$5	6	0	5.00	95	106	20	52	1.32
Jack Cressend	CLE	$5	2	0	2.51	43	40	9	28	1.14
Victor Zambrano	TB	$5	7	0	4.34	104	99	55	80	1.49
Felix Heredia	NYY	$5	2	1	2.75	39	34	16	17	1.27
Kyle Lohse	MIN	$5	8	0	5.33	96	112	22	54	1.39
Brendan Donnelly	ANA	$5	2	2	3.07	32	31	13	30	1.36
Mike Timlin	BOS	$5	3	0	3.61	37	34	5	31	1.04
Chris Mears	DET	$4	1	5	5.83	39	50	11	21	1.58
Travis Harper	TB	$4	4	1	4.26	38	36	13	24	1.29
Danny Patterson	DET	$4	0	3	4.07	18	15	4	19	1.07
David Wells	NYY	$4	5	0	4.98	99	120	16	43	1.37
Derrick Turnbow	ANA	$4	2	0	0.00	13	4	0	12	0.31
Ben Weber	ANA	$4	3	0	2.35	38	41	11	23	1.36
Scott Williamson	BOS	$4	1	3	4.69	31	28	14	36	1.37
Rob Bell	TB	$4	5	0	4.91	88	93	28	37	1.38
Ron Mahay	TEX	$4	3	0	3.51	41	32	19	34	1.24
Juan Rincon	MIN	$4	4	0	4.03	45	40	18	38	1.30
Ricardo Rincon	OAK	$3	4	0	2.08	26	21	16	16	1.42
B.j. Ryan	BAL	$3	1	0	1.02	27	17	14	30	1.17
Doug Waechter	TB	$3	3	0	3.31	35	29	15	29	1.25
Cliff Lee	CLE	$3	2	0	4.08	46	38	17	39	1.19
Bronson Arroyo	BOS	$3	0	1	2.08	17	10	4	14	0.81
Rich Harden	OAK	$3	5	0	4.46	75	72	40	67	1.50

Second Half Dollar Values - A.L. Pitchers

NAME	TEAM	$VAL	W	SV	ERA	IP	H	BB	K	RATIO
Jorge Sosa	TB	$3	4	0	4.35	81	82	37	51	1.47
Scott Schoeneweis	CHW	$3	2	0	3.61	37	34	11	36	1.20
Jason Stanford	CLE	$3	1	0	3.60	50	48	16	30	1.28
Jimmy Gobble	KC	$3	4	0	4.61	53	56	15	31	1.35
Kerry Ligtenberg	BAL	$3	4	0	3.91	28	29	6	22	1.27
Jeff Nelson	NYY	$3	1	1	3.21	28	24	11	37	1.25
Kevin Gregg	ANA	$3	2	0	3.28	25	18	8	14	1.05
Jake Westbrook	CLE	$3	4	0	4.14	72	74	34	34	1.51
Fernando Rodney	DET	$2	1	3	4.44	28	31	17	31	1.69
Freddy Garcia	SEA	$2	3	0	4.97	92	94	32	75	1.37
Chad Gaudin	TB	$2	2	0	3.60	40	37	16	23	1.33
Rodrigo Lopez	BAL	$2	6	0	5.05	103	127	28	80	1.50
Brian Shouse	TEX	$2	0	1	2.49	25	26	7	21	1.30
Scott Sullivan	CHW	$2	0	0	2.52	25	14	10	18	0.96
John Parrish	BAL	$2	0	0	1.90	24	17	8	15	1.05
Chris Hammond	NYY	$2	1	0	2.77	26	26	5	16	1.19
Jorge Depaula	NYY	$1	0	0	0.80	11	3	1	7	0.35
Eric Milton	MIN	$1	1	0	2.65	17	15	1	7	0.94
Jason Davis	CLE	$1	1	0	4.90	68	69	20	33	1.31
Alan Embree	BOS	$1	1	1	4.74	25	26	5	21	1.26
Jose Lima	KC	$1	6	0	5.40	55	65	19	27	1.53
Cliff Politte	TOR	$1	0	1	4.04	16	10	6	12	1.03
Rick Reed	MIN	$1	3	0	5.37	59	70	10	33	1.36
Gabe White	NYY	$1	2	0	4.35	12	8	2	6	0.81
Casey Fossum	BOS	$1	2	1	4.57	20	21	10	13	1.57
Jose Santiago	CLE	$1	1	0	1.72	16	12	7	7	1.21
Pete Walker	TOR	$1	1	0	3.52	23	19	8	12	1.17
John Halama	OAK	$1	1	0	4.31	48	55	11	19	1.38
Kris Wilson	KC	$1	3	0	4.69	31	38	6	18	1.43

Second Half Dollar Values - N.L. Pitchers

NAME	TEAM	$VAL	W	SV	ERA	IP	H	BB	K	RATIO
Eric Gagne	LA	$48	1	26	0.42	43	18	11	68	0.67
Billy Wagner	HOU	$39	0	22	1.33	41	21	12	45	0.81
Matt Mantei	AZ	$37	1	22	1.42	32	16	10	38	0.82
Dan Kolb	MIL	$33	1	21	1.80	35	29	12	30	1.17
Tim Worrell	SF	$30	2	21	4.21	36	38	14	35	1.43
Jason Isringhausen	STL	$29	0	20	2.85	35	28	15	35	1.24
Joe Borowski	CHC	$28	1	18	2.74	30	25	7	26	1.08
Livan Hernandez	MON	$27	9	0	2.42	130	104	33	115	1.05
Rod Beck	SD	$26	2	16	1.42	25	19	8	22	1.07
John Smoltz	ATL	$24	0	16	1.64	22	19	1	25	0.91
Javier Vazquez	MON	$24	7	0	2.45	117	93	27	114	1.02
Ugueth Urbina	FLA	$22	3	10	1.67	43	28	15	45	1.00
Mark Prior	CHC	$22	10	0	2.23	101	87	24	118	1.10
Greg Maddux	ATL	$21	10	0	3.00	105	102	11	55	1.08
Jason Schmidt	SF	$20	9	0	2.61	90	70	18	86	0.98
Julian Tavarez	PIT	$20	3	11	3.49	49	40	17	25	1.16
Braden Looper	FLA	$18	3	14	5.35	37	39	17	25	1.51
Matt Clement	CHC	$18	9	0	3.42	110	79	46	94	1.13
Chris Reitsma	CIN	$18	2	12	3.89	39	43	8	28	1.30
Brad Penny	FLA	$16	8	0	3.42	95	82	21	63	1.09
Kip Wells	PIT	$16	8	0	3.05	112	101	39	81	1.25
Steve Trachsel	NYM	$16	9	0	3.21	101	96	25	58	1.20
Al Leiter	NYM	$16	7	0	2.15	84	67	31	68	1.17
Josh Beckett	FLA	$15	7	0	2.75	101	89	36	107	1.23
Curt Schilling	AZ	$15	4	0	2.88	97	91	15	112	1.09
Wilson Alvarez	LA	$14	6	0	2.55	81	71	20	68	1.12
Sidney Ponson	SF	$14	7	0	3.53	107	100	27	55	1.19
Kevin Brown	LA	$14	4	0	2.55	99	90	30	88	1.22
Carlos Zambrano	CHC	$14	7	0	3.10	110	99	45	85	1.31
Vicente Padilla	PHI	$13	7	0	3.57	106	99	32	65	1.24
Rheal Cormier	PHI	$13	6	1	1.76	46	31	11	34	0.91
Mike Hampton	ATL	$13	11	0	3.84	117	124	37	70	1.37
Jerome Williams	SF	$12	5	0	3.16	94	84	30	68	1.21
Guillermo Mota	LA	$12	4	0	2.01	58	42	14	55	0.96
Brandon Webb	AZ	$12	6	0	3.38	104	86	46	114	1.27
Rocky Biddle	MON	$12	2	12	6.02	31	39	20	15	1.88
Adam Eaton	SD	$12	7	0	3.55	94	86	30	67	1.24
Wade Miller	HOU	$11	9	0	3.70	90	77	42	84	1.32
Roy Oswalt	HOU	$11	6	0	2.85	54	43	9	37	0.97
Kerry Wood	CHC	$11	6	0	3.56	96	70	51	123	1.26
Brian Lawrence	SD	$11	6	0	3.48	101	105	27	50	1.31
Tim Redding	HOU	$11	6	0	3.36	86	80	27	61	1.25
Oscar Villarreal	AZ	$11	5	0	1.98	50	34	17	44	1.02
Kevin Millwood	PHI	$10	5	0	4.00	110	102	36	76	1.25

Second Half Dollar Values - N.L. Pitchers

NAME	TEAM	$VAL	W	SV	ERA	IP	H	BB	K	RATIO
Justin Speier	COL	$10	1	8	4.94	31	31	9	31	1.29
Mark Redman	FLA	$10	8	0	4.26	103	97	37	87	1.30
Russ Ortiz	ATL	$10	11	0	4.35	97	85	48	81	1.37
Dave Weathers	NYM	$10	0	7	2.74	43	43	22	37	1.52
Randy Johnson	AZ	$9	5	0	3.57	91	95	22	94	1.29
Carl Pavano	FLA	$9	6	0	3.83	96	94	33	64	1.32
Joe Nathan	SF	$9	5	0	1.50	36	19	15	39	0.94
Odalis Perez	LA	$9	8	0	4.61	84	84	20	62	1.24
Dontrelle Willis	FLA	$8	6	0	3.99	97	92	38	80	1.34
Luis Ayala	MON	$8	4	3	2.75	36	39	10	29	1.36
Paul Quantrill	LA	$8	1	1	1.88	43	34	10	24	1.02
Brian Fuentes	COL	$8	2	4	2.98	36	34	14	39	1.32
Jim Brower	SF	$7	5	0	3.81	57	47	17	35	1.13
Horacio Ramirez	ATL	$7	5	0	4.02	103	101	41	52	1.38
Woody Williams	STL	$7	8	0	4.80	109	119	31	76	1.38
Mike Lincoln	PIT	$7	3	5	5.21	36	38	13	28	1.41
Hideo Nomo	LA	$6	7	0	3.98	95	92	48	74	1.47
Octavio Dotel	HOU	$6	0	2	2.93	40	27	14	42	1.03
Mike Stanton	NYM	$6	0	5	4.44	24	18	10	21	1.15
Brett Tomko	STL	$6	9	0	4.84	97	114	23	59	1.42
Will Cunnane	ATL	$6	2	3	2.70	20	14	6	20	1.00
Tomokazu Ohka	MON	$6	3	0	3.88	107	125	23	68	1.39
Jose Valverde	AZ	$6	1	1	2.48	36	16	20	53	0.99
Ron Villone	HOU	$6	6	0	4.48	88	77	43	75	1.36
Matt Herges	SF	$6	2	0	2.46	40	33	9	34	1.04
Matt Morris	STL	$6	3	0	3.59	58	55	13	33	1.18
Jae Seo	NYM	$5	4	0	4.55	95	96	28	61	1.31
Miguel Batista	AZ	$5	4	0	4.16	97	103	32	75	1.39
Jake Peavy	SD	$5	4	0	4.45	87	76	39	74	1.32
Ben Sheets	MIL	$5	5	0	4.64	97	113	19	69	1.36
Brian Meadows	PIT	$5	2	1	3.73	48	53	6	25	1.22
John Riedling	CIN	$5	2	0	3.02	48	40	16	39	1.17
Jeriome Robertson	HOU	$5	9	0	4.91	81	86	33	48	1.47
Tom Glavine	NYM	$4	4	0	4.14	91	99	31	40	1.42
Rick Helling	FLA	$4	3	0	4.34	64	67	12	46	1.23
Cal Eldred	STL	$4	4	0	2.83	35	27	16	36	1.23
Glendon Rusch	MIL	$4	0	1	2.87	47	47	11	35	1.23
Jose Acevedo	CIN	$4	2	0	2.67	27	17	6	23	0.85
Doug Davis	MIL	$4	3	0	2.88	56	58	22	39	1.42
Darren Oliver	COL	$4	8	0	5.26	87	99	25	43	1.42
Mike Williams	PHI	$4	1	7	6.69	32	36	22	26	1.80
Felix Rodriguez	SF	$4	4	1	2.19	25	21	14	16	1.42
Ricky Stone	HOU	$4	2	1	3.52	38	32	15	25	1.23
Dustin Hermanson	SF	$4	2	0	3.00	39	35	10	27	1.15

Second Half Dollar Values - N.L. Pitchers

NAME	TEAM	$VAL	W	SV	ERA	IP	H	BB	K	RATIO
Sterling Hitchcock	STL	$4	6	0	4.54	61	60	26	46	1.40
Jason Simontacchi	STL	$4	4	1	4.06	51	61	13	34	1.45
Michael Tejera	FLA	$4	2	1	3.03	27	19	11	17	1.12
Mike Dejean	STL	$3	3	3	4.85	43	42	23	39	1.52
Shane Reynolds	ATL	$3	6	0	4.96	93	107	24	49	1.41
Danny Miceli	HOU	$3	1	0	2.45	33	26	8	21	1.03
Garrett Stephenson	STL	$3	3	0	4.97	74	75	19	38	1.27
Dan Plesac	PHI	$3	1	2	2.90	19	15	6	21	1.13
Javier Lopez	COL	$3	3	1	3.38	29	32	7	18	1.33
Nelson Figueroa	PIT	$3	2	0	3.31	35	28	13	23	1.16
Luis Vizcaino	MIL	$3	2	0	3.69	32	21	11	31	1.01
Joey Eischen	MON	$3	1	1	3.68	22	17	3	16	0.91
Amaury Telemaco	PHI	$3	1	0	3.97	45	41	11	29	1.15
Chris Capuano	AZ	$2	2	0	2.88	25	20	5	20	1.00
Kent Mercker	ATL	$2	0	1	1.52	30	26	13	21	1.32
Randy Wolf	PHI	$2	7	0	5.36	97	103	39	84	1.46
Jose Jimenez	COL	$2	2	1	4.10	64	78	16	24	1.48
Todd Vanpoppel	CIN	$2	2	0	4.55	36	31	6	25	1.04
Dave Veres	CHC	$2	2	1	4.00	27	28	4	22	1.19
Jared Fernandez	HOU	$2	3	0	3.99	38	37	12	19	1.28
Scott Linebrink	SD	$2	2	0	3.16	37	33	15	37	1.30
Ryan Wagner	CIN	$2	2	0	1.66	22	13	12	25	1.15
Chad Cordero	MON	$2	1	1	1.64	11	4	3	12	0.64
Steve Kline	STL	$2	2	0	3.94	32	27	9	19	1.13
John Franco	NYM	$2	0	2	2.93	25	24	12	13	1.46
Paul Wilson	CIN	$2	3	0	4.66	75	80	28	43	1.43
Mike Remlinger	CHC	$1	2	0	3.34	35	30	16	34	1.31
Dan Wheeler	NYM	$1	1	1	4.10	42	43	15	30	1.39
Chad Fox	FLA	$1	2	0	2.91	34	27	21	37	1.41
Stephen Randolph	AZ	$1	5	0	4.32	33	27	24	27	1.53
Edwin Jackson	LA	$1	2	0	2.45	22	17	11	19	1.27
Brad Lidge	HOU	$1	2	0	4.58	37	27	18	44	1.21
Kyle Farnsworth	CHC	$1	1	0	4.12	39	30	18	48	1.22
Kevin Correia	SF	$1	3	0	3.66	39	41	18	28	1.50
Zach Day	MON	$1	5	0	4.91	66	73	27	31	1.52
Mike Gallo	HOU	$1	1	0	3.00	30	28	10	16	1.27
Salomon Torres	PIT	$1	2	1	4.81	58	62	23	42	1.47
Leo Estrella	MIL	$1	5	3	6.58	38	51	17	11	1.78
Brian Boehringer	PIT	$1	2	0	3.66	32	28	15	28	1.34
Dave Burba	MIL	$1	1	0	3.35	38	33	18	32	1.36
Valerio Delossantos	PHI	$1	4	0	4.66	29	23	18	24	1.41
Kevin Gryboski	ATL	$1	2	0	1.50	18	16	10	13	1.44

3-Year Dollar Values - A.L. Hitters

NAME	TEAM	$VAL	AB	RUN	HR	RBI	SB	AVG	OBA	SLG
Ichiro Suzuki	SEA	$48	673	116	10	61	40	.328	.374	.440
Alex Rodriguez	TEX	$44	621	127	52	132	15	.305	.396	.615
Alfonso Soriano	NYY	$44	651	106	32	89	40	.287	.326	.506
Carlos Beltran	KC	$43	592	107	26	102	36	.294	.364	.512
Magglio Ordonez	CHW	$39	596	103	33	116	14	.314	.381	.558
Bret Boone	SEA	$34	618	106	32	122	11	.301	.359	.526
Manny Ramirez	BOS	$33	511	98	37	112	1	.325	.426	.612
Derek Jeter	NYY	$33	580	107	16	67	23	.309	.380	.450
Garret Anderson	ANA	$33	649	85	29	121	8	.303	.330	.519
Jason Giambi	NYY	$31	538	109	40	116	2	.302	.441	.594
Miguel Tejada	OAK	$29	640	104	31	117	9	.285	.339	.486
Shannon Stewart	MIN	$29	597	99	12	59	15	.309	.369	.455
Johnny Damon	BOS	$28	625	110	12	60	29	.271	.342	.403
Bernie Williams	NYY	$27	532	94	20	87	8	.305	.395	.480
Mike Cameron	SEA	$27	540	86	23	89	27	.253	.346	.451
Carlos Delgado	TOR	$27	550	107	38	118	1	.286	.414	.561
Eric Chavez	OAK	$26	575	91	32	108	8	.282	.346	.522
Randy Winn	SEA	$26	545	81	10	67	21	.290	.349	.432
Mike Sweeney	KC	$26	474	80	23	89	7	.313	.393	.528
Carlos Lee	CHW	$25	558	86	27	92	12	.276	.336	.484
Rafael Palmeiro	TEX	$24	569	96	43	113	2	.269	.377	.547
Torii Hunter	MIN	$24	569	85	27	96	13	.266	.317	.484
Roberto Alomar	CHW	$24	560	87	12	64	19	.287	.361	.424
Jacque Jones	MIN	$23	523	76	19	68	10	.294	.337	.467
Aaron Boone	NYY	$22	526	76	21	82	20	.264	.328	.455
Corey Koskie	MIN	$22	507	82	18	80	16	.278	.374	.464
Nomar Garciaparra	BOS	$22	459	78	19	78	8	.304	.349	.523
Trot Nixon	BOS	$21	503	87	26	90	5	.279	.369	.514
Jorge Posada	NYY	$21	492	74	24	98	2	.275	.380	.487
Vernon Wells	TOR	$21	461	73	19	74	6	.298	.335	.501
David Eckstein	ANA	$20	547	83	5	45	22	.279	.350	.360
Alex Sanchez	DET	$20	340	40	1	23	32	.282	.324	.357
Cristian Guzman	MIN	$19	550	79	7	54	18	.280	.312	.406
Aubrey Huff	TB	$19	500	67	22	70	2	.294	.345	.494
Edgar Martinez	SEA	$19	432	65	21	91	2	.294	.411	.508
Raul Ibanez	KC	$19	461	70	18	82	4	.291	.347	.492
Kevin Millar	BOS	$19	477	68	20	79	1	.297	.362	.510
John Olerud	SEA	$19	555	80	18	93	1	.291	.392	.451
Juan Gonzalez	TEX	$19	379	61	22	82	1	.306	.348	.551
Todd Walker	BOS	$19	583	88	14	75	3	.293	.347	.439
Darin Erstad	ANA	$18	504	74	8	51	19	.267	.320	.367
Troy Glaus	ANA	$18	492	84	29	90	9	.250	.356	.486
Adam Kennedy	ANA	$18	467	61	9	47	17	.284	.335	.407
Frank Catalanotto	TOR	$17	388	67	9	45	9	.306	.369	.474

3-Year Dollar Values - A.L. Hitters

NAME	TEAM	$VAL	AB	RUN	HR	RBI	SB	AVG	OBA	SLG
Dmitri Young	DET	$17	434	57	19	60	4	.297	.357	.502
A.J. Pierzynski	MIN	$17	436	56	8	59	2	.301	.340	.449
Paul Konerko	CHW	$17	532	74	26	89	0	.276	.340	.474
Matt Lawton	CLE	$17	450	74	14	58	16	.257	.359	.411
Ellis Burks	CLE	$16	385	67	22	64	3	.286	.364	.520
Bob Higginson	DET	$16	485	65	14	62	13	.265	.345	.412
Carl Everett	CHW	$16	436	67	19	71	6	.272	.343	.467
Brad Fullmer	ANA	$15	385	59	15	59	7	.285	.349	.486
Tim Salmon	ANA	$15	495	75	19	70	6	.263	.373	.451
Michael Tucker	KC	$15	433	63	12	57	16	.254	.328	.419
Mike Young	TEX	$15	542	80	11	61	7	.277	.318	.413
Doug Mientkiewicz	MIN	$14	499	68	12	68	2	.290	.382	.437
Scott Spiezio	ANA	$14	490	69	14	73	6	.274	.342	.443
Mark McLemore	SEA	$14	352	55	5	45	21	.265	.364	.375
Melvin Mora	BAL	$14	446	68	14	53	11	.260	.356	.416
Marlon Anderson	TB	$14	514	64	8	59	11	.274	.326	.393
Travis Lee	TB	$14	544	68	17	77	5	.266	.340	.429
Jose Valentin	CHW	$14	472	74	27	72	7	.248	.320	.483
Luis Rivas	MIN	$14	451	62	6	42	19	.261	.312	.376
Carl Crawford	TB	$13	297	34	2	28	21	.275	.303	.365
Jason Varitek	BOS	$13	364	47	14	57	2	.273	.346	.457
Gabe Kapler	BOS	$13	341	51	8	44	13	.272	.335	.408
Joe Randa	KC	$13	544	67	13	78	2	.274	.331	.420
Chris Singleton	OAK	$13	388	54	6	44	13	.270	.309	.399
Rondell White	KC	$13	422	55	18	66	1	.276	.330	.459
Desi Relaford	KC	$12	377	56	7	46	14	.271	.335	.401
Tony Batista	BAL	$12	608	79	27	91	5	.239	.287	.428
Terrence Long	OAK	$12	567	75	14	71	5	.257	.310	.397
David Ortiz	BOS	$12	388	59	23	75	1	.268	.347	.529
Julio Lugo	TB	$12	444	67	11	42	11	.266	.328	.390
Jerry Hairston	BAL	$12	392	48	5	33	21	.253	.323	.361
Omar Vizquel	CLE	$11	481	71	6	47	13	.261	.330	.368
Jermaine Dye	OAK	$11	436	64	18	71	4	.252	.327	.428
Bill Mueller	BOS	$11	367	58	11	49	1	.299	.383	.474
Ruben Sierra	NYY	$11	357	45	15	57	3	.277	.322	.465
Jay Gibbons	BAL	$11	447	59	22	68	0	.259	.318	.470
Frank Thomas	CHW	$11	379	57	25	69	1	.257	.372	.513
Ramon Hernandez	OAK	$11	446	59	14	60	0	.255	.320	.404
Milton Bradley	CLE	$10	313	44	7	38	10	.271	.354	.425
Eric Hinske	TOR	$10	338	58	12	49	8	.263	.349	.462
Eric Owens	ANA	$10	342	41	3	28	15	.263	.310	.340
Jose Guillen	OAK	$9	287	39	14	43	2	.285	.332	.483
Jeff Cirillo	SEA	$9	424	49	8	53	7	.267	.324	.377
Dan Wilson	SEA	$8	351	37	7	43	1	.268	.302	.381

3-Year Dollar Values - A.L. Hitters

NAME	TEAM	$VAL	AB	RUN	HR	RBI	SB	AVG	OBA	SLG
Ben Grieve	TB	$8	396	54	11	51	5	.254	.364	.399
Carlos Guillen	SEA	$8	440	69	7	54	4	.265	.338	.381
Ben Molina	ANA	$8	387	34	8	53	0	.262	.294	.373
Rocco Baldelli	TB	$8	213	30	4	26	9	.289	.326	.416
Marty Cordova	BAL	$8	299	40	13	46	1	.274	.339	.465
Toby Hall	TB	$8	327	38	7	40	1	.263	.299	.391
Damian Jackson	BOS	$8	282	44	2	25	17	.249	.313	.344
Brian Roberts	BAL	$7	287	42	3	23	15	.258	.316	.348
Matt Lecroy	MIN	$7	189	21	9	34	0	.288	.336	.497
Rube Durazo	OAK	$7	312	57	16	54	0	.261	.379	.478
Greg Myers	TOR	$7	211	30	11	35	0	.267	.351	.461
Angel Berroa	KC	$7	232	36	6	27	9	.282	.334	.431
Brian Daubach	CHW	$7	345	47	16	57	1	.258	.350	.468
Bobby Kielty	TOR	$7	273	43	9	39	5	.261	.367	.428
BJ Surhoff	BAL	$7	293	35	5	36	4	.282	.337	.401
Josh Phelps	TOR	$7	225	34	12	42	1	.279	.356	.498
Ben Davis	SEA	$6	307	35	8	47	2	.243	.318	.375
Luis Matos	BAL	$6	190	29	6	19	8	.278	.333	.433
Brent Mayne	KC	$6	341	34	4	35	2	.255	.316	.333
Bubba Trammell	NYY	$6	316	41	14	51	1	.250	.328	.434
Jason Tyner	TB	$6	218	27	0	12	13	.263	.301	.308
Hank Blalock	TEX	$5	238	35	11	36	1	.282	.340	.482
Jeremy Giambi	BOS	$5	270	46	12	39	0	.260	.393	.456
Scott Hatteberg	OAK	$5	437	52	10	49	0	.261	.352	.394
Deivi Cruz	BAL	$5	492	50	9	55	2	.256	.284	.374
Rey Sanchez	SEA	$5	415	45	0	33	5	.274	.301	.324
Sandy Alomar	CHW	$5	232	23	5	28	0	.265	.292	.389
Einar Diaz	TEX	$5	364	39	3	36	1	.250	.297	.343
Ricky Gutierrez	CLE	$5	310	39	5	36	1	.283	.336	.376
Ron Gant	OAK	$4	201	36	10	33	3	.252	.331	.455
Hideki Matsui	NYY	$4	208	27	5	35	1	.287	.353	.435
Dustan Mohr	MIN	$4	261	37	7	28	4	.258	.318	.408
Shane Spencer	TEX	$4	322	37	9	43	2	.252	.323	.397
Herbert Perry	TEX	$4	253	34	10	37	2	.265	.326	.445
Mike Bordick	TOR	$4	313	36	7	40	6	.252	.319	.379
Karim Garcia	NYY	$4	164	21	11	32	0	.281	.312	.511
Nick Johnson	NYY	$4	256	41	10	38	2	.256	.377	.424
Eric Byrnes	OAK	$4	182	32	6	22	5	.258	.325	.456
Dave Dellucci	NYY	$4	221	29	7	31	5	.249	.329	.411
David Segui	BAL	$4	204	28	6	29	1	.281	.372	.424
Tom Wilson	TOR	$4	181	25	5	25	0	.255	.329	.391
Joe Crede	CHW	$3	262	32	10	39	1	.264	.306	.444
John Flaherty	NYY	$3	211	21	4	25	1	.253	.286	.383
Shane Halter	DET	$3	407	44	11	45	2	.249	.310	.406

3-Year Dollar Values - A.L. Hitters

NAME	TEAM	$VAL	AB	RUN	HR	RBI	SB	AVG	OBA	SLG
Mike Lamb	TEX	$3	212	33	4	23	1	.284	.342	.395
Damian Rolls	TB	$3	233	30	3	21	8	.262	.301	.359
Jeff Davanon	ANA	$3	150	22	6	19	6	.257	.336	.433
Tony Graffanino	CHW	$3	208	36	5	23	5	.271	.339	.423
Carlos Febles	KC	$3	280	40	4	21	10	.240	.312	.333
Carlos Pena	DET	$3	304	33	13	38	2	.246	.327	.448
Aaron Rowand	CHW	$3	194	28	6	24	2	.273	.325	.417
Jody Gerut	CLE	$3	160	22	7	25	1	.279	.336	.494
Doug Mirabelli	BOS	$3	168	20	8	24	0	.236	.318	.439
Terry Shumpert	TB	$3	187	27	4	17	6	.252	.316	.400
Mark Ellis	OAK	$3	300	45	5	29	3	.257	.331	.380
Chris Gomez	MIN	$2	312	34	6	35	2	.260	.298	.397
Reed Johnson	TOR	$2	138	26	3	17	2	.294	.353	.427
Larry Bigbie	BAL	$2	151	20	4	15	4	.272	.339	.398
Coco Crisp	CLE	$2	181	24	1	12	6	.265	.305	.361
Geronimo Gil	BAL	$2	216	19	5	22	1	.239	.287	.347
Aaron Guiel	KC	$2	198	31	6	30	1	.259	.326	.428
Kevin Mench	TEX	$2	164	22	6	24	1	.275	.341	.452
Brook Fordyce	BAL	$2	257	22	4	19	1	.242	.293	.343
Todd Greene	TEX	$2	138	16	7	17	0	.235	.253	.438
Mark Teixeira	TEX	$2	177	22	9	28	0	.259	.331	.480
Chris Woodward	TOR	$2	241	35	7	32	1	.261	.313	.427
Shawn Wooten	ANA	$2	202	21	6	28	1	.277	.318	.409
Orlando Hudson	TOR	$1	222	25	4	27	2	.270	.325	.409
Miguel Olivo	CHW	$1	112	13	2	11	2	.236	.287	.363
Casey Blake	CLE	$1	205	28	6	24	3	.254	.311	.402
Bill Haselman	BOS	$1	104	9	2	14	0	.260	.308	.359
Tom Prince	KC	$1	123	13	4	15	2	.219	.299	.371
Josh Bard	CLE	$1	131	11	4	16	0	.239	.285	.374
Rusty Greer	TEX	$1	148	21	3	15	1	.283	.348	.419
Armando Rios	CHW	$1	210	21	6	28	1	.253	.314	.393
Brent Abernathy	KC	$1	267	31	2	25	6	.245	.295	.327
Greg Colbrunn	SEA	$1	109	16	6	17	0	.310	.367	.562
Damion Easley	TB	$1	332	38	7	34	4	.235	.306	.357
Chone Figgins	ANA	$1	84	13	0	9	5	.290	.337	.361
A.J. Hinch	DET	$1	131	14	5	18	1	.212	.278	.378
Robert Machado	BAL	$1	132	13	2	13	0	.248	.303	.362
Al Martin	TB	$1	174	20	3	23	4	.245	.319	.371
Victor Martinez	CLE	$1	64	6	1	7	0	.288	.343	.345
Craig Monroe	DET	$1	168	21	9	25	2	.231	.281	.430
Rey Ordonez	TB	$1	346	33	2	36	2	.258	.299	.348
Mike Difelice	KC	$1	178	20	3	18	1	.225	.279	.344
Benji Gil	ANA	$1	172	19	4	23	3	.268	.296	.416
John Mabry	SEA	$1	157	18	7	26	1	.240	.311	.426

3-Year Dollar Values - N.L. Hitters

NAME	TEAM	$VAL	AB	RUN	HR	RBI	SB	AVG	OBA	SLG
Vladimir Guerrero	MON	$43	536	95	33	99	29	.324	.405	.581
Juan Pierre	FLA	$43	626	99	1	44	53	.307	.358	.377
Barry Bonds	SF	$42	423	119	55	112	10	.345	.542	.808
Todd Helton	COL	$39	574	125	37	124	4	.341	.440	.632
Bob Abreu	PHI	$39	579	106	24	99	30	.299	.405	.511
Albert Pujols	STL	$38	590	122	38	127	3	.334	.412	.613
Gary Sheffield	ATL	$35	528	102	33	105	13	.317	.414	.569
Sammy Sosa	CHC	$33	550	122	51	124	1	.299	.400	.631
Lance Berkman	HOU	$32	564	109	34	116	7	.304	.416	.572
Luis Gonzalez	AZ	$32	571	103	37	116	5	.307	.411	.576
Chipper Jones	ATL	$32	558	102	30	103	6	.321	.421	.553
Shawn Green	LA	$31	604	105	37	108	11	.287	.371	.539
Jeff Bagwell	HOU	$30	592	110	36	109	10	.286	.390	.537
Larry Walker	COL	$30	476	96	27	102	9	.325	.431	.583
Brian Giles	SD	$30	522	101	32	95	11	.302	.427	.576
Edgar Renteria	STL	$29	541	76	11	80	24	.300	.360	.433
Jim Thome	PHI	$29	528	104	49	124	0	.286	.414	.621
Luis Castillo	FLA	$28	579	87	3	41	34	.295	.364	.367
Cliff Floyd	NYM	$27	480	89	26	83	12	.300	.386	.547
Jimmy Rollins	PHI	$26	640	88	11	59	32	.261	.316	.396
Jeff Kent	HOU	$26	578	88	27	102	6	.303	.363	.528
Scott Rolen	STL	$26	564	94	28	107	12	.280	.372	.510
Orlando Cabrera	MON	$25	605	74	13	77	23	.279	.331	.424
Preston Wilson	COL	$25	526	81	27	92	18	.267	.335	.489
Derrek Lee	FLA	$25	560	90	26	84	15	.274	.368	.492
Ivan Rodriguez	FLA	$25	454	76	20	70	8	.306	.357	.516
Kenny Lofton	CHC	$24	532	95	12	54	25	.273	.342	.421
Andruw Jones	ATL	$24	593	99	35	105	8	.264	.338	.495
Raul Mondesi	AZ	$24	555	87	26	81	22	.251	.331	.456
Rafael Furcal	ATL	$24	541	88	9	46	25	.282	.335	.407
Richie Sexson	MIL	$24	591	92	40	117	1	.274	.362	.534
Jim Edmonds	STL	$24	474	93	32	94	3	.297	.406	.580
Roger Cedeno	NYM	$24	506	71	7	42	31	.274	.325	.373
Reggie Sanders	PIT	$24	466	78	29	87	16	.265	.335	.521
Ryan Klesko	SD	$23	492	81	27	92	10	.282	.377	.516
Steve Finley	AZ	$23	505	77	20	77	14	.283	.357	.477
Eric Young	SF	$22	525	78	8	35	30	.271	.335	.385
Ray Durham	SF	$21	528	93	14	56	19	.279	.358	.454
Jason Kendall	PIT	$21	579	76	6	52	12	.291	.362	.377
Moises Alou	CHC	$21	521	71	21	87	5	.295	.364	.479
Jose Vidro	MON	$21	533	87	16	73	3	.315	.382	.482
Jose Cruz	SF	$20	527	82	24	75	15	.257	.338	.463
Juan Encarnacion	FLA	$20	534	70	18	77	16	.263	.312	.437
Jeff Conine	FLA	$20	517	69	16	85	8	.289	.346	.450

3-Year Dollar Values - N.L. Hitters

NAME	TEAM	$VAL	AB	RUN	HR	RBI	SB	AVG	OBA	SLG
Craig Biggio	HOU	$19	607	105	17	63	10	.270	.355	.424
Mike Piazza	NYM	$19	405	62	27	75	0	.289	.373	.544
Paul Loduca	LA	$18	536	70	14	69	2	.289	.345	.433
Mike Lowell	FLA	$18	547	76	25	99	3	.278	.345	.481
Rich Aurilia	SF	$18	560	85	22	72	1	.288	.335	.472
Placido Polanco	PHI	$17	535	83	9	50	10	.295	.341	.409
Richard Hidalgo	HOU	$17	471	72	21	72	6	.276	.356	.487
Jay Payton	COL	$17	469	69	17	61	6	.290	.339	.468
Aramis Ramirez	CHC	$17	577	70	26	96	3	.270	.319	.466
Javy Lopez	ATL	$17	414	55	24	76	0	.280	.336	.507
Phil Nevin	SD	$16	393	60	22	76	3	.294	.364	.508
J.D. Drew	STL	$16	362	67	20	57	8	.286	.378	.514
Mark Kotsay	SD	$16	489	71	11	52	10	.283	.356	.427
Tino Martinez	STL	$16	525	73	23	86	2	.272	.339	.459
Marquis Grissom	SF	$15	459	65	19	66	8	.269	.299	.458
Tony Womack	CHC	$15	473	66	3	36	23	.258	.301	.339
Fred McGriff	LA	$15	444	55	25	82	1	.280	.359	.503
Dave Roberts	LA	$15	274	41	2	17	28	.265	.343	.338
Sean Casey	CIN	$14	510	65	11	70	3	.289	.352	.413
Shea Hillenbrand	AZ	$14	539	69	17	76	3	.280	.314	.442
Pat Burrell	PHI	$14	549	74	28	90	1	.251	.345	.475
Brian Jordan	LA	$14	418	58	16	68	2	.292	.343	.472
Fernando Vina	STL	$14	504	68	5	44	13	.281	.339	.379
Adam Dunn	CIN	$13	387	69	24	57	10	.241	.379	.484
Jeromy Burnitz	LA	$13	502	77	28	77	5	.236	.321	.455
Benito Santiago	SF	$13	452	49	11	58	3	.273	.312	.414
Doug Glanville	CHC	$12	434	49	8	33	17	.258	.287	.359
Alex S. Gonzalez	CHC	$12	562	69	18	65	9	.244	.303	.406
Edgardo Alfonzo	SF	$12	487	66	15	62	5	.270	.350	.418
Adrian Beltre	LA	$12	540	60	19	72	7	.253	.301	.421
Mark Grudzielanek	CHC	$12	519	71	8	48	5	.284	.327	.390
Jose Hernandez	PIT	$11	529	66	21	69	3	.254	.314	.423
Geoff Jenkins	MIL	$11	376	59	19	62	2	.273	.349	.495
Corey Patterson	CHC	$11	351	49	10	41	13	.263	.296	.422
Craig Wilson	PIT	$11	278	41	16	46	3	.272	.363	.496
Mike Lieberthal	PHI	$11	368	45	10	48	0	.289	.356	.437
Randall Simon	CHC	$11	383	42	14	64	0	.293	.321	.447
Vinny Castilla	ATL	$10	541	63	20	76	2	.256	.295	.425
Robert Fick	ATL	$10	455	60	16	68	0	.270	.335	.441
Brad Wilkerson	MON	$10	376	60	13	47	7	.261	.368	.452
Marcus Giles	ATL	$10	336	55	13	41	6	.285	.362	.476
Gary Matthews	SD	$10	406	63	9	41	12	.249	.330	.385
Junior Spivey	AZ	$10	355	63	11	50	6	.279	.363	.453
Scott Podsednik	MIL	$10	195	34	3	22	14	.309	.375	.440

3-Year Dollar Values - N.L. Hitters

NAME	TEAM	$VAL	AB	RUN	HR	RBI	SB	AVG	OBA	SLG
Mark Loretta	SD	$9	419	49	6	43	2	.304	.366	.407
Tom Goodwin	CHC	$8	204	33	2	17	19	.254	.307	.344
Eric Karros	CHC	$8	433	44	13	59	3	.263	.321	.407
Craig Counsell	AZ	$8	399	60	3	37	8	.267	.347	.343
Robin Ventura	LA	$8	438	60	21	70	2	.242	.357	.427
Dangelo Jimenez	CIN	$8	433	58	7	45	6	.267	.344	.381
Matt Stairs	PIT	$8	305	46	18	53	1	.262	.366	.500
Neifi Perez	SF	$7	488	58	4	42	7	.258	.285	.350
Todd Hollandsworth	FLA	$7	258	36	8	35	5	.288	.345	.481
Jason Larue	CIN	$7	365	44	13	48	2	.238	.316	.411
Juan Uribe	COL	$7	385	49	8	45	6	.258	.298	.408
Todd Zeile	MON	$7	445	56	13	64	1	.260	.345	.395
Charles Johnson	COL	$7	350	39	15	57	0	.239	.316	.433
Austin Kearns	CIN	$7	221	35	9	38	4	.293	.388	.480
Jose Macias	MON	$7	366	45	6	37	11	.255	.298	.378
Royce Clayton	MIL	$7	419	54	9	45	7	.246	.304	.362
John Vanderwal	MIL	$7	333	46	11	45	3	.264	.351	.448
Andres Galarraga	SF	$7	321	39	13	50	1	.270	.339	.448
Timoniel Perez	NYM	$7	343	37	6	37	5	.275	.311	.394
Michael Barrett	MON	$6	358	39	9	39	3	.246	.303	.391
Damian Miller	CHC	$6	343	40	11	42	0	.252	.329	.408
Geoff Blum	HOU	$6	414	51	10	51	4	.259	.324	.387
Eli Marrero	STL	$6	236	37	9	36	7	.257	.314	.433
Brad Ausmus	HOU	$6	440	48	5	44	4	.239	.304	.328
Pokey Reese	PIT	$6	318	35	5	34	14	.241	.303	.338
Ken Griffey	CIN	$5	242	36	14	38	1	.271	.364	.512
Kevin Young	PIT	$5	333	40	11	41	7	.236	.315	.397
Rob Mackowiak	PIT	$5	258	36	9	29	6	.256	.329	.426
David Bell	PHI	$5	440	59	13	58	1	.246	.314	.391
Mark Grace	AZ	$5	303	41	8	47	1	.268	.359	.416
Ron Belliard	COL	$5	367	57	7	37	5	.255	.322	.392
Chris Stynes	COL	$4	333	49	8	44	3	.261	.326	.404
Jack Wilson	PIT	$4	492	60	5	45	4	.246	.292	.330
Rickey Henderson	LA	$4	210	39	5	21	12	.224	.362	.346
Danny Bautista	AZ	$4	220	26	5	28	3	.296	.344	.433
Wil Cordero	MON	$4	288	36	9	41	1	.267	.338	.414
Alex Gonzalez	FLA	$4	398	41	10	48	2	.250	.307	.400
Barry Larkin	CIN	$4	301	47	4	27	6	.257	.328	.372
Brian Buchanan	SD	$4	207	29	10	30	3	.269	.336	.470
Orlando Palmeiro	STL	$4	270	34	2	29	5	.272	.341	.342
Tony Clark	NYM	$4	319	40	12	49	0	.249	.324	.424
Mike Matheny	STL	$4	379	38	6	41	1	.238	.304	.328
Ramon Vazquez	SD	$4	293	37	2	22	6	.266	.339	.347
Jason Phillips	NYM	$3	143	17	4	20	0	.299	.371	.443

3-Year Dollar Values - N.L. Hitters

NAME	TEAM	$VAL	AB	RUN	HR	RBI	SB	AVG	OBA	SLG
J.T. Snow	SF	$3	346	46	7	46	0	.255	.365	.384
Jose Vizcaino	HOU	$3	284	35	3	26	2	.283	.323	.374
Matt Williams	AZ	$3	252	35	11	40	1	.266	.319	.459
Julio Franco	ATL	$3	208	31	5	24	2	.289	.364	.413
Russ Branyan	CIN	$3	290	40	18	45	2	.227	.319	.464
Marlon Byrd	PHI	$3	177	29	3	15	4	.298	.359	.415
Chris Richard	COL	$3	221	31	7	28	4	.256	.324	.423
Lee Stevens	MIL	$3	300	42	13	51	1	.229	.325	.422
Cesar Izturis	LA	$3	377	36	1	27	8	.246	.270	.319
Morgan Ensberg	HOU	$3	173	28	9	26	3	.279	.369	.495
Mike Redmond	FLA	$3	174	17	2	18	0	.291	.356	.380
Kerry Robinson	STL	$3	192	27	1	15	8	.264	.303	.341
Ty Wigginton	NYM	$3	230	30	6	30	5	.263	.324	.418
Endy Chavez	MON	$2	229	30	2	20	7	.254	.293	.361
Wes Helms	MIL	$2	301	35	13	42	1	.247	.310	.436
Marvin Benard	SF	$2	195	30	5	20	5	.259	.310	.412
Mark Derosa	ATL	$2	214	30	5	22	2	.280	.332	.400
Orlando Merced	HOU	$2	200	25	5	28	4	.262	.323	.417
Abraham O. Nunez	PIT	$2	288	32	2	24	7	.248	.316	.339
Troy O'Leary	CHC	$2	263	32	7	38	2	.251	.319	.398
Gary Bennett	SD	$2	243	22	3	26	1	.250	.305	.333
Brady Clark	MIL	$2	174	21	4	23	6	.259	.332	.385
Ramon E. Martinez	CHC	$2	288	35	4	32	1	.267	.329	.373
Mark Quinn	SD	$2	176	22	6	24	4	.264	.298	.446
Brian Schneider	MON	$2	194	20	5	27	0	.252	.326	.422
Tsuyoshi Shinjo	NYM	$2	292	33	7	33	3	.246	.299	.370
Greg Vaughn	COL	$2	257	37	12	39	5	.208	.317	.399
Alex Cintron	AZ	$2	177	27	4	18	1	.302	.353	.462
Jolbert Cabrera	LA	$2	239	34	2	28	6	.257	.310	.370
Jeffrey Hammonds	SF	$2	251	30	6	25	3	.252	.327	.408
Gregg Zaun	COL	$2	159	16	4	21	1	.250	.314	.386
Mark Bellhorn	COL	$1	256	41	10	29	4	.234	.352	.415
Sean Burroughs	SD	$1	237	27	3	23	3	.282	.343	.381
Joe McEwing	NYM	$1	252	31	4	24	5	.246	.304	.351
Kelly Stinnett	PHI	$1	155	17	5	19	1	.243	.321	.401
Daryle Ward	LA	$1	258	23	7	40	0	.259	.308	.401
Andy Fox	FLA	$1	208	25	2	19	11	.233	.325	.319
Tyler Houston	PHI	$1	217	26	7	31	0	.283	.330	.440
Brian L. Hunter	HOU	$1	148	22	2	16	6	.264	.323	.378
Vance Wilson	NYM	$1	163	17	4	24	0	.250	.301	.373
Chad Moeller	AZ	$1	133	16	3	16	0	.268	.345	.427
Carlos Baerga	AZ	$1	130	16	2	19	2	.316	.360	.424
Alex Cora	LA	$1	380	38	4	30	4	.247	.306	.348
Felipe Lopez	CIN	$1	219	28	5	23	6	.232	.300	.369

3-Year Dollar Values - N.L. Hitters

Quinton McCracken	AZ	$1	205	28	1	20	3	.273	.328	.381
Greg Norton	COL	$1	191	23	9	36	2	.252	.320	.462
Josh Paul	CHC	$1	89	12	1	11	3	.255	.319	.346
Todd Pratt	PHI	$1	135	16	4	16	1	.245	.383	.404
Ricky Ledee	PHI	$1	233	34	8	35	1	.236	.326	.416
Eddie Perez	MIL	$1	159	11	4	16	0	.258	.291	.386
Reggie Taylor	CIN	$1	158	20	5	19	6	.236	.279	.393
Mo Vaughn	NYM	$1	189	26	10	29	0	.249	.345	.438
Robby Hammock	AZ	$1	65	10	3	9	1	.282	.343	.477
Yorvit Torrealba	SF	$1	113	13	2	15	0	.270	.331	.400
Eduardo Perez	STL	$1	136	23	7	22	2	.253	.337	.469
Wiki Gonzalez	SD	$0	130	11	3	19	1	.239	.321	.363
Todd Hundley	LA	$0	182	19	10	26	0	.198	.289	.398
Jose Reyes	NYM	$0	92	16	2	11	4	.307	.334	.434
Bobby Estalella	COL	$0	116	15	6	19	1	.200	.292	.418
Dave Ross	LA	$0	45	7	4	7	0	.254	.340	.559
Ruben Rivera	SF	$0	157	20	5	17	4	.232	.308	.378
Adam Everett	HOU	$0	160	21	3	18	4	.243	.314	.350
Ramon Castro	FLA	$0	55	6	4	9	0	.249	.321	.485
Miguel Cairo	STL	$0	200	31	3	24	2	.259	.315	.379

3-Year Dollar Values - A.L. Pitchers

NAME	TEAM	$VAL	W	SV	ERA	IP	H	BB	K	RATIO
Mariano Rivera	NYY	$38	3	39	2.18	66	52	10	62	0.95
Keith Foulke	OAK	$35	5	32	2.42	82	60	18	74	0.95
Troy Percival	ANA	$33	3	37	2.64	54	37	22	62	1.08
Eddie Guardado	MIN	$31	4	33	3.10	67	50	18	66	1.02
Byung Kim	BOS	$30	7	24	2.84	102	75	34	102	1.08
Armando Benitez	SEA	$29	4	32	3.03	72	55	35	82	1.24
Pedro Martinez	BOS	$29	14	0	2.27	168	125	36	203	0.96
Kazuhiro Sasaki	SEA	$27	2	31	3.13	54	41	15	55	1.04
Tim Hudson	OAK	$27	16	0	3.01	238	217	64	165	1.18
Barry Zito	OAK	$26	18	0	3.17	225	184	79	178	1.17
Jamie Moyer	SEA	$25	18	0	3.33	219	195	52	132	1.13
Mike Mussina	NYY	$25	17	0	3.52	220	201	43	197	1.11
Roy Halladay	TOR	$24	15	0	3.10	204	191	39	156	1.13
Billy Koch	CHW	$23	6	30	4.37	72	67	35	63	1.42
Mark Mulder	OAK	$23	18	0	3.36	208	192	47	147	1.15
Derek Lowe	BOS	$22	14	8	3.49	172	162	49	106	1.23
Mark Buehrle	CHW	$20	16	0	3.67	230	225	56	126	1.22
Bartolo Colon	CHW	$19	16	0	3.62	233	221	75	174	1.27
Freddy Garcia	SEA	$17	15	0	3.94	221	207	67	163	1.24
Roger Clemens	NYY	$16	17	0	3.89	204	192	63	198	1.25
Jarrod Washburn	ANA	$16	13	0	3.78	202	195	54	128	1.23
Jorge Julio	BAL	$16	2	20	3.22	50	47	23	43	1.39
Joel Pineiro	SEA	$16	12	0	3.28	161	144	50	114	1.21
Kelvim Escobar	TOR	$15	8	14	4.02	128	119	58	122	1.38
Tim Wakefield	BOS	$15	10	2	3.63	178	157	64	150	1.24
Bob Wickman	CLE	$14	2	17	3.08	34	34	8	34	1.24
Andy Pettitte	NYY	$13	16	0	3.82	181	198	41	147	1.32
Tom Gordon	CHW	$13	3	13	3.27	54	44	21	69	1.19
Latroy Hawkins	MIN	$13	5	10	2.96	70	64	23	58	1.24
Brad Radke	MIN	$13	13	0	4.31	186	200	24	106	1.21
David Wells	NYY	$12	13	0	4.04	173	191	28	99	1.26
Danys Baez	CLE	$12	6	10	3.92	97	86	41	83	1.31
Rick Reed	MIN	$12	11	0	4.21	175	186	28	111	1.22
Arthur Rhodes	SEA	$11	7	3	2.62	64	48	14	71	0.97
C.C. Sabathia	CLE	$11	14	0	4.11	196	179	82	154	1.33
Jon Lieber	NYY	$11	9	0	3.76	124	126	17	78	1.15
John Burkett	BOS	$10	12	0	4.15	191	196	55	139	1.31
Damaso Marte	CHW	$10	2	7	2.65	59	43	21	66	1.08
Ryan Franklin	SEA	$10	8	0	3.69	136	131	36	75	1.22
Shigetoshi Hasegawa	SEA	$10	5	6	2.80	66	58	22	37	1.21
Cory Lidle	TOR	$10	11	0	4.41	191	192	48	114	1.26
Kevin Appier	KC	$9	11	0	4.10	169	164	56	120	1.30
Esteban Loaiza	CHW	$9	14	0	4.35	189	209	43	135	1.33
Steve Karsay	NYY	$9	3	7	2.80	59	53	18	49	1.22

3-Year Dollar Values - A.L. Pitchers

NAME	TEAM	$VAL	W	SV	ERA	IP	H	BB	K	RATIO
Ramon Ortiz	ANA	$9	15	0	4.39	202	207	68	130	1.36
Mike Timlin	BOS	$9	5	2	3.48	84	77	14	54	1.07
Scott Williamson	BOS	$9	3	10	3.47	46	34	24	53	1.25
Johan Santana	MIN	$9	7	0	3.27	104	87	37	111	1.20
Francisco Cordero	TEX	$8	2	8	2.55	44	35	18	44	1.22
Lance Carter	TB	$8	3	9	3.71	33	29	8	20	1.11
Eric Milton	MIN	$8	10	0	4.46	136	137	30	95	1.22
Jeff Zimmerman	TEX	$8	1	9	2.40	24	16	5	24	0.90
Jeff Weaver	NYY	$8	10	1	4.40	196	213	54	126	1.36
Ben Weber	ANA	$7	6	2	2.86	76	73	25	43	1.30
Buddy Groom	BAL	$7	2	5	3.32	58	55	12	45	1.16
Juan Acevedo	TOR	$7	1	11	4.05	58	63	25	39	1.52
Jeff Nelson	NYY	$6	4	5	3.41	55	39	31	70	1.27
John Thomson	TEX	$6	9	0	4.64	164	173	39	104	1.29
Joe Mays	MIN	$6	10	0	4.51	153	159	41	70	1.31
Scot Shields	ANA	$6	3	0	2.54	70	59	22	49	1.16
Jeff Suppan	BOS	$6	11	0	4.62	210	224	64	113	1.37
Chad Bradford	OAK	$6	4	2	3.00	63	60	17	51	1.22
Al Levine	KC	$6	5	3	3.08	70	66	30	37	1.37
Brian Anderson	KC	$6	8	0	4.49	162	181	34	74	1.32
Curt Leskanic	KC	$5	2	6	3.02	41	34	20	38	1.32
Jon Garland	CHW	$5	10	0	4.34	167	166	71	94	1.42
Kyle Lohse	MIN	$5	10	0	4.66	157	165	48	106	1.35
Mike Macdougal	KC	$5	1	9	4.28	30	29	14	25	1.47
Chris Hammond	NYY	$5	3	0	1.81	46	39	14	36	1.15
Brendan Donnelly	ANA	$5	1	1	1.81	41	29	14	44	1.05
Ted Lilly	OAK	$5	7	0	4.48	133	128	46	112	1.31
Ramiro Mendoza	BOS	$5	6	3	4.41	86	96	19	56	1.34
Aaron Sele	ANA	$4	10	0	4.54	166	180	51	83	1.40
Jason Johnson	BAL	$4	8	0	4.24	172	184	65	110	1.44
David Riske	CLE	$4	2	3	3.22	51	40	24	59	1.26
Ricardo Rincon	OAK	$4	4	1	3.42	55	45	21	46	1.20
Kerry Ligtenberg	BAL	$4	3	1	3.10	62	54	25	51	1.28
Darrell May	KC	$4	5	0	4.37	114	114	34	70	1.30
Cliff Politte	TOR	$4	2	4	4.10	50	44	17	45	1.24
Ismael Valdes	TEX	$4	8	0	4.73	158	173	42	83	1.36
Chan Ho Park	TEX	$3	8	0	4.59	136	124	63	118	1.37
John Rocker	TB	$3	2	8	4.99	31	30	18	36	1.56
Matt Anderson	DET	$3	2	8	5.48	30	33	12	24	1.47
Omar Daal	BAL	$3	9	0	4.65	147	158	46	88	1.39
Giovanni Carrara	SEA	$3	5	0	3.73	68	65	23	46	1.29
Victor Zambrano	TB	$3	9	1	4.48	118	108	63	88	1.45
Francisco Rodriguez	ANA	$3	3	1	2.84	31	18	12	36	0.98
Rodrigo Lopez	BAL	$3	7	0	4.53	115	120	35	80	1.35

3-Year Dollar Values - A.L. Pitchers

NAME	TEAM	$VAL	W	SV	ERA	IP	H	BB	K	RATIO
Kenny Rogers	MIN	$3	10	0	4.64	176	196	56	99	1.44
Steve W. Sparks	OAK	$3	7	1	4.56	176	199	55	89	1.44
Aquilino Lopez	TOR	$3	0	5	3.42	25	19	11	21	1.25
John Lackey	ANA	$2	6	0	4.29	104	112	33	73	1.39
Robert Person	BOS	$2	6	0	4.67	103	90	46	85	1.32
Rafael Soriano	SEA	$2	1	1	2.96	34	25	9	33	1.02
John Halama	OAK	$2	6	0	4.18	107	120	31	57	1.42
Scott Sullivan	CHW	$2	6	0	4.28	82	78	32	72	1.35
Jamie Walker	DET	$2	2	1	3.47	36	31	9	28	1.09
Damian Moss	BAL	$2	7	0	4.22	118	109	63	66	1.46
Pat Hentgen	BAL	$2	3	0	4.26	82	77	28	48	1.29
Antonio Osuna	NYY	$2	3	4	4.40	41	43	16	40	1.46
Alan Embree	BOS	$2	3	1	4.41	57	54	18	62	1.25
Casey Fossum	BOS	$2	5	1	4.42	77	80	28	63	1.40
Jim Mecir	OAK	$2	3	2	4.23	56	54	23	46	1.38
Willis Roberts	BAL	$2	6	2	4.56	82	87	34	57	1.48
Julio Mateo	SEA	$1	1	0	3.37	36	30	8	29	1.06
Gabe White	NYY	$1	4	0	4.58	56	54	14	39	1.22
Jeremy Affeldt	KC	$1	3	1	4.19	68	70	25	55	1.40
Josh Towers	TOR	$1	5	0	4.88	77	91	9	38	1.30
Felix Heredia	NYY	$1	3	0	3.66	58	57	25	35	1.40
Scott Schoeneweis	CHW	$1	7	0	4.87	129	136	47	75	1.42
Tony Fiore	MIN	$1	4	0	3.94	46	38	22	29	1.33
Jeremi Gonzalez	TB	$1	2	0	3.92	52	44	23	32	1.28
Danny Patterson	DET	$1	2	1	3.68	29	28	6	16	1.18
Jason Bere	CLE	$1	4	0	4.71	93	91	35	80	1.35
Gil Meche	SEA	$1	5	0	4.59	62	62	21	43	1.34
Jason Davis	CLE	$1	3	0	4.44	60	61	17	32	1.30
Joe Kennedy	TB	$1	6	0	4.98	149	164	45	88	1.40
Brandon Lyon	BOS	$1	3	3	4.98	61	71	18	38	1.45
J.C. Romero	MIN	$1	4	0	4.17	70	66	33	55	1.43
B.J. Ryan	BAL	$1	3	1	4.13	54	47	30	58	1.42
Mark Wohlers	CLE	$1	2	2	4.53	46	47	17	33	1.37

3-Year Dollar Values - N.L. Pitchers

NAME	TEAM	$VAL	W	SV	ERA	IP	H	BB	K	RATIO
Billy Wagner	HOU	$40	2	39	2.29	75	49	21	91	0.94
Eric Gagne	LA	$40	4	36	3.10	105	79	27	127	1.00
John Smoltz	ATL	$36	2	37	2.60	68	53	14	72	0.99
Curt Schilling	AZ	$32	18	0	3.06	228	200	35	268	1.03
Jose Mesa	PHI	$30	4	37	3.77	68	67	30	56	1.43
Ugueth Urbina	FLA	$30	2	32	3.13	68	53	25	79	1.14
Randy Johnson	AZ	$29	17	0	2.74	208	168	55	277	1.07
Jason Isringhausen	STL	$28	2	29	2.51	60	44	19	61	1.06
Robb Nen	SF	$27	3	29	2.61	50	41	14	58	1.08
Greg Maddux	ATL	$24	16	0	3.22	217	213	34	138	1.14
Mike Williams	PHI	$24	3	32	4.30	63	60	32	47	1.46
Trevor Hoffman	SD	$23	2	27	3.00	43	36	14	48	1.15
Javier Vazquez	MON	$22	13	0	3.52	228	213	50	209	1.15
Jason Schmidt	SF	$21	14	0	3.19	181	146	59	182	1.13
Roy Oswalt	HOU	$20	14	0	2.92	167	152	38	153	1.14
Danny Graves	CIN	$20	6	22	4.45	116	129	28	56	1.35
Jose Jimenez	COL	$19	3	26	4.42	77	90	21	43	1.45
Matt Morris	STL	$18	17	0	3.42	200	197	52	159	1.25
Kerry Wood	CHC	$18	13	0	3.41	200	149	94	233	1.22
Octavio Dotel	HOU	$17	6	4	2.33	96	63	34	120	1.01
Russ Ortiz	ATL	$16	17	0	3.57	215	185	95	152	1.30
Randy Wolf	PHI	$16	12	0	3.70	191	166	63	167	1.20
Tim Worrell	SF	$16	5	13	2.87	76	67	30	61	1.27
Braden Looper	FLA	$16	4	15	3.44	79	73	29	54	1.28
Woody Williams	STL	$15	14	0	3.68	181	176	45	128	1.22
Hideo Nomo	LA	$15	15	0	3.63	212	178	98	197	1.30
Wade Miller	HOU	$15	15	0	3.60	188	167	71	163	1.27
Kevin Millwood	PHI	$14	13	0	3.77	187	172	57	144	1.23
Mike Dejean	STL	$14	3	16	3.53	81	76	39	68	1.42
Kevin Brown	LA	$14	9	0	2.85	130	115	38	116	1.18
Roberto Hernandez	ATL	$13	4	18	4.25	60	64	26	43	1.51
Joe Borowski	CHC	$13	2	12	2.99	55	47	15	55	1.14
Mark Prior	CHC	$13	8	0	2.74	109	94	29	131	1.12
Al Leiter	NYM	$13	13	0	3.58	191	183	69	151	1.32
Odalis Perez	LA	$13	11	0	3.92	168	160	41	122	1.20
Antonio Alfonseca	CHC	$12	3	16	4.31	67	72	25	51	1.45
Vicente Padilla	PHI	$12	10	0	3.51	150	143	42	97	1.24
Tom Glavine	NYM	$12	14	0	3.62	209	209	79	108	1.38
Steve Trachsel	NYM	$11	13	0	3.86	184	181	60	120	1.31
Miguel Batista	AZ	$11	10	0	3.75	173	161	62	115	1.29
Brian Lawrence	SD	$11	9	0	3.83	179	181	47	116	1.28
Estaban Yan	STL	$10	4	14	4.86	66	73	20	57	1.41
Matt Clement	CHC	$10	12	0	4.20	192	168	82	173	1.30
Brad Penny	FLA	$10	11	0	4.08	177	175	53	128	1.29
Paul Quantrill	LA	$9	6	1	2.50	79	76	17	52	1.17

3-Year Dollar Values - N.L. Pitchers

NAME	TEAM	$VAL	W	SV	ERA	IP	H	BB	K	RATIO
Steve Kline	STL	$9	3	6	2.92	66	54	26	42	1.23
Kip Wells	PIT	$9	11	0	3.77	176	171	69	127	1.36
Rod Beck	SD	$9	3	9	3.25	39	34	13	32	1.21
A.J. Burnett	FLA	$9	8	0	3.70	133	105	63	117	1.26
Matt Mantei	AZ	$9	2	10	3.24	30	24	11	35	1.18
Dave Weathers	NYM	$9	4	4	2.79	84	74	36	67	1.31
Rocky Biddle	MON	$8	5	12	4.81	93	93	43	68	1.47
Felix Rodriguez	SF	$8	8	1	2.90	70	55	28	65	1.19
Kirk Rueter	SF	$8	13	0	4.00	182	196	55	67	1.38
Vladimir Nunez	FLA	$8	3	7	3.77	67	60	24	49	1.26
Livan Hernandez	MON	$8	13	0	4.26	225	241	70	150	1.38
Mark Redman	FLA	$8	8	0	3.98	151	150	44	98	1.29
Scott Stewart	MON	$8	3	7	3.54	52	48	15	45	1.23
Mike Stanton	NYM	$8	6	4	3.18	68	63	25	52	1.30
Sidney Ponson	SF	$8	10	0	4.17	177	181	54	113	1.33
Dave Veres	CHC	$8	3	7	3.77	60	53	23	52	1.27
Paul Byrd	ATL	$7	8	0	4.06	110	115	21	60	1.23
Ben Sheets	MIL	$7	11	0	4.41	196	212	53	140	1.35
Tomokazu Ohka	MON	$6	9	0	4.06	166	187	39	101	1.36
Josh Beckett	FLA	$6	6	0	3.31	91	80	36	96	1.27
Mike Remlinger	CHC	$6	5	0	2.80	71	56	30	82	1.22
Elmer Dessens	AZ	$6	8	0	4.20	186	202	53	111	1.37
Rheal Cormier	PHI	$6	6	1	3.44	65	55	24	51	1.21
Chris Reitsma	CIN	$6	7	4	4.51	135	148	38	78	1.38
Matt Herges	SF	$6	5	3	3.32	81	82	33	65	1.42
Guillermo Mota	LA	$5	3	0	3.33	72	58	23	60	1.13
Paul Shuey	LA	$5	6	1	3.05	64	53	29	64	1.29
Justin Speier	COL	$5	5	3	4.32	71	65	21	58	1.21
Steve Reed	COL	$5	3	1	2.90	63	56	20	45	1.21
Tony Armas	MON	$5	8	0	4.08	131	118	58	110	1.35
Scott Strickland	NYM	$5	3	4	3.23	57	48	28	57	1.34
Brandon Webb	AZ	$5	3	0	2.84	60	47	23	57	1.15
Dan Kolb	MIL	$5	1	7	3.24	30	25	17	25	1.43
Carlos Zambrano	CHC	$5	6	0	3.57	110	98	54	88	1.38
Terry Adams	PHI	$4	7	0	4.02	124	124	44	96	1.36
Jim Brower	SF	$4	6	1	4.07	103	95	43	72	1.34
Adam Eaton	SD	$4	6	0	4.29	111	103	41	93	1.30
Jay Witasick	SD	$4	4	1	3.26	64	59	26	67	1.33
Kyle Farnsworth	CHC	$3	4	1	3.99	68	57	30	82	1.27
Orlando Hernandez	MON	$3	4	0	4.11	80	74	25	63	1.23
Chad Fox	FLA	$3	3	2	2.51	38	28	24	43	1.36
Joey Eischen	MON	$3	3	1	2.77	46	43	16	37	1.29
Luis Vizcaino	MIL	$3	4	2	4.50	60	52	22	57	1.24
Mark Guthrie	CHC	$3	4	1	3.27	48	41	20	40	1.29

3-Year Dollar Values - N.L. Pitchers

NAME	TEAM	$VAL	W	SV	ERA	IP	H	BB	K	RATIO
Dontrelle Willis	FLA	$3	5	0	3.30	54	49	19	47	1.28
Wilson Alvarez	LA	$3	3	1	3.65	57	53	19	46	1.28
Jake Peavy	SD	$3	6	0	4.24	98	93	38	82	1.34
Luis Ayala	MON	$3	3	2	2.92	24	22	4	15	1.10
Jose Valverde	AZ	$3	1	3	2.15	17	8	9	24	0.99
Joe Nathan	SF	$3	4	0	2.82	28	17	11	28	1.02
Jeff Fassero	STL	$3	4	5	4.82	74	80	28	63	1.47
Julian Tavarez	PIT	$3	8	4	4.67	133	145	56	71	1.51
Jae Seo	NYM	$3	3	0	3.79	63	64	15	37	1.26
Mike Koplove	AZ	$2	3	0	2.95	37	29	14	29	1.16
Mike Lincoln	PIT	$2	2	2	3.50	50	51	17	34	1.36
Ray King	ATL	$2	2	0	3.37	60	52	25	47	1.29
Dan Plesac	PHI	$2	3	1	3.52	38	30	17	49	1.24
Ricky Stone	HOU	$2	3	1	3.59	56	54	22	38	1.36
Rick Helling	FLA	$2	10	0	4.95	182	201	52	124	1.39
Brian Boehringer	PIT	$2	3	1	4.09	70	65	30	57	1.36
Andy Ashby	LA	$2	5	0	4.25	89	94	27	52	1.37
Josh Fogg	PIT	$2	7	0	4.63	117	125	37	67	1.39
Mike Matthews	SD	$2	4	0	3.79	67	61	30	50	1.36
Oscar Villarreal	AZ	$2	3	0	2.57	33	27	15	27	1.29
Brian Fuentes	COL	$2	2	1	3.40	38	32	18	43	1.31
Shane Reynolds	ATL	$2	9	0	4.85	141	160	40	81	1.41
Carlos Silva	PHI	$2	3	1	3.83	57	60	19	30	1.39
Jerome Williams	SF	$2	2	0	3.30	44	39	16	29	1.26
Darren Holmes	ATL	$1	1	0	2.88	32	29	7	31	1.14
Tim Spooneybarger	FLA	$1	1	0	3.23	32	23	13	23	1.11
John Riedling	CIN	$1	2	1	3.87	61	56	29	39	1.40
Mike Crudale	MIL	$1	1	0	2.08	25	18	11	20	1.18
Kevin Jarvis	SD	$1	6	0	5.06	107	113	29	69	1.33
Horacio Ramirez	ATL	$1	4	0	4.00	61	60	24	33	1.39
Jason Simontacchi	STL	$1	7	0	4.74	90	96	31	49	1.41
Cal Eldred	STL	$1	2	3	4.53	25	25	11	24	1.47
Brett Myers	PHI	$1	6	0	4.38	88	93	35	59	1.44
Rick White	HOU	$1	3	1	4.65	67	69	19	49	1.33
Zach Day	MON	$1	4	0	4.05	56	53	24	29	1.38
Dustin Hermanson	SF	$1	6	0	4.61	94	100	34	58	1.42
Turk Wendell	PHI	$1	2	1	3.91	44	39	20	28	1.36
Gene Stechschulte	STL	$1	2	2	4.14	34	33	16	24	1.42
Salomon Torres	PIT	$1	3	1	4.35	50	52	18	32	1.40
Dave Williams	PIT	$1	2	0	4.06	52	46	23	30	1.31
Chris Carpenter	STL	$1	5	0	4.39	96	106	34	67	1.45
John Franco	NYM	$1	2	1	3.48	29	30	11	22	1.39
Grant Roberts	NYM	$1	1	0	3.00	30	29	9	23	1.25
Brett Tomko	STL	$1	9	0	4.90	147	169	43	87	1.44

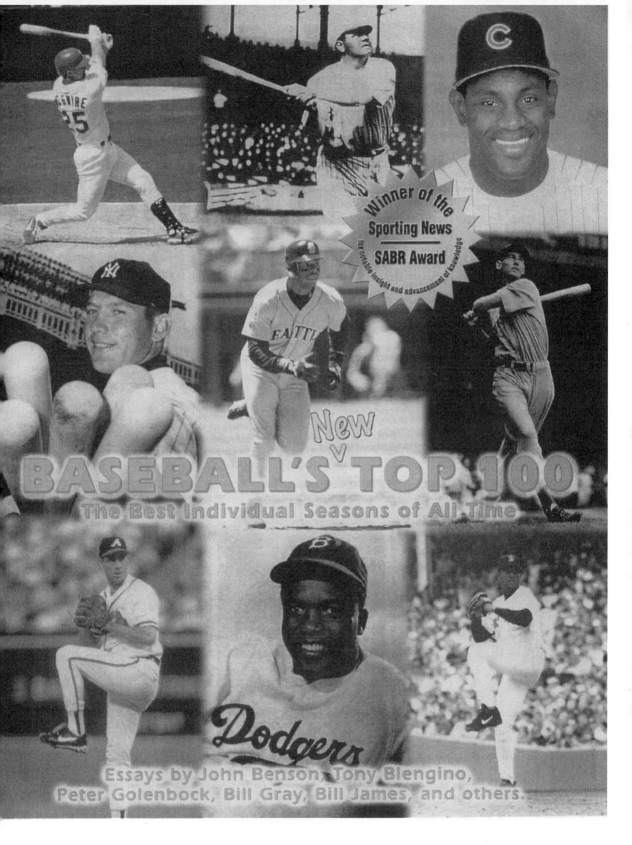

New
BASEBALL'S TOP 100
The Best Individual Seasons of All Time

Winner of the Sporting News SABR Award for notable insight and advancement of knowledge

Essays by John Benson, Tony Blengino, Peter Golenbock, Bill Gray, Bill James, and others.

ISBN # 1-880876-95-7
352 pages, hard cover, 8.5" x 11"
Retail Price: $24.95

John Benson's 2004 Baseball Player Forecasts

Continuous Updates
December 10 (or sooner) until April 10
Access via the Internet at johnbenson.com

Improved with 100% all-new player comments, new sleeper lists, new surge/fall alerts, and more!
The point is simple: winning!

Includes FREE 2004 Draft Software Program Upgrad

John Benson was the first person ever to publish NEX
YEAR'S baseball statistics before they happen. When e
eryone thought a "baseball forecast" meant predictior
of pennant-winners, Benson was issuing detailed individu
baseball player stats for the coming year, Rotisserie Do
lar Values, and customizing values for your unique leagu

The first is still the best. And for Baseball Draft Softwar
there is simply no competition. The original one is st
the only one.

Order now to get your PIN for continuous access from 1
10/03 until 4/10/04. Don't wait, because John just mig
begin issuing earlier than promised. (He's done it before

Or ... you can wait ... and get a busy signal when everyor
else is calling. To stay ahead of your competition, a
now. The best homework is always the work that begir
early. Start first, to finish first.

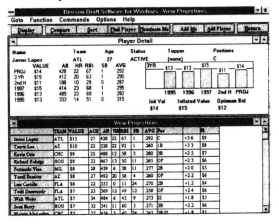

DIAMOND LIBRARY PUBLISHERS
15 CANNON RD.
WILTON CT, 06897

Customer Service: 203.834.1231
Order Line: 1-800-707-9090
Fax line: 203.834.1285

Name _____

Address_____

City _____ State _____ Zip _____ Phone_____

Mastercard / Visa # _____ - _____ - _____ - _____ Expiration _____

How did you hear about us?_____

Title:	Quantity	Price	Total
Pre-Season Guides:			
The Rotisserie Baseball Annual 2004	_____	$22.95	_____
Future Stars - The Rookies of 2004-2005	_____	$19.95	_____
Rotisserie League Baseball – 2004 **Official Manual and A to Z Scouting Guide**	_____	$19.95	_____
How-to-Win Guides:			
Rotisserie Baseball - Volume I - **Getting Ready for Draft Day**	_____	$12.95	_____
Rotisserie Baseball - Volume II – **Drafts, Auctions & Roster Management**	_____	$12.95	_____
Baseball History:			
Baseball's New Top 100 **HARDCOVER COLLECTORS EDITION**	_____	$19.95	_____
Baseball Wisdom (Spring 2004)	_____	$17.95	_____

SHIPPING: $4 per book, $16 maximum (Canada $8 per book $40 Max., Intl $9 per Book

John Benson's *Private Pages (Formerly the Baseball Monthly)*

Six Months $ 49   One Year $69   Two Years $99

CALL For Username and Password

Draft Software   Repeat Customer $69   New Customer $99
CALL For PinCode
Diamond Consulting Services with John Benson in Person on Phone
$150 per hour by Appointment.

Sub Total Books (Including Shipping)* _____

* **Tax (CT Residents please add 6% Sales Tax to this Sub Total)** .... _____

Sub Total Phone .... _____

Sub Total Private Pages .... _____

Sub Total Baseball Forecasts and Draft Software............... .... _____
ORDER TOTAL .... _____